ACID RAIN

AND
TRANSPORTED
AIR POLLUTANTS

IMPLICATIONS FOR PUBLIC POLICY

Office of Technology Assessment
Congress of the United States
Washington, D.C.

UNIPUB New York

Library of Congress Catalog Card Number 84-52370

ISBN 0-89059-044-3

Published in cooperation with the Office of Technology Assessment, Congress of the United States, 1985

Printed in the United States of America

Foreword

Transported air pollutants have been the topic of much debate during the Clean Air Act deliberations of the 97th and 98th Congresses. The current controversy over acid rain—the most publicized example of transported pollutants—focuses on the risks to our environment and ourselves versus the costs of cleanup. Since 1980, the committees responsible for reauthorizing the Clean Air Act—the House Committee on Energy and Commerce and the Senate Committee on Environment and Public Works—have called on OTA many times for information about the movements, fate, and effects of airborne pollutants, the risks that these transported air pollutants pose to sensitive resources, and the likely costs of various proposals to control them. Over the course of the debate, OTA has provided extensive testimony and staff memoranda to the requesting committees, and published a two-volume technical analysis, *The Regional Implications of Transported Air Pollutants,* in July 1982. This report synthesizes OTA's technical analyses of acid rain and other transported pollutants, and presents policy alternatives for congressional consideration.

OTA's work over the last several years has enabled us to forecast with reasonable accuracy the cost of controlling pollutant emissions, and, for each of the many pending legislative proposals, who will pay those costs. We also know a great deal about the transport, fate, and effects of transported air pollutants—vastly more than was known several years ago when Congress last considered the Clean Air Act. Still, it is not yet possible to accurately evaluate the damages wrought by the pollutants or the benefits to be gained by reducing emissions, though we can say that both the risks of harm and the costs of control are substantial.

The issue of transported pollutants poses a special problem for policymakers: assuring regional equity while balancing concerns for economic well-being with concerns for natural and human resources across large regions of the Nation. Scientific uncertainties surrounding many aspects of the problem complicate the decision of whether, or when, to control transported air pollutants. Additional complexities arise from our inability to treat costs, damages, and benefits in a uniform, quantitative way. Moreover, in OTA's judgment, even substantial additional scientific research is unlikely to provide significant, near-term policy guidance, or resolve value conflicts.

How, then, can Congress address *current damage,* consider *potential harm* to recipients of transported air pollutants, yet not enforce an *unnecessarily high cost* on those who would be required to reduce pollutant emissions? OTA's analysis cannot provide an unambiguous answer to this dilemma. It does, however, lay out some carefully weighed estimates of costs, some carefully reasoned conclusions about the nature and extent of downwind damages and risks, and several policy options that merit consideration. We hope that this information will help to narrow the issues of contention for this important environmental concern.

OTA is grateful for the assistance of the advisory panel, contractors, and the over 200 reviewers who provided advice and information throughout the course of this assessment.

JOHN H. GIBBONS
Director

Transported Air Pollutants Advisory Panel

Norton Nelson, *Chairman*
New York University Medical Center

Thomas H. Brand
Edison Electric Institute

Gene E. Likens
Cornell University

Robert Wilbur Brocksen
Electric Power Research Institute

Anne LaBastille
Adirondack Park Agency

Jack George Calvert
National Center for Atmospheric Research

Donald H. Pack
Private Consultant

David Hawkins
National Resources Defense Council, Inc.

Carl Shy
University of North Carolina

Edward A. Helme
National Governors' Association

George H. Tomlinson, II
Domtar, Inc.

Richard L. Kerch
Consolidation Coal

Principal Contractors

Brookhaven National Laboratory
Kathleen Cole, Duane Chapman,
  Clifford Rossi
Energy & Resource Consultants
Environmental Law Institute
Barbara J. Finalyson-Pitts,
  James N. Pitts, Jr.

Brand L. Niemann
Oak Ridge National Laboratory
E. H. Pechan & Associates
Perry J. Sampson
Jack Shannon
The Institute of Ecology

Additional Contributors

A. S. L. & Associates
Sanford Berg
Daniel Bromley
Thomas Crocker
Energy & Environmental Analysis, Inc.
Yacov Haimes
Perry Hagenstein
David Harrison
Walter Heck
IR & T Corp.

Steven Olson
James Reagan
Larry Salathe
John P. Skelly
SRI International
TRC Environmental Consultants
Michael P. Walsh

OTA Project Staff—Transported Air Pollutants Assessment

John Andelin, *Assistant Director, OTA*
Science, Information, and Natural Resources Division

Robert W. Niblock, *Oceans and Environment Program Manager*

Robert M. Friedman, *Project Director*
Rosina M. Bierbaum, *Assistant Project Director*
Patricia A. Catherwood, *Research Analyst*
Stuart C. Diamond,* *Editor/Writer*
George C. Hoberg, Jr.,* *Policy Analyst*
Valerie Ann Lee, *Policy Analyst*

Contributing Staff

Linda Garcia   Iris Goodman   Nancy Greenbaum   Jennifer N. Marsh

Administrative Staff

Kathleen A. Beil   Jacquelynne R. Mulder   Kay Senn

---

*OTA consultants.

Contents

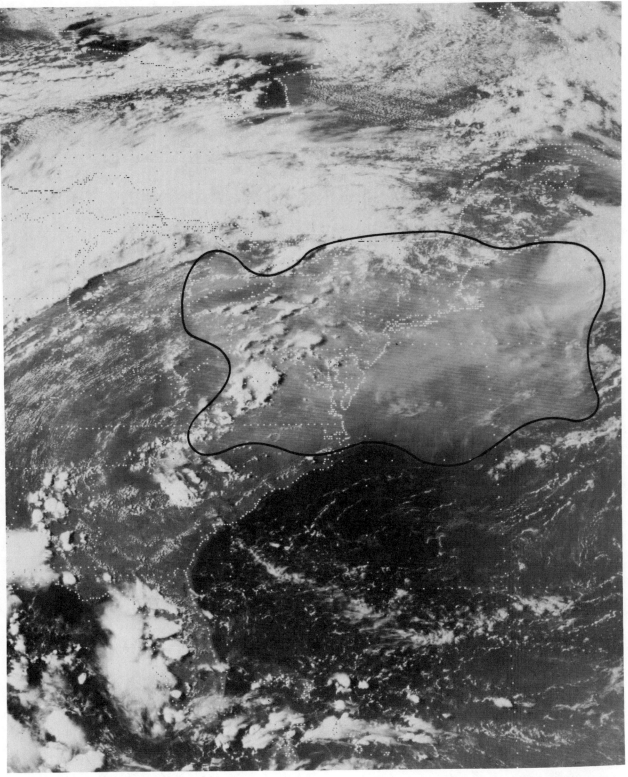

A hazy, polluted air mass is outlined on this July 1978 enhanced satellite photo. High levels of airborne sulfate and ozone, along with low visibility, persisted for about a week over much of the Eastern United States and Canada. The polluted air mass extends far offshore—at least 500 miles from manmade emissions sources—visible evidence of long-distance transport of air pollution.

Chapter 1
Summary

Contents

FIGURES

Summary

Until recently, air pollution was considered a local problem. Now it is known that winds can carry air pollutants hundreds of miles from their points of origin. These *transported* air pollutants can damage aquatic ecosystems, crops, and manmade materials, and pose risks to forests and even to human health. Throughout this report we discuss three of these pollutants: acid deposition (commonly called acid rain), atmospheric ozone, and airborne fine particles.

The Clean Air Act—the major piece of Federal legislation governing air quality in the United States—addresses local air pollution problems but does not directly apply to pollutants that travel many miles from their sources. However, reports of natural resource damage in this country, Canada, Scandinavia, and West Germany have made transported air pollutants—particularly acid rain—a focus of scientific and political controversy. Many individuals and groups, pointing to the risk of irreversible damage to resources, are calling for more stringent Federal pollution controls. Others, emphasizing scientific uncertainties about transported air pollutants and drawing different conclusions about how to balance risks against costs, contend that further pollution controls are premature, may waste money, and would impose unreasonable burdens on industry and the public.

OTA's analysis of acid deposition and other transported air pollutants concludes that these substances pose substantial risks to American resources. Thousands of lakes and tens of thousands of stream miles in the Eastern United States and Canada are vulnerable to the effects of acid deposition. Some of these have already been harmed. Elevated levels of atmospheric ozone have reduced crop yields on American farms by hundreds of millions of bushels each year. Acid deposition may be adversely affecting a significant fraction of Eastern U.S. forests; it, along with such other stresses as ozone and natural factors such as drought, may account for declining forest productivity observed in parts of the East. Both sulfur oxides and ozone can damage a wide range of manmade materials. Airborne fine particles such as

sulfate reduce visibility and have been linked to increased human mortality in regions with elevated levels of air pollution.

The costs of reducing pollutant emissions are likewise substantial. Most current legislative proposals to control acid deposition would cost about $3 billion to $6 billion per year. Adding these new emissions control proposals to our Nation's current environmental laws would increase the total costs of environmental regulation by about 5 to 10 percent. Average electricity costs would rise by several percent—as high as 10 to 15 percent in a few Midwestern States under the most stringent proposals. Additional emissions controls could also have important indirect effects, such as job dislocations among coal miners and financial burdens on some utilities and electricity-intensive industries.

Any program to reduce emissions significantly would require about 7 to 10 years to implement. If *no* further action is taken to control emissions, 30 to 45 years will elapse before most existing pollution sources are retired and replaced with facilities more stringently regulated by the Clean Air Act. **The effective time frame of most proposals to control acid deposition, therefore, is the intervening period of about 20 to 40 years—long enough to be significant to natural ecosystems.**

If all the *risks* posed by transported air pollutants were realized over this time period, resulting resource damage would outweigh control costs. The risks discussed throughout this report, however, are *potential* consequences, not necessarily the consequences that will, in fact, occur.

One of the most difficult questions facing Congress, therefore, is whether to act *now* to control acid deposition or *wait* for results from ongoing multimillion-dollar research programs. Both involve risks. *Delaying action* for 5 or 10 years will allow emissions to remain high for at least a decade or two, with the risk of further ecological damage. But predicting the magnitude and geographic extent of additional resource damage while waiting is not possible. *Acting now* involves the risk that the control program will be less cost effective or efficient than one designed 5 or 10 years from now. Significant advances in scientific understanding over this time period, however, are by no means assured.

The distributional aspects of transported air pollutants further complicate the congressional dilemma. Because these pollutants cross State and even international boundaries, they can harm regions far downwind of those benefiting from the activities that produce pollution. Moreover, different economic sectors bear the risks of waiting or acting now to control.

The policy decision to control or not to control transported air pollutants must be based on **the risks of resource damage, the risks of unwarranted control expenditures, and the distribution of these risks among different groups and regions of the country.** This study describes the tradeoffs implicit in this choice by characterizing the *extent* of the risks, their *regional distribution,* and the *economic sectors* that bear them. It concludes with a list of policy options available to Congress for addressing transported air pollutants.

THE POLLUTANTS OF CONCERN

The transported air pollutants considered in this study result from the emission of three *primary* pollutants: sulfur dioxide, nitrogen oxides, and hydrocarbons. As these pollutants are carried away from their sources, they can be transformed through complex chemical processes into *secondary* pollutants: ozone and airborne fine particles such as

sulfate and nitrate. Acid deposition results when sulfur and nitrogen oxides and their transformation products return from the atmosphere to the Earth's surface. Elevated levels of ozone are produced through the chemical interaction of nitrogen oxides and hydrocarbons (see fig. 1). Numerous chemical reactions—not all of which are

Figure 1.—Transported Air Pollutants: Emissions to Effects

The transported air pollutants considered in this study result from emissions of three pollutants: sulfur dioxide, nitrogen oxides, and hydrocarbons. As these pollutants are carried away from their sources, they form a complex "pollutant mix" leading to acid deposition, ozone, and airborne fine particles. These transported air pollutants pose risks to surface waters, forests, crops, materials, visibility, and human health.

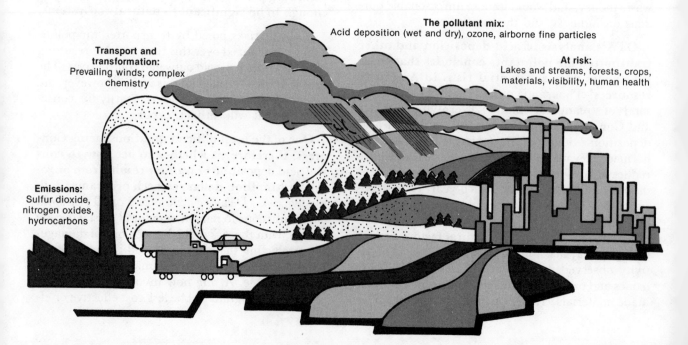

completely understood—and prevailing weather patterns affect the overall distribution of acid deposition and ozone concentrations.

Current levels of precipitation acidity and ozone concentrations are shown in figures 2 and 3, respectively. Peak levels of acid deposition—as measured by precipitation acidity, or pH*—center around Ohio, West Virginia, and western Pennsylvania. High levels of acid deposition are found throughout the United States and southeastern Canada. Peak values for ozone are found further south than for acid deposition, centering around the Carolinas. A band of elevated ozone concentrations extends from the mid-Great Plains States to the east coast.

During 1980 some 27 million tons of sulfur dioxide and 21 million tons of nitrogen oxides were emitted in the United States. Figure 4 displays the regional pattern of emissions. About 80 percent of the sulfur dioxide and 65 percent of the nitrogen oxides came from within the 31 States bordering or east of the Mississippi River. Figure 5 shows how these emissions have varied since 1900. Since 1940, sulfur dioxide emissions increased by about 50 percent and nitrogen oxides emissions about tripled. Throughout the same period, taller emission stacks became common, allowing pollutants to travel farther.

Figure 5 also shows a range of *projected* future emissions of these pollutants, assuming that current air pollution laws and regulations remain unchanged. *Actual* future emissions will depend on such factors as the demand for energy, the type of energy used, and the rate at which existing sources of pollution are replaced by newer, cleaner facilities. By 2030—the end of the projection period— most existing facilities will have been retired. Despite relatively strict pollution controls mandated for new sources by the Clean Air Act, **emissions of both sulfur and nitrogen oxides are likely to remain high for at least the next half century.**

The pollutants responsible for acid deposition can return to Earth in rain, snow, fog, or dew—col-

lectively known as acid precipitation—or as dry particles and gases. **Averaged over the Eastern United States, about equal amounts of sulfur compounds are deposited in wet and dry forms.** However, in areas remote from pollution sources, such as the Adirondacks, wet deposition may account for up to 80 percent of the sulfur deposited; in urban areas near many sources of pollution the situation is reversed.[1]

Pollutants emitted into the atmosphere can return to Earth almost immediately or remain aloft for longer than a week, depending on weather patterns and the pollutants' chemical interactions. During this time they move with prevailing winds, which in the Eastern United States tend to move from west to east and from south to north.

Preliminary analyses suggest that about one-third of the total amount of sulfur compounds deposited over the Eastern United States as a whole originates from sources over 500 kilometers (km) (300 miles) away from the region in which they are deposited. Another one-third comes from sources between 200 and 500 km (120 to 300 miles) away, and the remaining one-third comes from sources within 200 km (120 miles).[2]

Because pollution sources are unevenly distributed across the Eastern United States and Canada, the *relative* contribution of emissions from local, midrange, and distant sources varies by region. As shown in figure 6, sulfur deposition in the Midwest—a region with high emissions—is dominated by emissions from sources within 300 km (180 miles). The sulfur compounds that reach the less-industrialized New England region typically have traveled farther. The "average" distance—considering the contribution from both local and distant sources—is about 500 to 1,000 km (300 to 600 miles).

---

*Acidity is measured in pH units. Decreasing pH corresponds to increasing acidity, but in a nonlinear (logarithmic) way. Across the United States, average annual rainfall pH varies between about 4 and 6. Compared to a pH of 6, pH 5 is 10 times more acidic; pH 4 is 100 times more acidic; and so on. Referring to the shading in figure 2, pH 4.2 is twice as acidic as pH 4.5; about 6 times more acidic than pH 5; and about 20 times more acidic than pH 5.5.

[1]E. Altwicker and A. Johannes, "Wet and Dry Deposition in Adirondack Watersheds," *The Integrated Lake-Watershed Acidification Study: Proceedings of the ILWAS Annual Review Conference,* Electric Power Research Institute, EPRI EA-2827, 1983; and D. Fowler, "Removal of Sulfur and Nitrogen Compounds From the Atmosphere," *Ecological Impact of Acid Precipitation,* SNSF Project, Norway, 1980.

[2]J. Shannon, "Estimation of North American Anthropogenic Sulfur Deposition as a Function of Source-Receptor Separation," paper presented at the *NATO 14th International Technical Meeting on Air Pollution Modeling and Its Application,* Copenhagen, 1983.

Figure 2.—Precipitation Acidity—Annual Average pH for 1980

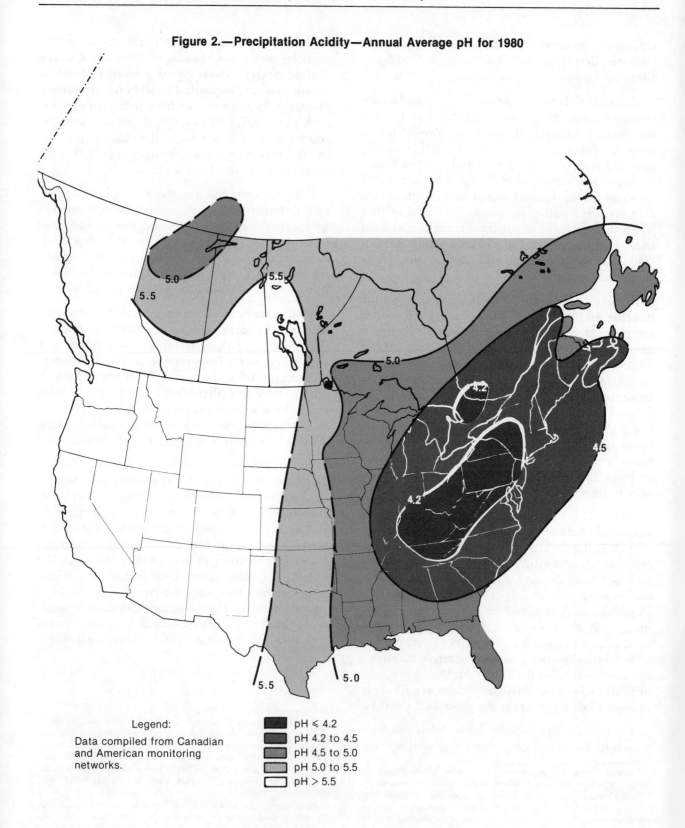

Legend:

Data compiled from Canadian and American monitoring networks.

	pH ≤ 4.2
	pH 4.2 to 4.5
	pH 4.5 to 5.0
	pH 5.0 to 5.5
	pH > 5.5

Figure 3.—Ozone Concentration—Daytime Average for Summer 1978

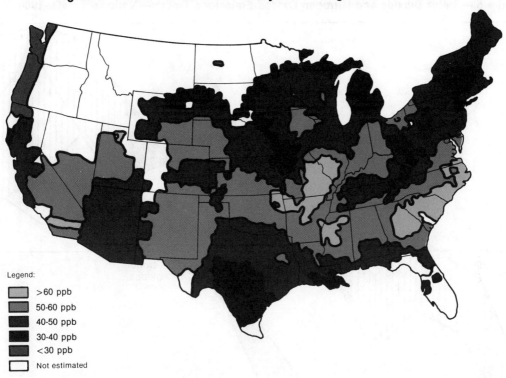

Legend:

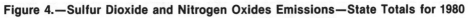

- >60 ppb
- 50-60 ppb
- 40-50 ppb
- 30-40 ppb
- <30 ppb
- Not estimated

Figure 4.—Sulfur Dioxide and Nitrogen Oxides Emissions—State Totals for 1980

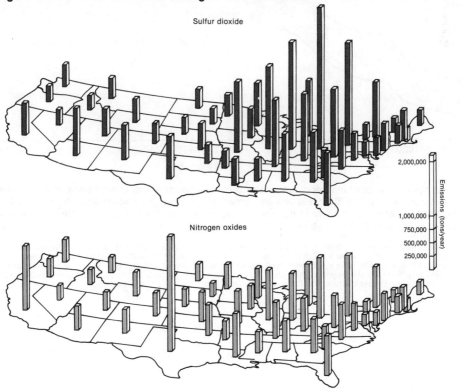

SOURCE: G. Gschwandtner, et al., "Historic Emissions of Sulfur and Nitrogen Oxides in the United States From 1900 to 1980," draft report to EPA, 1983.

Figure 5.—Sulfur Dioxide and Nitrogen Oxides Emissions Trends—National Totals, 1900-2030

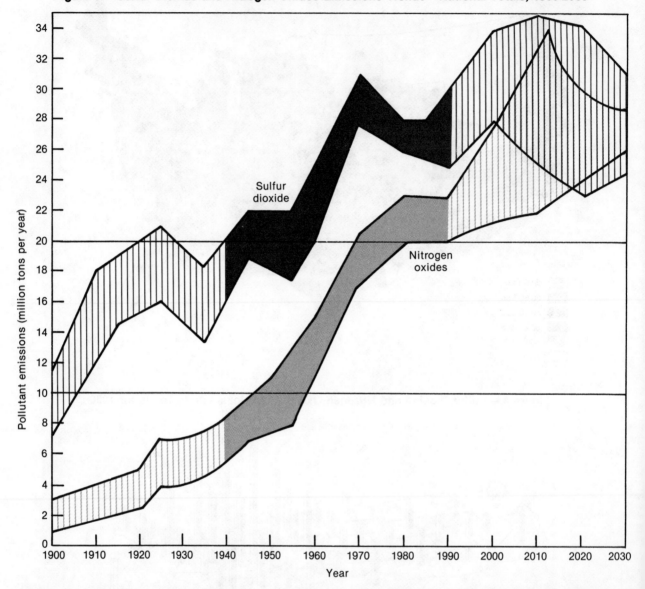

The graph above displays estimates of historical emissions, and projections of future emissions of sulfur dioxide and nitrogen oxides. Pre-1940 estimates and post-1990 projections are subject to considerable uncertainty. Projections of future emissions incorporate a wide range of assumptions about future economic growth, energy mix, and retirement of existing facilities; they assume no change in current air pollution laws and regulations.

SOURCES: Office of Technology Assessment. Composite from: U.S. Environmental Protection Agency, "National Air Pollution Emission Estimates, 1940-1980," 1982; G. Gschwandtner, et al., "Historic Emissions of Sulfur and Nitrogen Oxides in the United States From 1900 to 1980," draft report to the U.S. Environmental Protection Agency, 1983; *Emissions, Costs and Engineering Assessment*, Work Group 3B, United States-Canada Memorandum of Intent on Transboundary Air Pollution, 1982; and "Summary of Forecasted Emissions of Sulfur Dioxide and Nitrogen Oxides in the United States Over the 1980 to 2010 Period," ICF Inc. and NERA for the Edison Electric Institute, 1982; forecasts 1980 to 2030 by E. H. Pechan & Associates, Inc., for the Office of Technology Assessment, 1984.

Figure 6.—Average Sulfur Transport Distances Across Eastern North America

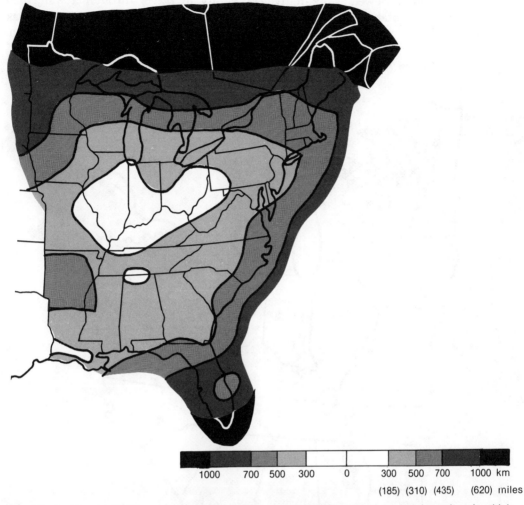

1000	700	500	300	0	300	500	700	1000 km
					(185)	(310)	(435)	(620) miles

The map above displays the "average" distance between the sources of sulfur dioxide emissions and the regions in which the sulfur compounds are eventually deposited. For each region of the Eastern United States and Canada, estimates of the sulfur deposited from all local, midrange, and distant emission sources are averaged to produce this map of typical transport distances. Such model-generated maps illustrate general patterns which will vary somewhat from year to year and model to model.

SOURCE: Jack Shannon, Argonne National Laboratory, 1984.

THE RISKS FROM TRANSPORTED AIR POLLUTANTS

The best documented and best understood effects of acid deposition are those on aquatic ecosystems. The sensitivity of a lake or stream to acid deposition depends largely on the ability of the soil and bedrock in the surrounding watershed to neutralize acid. Where the soil is very thin or has little neutralizing capacity, or where the terrain is so steep or rocky that rainfall runs right over it, the bodies of water within a watershed are at risk. When the waters of a lake or stream become more acidic than about pH 5, many species of fish die and the ecosystem changes dramatically. This may be due to the acidity, to the metals (especially aluminum) released under acidic conditions, or to a combination of both.

By categorizing the predominant soil and geological characteristics in each county of the Eastern United States, this study estimates the *potential* number of lakes and streams at risk from acid deposition. Because of the uncertainties involved, these numbers should be viewed as qualitative estimates only. In the 31 States bordering and east of the Mississippi River, roughly 25 percent of the land area contains soils and bedrock that allow acidity to travel through a watershed to lakes and streams (see fig. 7). About 17,000 lakes and 112,000 miles of streams lie within these sensitive areas. As

Figure 7.—Regions of the Eastern United States With Surface Waters Sensitive to Acid Deposition

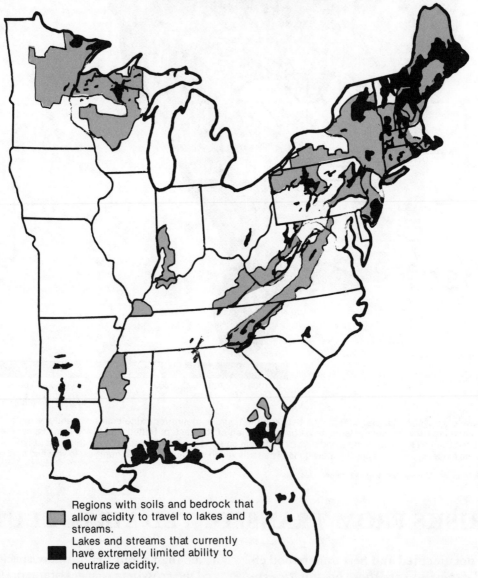

Regions with soils and bedrock that allow acidity to travel to lakes and streams.

Lakes and streams that currently have extremely limited ability to neutralize acidity.

The regions shaded light grey contain soils and bedrock that allow acidity to travel through a watershed to lakes and streams. Due to local variations, however, not all water bodies within these areas are sensitive to acid deposition. Likewise, some sensitive water bodies may be located outside the light grey areas. The dark areas contain lakes and streams that currently have such limited ability to neutralize acid[a] (as measured by water quality surveys) that they are now extremely vulnerable to further acid deposition or are already acidic.

[a]Regions with surface waters that have mean annual alkalinity less than 100 microequivalents per liter.

SOURCES: Office of Technology Assessment. Composite map from the Institute of Ecology, "Regional Assessment of Aquatic Resources at Risk From Acid Deposition," OTA contractor report, 1982; and J. Omernik, "Total Alkalinity of Surface Water," draft map prepared fo the U.S. Environmental Protection Agency, 1983.

a "best guess," about half of these lakes and streams have such limited ability to neutralize acid that they will acidify if enough acid-producing pollutants are deposited. **We estimate that about 3,000 lakes and 23,000 miles of streams—or about 20 percent of those in the sensitive areas— are now extremely vulnerable to further acid deposition or have already become acidic.** New England has the greatest percentage of lakes and streams considered sensitive to acid deposition. The Upper Midwest also has large numbers of sensitive lakes, and many sensitive streams are found in the Central Appalachian region.

In addition to the acidification of aquatic ecosystems, transported air pollutants have been linked to harmful effects to terrestrial ecosystems. **Broad forested areas subjected to elevated levels of acid deposition, ozone, or both have been marked by declining productivity and dying trees, although it is uncertain how much of this is due to airborne pollutants.** Figure 8 documents significant

Figure 8.—Recent Forest Productivity Declines Throughout the Eastern United States

The photograph shows corings from three softwood tree species growing on six sites across the East from Vermont to Tennessee. The corings show normal growth—widely spaced tree rings—until about 1960 (marked with a stripe). From about 1960 to the present the tree rings have markedly narrowed, evidence of decreased growth. Concerns have been raised that elevated levels of ozone and acid deposition in these regions may be involved in the observed declining productivity. As of now, the cause is unexplained.

SOURCE: Arthur Johnson, University of Pennsylvania; Samuel McLaughlin, Oak Ridge National Laboratory.

growth declines in several tree species beginning about 1960 throughout the East from Vermont to Tennessee. Acid deposition, ozone, heavy-metal deposition, drought, severe winters, or a combination of these stresses are possible causes under investigation.

Acid deposition might be harming trees in two ways: either directly (e.g., by removing nutrients from leaves), or indirectly, by altering the soils on which trees grow. If acid deposition harms trees directly, much of the forested area of the Eastern United States is at risk, with the greatest risk in high elevation areas where deposition is often greatest. If acid deposition affects forest soils, forests growing on nutrient-poor, naturally acidic soils are of greatest concern. This study estimates that such soils cover about 15 to 20 percent of the land area of the Eastern United States, primarily parts of New England, the Upper Midwest, and the South. Acid deposition might be stripping such essential nutrients as calcium and magnesium from these soils, or releasing metals, such as aluminum, that are toxic to plants. Whether this nutrient loss or release of metals from the soil is large enough to affect forest productivity at current levels of acid deposition is unknown.

A large area of U.S. forests is also exposed to elevated ozone concentrations. Ozone has been shown to damage tree foliage and reduce the growth rates of certain sensitive tree species. But its cumulative effect on *forest productivity* over the lifetime of trees—half a century or more—is difficult to predict.

Transported air pollutants adversely affect agricultural productivity. Up to 90 percent of the damage to crops from air pollutants may be due to ozone. Large areas of the United States, including much of the Midwestern Corn and Soybean Belts, are exposed to high levels of ozone. This study estimates that if ozone levels were reduced to their natural background levels, corn yields would have been 2 percent higher, wheat yields 5 percent higher, soybean yields 13 percent higher, and peanut yields 24 percent higher. Based on the value of these crops, **ozone causes about a 6- to 7-percent loss of U.S. agricultural productivity.**

Many areas of abundant agricultural production, such as Illinois, Indiana, and Ohio, also receive high levels of acid deposition. Some experiments using simulated acid rain have demonstrated reduced yields of agricultural crops, but others have found no effect.

Airborne pollutants accelerate the deterioration of many economically important materials. Sulfur oxides damage iron and steel, zinc, paint, and stone; certain types of rubber are susceptible to ozone. Pollution-induced damage is difficult to quantify because it cannot be distinguished readily from the weathering effects of the natural environment. The bulk of materials damage is thought to be caused by pollutants emitted *locally*. Regions at greatest risk are urban areas (especially those in industrial regions) and areas with historically significant buildings and monuments. One recent study estimated that reducing sulfur dioxide emissions in selected urban areas to achieve concentrations 25 to 30 percent below the current air quality standard could yield materials-related benefits of hundreds of millions of dollars annually.[3] Pollutant effects on unique or historic structures may be irreparable, and thus cannot be evaluated solely in monetary terms.

Air pollutants—along with natural causes such as humidity, fog, and dust—can significantly impair visibility. They reduce contrast, discolor the atmosphere, and obscure distant objects. **In the Eastern United States, airborne sulfates appear to be the single greatest contributor to reduced visibility, causing about 50 percent of visibility impairment annually, and about 70 percent during the summer.[4]** In the West, windblown dust and nitrogen oxides can also impair visibility significantly.

Air concentrations of sulfur dioxide, nitrogen oxides, and ozone are currently regulated to protect human health. No standards exist for airborne sulfates, which may also pose a threat to human health. At high exposure levels, sulfates can ag-

---

[3]E. H. Manuel, Jr., et al., "Benefits Analysis of Alternative Secondary National Ambient Air Quality Standards for Sulfur Dioxide and Total Suspended Particulates," Mathtech, Inc., report submitted to the U.S. Environmental Protection Agency, OAQPS, 1982.

[4]For example, see M. Ferman, et al., "The Nature and Source of Haze in the Shenandoah Valley/Blue Ridge Mountain Area," *J. Air Pollution Control Assoc.* 31:1074-1082, 1981; and U.S. Environmental Protection Agency, *Protecting Visibility, An EPA Report to Congress,* EPA 450/5-79-008, 1979.

gravate existing heart and lung conditions such as asthma. Several statistical studies comparing historical air pollution data and health records found a correlation between airborne sulfate levels and mortality, but whether there is a causal link between the two is not clear. For instance, elevated sulfate levels often occur with other airborne fine particles, one or more of which might be causing harm.

Disagreement exists within the scientific community over the significance of airborne sulfates to human health. **Some researchers conclude that there is a negligible effect at prevailing concentrations; others have found a significant association—several percent of annual mortality, primarily among people with preexisting cardiac or respiratory problems.** By combining the various estimates, this study concludes that a reasonable estimate of the magnitude of health risk posed by current levels of sulfates and other particulates is about 50,000 premature deaths (2 percent of total deaths) per year in the United States and Canada. This estimated health risk from transported air pollutants is a measure of *possible* harm. It can neither be confirmed nor disproven until further research is conducted.

Acidified waters can dissolve metals and toxic substances from soils, rocks, conduits, and pipes, and subsequently transport them into drinking water systems. Municipal water supplies can be monitored and corrected quite easily; potential problems with well water in rural areas are more difficult to detect and mitigate. Although acid deposition has not been proven to be the cause, water samples from a few areas in the Adirondacks and New England receiving high levels of acidity have contained lead concentrations exceeding the health-based standards.

THE RISKS OF CONTROLLING TRANSPORTED AIR POLLUTANTS

The above discussion of the risks from transported air pollutants relies heavily on such words as "could" and "might" because at present, we can only make educated guesses about the scope and severity of the problem. For example, scientists are certain that acid deposition damages lakes and streams, and that ozone damages crops. But they cannot say with certainty how many lakes and streams and what quantity of crops have been damaged. Nor can they forecast with confidence what these damages will be in the future. Part of the difficulty is the uncertainty about the extent to which resource damage is cumulative—some types of resource damage might worsen even if levels of acid deposition remain about the same.

These uncertainties are compounded by imprecise knowledge of the transport and transformation of pollutants emitted throughout the Eastern United States and Canada. Scientists have devised atmospheric transport models to simulate the movement of sulfur emissions. But even with these sophisticated tools, scientists can only *estimate* the amount of sulfur pollution transported from one large region to another, over seasonal to annual time scales. Similarly, scientists cannot confidently predict the degree to which emissions reductions in one region would reduce deposition in another.

Intertwined with the scientific uncertainties about the benefits of a control program are disagreements over values. Few would deny that there are significant environmental risks associated with transported air pollutants. **But there are also risks associated with controlling these pollutants—the risks that the benefits from reducing emissions do not justify the economic and social costs.**

Various groups and individuals differ sharply on where the balance should be struck between protecting the environment and protecting other areas of economic well-being. There is little agreement on the intrinsic worth of resources or the equitable distribution of costs to protect those resources. Unfortunately, more accurate atmospheric transport models or a better understanding of the level of emissions required to protect sensitive resources will do little to solve such questions of values.

To put the risks and uncertainties of controlling transported air pollutants into context, this study examines a range of programs to reduce emissions, focusing on the direct and indirect costs for specific regions of the United States and the country as a whole.

Most of the proposals introduced during recent sessions of Congress would control sulfur dioxide emissions, since sulfur compounds contribute twice as much acidity to rainfall in the Eastern United States as nitrogen compounds and are more strongly implicated with a variety of adverse effects. This study estimates that the annual costs to reduce sulfur dioxide emissions in the 31 States bordering and east of the Mississippi River could range from about $1 billion (or less) for about a 10- to 20-percent reduction, to about $3 billion to $6 billion for a 35- to 45-percent reduction below 1980 emissions levels by 1995.

The larger control programs could have several significant consequences. The average cost of electricity will increase by several percent. Certain utilities and electricity-intensive industries might be financially strained. And, if utilities achieve emissions reductions in part by switching to low-sulfur coal, jobs would be displaced from areas where coal high in sulfur content is mined to areas producing low-sulfur coal.

Because electric utilities account for about three-fourths of the sulfur dioxide emitted in the Eastern United States, most current legislative proposals would require significant reductions in utility emissions. In particular, utilities in the Midwestern States, which tend to burn high-sulfur coal, would bear the greatest impact of an emissions control program. Ultimately, these costs would be passed on to consumers in the form of higher utility bills. For example, this study estimates that **10 million tons of sulfur dioxide emissions could be eliminated from existing sources nationwide for about $3 billion to $4 billion per year, increasing average electricity rates by 2 to 3 percent.** These rate increases would vary by State, as shown in figure 9. Consumers in some States would see no in-

creases, while others would pay increases over three times the national average. **If the projected future growth in emissions must also be offset through reductions from current emitters (an additional 1 million to 3 million tons per year by 2000), average residential electricity costs could rise by about 4 to 5 percent, with increases of 10 to 15 percent in several States.**

An emissions control program could strain the financial resources of a number of electric utilities, particularly if State regulatory policies prohibit them from quickly passing on control costs to consumers. Based on selected economic ratings and the range of current State policies, utility sectors in several States might be relatively vulnerable to the additional capital requirements for pollution control equipment. Few of the States with the highest percentages of economically vulnerable utilities, however, are allocated extensive emissions reductions under current acid rain proposals.

Some firms and industries that rely heavily on electricity could become less competitive if their electricity rates were to increase substantially above rates in other parts of the country. Of greatest concern are those that produce electrometallurgical products, zinc and aluminum, alkali- and chlorine-based chemicals, and industrial gases.

If a control program is enacted that allows each utility to freely choose its own method of achieving emissions reductions, some utilities will choose to switch from burning high-sulfur coal to low-sulfur coal. **Under such a "freedom-of-choice" program to eliminate 10 million tons of emissions per year, future levels of high-sulfur coal production could fall 10 to 20 percent below 1980 levels.** Employment in regions that mine high-sulfur coal could be 20,000 to 30,000 jobs below projected levels. An equivalent number of jobs would open up in Eastern and Western States that mine low-sulfur coal. **Legislation that mandates the use of high-removal control technology could minimize such dislocations, but could increase total program costs by about $1.5 billion per year.**

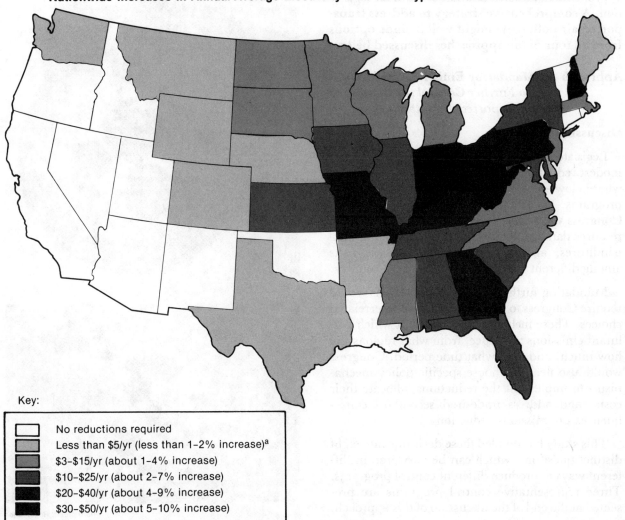

Figure 9.—Cost of Reducing Sulfur Dioxide Emissions by 10 Million Tons per Year, Nationwide Increases in Annual-Average Electricity Bills for a Typical Residential Consumer

Key:

☐	No reductions required
☐	Less than $5/yr (less than 1–2% increase)[a]
☐	$3–$15/yr (about 1–4% increase)
☐	$10–$25/yr (about 2–7% increase)
☐	$20–$40/yr (about 4–9% increase)
☐	$30–$50/yr (about 5–10% increase)

[a]Average annual cost increase (1982 dollars) for a typical residence consuming 750 kWh/month electricity. Percentage rate increases in each State are calculated from State-average 1982 electricity costs (ranging from about $200 to $900/yr; United States average about $600/yr).

SOURCE: Office of Technology Assessment, based on analyses by E. H. Pechan & Associates, Inc.

POLICY OPTIONS

Four approaches for congressional action on acid deposition and other transported air pollutants are discussed below:

A. Mandating emissions reductions to further *control the sources* of transported pollutants.

B. Liming lakes and streams to *mitigate some of the effects* of acid deposition.

C. Modifying the Federal acid deposition research program to *provide more timely guidance* for congressional decisions.

D. Modifying existing sections of the Clean Air Act to *enable the Environmental Protection Agency, States, and countries to more effectively address transported air pollutants other than acid deposition.*

Congress could choose to adopt some or all of these approaches in its consideration of clean air legislation. **A comprehensive strategy to address transported air pollutants might well include options from all four of the approaches discussed below.**

Approach A: *Mandating Emissions Reductions To Further Control the Sources of Transported Pollutants.*

Discussion

Legislated emissions reductions could range from modest reductions to keep emissions at—or somewhat below—current levels, to large-scale control programs. In choosing an appropriate program, Congress will need to weigh the risks of potential resource damage, the risks of inefficient control expenditures, and the distribution of these risks among different groups and regions of the country.

Mandating further emissions reductions would require Congress to make a number of interrelated choices. These include decisions about which pollutant emissions to reduce, from what regions, by how much, and over what time period. Congress would also need to choose specific policy mechanisms to implement the reductions, allocate their costs, and address undesired secondary consequences of emissions reductions.

This study has divided these decisions into eight distinct questions, which can be answered in different ways to produce different control programs. Three representative control programs are presented at the end of the discussion of this approach.

• Which Pollutants Should Be Further Controlled?

In the East, sulfur compounds currently contribute about twice as much acidity to precipitation as nitrogen compounds. Moreover, throughout the growing season, plants use much of the deposited nitrogen as a nutrient, making sulfur compounds responsible for a still larger share of acidity reaching lakes and streams. Sulfur compounds damage materials and in the particulate form (sulfate) reduce visibility and pose risks to human health. Both this study and a recent report from the National Academy of Science conclude that decreasing sulfur di-oxide *emissions* would reduce sulfur *deposition* by roughly the same proportion. For these reasons,

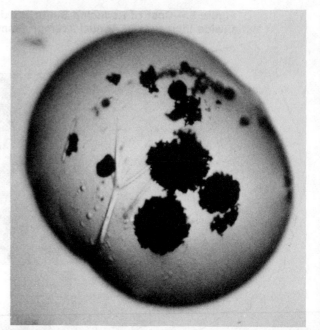

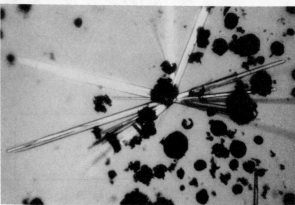

Photo credit: Roger Chen

A sulfate particle transformed from sulfur dioxide gas in a water droplet. The black soot (fly ash) speeds the conversion. Sulfate particles, when airborne, are part of a "pollutant mix" that degrades visibility and poses risks to human health. These small particles can be suspended for several days, gradually settling to Earth during dry periods, or rapidly washed from the air if it rains. In either form—wet or dry—sulfur compounds are major contributors to acid deposition.

sulfur dioxide is the logical focus for a program to control acid deposition in the Eastern United States.

Adding nitrogen oxides controls to the program is a reasonable next step if additional resource protection is desired. Nitrogen oxides emissions are expected to increase more rapidly over the next few decades than sulfur dioxide emissions. During the spring—a vulnerable period for aquatic life—both nitrogen and sulfur compounds found in melting snow travel freely through watersheds to bodies of water and contribute to acidification. Reducing nitrogen oxides emissions would also help lower regional ozone levels.

In the West, nitrogen compounds may contribute as much or more to precipitation acidity as sulfur and, thus, should be considered if a nationwide control program is desired.

• **How Widespread Should a Control Program Be?**

Both pollutant sources and resources sensitive to the effects of transported air pollutants are scattered across the Eastern United States. Because pollutants can travel hundreds of miles, programs to protect sensitive resources must encompass much of this area. Four regions are potential candidates:

1. The 21 States east of the Mississippi River and north of (and including) Tennessee and North Carolina, which receive the greatest levels of acidity. This region excludes several contiguous States that are large emitters.
2. The 31 States bordering and east of the Mississippi River, which emit 83 percent of the Nation's sulfur dioxide and 66 percent of its nitrogen oxides. This region has been the focus of most legislative proposals to date.
3. The 37 States east of the Rocky Mountains, which emit 89 percent of the Nation's sulfur dioxide and 85 percent of its nitrogen oxides.
4. The 48 contiguous States.

• **What Level of Pollution Control Should Be Required?**

Possible choices for further emissions control programs range from modest control (which would hold overall emissions at current levels) to large-scale emissions reductions. The decision of how much to reduce emissions involves two important components: the *scientific* question of the relationship between emissions reductions and resource protection, and the *policy* question of the socially desirable level of protection.

Most of the control programs proposed in recent sessions of Congress have aimed at reducing emissions by 8 million to 10 million tons per year below 1980 levels. Although the effects of such reductions are hard to predict, this study estimates that **reductions of 8 million to 10 million tons per year below 1980 levels are likely to protect *all but the most sensitive aquatic resources* in many areas receiving high levels of acid deposition. Those areas now receiving the *highest* levels of deposition—western Pennsylvania, for instance—would also benefit from reductions of this magnitude, though some risk of damage would still be present.** Risks of damage to forests, agriculture, materials, and health would likewise be reduced, and visibility would improve. A control program of this magnitude would cost about $3 billion to $6 billion per year. Costs would rise steeply if greater resource protection were desired.

More modest reductions, eliminating 2 million to 5 million tons of sulfur dioxide per year from existing sources, could be achieved for about $1 billion per year. Such a program would, at a minimum, offset expected emissions increases from utility and industrial growth, and might decrease emissions by 2 million to 3 million tons per year by the year 2000. Some resource improvement might result, or degradation might be slowed, but it is impossible at present to gauge by how much.

• **By What Time Should Reductions Be Required?**

Significant emissions reductions from existing sources would take at least 6 or 7—and possibly 10 or more—years to implement, given the planning, contracting, construction, and other steps that would be necessary. Waiting 4 to 6 years for the results of the Federal research program could increase the time required to reduce deposition to 10 to 16 years or more. Although resource damage will continue, it is impossible to predict how much damage might occur to resources during this additional delay, or how much more efficient a control program designed at the end of the decade might be. Because of the time needed for planning, **a control program initiated in the near future would not involve major expenditures for at least 5 years.** Control legislation could be modified with relatively modest cost penalties until 2 to 3 years before the compliance date, at which point major construction expenditures would have to begin.

• What Approach to Control Should Be Adopted?

Two general approaches are currently used for environmental regulation: "source-based" regulations and "environmental quality" standards. Source-based programs directly regulate the quantity of pollution allowed from emission sources. Programs based on environmental quality standards set goals or standards for resource exposure to pollutants; steps are then taken to meet these goals. Such a program requires a well-developed understanding of the transport, transformation, and effects of pollutants. **The knowledge needed to _implement_ an environmental quality standard for acid deposition is not yet available and may not be for at least a decade. This study therefore concludes that a source-based program, which regulates emissions directly, is the only approach available now for controlling acid deposition.** Such a program could specify, for example, maximum allowable emission rates (in pounds of pollutants per quantity of fuel burned) or maximum allowable statewide emissions (in tons of pollutants per year). A source-based approach could also limit emissions by mandating the use of specific technologies such as scrubbers or coal washing.

• How Should Emissions Reductions Be Allocated?

If Congress decides to mandate emissions reductions directly, it can either set a reduction formula that applies to all or some of the sources within a State, or it can set an overall reduction level for each State and allow the State to allocate emissions reductions within its borders. Congress could also set specific environmental protection goals, including economic considerations, and direct the Environmental Protection Agency (EPA) to develop an allocation plan to meet those goals.

Allocation formulas can take many different forms. For example, emissions could be reduced by an equal percentage in each State regardless of whether the State is a relatively high or low emitter. Alternatively, allowable emission _rates_ could be set, requiring the greatest reductions from sources that emit the greatest amounts of pollution per unit of fuel burned or similar measure. Most legislative proposals to date have followed the latter approach. A formula could be based on utility emissions alone or statewide total emissions. Allocation formulas differ in their resulting geographic patterns of emissions reductions and administrative complexity.

• Who Pays the Costs of Emissions Reductions?

The full costs of pollution control could be borne by those sources required to reduce emissions. **This "polluter pays" philosophy is the traditional approach to environmental regulation; in the case of transported air pollutants, however, the culpability of particular sources for specific resource damage is difficult to assess. Thus, some advocate spreading the costs of a control program to a larger group through such mechanisms as a tax on electricity or emissions.** Revenues would go to a trust fund, to be used to help finance control technology. Such cost-sharing mechanisms, however, can impose costs on areas that have taken action in the past to control emissions or that already have low emissions.

• What Can Be Done To Mitigate Employment and Economic Effects of a Control Policy?

To reduce employment dislocations resulting from increased demand for low-sulfur coal, Congress could require the use of control technologies designed for high-sulfur coal or require plants to use locally mined coal. Mandating the use of scrubber technologies could increase the costs of emissions reductions by about 25 to 50 percent for a large-scale program. Alternatively, if utilities are allowed to switch from high- to low-sulfur coal, workers or communities affected by the switch could be compensated.

To reduce the financial strain on specific utilities or their customers, Congress could establish a trust fund (as described under the previous question) to help pay for pollution control equipment.

Options

Congress could design a control program by selecting alternatives from each of the eight decision areas summarized above. Obviously, many combinations are possible; three representative options are presented below.

Option A-1: Mandate small-scale emission reductions.

A small-scale program would logically focus on further controlling sulfur dioxide emissions—the major manmade acidifying pollutant in the Eastern United States—within a 20- to 30-State region producing and receiving the greatest acid deposition. Two million to three million tons of sulfur dioxide emissions could be eliminated from existing sources for under $1 billion annually; 5 million tons per year could be eliminated for about $1 billion to $1.5 billion annually.

Control programs of this size would offset expected emissions increases of 2 million to 3 million tons per year by the year 2000, holding levels of acid deposition about constant or reducing them slightly below current levels. Such a program could be enacted alone, or as the first phase of larger programs discussed below, making the latter phase contingent on results of ongoing research.

Option A-2: Mandate large-scale emissions reductions.

A large-scale program similar to those proposed during recent sessions of Congress would reduce sulfur dioxide emissions by 8 million to 12 million tons per year. It could be confined to the Eastern United States or applied nationwide and could also include reductions in nitrogen oxides emissions.

We estimate that such a program would protect all but the most sensitive lakes and streams in many areas receiving high levels of acid deposition. Areas receiving the greatest levels of acidity, however, still might not be completely protected. Risks of damage to forests, crops, materials, and health would also be reduced and visibility would improve.

The costs of such a program could range from $2 billion to $3 billion per year to $6 billion to $8 billion per year, depending on its size and design. Congress might choose to spread some portion of control costs across a larger group than just those sources required to reduce. A trust fund generated by a tax on electricity or pollutant emissions could be established for this purpose. Congress could also mandate or subsidize the use of control technology to minimize job dislocations associated with switching from high- to low-sulfur coal.

Option A-3: Specify environmental quality goals or standards.

Rather than mandating specific emissions reductions, Congress could set environmental protection goals (including economic considerations, if desired) and direct EPA to establish a plan to achieve them. Because the tools needed to establish such a program are not yet available, this approach would not be feasible in the near future. It could, however, be preceded by small-scale, mandated reductions described earlier if Congress desired some emissions reductions within a decade. The compliance date for the remainder of the program might be set for early in the next century, which might allow enough time to develop the necessary modeling techniques, establish the standard, and achieve the required reductions.

Approach B: Liming Lakes and Streams To Mitigate Some of the Effects of Acid Deposition.

Discussion

Several chemicals can be used to temporarily treat acidified aquatic ecosystems. Mitigating the effects of acid deposition on other sensitive resources (e.g., forest soils) is not yet technically or economically feasible.

Adding large quantities of lime to water bodies has been effective in counteracting surface water acidification in parts of Scandinavia, Canada, and the United States. These programs have significantly improved water quality at a number of lakes

Photo credit: Ted Spiegel

Sulfur dioxide being emitted from the Kingston powerplant in Tennessee. Sulfur dioxide gas is invisible to the naked eye, but can be seen in the inset (upper right) with the aid of a special camera filter. The two 1,000-ft smokestacks were built in 1976, replacing the nine smaller stacks built with the plant during the mid-1950's. The tall stacks help the plant comply with local air-quality regulations, but disperse pollutants more widely.

and ponds, permitting fisheries to be maintained. Once begun, liming must be repeated every few years to prevent reacidification and buildup of toxic metal concentrations. Not all lakes and streams, however, respond sufficiently to liming to reestablish aquatic life, and little is known about the ecological consequences of continued liming.

Federal funding over the last several years permitted only a few research projects on the effects of liming to be undertaken each year. Several bills introduced during recent sessions of Congress proposed additional Federal support for mitigation programs. The Administration recently proposed about $5 million for liming research for fiscal year 1985. Funding at this level would provide more information on the feasibility of liming as a way to counteract the effects of acid deposition on sensitive lakes and streams. Such information would be extremely useful *regardless* of whether an emissions control program is adopted. Specific options available to Congress for promoting mitigation research are listed below.

Options

Option B-1: Expand current Federal mitigation research efforts under the National Acid Precipitation Assessment Program (NAPAP).

Federal funding through NAPAP for research on mitigation techniques—primarily liming—has been very modest. Congress could make more research funds available to expand this program so that it would include lakes and streams of varying geological, geographic, and biological conditions. Long-term monitoring of biological and chemical changes in limed water bodies should be an integral part of the program to determine frequency and effectiveness of liming, as well as secondary effects of this chemical alteration. Such a program could aid the Fish and Wildlife Service in developing guidelines that States, local communities, and private interests could use to mitigate the effects of acidification.

Option B-2: Expand Federal-State cooperative efforts for treating acidified surface waters and assessing results.

Funds to assess the effectiveness of water treatments are available under the existing Dingell-Johnson Act, which imposes a 10-percent tax on the wholesale cost of fishing tackle for projects to benefit recreational fishing. However, States currently do little mitigation-related work with these funds. Congress could direct additional resources towards mitigation activities by placing requirements on the use of these funds, by making more funds available, or by establishing new Federal-State cooperative programs.

Option B-3: Establish demonstration projects for acidified water bodies on Federal lands.

Congress could direct the Fish and Wildlife Service or the Forest Service to establish programs to treat selected lakes and streams on Federal lands and monitor their chemical and biological responses.

Approach C: Modifying the Current Research Program (NAPAP) To Provide More Timely Guidance to Congress.

Discussion

Under the Acid Precipitation Act of 1980 (Title VII of the Energy Security Act of 1980, Public Law 96-294), Congress created an interagency task force to carry out a comprehensive 10-year research and assessment program on acid deposition. After 2 years of planning, the task force presented Congress with the National Acid Precipitation Assessment Plan. According to this plan, an integrated, policy-related assessment is to be completed by 1987 and updated by 1989—a schedule that many members of Congress and public interest groups feel is too slow.

Several bills have proposed accelerating the plan. Such action has several disadvantages and is un-

Photo credit: Ted Spiegel

This researcher is measuring the acidity of a lake in the Adirondack Mountains, N.Y. Research sponsored by both the Federal interagency research program and such private groups as the Electric Power Research Institute has helped scientists understand some of the causes and consequences of acid deposition. A continuing, strong research program is needed, regardless of the outcome of emissions control legislation. Two important areas include: 1) effective methods to treat already damaged lakes and streams (options B-1 to B-3), and 2) research on combined air pollution stresses to forests (option C-3).

likely to provide guidance to policymakers in the short term. Redesigning the research schedule would consume a substantial amount of time and effort; moreover, many of the currently planned studies cannot be completed in the shorter times suggested. Accelerating the program might limit longer term studies, which are of great importance for evaluating and implementing any control program eventually put in place.

A strong, continuing research program is a necessary part of *any* strategy Congress might choose to address the problem of acid deposition. Current Federal research efforts could be strengthened in several ways. Option C-1 below is appropriate if Congress decides to wait several years to reconsider

an emissions control program; option C-2 is appropriate if Congress acts now to control acid deposition. Option C-3 could be adopted in either event.

Options

Option C-1: Establish a two-track research program.

In the absence of a legislated emissions control program, Congress could establish a policy assessment effort to be completed at an earlier date. The program could be assigned to either the existing interagency task force, or to a separate group entirely. Such a ''two-track'' program, leaving the current program largely intact, could analyze a series of control options within 2 or 3 years. This effort would need to begin almost immediately and therefore rely primarily on currently available information. Though this assessment would, by necessity, be based on less complete information than one begun several years from now, it could provide a common set of control costs estimates, deposition reductions, and similar information about alternative scenarios for policymakers to consider. The assessment could provide important information for considering the *initiation* of a control program; the present, longer term effort would be completed in time to reevaluate a control program, if enacted, before major expenditures occurred.

Option C-2: Redirect the research program if a control program is legislated.

Though the National Acid Precipitation Program was established as a long-term (10-year) effort, the enabling legislation does not explicitly address its fate if control legislation is passed. Maintaining the program in such a case, with some modifications, would have several benefits. Continued long-term monitoring and research will be necessary to evaluate the effectiveness of a control program after its passage, providing the opportunity to modify the control strategy if necessary. Also, with some redirection, the program would provide valuable guidance on implementing the control plan through the 1990's.

Option C-3: Broaden the ongoing research to include other transported air pollutants.

The Acid Precipitation Act of 1980 established an innovative, interagency research program addressing acid deposition. However, the effects of acid deposition on many resources—in particular, forests, crops, and materials—are difficult to separate from other pollutant stresses. Similarly, reducing emissions provides benefits in addition to those associated with reduced levels of acid deposition, for example, improved visibility. Congress could use the existing interagency structure and broaden NAPAP's mandate (and funding) to include research on other air pollutants. For example, recent studies showing forest productivity declines in the Eastern United States have raised

concerns about the combined stress from acid deposition, ozone, and heavy-metal deposition. An integrated approach to studying such pollutant mixes could both strengthen the current research effort, and, perhaps more important, provide guidance to Congress about the more general problem of transported air pollutants.

Approach D: Modifying Existing Provisions of the Clean Air Act To Enable EPA, States, and Countries To More Effectively Address Transported Air Pollutants Other Than Acid Deposition.

Discussion

The Clean Air Act was designed to control *airborne* concentrations of pollutants known to endanger public health and welfare. No provisions in the act provide a direct means of controlling the *deposition* of air pollutants or their transformation products.

Provisions were added to the act during its 1977 reauthorization to prevent a State's emissions from causing violations of National Ambient Air Quality Standards in other States or contributing to a pollution problem in other countries (secs. 110(a)(2)(E) and 115, respectively). These provisions are worded very generally and contain no guidelines for determining the sources or effects of transported air pollutants.

Several States have attempted to use these provisions, either through petitions to EPA or litigation in Federal courts, to force other States to curb emissions. To date, few of these suits or petitions have been settled. Recent decisions by Federal courts suggest that they are not prepared to require EPA to give broader consideration to interstate pollution than it does now.

To make the Clean Air Act a more effective means of controlling interstate and international pollution transport, Congress could modify the act in several ways. The changes discussed below would be helpful for addressing many transported air pollution disputes, but would probably be of limited use for such geographically widespread problems as acid deposition.

Options

Option D-1: Amend requirements for considering interstate pollution under the Clean Air Act.

Section 110(a)(2)(E) of the Clean Air Act is a very general provision that offers little guidance on how much interstate pollution is permissible, whether the law applies to the individual sources or to the cumulative sources throughout a State, and how interstate effects are to be demonstrated. Congress could amend the section to clarify EPA responsibilities for assessing and regulating interstate pollution. In addition, Congress could modify procedures for review of interstate pollution petitions (contained in sec. 126 of the act) to allow States to move on to the judicial appeals process if EPA does not act on the petitions before it. Such action would help eliminate the current bottleneck of States' petitions within EPA. Again, such changes would probably not make the Clean Air Act more effective in dealing with *acid deposition,* as the section applies only to pollutants for which National Ambient Air Quality Standards exist. Such changes might, however, assist States seeking relief from transported air pollutants currently regulated under the Clean Air Act.

Option D-2: Amend the international provisions of the Clean Air Act.

Section 115 of the Clean Air Act was designed to address local pollution effects occurring across an international boundary. As with section 110(a)(2)(E), its lack of specificity makes it an unwieldy tool for controlling air pollutants transported over long distances. Congress could amend this section to make it a more effective means of controlling these pollutants, for example, by identifying an appropriate international agency (e.g., the International Joint Commission) or providing a mechanism to establish bilateral commissions to address such problems. Such mechanisms might assist efforts to settle future international air pollution disputes.

Chapter 2
The Policy Dilemma

Contents

FIGURE

The Policy Dilemma

Fossil fuels are vital to the U.S. economy's production of goods and services. However, burning these fuels also produces large quantities of pollutants—substances that, once released into the atmosphere, can damage natural resources, health, agricultural crops, manmade materials, and visibility. Consequently, our Nation's laws and policies must strike a balance between the economic benefits and the environmental risks of fossil fuel combustion and other pollution-producing activities.

This assessment focuses on one class of air pollutants: those that are transported over large regions, either in their original form or as chemically transformed products. Such pollutants include acid deposition, ozone, and airborne sulfate. The current Clean Air Act[1] was designed to ameliorate

[1]Clean Air Act Amendment of 1977, Public Law 95-95 (Aug. 7, 1977), as amended.

local-scale pollution problems, and does not directly control pollution transport across hundreds of miles.

Over the past several years, controlling pollutants that contribute to acid rain has become a major policy issue. The House Committee on Energy and Commerce and the Senate Committee on Environment and Public Works—the committees that oversee the Clean Air Act—requested OTA to assess what is known about transported air pollutants, including the benefits and costs of controlling them. OTA's assessment primarily addresses potential effects in the eastern half of the United States, focusing on the risks of damage to sensitive resources, the economic risks that arise from further controlling pollution emissions, and how these risks are distributed among different groups and regions of the country. Policy alternatives available to Congress are also presented.

THE POLLUTANTS ADDRESSED IN THIS STUDY

Acid deposition, ozone, and airborne sulfate are produced from three air pollutants: sulfur dioxide, nitrogen oxides, and hydrocarbons. Acid deposition, commonly referred to as "acid rain," involves a variety of pollutants deposited in both wet and dry forms; it results from sulfur and nitrogen oxide gases, sulfates and nitrates (transformation products of these gases), and from interactions with other chemicals in the atmosphere. Figure 10 illustrates the pathways these pollutants travel through the environment. Both *directly emitted or "primary"* pollutants and *transformed or "secondary"* pollutants contribute to acid deposition. Both can be of concern on the local scale as well as on a regional scale. A pollutant can be returned to the Earth's surface within an hour or travel in the atmosphere for longer than a week, depending on its chemical properties, and factors such as weather patterns and other pollutants present in the atmosphere.

Besides contributing to acid deposition, the secondary pollutants addressed in this study—sulfates, nitrates, and ozone—are of concern for other reasons. Regional visibility degradation is closely correlated with concentrations of airborne sulfate particles. Sulfate particles in the atmosphere are also small enough to be deeply inhaled, and are thus of concern for their effects on human health. Ozone—formed in the atmosphere from nitrogen oxides and hydrocarbons—is injurious to plant life and of concern to human health.

Secondary air pollutants have several factors in common:

1. they can form over periods ranging from hours to days and travel hundreds to possibly thousands of kilometers;
2. they cannot be controlled directly, but only by controlling the pollutants from which they

Figure 10.—Processes and Environmental Effects of Acid Deposition

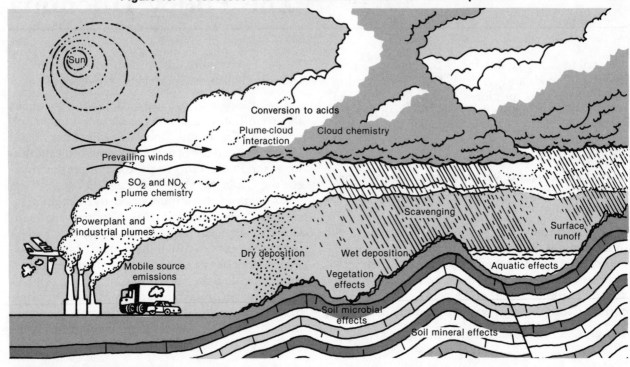

SOURCE: Adapted from *The Acid Precipitation Problem* (Corvallis, Oreg.: U.S. Environmental Protection Agency, Environmental Research Laboratory, 1976).

are formed (and possibly other pollutants that determine their rates of transformation);

3. different secondary pollutants result from the same primary pollutants—e.g., nitrogen oxides can react to form both nitrates and ozone; and

4. they manifest themselves in several ways—e.g., sulfate contributes both to acid deposition and to reductions in visibility.

WHY TRANSPORTED AIR POLLUTANTS ARE AN ISSUE

Public Concerns

Current evidence indicates that acid deposition has significant adverse effects on lakes and streams. Additionally, scientific concerns have been voiced over potentially significant effects on forests and soils, agricultural crops, manmade and natural materials, visibility, and human health. Recognizing this risk of damage, some individuals and groups have called on the Federal Government to control pollutant emissions more stringently than

current laws require. They cite large numbers of acidified lakes and streams, observed forest declines in polluted areas of Western Europe and Eastern North America, experiments showing crop damage, and deterioration of historic structures as evidence that air pollutants are causing widespread damage to important natural, economic, and cultural resources. Recommendations for additional emissions control have come, for example, from the National Commission on Air Quality, the National Governors' Association, the State and Territorial

Air Program Administrators, study groups of the National Academy of Sciences, and the 1982 Stockholm Conference on the Acidification of the Environment.

Others, pointing to uncertainties about the causes and consequences of transported pollutants, are concerned that further emissions controls may be mandated prematurely. They suggest that pollution transport processes, potential effects, and alternative mitigation strategies are poorly understood; thus, further controlling emissions now may waste money and impose unreasonable costs on industry and the public. Over the past several years, such concerns have been voiced by the U.S. Environmental Protection Agency (EPA), the Department of Energy, the Business Roundtable, and the U.S. Chamber of Commerce. Reducing total sulfur dioxide emissions by more than about 25 percent in the Eastern United States is estimated to cost in the billions of dollars annually. Efforts to control transported air pollutants through stringent sulfur dioxide emissions controls could increase electricity rates as well as displace mining jobs by reducing demand for high-sulfur coal.

Transported air pollutants also raise significant equity issues. Those served by the activities generating acid rain and ozone can be different from those who incur resource damage. Similarly, particular groups and regions might bear an unequal share of the costs of controlling transported air pollutants.

Why Transported Pollutants Are a Federal Concern

Transported air pollutants have become an issue for potential *Federal* action because they cross political boundaries. The current Federal system of pollution control relies on State-level abatement programs to limit pollution levels within individual States.* However, no effective means of control-

*National emissions limits for new sources of pollution (New Source Performance Standards) are in place to control future pollution emissions.

ling extensive pollution transport across State lines currently exists. Transported pollutants also cross the *international* boundary both into and from Canada. Article 1, Section 10 of the Constitution prohibits States from entering into agreements with foreign nations without the consent of Congress; thus, any pollution control agreements with Canada would require Federal action.**

Existing Federal air pollution control mechanisms are governed primarily by the Clean Air Act, which Congress is now considering for reauthorization. To date, control strategies developed under the Act have focused on controlling local ambient air concentrations. However, many observers have questioned the effectiveness of this approach for controlling transported air pollutants.

**The United States and Canada signed a Memorandum of Intent in August 1980, establishing a bilateral research plan to investigate transboundary air pollution and pledging work toward a bilateral accord on transboundary air pollution. Negotiations began on June 23, 1981, and are still in progress.

Photo credit: Canadian Government

Acid rain is a frequent topic of discussion among key environmental and diplomatic officials from the United States and Canada. From left to right: EPA Administrator, W. Ruckelshaus; Secretary of State, G. Schultz; American Ambassador, P. Robinson; Deputy Prime Minister, A. MacEachen; Canadian Ambassador, A. Gottlieb; and Minister of the Environment, C. Caccia

CHARACTERISTICS OF THE POLICY DEBATE

Several aspects of transported air pollutants have shaped the public policy debate over whether or not to further control pollutant emissions at this time. First, *scientific uncertainty* exists over the current severity and geographic extent of the damages attributable to transported air pollutants, as well as over the timeframe in which further damage might occur. Second, and of great political importance, transported air pollutants pose a *distributional problem,* having intersectoral, interregional, international, and intergenerational equity aspects. Third, significant *disagreements in values* exist over how to balance the costs of controlling pollutants and the environmental risks posed by pollution.

Disagreements Over Facts

Debate over scientific understanding of transported air pollutants is perhaps the most visible aspect of the policy controversy. Many assert that the causes and consequences of acid deposition are both sufficiently understood and significant to warrant immediate action to control it. Others emphasize the complexity of the phenomena involved, and argue that no regulatory strategy can be justified on the basis of existing scientific knowledge.

Scientific uncertainty is not new to air pollution policy. The continuing controversy over the nature and magnitude of health risks—the critical measure for setting local air quality standards—illustrates the difficulty of unambiguously documenting the scientific basis for regulation. Similarly, the extent to which transported air pollutants affect health, crops, visibility, materials, forests and soils, and lakes and streams is uncertain. Current inability to quantify these relationships precludes agreement as to whether the benefits of reducing pollutant levels would justify the costs involved in further controlling emissions.

Because some types of air pollutants can be transformed, dispersed, and transported over long distances, identifying the specific emission sources responsible for resource damage in a particular area is extremely difficult. Consequently, designing emission control policies for transported pollutants

becomes difficult both analytically and politically: analytically, because the sources that can most efficiently reduce deposition in the affected areas may not be readily identifiable; politically, because placing the burden of control on certain regions may appear to be arbitrary or inequitable.

Distributional Issues

The distributional aspects of transported air pollutants further complicate the policy dilemma. Pollution control, by affecting the relative prices of various products, benefits economic activities that are inherently less polluting, or that can reduce pollution less expensively, at the expense of more pollution-intensive goods and services. But the geographical scope of transported air pollutants creates several distributional issues not present in conventional, local air pollutant problems.

Within the United States, winds carry pollutants over long distances, so that activities in one region of the Nation may contribute to resource damage in other regions. Many of these activities primarily benefit the source region, while some of their costs, in terms of resource damage caused by their waste products, fall elsewhere. Long-range pollution transport thus redistributes benefits and costs among regions. Programs to control transported air pollutants would also have *interregional* distribution aspects. The costs of controlling emissions might be imposed primarily on source regions (depending on the scheme for allocating costs), while the major benefits of reducing emissions might accrue primarily to downwind, receptor regions.

Winds also carry pollutants over national borders, posing an *international* as well as an interregional distribution problem. About three to five times more pollution is transported from the United States to Canada than reaches this country from Canada.[2] The Canadian Government asserts that fossil fuel combustion in the United States is damag-

---

[2]United States-Canada Memorandum of Intent on Transboundary Air Pollution, Executive Summary, Work Group Reports, February 1983.

ing lakes and streams, and might damage forests, in Eastern Canada; consequently, Canada is paying some of the costs of U.S. economic activities. Federal and provincial Ministers of the Environment have pledged to reduce sulfur dioxide emissions by 50 percent in Eastern Canada by 1994 and urged the United States to undertake parallel emissions reductions. Distributional equity questions would still exist if the two nations undertake further control programs, in that the United States and Canada might benefit differentially from reduced transboundary pollution.

The *intergenerational* aspects of transported air pollutants raise yet another equity issue. Both the appearance of harmful effects and the recovery of damaged resources may lag behind changes in pollution levels. For instance, lake and stream acidification and forest damage may take on the order of decades to occur. Because acid deposition may diminish a watershed's ability to neutralize future acid inputs, *future* resource damages may depend on the total amount of deposition an area has already received. In addition, resources may require a relatively long period of time to recover following a reduction in the level of acidic inputs. If both the onset and amelioration of adverse effects involve extensive delays, the amount of acid deposition produced by one generation could affect the quality of ecological and other societal resources available to future generations.

Disagreements Over Values

Even if a scientific consensus existed on the magnitude of the problem of transported pollutants, policy choices would still be complicated by lack of agreement over how to promote economic development while protecting the environment. Although the concept of a tradeoff between these two values is widely accepted, various individuals and groups differ sharply on where the balance should be struck.

Disagreements over facts and values are intertwined. Differing value structures lead various individuals and groups to draw quite different conclusions from the same body of scientific information. Widespread recognition of scientific uncertainties has focused the policy debate on whether both the magnitude of damage involved and the effectiveness of control efforts are sufficiently known to pursue emissions reductions. This dispute involves both relatively objective issues of science, e.g., how reducing sulfur emissions might affect sulfur deposition in certain areas, and subjective issues of values, e.g., what level of scientific certainty and/or what degree of damage is required to justify undertaking a control program.

RISK AND UNCERTAINTY

Scientists can describe potential resource damage and regions of the United States most susceptible to damage from transported pollutants, but they cannot *precisely quantify* what levels of damage have already occurred or could occur in the future. Similarly, analysts can estimate the costs of alternative control strategies, and who might bear these costs, but how *effective* these control strategies would be for avoiding resource damage cannot be calculated with confidence. Given the difficulty of quantifying the relationship between reducing emissions and preventing resource damage, **Congress must base near-term policy decisions on the risks of resource damage, the risks of unwarranted** **control expenditures, and the distribution of these risks among different groups and regions of the country.**

Risk, in the sense used in this report, refers to some possible, harmful outcome—either resource damage or excessive control costs. Three concepts are important:

1. a potential for harm exists;
2. there is some uncertainty about whether the harm will actually come to pass; and
3. if it does, there is uncertainty about how extensive it will be.

Throughout this report, OTA describes the risks of controlling or not controlling transported air pollutants, emphasizing those risks with potentially significant consequences for society. To put this information in perspective, wherever possible, we have tried to describe the uncertainty in estimates of the *magnitude and extent* of the potential harm, as well as how likely such harm is to occur.

Assessments of risk such as those presented in chapter 3, and the regional descriptions presented in chapter 5, focus on *potential* consequences, not necessarily the consequences that will, in fact, occur. Uncertainty—stemming from limitations in data and understanding—precludes drawing definitive scientific conclusions. **Nonetheless, uncertainty does not remove the risks to which society is actually subjected, although it makes these risks substantially more difficult to describe.** Five key uncertainties, chosen for their relevance to the policy debate, are presented below.

KEY SCIENTIFIC UNCERTAINTIES

Later chapters of this report will describe what is at stake in decisions to control or not to control transported air pollutants. This chapter outlines key uncertainties to provide an overview of current debates within the technical and scientific community. Each of these uncertainties will also be discussed throughout the report as appropriate to the issue being addressed.

Five key uncertainties are especially relevant to congressional decisions about transported air pollutants. These include controversies about:

1. the extent and location of current damages,
2. future damages (whether they are cumulative and/or irreversible),
3. the geographic origins of observed levels of pollution,
4. the effectiveness of emissions reductions for reducing current levels of transported pollutants, and
5. whether a research program will provide significant new results.

These scientific uncertainties affect several policy concerns, including:

- making air pollution control policy as fair as possible, i.e., providing some legal recourse to those bearing the risks of damage, and (if a control program is adopted) distributing costs of control fairly;
- minimizing cumulative and irreversible damage, and their intergenerational implications;
- weighing the risk of damage against gains that might be achieved by waiting for better information or improved technology; and
- assuring that the societal benefits of a control program justify the cost.

Uncertainty About the Extent and Location of Current Damages

Scientists are certain that transported air pollutants have caused *some* damages. At issue is the severity of the damage, whether it is fairly localized or widespread, and which resources are affected. For example, there is little question that acid deposition damages lakes, and ozone harms crops. The uncertainties revolve around *how many* lakes and streams and *what quantity* of crops. For these and other resources, the *risks* of extensive damage over large parts of the United States are substantial. Chapter 3 summarizes the aggregate risks in the Eastern United States for a number of affected resources; chapter 5 describes the regional *patterns* of these risks using an extensive series of maps. Appendixes discuss each resource of concern in greater detail.

For certain concerns, such as the extent of damage to forests from acid deposition, the uncertainties are so large that it is difficult to describe the patterns or magnitude of the risk. Damage to forests from ozone, and the effects of toxic metals released into drinking water due to acid deposition, also fall into this category. The report also discusses these types of risks, presenting geographical patterns where possible.

Uncertainty About Future Damages

Growing scientific recognition that transported pollutants are linked to observed damages intensifies concern over the potential for future damage, even if current damages are not extensive. Of particular importance is the extent to which damages are *cumulative* and/or *irreversible*.

The Extent to Which Damages Are Cumulative

For some resources, pollution-related damages might *worsen* over time if pollution remains at about current levels. For short-lived species, such as crops harvested annually, this is not a relevant concern. Damage to this year's crops from ozone— and potentially from acid deposition—is caused only by current levels of pollution. However, for longer lived species such as trees, *cumulative* damage is of concern. Ozone injury and potential acid deposition-related damage to forests may be small in any one year, but continued stress over many years could ultimately reduce productivity.

The portion of *current* aquatic resource damage attributable to the cumulative effects of deposition over many years is also uncertain. One major unknown is the degree to which years of exposure to acid deposition deplete the neutralizing capability of soils in the surrounding watersheds.

The extent to which damages accumulate—and over what time scale—has played a major role in the policy debate over the risks of delaying control action. If damages are not significantly cumulative, delaying control action while awaiting further information would not increase the level of damage

Photo credit: New England Interstate Water Pollution Control Commission

Much of the acid deposition that eventually enters a lake or stream first reaches the ground in the surrounding watershed, and travels with runoff water over soils and bedrock

from year to year (assuming that the level of pollution remains fairly constant). However, for those effects of transported pollutants that are cumulative, the longer control actions are delayed, the greater the severity of the damage.

The Extent to Which Damages Are Irreversible

A closely coupled concern is whether damage can easily be reversed, and if so, over what time period? Again, once ozone concentrations are reduced below damaging levels, direct crop damage is easily eliminated the following year. At the other extreme, damage to monuments or other unique art objects from air pollution would be irreversible.

If acid deposition is reduced, fish populations may be restored either by restocking or by natural means. However, if surrounding soils have lost their

Photo credit: New England Interstate Water Pollution Control Commission

Acid deposition might harm trees directly or alter the soils in which they grow. However, more research is necessary to determine to what extent current levels of acid deposition and other transported pollutants are involved in observed declines in Eastern U.S. forest productivity

acid-neutralizing capability, even moderate inputs of acid may prevent fish from returning for decades unless the water body is periodically treated with lime. Similarly, if acid deposition causes nutrients to be lost from a forest floor, forest productivity may be impaired for many decades. The effects of a severe series of ozone episodes, or the potential cumulative effects of acid deposition, will persist in the forest community until a new forest grows.

The potential irreversibility of resource damage makes delaying control action until better information is obtained highly controversial. For those damages that are reversible, it is important to know how alternative levels of pollution reduction would affect the extent of resource improvement. Chapters 3 and 5 present estimates of the benefit to crops and aquatic resources of reducing ozone and acid deposition levels, although considerable uncertainty surrounds these preliminary estimates. However, to the extent that damages are *both* significantly cumulative and irreversible, waiting for better information would irreparably harm resources for this generation and the next several to follow.

Uncertainty About the Origin of Observed Levels of Transported Pollutants

Pollutants Leading to Acid Deposition

The previous sections have outlined uncertainties concerning the potential benefits of reducing current levels of transported pollutants. If policymakers wish to reduce current levels of pollutants, the next logical question is, "Where are they coming from?" Three questions are important: 1) whether the precursor pollutants are of natural or manmade origin; 2) whether they come from local sources or from distances exceeding hundreds of kilometers; and 3) whether it is possible to define the geographic origin of pollutants deposited in a particular region. These questions are addressed briefly in chapter 4, and in greater detail in appendix C.

The first two questions are *not* key uncertainties. Though pollutants of natural origin cause some acid deposition, deposition over large areas of the Eastern United States far exceeds the level attributable to natural sources of pollutants. In addition, while local sources (i.e., within 30 miles) do contribute to acid deposition, most analyses indicate that a large share of the deposition—in some cases, over half—originates from both medium-range and distant sources (i.e., greater than 300 miles away) as well.

The key uncertainty is whether scientists can reliably determine *how much* of the deposition in any one region originates from emissions in any other. Computer models of varying sophistication are available to perform such analyses, but their accuracy in portraying this relationship is uncertain. **The inherent variability of weather patterns and the complexity of atmospheric chemistry make it unlikely that models will *ever* be able to predict how much one individual source of emissions contributes to deposition in a small area.** However, these models can be used to assess current *annual average* patterns of pollutant transport over *large* geographic regions—on this scale, models reproduce observed patterns of annual sulfur deposition in rainfall reasonably well. Their capacity to synthesize extensive meteorological data makes these models the best available tools for describing the current relationship between emissions in one area and deposition in another. Model-based estimates of the extent of interregional transport for sulfur pollution are presented in chapter 4.

Model adequacy is a critical element in several suits and petitions by States to control transported air pollutants under the interstate provisions of the current Clean Air Act. EPA considers available models inadequate to reliably analyze long-range pollution transport; consequently, the Agency does not assess the effects of pollution that travels beyond 50 kilometers (30 miles). However, the petitioning States assert that available "long-range transport" models reflect the state of the art and should therefore be used by EPA.

In addition, policy-level attempts to reduce pollutant deposition *in identified, sensitive regions* would rely to a large extent on model-based abilities to determine the sources of such deposition. However, no amount of accurate, detailed modeling information would be sufficient to eliminate policy disputes over which region's resources *should* be protected, or which region's emissions *should* be controlled.

Photo credit: Ted Spiegel

Tracking this weather balloon by radar helps to determine how air masses travel and mix under a variety of atmospheric conditions. Such data are important for understanding how pollutants are transported and transformed when they are aloft

Because many regions have sensitive resources, and all of them receive some deposition from each of many emitting regions, a variety of possible strategies could be used to reduce deposition on sensitive resources. For example, decisionmakers, in response to equity concerns, could develop control programs under which multi-state regions responsible for "large" shares of deposition in "several" sensitive areas bear the "greatest share" of emissions reductions. Whether the broad regional patterns of transport described by the models are accurate enough for this purpose is as much a policy question as a scientific one.

Pollutants Leading to Ozone Formation

The same three questions apply to ozone: whether the precursor pollutants are of natural or manmade origin, whether they are of local or distant origin, and whether it is possible to pinpoint the geographic source of deposition in a specified region. As with acid deposition, ozone levels over broad regions of the United States exceed natural background levels. Though locally produced ozone is a problem in many of the Nation's urban areas, ozone's chemical precursors can travel long distances, and elevated ozone levels are found in rural areas downwind from emission sources. However, models of long-range ozone transport are in a rudimentary stage of development. Because the chemistry of ozone formation is very complex, major uncertainties exist over the geographic origin of elevated ozone concentrations in rural areas.

Uncertainty About the Effectiveness of Emissions Reductions for Reducing Levels of Transported Pollutants at Desired Locations

Uncertainty about the *effectiveness* of reducing emissions as a means of controlling transported pollutants stems from two factors. The first—uncertainty about how well current models describe the relative contribution of one area's emissions to another's pollution—has been explained in the previous section. While this "source-receptor" relationship cannot be defined precisely, existing models can synthesize extensive meteorological information to provide broad regional descriptions. Still, the remaining uncertainty raises questions about the extent to which emissions reductions in any specific area would reduce pollution in another area.

The second unknown concerns the chemical processes that transform pollutants in the atmosphere. It is known that numerous complex chemical reactions are involved in forming ozone, airborne sulfates, and acid deposition. Uncertainties exist about how effective reducing emissions of each precursor pollutant will be in controlling the transformed products.

For example, sulfur dioxide emissions are transformed to sulfate, a major constituent of acid deposition. Reducing the total amount of sulfur dioxide emitted will undoubtedly reduce the overall amount of deposited sulfate, but it is difficult to quantify the reduction in deposition that a specific emissions cutback will produce *in a specific area.* **Most analyses indicate that reducing sulfur dioxide emissions within a broad control region will significantly, but not quite equally, reduce the amount of sulfur deposited in various forms in that region.** However, some scientists are uncertain that reducing sulfur dioxide emissions *alone* is the most efficient way to control acid deposition. Because other pollutants (e.g., hydrocarbons and nitrogen oxides) can enhance or impede chemical transformations of sulfur dioxide, these other pollutants might also be controlled simultaneously to reduce acid deposition in specific geographic regions. Chapter 4 and appendix C discuss this in greater detail.

Uncertainties about which pollutants to control, as well as the uncertain relationship between emissions reductions and deposition reductions, complicate the policy objective of reaping the greatest possible benefit from the costs of controlling emissions. Scientists are unable to confidently project the precise pattern of deposition reductions that would result from a specified emissions control plan. Under these circumstances, a control program designed and implemented today might not produce the maximum benefits achievable for a given cost.

Uncertainty About Whether a Research Program Will Provide Significant New Information

One of the most difficult decisions facing Congress is whether to act during this reauthorization of the Clean Air Act, or to await results from ongoing, multimillion dollar Federal and private research efforts on acid deposition. While the research efforts are intended to reduce the uncertainty discussed above, how much new insight 4 to 6 years of further research will provide is unknown.

For example, years to decades are required to observe changes in many ecological processes. Patterns of crop yield and forest productivity typically vary from year to year; separating the effect of acid deposition from normally expected year-to-year fluctuations requires many years of data. The processes of soil formation and depletion proceed on the time scale of decades. These mechanisms

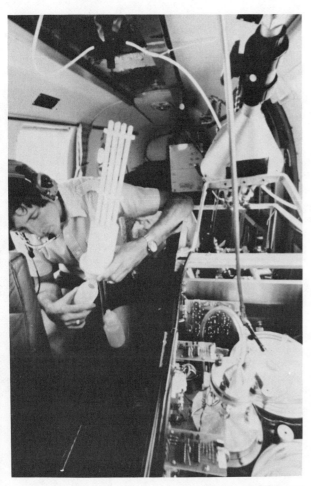

Photo credit: Ted Spiegel

Collecting and testing water droplets from clouds high above the ground in southern Ohio. Researchers also use this airborne laboratory to analyze gaseous and particulate pollutants in the atmosphere

can be artificially accelerated and studied in laboratories, but the extent to which such experiments reflect real-world conditions is uncertain.

While scientists understand the basic mechanisms of acid formation and deposition, detailed knowledge of the complex chemistry and meteorology involved will require many more years of research. Ongoing efforts to evaluate the current generation of computer models that simulate atmospheric processes have already taken several years. Efforts to develop new transport and transformation models are underway; the number of years needed to significantly improve existing models is unknown.

Uncertainties about the progress of research programs are important in considering the timetable for policy decisions. Given the planning and construction efforts required to significantly reduce pollutant emissions, a decision to control emissions now may still require 6 to 10 or more years to implement. **Waiting another 4 to 6 years for the results of a research program before making control decisions increases the time required to reduce deposition to 10 to 16 years. Delaying control action increases the risk of resource damage but reduces the risk of inefficient control expenditures.** Congress could avoid this delay by mandating controls now, while retaining the option to change the law if new research results point to alternative courses of action. To achieve compliance within a decade, however, expenditures would have to begin within 6 to 8 years. If results suggesting an alternative control strategy appear much after this time, major expenditures may be irrevocable.

Chapter 3
Transported Air Pollutants: The Risks of Damage and the Risks of Control

Contents

Transported Air Pollutants: The Risks of Damage and the Risks of Control

As discussed previously, the risks of transported air pollutants are amenable only to qualitative descriptions. Certain aspects can be described numerically—for example, the numbers of lakes and streams currently altered by acid deposition, or people exposed to health risks from airborne sulfates and other small particles. Wherever possible, this report also presents numerical estimates of the risks to a region's resources, industry, jobs, and consumer pocketbooks. However, the substantial uncertainties associated with available data and theory mean that these numerical descriptions should be viewed as qualitative estimates, rather than exact, quantitative answers. One should not be misled by the apparent precision of the numbers. The information presented is intended to convey approximate outcomes—in some cases with unknown margins of error—and broad regional patterns.

This chapter summarizes the OTA estimates of risk to the Eastern United States as a whole. OTA-sponsored or in-house work provides the basis for most of these estimates. Chapter 5 will examine who bears these risks, by State and by economic sector. These chapters use the somewhat artificial dichotomy of *mandating further emissions reductions* vs. *maintaining the status quo* as a framework for describing potential consequences. Chapters 6 and 7 of this report present congressional options, including interim decisions, in greater detail.

NO CONGRESSIONAL ACTION

Resources at Risk

Two factors determine the potential for resource damage from transported air pollutants: 1) the *amount* of pollution to which the resource is exposed, and 2) the *sensitivity* of resources to acid deposition and ozone. Resource sensitivity varies from resource to resource—and among the specific plants, animals, soils, and materials within each resource category. Some resources are *directly affected* by the pollution received. For example, crops are affected by exposure to ozone, and some building materials are affected by acid-producing substances deposited on their surfaces.

For other resources, sensitivity also depends on characteristics of the local environment. For example, lakes and streams are affected primarily by the amount of acid-producing substances that eventually travels through the watersheds to lakes and streams, as well as by the acid deposition that falls directly onto the surface of the water. The acid-neutralizing capabilities of the soil and bedrock in the surrounding watershed help determine the susceptibility of water bodies to acid deposition. Acid deposition may affect forests through subtle soil chemical changes—here again, the sensitivity of the forest resource could largely depend on soil characteristics.

Aquatic Ecosystems[1]

More is known about how acid deposition affects aquatic ecosystems—and the current extent of these effects—than for any other resource. Substantial evidence indicates that acid deposition alters water chemistry in sensitive lakes and streams. Most vulnerable are small lakes and streams in watersheds that have little capability to neutralize acid, due either to the chemical composition and/or thinness of the soils, or to terrain that is so steep or rocky

---

[1]This section is based primarily on material from: The Institute of Ecology, "Regional Assessment of Aquatic Resources at Risk From Acid Deposition," contractor report submitted to the Office of Technology Assessment, 1982.

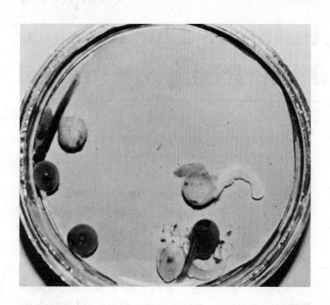 

Photo credit: Lars Overrein

Highly acidified waters, and water chemistry changes caused by acidity, may prevent fish from developing. In the experiment illustrated above. Brown trout eggs were placed simultaneously in waters of differing acidity. The embryos shown at left failed to develop in acidic water (pH 4.6). The fry at right were raised in less acid water (pH 5.5) and appear normal

that rainfall runs over it before acid can be neutralized.

Fish are sensitive both to the acidity of water, and to toxic metals—primarily aluminum—that are released from the watershed under acid conditions. When waters become more acid than pH 5, many fish species are eliminated and major changes in lake ecosystem processes frequently occur. High acidity, toxic concentrations of metals such as aluminum, or some combination of the two appear to cause these changes.

Based on the predominant soil and geological characteristics in each county, OTA classifies about 25 percent of the land area of the Eastern 31-State region as "sensitive," i.e., allowing the transport of acidity through a watershed to lakes and streams. Within these identified sensitive regions are approximately 17,000 lakes and 112,000 miles of streams —these figures provide an upper bound of the aquatic resources at risk. Only a portion of the total number of lakes and streams in the sensitive regions should currently be considered vulnerable to acid

inputs. Small lakes and stream segments are, in general, most susceptible to change. While some areas have geologic characteristics that make them sensitive to acidification, they may not receive enough acid deposition to alter the water quality of lakes and streams. In addition, local variations in geology, soil conditions, and topography affect the land's ability to prevent acidification of water bodies.

OTA used available water quality data from about 800 lakes and 400 streams throughout eight States in the Eastern half of the United States to estimate the number of lakes and streams currently vulnerable to acid deposition. OTA estimates that about 9,500 lakes and 60,000 miles of streams currently have limited acid neutralizing capabilities such that, given sufficient acid deposition, they might acidify—a "best guess" encompassing about half the upper-bound estimate presented earlier.

OTA also used available water quality data, correcting for a percentage of lakes and streams that may be naturally acidic, to estimate that about

3,000 lakes and 23,000 miles of streams have already become acidified, or have so little acid-neutralizing capability left that they are extremely vulnerable to further acid deposition. This corresponds to about 20 percent of the lakes and streams found in identified sensitive areas.

Of the approximately 50,000 lakes in Eastern Canada, the Ontario Ministry of the Environment estimates that about 20 percent, or 10,000, are currently acid-altered.*

Scientists cannot yet estimate how many more lakes and streams could become acidified if current levels of acid deposition continue into the future. Two cumulative processes are important: 1) the potential loss of the soil's ability to neutralize acid inputs, and 2) for lakes, the accumulation of acidifying substances over years to decades, until lake waters come into equilibrium with the level of deposition received from the watershed. The latter process delays lake response to acid deposition, with greater time delays in larger lakes and lakes with slow rates of water replacement.

Many smaller acid-altered lakes and streams in the Northeast are probably in equilibrium with present deposition levels. By assuming that continued acid deposition will not further degrade the soil's neutralizing capability—the "best-case" situation—one can estimate improvements in water quality that reduced levels of acid deposition might produce. OTA used a simple, theoretical model to project how future changes in acid deposition levels might change the numbers of acid-altered lakes and streams in the Eastern United States. If sulfate deposition were decreased by 20 percent, OTA estimates that 10 to 25 percent of these water bodies might show improvement. If sulfate deposition were reduced by 30 percent, about 15 to 40 percent might show improvement. If sulfate deposition were increased by 10 percent, OTA estimates that acid-alteration of lakes and streams might intensify by about 5 to 15 percent.

Again, these are best-case estimates, assuming that the effects of acid deposition are not cumulative. However, in those areas that are not in

equilibrium with above-normal deposition levels, some lakes and streams might still continue to acidify slowly despite the reduction levels discussed above. Such effects might be most pronounced in the Southeast and upper Midwest.

Terrestrial Ecosystems[2]

A variety of transported air pollutants affects both croplands and forested ecosystems. Ozone, a gaseous pollutant toxic to plants, may account for up to 90 percent of air pollution-related damage to crops. How much crop damage is due to transported rather than locally produced ozone is uncertain. Observed effects include both damage to the quality of crops (e.g., leaf spotting) and reductions in crop yield.

Damage to crops from acid deposition under *natural* conditions has not yet been observed, although experiments using simulated acid rain have shown reduced yields and altered crop quality. Since the chemistry of agricultural soils is already highly controlled with fertilizers and other chemicals, the primary effects of acid deposition would likely be on the above-ground portions of plants. The role of pollutant *mixes* may also be significant, since acid deposition seldom occurs in the absence of other pollutants. In some cases, it appears that the presence of sulfur or nitrogen oxides in the atmosphere makes crops more susceptible to ozone damage.

To assess the risks to crops from transported air pollutants, OTA has estimated the benefits that might result from reducing *ozone* concentrations to natural "background" levels. Similar estimates of the effects of acid deposition on crops, or of the effects of pollutant mixes, are not yet possible.

Data from field experiments were used to estimate ozone effects on crop productivity for peanuts (a sensitive crop), soybeans (sensitive/intermediate), wheat (intermediate), and corn (tolerant). These "dose-response" relationships were then combined with 1978 ozone monitoring data and 1978 agricultural statistics. Results suggest that if ozone con-

---

*U.S.-Canada Memorandum of Intent on Transboundary Air Pollution, Impact Assessment, Work Group 1, February 1983.

[2]This section is based primarily on material from: Oak Ridge National Laboratory, Environmental Sciences Division, "An Analysis of Potential Agriculture and Forest Impacts of Long-Range Transport Air Pollutants," contractor report submitted to the Office of Technology Assessment, 1982.

Photo credit: Ted Spiegel

Technicians at Oregon State University move a plastic cage that provides a controlled environment for spraying crops with simulated acid rain. Results from such experiments can help scientists understand if, and how, acid rain affects crops

centrations had been reduced to natural, background levels in 1978, corn yields would have increased by 2 percent, wheat by 5 percent, soybeans by 13 percent, and peanuts by 24 percent. As measured by 1978 crop prices, ozone caused about a 6- to 7-percent loss of agricultural productivity, of which almost two-thirds stemmed from soybean losses.

In forest ecosystems, transported pollutants may directly damage trees, as well as affect the soils in which trees grow. Because trees are long-lived species, they are vulnerable to long-term chronic effects. Scientists have documented ozone damage to the foliage of many tree species, but the concentrations of ozone necessary to cause damage is not well known. About one-quarter to one-third of the forested land area in the Eastern United States is exposed to ozone concentrations about twice the natural background levels.

Concern over the effects of acid deposition and ozone on forests stems from observed productivity declines and tree death in areas with elevated pollution levels. Pests or disease—common causes of forest declines—do not appear to be responsible for damage in such areas as the Adirondack Mountains in New York, the White Mountains in Vermont, the Pine Barrens in New Jersey, the Shenandoah Mountains in Virginia, the Smoky Mountains in Tennessee, and forested areas of West Germany. Acid deposition, ozone, heavy-metal deposition, severe winters, drought, or a combination of these are possible causes under investigation. Acid deposition might be a factor either by affecting trees directly or by altering the soils on which trees grow.

Acid deposition can remove essential nutrients such as calcium and magnesium *directly* from tree foliage. If the rate of nutrient loss is greater than can be replaced through the roots, nutrient defi-

Photo credit: Arthur Johnson

Dead and dying red spruce at Camel's Hump in the Green Mountains of Vermont. Tree death and growth decline of red spruce in Northeastern forests have led some researchers to speculate about potential links between forest damage and acid deposition. Scientific investigations cannot yet confirm or rule out acid deposition as a contributor to the observed damages

ciency will result. Scientists do not know which tree species are most susceptible to foliar nutrient loss, or the level of acid deposition at which such loss becomes harmful.

Forest soils may be altered by acid deposition with either beneficial or harmful results. The nitrates and sulfates from acid deposition can supply essential plant nutrients. In many areas, nitrogen in the soil is in short supply; on these soils nitrates in acid rain might improve forest productivity. Sulfur-deficient soils, however, are quite rare.

Nonacidic or weakly acidic soils typically contain such large quantities of neutralizing substances (e.g., calcium) that harmful changes to these soils seem unlikely. Of greatest concern are forest ecosystems with naturally acidic soils. The major soil-mediated risks from acid deposition include:

1. mobilization of metals such as aluminum that are toxic to plants in sufficient quantity, and
2. the potential stripping of calcium, magnesium, and other nutrients essential for plant growth from the soil.

Naturally acidic soils occur fairly extensively, being the predominant soil type in about half the counties east of the Rocky Mountains covered by forest or rangeland. In about one-third of these acidic soils, the strong, freely moving acids from acid deposition can release aluminum and other toxic metals from the soil. However, whether toxic metals are released in sufficient quantities to affect forest productivity is unknown. The remaining two-thirds of Eastern acidic soils are underlain with surface layers that can trap sulfate, possibly preventing the release of aluminum in these areas.

Acid deposition can remove essential nutrients such as calcium and magnesium from the soil, but the *rate* of removal—and the importance relative to other factors—is difficult to determine. Moderately acid soils are thought to lose nutrients at a faster rate than more acid soils, but the more acid soils typically have less nutrients. On nutrient-poor acid soils, especially those where sulfate can travel freely through the soil, further nutrient loss—even at a slow rate—from the soil, forest canopy, and decomposing plant material might be significant. About 15 to 20 percent of the Eastern counties meet these criteria, but whether nutrient loss is significant enough to affect near-term forest productivity is unknown.

Though relatively rare in the Eastern United States, some moderately acid soils might further acidify from nutrient loss over decades of exposure to acid deposition. About 1 to 5 percent of the Eastern counties (depending on the soil criteria used) are dominated by soils of this type.

Data and knowledge limitations prevent a more detailed description of the risks of transported air pollutants to forests than given above. Of concern are forested lands exposed to: 1) high ozone concentrations, 2) high levels of acid deposition, or 3) underlain with soils that may be sensitive to acid deposition.

Other Resources

Air pollution damages a broad range of materials—including building stone, rubber, zinc, steel, and paint. Ozone is the pollutant that most affects rubber, while many other materials are chiefly affected by sulfur oxides. Humidity plays a key role in materials damage—dry-deposited sulfur dioxide and sulfate that dissolve on moist surfaces (forming concentrated sulfuric acid) may cause greater damage than relatively less acidic rain. Since air pollution is only one of many environmental factors (e.g., temperature fluctuations, sunlight, salt, micro-organisms) that cause materials damage, it is difficult to determine what proportion of damage it accounts for. Moreover, it is difficult to determine the proportion of materials damage caused by transported pollutants as opposed to local pollution sources.

Analyses of the monetary costs of materials damage frequently make assumptions about the quantity of sensitive materials exposed to elevated pollution levels and the effects of damage on replacement or repair rates. A recent EPA-funded study employed an alternative approach, using data on expenditures in 24 metropolitan areas and 6 manufacturing sectors to estimate the extra materials-related costs attributable to sulfur pollution.[3] It concluded that reducing sulfur dioxide emissions in urban areas to meet concentrations about 25 to 30 percent below the national primary standard would create benefits of approximately $300 million annually for about one-half the households and about 5 to 10 percent of the producing sector in the United States. These results cannot be extrapolated to provide estimates of benefits to the Nation overall, as the lack of necessary data precludes analyzing the rest of the economy in this manner.

Photo credit: Ted Spiegel

Statues in a Kentucky cemetery illustrate one of the difficulties in assessing pollution-related damages to materials. Acidic pollutants and natural weathering have helped erode both the covered and uncovered marble statues shown above. However, rainfall also washes away some of the dry-deposited pollutants from the uncovered statue at right

Yet another resource at risk from transported air pollutants is visibility.[4] Visibility levels depend on a number of factors, including humidity, manmade pollutant emissions, and such other factors as fog, dust, sea spray, volcanic emissions, and forest fires.

Pollutants impair visibility by scattering and absorbing light. Concentrations of fine particles—primarily sulfates and nitrates—can sufficiently inter-

[3]E. H. Manuel, Jr., et al., "Benefits Analysis of Alternative Secondary National Ambient Air Quality Standards for Sulfur Dioxide and Total Suspended Particulates," Mathtech, Inc., report submitted to the U.S. Environmental Protection Agency, OAQPS, 1982.

[4]This subsection is based primarily on: B. L. Niemann, "Review of the Long-Range Transport of Sulfate Contribution to Regional Visibility Impairment," contractor report submitted to the Office of Technology Assessment, 1983.

fere with the transmission of light to reduce visibility levels significantly. Elevated levels of these and other particles in the atmosphere periodically create regional haze conditions, reducing contrast, distorting nearby objects and causing distant ones to disappear, discoloring the atmosphere, and decreasing the number of stars visible in the night sky. Examination of airport data, pollution measurements, and satellite photography also indicates that regional-scale hazy air masses move across large geographic areas, and cause significant visibility reduction in areas with little or no air pollutant emissions. Episodic haze conditions during summer currently make it the worst season for visibility.

Sulfate concentrations correlate well with visibility impairment over large regions of the United States; in the East, sulfate appears to be the single most important contributor to visibility degradation. Recent studies suggest that sulfates account for 70 percent of visibility impairment during the summer, and 50 percent annually, in the Eastern United States. Nitrates rarely contribute substantially to visibility degradation in the East. However, in the Western United States, windblown dust and nitrogen oxides can also reduce visibility significantly.

Risks of Health Effects[5]

Extremely small particles, including airborne sulfates, are the component of transported air pollutants of greatest concern for human health. These small particles can travel long distances through the atmosphere and penetrate deeply into the lung if inhaled. Statistical (cross-sectional) studies of death rates throughout the United States have found some correlation between elevated mortality levels and elevated ambient sulfate levels. Whether sulfate is actually linked to premature mortality, or merely indicates other harmful agents (e.g., other particulates) associated with sulfates, is unknown.

To estimate damages caused by transported air pollution quantitatively, OTA used sulfate concentrations as an *index* of this "sulfate/particulate mix." The analysis projected a *range* of mortality

Photo credit: John Skelly

View of the Peaks of Otter in the Shenandoah National Park under different visibility conditions. The picture at top was taken on a relatively pollution-free day; the picture on the bottom shows the same scene when a regional-scale hazy air mass obscures the view

estimates for a given population exposure level, in order to incorporate disagreements within the scientific community over the significance of sulfates to human health. While some researchers conclude there is a negligible effect, others have found a significant association, ranging up to 5 percent of the deaths per year in the United States and Canada attributed to current airborne sulfate/particulate pollution. Though further research and data are needed to resolve this controversy, this pollutant mix could be responsible for about 50,000 premature deaths per year (about 2 percent of annual mortality), particularly among people with preexisting respiratory or cardiac problems. If pollutant emissions remained the same through the year 2000, increases in population might cause slightly higher numbers of premature deaths; a 30-percent decrease in emission levels by 2000 might reduce the percentage of deaths annually attributable to air pollution to 1.6 percent (40,000 persons). In each of these cases, ranges of mortality are estimated to extend from zero deaths to about three times the number reported above.

[5]This section is based primarily on: Brookhaven National Laboratory, Biomedical and Environmental Assessment Division, "Long-Range Transport Air Pollution Health Effects," contractor report submitted to the Office of Technology Assessment, 1982.

Researchers have not found consistent associations between health effects and outdoor concentrations of nitrogen oxides. High localized concentrations of nitrogen dioxide are considered greater cause for concern than ambient levels of transformed and transported nitrogen oxide pollutants. However, quantitative estimates of health-related damages due to nitrogen oxides, or of the populations at risk from these pollutants, cannot yet be developed.

Acidified waters can dissolve such metals as aluminum, copper, lead, and mercury, and release such toxic substances as asbestos, from pipes and conduits in drinking water distribution systems as well as from soils and rocks in watersheds. Water samples from some areas receiving high levels of acid deposition show elevated metal concentrations, raising concern about a possible connection between acid deposition and degradation of drinking water quality. Drinking water samples in the Adirondacks have shown lead concentrations of up to 100 times health-based water quality standards. Mercury concentrations above public health standards have been found in fish from acidified lakes in Minnesota, Wisconsin, and New York. Elevated levels of aluminum and copper, two metals not considered toxic to the general public, have also been found both in Adirondack well water and in surface water samples throughout New England. Acidified municipal water supplies can be monitored and corrected quite easily. However, acidified well water in rural areas is more difficult to detect and mitigate. Potential health effects due to acidification of these water supplies and subsequent leaching of toxic substances remain of concern.

Potential for the Courts or EPA To Rule in the Absence of Congressional Direction[6]

The existing Clean Air Act does not directly address long-range pollution transport; however, provisions added to the Act during a previous reauthorization (1977) require States and EPA to ensure that stationary sources of pollution in any given State do not prevent attainment of air quality standards in another State. These provisions are worded very generally; the act contains no procedures or guidelines for determining how interstate pollution effects are to be measured, or what levels of interstate transport are impermissible.

A number of States have sought to use these interstate pollution provisions as a vehicle for compelling other States to curb emissions of transported pollutants. These States have challenged EPA-approved pollution control plans in court, and have petitioned EPA to require reductions in cumulative emissions from upwind States in order to abate present levels of interstate pollution. EPA has made no determinations on petitions requesting relief from long-range pollution effects; however, in legal proceedings the Agency has taken the position that no reliable analytic tools are currently available to assess long-range pollution transport. Affected parties are likely to challenge any future EPA determination on these petitions in court; thus, in the absence of further congressional action, the judicial branch could ultimately be required to arbitrate the long-range transport controversy.

Risk of Strained International Relations[7]

Present Federal policies on transported pollutants have also strained relations between the United States and Canada. Bilateral efforts are proceeding under a Memorandum of Intent (MOI) to develop an accord on the acid deposition issue. However, the Canadian Government has not been pleased by the progress of these negotiations. A dissatisfied Canada could choose to link the acid rain issue to other important areas of bilateral concern. The Clean Air Act currently provides Canada no explicit means of legal recourse for abating long-range transported air pollution from the United States. However, the previous administration took actions under the international provision of the Clean Air Act that may have created a legal obligation for this country to reduce emissions.

---

[6]This section is based primarily on material from: "Avenues for Controlling Interstate Pollution Under the Current Clean Air Act," the Office of Technology Assessment staff paper, 1982.

[7]This section is based primarily on material from: Environmental Law Institute, "Long-Range Air Pollution Across National Boundaries: Recourses in Law and Policy," contractor report submitted to the Office of Technology Assessment, 1981.

IF FURTHER EMISSIONS REDUCTIONS ARE MANDATED

Of the major transported pollutants, congressional attention has focused on controlling acid deposition. Acid deposition results from both sulfur and nitrogen oxides; however, in the Eastern United States, sulfur oxides currently contribute about twice as much acidity as nitrogen oxides. Several bills proposed during the 97th and 98th Congresses would mandate reducing sulfur dioxide emissions by about one-third to one-half either throughout the continental United States or in the 31 States bordering and east of the Mississippi River.

Of the 26 to 27 million tons of sulfur dioxide emitted in the United States during 1980, about 22 million tons were emitted in the Eastern 31 States. Electric utilities emitted about 70 to 75 percent of the total eastern, approximately 16 million tons. Non-utility combustion (primarily industrial boilers) accounted for about 10 to 15 percent of the total, with the remainder coming from industrial processes and other sources. Each of three States—Ohio, Pennsylvania, and Indiana—emitted in excess of 2 million tons of sulfur dioxide per year, totaling 30 percent of the region's emissions. Six additional States—Illinois, Missouri, Kentucky, Florida, West Virginia, and Tennessee—emitted in excess of 1 million tons each, together producing an additional 30 percent of the 31-State total.

Most current legislative proposals would place the greatest burden of emissions reductions on the utility sector and the Midwestern States. The costs likely to result from a control program include:

1. increased electricity costs to consumers,
2. loss of coal production and subsequent unemployment in regions where high-sulfur coal is mined, and
3. financial strain to certain vulnerable utilities and industrial corporations.

The *risk* imposed by a control program is that some of these costs might be unnecessary. A control program designed 10 years hence might achieve the same level of protection at lower cost than one designed today; similarly, the level of required protection might be more accurately identified. This section first presents the potential costs of control, and then discusses the risk that the control program might not be as efficient or cost effective as desired.

Utility Control Costs

Both the *total* tonnage of sulfur dioxide to be eliminated, and control costs per ton, determine the cost of controlling utility sulfur dioxide emissions. Costs rise as greater removal is sought, both because more emissions are being controlled and because the cost of eliminating each additional ton of sulfur dioxide increases. OTA estimates the costs of reducing sulfur dioxide emissions in the 31 Eastern States, in 1982 dollars, to be about:

- $0.5 to $1 billion/year to eliminate about 4 to 5 million tons/year
- $1 to $2 billion/year to eliminate about 6 to 7 million tons/year
- $2 to $2.5 billion/year to eliminate about 8 million tons/year
- $2.5 to $3.5 billion/year to eliminate about 9 million tons/year
- $3 to $4 billion/year to eliminate about 10 million tons/year
- $4 to $5 billion/year to eliminate about 11 million tons/year

The estimates above are based on the costs of controlling utility emissions, and *do not* include costs to offset any *future emissions increases* from utilities and industry. These costs can also be presented as percent increases in average residential rates for electricity, on both a regional and State basis. For example, a 50-percent reduction in utility sulfur dioxide emissions (8 million tons per year, about 35 percent below *total* regional emissions) would increase *average* residential rates by about 2 to 3 percent. Rate increases would vary by State, of course—consumers in some States would pay no increases, while others would pay over twice the regional average. For specific utilities, costs may be somewhat higher—several utilities have asserted that their residential rates might increase by 25 percent or more.[8]

These cost estimates are for control strategies that limit *rates* of emissions—sulfur dioxide emitted per quantity of fuel burned—similar to provisions in several bills proposed during the 97th and 98th Congresses. The range of cost estimates for each reduction level presented above reflects alternative methods of allocating emissions reductions *within* a State. In addition, the estimates assume that each utility chooses the most cost-effective method applicable to plant conditions. This results in a mix of scrubber use and fuel switching throughout the region.

The cost of removing a ton of sulfur dioxide is generally lower when a plant's emission rate is high. Consequently, total regional control costs are lower when emissions cutbacks are allocated to States on the basis of their emissions rates than when equal percentage reductions are required for all States. As discussed in chapters 6 and 7, this method of allocating reductions concentrates a higher proportion of reductions on Midwestern States whose utilities burn high-sulfur coal. However, many areas that currently have lower sulfur dioxide emissions rates already pay higher electricity costs than prevail in the Midwest.

Effects on the U.S. Coal Market

Switching from high- to low-sulfur coal is one of the major available options for achieving substantial emissions reductions. Consequently, mandating further emissions reductions creates the risk of significant coal-market disruptions by increasing the demand for low-sulfur coals at the expense of high-sulfur coals. Risks of production and employment losses occur almost exclusively in the Eastern United States, where coal reserves are primarily of high-sulfur content. The Western coal-producing States, and parts of Kentucky and West Virginia, contain low-sulfur coal reserves and might therefore benefit from acid deposition controls. For the nation as a whole, regulations designed to control acid

deposition would probably not affect total coal production.

The extent to which utility and industrial users would shift to low-sulfur coal depends on the relative cost advantage of fuel switching as opposed to removing sulfur dioxide by technological means (e.g., scrubbers). Each method has clear advantages for some situations, but for many plants, the cost difference is modest enough to make predictions of future preferences highly uncertain. The following projections of future coal production and employment shifts are based on current costs, and might change significantly if new control technologies become available or coal prices change.

OTA estimated the extent to which coal production and employment would be affected by an emissions reduction program of 10 million tons or more that neither mandates nor provides financial incentives for using particular control technologies. Under such a program, 1990 levels of production in the high-sulfur coal areas of the Midwest (Illinois, Indiana, and western Kentucky) and Northern Appalachia (Pennsylvania, Ohio, and northern West Virginia) might decline to about 10 to 20 percent below 1979 levels. Estimates of production declines are averaged over these regions, and thus may be greater or less in some States and counties than others.

For the low-sulfur coal areas of Central Appalachia (eastern Kentucky, southern West Virginia, Tennessee, and Virginia) and the Western United States, acid rain control measures are projected to expand coal production beyond currently projected 1990 levels. This effect is more pronounced in Central Appalachia than in the West, due to its proximity to Eastern markets.

In general, *employment* changes would follow changes in production. A 10-million-ton emissions cutback is projected to reduce employment in *high-sulfur coal-producing areas* by between 20,000 and 30,000 jobs from projected 1990 levels. About 15,000 to 22,000 additional jobs would open up in Eastern low-sulfur coal-producing areas, and an additional 5,000 to 7,000 jobs in the West. The risk of unemployment is most severe in Illinois, Ohio, northern West Virginia, and western Kentucky— for these areas, coal-mining employment is projected to decline more than 10 percent below current levels.

[8]"A Report on the Results From the Edison Electric Institute Study of the Impact of the Senate Committee on Environment and Public Works Bill on Acid Rain Legislation (S. 768)," National Economic Research Associates, Inc., report submitted to Edison Electric Institute, 1983.

Photo credit: Douglas Yarrow

Last shift comes out at Eccles #5 before the 1977 contract strike

These employment shifts would cause proportional changes in direct miner income. At the national level, benefits to low-sulfur regions are projected to balance out losses to high-sulfur regions. This level of aggregation, however, obscures the regional distribution of coal-related economic costs. Direct income effects for a 10-million-ton emissions reduction are estimated below:

- Northern Appalachia: $250 to $350 million per year *loss*;
- Central Appalachia: $400 to $550 million per year *gain*;
- Midwest: $250 to $400 million per year *loss*;
- West: $100 to $200 million per year *gain*.

The total economic impacts of coal-market shifts—reflecting, in addition, indirect employment and income effects on other economic activities—may be two to three times greater.

Effects on Utility and Industrial Financial Health

While the costs of further controlling utility sulfur emissions are ultimately passed on to electricity consumers, they can strain the resources of financially troubled utilities that must initially pay them. Additionally, reducing industrial process and boiler emissions imposes the risk of rendering sulfur dioxide-emitting industries in controlled regions less competitive than their less or uncontrolled counterparts in other geographic areas.

On the basis of average 1980 utility bond ratings and stock indicators, utility sectors in eight States appeared to be relatively vulnerable to the additional capital requirements that could result from further sulfur dioxide control: Arkansas, Connecticut, Florida, Maine, Michigan, Pennsylvania, Vermont, and Virginia.* If cutbacks are allocated on the basis of emissions rates, three of these States—Pennsylvania, Florida, and Michigan—are likely to be required to reduce emissions significantly. Greatest reductions would be required in Pennsylvania, where present State regulatory policies also cause substantial delays before utilities can pass increased fuel costs and/or construction costs on to consumers.

Several other States have regulatory policies considered unfavorable to utility pollution control expenditures, although their utilities showed better average financial health in 1980. The regulatory policies set by public utility commissions in each State can significantly affect the financial burden of raising additional capital to further control sulfur dioxide emissions. Such policies vary substantially from State to State. Moreover, these policies are subject to change, and might themselves be affected by the passage of new pollution control legislation.

Major increases in electricity costs due to increased controls might also hurt utilities by reducing demand for electricity. However, OTA-projected increases in average electricity rates resulting from stricter sulfur dioxide emissions controls are not high enough to affect demand for electrical power appreciably.

OTA also identified industries in which electricity is a major component of production costs. For about 15 industries, concentrated primarily in the areas of primary metals, chemicals and allied products, and stone, clay, and glass products, electricity costs exceed 10 percent of the value added* by the manufacturer—nearly four times the national average. Electricity costs are equal to about 40 percent or more of the value added in industries that produce electrometallurgical products, primary zinc, primary aluminum, alkali- and chlorine-based chemicals, and industrial gases—these five industries alone use about 16 percent of the electricity consumed by industry in this country. Within these energy-intensive industries, manufacturers served by utilities with high control costs might be rendered less competitive than those in regions that are either uncontrolled or incur lower control costs.

Preliminary analyses of industrial process emissions also suggest some potential for economic dislocation in the iron and steel and cement industries if their emissions were to be strictly controlled. Stricter sulfur dioxide emissions controls, if imposed in the Southwestern United States, could also create hardships for the region's currently depressed copper smelting industry.

---

*Individual utilities in relatively weak financial conditions were also found in Massachusetts, Indiana, Ohio, Georgia, New Jersey, and West Virginia.

*"Value added" is the difference between the selling price of the product and the cost of energy and materials to manufacture it.

RISK THAT CONTROL MAY NOT BE AS EFFECTIVE OR EFFICIENT AS DESIRED

Proposals for controlling sulfur dioxide emissions aim to reduce sulfur deposition—a major contribution to acidification—in areas sensitive to its effects. However, as discussed previously, incomplete understanding of pollutant transport and transformation creates the risk that any control strategy designed at this time: 1) will not reduce deposition to the extent, and in the specific locations, desired; and 2) may not be as cost-effective as possible.

This section reviews estimates of the reduction in acid deposition needed to minimize further damage to sensitive resources—and the likelihood of reaching these "deposition targets" under alternative control strategies. In addition, the section discusses the potential for designing a more cost-effective strategy to reduce acid deposition by controlling nonsulfur pollutants in addition to sulfur dioxide.

Effectiveness of Emissions Reductions for Achieving Desired Deposition Reductions

While any major reduction in acid deposition levels would likely benefit some sensitive resources, scientists have attempted to define "target" deposition levels—the maximum level of deposition for avoiding further damage to all but the most sensitive resources.* Target deposition values have been presented in reports by the National Academy of Sciences (NAS), the Impact Assessment Work Group established by the United States-Canada Memorandum of Intent on Transboundary Air Pollution,** a working group at the 1982 Stockholm Conference on the Acidification of the Environment, and others. These have been expressed as levels of acidity, levels of sulfate in rainfall, or total deposited sulfur.

OTA estimated the reductions in "wet sulfur deposition"—the sulfur deposited in rain and snow—necessary to reach these target deposition levels. As outlined in chapter 5 and appendix C, the estimates range from eliminating about 50 to 80 percent of deposition in those areas receiving highest levels, to eliminating about 20 to 50 percent of deposition over large regions of Eastern North America identified as having sensitive aquatic resources.

Several bills introduced during the 97th and 98th Congresses proposed cutting sulfur dioxide emissions back by about 8 to 10 million tons per year—about a 35 to 45 percent reduction in Eastern U.S. emissions. Using two different types of computer models, OTA estimated the sulfur deposition reductions that might result if these legislative proposals were enacted. The more optimistic model estimate suggests that both wet and dry sulfur deposition would be reduced by as much as 45 to 60 percent in the areas of greatest deposition. Both wet and dry sulfur deposition would be reduced by about 30 to 50 percent annually over large regions of Eastern North America. The second model projection—based on conditions that prevail during extreme pollution episodes—suggests that emissions reductions of 35 to 45 percent would comparably reduce *dry* sulfur deposition. However, the model predicts that *wet* sulfur deposition would respond less directly, decreasing by about 25 to 35 percent in areas of greatest deposition, and by 20 to 30 percent over much of Eastern North America, during high pollution episodes.[9]

These estimates provide a plausible range of deposition reductions that might result from reducing emissions by 35 to 45 percent. The reductions in total sulfur deposition estimated above are difficult to compare to target deposition levels, because these targets have been expressed in a variety of ways. However, the following preliminary conclusions can be drawn, subject to a large degree of uncertainty: In areas of greatest deposition, for example, western Pennsylvania, reducing Eastern United States sulfur dioxide emissions by 8 to 10 million tons per year might not be sufficient to bring deposition levels within the targeted maximum for protecting all but the most sensitive resources. In areas receiving less deposition, such as northern New England, the southern Appalachians, and the upper Midwest, sulfur dioxide emissions reductions of this magnitude are likely to achieve the target deposition levels.

Efficiency Concerns

Because large-scale cutbacks in sulfur dioxide emissions will cost billions of dollars annually, some have suggested that even if the deposition reduction goals could be achieved now, a more cost-effective program might be designed when atmospheric processes are better understood. Such concerns raise the following questions:

1. Can specific sources or source areas affecting sensitive resource areas be identified for emissions control?

---

*Maximum deposition targets are based on protecting *aquatic* resources, as too little is known about the sensitivity of other resources to allow similar levels of protection to be defined. In addition, most targets are based on amounts of *wet* deposition, since current data are insufficient for considering dry deposition.

**Only the Canadian members of the Work Group recommended a target deposition value.

[9]A recent NRC study for the National Academy of Sciences used slightly modified model assumptions to reexamine the OTA analysis. The NRC committee concluded that reductions in wet sulfur deposition would more closely approximate the reductions in sulfur dioxide emissions than OTA had estimated. *Acid Deposition: Atmospheric Processes in Eastern North America,* Committee on Atmospheric Transport and Chemical Transformation in Acid Deposition, National Research Council, National Academy Press, Washington, D.C., 1983.

2. Can cutbacks in other acidifying pollutants, such as nitrogen oxides, eliminate acid deposition for lower cost?
3. Can sulfur deposition be controlled more cost effectively by controlling co-pollutants such as reactive hydrocarbons concurrently with sulfur dioxide emissions?

Atmospheric transport models for linking source regions and receptor regions have been available for several years, but their accuracy is subject to debate. Current understanding suggests that, given the widespread distribution of sensitive resources, a program to bring deposition within the previously mentioned target rates in all sensitive areas would have to encompass most of the Eastern United States. Within some bounds, emissions reductions from one area can be substituted for reductions from another without jeopardizing the desired pattern of deposition, but the goal of minimizing total costs is likely to conflict with cost distribution goals. The dual problems of defining the value of one resource area relative to others, and equitably distributing costs, are difficult political questions that could not be solved through more accurate modeling capabilities.

Controlling nitrogen oxides may be less expensive for some sources than controlling sulfur ox-ides, but whether it is as efficient for preventing resource damage is subject to question. Currently, twice as much rainfall acidity comes from sulfur oxides as from nitrogen oxides. In addition, plants often take up nitrogen oxides as nutrients, further increasing the proportion of lake and stream acidity produced by sulfur oxides. Though future research may reveal that intermittent events—such as spring snow melts containing high levels of both deposited nitrogen oxides and sulfur oxides—are responsible for the greatest share of damage, current understanding suggests that sulfur oxides are the first choice for control.

Future research may reveal more cost-effective opportunities for reducing sulfur deposition by controlling co-pollutants concurrently with sulfur dioxide emissions. Preliminary modeling results indicate that the ratio of reactive hydrocarbons to nitrogen oxides is an important determinant of the atmospheric transformation of sulfur oxides. Though broad regional sulfur oxide deposition overall might remain relatively constant, reducing emissions of these co-pollutants along with sulfur dioxide might achieve more desirable patterns of deposition than would result from reducing sulfur dioxide emissions alone.

Chapter 4
The Pollutants of Concern

Contents

The Pollutants of Concern

This chapter: 1) provides estimates of pollutant emissions, 2) describes current geographic patterns of *emitted* pollutants, and concentrations and deposition of *transformed* pollutants, and 3) analyzes the *patterns and processes* of pollutant transport and transformation. The pollutants of concern and their transformation products are:

- sulfur dioxide—both as sulfur dioxide gas and as the transformation product, sulfate;
- nitrogen oxides—as a gas, as the transformation product, nitrate, and as a precursor of ozone; and
- reactive hydrocarbons—as precursors of ozone.

OTA has assembled estimates of current emissions and historical and projected emissions trends for these three pollutants. Projections of sulfur dioxide and nitrogen oxides emissions are provided for the United States overall, for the Eastern 31-State region, and by major producing sector. The chapter examines future utility emissions of sulfur dioxide in greater detail.

To show where these emissions originate, current emissions levels are described in a series of maps. The chapter then presents maps of measured *deposition levels* for acidity and sulfate, and *air concentrations* for ozone and airborne sulfate. These maps can be used to compare the *origins* of the three emitted pollutants to the eventual *destinations* of the transformed pollutants on which the assessment focuses.

Finally, the chapter presents model-based estimates of the regional *transport* of sulfur oxides—the most abundant acid-producing pollutant, and the pollutant for which the greatest amount of information about transport, transformation, and deposition patterns is available. In addition, the section briefly describes the chemical processes that *transform* the three emitted pollutants, to aid in understanding how changes in emissions levels might affect resulting levels of transported pollutants.

EMISSIONS

Current and Historical

In the United States during 1980 approximately 26 million tons of sulfur dioxide, 21 million tons of nitrogen oxides, and about 24 to 28 million tons of hydrocarbons (volatile organic carbon) were emitted by manmade sources. Of this total, about 22 million tons of sulfur dioxide, 14 million tons of nitrogen oxides, and about 19 to 20 million tons of hydrocarbons were emitted in the 31 States east of or bordering the Mississippi River. For the Nation overall, the major sources of sulfur dioxide emissions—about 90 to 95 percent of the total—are electric-generating utilities, industrial boilers, and industrial processes. Similarly, three sectors—utilities, mobile sources, and industry—produce more than 95 percent of the country's manmade nitrogen oxides emissions. Mobile sources and industrial processes produce about 80 to 85 percent of U.S. hydrocarbon emissions, while the remainder comes from a wide variety of sources.

Table 1 presents current (1980) estimated emissions of sulfur dioxide, nitrogen oxides, and hydrocarbons for each of the 50 States.[1] To place the current level of emissions into historical perspective, table 2 shows estimated total U.S. and Eastern 31-State emissions of sulfur dioxide and nitrogen oxides, and estimated total U.S. hydrocarbon emissions, for selected years between 1940 and 1980. Between 1940 and 1970, nationwide sulfur dioxide emissions increased by roughly 50 percent, from about 19 million to 30 million tons per year. From

---

[1]Estimates are from *Emissions, Costs, and Engineering Assessment,* Work Group 3B, United States-Canada Memorandum of Intent on Transboundary Air Pollution, June 15, 1982. Tables 3 and 4 compare the 50-State and Eastern 31-State region totals, by utility and industrial sector, with other estimates of sulfur dioxide and nitrogen oxides emissions.

Table 1.—1980 Total Emissions of Sulfur Dioxide, Nitrogen Oxides, and Hydrocarbons in the United States
(1,000 tons/year)

State	SO₂	NOₓ	HC	State	SO₂	NOₓ	HC
Alabama	760	450	530	Montana	160	120	160
Alaska	20	55	50	Nebraska	75	190	200
Arizona	900	260	250	Nevada	240	80	70
Arkansas	100	220	270	New Hampshire	90	60	100
California	445	1,220	2,550	New Jersey	280	400	810
Colorado	130	275	360	New Mexico	270	290	195
Connecticut	70	135	370	New York	950	680	1,250
Delaware	110	50	70	North Carolina	600	540	680
District of Columbia	15	20	35	North Dakota	100	120	70
Florida	1,100	650	880	Ohio	2,650	1,140	1,280
Georgia	840	490	580	Oklahoma	120	520	460
Hawaii	60	45	75	Oregon	60	200	330
Idaho	50	80	170	Pennsylvania	2,020	1,040	1,360
Illinois	1,470	1,000	1,200	Rhode Island	15	40	120
Indiana	2,000	770	700	South Carolina	330	200	550
Iowa	330	320	300	South Dakota	40	90	110
Kansas	220	440	350	Tennessee	1,100	520	580
Kentucky	1,120	530	430	Texas	1,270	2,540	3,400
Louisiana	300	930	790	Utah	70	190	160
Maine	100	60	120	Vermont	7	25	45
Maryland	340	250	370	Virginia	360	400	530
Massachusetts	340	250	600	Washington	270	290	500
Michigan	900	690	1,100	West Virginia	1,100	450	150
Minnesota	260	370	500	Wisconsin	640	420	530
Mississippi	280	280	330	Wyoming	180	260	110
Missouri	1,300	570	690	U.S. total	26,500	21,220	28,350

SOURCE: *Emissions, Costs and Engineering Assessment*, Work Group 3B, United States—Canada Memorandum of Intent on Transboundary Air Pollution, June 15, 1982.

Table 2.—Historical Trends in Sulfur Dioxide, Nitrogen Oxides, and Hydrocarbon Emissions (millions of tons)

Year	Sulfur dioxide National[a,b]	Eastern 31 States[b]	Nitrogen oxides National[a,b]	Eastern 31 States[b]	Hydrocarbons National[a]
1940	19.1	—	7.2	—	15.3
1950	18.1-21.6	14.6	7.4-10.3	5.4	19.3
1955	17.7	14.3	8.5	6.4	—
1960	21.2-22.2	18.9	11.5-14.0	8.5	23.8
1965	26.7	22.8	14.2	10.4	—
1970	28.7-30.8	24.0	17.7-20.4	12.4	29.8
1975	27.3-28.2	23.4	19.3-21.6	13.3	25.1
1980	25.2-26.1	21.2	21.0-22.8	13.9	24.0-28.3[c]

SOURCES: [a]*National Air Pollution Emission Estimates, 1940-1980*, U.S. Environmental Protection Agency, January 1982, EPA-450/4-82-001.
[b]"Historic Emissions of Sulfur and Nitrogen Oxides in the United States from 1900 to 1980," G. Gschwandtner, et al., 1980. Draft reports to EPA from Pacific Environmental Services, Inc.
[c]*Emissions, Costs and Engineering Assessment*, Work Group 3B, United States-Canada Memorandum of Intent on Transboundary Air Pollution, June 15, 1982.

1970 to 1980 emissions totals show a decline from about 30 million to 26 million tons per year, and from about 24 million to 21 to 22 million tons for the Eastern 31-State region. Estimates are available for pre-1940 emissions levels, but these are based on incomplete data. These data suggest that throughout the period 1920-40, nationwide sulfur dioxide emissions averaged roughly 17 million tons per year.[2] Appendix A presents historical emissions estimates in greater detail.

Over the period 1940-80, nitrogen oxides emissions grew much more rapidly than sulfur dioxide—virtually tripling—but have declined slightly from 1978 to 1980. Hydrocarbon emissions are estimated to have doubled, from about 15 million tons in 1940 to about 30 million tons per year in 1970. From 1970 to 1980, hydrocarbon emissions declined—according to various estimates, to about 24 to 28 million tons per year.[3]

Future Emissions Under Current Laws and Regulations

Assuming that current air pollution laws and regulations remain unchanged, future emissions of both sulfur dioxide and nitrogen oxides will depend primarily on three factors:

- future demand for energy, including energy for electricity generation, industrial fuel use, and automobiles;
- the type of energy used to meet future demand, for example, the extent of such nonfossil energy use as nuclear and hydropower, and less polluting fuels such as natural gas; and
- the rate at which existing pollution sources—both stationary sources and highway vehicles—are replaced with newer sources more tightly controlled under the Clean Air Act.

---

[2] "Historic Emissions of Sulfur and Nitrogen Oxides in the United States From 1900 to 1980," G. Gschwandtner, et al., 1983. Draft report to EPA from Pacific Environmental Services, Inc.

[3] Hydrocarbon emissions are difficult to estimate, in part because a major source of their production is the evaporation of chemical solvents. As shown in tables 1 and 2, the 24-million-ton estimate is derived from U.S. Environmental Protection Agency, *National Air Pollutant Emission Estimates, 1940-1980,* while the 28-million-ton figure is from the U.S.-Canada MOI, Work Group 3B, *Emissions, Costs and Engineering Assessment.*

Each of these factors is, of course, uncertain, but analysts can estimate pollutant emissions that would result from plausible future trends. The first three parts of this section will present several projections of future sulfur dioxide, nitrogen oxides, and hydrocarbon emissions over the next two to three decades. The fourth part will discuss how these factors, as well as further emission controls, affect future sulfur dioxide emissions from the *utility* sector.

Sulfur Dioxide Emissions

Table 3 presents various projections of sulfur dioxide emissions through the year 2010. For the United States as a whole, sulfur dioxide emissions are projected to increase over 1980 levels by 10 to 25 percent by 2000, and by 20 to 30 percent by 2010. The greatest projected rate of increase is in the industrial sector—25 to 40 percent by 2000.

Within the 31 Eastern States, the industrial sector is again projected to account for the fastest growth in emissions. By 2000, total sulfur dioxide emissions are projected to increase by 10 to 30 percent, while emissions from the industrial sector alone increase between 50 to 90 percent. By 2010, total emissions are projected to increase by about 15 to 25 percent over 1980 levels. These projections assume that rising oil and natural gas prices will cause many current users of these cleaner fuels to switch to coal. Utility emissions are forecast to increase slightly through about 2000 and then to begin declining slightly. Because of the growth increase projected for the industrial sector, utility emissions will drop from about 75 percent of the total in 1980 to about 60 to 65 percent of the total by 2010.

Nitrogen Oxides Emissions

While mobile sources are currently the single largest nitrogen oxides-producing sector, by 2010 rapid growth in emissions from the utility sector is expected to make utilities the single largest source of nitrogen oxides. Table 4 presents various projections of nitrogen oxides emissions for utilities, mobile sources, and industry.

For the United States, nitrogen oxides emissions by 2000 are expected to increase over 1980 levels by about 25 percent; by 2010, emissions are forecast

Table 3.—Projected Sulfur Dioxide Emissions (million tons/year)

	United States							Eastern 31 States						
	1980	1985	1990	1995	2000	2005	2010	1980	1985	1990	1995	2000	2005	2010
Total:														
MOI[1]	26.5	—	25.3	—	29.3	—	—	21.8	—	21.4	—	24.3	—	—
EEI[2a]	27.3	26.9	27.2	29.4	31.1	—	33.4	21.7	21.2	21.6	23.5	23.9	—	24.6
EEI[2b]	27.3	28.7	29.4	32.0	34.6	—	35.0	21.7	23.5	24.2	26.6	27.9	—	26.7
Utility:														
MOI[1]	17.3	—	17.5	—	17.9	—	—	16.0	—	15.9	—	16.1	—	—
EEI[2a]	17.5	17.6	17.9	18.6	18.2	—	18.2	16.2	15.5	15.7	15.9	15.1	—	14.5
EEI[2b]	17.5	19.3	20.1	21.2	21.6	—	19.8	16.2	17.8	18.3	19.0	19.1	—	16.6
EPA[3]	17.4	18.8	20.0	20.2	19.6	—	18.7	16.2	17.1	17.9	18.0	17.1	—	15.8
NWF[4]	—	—	19.6	—	21.0	—	—	—	—	17.8	—	18.1	—	—
EEI[5]								—	—	18.3	—	—	—	—
Industry:														
MOI[1]	7.4	—	5.9	—	9.3	—	—	4.4	—	4.1	—	6.7	—	—
EEI[2c]	7.5	7.4	7.2	8.6	10.5	—	12.2	3.8	4.2	4.4	6.3	7.2	—	8.2
EEI[5]								—	—	4.4	—	—	—	—

Sources of estimates:
1. MOI—*Emissions, Costs and Engineering Assessment,* Work Group 3B, United States-Canada Memorandum of Intent on Transboundary Air Pollution, June 15, 1982.
2. EEI—"Summary of Forecasted Emissions of Sulfur Dioxide and Nitrogen Oxides in the United States Over the 1980 to 2010 Period," prepared by ICF Inc. and National Economic Research Associates for the Edison Electric Institute and Utility Air Regulatory Group, April 1982.
   2a—National Economic Research Associates (NERA) estimate.
   2b—ICF Inc. estimate.
   2c—Joint NERA/ICF estimate.
3. EPA—Personal communication from J. Austin, EPA. Projections prepared for EPA by ICF Inc., using assumptions stated in "Analysis of a 10 Million Ton Reduction in Emissions From Existing Utility Powerplants," ICF Inc., June 1982.
4. NWF—"Cost and Coal Production Effects of Reducing Utility Sulfur Dioxide Emissions," prepared for National Wildlife Federation and National Clean Air Coalition by ICF Inc., Nov. 14, 1981.
5. EEI—"January 25, 1982 Preliminary ICF Analysis of the Mitchell Bill Prepared for the Edison Electric Institute," Edison Electric Institute letter, Feb. 8, 1982.

Table 4.—Projected Nitrogen Oxides Emissions (million tons/year)

	United States							Eastern 31 States						
	1980	1985	1990	1995	2000	2005	2010	1980	1985	1990	1995	2000	2005	2010
Total:														
MOI[1]	21.2	—	21.2	—	26.6	—	—	14.0	—	15.0	—	18.5	—	—
EEI[2a]	21.0	22.2	22.3	23.9	26.2	—	32.8	14.9	15.6	15.6	16.4	17.7	—	21.8
EEI[2b]	21.0	21.7	22.3	24.0	26.5	—	31.8	14.9	15.5	15.8	16.8	18.4	—	21.3
Utility:														
MOI[1]	6.4	—	7.5	—	9.6	—	—	4.8	—	5.7	—	6.9	—	—
EEI[2a]	7.2	8.8	9.3	10.2	11.1	—	14.8	5.4	6.5	6.8	7.2	7.6	—	9.9
EEI[2b]	7.2	8.3	9.3	10.3	11.4	—	13.8	5.4	6.4	7.0	7.6	8.3	—	9.4
EEI[3]								—	—	6.2	—	—	—	—
Industry:														
MOI[1]	4.6	—	4.2	—	5.6	—	—	2.4	—	3.0	—	3.7	—	—
EEI[2c]	3.5	3.7	4.2	4.7	5.3	—	6.0	2.3	2.5	2.8	3.2	3.7	—	4.1
EEI[3]								—	—	2.6	—	—	—	—
Mobile:														
MOI[1]	9.4	—	8.6	—	10.7	—	—	6.2	—	5.8	—	7.3	—	—
EEI[2c]	9.4	8.9	8.2	8.4	9.2	—	11.5	6.5	6.0	5.5	5.5	6.0	—	7.4

Sources of estimates:
1. MOI—*Emissions, Costs and Engineering Assessment,* Work Group 3B, United States-Canada Memorandum of Intent on Transboundary Air Pollution, June 15, 1982.
2. EEI—"Summary of Forecasted Emissions of Sulfur Dioxide and Nitrogen Oxides in the United States Over the 1980 to 2010 Period," prepared by ICF Inc. and National Economic Research Associates for the Edison Electric Institute and Utility Air Regulatory Group, April 1982.
   2a—National Economic Research Associates (NERA) estimate.
   2b—ICF Inc. estimate.
   2c—Joint NERA/ICF estimate.
3. EEI—"January 25, 1982 Preliminary ICF Analysis of the Mitchell Bill Prepared for the Edison Electric Institute," Edison Electric Institute letter, Feb. 8, 1982.

to increase by about 50 to 55 percent. The utility sector is projected to account for most of this increase (about 60 to 75 percent). For the 31 Eastern States, nitrogen oxides emissions are projected to increase by about 20 to 30 percent by 2000, and by about 45 percent by 2010.

Hydrocarbon Emissions

Reliable quantitative estimates of future hydrocarbon emissions are not available at this time. However, in general, hydrocarbon emissions are projected to decline somewhat from 1980 levels, and then to remain relatively constant. Petroleum refining and storage is the only major source of hydrocarbons projected to significantly increase emissions through 2000; expected improvements in abatement practices and potential shifts away from liquid hydrocarbon fuels toward coal use might partially or completely offset such increases.[4] Emissions from industrial processes—a major source of hydrocarbons—depend heavily on the specific process in use, making these emissions very difficult to estimate.

Utility Sulfur Dioxide Emissions in the 31 Eastern States

As demonstrated by the variations among the projections presented in tables 3 and 4, forecasting pollutant emissions is not an exact science. Emissions scenarios depend on numerous assumptions about future economic conditions. For example, projections of rapid growth of sulfur dioxide emissions from the industrial sector assume increased industrial output, along with a change from oil use to coal. The range of the projections reflects different plausible assumptions about future rates of industrial growth and the relative future price of oil and coal.

OTA used a simple projection model to examine how various factors affect forecasts of utility sulfur dioxide emissions in the Eastern half of the country. The major factors affecting utility emissions are: 1) demand for electricity (for this analysis, OTA assumes growth to be 2.5 percent per year, with a range of 2.0 to 3.0 percent per year); and 2) retirement age of existing plants (for this analysis,

---

[4]*Environmental Outlook 1980*, U.S. Environmental Protection Agency, July 1980, EPA-600/8-80-003.

OTA assumes the useful life of a plant to be 50 years, with a range of 40 to 60 years). Other factors include reliance on nonfossil energy sources (assumed to provide the same proportion of electricity generation as in 1980), emission rates from new sources regulated under the New Source Performance Standards (NSPS) (assumed to average 0.6 lb sulfur dioxide per million Btu), and reductions required to comply with State Implementation Plans (SIPs) (assumed to be about 1 million tons of sulfur dioxide; possible SIP relaxations might reduce this amount).

Figure 11 shows how these factors affect emissions forecasts, using a 60-year forecast period to allow for replacement of all utility plants operating in 1980. Figure 11A illustrates the sensitivity of emissions forecasts to demand for electricity. The lowest curve shows emissions in the unlikely event that no growth in demand occurs. Under such a scenario, emissions would decline to 20 percent of the current 16 million tons of utility sulfur dioxide emissions when all existing sources are replaced by new sources regulated under NSPS.

Existing facilities are assumed to retire after 50 years of service. Assuming an increase in demand for electricity ranging from 2 to 3 percent per year, emissions will increase to 7 to 11 percent above current levels by 2000, decline to about 50 to 75 percent of current levels by 2025 to 2030, and then begin to climb again. However, as figure 11B shows, these trends are extremely sensitive to the average life of existing sources, assumed to be 50 years for the estimates presented above. Figure 11B illustrates emissions trends assuming 2.5 percent growth per year, but varying the average retirement age of existing utility plants. A 40-year retirement age would cause emissions to decline steadily to about 50 percent of current levels by 2015 to 2020, and subsequently rise. If the useful life of existing plants is extended to 60 years, emissions might rise to about 20 percent above current levels by 2010, decline to about 80 percent of current amounts by 2030, and then begin to rise again.

Figure 11C shows the effect of limiting allowable emission rates now, as opposed to waiting for NSPS-regulated new sources to replace existing utilities. The distance between the "base case" curve (no change in current laws and regulations) and the "emissions rate limitation" curves repre-

Figure 11.—Forecasts of Utility Sulfur Dioxide Emissions for the Eastern 31-State Region of the United States

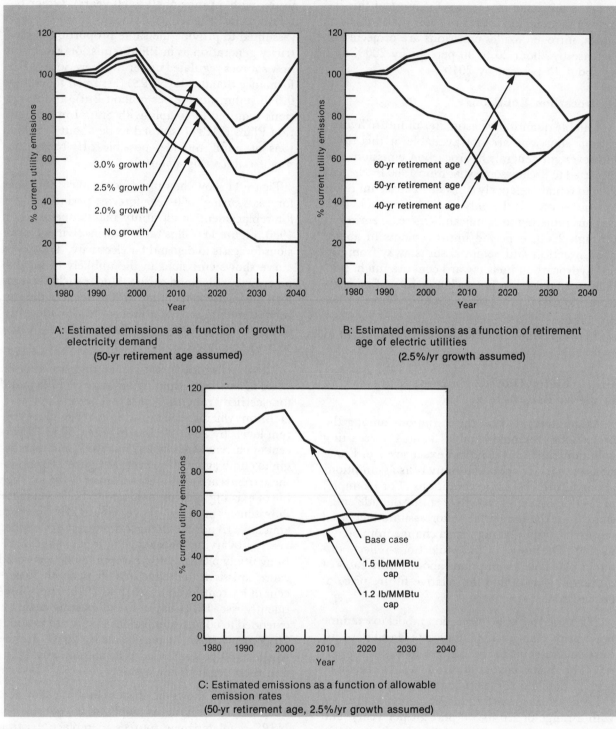

A: Estimated emissions as a function of growth
    electricity demand
    (50-yr retirement age assumed)

B: Estimated emissions as a function of retirement
    age of electric utilities
    (2.5%/yr growth assumed)

C: Estimated emissions as a function of allowable
    emission rates
    (50-yr retirement age, 2.5%/yr growth assumed)

SOURCE: Office of Technology Assessment.

sents the difference in emissions at any point in time. A 1.5 lb sulfur dioxide per million Btu "emissions cap" on all Eastern utility sources by 1990 would reduce emissions to about 50 percent of current levels. Emissions would then increase to about 60 percent of current levels by 2025 and (after all existing sources retired) follow the same growth trend as the base case by 2030. Under a 1.2 lb per million Btu cap by 1990, emissions would decrease to 40 percent of current emissions by 1990, and then rise to about 60 percent of current levels by 2025. Assuming a shorter retirement age would, of course, decrease the length of time during which

the base case and the emissions cap scenarios substantially differed, and a longer retirement age would increase that time.

The range of projections from the simple model discussed above agrees reasonably well with the more sophisticated projections presented earlier in this section. Projections beyond 2000 to 2010 are presented to illustrate how emissions levels might respond to plausible changes in electricity demand and utility operating procedures, but should not be considered accurate forecasts, as many other factors may change over so long a time.

PATTERNS OF POLLUTANT EMISSIONS, AIR CONCENTRATIONS, AND DEPOSITION

Geographical Emissions Patterns

Figures 12, 13, and 14 display maps of emissions densities (in tons per square mile per year) for sulfur dioxide, nitrogen oxides, and reactive hydrocarbons, respectively. For all three pollutants, emissions densities are generally greater in the East than in the West.

Geographical Patterns of Deposition and Air Concentrations for Transformed Pollutants

Figures 15 through 18 display maps of deposition levels for acidity and sulfate in precipitation, and air concentrations for airborne sulfate and ozone— each of which is a major determinant of potential damage from transported air pollutants. Patterns of rainfall acidity and sulfate deposition, and airborne sulfate concentrations, are similar over the Eastern United States. The regional distribution of ozone differs substantially from the other three.

The best information available on patterns of acidic deposition comes from monitoring networks that collect rainfall samples. Though only about *half* of all acid deposition over the Eastern United States

comes from precipitation, dry deposition of gaseous and particulate pollutants is not extensively monitored. Figure 15 shows average annual precipitation acidity (measured as ph*) throughout North America during 1980. Figure 16 shows the geographical patterns of of wet-deposited sulfate. The highest deposition rates center around eastern Ohio, western Pennsylvania, and northern West Virginia. A band surrounding this area—from the Atlantic Ocean west to the Mississippi River, and from southern Ontario to northern Mississippi, Alabama, and Georgia—receives from 50 to 80 percent of these peak deposition rates. The data used to construct this map are from 1980; deposition will vary from year to year at any given location, but the broad pattern will probably remain quite similar.

Figure 17 displays airborne sulfate concentrations in rural and remote areas, illustrating large-scale, regional patterns. The highest concentrations occur in a broad band covering the Midwest and Middle Atlantic States.

---

*Acidity is measured in pH units. Decreasing pH corresponds to increasing acidity. The pH scale is not linear; compared to a pH of 6, pH 5 is 10 times more acid, pH 4 is 100 times more acid, and so on.

Figure 12.—Sulfur Dioxide Emissions Density (tons/mile², 1980)

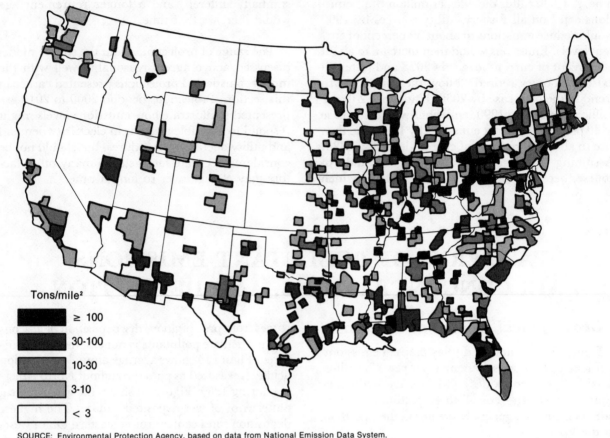

Tons/mile²

≥ 100
30-100
10-30
3-10
< 3

SOURCE: Environmental Protection Agency, based on data from National Emission Data System.

Patterns of ozone concentration are also available from monitoring data. Figure 18 displays growing-season average ozone concentrations, after eliminating local-scale variations due to urban influences. In the Eastern United States, peak values for ozone are found further south than for acid deposition, centering on North and South Carolina. A band of elevated ozone extends from the Mid-Great Plains States to the east coast, as far north as central Indiana and south to the central Gulf Coast States.

THE REGIONAL PATTERNS OF SULFUR OXIDES TRANSPORT

How pollutant emissions from a particular region (or group of regions) affect ambient air quality and pollutant deposition at some other location is a major controversy in the long-range transport debate. Emitted pollutants are transformed, transported, and deposited through a complex chain of chemical and physical processes.

Figure 19 schematically illustrates the gradual transformation and deposition of sulfur pollution as an air mass travels downwind over several days. Sulfur pollution can be deposited in both its emitted form, sulfur dioxide (lighter shading), and as sulfate (darker shading), after being chemically transformed in the atmosphere. Both forms can be de-

Figure 13.—Nitrogen Oxide Emissions Density (tons/mile²)

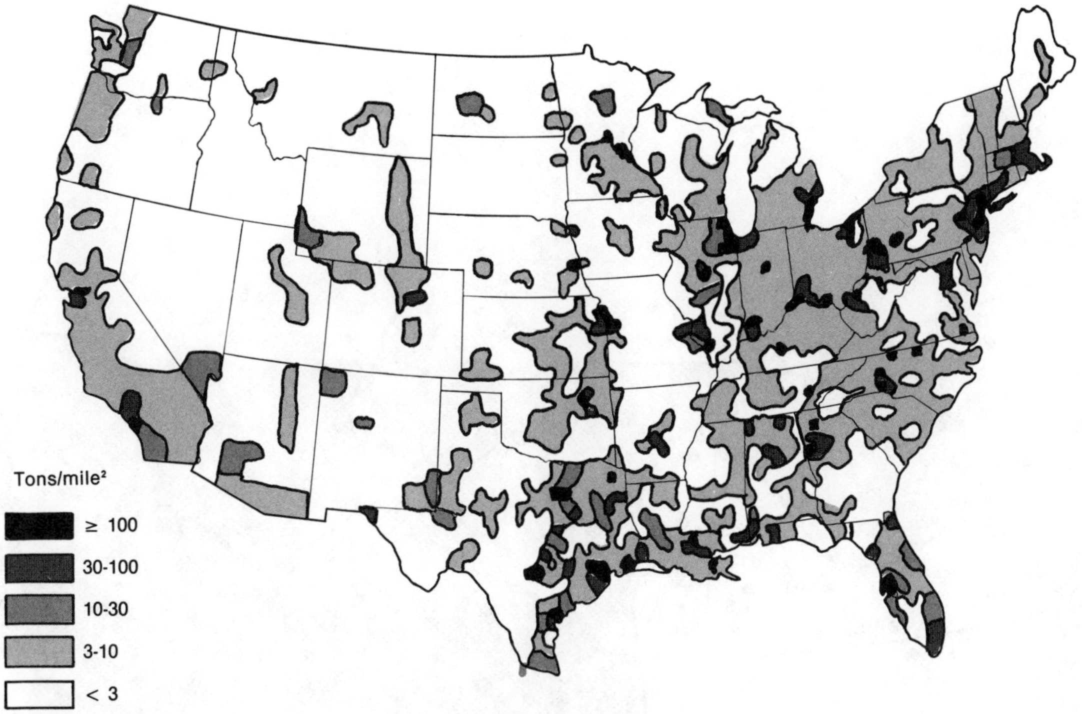

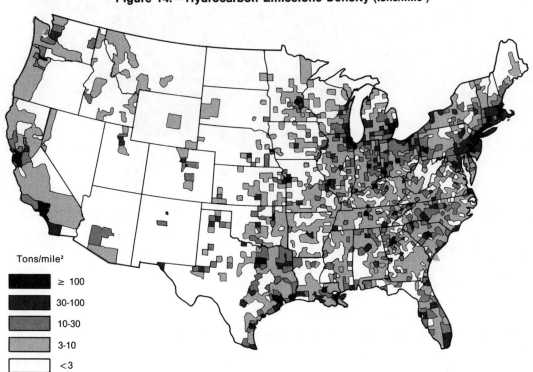

Tons/mile²

≥ 100

30-100

10-30

3-10

< 3

SOURCE: Environmental Protection Agency, based on data from National Emission Data System.

Figure 14.—Hydrocarbon Emissions Density (tons/mile²)

Tons/mile²

≥ 100

30-100

10-30

3-10

<3

SOURCE: Environmental Protection Agency, based on data from National Emission Data System.

Figure 15.—Precipitation Acidity—Annual Average pH for 1980, Weighted by Precipitation Amount

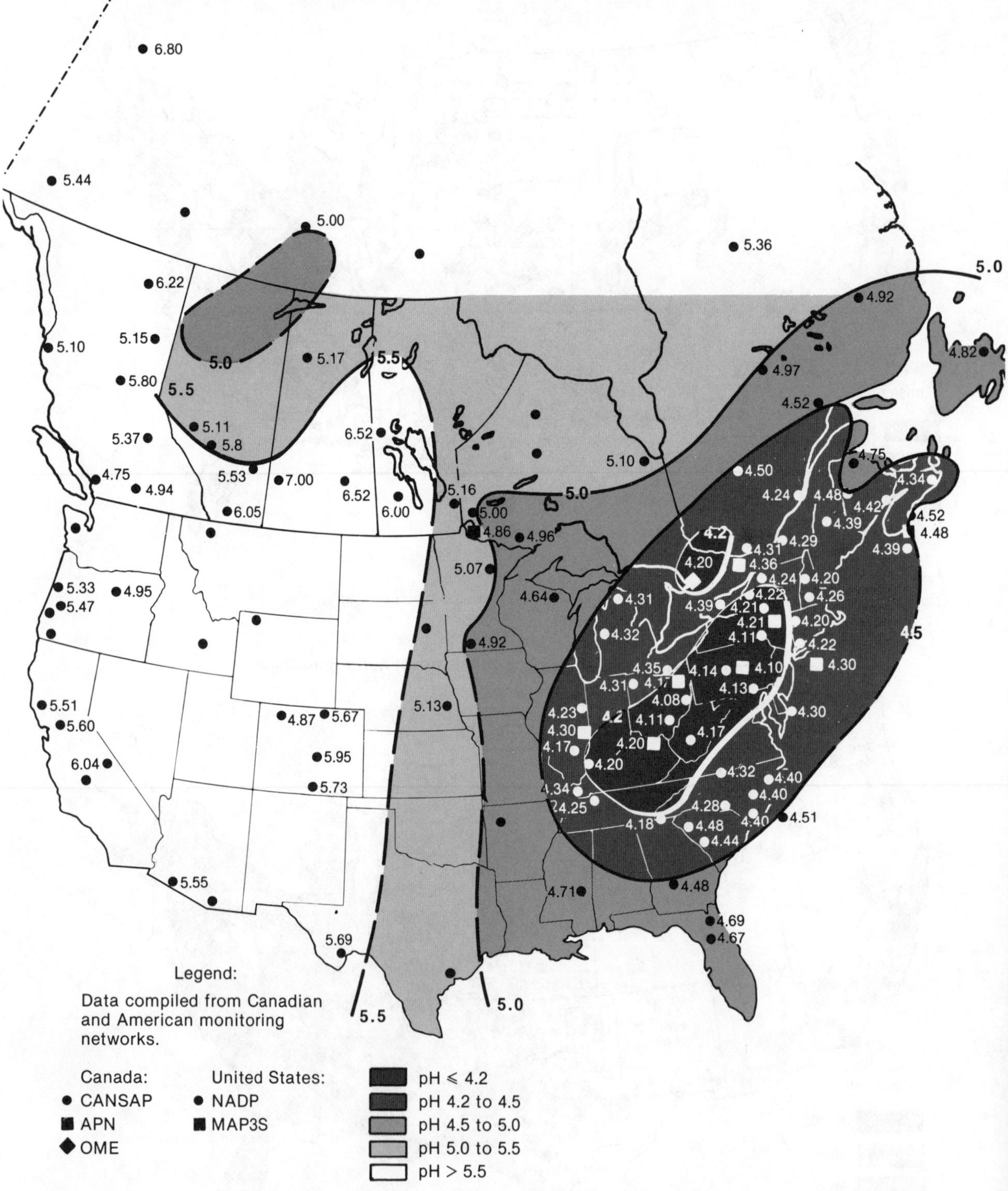

Legend:

Data compiled from Canadian and American monitoring networks.

Canada:	United States:
● CANSAP	● NADP
■ APN	▤ MAP3S
◆ OME	

pH ≤ 4.2
pH 4.2 to 4.5
pH 4.5 to 5.0
pH 5.0 to 5.5
pH > 5.5

SOURCE: *Impact Assessment,* Work Group 1, United States-Canada Memorandum of Intent on Transboundary Air Pollution, final report, January 1983.

Figure 16.—Sulfate in Precipation, 1980 (annual deposition in milliequivalents/meter²)

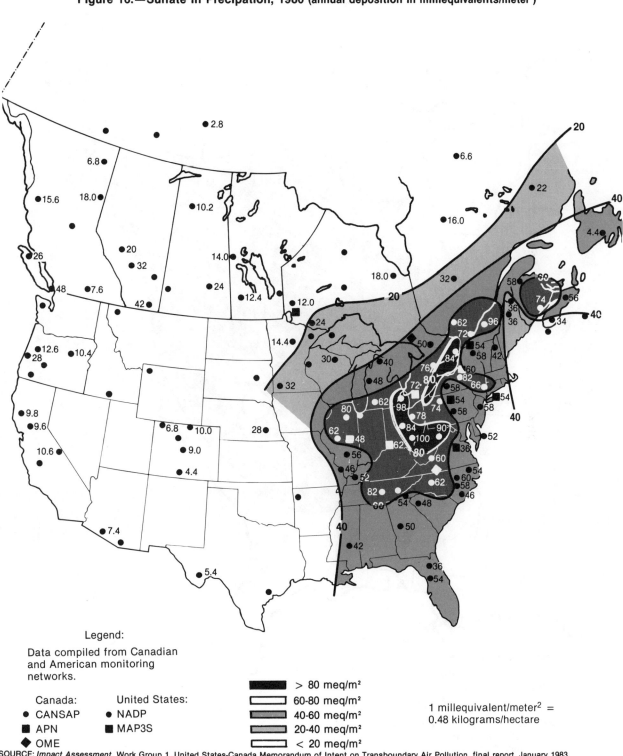

Legend:

Data compiled from Canadian
and American monitoring
networks.

Canada:	United States:
● CANSAP	● NADP
■ APN	■ MAP3S
◆ OME	

■ > 80 meq/m²
☐ 60-80 meq/m²
▨ 40-60 meq/m²
▨ 20-40 meq/m²
☐ < 20 meq/m²

1 millequivalent/meter² =
0.48 kilograms/hectare

SOURCE: *Impact Assessment*, Work Group 1, United States-Canada Memorandum of Intent on Transboundary Air Pollution, final report, January 1983.

Figure 17.—Airborne Sulfate—Annual Average Concentration for 1977-78 (micrograms/meter³)

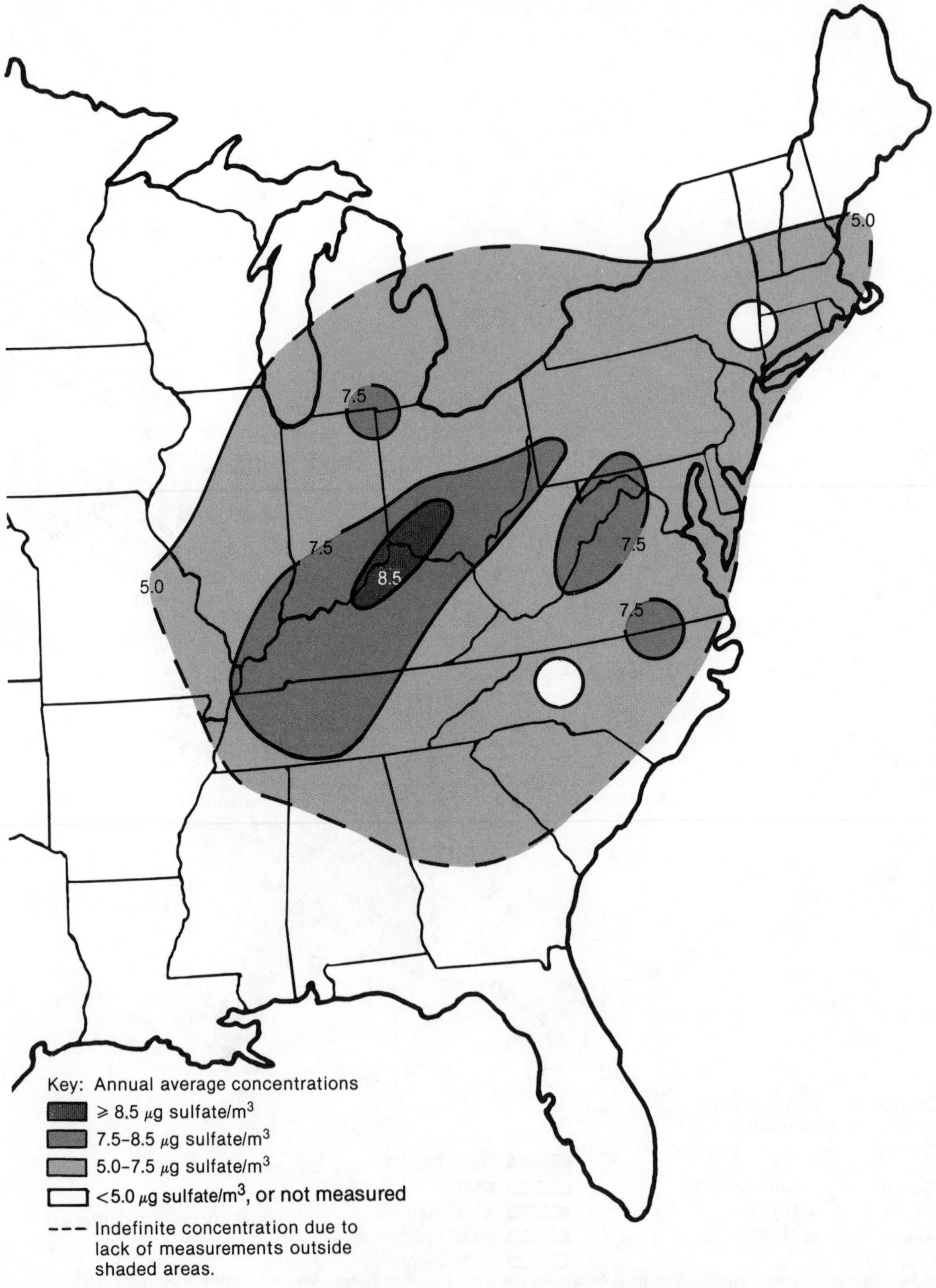

Key: Annual average concentrations

⬛ ≥ 8.5 μg sulfate/m³

⬛ 7.5–8.5 μg sulfate/m³

⬛ 5.0–7.5 μg sulfate/m³

⬜ <5.0 μg sulfate/m³, or not measured

- - - Indefinite concentration due to lack of measurements outside shaded areas.

NOTE: Contours are based on data collected during selected months to represent seasonal averages between August 1977 and June 1978 at SURE II stations.

SOURCE: B. L. Neimann, "Data Bases for Regional Air Pollution Modeling," presented at the EPA Regional Air Pollution Modeling Workshop, Port Deposit, Md., October 1979.

Figure 18.—Ozone Concentration—Daytime, Growing Season Average for 1978
(parts per billion, June to September daily 7-hr average)

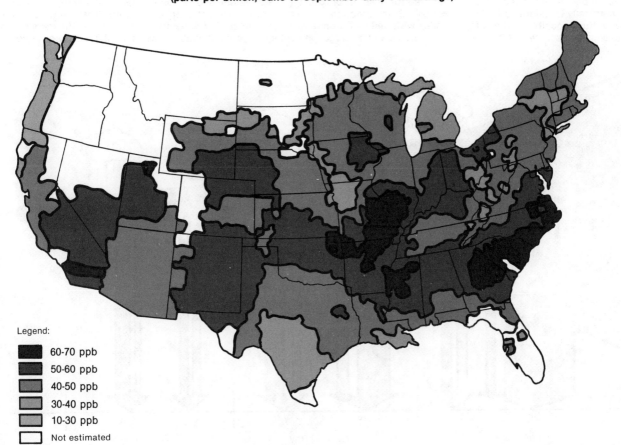

Legend:

■	60-70 ppb
■	50-60 ppb
▨	40-50 ppb
▨	30-40 ppb
▨	10-30 ppb
□	Not estimated

SOURCE: J. Reagan, personal communication, Environmental Protection Agency, 1983.

posited "wet" (i.e., by removal from the air during periodic precipitation events) and "dry" (by the slow, continuous removal of gaseous and particulate sulfur oxides).

As distance from the emission source increases, the relative amount of sulfur deposited in each of these forms changes. Dry deposition predominates close to the emission source; wet deposition predominates in distant areas. Most scientists estimate that these two processes deposit about *equal* amounts of sulfur *when averaged annually over the Eastern United States.* Both wet and dry deposition contribute to the *total* acidity received by ecosystems.

Computer models of pollution transport attempt to describe this process mathematically. Transport models are currently the only practical procedure

available to estimate the relationship between areas of origin and areas of deposition.* Transport models for sulfur oxides have been available for several years, though their accuracy is still a subject of scientific debate. Appendix C discusses the strengths and weaknesses of these models. Preliminary models of nitrogen oxides transport are just now being developed.

The model results are best used to estimate one region's *relative* contribution to deposition in another, rather than for projecting the magnitude of deposition quantitatively. The discussion that fol-

---

*Newly developed tracer techniques may provide additional information on pollution transport. The U.S. and Canadian Governments are jointly conducting the "cross-Appalachian tracer experiment" (CAPTEX), using a chemical called perfluorocarbon to trace the flow of acidic pollutants from sources in Ohio and Ontario.

Figure 19.—The Effects of Time and Distance on Conversion and Deposition of Sulfur Pollution

Sulfur can be deposited in both its emitted form, sulfur dioxide (lighter shading), and as sulfate (darker shading), after being chemically transformed in the atmosphere. Both compounds can be deposited in either dry or wet form. The relative amount of sulfur deposited in these forms varies with distance from emission sources. Dry deposition predominates in areas close to emission sources. Wet deposition is responsible for a larger percentage of pollutant load in areas distant from source regions.

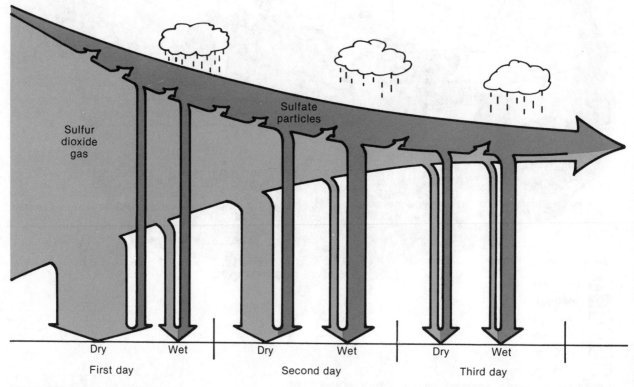

Sulfur dioxide gas

Sulfate particles

| Dry | Wet | Dry | Wet | Dry | Wet |

First day   Second day   Third day

SOURCE: Office of Technology Assessment.

lows characterizes current *patterns* of sulfur oxide transport, but should not be considered a quantitative description.

The results of transport models suggest that pollutants travel from one region to another, in *all* directions, with greater movements of pollutants from west to east and from south to north than in other directions. In addition, while pollutants can travel long distances, emissions *within* a region contribute a large share to total deposition in that region.

To illustrate these points, Eastern North America can be divided into four regions as shown in figure 20. These regions were chosen to intersect at the area of peak wet sulfur deposition in 1980, to minimize deposition biases for any one region. Figure

20 also displays the percentage of sulfur dioxide emitted in each region, and model-based estimates of the percentage of *total* (wet plus dry) sulfur deposited. Sulfur dioxide *emissions* are roughly comparable in the northeastern region (I), southeastern region (II), and southwestern region (III). Emissions in the northwestern region (IV) are over twice the amount of any of the other regions. Total sulfur *deposition* is lowest in the southern regions (II and III) and highest in the northern regions (I and IV).

Figure 21 presents model-based estimates of how much deposition in each region originates from *within* its borders, and from each of the *other* regions. For example, the pie chart in the upper right shows that, of the total sulfur deposited in

Figure 20.—1979 Sulfur Dioxide Emissions and Estimated Sulfur Deposition—Percent Contributed and Received in Four Subregions Covering the Eastern Half of the United States

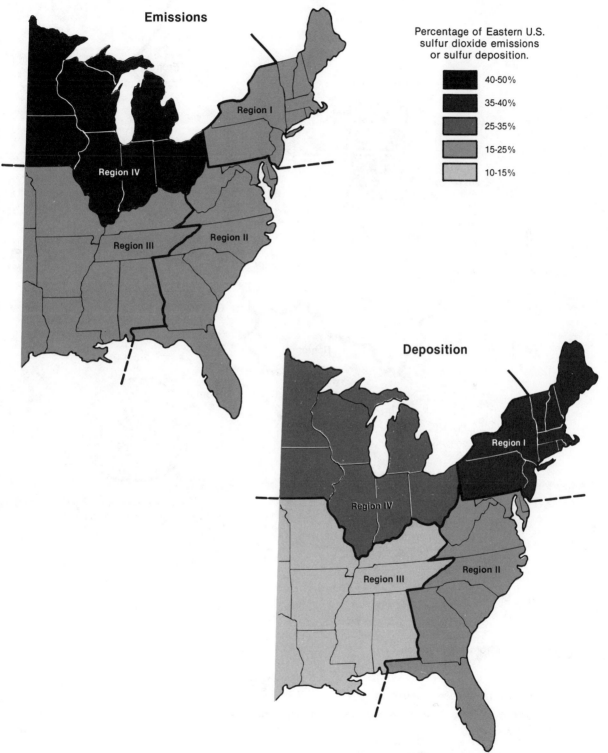

SOURCE: J. Shannon, personal communication, Argonne National Laboratory and E. H. Pechan & Associates, Inc., 1982.

Figure 21.—Percent of Sulfur Deposition Estimated To Originate From Within Each Region and From Other Regions (winter and summer 1979)

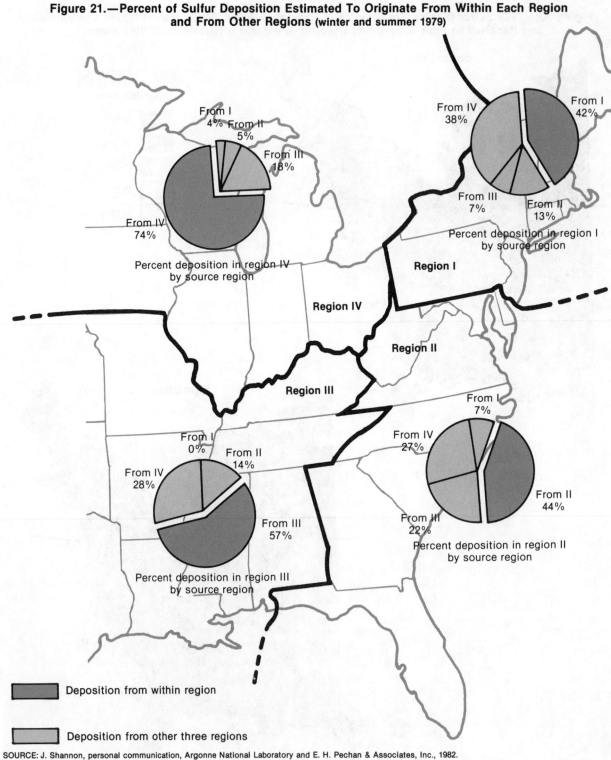

Deposition from within region

Deposition from other three regions

SOURCE: J. Shannon, personal communication, Argonne National Laboratory and E. H. Pechan & Associates, Inc., 1982.

region I (northeastern), approximately 40 percent originates within its own borders, about 40 percent comes from region IV (northwestern), and about 20 percent from the other two regions combined.

When regions as large as these are analyzed, each contributes as much or more to its own deposition as any other single region contributes to it. However, because all regions contribute to deposition in all other regions, a large percentage of deposition in any given region (in some cases over 50 percent) comes from outside. The greatest amounts of interregional transport follow the direction of prevailing winds—generally west to east and south to north.

While the analysis above indicates the magnitude and direction of interregional transport, it does not show the average distances sulfur pollutants can travel. Figure 22 displays model-based estimates of the *percentage of deposition due to long-distance transport,* arbitrarily defined as greater than 500 km (300 miles). A 500-km radius circle is shown to illustrate the scale of transport being discussed. Because wet deposition predominates in remote areas and dry deposition predominates close to emission sources, the two processes are illustrated separately.

In general, long-distance transport accounts for a greater percentage of wet deposition than of dry deposition. Throughout the Midwest and Central Atlantic States, about 30 to 50 percent of the wet deposition originates from emissions greater than 500 km away, as compared to 10 to 30 percent for dry deposition. Throughout New York and New England, long-distance pollutant transport contributes 50 to 80 percent of the wet deposition and 30 to 60 percent of the dry deposition. Over much of the South, most of the deposition originates from sources within 500 km—about 10 to 30 percent of both wet and dry deposition is due to long-distance transport.

These results are model-based simulations of the 1980 summer season. The percentages will vary for other seasons and years, but the broad patterns should be similar.

The accuracy of pollution transport models, which use detailed emissions data and sophisticated meteorology, is a subject of scientific debate.

Measured levels of wet sulfur deposition for 1980 agree fairly closely with OTA's model-based calculations, averaging over large regions on an annual basis. Dry deposition is not monitored routinely enough to compare with model estimates. The model does not include nitrogen oxides, the other major contributor to acid deposition, nor does it portray the complex chemistry involving other atmospheric pollutants.

The chemical reactions that produce acid deposition involve a mix of pollutants present in gas form, dissolved in liquids (e.g., in clouds), and adhering to particles. Sulfur dioxide, nitrogen oxides, and hydrocarbons undergo transformations that may follow many complex chemical pathways. The sequence actually followed depends on concentrations of other chemicals that may inhibit, compete with, or enhance production and deposition of acidity. The same chemicals that transform or "oxidize" sulfur dioxide and nitrogen oxides to acid are also essential for forming ozone. In addition, the physical characteristics of the atmosphere—windspeed, sunlight intensity, and rainfall frequency—affect these transformations.

Predicting quantities of deposition at a *specific* time and place is not yet possible, and may not be for many years. Making such predictions would require detailed information on the current concentrations of sulfur dioxide, nitrogen oxides, and hydrocarbons, as well as on the history of the air mass, including the frequency and amounts of fresh pollutant inputs, the frequency and duration of recent rainfall events, and other specific chemical and physical information.

However, current understanding of the various chemical and physical processes involved permits scientists to characterize very generally—over large spatial scales, and seasonal time scales—the effects of reducing emitted quantities of various pollutants. The deposition changes that would result from reducing emissions of sulfur dioxide, nitrogen oxides, and hydrocarbons are discussed in appendix C, and are summarized briefly below:

- Reducing sulfur dioxide emissions will reduce the total amount of acid formed in the atmosphere, *if* levels of nitrogen oxides and hydrocarbons remain constant, and chemical reactions are not limited by a shortage of ox-

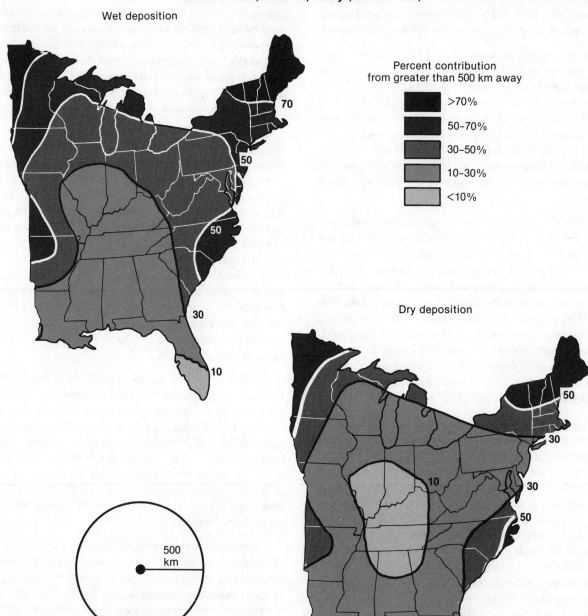

Figure 22.—Estimated Percentage of Sulfur Deposition From Emissions Over 500 km (300 miles) Away (summer 1980)

Wet deposition

Percent contribution from greater than 500 km away

>70%
50-70%
30-50%
10-30%
<10%

Dry deposition

SOURCE: J. Shannon, personal communication, Argonne National Laboratory, 1982.

idizing agents. Furthermore, given these conditions, a decrease in sulfur dioxide emissions should decrease total sulfur deposition by an approximately equal proportion. *Where* deposition will decrease can only be estimated on a regional scale.

- Decreasing nitrogen oxides emissions—while holding hydrocarbon emissions constant—would decrease the amount of ozone produced over a large region, as well as the amount of nitric acid ultimately deposited. The total amount of sulfur deposited would probably not be affected, although the conversion of sulfur dioxide to sulfate might accelerate somewhat, affecting the regional distribution of deposition.

- Reducing hydrocarbon emissions can decrease the production of ozone, and of some key chemicals responsible for transforming sulfur dioxide and nitrogen oxides to acids. This would slow the production of sulfuric and nitric acids, again altering the patterns of deposition, but probably would not affect total *amounts* of deposition.

If current regulations remain unchanged, sulfur dioxide emissions are projected to remain about constant or increase slightly, hydrocarbon emissions to remain about constant, and nitrogen oxides emissions to increase. Local acid deposition due to nitric acid would probably increase. The amount of total sulfur deposited might remain about constant, but reactions involving increased nitrogen oxides emissions might cause the geographic patterns of sulfur deposition to change.

Given the complexities of atmospheric chemistry, and inherent meteorological variability, as well as the need to develop detailed emissions inventories (especially for nitrogen oxides and hydrocarbons), it is unlikely that a definitive model linking particular sources to specific receptors will be developed in the next decade. Policy decisions to control or not to control precursor emissions will have to be made without the benefit of such precise information.

Chapter 5
The Regional Distribution of Risks

Contents

FIGURES

Chapter 5
The Regional Distribution of Risks

INTRODUCTION

Chapter 3 presented the risks of controlling and not controlling transported air pollutants for the Eastern 31-State region overall. However, the ways in which these risks are distributed throughout the region are of prime significance to the policy debate. Most importantly, considerable variation is found in:

- the distribution of pollution sources, and hence, the distribution of potential control costs;
- the distribution and extent of resources at risk, their levels of exposure, and their inherent sensitivity to transported pollutants; and
- the relative importance of the economic sector at risk to each State's economy.

Scientific uncertainties complicate the task of describing the distribution of risk. However, even if scientists attained "perfect knowledge" of the causes and consequences of transported air pollutants, different *groups* and *regions of the country* would bear these risks. Thus, while it is impossible to precisely specify these groups and regions at present, the distributional aspects of transported pollutants are *inherently* part of the policy problem.

This chapter describes how the risks associated with three pollutants—acid deposition, ozone, and airborne sulfate—are distributed. The order of discussion closely follows the presentation in chapter 3 of the aggregate risks to the Eastern 31-State region. This chapter, however, focuses on the regional distribution of these risks, and is extensively illustrated with maps.

Two situations are described: 1) the risk of resource damage and adverse health effects if Con-

gress maintains the status quo for pollutant emissions, and 2) the costs and economic effects of additional pollution-control measures that might be adopted.

Some of the risks of controlling or not controlling transported air pollutants can be thought of as "localized" risks. For example, fewer than half the States contain deposits of high sulfur-content coal; only in these States could current coal production be lost due to additional pollution-control requirements. Similarly, only parts of the Eastern United States contain lakes and streams considered potentially sensitive to acid deposition. Other risks can be characterized as "distributed"—risks that are present in virtually all States in the Eastern region. For example, crops are grown in all States. Three factors determine the relative importance of ozone-caused crop damage: 1) the concentration of ozone in a State, 2) the sensitivities of a State's crops to ozone, and 3) the importance of agriculture to the State economy. Likewise, the effects of utility pollution-control costs depend both on the amount of the State income spent on electricity and on a State's pollutant emissions.

In addition to describing the geographic patterns of risk from transported air pollutants, this chapter assesses the relative importance of five economic sectors of concern: agriculture, forestry and forest product-related industries, freshwater recreational fishing, coal mining, and electricity generation. The first four sectors vary considerably in economic importance from State to State—from a small percentage of the regional average to several times that average. The last sector, electricity generation, is much more uniformly distributed.

NO CONGRESSIONAL ACTION

Aquatic Ecosystems

As discussed in chapter 3, lakes and streams are affected not only by the acid deposition falling directly on them, but also by the amount of acid-producing substances entering them from surrounding watersheds. Regions with soils and bedrock that neutralize acidic deposition are not likely to be affected. The areas outlined in figures 23 and 24 are thought to allow acidity to travel through watersheds to lake and streams. These areas contain soils that either cannot neutralize acidity, or are so steep and rocky that rainfall has little contact with soils and runs directly into lakes or streams. The *size* of the circles on each map illustrates the extent of lake and stream resources in each region. The greatest number of lakes is found in the upper Midwest, followed by New England. The greatest mileage of small streams is found in New England, followed by the mountain region of

Figure 23.—Estimated Percentages of Lakes Vulnerable to Acid Deposition in Sensitive Regions of the Eastern United States

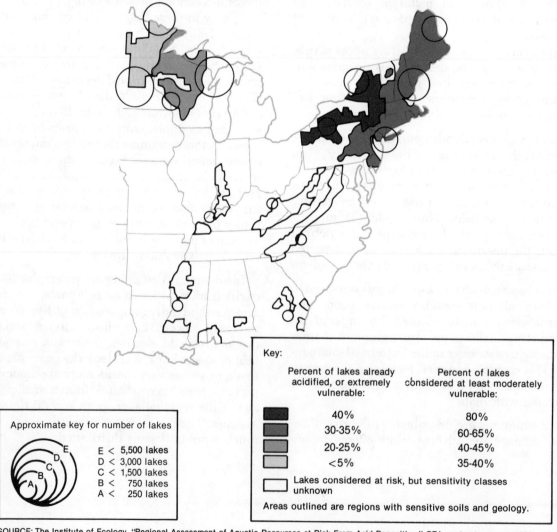

Approximate key for number of lakes

E < 5,500 lakes
D < 3,000 lakes
C < 1,500 lakes
B <   750 lakes
A <   250 lakes

Key:

Percent of lakes already acidified, or extremely vulnerable:	Percent of lakes considered at least moderately vulnerable:
40%	80%
30-35%	60-65%
20-25%	40-45%
<5%	35-40%

Lakes considered at risk, but sensitivity classes unknown

Areas outlined are regions with sensitive soils and geology.

SOURCE: The Institute of Ecology, "Regional Assessment of Aquatic Resources at Risk From Acid Deposition," OTA contractor report, 1982.

Figure 24.—Estimated Percentages of Streams Vulnerable to Acid Deposition in Sensitive Regions of the Eastern United States

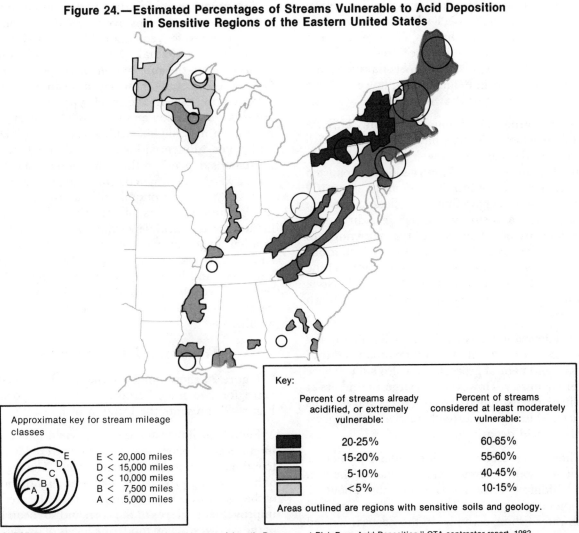

Approximate key for stream mileage classes

E < 20,000 miles
D < 15,000 miles
C < 10,000 miles
B < 7,500 miles
A < 5,000 miles

Key:

	Percent of streams already acidified, or extremely vulnerable:	Percent of streams considered at least moderately vulnerable:
	20-25%	60-65%
	15-20%	55-60%
	5-10%	40-45%
	<5%	10-15%

Areas outlined are regions with sensitive soils and geology.

SOURCE: The Institute of Ecology, "Regional Assessment of Aquatic Resources at Risk From Acid Deposition," OTA contractor report, 1982.

West Virginia, Kentucky, western Virginia, North Carolina, and eastern Tennessee.

However, because of local variation in soil and watershed characteristics, not all the lakes and streams within these regions will be vulnerable to acidic deposition. The intensity of shading within each outlined area indicates the percentage of lakes and streams estimated to be vulnerable to acid deposition, based on water quality characteristics. The northeastern regions have the greatest percentages of "extremely" vulnerable lakes and streams—we estimate about 30 to 40 percent of the over 5,000 lakes and 10 to 20 percent of the 65,000 stream miles in the area. These regions also receive high levels of acidic deposition. In addition, large

numbers of moderately vulnerable lakes are found in the upper Midwest, and extensive mileages of moderately vulnerable streams are found in the central Appalachian/Blue Ridge regions.

Directly comparing current conditions to historical data, only a small number of surface waters in North America are *known* to have acidified. Data from several decades ago are sparse; in addition, differences in sampling and measurement techniques make comparisons with current data difficult. A review of the available evidence for acidification found significant changes in water body chemistry in studies of: 250 lakes in Maine, 94 lakes in New England, 40 lakes in the Adirondacks, and two streams in the New Jersey Pine Barrens, as well as in 16 lakes near Halifax, Nova Scotia, 22 lakes in the LaCloche Mountains, Ontario, and Clear Lake, Ontario. Changes in water chemistry over time have also been reported for 38 North Carolina streams, 6 Nova Scotia rivers, and 314 surface waters in Pennsylvania; however, firm conclusions cannot be drawn from these studies.[1]

In the Adirondack Mountains, the only U.S. location in which scientists have documented *fish population* declines, the New York State Department of Environmental Conservation has reported the disappearance of fish populations in about 180 lakes. Researchers have found correlations between acidity levels and survival of fish in Adirondack lakes and streams. Four other areas are known to have experienced losses of fish populations associated with surface water acidification: 1) the LaCloche Mountain region of Ontario, 2) Nova Scotia, 3) Southern Norway, and 4) Southern Sweden.

Acid deposition may not be the sole cause of the changes discussed above. Other man-induced stresses and natural processes can also alter surface water chemistry. However, the largest numbers of acidified and extremely sensitive lakes and streams are located in regions currently receiving the highest levels of acid deposition.

Though the economic value of these particular sensitive resources cannot yet be estimated, the Fish and Wildlife Service has estimated that about 21 million people spent $6.3 billion on all recreational freshwater fishing activities in the Eastern United States during 1980. Figure 25 illustrates how these expenditures vary by State, displaying the importance of recreational fishing to each State's economy *relative* to the 31-State regional average.

Because there are few data to determine whether lakes and streams sensitive to acid deposition are those preferred for recreational fishing, OTA cannot estimate potential regional economic losses resulting from the elimination of fish populations. One local-scale study, however, has estimated losses to New York resident anglers of approximately $1.7 (1982 dollars) million annually from lost fishing opportunities in about 200 acidified Adirondack lakes and ponds.[2] Potential losses to individuals whose livelihoods depend on the recreational fishing industry were not estimated. On a regional scale, the States at greatest economic risk are those with: 1) the greatest numbers of sensitive lakes, 2) the highest levels of acid deposition, and 3) the highest relative expenditures for recreational fishing. Among these are the New England States of Maine, Vermont, and New Hampshire; the Appalachian region of West Virginia and eastern Kentucky; and parts of the Midwestern States of Wisconsin and Minnesota.

Terrestrial Ecosystems

Figure 26 shows major agricultural production areas for two major crops, corn and soybeans. Figure 27 presents the location of forests.

Figure 28 illustrates the crop yield gains that might occur if ozone concentrations were lowered to estimated natural background levels. The regions of highest crop production—an area slightly north of the peak ozone concentrations—show the greatest improvement. Here, in the corn and soybean belt of the Midwest, even moderate levels of ozone can cause substantial crop damage. For Iowa, Indiana, and Illinois, reducing ozone concentrations to background levels might cause both soybean and corn yields to increase by about 20 to 40 million bushels per year in each State. (See app. B for potential productivity gains in wheat and peanuts with decreased ozone concentrations.)

Comparing figures 15 (patterns of acidity) and 26 (current corn and soybean yields) indicates that elevated levels of acid deposition occur within several major crop-producing States, including Illinois, Indiana, and Ohio. Reductions in both soy-

[1]R. A. Linthurst, J. P. Baker, and A. M. Bartuska, "Effects of Acidic Deposition: A Brief Review," *Proceedings of the APCA Specialty Conference on Atmospheric Deposition,* Air Pollution Control Association, November 1982, reviewing International Electric Research Exchange, *Effects of SO₂ and Its Derivatives on Health and Ecology,* Central Electricity Generating Board, Leatherhead, England; National Research Council of Canada, *Acidification in the Canadian Aquatic Environment: Scientific Criteria for Assessing the Effects of Acidic Deposition on Aquatic Ecosystems,* Associated Committee on Scientific Criteria for Environmental Quality, National Research Council of Canada, NRCC No. 18475, 1981; and J. Baker, "Effects on Aquatic Biology," *Draft Critical Assessment Document: The Acidic Deposition Phenomenon and Its Effects,* Chapter E-5, 5.6 Fishes (October 1982).

[2]F. C. Menz and J. K. Mullen, "Acidification Impact on Fisheries: Substitution and the Valuation of Recreational Resources," *Economic Perspectives on Acid Deposition,* T.D. Crocker (ed.) (Ann Arbor: Butterworth Press, 1984).

Figure 25.—Freshwater Recreational Fishing—Relative Economic Importance

1980 recreational fishing expenditures by State (expenditures on freshwater recreational fishing, scaled by State income, compared to regional average)

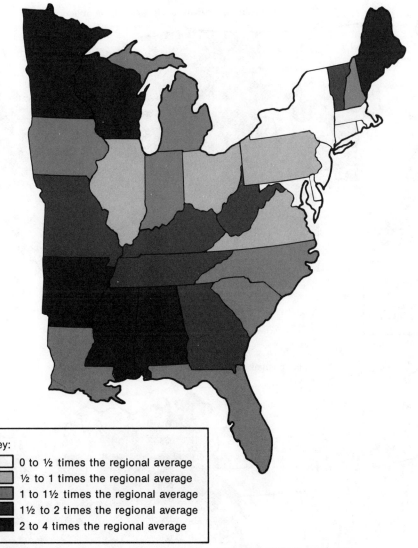

Key:
- 0 to ½ times the regional average
- ½ to 1 times the regional average
- 1 to 1½ times the regional average
- 1½ to 2 times the regional average
- 2 to 4 times the regional average

SOURCE: Office of Technology Assessment, from U.S. Census Bureau and U.S. Fish and Wildlife Service data.

bean and corn productivity have been observed in field experiments with simulated acid rain, but other experiments have yielded contradictory results.

Scientists have recently discovered productivity declines in several tree species throughout the Eastern United States from New England to Georgia. Acid deposition, ozone, heavy-metal deposition,

drought, severe winters or a combination of these are possible causes under investigation.

By coring trees and measuring the thickness of annual growth rings, scientists have observed marked reductions in productivity beginning about 1960 in red spruce, shortleaf pine and pitch pine. Corings from about 30 other species at 70 sites throughout the East are currently being analyzed to deter-

Figure 26.—Production of Corn and Soybeans in 1978

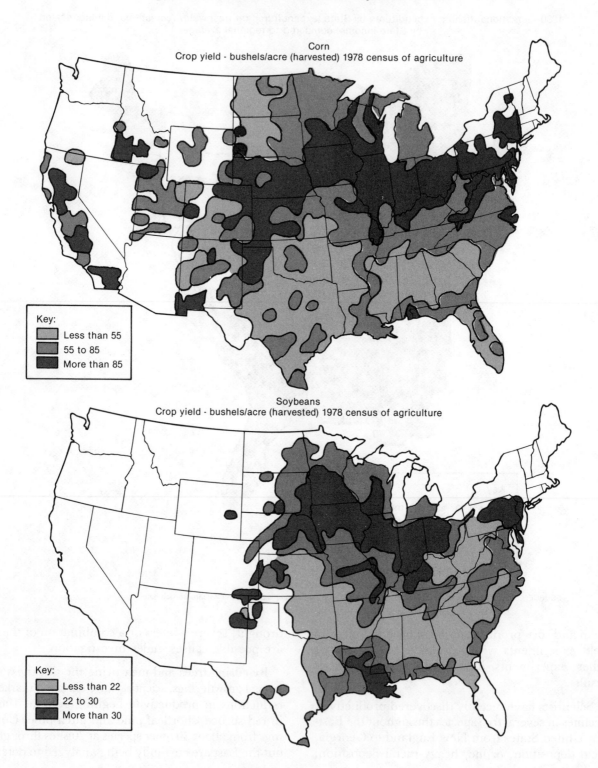

Corn
Crop yield - bushels/acre (harvested) 1978 census of agriculture

Key:
Less than 55
55 to 85
More than 85

Soybeans
Crop yield - bushels/acre (harvested) 1978 census of agriculture

Key:
Less than 22
22 to 30
More than 30

SOURCE: Oak Ridge National Laboratory, from 1978 Census of Agriculture.

Figure 27.—Percent of Land Area Capable of Commercial Timber Production[a]

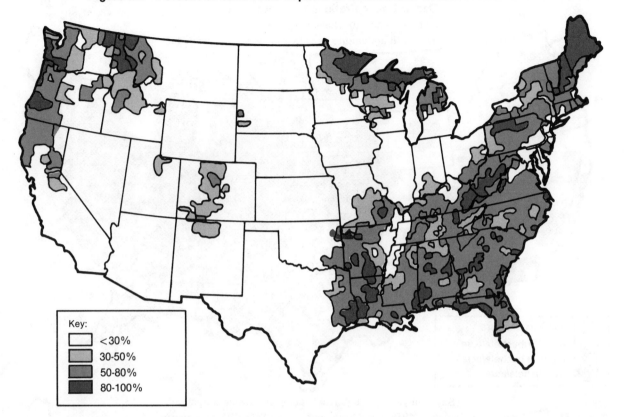

Key:
- <30%
- 30-50%
- 50-80%
- 80-100%

[a]The U.S. Forest Service defines commercial timberland as lands capable of producing greater than 20 cubic feet of industrial roundwood per acre per year, in natural stands.

SOURCE: Oak Ridge National Laboratory, 1981; U.S. Forest Service State forest inventory.

mine the geographic extent and severity of the problem. Routine measurements of tree growth by the U.S. Forest Service have shown productivity declines in loblolly pine and shortleaf pine during the 1970s in the Piedmont region of South Carolina and Georgia.

Although ozone is known to harm trees, quantitative estimates of forest productivity losses due to ozone are lacking because of the difficulty of performing experiments on long-lived species. By comparing figures 18 and 27, one can observe that elevated ozone concentrations coincide with forested regions in the southern Appalachian Mountains, the Ozark Mountains, and parts of the southern softwood area of the Southeastern and South Central States.

Much of the forested area of New England, the Appalachian Mountains, and parts of the southern softwood forests of Alabama and Georgia receive elevated levels of acid deposition, as can be seen in figures 15 and 27. However, the relationships between forest health and levels of deposition are not well known. The nitrogen deposited is a beneficial nutrient, but the acidity might damage leaf surfaces, remove nutrients from foliage, alter susceptibility to pests (either beneficially or detrimentally), or alter forest soil chemistry.

Forest soils are at risk from acid deposition due to: 1) release (mobilization) of soil-bound metals, such as aluminum, that are toxic to plants if present in sufficient quantity, 2) potential leaching of calcium, magnesium, and other nutrients essential for plant growth from the soil, and 3) further acidification of soils. Figure 29 displays the geographic distribution of these risks. Available information allowed OTA to identify those counties in which soils susceptible to these effects predominate; other locations where they occur to a lesser extent could not be determined.

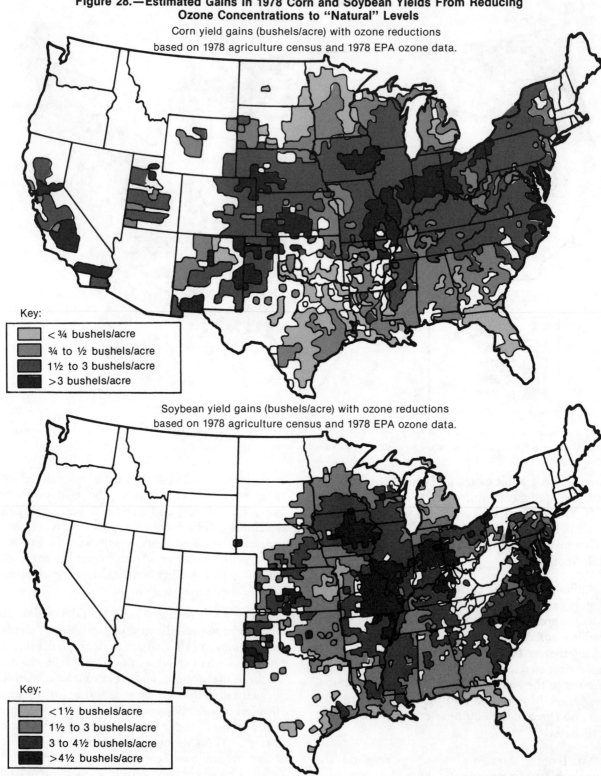

Figure 28.—Estimated Gains in 1978 Corn and Soybean Yields From Reducing Ozone Concentrations to "Natural" Levels

Corn yield gains (bushels/acre) with ozone reductions based on 1978 agriculture census and 1978 EPA ozone data.

Key:
- < ¾ bushels/acre
- ¾ to ½ bushels/acre
- 1½ to 3 bushels/acre
- >3 bushels/acre

Soybean yield gains (bushels/acre) with ozone reductions based on 1978 agriculture census and 1978 EPA ozone data.

Key:
- <1½ bushels/acre
- 1½ to 3 bushels/acre
- 3 to 4½ bushels/acre
- >4½ bushels/acre

SOURCE: Oak Ridge National Laboratory, "An Analysis of Potential Agriculture and Forest Impacts of Long-Range Transport Air Pollutants," OTA contractor report, 1983.

Figure 29.—Soil Sensitivity to Acid Deposition (nonagricultural)

Forested and range areas with soils thought to be susceptible to the effects of acid deposition. Shaded areas represent counties in which a susceptible soil type predominates. The three levels of shading correspond to different soil types, and potential effects, rather than to degrees of susceptibility.

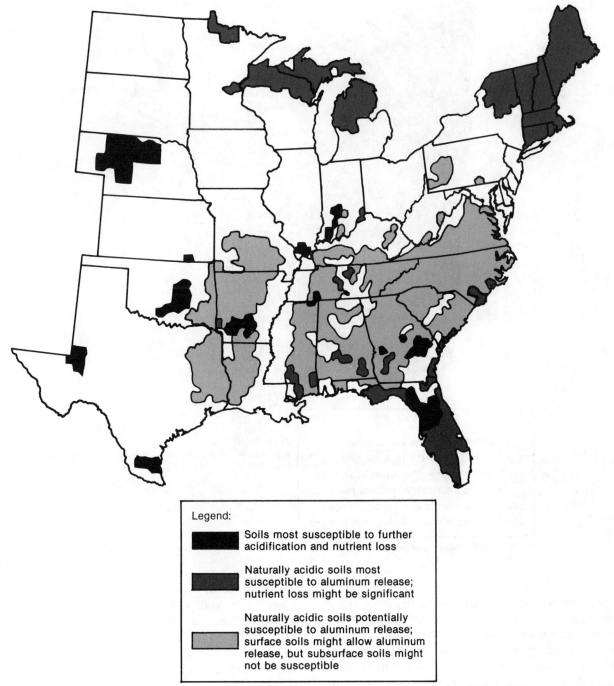

Legend:

Soils most susceptible to further acidification and nutrient loss

Naturally acidic soils most susceptible to aluminum release; nutrient loss might be significant

Naturally acidic soils potentially susceptible to aluminum release; surface soils might allow aluminum release, but subsurface soils might not be susceptible

SOURCE: Oak Ridge National Laboratory, "An Analysis of Potential Agriculture and Forest Impacts of Long-Range Transport Air Pollutants," OTA contractor report, 1983.

Figure 30.—Agriculture—Relative Economic Importance

elative importance of agriculture-related income to State income, 1978-80

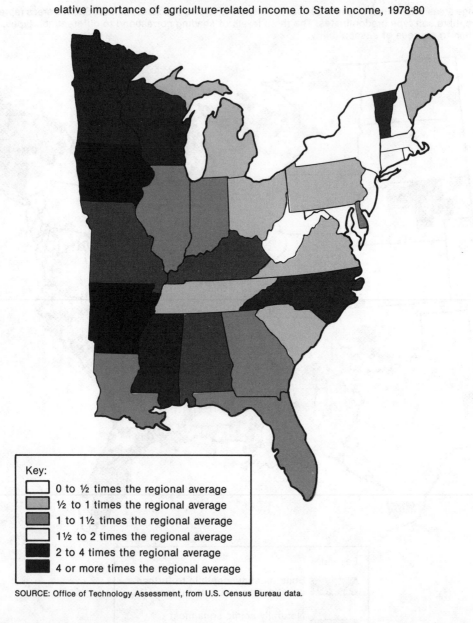

Key:

☐	0 to ½ times the regional average
▧	½ to 1 times the regional average
▨	1 to 1½ times the regional average
☐	1½ to 2 times the regional average
■	2 to 4 times the regional average
■	4 or more times the regional average

SOURCE: Office of Technology Assessment, from U.S. Census Bureau data.

Soils must already be acidic—about pH 5 or lower—to release aluminum in the presence of the strong acids in acid deposition. Regions where naturally acid soils predominate are shown as the medium and light gray areas in figure 29. However, the soils in the light gray areas trap sulfate in their lower layers, which somewhat reduces the amount of this strong acid available for releasing aluminum.

Soils that are both acidic and do not impede the flow of sulfate (shaded a medium gray in fig. 29)

predominate in New England and northern New York State, and parts of the upper Midwest and Florida. These regions are considered most susceptible to the toxic effects of aluminum; however, whether resulting aluminum concentrations will be high enough to significantly alter forest productivity is not yet known.

Figure 29 also displays regions of the Eastern United States where nutrient loss is of concern. The dark patches are areas with moderately acid soils.

Figure 31.—Forestry—Relative Economic Importance

Relative importance of forestry-related income to State income, 1978-80

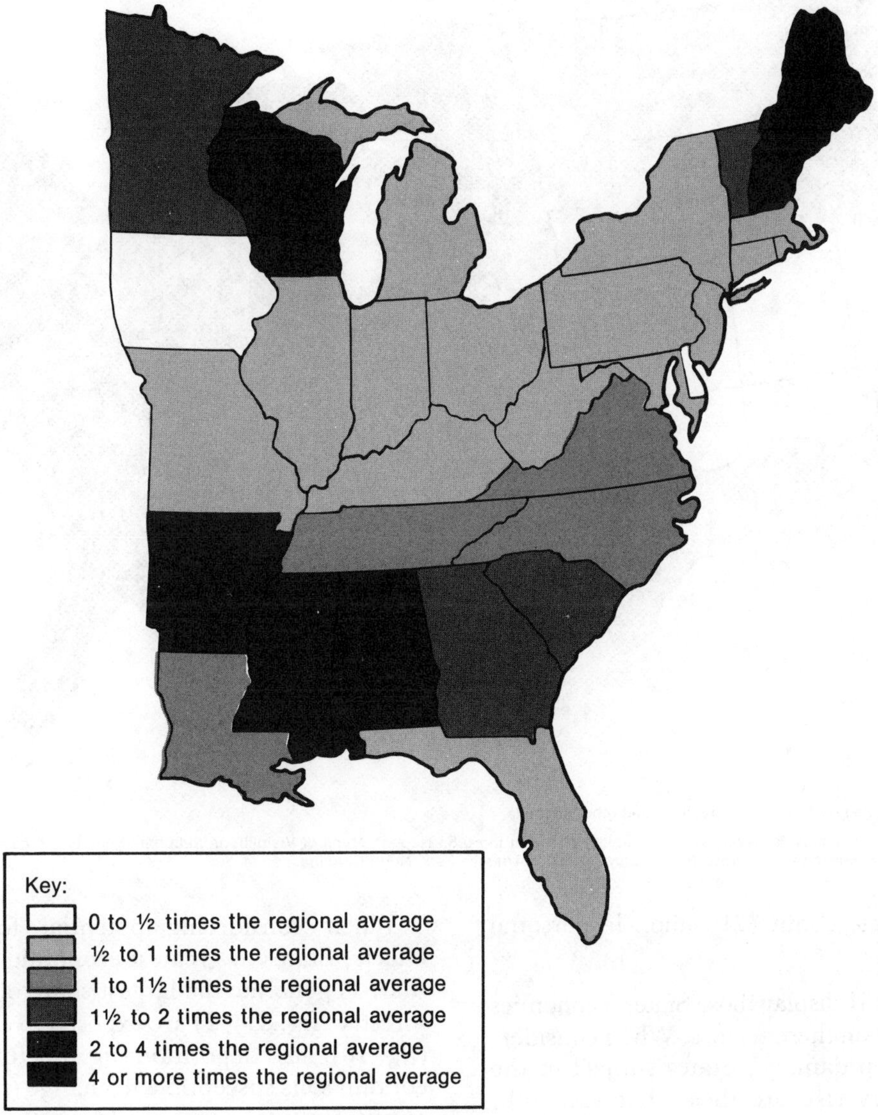

Key:

☐ 0 to ½ times the regional average

▨ ½ to 1 times the regional average

▨ 1 to 1½ times the regional average

▨ 1½ to 2 times the regional average

■ 2 to 4 times the regional average

■ 4 or more times the regional average

SOURCE: Office of Technology Assessment, from U.S. Census Bureau data.

Loss of calcium, magnesium, and other nutrients from these relatively uncommon soils through decades of exposure to acid deposition might cause these soils to further acidify. Nutrients can also be lost from more acidic soils—typically already nutrient poor—but probably at a slower rate. Most susceptible are those regions (shaded medium gray) with nutrient-poor acid soils that allow sulfate to move freely, potentially carrying away nutrients from the soil, plant canopy, and decaying plant material. However, whether the *rate* of nutrient loss from these soils is more rapid than replacement by weathering is unknown.

Both agriculture and forestry are important to the overall economy of the Eastern United States, each providing about 3.7 percent of the total regional income. Agriculture and related services are responsible for about $22 billion of the region's income; forestry, wood, lumber, paper, and allied

Figure 32.—Median Yearly Visual Range (miles) for Suburban and Nonurban Areas

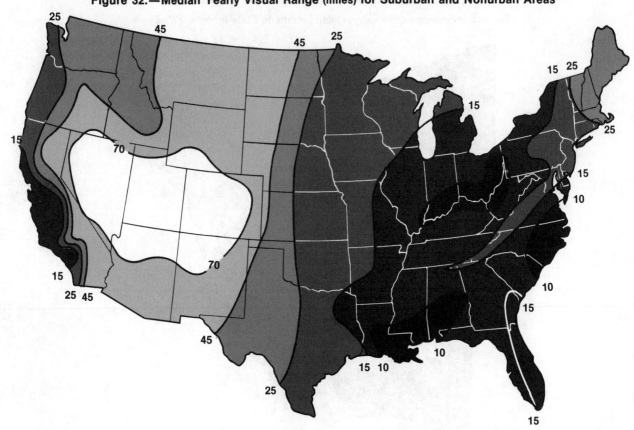

Data from 1974–76, estimated from visual observations and other methods.

SOURCE: Trijonis, J., and Shapland, R., 1979: Existing Visibility Levels in the U.S.: Isopleth Maps of Visibility in Suburban/Nonurban Areas During 1974–76, EPA 450/5-79-010, U.S. Environmental Protection Agency, Research Triangle Park, North Carolina.

industries generate about $21 billion in personal income.

Figures 30 and 31 display those States' economies that depend most on these sectors. When considering potential crop damage, States subject to the greatest monetary risk are those that are both: 1) exposed to elevated ozone (fig. 18), acid deposition (fig. 15), or both; and 2) generate the largest share of State income from agriculture (fig. 30). Iowa, Illinois, Indiana, Missouri, Arkansas, Mississippi, Alabama, and North Carolina are at greatest economic risk from ozone damage. If acid deposition affects crops, the above States plus Vermont would be at greatest risk.

When considering potential forestry-related effects, States at greatest economic risk are those that: 1) generate the largest share of income from forestry (fig. 31); 2) are exposed to elevated ozone (fig. 18), acid deposition (fig. 15), or both; and 3) contain soils susceptible to change (fig. 29). States at greatest economic risk from ozone include the southern softwood region extending from Arkansas to North Carolina. Many of these States receive high levels of acid deposition and have soils considered susceptible to mobilization of toxic aluminum or nutrient loss, as do the New England States of Vermont, New Hampshire, and Maine.

Figure 33.—Population Exposure to Airborne Sulfate (an indicator of potential health effects from sulfates and other airborne particulates in each State)

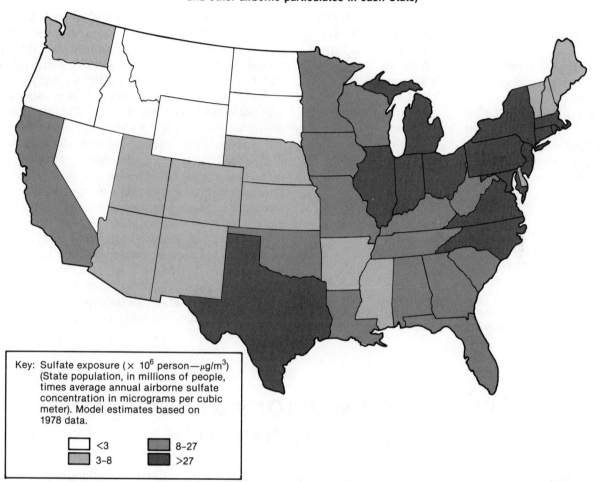

Key: Sulfate exposure ($\times$ 10^6 person—μg/m^3) (State population, in millions of people, times average annual airborne sulfate concentration in micrograms per cubic meter). Model estimates based on 1978 data.

☐ <3   ▨ 8–27
▨ 3–8   ■ >27

SOURCE: Brookhaven National Laboratory, Biomedical and Environmental Assessment Division, "Long Range Transport Air Pollution Health Effects," OTA contractor report, May 1982.

OTHER RISKS

Materials

Materials at greatest risk from exposure to acidic deposition include metals, such as steel and zinc, and stone masonry. Regions at greatest risk correspond to those with the greatest population densities and areas with historically significant buildings and monuments. Scientists estimate that the bulk of materials damage is caused by *local-scale* pollutants, and that sulfur dioxide emissions are responsible for a major share of pollutant-induced damages to a broad range of materials. Elevated ozone concentrations are harmful to such materials as paint on home exteriors and rubber. The distribution of materials sensitive to air pollutants is not well known, since inventories have been taken in very few areas.

Visibility

For the Eastern United States, sulfate is the single most important contributor to visibility degradation; patterns of impairment in the region correlate fairly well to airborne sulfate concentrations (presented earlier as fig. 17). Sulfate is currently estimated to account for 50 percent of visibility degradation annually, and 70 percent of summer visibility degradation in the East. In the West, nitrates may play a larger role than sulfates in visibility impairment. Figure 32 shows annual average visibilities throughout the Nation for the mid-1970's, the most recent information available to OTA. Visibility in the Eastern United States has improved slightly over the past decade, but is still less than pre-1960 levels.

Current Eastern visibility levels are generally far lower than those in the West. However, it should be noted that *unimpaired* Eastern visibility levels would be significantly lower than in the West, due to higher Eastern humidity levels. In addition, where visibility is already low, an increment of additional sulfate may not reduce visibility much further; in more pristine areas, the same increment of additional sulfate may significantly decrease visibility.

Risk of Health Effects

The health risk to any *individual* is thought to be correlated to sulfate concentrations in the atmosphere. However, whether premature mortality observed in statistical studies actually results from sulfate in air pollution, from different components of the sulfate-particulate mix, or from other factors not considered, is unknown. This risk varies from increases of less than 1 percent in excess mortality in the West to about 4 percent (a range from about 0 to 10 percent) in the regions of highest sulfate concentration. The health risk to a State is determined both by the potential increase in mortality and by the State's population. Some of the Northeastern States with the highest population densities (e.g., New York, Pennsylvania, and Ohio) are also exposed to the highest airborne sulfate concentrations, and are therefore at greatest risk. Figure 33 displays the total exposure of each State's population to airborne sulfate, an indicator of the relative risk of premature mortality in each State.

IF FURTHER EMISSIONS REDUCTIONS ARE MANDATED

Rates of Pollutant Emissions

The regional patterns of pollutant emissions are perhaps the best indicator of how costs to control transported air pollution might be distributed. Figures 12 and 13 in chapter 4 display maps of emissions *densities* (in tons per square mile) for sulfur dioxide and nitrogen oxides. This section discusses another measure of pollutant emissions more directly related to potential control costs—emission *rates,* expressed as pounds of pollutants per quantity of fuel burned.

To date, the major legislative proposals to control acid deposition have focused primarily on sulfur dioxide emissions. Though emissions reductions can be allocated to States in many ways, most of these bills propose reductions based on emission rates. This approach avoids penalizing areas emitting large quantities of sulfur dioxide because of

high electrical or industrial productivity; instead, reductions are concentrated in areas that emit greater-than-average amounts of sulfur dioxide for a given amount of production.

Sulfur dioxide emission rates vary widely among States. Emission rates can be decreased either by using: 1) a lower sulfur fuel, or 2) technological means, such as capturing the sulfur dioxide gas with "scrubbers" after the fuel is burned.

Figure 34 displays estimates of statewide average sulfur dioxide emission rates from utilities and industrial boilers. Within the Eastern 31-State region, utilities account for about 70 to 75 percent of sulfur dioxide emissions, and industrial boilers for about 10 to 15 percent.

The Midwestern States have the highest utility emission rates, and are therefore at greatest risk from additional pollution control regulations. In-

Figure 34.—Average 1980 Emission Rates for Sulfur Dioxide From Utility and Industrial Sources (lb SO₂/MMBtu)

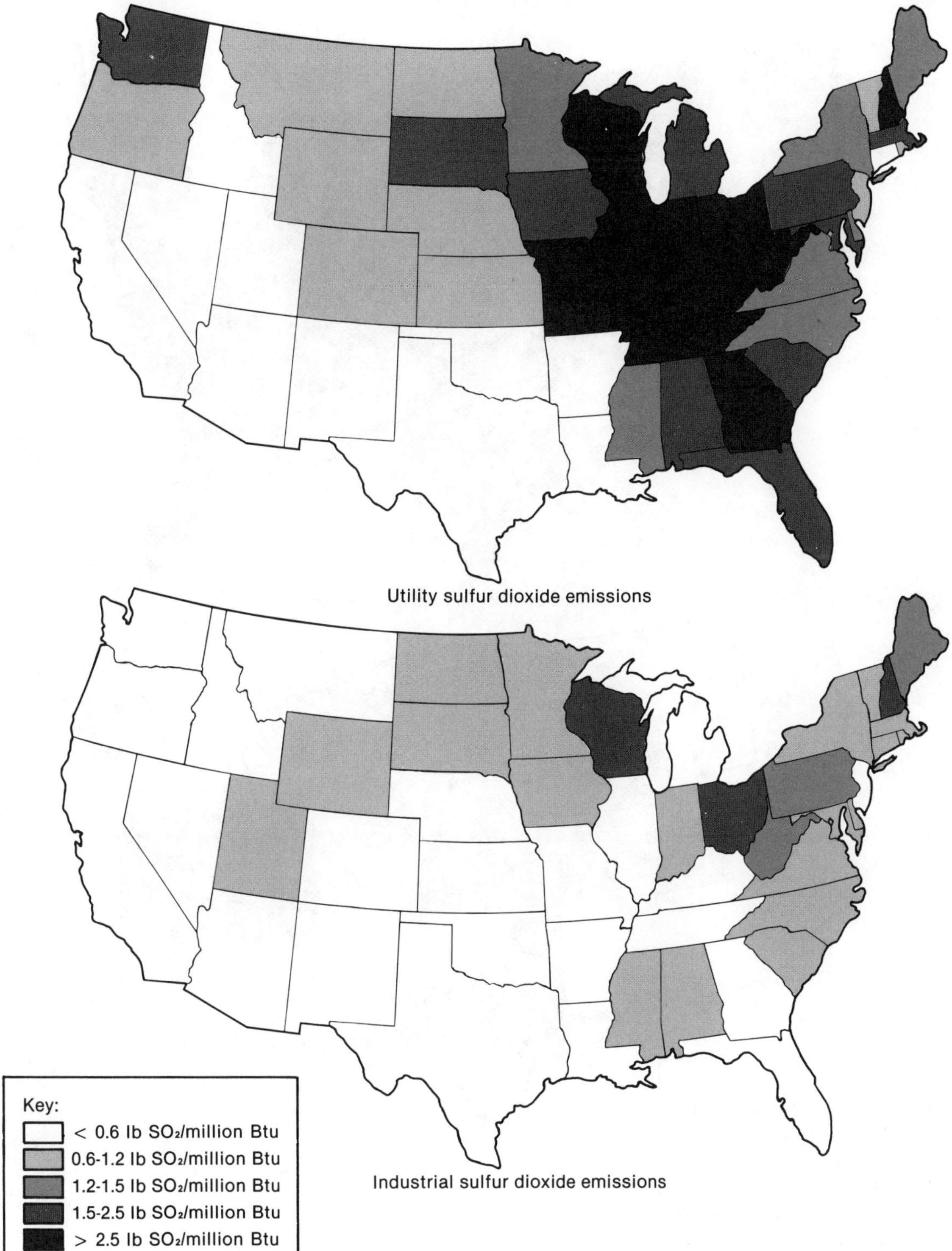

Utility sulfur dioxide emissions

Industrial sulfur dioxide emissions

Key:
- < 0.6 lb SO₂/million Btu
- 0.6-1.2 lb SO₂/million Btu
- 1.2-1.5 lb SO₂/million Btu
- 1.5-2.5 lb SO₂/million Btu
- > 2.5 lb SO₂/million Btu

SOURCE: E. H. Pechan & Associates, from Energy Information Administration data (EIA forms 4 and 423), and EPA National Emissions Data System (NEDS).

Figure 35.—Average 1980 Emission Rates for Nitrogen Oxides From Utility and Industrial Sources (lb NO₂/MMBtu)

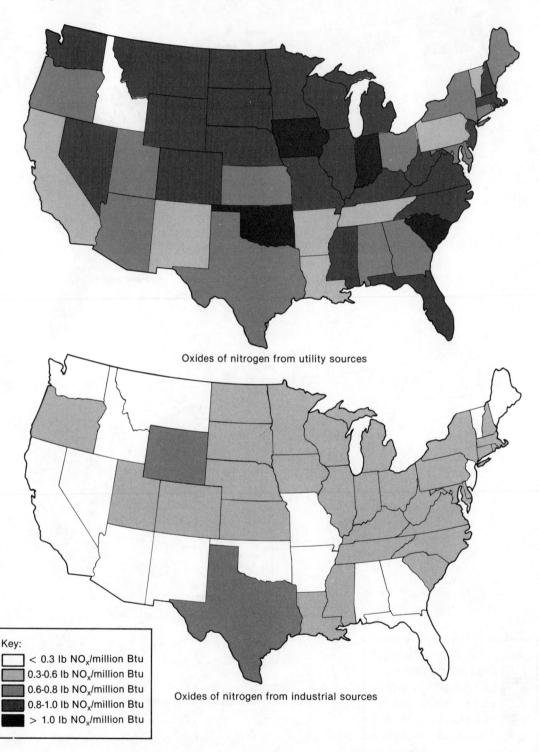

Oxides of nitrogen from utility sources

Key:
- ☐ < 0.3 lb NO_x/million Btu
- ☐ 0.3-0.6 lb NO_x/million Btu
- ☐ 0.6-0.8 lb NO_x/million Btu
- ☐ 0.8-1.0 lb NO_x/million Btu
- ☐ > 1.0 lb NO_x/million Btu

Oxides of nitrogen from industrial sources

SOURCE: E. H. Pechan & Associates, from Energy Information Administration data (EIA forms 4 and 423), and EPA National Emissions Data System (NEDS).

dustrial boiler emission rates are more evenly distributed, with highest average rates occurring in the Midwestern and Central Atlantic States.

Nitrogen oxides are both a component of acid deposition and a precursor to ozone. Reducing nitrogen oxides emissions from existing sources has not been proposed to date, although some bills have prohibited further increases in nitrogen oxides emissions or allowed reductions to substitute for sulfur dioxide reductions.

The three major sources of nitrogen oxides in the 31-State region are mobile sources (45 percent), utilities (35 percent), and industrial boilers (15 to 20 percent). Highway vehicles account for about 75 percent of the emissions from mobile sources, or about one-third of total Eastern U.S. nitrogen oxides emissions.

Figure 35 displays State-average nitrogen oxides emission rates from utilities and industrial boilers, respectively. As with sulfur dioxide emissions, proposals for controlling nitrogen oxides might allocate reductions on the basis of emission rates. Emission rates are more evenly distributed for nitrogen oxides than for sulfur dioxide. Additional mobile-source controls would regionally distribute costs according to patterns of new vehicle purchases.

Utility Control Costs

Figure 36 displays the effects of further pollution control on the cost of electricity. Annual increases in a typical residential consumer's electricity bills are estimated for a 10-million-ton reduction in sulfur dioxide emissions from existing utility sources. Total costs of such a program would be about $3 to $4 billion per year (1982 dollars), assuming each utility chooses the most cost-effective method of reducing emissions. Emissions reductions are allocated to States on the basis of 1980 utility emission rates. (Similar to several legislative proposals, reductions are based on each State's share of sulfur dioxide emitted in excess of 1.2 lb per million Btu of fuel burned.) For this hypothetical pollution-control plan, the reduction formula applies to the contiguous 48 States; however, reductions, in the Eastern 31 States would be quite similar if the formula applied only to these Eastern States.* The

highest rate increases occur in the Midwestern States and a few Southeastern and New England States.

Figure 37 displays the cost of a smaller pollution control program. About 6 million tons of sulfur dioxide could be eliminated annually in the Eastern 31 States by limiting utility emission rates to 2 lb per million Btu, at a cost of about $1 to $1.5 billion per year. If the control program was confined to the 22-State region receiving the highest levels of acid deposition, about 4.8 million tons per year could be eliminated for annual costs of $1 billion or less.

These cost estimates assume that all required emissions reductions would come from utilities, and that additional emissions coming from new utility plants or increased use of existing plants are not offset by further reducing existing plant emissions. In addition, these cost estimates assume that the use of control technology (e.g., scrubbers) is not required.

Similar to the maps presented earlier depicting the relative economic importance of recreational fishing, agriculture, and forestry, figure 38 displays the relative share of State income spent on residential electricity. For the region as a whole, about 2.3 percent of personal income, or $26 billion, is spent on electricity. The distribution of these expenditures by State is much more uniform than for the sectors discussed above, but is somewhat higher throughout the South.

Risk to the Utility Industry

Additional expenditures to control emissions could potentially affect the financial health of individual utilities. Three major factors determine the extent to which utility companies could be affected: 1) the extent of emissions reductions required under a given control program, 2) the utility's financial position, and 3) State-level regulatory policies that affect a utility's short- and medium-term ability to pass on the costs of pollution control to consumers. OTA did not attempt to analyze how these factors would affect the financial health of the more than 100 major publicly owned utilities in the 31 Eastern States, but drew on available information to assess the *relative* sensitivity of each *State's* utility sector to further emissions control.

---

*Western sulfur dioxide emissions in excess of 1.2 lb per million Btu are less than 5 percent of the allocated reductions.

Figure 36.—Cost of Reducing Sulfur Dioxide Emissions 10 Million Tons per Year, Nationwide Increases in Annual-Average Electricity Bills for a Typical Residential Consumer

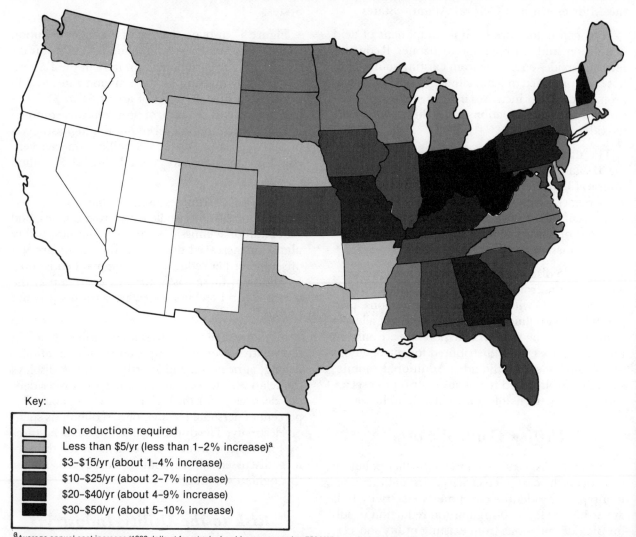

Key:

☐	No reductions required
▨	Less than $5/yr (less than 1–2% increase)[a]
▨	$3–$15/yr (about 1–4% increase)
▨	$10–$25/yr (about 2–7% increase)
▨	$20–$40/yr (about 4–9% increase)
■	$30–$50/yr (about 5–10% increase)

[a]Average annual cost increase (1982 dollars) for a typical residence consuming 750 kWh/month electricity. Percentage rate increases in each State are calculated from State-average 1982 electricity costs (ranging from about $200 to $900/yr; United States average about $600/yr).

SOURCE: Office of Technology Assessment, based on analyses by E. H. Pechan & Associates, Inc.

Figure 39 displays patterns of utility earnings and bond ratings for 1980 in each State, two indicators of the financial health of a State's utility sector. Figure 34 shows statewide average 1980 utility emission rates for sulfur dioxide—the best indicator of the extent of utility-sector reductions likely to be required under most of the control proposals introduced in the 97th and 98th Congresses.

Comparing figures 34 and 39 shows that few States *both:* 1) had high emission rates, and 2) fell

into the least favorable financial category, in 1980. However, several Midwestern States with high emission rates (and, therefore, potentially subject to extensive control requirements) fell into the moderately favorable financial categories.

Policies established by State public utility commissions can affect an individual utility's near-term ability to pass on the costs of pollution control to consumers. For example, for coal-burning utilities that might choose to use scrubbers, the State's pol-

Figure 37.—Cost of Reducing Sulfur Dioxide Emissions 6 Million Tons per Year, Eastern 31 States Increases in Annual-Average Electricity Bills for a Typical Residential Consumer

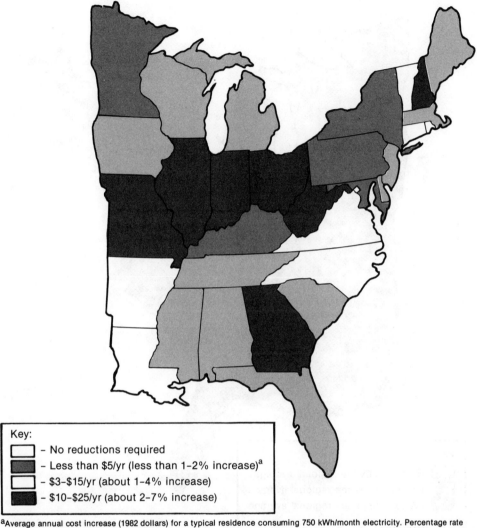

Key:
- [ ] – No reductions required
- [ ] – Less than $5/yr (less than 1–2% increase)[a]
- [ ] – $3–$15/yr (about 1–4% increase)
- [ ] – $10–$25/yr (about 2–7% increase)

[a]Average annual cost increase (1982 dollars) for a typical residence consuming 750 kWh/month electricity. Percentage rate increases in each State are calculated from State-average 1982 electricity cost (ranging from about $200 to $900/yr, United States average about $600 yr).

SOURCE: Office of Technology Assessment, based on analyses by E. H. Pechan & Associates, Inc.

icies regarding capital investment, in combination with the utilities' current financial ratings, determine the burden of raising capital for constructing scrubbers. Results of a survey of current State regulatory policies, and a discussion of their relative importance, are presented in appendix A. However, these policies might change considerably if a major Federal program to further limit pollution emissions is enacted.

Risks of Shifts in Coal Production

Because switching to lower sulfur fuel is often a cost-effective way to reduce sulfur dioxide emissions, emission-reduction schemes could cause coal production to shift from high-sulfur coal regions to low-sulfur coal regions.

Figure 40 displays coal production by State for both high- and low-sulfur coal. The size of each

Figure 38.—Expenditures for Residential Electricity—Relative Economic Importance

Relative share of State income spent for residential electricity, 1980

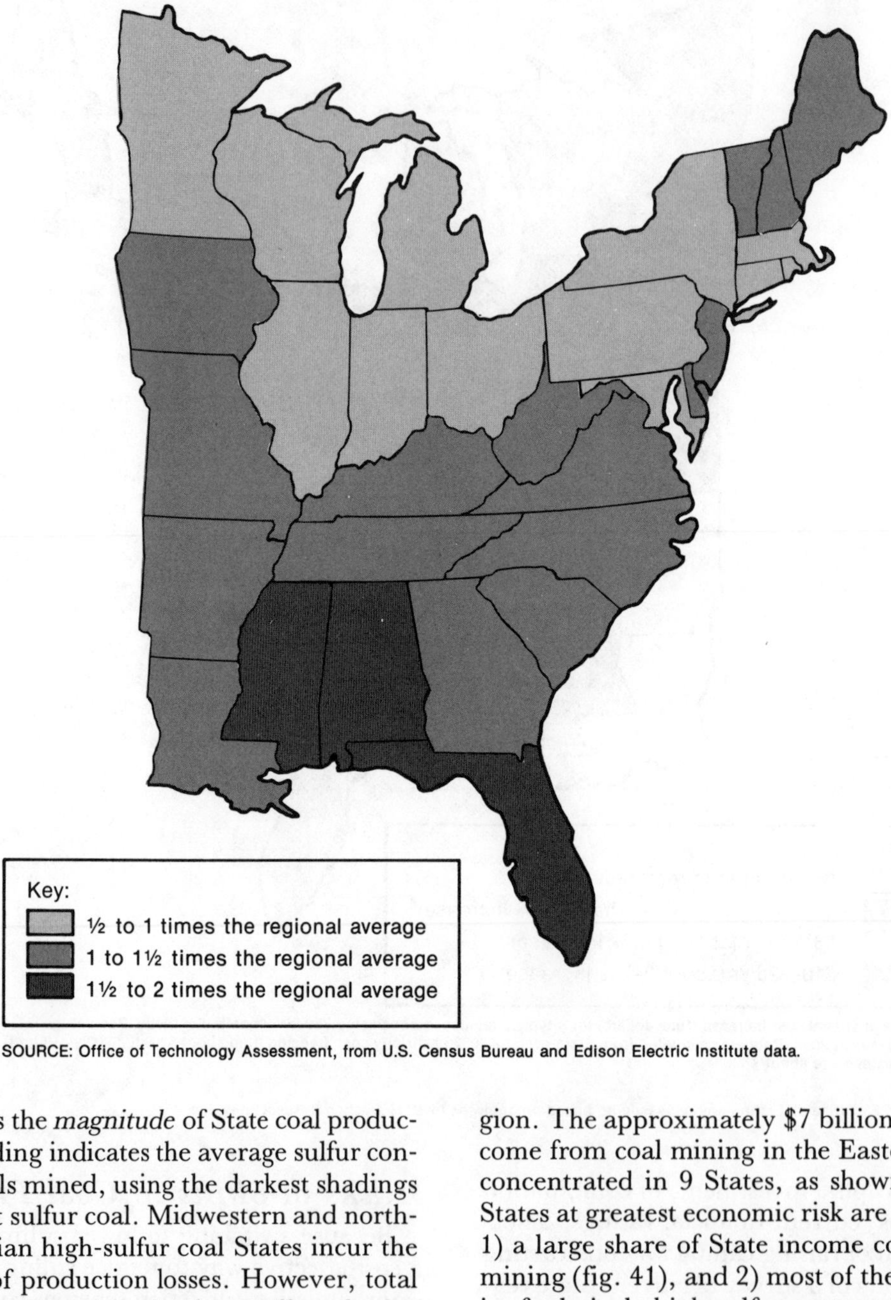

Key:
■ ½ to 1 times the regional average
■ 1 to 1½ times the regional average
■ 1½ to 2 times the regional average

SOURCE: Office of Technology Assessment, from U.S. Census Bureau and Edison Electric Institute data.

circle indicates the *magnitude* of State coal production. The shading indicates the average sulfur content of the coals mined, using the darkest shadings for the highest sulfur coal. Midwestern and northern Appalachian high-sulfur coal States incur the greatest risk of production losses. However, total coal production is projected to be unaffected; production gains of similar magnitudes would occur in the low-sulfur coal regions of Central Appalachia and the West.

Of all the economic sectors at risk, coal mining is the least evenly distributed across the Eastern re-

gion. The approximately $7 billion of regional income from coal mining in the Eastern 31 States is concentrated in 9 States, as shown in figure 41. States at greatest economic risk are those in which: 1) a large share of State income comes from coal mining (fig. 41), and 2) most of the coal produced is of relatively high-sulfur content (fig. 40). States meeting these criteria include West Virginia, Kentucky, Pennsylvania, Alabama, and Virginia. For these States, the income from coal mining is more than twice the regional average, and more than 80 percent of the coal produced emits greater than 1.2 lb sulfur dioxide per million Btu when burned.

Figure 39.—Electric Utilities—Selected Financial Indicators of Sensitivity to Control Expenditures

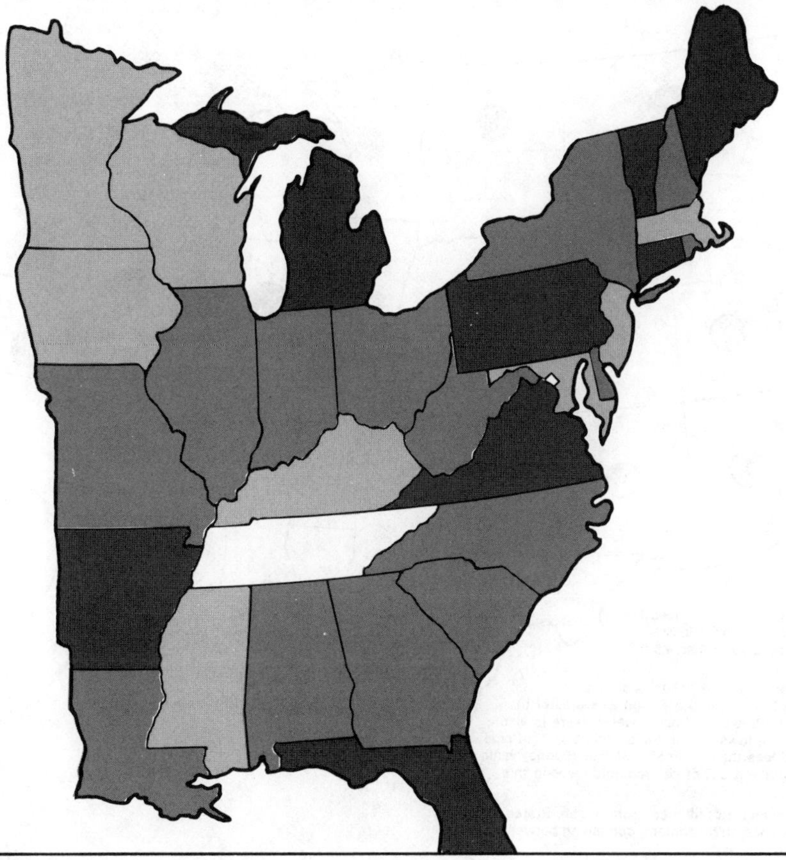

Key for financial indicators

Sensitive to additional air pollution control requirements: relatively poor bond ratings *and* below-average return on common equity in 1980.

Moderately sensitive to additional air pollution control requirements: poor bond ratings *or* below-average return on common equity in 1980.

Insensitive to additional air pollution control requirements: relatively good bond ratings *and* above-average return on common equity in 1980.

SOURCE: K. Cole, et. al., "Financial and Regulatory Factors Affecting the State and Regional Economic Impact of Sulfur Oxide Emissions Control," OTA contractor report, 1982.

Figure 40.—Quantities and Sulfur Content of Coals Produced for Electric Utilities, by State—1980

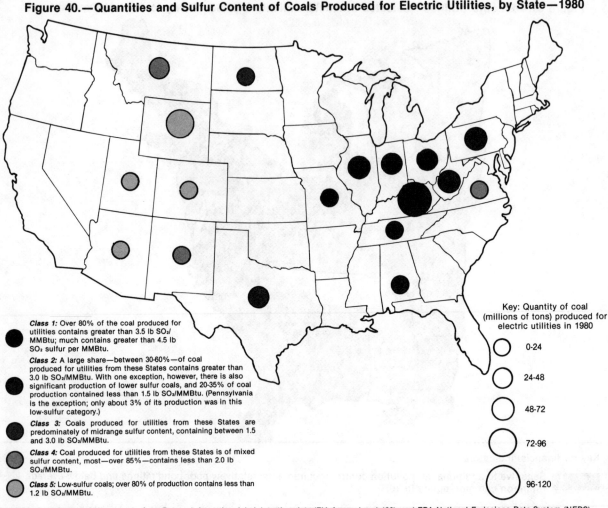

Class 1: Over 80% of the coal produced for utilities contains greater than 3.5 lb SO₂/MMBtu; much contains greater than 4.5 lb SO₂ sulfur per MMBtu.

Class 2: A large share—between 30-60%—of coal produced for utilities from these States contains greater than 3.0 lb SO₂/MMBtu. With one exception, however, there is also significant production of lower sulfur coals, and 20-35% of coal production contained less than 1.5 lb SO₂/MMBtu. (Pennsylvania is the exception; only about 3% of its production was in this low-sulfur category.)

Class 3: Coals produced for utilities from these States are predominately of midrange sulfur content, containing between 1.5 and 3.0 lb SO₂/MMBtu.

Class 4: Coal produced for utilities from these States is of mixed sulfur content, most—over 85%—contains less than 2.0 lb SO₂/MMBtu.

Class 5: Low-sulfur coals; over 80% of production contains less than 1.2 lb SO₂/MMBtu.

Key: Quantity of coal (millions of tons) produced for electric utilities in 1980

0-24

24-48

48-72

72-96

96-120

SOURCE: E. H. Pechan & Associates, from Energy Information Administration data (EIA forms 4 and 423), and EPA National Emissions Data System (NEDS).

Figure 41.—Coal—Relative Economic Importance

Relative importance of coal-related income to State income, 1978-80

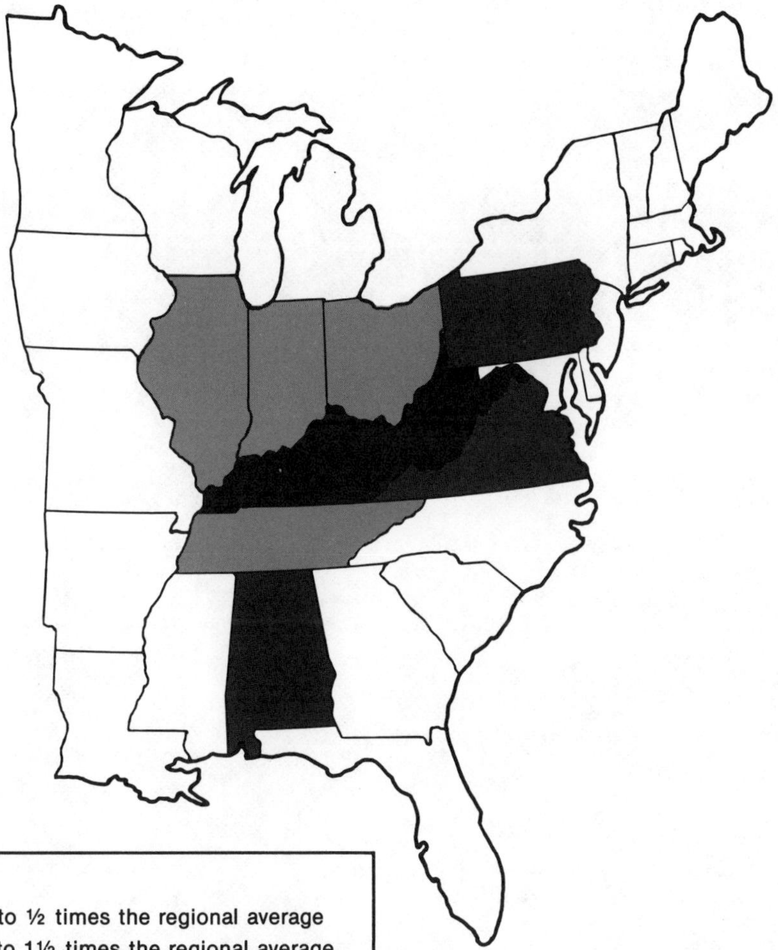

Key:
- 0 to ½ times the regional average
- 1 to 1½ times the regional average
- 2 to 4 times the regional average
- 4 or more times the regional average

SOURCE: Office of Technology Assessment, from U.S. Census Bureau data.

Chapter 6
Policy Options

Contents

TABLE

Policy Options

This chapter presents options for congressional action on acid deposition and other transported air pollutants. As background, it first describes existing Federal statutes relating to transported air pollutants, and summarizes the legislative proposals introduced during the 97th and 98th Congresses.

CURRENT LAW AND RECENT LEGISLATIVE PROPOSALS

The present Clean Air Act is designed to control *airborne concentrations* of pollutants that endanger public health and welfare. The act requires EPA to set National Ambient Air Quality Standards (NAAQS), and makes each State responsible for bringing its air pollutant concentrations down to or below the NAAQS.* Despite these limitations on allowable concentrations, large quantities of pollutants are still emitted and eventually deposited. Provisions were added to the act in 1977 to prohibit a State's emissions from contributing to violations of NAAQS *in other States,* or to any pollution problem *in other countries.* These provisions, however, appear to be ineffective for dealing with problems of the geographic scope of acid deposition.

The act further restricts *future* emissions by placing stringent emission limits on new sources of pollution, such as electric utilities and motor vehicles. These New Source Performance Standards (NSPS) are expected to achieve reductions in total emissions within 30 to 50 years. Continuing emissions from both old and new sources, however, will maintain or increase pollution levels during the next few decades unless additional controls are mandated.

To date, congressional action on acid deposition has been limited to funding research. The Acid Precipitation Act of 1980—Title VII of the Energy Security Act, Public Law 96-294—created an Interagency Task Force to conduct a comprehensive 10-year assessment of the causes and consequences of, and means and costs of controlling, transported acidic pollutants. The Task Force presented an Assessment Plan to Congress in June 1982. Under the plan, Congress would receive policy-related "integrated assessments" between 1987 and 1989.

Several bills were introduced during the 97th and 98th Congresses to accelerate the research program from 10 to 5 years; another bill would direct the Task Force to report to Congress on the progress of research, and provide recommendations for action, once every 2 years. Options for making the research plan more responsive to congressional (and potentially, regulatory) needs are presented later in this chapter under "Approach C: Modifying the Federal Acid Deposition Research Program."

Legislators have also introduced a variety of proposals to control acid deposition directly. Many would establish a 31-State control region, and mandate reductions of annual sulfur dioxide emissions in the region by 8 to 12 million tons below actual 1980 emission levels by the early 1990's. Individual States would be allocated reductions through formulas based primarily on utility sulfur dioxide emission rates. Variations on this approach include designating a smaller, 22-State control region, designating a 48-State control region, establishing a trust fund to pay some or all of the costs of emissions reductions, allocating reductions by considering *both* utility and industrial emissions, and allowing 2 tons of nitrogen oxides emissions to be substituted for each required ton of sulfur dioxide emissions reductions.

The bills vary in their treatment of new sources of emissions; some allow emissions from post-1980 sources to increase total emissions in the region, while others require further reductions to offset new emissions. Options for controlling the sources of

---

*National Ambient Air Quality Standards currently exist for six pollutants: sulfur dioxide, nitrogen dioxide, ozone, total suspended particulates, carbon monoxide, and lead.

transported air pollutants are discussed under "Approach A: Mandating Emissions Reductions."

Bills addressing other aspects of transported pollutants have also been introduced during the 97th and 98th Congresses. For example, several bills would tighten nitrogen oxide emission standards for utility and mobile sources, accelerate development of innovative pollution control technologies, and provide Federal funding to lime acid-altered bodies of water that have ceased to support some fish species. Alternatives for implementing the last of these proposals are presented under "Approach B: Liming Lakes and Streams."

Bills have also been introduced to amend the interstate and international provisions of the Clean Air Act. Clarifying the scope of these provisions could aid States, EPA, and affected foreign countries in dealing with transboundary pollution problems *other than acid deposition*—in particular, mid-distance transport of air pollution currently regulated under the act. Options for amending these sections of the current law are presented under "Approach D: Modifying the Existing International and Interstate Sections of the Clean Air Act."

APPROACHES AND OPTIONS

This section presents congressional options for addressing acid deposition and other transported air pollutants, grouped according to four major approaches:

- Approach A: Mandating emissions reductions to further *control the sources* of transported pollutants;
- Approach B: Liming lakes and streams to *mitigate some of the effects* of acid deposition;
- Approach C: Modifying the Federal acid deposition research program to provide *more timely guidance* for congressional decisions; and
- Approach D: Modifying existing sections of the Clean Air Act to *enable EPA, States, and countries to more effectively address transported pollutants other than acid deposition.*

Congress could choose to adopt some or all of these approaches in considering clean-air legislation. A comprehensive strategy for addressing transported air pollutants might well include options from all four approaches. The four are described below, along with their respective options.

APPROACH A:
Mandating Emissions Reductions

Discussion:

Additional legislated emissions reductions could range from modest, possibly interim, reductions to offset expected future emissions growth, to large-scale control programs. In choosing an appropriate program, Congress will need to weigh the risks of potential resource damage against those of inefficient control expenditures. These decisions are complicated by the scientific uncertainties, disagreement over values, and distributional issues discussed throughout this report.

Mandating further emissions reductions would require Congress to make a number of interrelated choices. These include decisions about which pollutant emissions to reduce, from what source regions, by how much, and over what time period. Congress would also need to choose specific policy mechanisms to implement the reductions, allocate their costs, and address undesired secondary consequences of emissions reductions.

OTA has outlined a series of eight control-policy decisions that must be made in order to design acid deposition control legislation. These are summarized below, to provide the framework for considering three representative emissions control options presented at the end of this section. Chapter 7 discusses the eight control-policy decisions in greater detail, and presents options available to Congress under each decision area.

- *Which Pollutants Should Be Further Controlled?*

Three pollutants are potential candidates: sulfur dioxide, nitrogen oxides, and hydrocarbons. Sulfur dioxide and nitrogen oxides (and their transformation products) are major sources of acidity to the environment. In the *Eastern* United States, sulfur compounds annually contribute about twice as much acidity to precipitation as nitrogen compounds. Moreover, during most times of the year, plants use much of the deposited nitrogen as a nutrient, making sulfur compounds responsible for a still larger share of acidity reaching water bodies. For these reasons, any control program for the Eastern United States would have to include provisions for reducing sulfur dioxide emissions.

If desired, additional resource protection can be achieved by also mandating reductions of nitrogen oxides emissions. Nitrogen oxides emissions are expected to increase more rapidly over the next few decades than sulfur dioxide emissions. During springtime snow melt, both sulfur and nitrogen compounds accumulated in the snow over the winter can reach water bodies unimpeded. In the West, nitrogen compounds may contribute as much as or more acidity to precipitation than do sulfur compounds, and thus should be considered if a nationwide control program is enacted.

Hydrocarbons can affect the geographic distribution of acid deposition. The atmospheric chemistry involved, however, is not sufficiently understood to ''fine-tune'' a sulfur dioxide or combined sulfur dioxide and nitrogen oxides control program with hydrocarbon emissions control.

• *How Widespread Should a Control Program Be?*

Four regions are potential candidates for emissions reductions, starting with the Northeastern United States and expanding southward and westward: 1) the approximately 21-State Northeastern region receiving the greatest levels of acid deposition; 2) a 31-State region (all States east of and bordering on the Mississippi River), incorporating a band of States around the region of greatest deposition; 3) a 37-State region, including all States east of the Rocky Mountains; and 4) the contiguous 48 States.

About 65 percent of the Nation's sulfur oxides and 45 percent of its nitrogen oxides are emitted in the 21-State region east of the Mississippi and north of and including Tennessee and North Carolina. About 85 percent of the Nation's sulfur ox-

ides and 65 percent of nitrogen oxides are emitted in the 31-State region.

• *What Level of Pollution Control Should Be Required?*

The congressional choice of how much pollution to eliminate must, of necessity, be based on incomplete information. Expected resource-protection benefits, control costs, and other potential risks and benefits are concerns that must be balanced to determine the socially desirable level of emissions reductions. The *costs* of various levels of control are relatively well-known, but only a few reference points are available for assessing the potential *benefits* of further emissions control.

An acid deposition control program could range in size from one that would prevent future increases in emissions—eliminating about 2 to 3 million tons of the 22 million tons of sulfur dioxide emitted annually in the Eastern 31-State region to offset expected growth through the year 2000—to one that would achieve large-scale reductions below current levels. Eliminating about 11 to 12.5 million tons of sulfur dioxide per year might be considered the upper end of this range; mandating even larger emissions reductions would require most *existing* utilities to adopt more stringent emissions controls than those governing emissions sources subject to NSPS.

Reducing sulfur dioxide emissions in the eastern United States by 8 to 10 million tons per year below current levels would probably protect all but the most sensitive aquatic resources in many areas receiving high levels of acid deposition, but not in those areas receiving the greatest amounts. Risks of damage to sensitive forests, materials, and crops would also be reduced. In addition, airborne fine-particle levels would be lower, improving visibility and reducing risks to human health. Such reductions—near the upper end of the feasible range—would cost about $3 to $6 billion per year, depending on the design of the control program. Costs would rise steeply if greater resource protection were desired; both control costs and the amount of resource protection would be less with lower emissions reductions.

About 2 to 5 million tons of sulfur dioxide emissions per year could probably be eliminated for about $1 billion per year or less. This would certainly be enough to prevent emissions from increasing through 2000 (i.e., offset expected industrial and utility growth), and could potentially decrease emissions 2 to 3 million tons below current levels by 2000. Risks of damage to sensitive aquatic resources, forests, agriculture, materials, and health would be reduced, but at present it is impossible to gauge by how much.

Congress could either specify the level of emissions reductions directly or state the policy goals to be met and instruct the Administrator of EPA to set the level of reductions.

• By What Time Should Reductions Be Required?

A congressional decision to require further controls is likely to take at least 6 or 7—possibly 10 or more—years to implement. Extensive Federal, State, and source-level planning will be required even before the contract and construction stages begin. Smaller levels of emissions reductions, if achieved primarily through fuel switching, might be implemented somewhat more quickly.

Alternatively, Congress might decide to wait for guidance from the National Acid Precipitation Assessment Program, thereby delaying controls an additional 4 to 6 or more years. Additional risks of resource damage would result from such a delay, but current understanding does not allow their quantification.

Congress could also direct Federal and State officials to begin control planning now, but make the contract and construction phase *conditional* on the results of further research. Control programs could be modified or specific implementation plans changed as late as about 2 years before the compliance date, at which point major construction expenditures would have to begin.

• What Approach to Control Should Be Adopted?

Existing environmental regulations focus on either: 1) pollution sources, i.e., directly regulating total emissions or emission rates from sources or regions; or 2) pollutant exposure, i.e., setting goals or standards to limit human or environmental exposure to pollutants.

The first approach, a source-oriented control program, could be implemented now, either by directly limiting emissions or emission rates or by requiring the use of control technologies.

Controlling acid deposition through the second approach would require a well-developed understanding of the transport, transformation, fate, and effects of pollutants. Such knowledge—accurate enough for a receptor-based regulatory program—does not yet exist for acid deposition. By the mid-1990's, however, models and similar tools might have accuracy sufficient for designing a receptor-based approach on a *regional scale* (i.e., with emissions reductions allocated to State-size or larger areas).

• How Should Emissions Reductions Be Allocated?

Congress could limit emissions directly by: 1) mandating a reduction formula that applies to all or a subset of *individual sources* within a control region; or 2) allocating emissions reductions to *States,* allowing the States to allocate source-level cutbacks within their borders. Alternatively, Congress could direct EPA to allocate emissions reductions to meet specified congressional goals.

Policy considerations pertinent to designing an allocation formula include: "Who is to gain the benefit of resource protection and who is to bear the burden of reductions?" and "How administratively and economically efficient is the plan?" Most legislative proposals to date have been based on: 1) *emission rates* (i.e., sulfur dioxide emitted per quantity of fuel burned) in order to reduce emissions most cost effectively, and 2) *utility emissions only,* to reduce the administrative complexity of determining each State's share. While fairly accurate data are available on the 70 percent of Eastern sulfur dioxide emissions from utilities, emissions from other sectors are difficult to estimate accurately.

Chapter VII and appendix A review a number of allocation approaches, some based on *total* State emissions, some on a State's utility emissions alone. Each allocation formula varies in the resulting geographic pattern of emissions reductions, total costs for equivalent regionwide reductions, and administrative complexity.

• **Who Pays the Costs of Emissions Reductions?**

Allocating reductions and allocating their costs are two distinct issues. Congress could: 1) require affected sources to pay the full costs of control, or 2) create a fee or tax to spread control costs over a larger group than those required to reduce emissions. While the former approach is consistent with the current Clean Air Act, the latter recognizes the difficulty of linking emissions from any given source to damage in areas far removed.

• **What Can Be Done to Mitigate Employment and Economic Effects of a Control Policy?**

Cutting back sulfur dioxide emissions could significantly affect two industries: coal mining and electric utilities. If utilities and other emitters are allowed to switch to lower sulfur fuels—often a cost-effective means of reducing emissions—some production will shift from regions producing high-sulfur coal to those producing low-sulfur coal, with associated employment and economic effects. Employment shifts might be reduced by requiring emitters to install control technologies designed for use with high-sulfur coals, or by restricting coal purchases according to location of coal supply. Such a program might increase total control costs considerably, however. For reductions in the range of 8 to 10 million tons per year, costs might rise by 25 to 50 percent, depending on the specifics of the plan. Special compensation to workers or communities affected by the new law would also be possible.

Those utilities that choose (or are required) to use control technologies for meeting major emissions reduction requirements would need to raise additional capital to build such equipment. Congress could reduce financial pressures on utilities by establishing a tax to help pay for the costs of control, or by funding research and demonstration projects to develop potentially cheaper control technologies.

Options:

Congress could design a control program by selecting alternatives from each of the eight decision areas summarized above. Obviously, many combinations are possible; the three options presented below represent portions of the decisionmaking spectrum ranging from modest reductions to large-scale control programs. Each strikes a different balance between the risks of future resource damage and the risks of inefficient pollution control.

Option A-1: Mandate Small-Scale Emissions Reductions.

A small-scale program would logically focus on controlling sulfur dioxide emissions—the major manmade acidic pollutant in the Eastern United States—within the broad region receiving greatest levels of acid deposition. Eliminating about 2 to 5 million tons of sulfur dioxide emissions per year would be feasible within about 5 to 7 years from the date of passage. Reductions of this magnitude would probably hold acid deposition levels about constant, or result in modest declines, through the end of the century.

The control region might encompass either the Northeastern 21 States or the 31 Eastern States. All States could be required to eliminate an equal percentage of emissions (e.g., 10 to 20 percent), or be allocated reductions based on emission rates (e.g., an emission rate limitation of between 2.5 and 4.0 lb of sulfur dioxide per million Btu of fuel burned). Each State might be responsible for determining which sources to control and how much pollution to eliminate from each source. Alternatively, Congress could mandate emission rate limitations for all sources emitting in excess of a specified rate.

Other possibilities for modest emissions reductions include mandatory coal washing for certain types of coal, or requiring selected sources to use emissions control technology. The former might eliminate up to about 2 million tons of sulfur dioxide per year, while the latter approach could be designed to achieve cutbacks of any desired magnitude in the range of 2 to 5 million tons per year. Either of these last two approaches would minimize losses of high-sulfur coal production and related employment, but would increase the cost of control.

A small-scale program could be accomplished for under $1 billion per year (1982 dollars) for a cutback of 2 to 3 million tons per year of sulfur dioxide, and for about $1 to $1.5 billion per year for about a 5-million-ton reduction. Costs could range, however, as high as $2.5 billion per year for a 5-million-ton program requiring the use of emissions control technology. Congress could require the sources allocated emissions reductions, and their customers, to pay the cost of reductions directly, or spread the costs more widely by establishing a fee on electricity or pollutant emissions.

Option A-2: Mandate Large-Scale Emissions Reductions.

Many of the acid deposition control proposals introduced during the 97th and 98th Congresses would reduce sulfur dioxide emissions by 8 to 12 million tons annually. Several include reductions in nitrogen oxide emissions as part of the control program as well.

As discussed in chapter 5, large-scale sulfur dioxide emissions reductions (8 to 10 million tons annually below 1980 levels) would probably protect all but the most sensitive lakes and streams in many areas receiving high levels of acid deposition. Areas currently receiving *the highest* levels of acid deposition (e.g., Western Pennsylvania) would also benefit, but to a lesser extent—a larger proportion of their aquatic resources might still be at risk.

The control region for a program of this scale might include the 31 Eastern States, all States east of the Rocky Mountains, or the 48 contiguous States. If the desired control region extends to the West, nitrogen oxides emissions become increasingly important, as nitrogen oxides contribute relatively larger shares of precipitation acidity in the West than in the East.

A large-scale program would require about 8 to 12 years to implement. By choosing a longer compliance time (e.g., 12 years), Congress could allow greater opportunity for modifying control plans to incorporate future research results or newly developed control technologies. The program could be altered or implementation plans changed until about 2 to 4 years before the scheduled compliance date. Although Federal, State, and source-level personnel would have spent considerable time and effort planning the program, few contracts would have been let before that time, and major capital expenditures would not have occurred. The program could either have a single compliance date or be implemented in phases, beginning with a first phase similar to option A-1.

Emissions reductions can be allocated to States in many ways. Major alternatives are discussed in detail in chapter 7 and appendix A. Each formula has distributional implications—for both who reduces and who receives the benefits of the reductions. In addition, the formulas vary in administrative complexity. For example, many recent acid rain control proposals have been based on utility emissions in excess of a specified rate—1.2 or 1.5 lb of sulfur dioxide per million Btu of fuel burned. This is perhaps the least expensive approach for reducing *regional* emissions, but it concentrates much of the required reduction in the Midwest. Such a program would cost from $2 to $5 billion per year, depending on the stringency and design. Offsetting future emissions growth, if required, might cost an additional $1 to $2 billion per year.

Because such an approach would be costly for electricity consumers in some States, Congress might want to create a trust fund to finance part of the program. A trust fund to pay for capital costs associated with emissions control technology would also assist an already capital-short utility industry. The trust fund could be based either on pollutant emissions or on a surrogate, such as electricity generated or fuel deliveries.

Paying part of the costs of pollution control technology through a trust fund (but not reimbursing fuel-switching costs) would also help to prevent losses in high-sulfur coal production and employment. However, encouraging the use of control technology through a trust fund, or mandating its use, would increase total control costs and reduce potential gains in Western coal production.

Option A-3: Mandate an "Environmental Quality" Standard.

Rather than mandating specific emissions reductions, Congress could direct the Administrator of EPA to develop a control plan to achieve congressionally specified environmental quality goals (including cost considerations, if desired). Though at present scientists cannot accurately predict the benefits of various levels and regional patterns of emissions reductions, such capability might be possible by 1995 or 2000. A control program could then be based in part on a better understanding of the relationship between emissions and deposition among State or multi-State regions. It is unlikely, however, that scientists will be able to relate emis-

Photo credit: Ted Spiegel

The lime in this Ohio mine will be used for flue gas de-sulfurization, or washing, which removes sulfur, ash and other impurities from coal. About one-third of the coal burned by Eastern and Midwestern utilities is washed, thereby preventing about 2 million tons of sulfur dioxide emissions each year. An additional 2 million tons could be eliminated by more extensive use of this technique

Photo credit: Ted Spiegel

At the Bruce Mansfield powerplant in Pennsylvania, lime is destined for use in the plant's flue-gas "scrubber." The lime is mixed with water and sprayed over the exhaust gas, removing over 90 percent of the sulfur dioxide that otherwise would have been emitted. The sulfur-laden lime slurry is discharged as a wet sludge that must be disposed with care to prevent water contamination. Newer technologies promise easier waste disposal or the possibility of reclaiming a usable product

sions from single sources to small receptor areas for the foreseeable future.

A concerted 10- to 15-year effort might produce a control program either less expensive or more effective than that outlined in option A-2. However, the longer time required to achieve compliance—it would be about 2005 to 2010 before the plan could be implemented—would also permit additional resource damage.

Congress might choose to precede such a program with mandated, small-scale emissions reductions, such as presented in option A-1. The reductions required under option A-1 are unlikely to

exceed those eventually required under the environmental quality standard; at a minimum, they would prevent acid deposition levels from increasing before the remainder of the plan is implemented.

APPROACH B: Liming Lakes and Streams.

Discussion:

OTA estimates that about 3,000 lakes and 23,000 miles of streams in the Eastern 31 States are extremely sensitive to acid deposition or are already acid-altered. Damage to or elimination of fisheries has been documented in several regions of eastern North America. Any congressional decision to reduce emissions that contribute to acid deposition would take at least a decade to implement, so it might be many years before lakes could be seen to improve. Moreover, while a significant portion of these lakes and streams would benefit from substantial emissions reductions, some might still not improve sufficiently to ensure support of self-sustaining fish populations.

Several forms of chemical treatment have been used for reducing acid-related damages to sensitive aquatic ecosystems. Most involve neutralizing acidic waters and sediments with large quantities of alkaline substances. One technique—temporarily restoring the buffering capacity of a lake or stream with lime—often improves water quality sufficiently to maintain reproducing fisheries. Treating terrestrial ecosystems has also been proposed; however, while alkaline materials are commonly added to acidic agricultural soils, little experimentation has occurred on forested ecosystems. Counteracting surface-water acidity cannot substitute for controlling transported pollutants at their source. Such measures can, however, provide short-term protection to some currently altered resources, by treating one of the *symptoms* of acid deposition.

Not all lakes and streams respond sufficiently to liming to maintain reproducing fisheries. In particular, lakes with short water-retention times (i.e., where water remains in the lake for less than a year), and streams with great variations in flow, are very difficult to lime effectively. Historically, such additional factors as demonstrated ability to support a significant, viable fishery, recreational potential and public access to waters, and degree of acidification have been used to guide the choice of liming targets. For those lakes where liming is effective, a single application of lime will restore buffering capacity for a period of 3 to 5 years; to prevent reacidification, lime must be reapplied every few years.

While liming has enhanced fish survival in a number of lakes and streams, its long-term implications for the food chain on which fish depend is uncertain. Scientists do not know how periodi

changes in water body chemistry through liming will affect aquatic ecosystems over the long term. Little research has been done on alternative measures or on minimizing adverse impacts of liming. Increased Federal and State efforts to develop and test aquatic treatment methods could help to increase availability of fishing recreation in highly sensitive areas over the next few decades.

Liming has been effective in counteracting surface-water acidification in parts of Scandinavia, Canada, and in the United States in New York and Massachusetts. The most extensive U.S. program was begun by the New York State Department of Environmental Conservation in 1959. It initially targeted small, naturally acidic ponds in heavily used recreational areas, and expanded to treating selected acidified lakes with significant potential to support recreational fishing during the mid-1970's. The program is quite small—only about 60 lakes in total (covering about 1,000 acres) have been treated since its inception. Following liming, water quality has improved at a number of lakes and ponds, and self-propagating sport fishing populations have been reintroduced and maintained.

Costs for liming ponds and lakes under the New York State program have ranged from approximately $30 to $300 per acre for each application, depending on the size and accessibility of the water body. A recent study of liming requirements in the Adirondack Mountain region of New York State estimated that a 5-year program for liming several hundred acidified lakes in the region could be implemented for between $2 and $4 million per year, depending on the desired buffering level.[1] This does not include the costs of restocking fish or continuing monitoring of lake water chemistry and biology, which would increase the cost considerably.

Federal funds have been available since 1950 under the Dingell-Johnson Act to aid States in carrying out ''projects having as their purpose the restoration, conservation, management, and enhancement of sport fish and the provision for public use and benefits from these resources.'' A 10-percent excise tax on the wholesale cost of fishing tackle

---

[1]Frederic C. Menz and Charles T. Driscoll, ''An Estimate of the Costs of Liming To Neutralize Acidic Adirondack Surface Waters,'' Contribution #13 of the Upstate Freshwater Institute, June 1983.

Adding lime to a lake can temporarily restore its ability to neutralize incoming acids, thereby preventing harm to aquatic life. Lakes near roads can often be limed by boat (shown above); for others, large quantities of lime must be transported by aircraft. Not all lakes and streams can be effectively limed

provides revenues under the act. States are reimbursed for 75 percent of their expenditures on projects approved by the U.S. Fish and Wildlife Service (FWS). About 60 percent of total Dingell-Johnson funds are currently used by States for survey, management, and research activities.

Dingell-Johnson funds have been used in the past to support individual liming projects; they provided startup money to the New York State Department of Environmental Conservation's liming program from 1959 to 1965. FWS program staff suggest that States able to demonstrate the potential cost-effectiveness of liming to meet a specific acidification problem could presently receive Federal funds for liming and follow-up monitoring.

A proposal to expand the coverage of the Dingell-Johnson excise tax to include additional recreational fishing equipment is currently before the Congress (H.R. 2163); if passed, the proposal would approximately double receipts collected under the act. Expanding the fund has been advocated as a means of allowing States to keep up with the costs of sport fish management in an era of rising costs and declining State resources. Such a move might also encourage States to include mitigation efforts among their project proposals for Federal funding.

Lack of funding for liming projects, however, may not be the most important impediment to expanding mitigation activities. Improving our current ability to restore or protect acid-altered waters will require extensive monitoring of the chemical and biological changes that follow liming applications. Until considerably greater resources are allocated to studying the ways in which liming affects various types of water bodies, the results of each application will remain uncertain.

Federal research on aquatic treatment methods, as specified in the Acid Precipitation Act of 1980, began in 1982 under the direction of the FWS. To date, the Federal research effort has produced a technical report on liming, and an agenda of further research needs determined by participants in an international mitigation conference. Total Federal funding for these efforts in fiscal year 1983 amounted to $225,000.

The administration recently proposed about $5 million dollars for liming research for fiscal year 1985. Such funding increases would permit researchers to study the effects of liming on water bodies with differing geological, chemical, and biological characteristics throughout the Eastern United States, and to investigate the effectiveness of alternative mitigation measures.

Options:

Specific options available to Congress for Federal support of research and implementation of techniques to mitigate some of the effects of acid deposition are described below.

Option B-1: Expand Federal Research on Aquatic (and Other) Treatment Methods.

Although researchers at the FWS have begun to investigate the effects of a few mitigation techniques—primarily liming—on aquatic life in acidified lakes, levels of funding are low and permit only a few research projects to be undertaken each year. Additional funding—for example, at the $5 million per year level proposed by the administration—would allow the FWS program to expand its coverage to a variety of lakes and streams being treated under differing geological, geographic, and biological conditions. Such expansion would aid the FWS in developing guidelines on liming and other mitigation techniques for use by States, local communities, and private interests.

Further research on treatment methods for terrestrial ecosystems and watersheds could also be undertaken through either the Forest Service or FWS.

Congress could provide additional funding specifically for mitigation research, or direct the Interagency Task Force (responsible for directing Federal acid deposition research under the Acid Precipitation Act of 1980) to allocate a greater portion of its existing budget to such activities.

Option B-2. Expand Federal-State Cooperative Efforts for Treating Acidified Surface Waters and Assessing Results.

While costs for liming acidified surface waters are relatively modest, assessing the effectiveness of these treatments can be much more expensive than liming itself, and requires substantial technical expertise. Federal funds to support liming and follow-up monitoring are potentially available under the existing Dingell-Johnson Act, although States currently carry out very little mitigation-related work with these funds.

Congress could instruct the FWS to provide guidelines to States on requirements for qualifying for Dingell-Johnson funds to treat acidified surface waters. Congress could also broaden the act's excise tax base to provide States with additional funds as an indirect means of encouraging State-level mitigation efforts. Alternatively, Congress could establish a new Federal-State cooperative program specifically to support surface-water treatment and subsequent monitoring activities.

Option B-3: Establish Demonstration Projects for Acidified Water Bodies on Federal Lands.

The Federal Government has extensive land holdings in areas of the Eastern United States that are considered sensitive to the effects of acid precipitation, including the White Mountain National Forest in New Hampshire, the Green Mountain National Forest in Vermont, and the Allegheny National Forest in northwestern Pennsylvania. Congress could direct the Forest Service and the FWS to establish cooperative demonstration programs to treat selected lakes and streams on Federal lands with significant recreational fishing potential or heritage fish populations, and subsequently monitor their chemical and biological responses. Funding could be provided through the existing interagency acid deposition research program to fund FWS monitoring activities, or be allocated to the Forest Service specifically for surface-water mitigation.

APPROACH C:
Modifying the Federal Acid Deposition Research Program

Discussion:

Under the Acid Precipitation Act of 1980 (Title VII of the Energy Security Act of 1980—Public Law 96-294), Congress created an Interagency Task Force* to conduct a comprehensive 10-year national assessment program on acid deposition. The goals of the research program are:

- to identify the causes and sources of acid precipitation,
- to evaluate the environmental, social, and economic effects of acid precipitation, and
- to determine the effectiveness of actions available to control the emissions responsible for acid deposition, and mitigate harmful effects of acid deposition on receptor systems.

The act requires the Task Force to submit annual reports to the President and Congress, describing the progress of the research program and recommending actions that Congress and appropriate Federal agencies might take to alleviate acid deposition and its effects.

The Task Force presented a detailed research program—the National Acid Precipitation Assessment Program (NAPAP)—to Congress in June 1982. NAPAP outlines the general strategy for organizing the research effort, using 10 working groups organized by scientific discipline. These working groups are composed of program managers and experts from the Federal agencies participating in the research effort. Areas of responsibility for each of the 10 working groups are outlined in table 5.

The plan specifies an ambitious research program requiring extensive coordination among groups. If the research continues on schedule, the Task Force expects to develop by 1985 preliminary estimates of current and potential resource damage due to acid deposition. It plans to use this information, along with models developed by the task

*The Interagency Task Force is composed of heads and representatives of various agencies and national laboratories and four members appointed by the President.

Table 5.—Organization of the National Acid Precipitation Assessment Program

Task Group A: Natural Sources
Coordinating agency—NOAA. Responsibility—assess the effect of natural emissions on acid deposition.

Task Group B: Man-Made Sources
Coordinating agency—DOE. Responsibilities—refine existing sulfur dioxide and nitrogen oxides emissions estimates, and develop improved models to estimate future sulfur and nitrogen emissions from major polluting sectors.

Task Group C: Atmospheric Processes
Coordinating agency—NOAA. Responsibilities—examine the link between emission of pollutants and acid deposition.

Task Group D: Deposition Monitoring
Coordinating agency—DOI. Responsibilities—develop a long-term national program to monitor the chemical composition of acid deposition (both wet and dry), and improve the reliability and accuracy of sampling techniques.

Work Group E: Aquatic Effects
Coordinating agency—EPA. Responsibilities—1) assess the resources at risk in the United States from acid deposition, 2) study the mechanisms by which biological damage can occur, 3) evaluate the risk of acidifying drinking water supplies through acid deposition, and 4) analyze strategies to mitigate the harmful effects of acid deposition.

Task Group F: Terrestrial Effects
Coordinating agency—DOA. Responsibilities—assess the nature and extent of the effects of acid deposition on crops, forests, and noncommercial terrestrial ecosystems.

Task Group G: Effects on Materials
Coordinating agency—DOI. Responsibilities—assess the effect of air pollution—in particular, acid deposition—on a range of economically important materials and historic monuments and structures.

Task Group H: Control Technologies
Coordinating agency—EPA. Although this group was referred to in the National Plan of June 1982, the latest draft operating plan does not contain a work statement for the control technology group, nor does it specify deliverable reports.

Task Group I: Assessments and Policy Analysis
Coordinating agency—EPA. Responsibilities—integrate the research results of the other work groups, and carry out cost-benefit analyses to assist the Task Force in formulating guidance for policymakers.

Task Group J: International Activities
Coordinating agency—DOS. Responsibility—ensure that the National Program is coordinated with ongoing U.S.-Canadian and other international activities related to acid deposition.

SOURCE: Office of Technology Assessment, based on information from the National Acid Precipitation Assessment Program, June 1982; and the Interagency Task Force on Acid Precipitation, January 1982.

groups, to produce integrated, policy-related assessments in 1987 and 1989. The 1985 damage estimates are expected to be used primarily for redirecting or fine-tuning the further research efforts. Since the planned assessment activity calls for extensive methods development and data collection before policy analysis begins, NAPAP does not anticipate "useful guidance to policymakers" until 1987 to 1989.

Many members of Congress and public interest groups have expressed concern about the length of time projected for NAPAP to produce a useful policy assessment. While such a research plan might produce more accurate analyses than those resulting from a shorter effort, many consider waiting until 1989 for this level of refinement unacceptable. Several bills introduced in the 97th and 98th Congresses proposed to accelerate the originally planned 10-year program to a 5-year effort.

Such a legislated acceleration could seriously compromise the scientific credibility of the results. Substantial time and effort would be needed to redesign the research schedule. (The present program required 2 years to plan.) Many currently planned research efforts are designed to build on results from work presently under way; these projects would have to be significantly redesigned so that they could begin more quickly. Moreover, many of the currently planned efforts simply could not be accelerated, even if additional funding were provided.

For many field experiments on lakes, forests, and soils, doubling the number of experiments in one year usually cannot substitute for 2 consecutive years of research. It is doubtful that a new generation of atmospheric transport models could be developed within a few years. Such modeling efforts involve years of trial and error—and require several more years of monitoring data to validate the results over a range of climatological conditions.

A strong, continuing research program is a necessary part of any strategy Congress might choose to address the problem of acid deposition. Several modifications, however, might make the current program more responsive to congressional information needs.

If a decision on an emissions control program is delayed for several years, Congress could estab-

Photo credit: Richard Linthurst

An extensive network of precipitation chemistry samplers (shown above) is part of the National Acid Precipitation Assessment Program—the Federal research program to better understand the causes and effects of acid deposition. Broadening the research program to include such other pollutants as ozone could provide information useful to Congress for addressing the more general problem of transported air pollutants

lish a new, separate assessment activity investigating a range of legislative options. Findings from ongoing Federal research could then be incorporated into policy guidance more quickly than is planned under the present timetable, without disturbing the longer term Federal plan.

If Congress acts to control acid deposition, the program could be redirected to support implementation and evaluation of the legislation. Concerns have been raised within the scientific community that if control legislation is enacted, important research efforts might not be adequately funded over the long term. At least 5 years would elapse between the time legislation is passed and emissions reductions are achieved. Continued research in a number of fields would be important for further evaluation of the control strategy throughout this period, and for designing and implementing the chosen control program into the 1990's.

Many within the scientific community are also concerned over the *breadth* of the research program, regardless of whether a control program is adopted. NAPAP's enabling legislation focuses on acid deposition. However, researchers have found this emphasis to be restrictive in two ways. Several resources—notably forests, crops, and materials—are exposed to multiple air pollutants; understanding the effect of any single pollutant requires research on all. Similarly, the potential benefits of emissions reductions are not limited to those associated with lowered levels of acid deposition.

For example, reductions of sulfur dioxide emissions will improve visibility and lower concentrations of airborne fine particles. It is difficult, however, to coordinate the various existing Federal air-pollution research programs addressing these problems with the NAPAP effort. The innovative research management framework established by the Acid Precipitation Act of 1980 could serve as the basis for a more encompassing Federal air-pollution research effort.

Options:

Specific options available to Congress for modifying the current acid deposition research program are described below.

Option C-1: Establish a ''Two-Track'' Research Program.

Concurrent with the existing research program, Congress could mandate a separate policy assessment—with separate funding—to be completed by a specified date. The current Plan could remain intact, although some modifications might be necessary to provide needed information to the policy assessment effort. Such a ''two-track'' program could provide Congress with timely policy guidance, without jeopardizing the longer term research currently under way.

Congress could require the assessment to evaluate a series of control alternatives within 2 or 3 years. Though the evaluation would have to be based on incomplete information (as might the currently planned integrated assessment), a common set of alternative scenarios would be available for policymakers to consider. This option would establish a research effort similar to this OTA assessment—a description of plausible outcomes from various policy alternatives—but with the benefit of a few more years of data and greater resources.

Such a research effort would use a consistent set of assumptions and models to evaluate:
- the costs of each control program,
- secondary effects of control (e.g., shifts in coal-mining related employment),
- expected deposition reductions (using several currently available atmospheric transport models),
- other air quality benefits (e.g., improvements in visibility and air concentrations for fine particulates), and
- resource benefits (e.g., percent of land area receiving deposition at or below levels thought to be safe for sensitive aquatic resources).

EPA (which currently coordinates the Assessments and Policy Analysis Task Group), might be designated to conduct the short-term evaluation, or another organization (e.g., the Council on Environmental Quality) might be chosen if two separate assessments are desired. One (or a consortium) of the national laboratories or the National Academy of Sciences are possible candidates from outside the Federal agencies.

Option C-2: Redirect the Research Program If a Control Program Is Legislated.

The Acid Precipitation Act of 1980 does not provide for modifying the research program if a control program were enacted. Continued research—with some redirection—would serve several purposes if control legislation were passed. Research results could be used in designing and implementing the details of the chosen control strategy through the 1990's. Because it might take about a decade to implement, the control program would require vigorous research support to reflect the most current, rather than 10-year-old, scientific information. In addition, the research program could provide data to evaluate the effectiveness of the legislation after passage.

The Interagency Task Force is already examining necessary changes to the research plan to be responsive to potential control legislation. Congress could direct the Task Force to modify the program to provide information appropriate for regulatory decisionmaking.

Option C-3: Broaden the Research Program To Address Other Transported Air Pollutants.

The Acid Precipitation Act of 1980 established an innovative, interagency research program to evaluate the effects of acid deposition and the effectiveness of means available to control it. The effects on many resources, however, are difficult to determine without active research on other pollutants. Similarly, the benefits of reducing pollutant emissions are not confined to those associated with reduced levels of acid deposition.

Congress could use the existing interagency structure and broaden its mandate to include research on other air pollutants. For example, research showing forest productivity declines in the United States and West Germany has led scientists to become concerned about the combined stress from acid deposition, ozone, and heavy-metal deposition. Broadening the research program could provide useful information to Congress for evaluating both current proposals to control acid deposition and, perhaps more importantly, future modifications to the Clean Air Act that might be desirable for addressing the more general problem of transported air pollutants.

APPROACH D: *Modifying Existing International and Interstate Sections of the Clean Air Act*

Discussion:

The 1977 Amendments to the Clean Air Act added provisions to regulate interstate and international air pollutant effects through the existing control mechanism of state implementation plans (SIPs). Section 110(a)(2)(E) requires SIPs to prevent a State's emissions from causing violations of air quality standards in *other States*.[2] The section further prohibits EPA from approving a SIP or a SIP revision that causes violations of National Ambient Air Quality Standards (NAAQS) in another State. Currently, however, this section applies only to air concentrations of pollutants for which NAAQS exist and therefore does not directly address acid deposition.

EPA has not issued regulations interpreting section 110(a)(2)(E) since it was enacted in 1977; however, agency reviews of potential interstate pollution violations to date have been limited to the portion of the SIP undergoing revision. When proposed SIP revisions would relax an individual source's emissions limitations, EPA assesses only how the source's proposed emissions *increase* would affect interstate air quality. EPA also takes the position that there are no adequate modeling tools to assess the long-range effects of either individual or multiple sources.

Several States and other petitioners have filed suit in the U.S. Circuit Courts to challenge EPA's approval of SIP relaxations, claiming that the resulting pollution increases would violate this interstate pollution provision. Few of these legal suits, however, have been settled. While some uncertainty remains over how the courts will interpret interstate pollu-

---

[2]Sec. 110(a)(2)(E) states that the SIP must contain: Adequate provisions (i) prohibiting any stationary source within the State from emitting any air pollution in amounts which will (a) prevent attainment or maintenance by any other State of any such national primary or secondary ambient air quality standard, or (b) interfere with measures required to be included in the applicable implementation plan for any other State under Part C to prevent significant deterioration of air quality or to protect visibility and, (ii) insuring compliance with requirements of sec. 126, relating to interstate pollution abatement. (sec. 110(a)(2)(E)).

tion control requirements, recent decisions suggest that the Federal courts are not prepared to interpret section 110(a)(2)(E) to require broader consideration of interstate pollution effects than occurs under current EPA practices.

Section 126 allows any State or political subdivision to petition the Administrator of EPA to remedy interstate pollution. The language of section 126 is relatively vague, and to date EPA has not issued interpretive regulations. The section relies on provisions of section 110(a)(2)(E) for determining the prohibited quantity of interstate pollution. A number of States seeking relief from long-range interstate pollution have filed section 126 petitions. EPA has consolidated the petitions of the States of New York, Pennsylvania, and Maine into a single proceeding. These States have requested far-reaching relief from alleged interstate pollution problems, including revision of EPA policies and broad-scale reductions in emissions throughout the Eastern United States.

EPA has not yet ruled on these petitions; despite the statutorily mandated deadline (60 days) for ruling on a State's petition, a number have been outstanding for years. States have the right to challenge an EPA determination on a section 126 petition in court, but no such challenge is possible until EPA acts on the petitions. In March 1984, six Northeastern States sued EPA to rule on the outstanding petitions but no court action has yet been taken.

Section 115 of the Clean Air Act provides an administrative mechanism for controlling pollution that crosses international boundaries. It is activated either by the Administrator of EPA or at the request of the Secretary of State. If the Administrator determines that the United States is causing or contributing to ''air pollution which may reasonably be anticipated to endanger public health or welfare in a foreign country,'' EPA must require revisions to SIPs in the States in which the emissions originate. Section 115 allows control of *any* air pollutant—unlike the interstate pollution provisions, which can be used only to control air concentrations of pollutants for which NAAQS have been issued. Thus, the section may be interpreted to per-

mit direct control of acid deposition caused by transboundary pollution.*

Acid deposition resulting from long-range pollution transport has become a major issue between the United States and Canada. At present, no agreement between the two nations directly addresses transboundary air pollution; however, the two countries have begun negotiations to reach a bilateral accord under a Memorandum of Intent signed Aug. 5, 1980.

Options:

Specific options to clarify Clean Air Act provisions controlling long-range pollution transport (sections 110(a)(2)(E), 126, and 115) are described below.

Option D-1: Amend the Interstate Pollution Provisions of the Clean Air Act.

Section 110(a)(2)(E) of the Clean Air Act is the major existing interstate pollution provision. It was designed to address local-scale interstate pollution problems. The section applies to air concentrations of pollutants for which NAAQS exist (e.g., airborne particulates); it does not directly address acid deposition.**

Currently, EPA reviews only the effects of SIP *revisions* on interstate pollution levels. States are also concerned, however, with the *cumulative* emissions from sources outside their border leading to potential air quality degradation within their State. Several States have protested to both EPA and the courts about EPA's interpretation of this and other aspects of the section.

---

*On Jan. 13, 1981, then EPA Administrator Douglas M. Costle announced a finding of endangerment with respect to acid deposition in Canada, and moved to activate this international provision. To date, however, EPA has sent no formal notification requiring revision of any State implementation plan.

**Amendments to sec. 110(a)(2)(E), if combined with, for example, a new deposition standard, or new NAAQS for sulfates and nitrates, could in theory be used to control acid deposition. However, such mechanisms would offer, at best, an indirect and uncertain means of doing so. They would leave to administrative discretion a wide range of political issues, including the size of the control region, the required amount of emission reductions, and the distribution of reductions among States or other regions. They would also require a lengthy standard-setting and allocation process, and could engender substantial legal and procedural battles among EPA, the States, and the Federal court system.

Clarification of EPA's responsibilities for restricting interstate pollution requires congressional guidance on several aspects of section 110(a)(2)(E). These include: 1) whether the section restricts interstate pollution from *individual sources only,* or from the cumulative emissions of sources throughout the State, 2) how much interstate pollution is permissible, 3) what constitutes proof of causation of interstate pollution effects, 4) whether EPA is required to review the *entire* SIP for compliance with section 110(a)(2)(E) when States revise a portion of their SIPs, and 5) whether EPA is required to review SIPs approved before the section went into effect.

Closely related to clarification of section 110(a)(2)(E), Congress could require EPA to develop guidelines for *reviewing* interstate pollution petitions (currently contained in section 126 of the Clean Air Act). Section 126 could also be modified to require EPA to resolve petitions within a specified amount of time. For example, Congress could retain the 60-day requirement for holding hearings on a section 126 petition, but allow EPA additional time from the close of the hearing to reach a determination. By further specifying *de facto* denial of the petition if the agency fails to make a determination within, for example, 6 months to a year, Congress could make it possible for States to receive *judicial* review of section 126 petitions in the absence of administrative review by EPA.

Such changes could be effective in ending the current bottleneck of States' petitions within EPA, permitting States to bypass stalled or inactive agency decisionmaking procedures and move on to the judicial-appeals process for section 126 petitions.

Option D-2: Amend the International Provisions of the Clean Air Act.

Section 115 of the Clean Air Act was designed to address local pollution effects occurring near an international border. However, an EPA administrator who chooses to implement section 115 can require further control of *any* air pollutant from any number of States that may contribute to an international pollution problem. The section provides no guidance on what levels or kinds of transboundary pollution are impermissible, how to allocate control responsibilities among States, or how to revise SIPs to require control of pollutants for which NAAQS do not exist. At present, the open-endedness of the authority delegated by section 115 makes it an unwieldy and potentially a politically volatile tool for controlling such long-range transported air pollutants as acid deposition and ozone.

The section could be amended to provide more specific instructions and guidelines to the EPA Administrator. For example, Congress could direct the Administrator to consult with the Department of State to designate an appropriate international agency or establish a bilateral commission to determine the magnitude of the problem and the levels of control to be required. For addressing air pollution transport to and from Canada, Congress might direct the Administrator to refer the problem to the International Joint Commission, established by Canada and the United States in 1909 to monitor transboundary pollution problems.

Activating section 115, however, could conflict with other bilateral mechanisms for dealing with transboundary pollution problems. In the case of U.S.-Canadian acid deposition problems, initiating action under section 115 might interfere with ongoing talks with Canada under the 1980 Memorandum of Intent on Transboundary Air Pollution.

Chapter 7
Legislating Emissions Reductions

Contents

TABLES

Legislating Emissions Reductions

Chapter 6 presented four approaches available to Congress for addressing transported air pollutants. Under the first approach—further controlling the sources of pollutant emissions—three options were discussed. These correspond to broad *strategies* for further emissions control: mandating a small-scale emissions reduction program; mandating a large-scale program; and establishing a control program based on an environmental quality standard.

If Congress decides to enact an emissions control program at this time, the choice of one of these three broad strategies is only the first step in designing legislation. Policymakers would also have to make a number of complex, interrelated decisions to specify the *details* of the chosen strategy. For example, more than 10 bills before the 98th Congress propose large-scale emissions reductions, but the differences among them are substantial.

Accordingly, this chapter is intended to serve as a guide for turning the broad emissions control strategies presented in chapter 6 into a legislative proposal. It also provides a framework for evaluating specific provisions of the many acid deposition control bills introduced to date. The chapter expands on the brief discussion of the eight control-policy decisions presented in the previous chapter. Table 6 summarizes the eight decisions, along with their corresponding options.

Other transported air pollutants, such as ozone and airborne sulfates, will be mentioned where appropriate, but detailed options for controlling them, either separately or in combination with acid deposition, are not presented. Where possible, each discussion will assess the current state of knowledge, the possibility of acquiring further relevant information in the near future, and the societal value choices involved.

Decision 1: Which Pollutants Should Be Further Controlled?

Discussion:

Most acid rain control proposals to date have focused on reducing emissions of sulfur dioxide. There are several reasons for this.

Table 6.—Summary of Control-Policy Decisions and Options

Decision 1: Which Pollutants Should Be Further Controlled?
Option 1a : Sulfur Dioxide Alone
Option 1b: Both Oxides of Sulfur and Nitrogen
Option 1c: Sulfur Dioxide, Nitrogen Oxides, and Hydrocarbons

Decision 2: How Widespread Should a Control Program Be?
Option 2a: 21 Northeastern States
Option 2b: 31 Eastern States
Option 2c: 36 Eastern States
Option 2d: 48 Contiguous States
Option 2e: Allow EPA to Define Appropriate Control Region

Decision 3: What Level of Pollution Control Should Be Required?
Option 3a: Mandate Emissions Reductions
Option 3b: Mandate Reductions, Including Offsets for Future Emissions Growth
Option 3c: Require EPA To Specify Reductions

Decision 4: By What Time Should Reduction Be Required?
Option 4a: 6 to 10 years
Option 4b: 10 to 16 years, Allowing a Delay for Research
Option 4c: 8 to 12 Years, With a "Mid-Course" Reevaluation
Option 4d: Stagger Compliance Schedules

Decision 5: What Approach to Control Should Be Adopted?
Option 5a: Directly Specify Emissions Reductions or Emission Rate Limitations
Option 5b: Specify Use of Control Technologies
Option 5c: Establish an "Environmental Quality" Standard

Decision 6: How Should Emissions Reductions Be Allocated?
Option 6a: Directly to Sources
Option 6b: To States
Option 6c: Responsibility of Governors in Control Region
Option 6d: Responsibility of EPA
Option 6e: Allow Trading of Emissions Reductions Requirements
Option 6f: Allow Substitution of Nitrogen Oxides Emissions Reductions

Decision 7: Who Will Pay the Costs of Emissions Reductions?
Option 7a: Sources Allocated Emissions Reductions
Option 7b: Establish a Trust Fund To Pay Part of Costs

Decision 8: What Can Be Done To Mitigate Employment and Economic Effects of a Control Policy?
Option 8a: Require Reductions by Technological Means
Option 8b: Strengthen Clean Air Act, Section 125
Option 8c: Establish Worker Assistance Program
Option 8d: Utility Tax Breaks
Option 8e: Pollution Control Technology R&D

SOURCE: Office of Technology Assessment.

Substantially greater amounts of sulfur dioxide are released into the atmosphere in the Eastern half of the United States than nitrogen oxides. Eastern U.S. sulfur dioxide emissions in 1980 were about

22 million tons, whereas nitrogen oxides emissions were about 14 to 15 million tons. Sulfur dioxide and its transformation products currently contribute about twice as much to *precipitation acidity* in the Northeast as do nitrogen oxides.

Once deposited, sulfur compounds are more likely to threaten natural ecosystems than nitrogen compounds. While sulfur and nitrogen are both essential nutrients in soil ecosystems, most Eastern forests require and retain far greater amounts of nitrogen than of sulfur. Consequently, sulfur compounds are more likely to travel through watersheds and increase the acidity of water bodies, while nitrogen compounds are more frequently taken up by plants before they reach lakes and streams.* Finally, approaches to controlling sulfur dioxide are more developed than for nitrogen oxides.

Nitrogen oxides emissions, however, are expected to contribute an increasing share to Eastern acid deposition, as nitrogen oxides emissions are projected to rise at a faster rate than sulfur dioxide emissions. In the Western United States, nitrogen compounds currently contribute as much to precipitation acidity as sulfur compounds do, and in many regions a greater amount. Nitrogen oxides are also involved in the production of ozone, a transported air pollutant known to damage crops and forests.

Air concentrations of both nitrogen oxides and hydrocarbons influence the rate at which sulfur dioxide is transformed to sulfates. Model-based studies indicate that altering nitrogen oxides and hydrocarbon concentrations does not affect *total* sulfur deposition nearly as much as does directly reducing sulfur dioxide concentrations. The presence of these ''co-pollutants'' can alter *wet* sulfur deposition, but does not significantly affect dry sulfur deposition. The limited understanding of atmospheric chemistry, however, provides little guidance for designing a control program involving these pollutants *along with* sulfur dioxide. Appendix C discusses how these other pollutants may potentially affect the amount of sulfur deposited within the Eastern United States.

---

*Nitrogen compounds deposited in snowfall are of greatest concern to aquatic ecosystems when they are released during spring snow melt. The ''acid shock'' caused by the acidity released from snow melt occurs during spawning periods, when fish populations are most susceptible to damage.

Conclusions and Options:

Three pollutants are possible candidates for acid deposition control: sulfur dioxide, nitrogen oxides, and hydrocarbons. Any program to control Eastern levels of acid deposition should include reductions in sulfur dioxide emissions. Depending on the desired degree of resource protection and geographic extent and scheduling of the control program, other pollutants might be included as well.

Options available to the Congress are described below.

Option 1a: Reduce Emissions of Sulfur Dioxide

Over the Eastern United States, deposition of sulfur oxides is generally greater than deposition of nitrogen oxides. In addition, sulfur oxides appear to have greater potential for damaging ecosystems and degrading visibility, and are of concern because of possible health effects from airborne sulfates. While co-pollutants may affect the *degree* to which cutting back sulfur dioxide reduces deposition, reducing sulfur dioxide emissions is the most plausible means of reducing acid deposition in the Eastern United States.

Option 1b: Reduce Emissions of Both Oxides of Sulfur and Nitrogen

While cutting back sulfur dioxide emissions *alone* may substantially reduce Eastern acid deposition, controlling nitrogen oxides emissions *in addition* to sulfur oxides would provide further protection to sensitive natural resources. Currently, nitrogen oxides are the second greatest manmade source of acidity. Nitrogen oxides emissions, however, have increased much more rapidly than sulfur dioxide emissions during the past few decades, and are projected to increase an additional 25 percent by 2010. Thus, they will contribute an increasing share of acid deposition. Reductions of nitrogen oxides emissions would also help lower regional ozone levels.

Congressional action to reduce acid deposition in the Western United States, if desired, must also address nitrogen oxides emissions. A nationwide acid deposition control program might therefore involve both pollutants.

Option 1c: Reduce Emissions of Sulfur Dioxide, Nitrogen Oxides, and Hydrocarbons

Sophisticated models of both the chemistry and meteorology of the atmosphere may eventually make it possible to design more cost-effective strategies relying on control of all three pollutants involved in acid deposition. The modeling capability to design such a strategy for a near-term control program, however, does not yet exist; and it is uncertain whether this capability will be available within the next decade. Such multiple-pollutant control might best be considered for future refinements to an ongoing acid deposition control program.

Decision 2: How Widespread Should a Control Program Be?

Discussion:

Most of Eastern North America—from southern Ontario and Quebec to northern Mississippi, Alabama, and Georgia, and from the Atlantic Coast as far west as the Mississippi River—receives precipitation more acidic than pH 4.5. This area includes large regions with lakes and streams considered sensitive to the effects of acid deposition at this level.

While a substantial fraction of pollutant emissions is deposited locally, the remainder travels with air masses moving over a region, and is deposited at distances and directions determined by prevailing chemical and meteorological conditions. Pollutants contributing to acid deposition may travel well over 500 miles. A large share of sulfur deposition—in some regions, over half—originates from sources over 300 miles away. For example, model analyses suggest that 50 to 70 percent of the sulfur deposited in northern New York State, New England, and parts of southeastern Canada is emitted from sources more distant than 300 miles.* Consequently, acid deposition is regional in scope: emissions sources in a multi-State region contribute to deposition in many other regions, depending on complex and variable atmospheric conditions.

Many legislative proposals to date have focused on a 31-State region encompassing the States east of, and the first tier of States west of, the Mississippi River. Of the 26 to 27 million tons of sulfur dioxide emitted in the continental United States in 1980, about 22 million tons, or 80 to 85 percent, came from this 31-State region. In addition, sulfur dioxide control proposals have focused on electric utilities, which emit about three-quarters of Eastern sulfur dioxide. In the West, utilities emit about 30 percent, while industrial sources emit about 60 percent (half of which comes from smelters). The prevailing use of low-sulfur coal in the West results in significantly lower sulfur dioxide emissions rates.

Of the 21 to 22 million tons of nitrogen oxides emitted in the continental United States in 1980, about two-thirds, or 14 million tons, came from the 31-State region. In the East, about 35 percent came from utility combustion and about 15 percent from nonutility combustion. In the West, utilities contribute about 20 percent and nonutility combustion about 30 percent of the total. Mobile sources emit about 45 percent of nitrogen oxides in both regions.

As discussed in Decision 1, either sulfur oxides, nitrogen oxides, or some combination of the two could be controlled uniformly across the chosen region, or separately for subregions within it. Table 7 shows emissions data for the United States as a whole and for several regional breakdowns.

Conclusions and Options:

All of the legislative proposals to control acid deposition to date have included emissions reductions in, at least, the 21 Northeastern States. We present four possible emissions control regions—all of which include this region, but extend south and west depending on the geographic extent of resource protection desired. Congress could specify the size of the control region directly in legislation, or require EPA to establish a control region that best meets congressional goals.

Congressional options are described below.

Option 2a: Require Emissions Reductions From 21 Northeastern States

Given the geographic extent of sensitive resources exposed to high levels of acid deposition and the

---

*These model-based analyses are discussed more thoroughly in ch. 3 and app. C.

Table 7.—Sulfur and Nitrogen Oxide Emissions by Region

	SO₂ emissions (thousand tons)	Percent of U.S. total	NOₓ emissions (thousand tons)	Percent of U.S. total
48 States	26,420	100%	21,120	100%
37 States	23,640	89	17,910	85
31 States	21,810	83	14,000	66
21 States	16,540	63	9,720	46
Rockies, west	2,780	11	3,210	15
17 Western States	4,620	17	7,120	34

SOURCE: *Costs, and Engineering Assessment*, Work Group 3B, United States-Canada Memorandum of Intent on Transboundary Air Pollution, June 15, 1982.

average distance of pollutant transport, we feel the smallest effective control region would consist of the States east of the Mississippi River and north of (and including) Tennessee and North Carolina. This region roughly covers the portion of the United States receiving the most acidic precipitation—in 1980 averaging lower than pH 4.5, a level thought to harm sensitive lakes and streams. About 65 percent of the Nation's sulfur oxides and 45 percent of its nitrogen oxides are emitted in this region.

The region excludes, however, several major emission-producing contiguous States—i.e., Missouri, the fifth largest sulfur dioxide-emitting State, and the southern States of Georgia, Alabama, and Florida. Major nitrogen oxide-emitting States that border the region are Louisiana, Missouri, and the above-mentioned Southern States.

Option 2b: Require Emissions Reductions From 31 Eastern States

This region consists of those States east of and bordering on the Mississippi River, and has been the focus of most legislative proposals and control strategies to date. It emits about 80 to 85 percent of the Nation's sulfur oxides and 65 percent of its nitrogen oxides. One large emitter, Texas, borders this region, ranking sixth-highest in sulfur dioxide and first in nitrogen oxide emissions among the 50 States. Texas utilities generally emit sulfur dioxide at relatively low rates, however, averaging 0.3 lb per million Btu fuel burned.

Option 2c: Require Emissions Reductions From the 37 Eastern States

This region encompasses all States east of the Mississippi, plus two tiers of Western States, i.e., the States east of the Rocky Mountains. This region emits about 90 percent of the Nation's sulfur oxides and 85 percent of its nitrogen oxides. Because emissions rates in the six additional States are relatively low, applying most of the current acid rain control proposals to this region would not appreciably change reductions required from the 31 Eastern States.

Option 2d: Require Emissions Reductions From the Entire 48 Contiguous States

This option treats acidic deposition as a national problem and requires all regions to further control emissions. While effects from acid deposition are currently of greatest concern in the East, highly acidic precipitation events have been observed in parts of the Western States. As discussed previously, different pollutants might be controlled in the East (where sulfur dioxide is the major pollutant) and the West (where nitrogen oxide emissions are greater).

Option 2e: Allow EPA To Define the Appropriate Control Region

Rather than legislating a specific control region, Congress could define the goals of a control program and require EPA to establish the control region by a specified date. EPA could then use information available at that time (e.g., pollution transport models, maps of sensitive regions, control cost estimates) to demarcate a region consistent with congressional guidelines.

Decision 3: What Level of Pollution Control Should Be Required?

Discussion:

The decision on how much to reduce emissions must take into account two important components:

1) the *scientific question* of the relationship between emissions reductions and resource protection, and 2) the *policy question* of what is the socially desirable level of resource protection. The latter involves such policy concerns as balancing the costs of reductions with the expected resource-protection benefits, and distributing the risks and costs equitably among different groups and geographic areas.

No unique "formula" exists for comparing the risks of resource damage with the costs of further emissions controls. Neither scientific nor economic methods can presently analyze the various policy concerns precisely. Moreover, differing priorities among regions and interest groups will lead each to weigh these concerns differently. Several reference points are available, however, for comparing both the benefits and costs of various levels of reduction.

Several groups[1] have estimated maximum levels of acid deposition that most sensitive lakes and streams could receive without undergoing further damage. Specifying deposition limits to protect against damage to such other resources as crops, forests, or materials is not yet possible.

OTA's analysis of how emissions reductions would affect deposition levels concludes that in areas of highest deposition—e.g., western Pennsylvania and northern West Virginia—reducing sulfur dioxide emissions 8 to 10 million tons per year below current levels *might not* be sufficient to bring deposition levels within these recommended targets for protecting *all but the most sensitive* aquatic resources. In areas of lower deposition, such as northern New England, the southern Appalachians, and the upper Midwest, the recommended deposition limits *might* be achievable through sulfur dioxide emissions cutbacks of this magnitude. Thus, reductions of this magnitude would probably *not overshoot* a possible congressional goal of protecting all but the most sensitive aquatic resources.

Risks of damage to sensitive forests, materials, and crops would also be reduced. In addition, airborne fine-particulate levels would be lower, improving visibility and reducing risks to human health.

Whether this is the *desired* level of protection must be addressed, however. Reducing emissions by about 8 to 10 million tons of sulfur dioxide per year below current levels (including offsets for expected new growth) would cost about $3 to $6 billion per year (1982 dollars), depending on the design of the program. Smaller, less expensive cutbacks will provide less protection for sensitive resources, but how much less is unknown. Larger emissions reductions might protect more resources, but the costs would rise steeply.

In addition to preventing potential future damages, reductions might improve water quality in currently acidified lakes and streams. Projections from a simple computer model have been used to estimate how reductions in sulfate deposition might improve water quality.[*] If sulfur dioxide emissions were reduced to 8 to 10 million tons below 1980 levels, about 15 to 40 percent of the aquatic resources already acidified or extremely sensitive to further acid deposition might experience some recovery.

With emissions about 4 to 5 million tons below 1980 levels, we estimate that water quality will improve in a maximum of 10 to 25 percent of these aquatic resources. Reductions of this magnitude, including offsets for emissions growth, might be achievable for $1 to $3 billion per year (1982 dollars).

Congress, however, might decide that the uncertain magnitude of benefits to be gained does not justify such multibillion-dollar expenditures. Holding emissions levels constant, or possibly decreasing them slightly below current levels, might be considered more appropriate until more is known about the extent of the risks to sensitive aquatic resources, forests, agriculture, materials, and human health. For expenditures of about $1 billion per year or less, about 2 to 5 million tons of sulfur dioxide can be

---

[1]Work Group I, Impact Assessment, U.S.-Canada Memorandum of Intent on Transboundary Air Pollution, *Phase II Summary Report,* October 1981; National Research Council, *Acid Deposition, Atmospheric Processes in Eastern North America,* Committee on Atmospheric Transport and Chemical Transformation in Acid Precipitation (Washington, D.C.: National Academy Press, 1983); L. S. Evans, et al., "Acidic Deposition: Considerations for an Air Quality Standard," *Water, Air and Soil Pollution* 16:469-509, 1981.

---

[*]This model assumes that the effects of acid deposition are *not* cumulative and *are* reversible in a short time period. If these conservative assumptions are incorrect, the level of recovery will be slower.

eliminated annually—certainly enough to offset projected emissions growth through 2000, and possibly to decrease emissions levels 2 to 3 million tons below 1980 levels by that time. This is likely to provide some benefit to sensitive resources but, again, such benefits cannot be quantified accurately.

Given the uncertainty that reducing emissions will decrease resource damage to the extent, and in the locations expected, and the resulting difficulty in estimating the benefits, policymakers may have to determine the level of emissions reductions qualitatively. Even if both the benefits and costs of emissions reductions could be rigorously quantified—e.g., by the multiyear research program currently under way in EPA and other agencies—several other factors would enter into the decision.

Many of the resources at risk from continued acid deposition, such as lakes and forests, provide benefits that cannot be calculated solely in economic terms. While these resources do generate income—e.g., freshwater fishing and forestry are multibillion-dollar industries—they are valued for noneconomic reasons as well. Similarly, losses in employment in the high-sulfur coal industry from emissions reductions may cause greater hardships than estimates of lost income indicate.

Finally, benefits and costs of controlling transported pollutants differ substantially among various economic sectors and geographic areas within a control region. Calculating aggregate benefits and costs for the entire affected region ignores these distributional effects.

Conclusions and Options:

Congress could specify emissions reductions to reach a socially desired level of resource protection, considering the costs of further emissions control, the potential resource protection benefits, and other policy concerns. The level of reduction chosen, however, must of necessity be a "best guess" based on incomplete information.

For expenditures of $1 billion per year or less, enough sulfur dioxide emissions could be eliminated to hold emissions constant (i.e., offset expected industrial and utility growth), or to reduce emissions levels 2 to 3 million tons below current levels by the year 2000. This would reduce future risks to

sensitive aquatic resources, forests, agriculture, materials, and health, but by how much is uncertain. Eliminating 8 to 10 million tons of sulfur dioxide annually from existing utilities by this date would cost $2 to $5 billion per year.

Reductions of this magnitude might protect *all but the most sensitive* aquatic resources in many areas, but might not afford this level of protection in areas currently receiving the highest levels of acidic deposition. The level of emissions reductions necessary to protect against potential damage to such other resources as crops, forests, or materials is not yet known.

Once the aggregate regional level of emissions reductions is chosen, Congress must further decide whether the control program should be designed to accomplish: 1) a "one-time" emissions reduction (i.e., eliminating a specified emissions tonnage from existing sources, but not restricting future emissions growth), or 2) an absolute "ceiling" on regional emissions, thus requiring further reductions as new sources are built.

An increase of about 1 to 3 million tons of sulfur dioxide emissions per year is projected by 1995. The highest rates of emissions growth are expected in the South and the West. Thus, an absolute ceiling on emissions would be difficult to achieve in these regions, as well as in those States that currently have low emissions rates.

Alternatively, Congress could give EPA responsibility for setting reduction levels.

Options available to Congress are described below.

Option 3a: Mandate Specific Levels of Emissions Reductions

A congressionally mandated emissions control program could range from preventing projected increases in emissions to large-scale reductions below current levels. In the Eastern 31-State region, a pragmatic estimate of about 11 to 12.5 million tons of sulfur dioxide per year constitutes the upper limit of feasible emissions reductions, given current technology and costs. Larger reductions would require stricter emission rate limitations for all *existing* utility plants than those currently applicable to *new* plants under New Source Performance Standards.

Table 8 presents estimates of the costs of controlling *utility* sulfur dioxide emissions in the Eastern 31 States. Cost estimates are for control strategies based on specified maximum allowable emission rates, assuming 1980 emissions and emission rates. The costs of other programs will vary, depending on how emissions reductions are allocated and implemented. However, both the amount of sulfur dioxide emissions eliminated from existing facilities and the extent of future emissions growth determine the *net* reductions at any future date. Future emissions growth in the region might shrink the reductions presented in table 8 by about 1 to 3 million tons per year by 2000.

Option 3b: Mandate Reductions, Including Offsets for Future Emissions Growth

If Congress specifies emissions reductions, it must also determine how to treat future growth in emissions. For example, added emissions from *new* sources would shrink an 8-million-ton cutback in sulfur dioxide emissions from *existing* sources to an overall reduction of 5.5 to 6.5 million tons below current levels by 1995. This might be considered adequate through about 2000, when the effectiveness of the program can be reevaluated.

However, to reduce overall emissions by, for example, 8 million tons below current levels by 1995, existing sources would have to reduce emissions by 9.5 to 10.5 million tons. To offset emissions from sources not yet built—already subject to tight control under current New Source Performance Standards—State plans would have to eliminate enough "extra" current emissions to accommodate potential future emission levels, or face the risk of discouraging new industrial or utility growth.

For the more stringent emissions control programs listed in table 8, offsetting future emissions growth as well might cost an additional $1 to $2 billion per year.

Option 3c: Require EPA To Specify Emissions Reductions To Meet Congressional Goals

Congress could give EPA responsibility for setting reduction levels by a given date, according to specified congressional goals for resource protection and economic considerations. EPA could then incorporate emerging research findings into its technical judgment of what level of reductions are consistent with congressional goals. The choice could be left completely to EPA discretion, or be bounded by the Congress (e.g., eliminating 2-to-5 million, or 5-to-10 million tons of sulfur dioxide emissions).

Scientists might soon be able to *estimate* the extent of aquatic resource protection afforded by various levels of emissions reductions, but might require many years to develop similar estimates for other resources. Nonetheless, such estimates, even for aquatic resources, are likely to remain controversial for many years, due to uncertainties over how reductions in emissions would affect deposition levels, and how reductions in deposition levels would affect aquatic resources. If Congress required EPA to weigh the benefits and costs of emissions reductions, it would also need to specify the economic goals to be met, the kinds of benefits to be included in calculations, and the treatment of regional differences in costs and benefits.

Table 8.—Costs of Reducing Sulfur Dioxide Emissions in the Eastern 31 States
(Excludes costs to offset future emissions growth; all costs in 1982 dollars)

Emission rate limitation (lbs. SO₂/million Btu)	Emissions reductions (million tons SO₂)	Total cost[a] ($ billions)	Average cost of reductions ($/ton)	Marginal cost of reductions[b] ($/ton)
2.5	4.6	0.6-0.9	170-240	320
2.0	6.2	1.1-1.5	200-280	440
1.5	8.0	1.8-2.3	260-330	700
1.2	9.3	2.6-3.4	310-400	740
1.0	10.3	3.2-4.1	350-440	830
0.8	11.4	4.2-5.0	400-480	1,320

[a]Excludes costs to meet current SIPs.
[b]Cost (in dollars per ton) to achieve the next increment of reductions.

SOURCE: Office of Technology Assessment, based on analyses by E. H. Pechan & Associates, Inc., 1983.

Decision 4: By What Time Should Reductions Be Required?

Discussion:

This decision focuses on the tradeoff between the risk of resource damage from continued levels of acid deposition, and the risk of inefficient or unnecessary control expenditures by acting on limited knowledge of many of the atmospheric and ecological processes involved. Throughout the discussion, it is necessary to keep in mind that further emissions controls would take at a minimum about 6 to 10 years to implement, given the planning, contracts, construction, and other steps necessary to significantly reduce pollutant emissions.

A "fast-track" program—one requiring emissions reductions in 6 to 10 years—could probably be met only if Congress directly specified the amount of reductions. Such a program would require individual control decisions to be made quickly; even then, if large-scale reductions were mandated, it might not be possible to install scrubbers and expand low-sulfur coal supplies rapidly enough to meet the deadline.

Waiting 4 to 6 years for further research results would increase the time required to reduce deposition to 10 to 16 years, but might lead to a better control program. During the waiting period, knowledge of acid deposition and its effects will advance, and more cost-effective control technologies might be developed. However, it is not possible to count on significant scientific breakthroughs in this relatively short time.

An intermediate schedule could mandate reductions now, but allow more time for implementation than the "fast-track" program. The program could be designed to incorporate results from the Federal acid deposition research program in about 3 to 5 years, to determine whether the control program should remain intact, be modified, or be discontinued. Federal and State planning processes could proceed without delay—recognizing that the research program might not substantially alter current understanding—but such a program would not require additional pollution control expenditures until *after* the reevaluation point.

Innovative approaches to pollution control—e.g., technologies such as LIMB (limestone injection multistage burners) or regenerable processes, discussed in appendix A—raise additional scheduling-related issues, as they may take longer to plan and install than more traditional approaches. Congress could provide incentives to try these potentially more cost-effective technologies by extending compliance deadlines when they are used.

Conclusions and Options:

A major emissions control program would require, at minimum, about 6 to 10 years to implement. A longer compliance period might be desired to allow policymakers the opportunity to consider the results of the Federal acid deposition research plan. The additional delay, however, might result in more extensive resource damage.

Options available to the Congress with regard to scheduling emissions reductions are described below.

Option 4a: Require Reductions in 6 to 10 Years

Achieving significant reductions within 6 to 10 years would probably require Congress to specify emissions reductions or emission rate limitations. State-level planning and source-level implementation of reductions would have to proceed rapidly. Federal and private-sector acid precipitation research findings might occur too late to be used for modifying the program.

Option 4b: Require Reductions in 10 to 16 Years, Allowing a Delay for Research

Delivery of Federal research results in 4 to 6 years could serve as the starting date for planning specified reductions or an environmental quality standard. Compliance with the program would then require an additional 6 to 10 years.

Option 4c: Require Reductions in 8 to 12 Years, With a "Mid-course" Reevaluation

Federal and State planning could begin immediately, but the compliance date could be set so that individual sources would not have to begin planning construction and contracts until after a reevaluation period in about 3 to 5 years. New research results, if any appeared, could be used to determine whether the control program should remain intact, be modified, or be eliminated.

Option 4d: Stagger Compliance Schedules

To promote potentially more cost-effective technologies, sources using innovative emissions control approaches could be given extra time to comply with any of the schedules outlined in options 4a through 4c.

If interim reductions are desired in conjunction with longer compliance schedules (e.g., options 4b and 4c), earlier reductions could be required from sources switching to low-sulfur fuels or from those sources emitting at the highest rates. Mandatory coal washing, though more expensive than approaches that allow each source to choose its least-expensive alternative, is another method for achieving interim reductions. This alternative has the advantage of being potentially less disruptive to the coal industry.

Decision 5: What Approach to Control Should Be Adopted?

Discussion:

Several regulatory frameworks are available to the Congress for controlling transported air pollutants. These fall into two broad categories:

1. "Environmental quality" approaches—setting goals or standards for *resource exposure* to pollutants—including:
   * Establishing environmental quality goals or standards based on *air concentrations* of pollutants.
   * Establishing environmental quality goals or standards based on pollutant *deposition rates*.
2. "Source-based" approaches—directly regulating *emissions* from sources or regions—including:
   * Specifying *total* emissions reductions (in tons of pollutants per year), or allowable pollutant emission *rates* (most commonly expressed as pounds of pollutant per unit

of fuel burned for stationary sources, and grams of pollutant per mile for automobiles).
   * Requiring either specific *types* of control technologies (e.g., scrubbers), or technology-based *performance* standards.

Air quality goals are currently implemented through both approaches. For example, National Ambient Air Quality Standards (NAAQS) are *environmental quality* standards. Allowable air concentrations of pollutants are set to protect the public health and welfare. New Source Performance Standards (NSPS) are *source-based* standards. They seek to minimize *future* pollutant emissions by regulating emission rates, even for cases in which NAAQS would be met without their use. NSPS for coal-fired utilities both set a maximum allowable emissions rate and require the removal of 70 to 90 percent of potential sulfur dioxide emissions by technological means.

NAAQS might be used as a framework for controlling transported pollutants. Welfare-based secondary standards for these pollutants could be made more stringent and enforced more rigorously. Such an approach might be effective for controlling resource damage from ozone. To address acid deposition, Congress could require EPA to establish NAAQS for sulfate and nitrate particulates, the principal transformation products of sulfur dioxide and nitrogen oxides. To make the NAAQS approach effective, EPA would have to broaden its consideration of long-range pollution transport.

The NAAQS are *air* concentration standards, however, designed to minimize human health effects from breathing pollutants, crop and forest damage from exposure to pollutant gases, or materials damage from exposure to gases or particles. A different type of environmental quality standard—a *deposition standard*—would be more consistent with our understanding of the environmental effects of acid deposition. Though conceptually attractive, a deposition standard would be quite difficult to implement. Natural variations in precipitation and wind patterns can cause an area's deposition to vary considerably from year to year.

Due to the many source regions and sensitive receptor regions involved, designing measures to comply with the standards, either at the Federal or State level, would be a difficult and time-consuming administrative and political process. Moreover, while existing models can link large source regions to large receptor regions, identifying specific sources responsible for deposition in specific areas far downwind is beyond their current capabilities.

A *source-based* approach—the one embodied in most of the acid rain control proposals to date—would *require emissions reductions throughout a broad region* believed to contribute to acidification in sensitive areas. Unlike deposition standards, the implementation of source-based approaches is not restricted by the major uncertainties and inherent characteristics of the acid deposition problem. Two types of source-based regulatory approaches are possible: 1) directly specifying emissions reductions or allowable emissions rates, and 2) limiting emissions by requiring the use of specific technologies or technology-based performance standards.

The first approach can be used either to directly control sources or to assign reductions to regions, leaving the choice of which sources to control to another decisionmaking body. The advantages and disadvantages of these alternatives are discussed in *Decision 6: How Should Emissions Reductions Be Allocated?*

Specified emissions or emissions rates give each emitter the option of choosing the least expensive control method, according to individual plant conditions. The second approach—technology-based standards—reduces or eliminates a plant's options. Technology-based standards, however, avoid some of the adverse effects of "nontechnological" methods of pollution control—i.e., switching to cleaner fuels. Technological standards would minimize production and employment losses in many Eastern U.S. coal regions. As discussed in detail in Decision 8, there is a tradeoff between minimizing these adverse, indirect effects of control, and allowing emitters to choose the least expensive control method.

Conclusions and Options:

If Congress decides that an acid deposition control program should be implemented in the near future—within about 10 to 15 years—several "source-based" approaches to control are feasible. A control program based on an "environmental

quality" standard (similar to the ambient air quality standards of the Clean Air Act) might be possible in the future, but the scientific tools needed to support such an approach are not yet available.

Options available to Congress are discussed below.

Option 5a: Directly Specify Emissions Reductions or Emissions Rate Limitations

Emissions limitations may be specified for either a class of sources or by region. Decision 6 discusses the distributional implications of various kinds of reduction programs. The approach presumes that the effects of acid deposition are significant enough to warrant emissions reductions, but that scientific uncertainties permit no more resolution in a control approach than to reduce aggregate, regional emissions. Limiting emissions by region or source category may involve inefficiencies in that it does not specifically seek to connect the location and amount of emissions to the location and sensitivity of areas of deposition. This approach, however, best reflects current knowledge about the relationship between emissions and acid deposition.

Option 5b: Specify the Use of Control Technologies

Emissions could also be reduced by specifying technology performance standards (e.g., 50-percent reduction, "best available," and so on) or mandating the use of specific technologies (e.g., coal washing). Like option 5a, the approach does not depend on linking source regions to receptor regions.

Technology-based standards are potentially more expensive than a control program that allows each emitter to meet the required reductions through the least-expensive (or otherwise advantageous) method of control. Technology standards are administratively simple, however, and would minimize coal market disruptions that might result from other approaches to control. (Potential effects on coal production are discussed in detail in Decision 8.)

Option 5c: Specify an "Environmental Quality Standard" Approach

Acid deposition control strategies could be pursued by: 1) establishing and enforcing more stringent secondary NAAQS for sulfur dioxide and nitrogen oxides, or 2) developing NAAQS for air concentrations of sulfates and nitrates. Secondary NAAQS for ozone are currently identical to the health-based primary standard—a 1-hour maximum allowable concentration. A secondary standard based on a longer averaging time might better reflect potential terrestrial resource damages from chronic ozone exposure.

Alternatively, to control acid *deposition,* standards could be developed to limit the rate of deposition of acidity or sulfur and nitrogen compounds over a given surface area. These standards could vary regionally, depending on the sensitivity of resources to acid deposition.

Because transported air pollutants routinely cross State boundaries, implementing an environmental quality standard to control transported pollutants would require Federal or regional mechanisms for revising State Implementation Plans to meet the new standards. This strategy is constrained by the problem of linking well-defined source areas to well-defined receptor areas—a scientific question that may not be resolved for many years. Even if transport models were improved, the inherent variability of the atmosphere would require limiting the total amount of pollutants emitted from a State or similar-size region, rather than setting emissions limits for individual sources. Moreover, this approach would involve a long and detailed standard-setting and implementation process.*

Decision 6: How Should Emissions Reductions Be Allocated?

Discussion:

Strategies for controlling transported air pollutants must address the following issues:

* Who is to allocate emissions reductions to sources or States?
* If Congress chooses to allocate reductions directly, what method should be used?

*For purposes of comparison, although Clean Air Act revisions in 1977 directed EPA to review and revise the existing NAAQS for five pollutants by 1980, as of 1983 only the standard for ozone had been revised. A revision had been proposed for carbon monoxide; the standards review of the remaining three pollutants will probably be completed by the end of 1984.

The question of who is to pay the control costs—a matter distinct from who is to reduce emissions—is discussed in Decision 7.

Two approaches are available to Congress for directly specifying emissions reductions: 1) mandating a reduction formula for all or a subset of individual sources within the region, or 2) allocating reductions to States or other subregions, allowing another decisionmaking group, such as a State or EPA, to allocate emissions reductions to individual sources.

Congress could also allocate emissions reductions indirectly by assigning responsibility for designing allocation schemes, either with or without accompanying guidelines. Congress might set a goal of reducing deposition within a specified region, recognizing that a wide variety of allocation formulas could achieve that goal. Reductions from one subregion could be substituted for those in a different subregion, within certain bounds, while still maintaining the same average pattern of deposition reductions.

Congress might provide additional guidelines—for example, that the eventual formula allocate reductions on the basis of the current best estimates of how much sources contribute to deposition in given areas. Other guidelines might include minimizing costs to the control region as a whole, limiting the percentage of emissions to be eliminated in any given region, or considering past pollution control efforts.

Four broad policy considerations are pertinent to designing an allocation formula for reducing emissions, or providing guidelines for others to follow:

* Who is to gain the benefit of resource protection,
* Who is to bear the burden of reductions,
* The plan's administrative efficiency, and
* The plan's economic efficiency.

In planning an allocation formula, tradeoffs among these various interrelated concerns must be considered. For example, a plan that attempts to maximize economic efficiency may be difficult to administer, or might concentrate reductions in one or more regions.

Political consideration of ''Who is to gain the benefit of resource protection'' is intertwined with several of the issues discussed previously. Congress could either attempt to reduce deposition in selected high-deposition areas with large concentrations of sensitive resources, or attempt broader-scale protection. A uniform deposition standard, for example, implies the goal of protecting all areas equally, regardless of their concentrations of sensitive resources. Targeting specific areas for deposition reductions, however, favors one State's resources over another's.

The decision on who reduces emissions must consider the scope of desired resource protection, as well as other aspects of any allocation scheme. A plan that provides uniform protection might disperse the required reductions over a larger area than one focusing on sensitive regions. In addition, each specific formula affects the relative share allocated to utilities as opposed to industries; regions whose local coals are higher or lower in sulfur content; and so on.

Allocating reductions on the basis of emissions per area differs in costs and distributional implications from a plan based on an allowable pollutant emission rate per amount of fuel burned. The first approach concentrates reductions in areas with a *high density of sources,* even if these sources are relatively pollution-free. The second approach focuses on sources with *high rates of pollution,* even though the sources might be few and far between. Neither approach directly addresses such factors as past emissions reductions or patterns of pollution deposition.

Appendix A presents eight alternative allocation formulas for reducing sulfur dioxide emissions, and the implicit rationales and distributional consequences of each. Three are based on *total emissions,* five on *utility emissions alone.* Variants include formulas based on: emissions per area; emissions per capita; equal percentage reductions per State; State-average utility emissions rates; emissions above a specified emissions rate; and emissions per quantity of electricity generated (including nonfossil energy).

Another aspect of choosing an allocation formula is administrative feasibility. For example, many control proposals have allocated emissions reductions based on utility emissions not only because they emit about three-quarters of the sulfur dioxide

in the 31 Eastern States, but also because the remaining emissions are difficult to characterize. Accurate estimates of emissions rates for many small industrial boilers are unavailable. Industrial process emissions would have to be regulated according to emissions per product, rather than per quantity of fuel burned, and separate standards would have to be set for each industry.

Finally, for a given overall reduction, each allocation formula results in a different *distribution* of costs, as well as different *total* costs. Controlling plants that emit at high rates is usually cheaper per ton of pollutant removed than controlling lower emitting plants. However, the potential cost to the particular source—or to the State with a large proportion of plants emitting at high rates—increases as the required reductions increase. Allocation formulas that minimize total program costs tend to concentrate reduction requirements on States with the highest average emissions rates.

Conclusions and Options:

If Congress decides to directly assign emissions reduction responsibilities to either sources or States, many reduction formulas are possible. Several policy considerations pertinent to designing an allocation formula include: 1) the resulting distribution of reductions (which determines both the distribution of costs and deposition reductions; 2) the plan's total costs, and 3) the plan's economic efficiency. Tradeoffs among these various interrelated concerns must be considered.

In addition to options for congressional allocation of emissions reductions, we also present options for: 1) assigning allocation responsibilities to either EPA or the governors of States in the control region, and 2) adding flexibility to the chosen formula by allowing trading of emissions reductions requirements.

Options available to Congress for allocating emissions reductions are described below.

Option 6a: Allocate Emissions Reductions Directly to Sources

Emissions reductions could be allocated directly to sources by two means:

1. *Legislating maximum allowable emissions rates.* Congress could set maximum allowable emis-

sions rates for electric utilities, industrial boilers, and industrial process emissions. Reductions achievable by specifying alternative maximum emissions rates for utilities, industrial and commercial boilers, and all large boilers are presented for the 31-State Eastern region in table 9 and for the contiguous 48 States in table 10.

2. *"Targeting" emissions reductions to specific sources.* Reductions could also be allocated to only the largest sources. Of the 16 million tons of sulfur dioxide emitted by utilities in the 31-State Eastern region during 1980, close to 60 percent came from the top 50 sources, about 70 percent from the top 75 sources, and close to 80 percent from the top 100 sources. Alternatively, Congress could target those plants emitting at the highest rates. About 75 percent of 1980 utility sulfur dioxide emissions came from plants emitting in excess of 2.5 lb of sulfur dioxide per million Btu, and 60 percent came from plants emitting in excess of 3.0 lb of sulfur dioxide per million Btu.

These relatively few sources could substantially reduce regional emissions by using scrubbers under procedures similar to the existing New Source Performance Standards. Each of these "targeted reduction" schemes, however, draws an arbitrary cutoff line—those just above it would be required to reduce emissions substantially (e.g., 90 percent

Table 9.—Sulfur Dioxide Emissions Reductions With Emission Rate Limitations—31 Eastern States

lbs. $SO_2/10^6$ Btu	1.0	1.2	1.5	2.0	2.5	3.0	4.0
All boilers (1980 emissions = 19,200 thousand tons/year)							
Thousand tons/year	11,600	10,400	8,900	6,800	5,100	3,700	2,000
Percent reduction in class	60	54	46	35	26	19	10
Percent reduction below total[a]	53	48	41	31	23	17	9
Utility boilers (1980 emissions = 16,070 thousand tons/year)							
Thousand tons/year	10,300	9,320	8,020	6,170	4,620	3,370	1,730
Percent reduction in class	64	58	50	38	29	21	11
Percent reduction below total[a]	47	43	37	28	21	15	8
Nonutility boilers (1980 emissions = 3,200 thousand tons/year)							
Thousand tons/year	1,300	1,100	900	640	460	360	220
Percent reduction in class	40	35	28	20	15	11	7
Percent reduction below total[a]	6	5	4	3	2	2	1

[a]1980 total sulfur dioxide emissions = 21,800 thousand tons/year.

SOURCE: E. H. Pechan & Associates, from Energy Information Administration data (EIA forms 4 and 423), and EPA National Emissions Data System (NEDS).

Table 10.—Sulfur Dioxide Emissions Reductions With Emission Rate Limitations—Entire United States

lbs. $SO_2/10^6$ Btu	1.0	1.2	1.5	2.0	2.5	3.0	4.0
All boilers (1980 emissions = 21,000 thousand tons/year)							
Thousand tons/year	11,900	10,600	9,000	6,900	5,100	3,700	2,000
Percent reduction in class	57	48	43	33	24	18	9
Percent reduction below total[a]	45	40	34	26	19	14	7
Utility boilers (1980 emissions = 17,380 thousand tons/year)							
Thousand tons/year	10,530	9,470	8,100	6,200	4,630	3,370	1,730
Percent reduction in class	61	55	47	36	27	19	10
Percent reduction below total[a]	40	36	31	23	17	13	7
Nonutility boilers (1980 emissions = 3,600 thousand tons/year)							
Thousand tons/year	1,300	1,100	930	660	480	370	230
Percent reduction in class	37	32	26	18	13	10	6
Percent reduction below total[a]	5	4	4	2	2	1	1

[a]1980 total sulfur dioxide emissions = 26,400 thousand tons/year.

SOURCE: E. H. Pechan & Associates, from Energy Information Administration data (EIA forms 4 and 423), and EPA National Emissions Data System (NEDS).

reduction by technological means), while those just below the cutoff would be exempt.

Option 6b: Allocate Emissions Reductions to States (or Other Jurisdictional Entities

Congress could allow States to achieve specified emissions reductions in any way they choose. Other appropriate jurisdictional units include Air Quality Control Regions (AQCRs) or even operating utilities (which often own several individual sources).

While this approach would add another layer of administrative complexity, allowing each State or other jurisdiction to allocate reductions offers potentially significant cost savings over uniform emissions rate requirements. For example, OTA estimates that for cutbacks of about 8 to 10 million tons per year, allowing States to design "least-cost" allocation plans could reduce costs by about 20 to 25 percent from those that impose uniform limits on emission rates.

Congress could allocate emissions reductions to States in many ways. The allocation formula could be based on: 1) utility emissions alone (the sector for which the most accurate emissions data exist, 2) emissions from both utility and nonutility combustion, or 3) total emissions (including industrial process emissions).

Reductions based on each State's utility emissions or combined utility, industrial, and commercial boiler emissions could be calculated from:

- emissions in excess of a specified rate (sulfur dioxide emitted per quantity of fuel burned), or
- average emission rates (giving credit to States for less polluting sources).

Reductions based on total emissions could be calculated from:

- emissions per unit area,
- emissions per capita,
- equal percentage reductions for each State, or
- a series of allowable emission rates set separately for each major sector (i.e., utilities, industrial boilers, and major industrial processes).

Other factors that could be incorporated into State-level allocation formulas include:

- extent of use of nonfossil or low-emitting energy sources, or
- upper limits on the extent of reductions required.

Table 11 compares the State-by-State emissions reductions required under several of these alternatives to achieve a total regional reduction of about 8 million tons of sulfur dioxide per year.

Option 6c: Direct the Governors of the States in the Control Region To Allocate Emissions Reductions

Rather than assigning specific reductions to States, Congress could require the governors of the States within the control region to design an allocation formula. Congress could either provide guidelines or allow the governors complete freedom to develop a plan. Congress would have to determine the number of governors necessary to reach agreement (e.g., either a simple or a two-thirds majority) and alternative mechanisms in the event that agreement is not reached.

Option 6d: Provide Control Program Guidelines and Direct the Administrator of EPA To Develop the Allocation Formula

This option must be used if Congress adopts an environmental quality standard approach, but could also be used for developing an allocation formula following more general principles. For example, Congress could legislate resource protection goals (specifying equal protection from pollutants for all regions or greater protection in areas with high concentrations of sensitive resources), upper and lower limits on any State's emissions reductions requirements, guidelines for considering past reductions, and so on. The Administrator of EPA would then translate these goals as closely as possible into regulatory language.

Option 6e: Allow Trading of Emissions Reductions Requirements

To reduce the cost of implementing emissions reductions, Congress could allow sources or States

Table 11.—Emissions Reductions Required by Alternative Allocation Approaches (percent below 1980 emissions)

	Utility emissions only				Total SO₂ emissions			
	1.5 lb/MMBtu rate limitation		1.3 lb/MMBtu average		35% reduction		16 tons/mi²	
	Percent below:		Percent below:		Percent below:		Percent below:	
State	Utility	Total	Utility	Total	Utility	Total	Utility	Total
Alabama	38	27	42	30	48	35	4	3
Arkansas	35	9	35	0	>100	35	35	9
Connecticut	0	0	0	0	78	35	0	0
Delaware	44	21	44	21	73	35	>100	70
District of Columbia	0	0	0	0	>100	35	>100	93
Florida	34	22	24	16	52	35	21	14
Georgia	47	41	53	47	39	35	0	0
Illinois	58	44	51	39	45	35	50	38
Indiana	65	50	67	52	45	35	93	71
Iowa	46	32	40	28	49	35	0	0
Kentucky	58	52	62	56	38	35	47	42
Louisiana	0	0	0	0	>100	35	0	0
Maine	8	1	8	1	>100	35	0	0
Maryland	34	22	38	25	53	35	75	50
Massachusetts	24	19	25	20	43	35	77	61
Michigan	31	19	28	17	56	35	0	0
Minnesota	24	16	13	9	51	35	0	0
Mississippi	44	20	0	0	77	35	0	0
Missouri	67	59	69	61	39	35	16	14
New Hampshire	47	41	53	46	40	35	3	3
New Jersey	24	9	0	0	88	35	>100	55
New York	33	17	7	3	68	35	31	16
North Carolina	4	2	11	8	48	35	0	0
Ohio	62	50	65	53	42	35	91	75
Pennsylvania	44	32	48	34	48	35	88	64
Rhode Island	0	0	0	0	>100	35	0	0
South Carolina	29	19	32	21	53	35	0	0
Tennessee	59	51	63	55	40	35	43	37
Vermont	3	0	0	0	>100	35	0	0
Virginia	5	1	5	2	77	35	2	1
West Virginia	49	43	51	44	40	35	74	64
Wisconsin	60	45	60	46	45	35	0	0
Eastern 31 state	50	37	50	37	48	35	50	37

SOURCE: Office of Technology Assessment, based on analyses by E. H. Pechan & Asssociated, Inc., 1983.

to purchase reductions, rather than requiring each source or State to meet its own requirement directly. This type of flexibility would allow sources with higher-than-average control costs—due, for example, to engineering design or poor availability of alternative fuels—to purchase the rights to more cost-effective reductions.

Congress could allow this type of trading throughout the entire control region, or permit it only within smaller areas (e.g., EPA Federal regions) to maintain a desired regional pattern of reductions. Such trading could be allowed freely on the open market, or through a marketable permit system to assist and monitor transactions.

If future emissions from sources not yet built must be offset by reductions from existing sources, allowing trading would be particularly helpful to States with high rates of utility or industrial growth.

Option 6f: *Allow Substitution of Nitrogen Oxides Emissions for Part of Required Sulfur Dioxide Emissions Reductions*

For some sources, reducing nitrogen oxide emissions costs less than reducing sulfur dioxide emissions. To lower the costs of implementing required reductions, Congress could allow sources to choose the mix of pollutant cutbacks that minimizes control costs, subject to a specified substitution formula. Substitution of nitrogen oxides could be allowed on a ton-for-ton basis, 1.4 to 1 (the ratio of the acidifying potential of the two pollutants), or be based on estimates of how the two pollutants affect natural ecosystems. Because much of the deposited nitrogen is used by plants, substitution ratios ranging from 2 tons of nitrogen oxides for each ton of sulfur dioxide, to ratios as high as 4 to 1, might be considered.

Because the current inventory of nitrogen oxide emissions is not very accurate, however, a substitution program based on historical emissions (e.g., 1980) would be difficult to administer. Given the uncertainties in nitrogen oxide emissions and in control cost data, OTA cannot estimate the extent of use or potential cost savings of such a provision.

Decision 7: Who Should Pay the Costs of Emissions Reductions?

Discussion:

Emissions control costs can be allocated according to two general approaches: 1) full costs of control could be paid by sources required to reduce emissions, or 2) control costs could be funded from a group larger than those required. For example, a tax on pollutant emissions or electricity sales could be used to generate a trust fund to pay for reductions.

Currently, sources of emissions incur lower costs of production through their ability to dispose of pollutants in the atmosphere. These pollutants create costs to people whose livelihoods depend on the resources at risk from acid deposition. The situation, however, is not a simple case of "polluting region" versus "receptor region." The benefits of lowered production costs are shared throughout the Nation in the form of lower product prices, although the greatest benefit accrues in the locale of the source. Likewise, people living outside regions that have resources at risk benefit from using those resources, but the people within these regions benefit most.

The first approach allocates the control costs to those who would be responsible for reductions. Yet since it is not possible to precisely link emissions from any given source to damage in areas far removed, some assert that this would be unfair.

The alternative approach would distribute the costs of reductions to a larger group. For example, imposing a pollution tax implies that *all* emissions contribute to the risk of resource damage, not just those from sources emitting in excess of a specified rate. Because so few sources are actually monitored, however, such an approach would be administratively complex.

Other trust fund approaches, such as a tax on electricity generation, are also possible. Because electricity generation is carefully monitored, this approach would be much easier to implement. Though an electricity tax approach is not based on the amount of pollution produced, it recognizes that energy consumption creates much of the pollution. This approach, however, spreads the burden of control costs to all energy consumers, even those in regions with lower polluting sources such as natural gas or hydropower, and those already paying for pollution control. Another alternative is an electricity tax that is graduated on the basis of a pollution emission rate, combining aspects of the two previous approaches.

A trust-fund approach has some undesirable economic and administrative aspects, though it is difficult to estimate how severe these may be. A fund that covered most or all of the costs of emissions control could reduce incentives for sources to minimize control costs. In addition, substantial plant-to-plant variations in scrubber costs and region-to-region variations in fuel-switching costs could create considerable difficulties in establishing allowable cost schedules.

OTA has compared the distributional implications of three tax approaches: 1) a tax on electricity generation; 2) a tax on sulfur dioxide emissions; and 3) a tax on both sulfur dioxide and nitrogen oxide emissions, set so that two-thirds of the revenues are generated from sulfur dioxide and one-third from nitrogen oxide emissions. This is roughly the ratio of sulfur and nitrogen compounds deposited in precipitation in the Eastern United States. All three tax approaches are assumed to apply to all 50 States.

A tax on electricity generation would collect *all* revenues from electricity consumers. A sulfur dioxide tax would collect about 70 percent of revenues from the utility sector, and about 30 percent from industry. Taxing both sulfur dioxide and nitrogen oxide emissions would collect 55 to 60 percent of the total revenues from utilities, 25 to 30 percent from industry, and 10 to 15 percent from highway vehicles. Emissions from residential and other miscellaneous sources were not included in either of the pollution-tax approaches.

OTA analyzed how the alternative tax approaches would affect costs for each State's *electricity consumers* only. Since many manufactured goods are distributed nationwide, industrial costs are often

borne by consumers over a much larger area than the State in which the industry is located. A tax on highway vehicles (e.g., a sales or registration tax) would be distributed on a roughly per-capita basis.

Table 12 displays estimates of percentage increases in residential electricity rates from an electricity tax raising $5 billion annually. State-to-State variations are due solely to differences in the average electricity rate currently paid by consumers in each State. Table 12 also shows residential electricity rate increases under both pollution-tax alternatives.

These approaches result in lower nationwide-average rate increases than an electricity tax because part of the costs is borne by other sectors. Because of the large variation in pollution emission rates among utility plants, however, costs would be less evenly distributed, both within each State and from State to State. Because utilities emit a larger share of nationwide sulfur dioxide than nitrogen oxide emissions, rate increases are typically somewhat lower for a tax on both sulfur dioxide and nitrogen oxide emissions (column 2) than on sulfur dioxide emissions alone (column 3).

Rate increases shown in table 12 illustrate the relative distribution of costs under 1980 conditions. Future changes in electricity demand and pollutant emissions could alter these estimates substantially. For example, reducing sulfur dioxide emissions by 10 million tons per year would reduce total revenues collected under a pollution tax by about 15 to 30 percent, depending on the tax approach. Further details can be found in appendix A.

Conclusions and Options:

Under the Clean Air Act, sources that are required to reduce pollutant emissions must pay the entire costs of control. Several acid deposition control bills introduced to date would maintain this policy. Others have proposed a cost-sharing mechanism, whereby a tax on electricity or pollutant emissions would be used to help fund the costs of control.

Options available to Congress are described below.

Table 12.—50-State Taxes Raising $5 Billion per Year During the Early 1980's (total in later years will vary with changes in emissions and electricity generated)

| State | Total electricity | Average residential electricity rate increase (percent) from alternate tax approaches (Before control, 1980 emissions) | |
		SO₂ and NOₓ	SO₂ only
Alabama	4.0	2.0	2.5
Alaska	4.0	0.9	1.4
Arizona	3.1	0.7	0.7
Arkansas	4.4	0.6	0.5
California	3.0	0.2	0.2
Colorado	3.7	1.3	1.2
Connecticut	2.5	0.3	0.3
Delaware	2.4	1.4	1.8
District of Columbia	4.5	2.2	2.7
Florida	3.1	1.7	2.2
Georgia	4.2	3.5	4.5
Hawaii	1.8	0.8	1.1
Idaho	8.2	0.0	0.0
Illinois	3.6	2.9	3.6
Indiana	3.8	5.9	7.7
Iowa	3.6	3.0	3.5
Kansas	3.7	1.8	2.0
Kentucky	4.5	5.7	7.3
Louisiana	4.2	0.5	0.2
Maine	3.3	0.4	0.6
Maryland	3.6	1.8	2.3
Massachusetts	2.9	1.6	2.1
Michigan	4.3	2.5	3.0
Minnesota	3.8	1.8	2.0
Mississippi	4.0	2.1	2.6
Missouri	4.1	6.6	8.8
Montana	6.4	0.9	0.9
Nebraska	4.7	1.3	1.3
Nevada	3.9	1.0	0.9
New Hampshire	2.9	2.9	3.6
New Jersey	2.6	0.8	0.9
New Mexico	2.9	1.0	0.9
New York	2.1	0.7	0.9
North Carolina	3.7	1.8	2.1
North Dakota	4.1	1.9	2.0
Ohio	3.3	4.5	5.9
Oklahoma	4.5	0.6	0.3
Oregon	7.2	0.1	0.1
Pennsylvania	3.1	2.7	3.5
Rhode Island	3.0	1.3	1.5
South Carolina	3.6	1.4	1.7
South Dakota	3.6	1.1	1.1
Tennessee	4.9	5.3	7.0
Texas	3.7	0.7	0.5
Utah	3.6	0.8	0.6
Vermont	3.5	0.1	0.0
Virginia	3.3	1.2	1.4
Washington	9.5	0.5	0.7
West Virginia	4.2	4.1	5.1
Wisconsin	4.4	4.1	5.2
Wyoming	6.1	3.0	2.9
U.S. total	3.3	1.9	2.3

SOURCE: Office of Technology Assessment.

Option 7a: Require the Sources Allocated Emissions Reductions, and Their Customers, To Pay the Cost of Those Reductions

This approach is simple to administer and provides the greatest incentives for each source to minimize control costs. Given the difficulty of precisely linking emissions in one region with resource damage in another, however, many have questioned the "fairness" of the cost allocation.

Option 7b: Establish a Trust Fund To Provide Some or All of the Necessary Funds for Reducing Emissions

Funds could be drawn from a tax on emissions, a tax on electricity production, or even from general revenues. This approach is administratively complex and might reduce incentives for minimizing control costs. Costs would be distributed more uniformly among States than under option A; still, this distribution of the costs and benefits of emissions reductions also raises regional equity concerns.

Decision 8: What Can Be Done To Mitigate Employment and Economic Effects of a Control Policy?

Discussion:

Two industries are likely to be most affected by legislated reductions in sulfur dioxide emissions: coal mining and electric utilities. In the absence of restrictions imposed by Congress, emissions reductions would be achieved through a mix of switching to lower sulfur fuels and installing flue-gas desulfurization units ("scrubbers"). Individual sources' control decisions—unless specified by Congress—will be determined by the relative cost effectiveness of the two approaches for that source and location.

Both control options have undesirable consequences: fuel switching is projected to cause some coal production to shift from high-sulfur to low-sulfur producing regions, affecting employment and economic patterns. Scrubbing allows the continued use of high-sulfur coal, but imposes high capital costs on a utility industry already requiring additional capital for continued growth and health.

As discussed in chapters 3 and 5, a program to reduce sulfur dioxide emissions by 10 million tons per year might reduce mining employment in high-sulfur coal regions by 20,000 to 30,000 jobs from otherwise projected future levels, and to cause economic activity in the range of $600 to $800 million per year to shift from high- to low-sulfur producing regions. These chapters also discuss the utility industry's recent financial situation, showing that during 1980 utilities in a number of Eastern States were in relatively poor positions to raise new capital either through bond-related borrowing or by issuing additional stock. An acid rain control program could have some effect on the financial health of these utilities, but the magnitude of the effect is unknown.

Two approaches are available to minimize the effects of an acid rain control program on the coal industry:

- The "technological approach," i.e, either directly or indirectly mandating the use of control technologies. For example, Congress could require that a set percentage of the sulfur potentially emitted from coals be removed by technological means, regardless of how much sulfur the coal contains.
- The "local coal approach," which would restrict utility coal consumption on the basis of the *location* of the coal supply, as in Section 125 of the Clean Air Act.

The technological approach could, in effect, require sources to achieve reductions via high-removal emissions control technologies, such as wet or dry flue-gas "scrubbers." Such an approach is the basis for current New Source Performance Standards, which require 70- to 90-percent removal of potential emissions by technological means. Because the use of scrubbers cannot be avoided by switching to lower-sulfur fuels, locally available higher sulfur coals—which tend to be cheaper because of lower transportation costs—would often be preferred.

Such a policy is not without additional costs, however. OTA analyzed the cost of installing scrubbers on 50 of the largest utility plants emitting sulfur dioxide at a rate greater than 3 lb per million Btu. These 50 plants emitted about 7.6 million tons of sulfur dioxide in 1980 and consume about 60 percent of the high-sulfur coal produced for utilities. Mandating the use of scrubbers on these plants would cost about $1.5 billion per year *more* than allowing each plant to use the most cost-effective method of achieving the same reductions.

In a control program eliminating 10 million tons of sulfur dioxide emissions per year, such a provision would increase total program costs by an additional one-third to one-half. Moreover, many available technology-based emissions reduction methods (e.g., wet scrubbing) produce large quantities of liquid or solid effluents. A typical 1,000 MW plant scrubbing high-sulfur coal produces about 200,000 tons of sludge per year. This must be disposed of—posing additional environmental risks—if useful products cannot be recovered economically.

If more modest sulfur dioxide emissions reductions are desired—less than 2.5 million tons per year—Congress could require physical cleaning for all coal above a specified sulfur content. This technology-based approach would also help prevent production and unemployment losses in high-sulfur coal regions.

Additional coal-cleaning could eliminate moderate amounts of sulfur emissions at a relatively low cost for existing boilers that use higher-sulfur coals. Costs range from about $250 to $350 per ton of sulfur dioxide removed for Midwestern high-sulfur coals to $1,000 to over $3,000 per ton removed for southern Appalachian low- and medium-sulfur coals. The low range of coal-cleaning costs is competitive with or slightly higher than costs for fuel-switching.

Generally, the higher the sulfur content of the coal, the more economically the sulfur can be removed from it. Depending on the type of coal, 10 to 40 percent of its sulfur can be fairly easily removed. If a greater percentage of the sulfur must be removed, physical coal washing alone becomes economically inefficient.

Coal washing is currently a widely used technique. One-third of the utility coal mined in the Eastern high-sulfur coal producing States was washed in 1979, removing about 10 percent of potential sulfur dioxide emissions (about 1.8 million tons) from these coals.

In many instances, the benefits of coal cleaning can partially offset the cost, because: 1) cleaning reduces the ash content of coal, reducing both costs of transportation to the powerplant and ash disposal requirements at the powerplant; 2) removal of impurities increases the heating value (energy per unit of weight) of coal; and 3) washing creates a more uniform fuel that can increase boiler operation efficiency.

The second major approach to mitigating the coal-market effects of proposed emissions reductions is based on section 125 of the Clean Air Act, which allows the States or EPA to restrict coal consumption to coals produced "locally or regionally," if such an action would "prevent or minimize significant local or regional economic disruption or unemployment." The potential effectiveness of the current section 125 is difficult to judge because neither the statute, nor EPA in its ongoing proceedings, has defined "locally or regionally" available coal or "significant" economic disruption. No ruling has yet been made under section 125, although EPA has *proposed* a ruling based on a petition filed by the United Mine Workers and others in the State of Ohio in 1978.

Appropriately defining "locally or regionally" available coal is extremely important for designing a workable local-coal policy. If, for example, "local or regional" was to be considered synonymous with State boundaries, invoking section 125 would leave interstate trade in high-sulfur coal vulnerable to control-induced disruption. Table 13 presents interstate exports of medium- and high-sulfur coal as a percentage of total utility coal production for each coal State. As much as 66 percent of Illinois' and 82 percent of Kentucky's high-sulfur coal would remain vulnerable under such a definition.

Protection can be increased only by expanding the area considered local or regional, thereby incorporating larger percentages of a State's high-sulfur coal market. For example, if the Illinois "region" were expanded to include Missouri, Indiana, and Michigan, the proportion of high-sulfur coal exported outside the "region" would fall from 66 percent (when considering only Illinois) to 21 percent (when considering all four States).

The variation in sulfur content of a "region's" coal reserves is another factor that must be con-

Table 13.—Interstate Coal Shipments

Major coal-producing States	1980 production for utility market (millions of tons)	Noncompliance[a] coal exported to other States (percent of State production)	Major destination States (shipments greater than 1 million tons)
Alabama	15.8	10	
Arizona	10.5	0	
Colorado	13.6	3	
Illinois	54.4	66	FL, GA, IN, IA, MO, WI
Indiana	27.3	22	GA, KY
Kentucky	112.4	73	AL, FL, GA, IN, MI, MS, NC, OH, SC, TN, VA, WV, WI
(East)	(73.9)	(75)	
(West)	(38.5)	(69)	
Missouri	5.0	34	KS
Montana	27.9	52	MN, WI
New Mexico	17.0	1	
North Dakota	15.3	21	SD
Ohio	34.3	27	AL, MI, PA
Pennsylvania	50.9	30	MD, NY, OH, WI
Tennessee	7.6	35	
Texas	27.0	0	
Utah	8.5	7	
Virginia	13.8	71	NC
West Virginia	53.1	39	MI, NJ, NC, OH, PA
(North)	(30.8)	(46)	
(South)	(22.3)	(30)	
Wyoming	89.7	10	IL, IA

[a]"Noncompliance" coal is defined as coal that would not permit utilities to comply with a 1.2 lb SO_2/million Btu emissions limit without applying control technology.
SOURCE: *DOE/EIA Form 423, supplied to OTA by E. H. Pechan & Associates.*

sidered when designing appropriate regional boundaries. Including reserves of vastly different sulfur content in the same region is unlikely to prevent disruption to the high-sulfur coal industry. For instance, defining a region to include southern West Virginia and Ohio would still permit dramatic shifts from high- to low-sulfur coal under the statutory constraints of section 125, since major quantities of low-sulfur reserves lie in southern West Virginia.

Thus, section 125 could effectively mitigate control-induced coal-market shifts only if regions could be designed to include a significant portion of a State's coal customers, while excluding large reserves of coal with differing sulfur content. In practice, a balance would have to be struck between defining regions large enough to protect sufficient amounts of coal, and small enough to exclude significantly different coal reserves.

The analysis above suggests that issues of definition may present significant problems for effective implementation of section 125. Moreover, restricting competition among coal suppliers on the basis that a given level of unemployment warrants Federal action could cause a great deal of political controversy. EPA concludes that its "experience with Section 125 casts considerable doubt on the workability of this portion of the statute."[2]

EPA suggested a third alternative, analogous to programs providing adjustment assistance to workers, firms, and communities injured by foreign competition resulting from free-trade laws. A program could be designed to provide special compensation to workers and communities seriously affected by environmental regulations.

As of 1980, Congress had established about 20 special worker-assistance laws that supplement regular Federal-State unemployment insurance programs. Most provide assistance to workers either unemployed or underemployed as a result of a Federal action or policy. Several of these programs are ongoing; for example, the Trade Act of 1974 provides assistance to workers adversely affected by foreign competition. Others have been established to help workers so affected by one-time Federal actions. These include temporary benefits for airline employees under the Airline Deregulation Act of

1978, for loggers affected by the expansion of the Redwoods National Park, and for railroad employees affected by the establishment of Amtrak and Conrail.

The largest special worker-assistance program, the Trade Adjustment Assistance program to help workers hurt by foreign competition, paid $1.6 billion to more than 500,000 workers during 1980. Most of the others are much smaller.

Benefits provided by these programs range from relocation, training, and job search benefits (but no direct monetary payments) to monetary benefits ranging from 60 to 100 percent of the worker's salary. Some programs are funded through congressional appropriations, while others receive funds from the public or private corporations involved (e.g., the railroads absorbed by Amtrak). Most of the programs provide benefits for between 1 and 6 years. Two programs provide benefits until age 65.

To assist coal miners adversely affected by acid rain legislation, Congress could establish a special worker-assistance program similar to those described above. The program could provide special retraining to help workers find jobs in other industries in their communities and assist workers that desire to move to other areas where greater employment opportunities may be available. It should be noted, however, that during past fluctuations in coal production, workers in the Appalachian area have tended to remain in their home communities without jobs rather than relocate to areas where employment opportunities may be greater.

Congress could also provide for direct payments to unemployed workers either for a set period (e.g., 1 to 6 years) or until retirement age. Funds for the program could come from congressional appropriations or through a trust fund established from a tax on electricity generation, pollution emissions, or coal sulfur content.

Measures for reducing economic incentives to switch to lower sulfur fuels, or for prohibiting the use of nonlocal fuel, would increase scrubber-related capital requirements for the utility industry. One method available to Congress to minimize the capital burden on utilities, and the subsequent cost to consumers, was discussed under the previous policy question, "Who Should Pay the Cost of Emis-

---

[2]46 Fed. Reg. 8109.

sions Reductions?'' A tax on electricity generation or pollution emissions could be used to reimburse utilities for all or part of the capital costs of pollution control technology. Annual operating and maintenance costs—about half the total costs of controls—might still be paid by each utility's consumers, but the burden of raising construction capital would be reduced.

Modifications to the Federal tax code have been proposed as another means of reducing the capital costs of pollution control. The Economic Recovery Tax Act of 1981 (Public Law 97-84) allows utilities to use accelerated depreciation to recover investment costs. This provides tax benefits to utilities, creating more favorable cash-flow conditions.[3] The availability of tax-exempt industrial development bonds to finance pollution control hardware (thereby allowing utilities to raise capital at lower interest rates) is another means by which the Federal Government currently offsets the additional capital costs of pollution control.

Additional changes to the tax laws—e.g., increasing tax deductions for pollution control investment—would help some, but not all, utilities to finance pollution control technology. About 20 percent of major privately owned utilities paid no Federal income tax in 1981. Over 50 percent paid some tax, but took the maximum allowable investment tax credit (85 percent of a company's tax liability).[4]

Another approach to reducing capital requirements for pollution control is to encourage development of potentially lower cost control technologies, such as LIMB (Limestone Injection Multistage Burners) or regenerable processes. At present, government and industry support for new pollution control technologies tends to emphasize technologies for sources yet unbuilt. Current law does not require existing plants to use technology-based pollution control for meeting ambient air quality standards.

Investments in research and development for pollution control technologies to retrofit existing

sources are subject to both: 1) the risks inherent in any R&D program and, 2) the unpredictable demand for these technologies, given uncertainties about future pollution control regulations. Federal cost-sharing of R&D for retrofitting existing sources would reduce investment risks and might encourage research on innovative, and potentially new, cost-saving technologies. The Federal Government could also increase its own research activities in this area.

Conclusions and Options

In addition to the direct costs of control, acid deposition control legislation could have undesirable secondary consequences. Three options are presented to minimize economic hardship to miners of high-sulfur coal. Two options are presented to help ease potential difficulties the utility industry might face in raising capital to pay for pollution control technology.

Options available to Congress to mitigate undesirable effects of a control policy are described below.

Option 8a: Require Sources To Reduce Emissions by Technological Means

Congress could mandate emissions reductions by technological means, to minimize potential production shifts within the U.S. coal industry and thereby minimize adverse regional employment and economic changes. For large-scale reductions, Congress could mandate control requirements similar to NSPS. Requiring emitters to remove a high percentage of potential sulfur dioxide emissions through such control technologies as scrubbers would minimize the economic advantage of switching to lower sulfur coal.

For smaller reductions—up to about 2.5 million tons of sulfur dioxide per year—Congress could direct EPA to require washing for particular coals. To minimize the costs of this option, Congress could direct EPA to exempt those coals for which washing is not cost effective.

Mandating emissions reductions through technological means would minimize unemployment in high-sulfur coal areas and stimulate the pollution control and construction industries. This approach, however, would also increase overall con-

---

[3]For a discussion of how this law benefits utilties, see D. W. Kiefer, "The Impact of the Economic Recovery Tax Act of 1981 on the Public Utility Industry," Congressional Research Service, 1982.

[4]D. W. Kiefer, "Tax Credits: Their Efficacy in Helping the Utility Industry Finance Retrofitting to Reduce Sulfur Dioxide Emissions," Congressional Research Service, 1983.

trol costs, limit the potential economic gains to areas that produce low-sulfur coal, and increase electricity costs to consumers.

Option 8b: Strengthen and Clarify the Local Coal Protection Provision of the Clean Air Act, Section 125

Section 125 of the Clean Air Act allows States or EPA to prohibit the use of coals that are not produced "locally or regionally," if such an action would "prevent or minimize significant local or regional economic disruption or unemployment." Congress provided no guidance, however, on the meaning of these terms, and no ruling has been made under the section to allow policymakers to determine its effectiveness.

Congress could enhance the section's effectiveness by defining "significant" economic disruption or unemployment (e.g., a threshold of projected increased unemployment of 10 percent, 20 percent, etc.). In addition, Congress could provide guidance on defining a region for use in implementing the section.

Assuming that the provision could be implemented effectively, it would achieve the same goal as option 8a—minimizing unemployment in high-sulfur coal regions—but would increase overall control costs. EPA has stated, however, that its "experience with Section 125 casts considerable doubt on the workability of this portion of the statute."

Option 8c: Establish a Special Worker-Assistance Program for Affected Coal Miners

Congress has established many special worker-assistance laws to help people that are either unemployed or underemployed as a result of a Federal action. A similar program could be established to assist high-sulfur coal miners adversely affected by acid rain legislation.

Such a program could provide direct monetary benefits or relocation, training, and job-search assistance. Funding for the program could come from either general tax revenues or a tax on electricity, sulfur dioxide emissions, or coal sulfur content.

Option 8d: Reduce Utility Capital-Raising Requirements for Pollution Control Equipment

Additional pollution control regulations would increase the capital requirements of the utility industry at a time when some utilities are in poor financial condition. Adopting either option 8a or 8b as part of an emissions reduction program would increase the use of control technology, thereby increasing capital requirements even further.

Several means are available to Congress to aid utilities in raising the necessary capital. Two measures already in use are industrial development bonds to finance pollution control equipment and tax breaks under the Economic Recovery Tax Act of 1981 (Public Law 97-84). Ensuring the continued availability of low-cost industrial development bonds can lower the costs of pollution control equipment to both utilities and consumers. Additional tax breaks, similar to the accelerated method of depreciation permitted by the Economic Recovery Tax Act of 1981, but specific to pollution control equipment, could also be provided. Because many utilities already pay little or no Federal income tax, however, such a policy would assist some, but not all, utilities that might choose technology-based controls.

A more direct approach to reducing the capital requirements of the utility industry was presented under Decision 7. Congress could establish a tax on electricity or pollutant emissions to pay for all or part of the capital costs of pollution control equipment.

Option 8e: Provide Federal Support for R&D on Pollution Control Technologies for Existing Sources

Congress could increase Federal research and development activities or take measures to encourage private-sector R&D. More specifically, Congress could establish a cost-sharing program for research on innovative methods of retrofitting existing sources with pollution control technologies. Focusing the program on retrofit technologies would direct limited Federal funds to pollution control methods for sources most affected by possible acid rain control legislation—existing sources that do not currently use pollution control technologies. A program to assume some or all of the risks of R&D might encourage development of cost-saving technologies that could reduce utility capital requirements and minimize production shifts within the coal industry.

Appendixes

Appendix A
Emissions and the Costs of Control

A.1 HISTORIC EMISSIONS OF SULFUR AND NITROGEN OXIDES

During 1980, about 25 million to 27 million tons of sulfur dioxide (SO_2) and about 21 million to 23 million tons of nitrogen oxides (NO_x) were emitted nationwide by electric utilities, industry, highway vehicles, and other sources. SO_2 emissions peaked around 1970 at about 29 million to 31 million tons per year; NO_x emissions peaked during the late 1970's at about 21 million to 24 million tons per year.

Estimates such as these are calculated from data collected by the Environmental Protection Agency (EPA) and the Department of Energy (DOE) on a large variety of emitting sources. Pertinent information includes, for example, fossil fuel consumption, sulfur content of fuels burned, and average NO_x emissions rates from various types of boilers and highway vehicles. Due to the extensive data collection and monitoring activities of both agencies, **current** emissions estimates are accurate to within 5 to 10 percent nationwide. However, the uncertainty around emissions estimates is larger for prior years. Reasonably complete data exist for the last three decades; emissions between 1900 and 1950 must be inferred using whatever historical records exist. Assumed values are necessary to fill in missing data to complete the calculations.

Tables A-1 and A-2 present estimates of 1980 SO_2 and NO_x emissions by State and sector. These estimates were calculated by EPA for the U.S.-Canada Memorandum of Intent on Transboundary Air Pollu-tion.[1] Nonutility combustion (table A-1, col. 3, table A-2, col. 4) includes emissions from industrial, commercial, and residential combustion sources. Industrial process emissions of SO_2 (table A-1, col. 4) include emissions from nonferrous smelters, petroleum refineries, cement plants, natural gas plants, iron and steel mills, and sulfuric acid plants. Transportation emissions of NO_x (table A-2, col. 2) include highway vehicles and such off-highway mobile sources as aircraft, railroads, vessels, and construction equipment.

Estimated historic emissions of SO_2 and NO_x from 1900 to 1980 are presented graphically below.[2] These estimates are from ongoing work by an EPA contractor, and are subject to further review and revision. (The estimates for 1980 agree to within about 5 percent with the emissions estimates presented in tables A-1 and A-2.)

Figure A-1 presents **State-level** SO_2 and NO_x emissions estimates for the period 1950 to 1980. Most of the data needed to calculate these estimates were available by State from various government reports;

---

[1]"Emissions, Costs and Engineering Assessment," Work Group 3B, *United States-Canada Memorandum of Intent on Transboundary Air Pollution,* June 1982.

[2]The maps and graphs presented in this section are from the draft report "Historic Emissions of Sulfur and Nitrogen Oxides in the United States From 1900 to 1980," G. Gschwandtner, K. C. Gschwandtner, and K. Eldridge, October 1983. The work was performed by Pacific Environmental Services, Inc., under contract to EPA.

Table A-1.—Estimated 1980 SO₂ Emissions (thousands of tons)

State	Total 1980 SO$_2$ emissions	Utility combustion	Nonutility combustion	Process emissions	Other SO$_2$ emissions
Alabama	759	543	86	95	35
Alaska	19	12	3	1	2
Arizona	900	88	9	787	17
Arkansas	102	27	32	29	14
California	446	78	56	197	116
Colorado	132	77	24	17	13
Connecticut	72	32	35	0	5
Delaware	109	52	26	25	6
District of Columbia	15	5	8	0	2
Florida	1,095	726	97	159	113
Georgia	840	737	44	14	45
Hawaii	58	42	8	6	3
Idaho	47	0	11	30	5
Illinois	1,471	1,126	188	119	38
Indiana	2,008	1,540	290	151	27
Iowa	329	231	57	27	13
Kansas	223	150	11	39	22
Kentucky	1,121	1,008	66	29	18
Louisiana	304	25	76	153	50
Maine	95	16	65	4	10
Maryland	338	223	56	42	17
Massachusetts	344	275	58	1	11
Michigan	907	565	154	152	35
Minnesota	260	177	44	18	22
Mississippi	285	129	48	75	32
Missouri	1,301	1,141	55	81	25
Montana	164	23	25	104	11
Nebraska	75	49	4	5	17
Nevada	243	34	2	203	5
New Hampshire	93	80	10	0	2
New Jersey	279	110	75	42	52
New Mexico	269	85	2	166	16
New York	944	480	335	71	59
North Carolina	602	435	116	23	28
North Dakota	107	86	13	4	5
Ohio	2,647	2,172	311	118	46
Oklahoma	121	38	15	52	16
Oregon	60	3	25	8	24
Pennsylvania	2,022	1,466	254	239	63
Rhode Island	15	5	8	0	2
South Carolina	326	213	84	13	16
South Dakota	39	29	3	3	4
Tennessee	1,077	934	83	27	33
Texas	1,277	303	106	719	148
Utah	72	22	16	27	6
Vermont	7	1	5	0	1
Virginia	361	164	142	14	41
Washington	272	69	41	132	29
West Virginia	1,088	944	84	43	16
Wisconsin	637	486	107	5	40
Wyoming	184	118	30	29	8
U.S. total	26,557	17,373	3,504	4,296	1,385
Percent of U.S. total	100	65	13	16	5

SOURCE: Emissions, Costs and Engineering Assessment, Work Group 3B, United States-Canada Memorandum of Intent on Transboundary Air Pollution, June 1982.

Table A-2.—Estimated 1980 NO$_x$ Emissions (thousands of tons)

State	Total 1980 NO$_x$ emissions	Transportation	Utility combustion	Nonutility combustion	Other NO$_x$ emissions
Alabama................	450	164	172	83	31
Alaska	58	27	0	27	4
Arizona.................	258	119	91	40	9
Arkansas	217	131	26	45	15
California..............	1,225	820	115	205	85
Colorado	276	115	86	67	9
Connecticut	134	90	20	23	1
Delaware	52	22	19	9	2
District of Columbia	22	14	2	6	1
Florida	648	347	214	52	35
Georgia	494	236	189	39	31
Hawaii	45	26	13	3	3
Idaho	81	52	0	15	15
Illinois	1,005	425	416	129	35
Indiana	773	280	361	99	33
Iowa	321	165	98	47	9
Kansas	437	176	86	151	24
Kentucky	531	183	272	67	9
Louisiana	928	190	98	552	89
Maine	59	42	1	13	3
Maryland	248	143	61	37	7
Massachusetts	254	158	57	37	2
Michigan	690	302	237	121	29
Minnesota	373	200	112	53	8
Mississippi	285	125	50	79	31
Missouri	568	254	237	49	27
Montana	126	63	23	22	18
Nebraska	195	124	40	22	8
Nevada	83	35	43	4	1
New Hampshire	56	27	25	4	1
New Jersey	406	246	66	68	25
New Mexico	290	97	80	109	4
New York	680	385	130	139	26
North Carolina	536	253	214	50	19
North Dakota	125	60	53	11	1
Ohio	1,145	438	516	162	29
Oklahoma	526	181	105	216	24
Oregon	192	144	3	25	20
Pennsylvania............	1,037	434	390	164	49
Rhode Island...........	36	28	3	5	0
South Carolina	260	127	84	39	10
South Dakota	89	58	21	4	7
Tennessee	517	224	200	69	25
Texas	2,544	745	522	1,113	163
Utah	144	65	39	33	7
Vermont	25	22	1	2	0
Virginia	405	250	62	65	28
Washington.............	289	193	25	32	39
West Virginia	452	87	302	55	9
Wisconsin	420	208	145	57	11
Wyoming	255	69	103	78	6
U.S. total	21,267	9,367	6,225	4,595	1,080
Percent of U.S. total	100	44	29	22	5

SOURCE: Emissions, Costs and Engineering Assessment, Work Group 3B, United States-Canada Memorandum of Intent on Transboundary Air Pollution, June 1982.

Figure A-1.—SO₂ and NOₓ Emissions From 1950 to 1980, By State

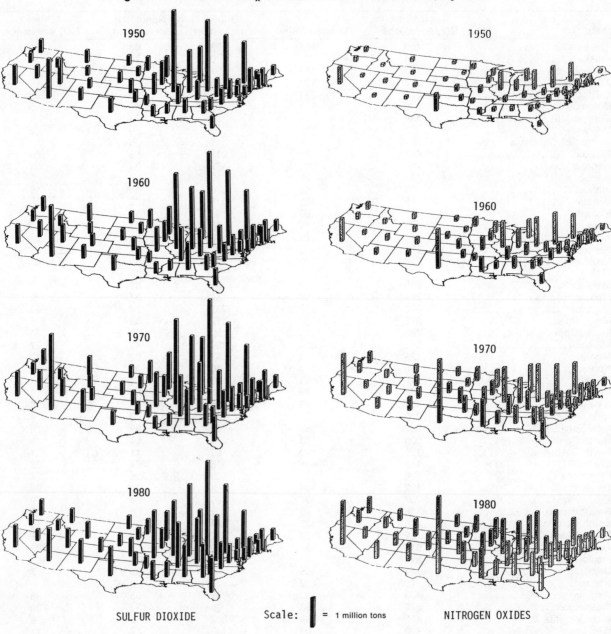

SULFUR DIOXIDE   Scale: █ = 1 million tons   NITROGEN OXIDES

when data were missing, information from the nearest year of record was used.

During 1950, between 18 million and 21 million tons of SO₂ were emitted nationwide. By 1970, annual SO₂ emissions had increased by about 10 million tons over 1950 levels; between 1970 and 1980, emissions declined by about 4 million tons per year.

Figure A-1 also illustrates the geographic pattern of NO_x emissions. During the 1950's, nationwide NO_x emissions were about 8 million to 10 million tons per year. By 1980, nationwide NO_x emissions were over twice 1950 levels.

Figure A-2 graphically illustrates SO₂ and NO_x emissions from 1900 to 1980 by sector and geographic (multi-State) region. For SO₂, the sectors include: electric utilities; industry (including industrial boilers and—for 1950 and later—copper smelters and cement plants); commercial and residential boilers; and other sources, including railroads, vessels, and off-highway vehicles. The sectors for which NO_x emissions are estimated include those listed above, plus highway vehicles and natural gas pipelines. The regions are single or grouped EPA Federal regions, as shown on the accompanying map.

Emission trends for SO₂ show a consistent pattern in each of the regions. While pre-1950 trends are uncertain, SO₂ emissions appear to have increased until about 1925, decreased during the Depression, increased once again during World War II, and then declined until the 1950's. After 1950, annual emissions increased through about 1970, and then declined. In some regions, for example, New York and New England (regions 1 and 2), this historic pattern of emissions increases and decreases appears as variations around a fairly constant long-term average. In other regions, for example, the Mid-Atlantic and Southeastern regions (regions 3 and 4), short-term variations accompany a longer term trend of increasing annual SO₂ emissions.

Annual NO_x emissions have increased throughout the century in all regions. New York and New England (regions 1 and 2) show the lowest rates of increase, while the Southeast and South Central regions (regions 4 and 6) show the most rapid increases.

A.2 CONTROL TECHNOLOGIES FOR REDUCING SULFUR AND NITROGEN OXIDE EMISSIONS

Acid deposition and ozone result primarily from the chemical transformation of three pollutants: oxides of sulfur, oxides of nitrogen, and hydrocarbons. This section discusses the techniques available for controlling emissions of oxides of sulfur and nitrogen. Where possible, for each emission control approach, the following information will be presented:
* the processes involved in the technique;
* its stage of development, i.e., whether the technology is currently commercially available or requires further research and development (R&D);
* the effectiveness of the technique, i.e., the degree of reduction it can reliably achieve;
* costs; and
* secondary effects.

The major source of nitrogen oxides and sulfur dioxide is the combustion of fossil fuels. During the combustion process, sulfur contained in the fuel reacts with oxygen to form sulfur oxides, primarily sulfur dioxide gas (SO₂) and, after sulfate. Nitrogen—contained in both the air used for combustion as well as in the fuel—reacts with oxygen to form gaseous nitrogen oxides (NO_x). There are three general approaches to controlling these emissions:

* **precombustion:** the amount of sulfur or nitrogen in the fuel being burned can be reduced, either by using fuels naturally lower in sulfur or nitrogen content, or by subjecting the fuels to some kind of physical or chemical process to remove sulfur and nitrogen;
* **during combustion:** the combustion process can be altered to reduce the amount of sulfur and nitrogen compounds released in the gas stream; and
* **postcombustion:** the products of combustion can be treated to remove pollutants before they are released into the atmosphere.

All three of these approaches have been successfully used to reduce emissions from existing sources.

In addition to these differences among approaches to control, the stage of development of the emissions control techniques discussed in this appendix varies considerably. Technologies may be characterized as:

* **In-use technologies.**—Those with demonstrated control capabilities currently sold on a commercial scale in the United States.
* **Available technologies.**—Those that have been tested and proven but are not currently operational in the United States on any significant scale.

Figure A-2.—Regional SO₂ and NOₓ Emissions by Source Category From 1900 to 1980

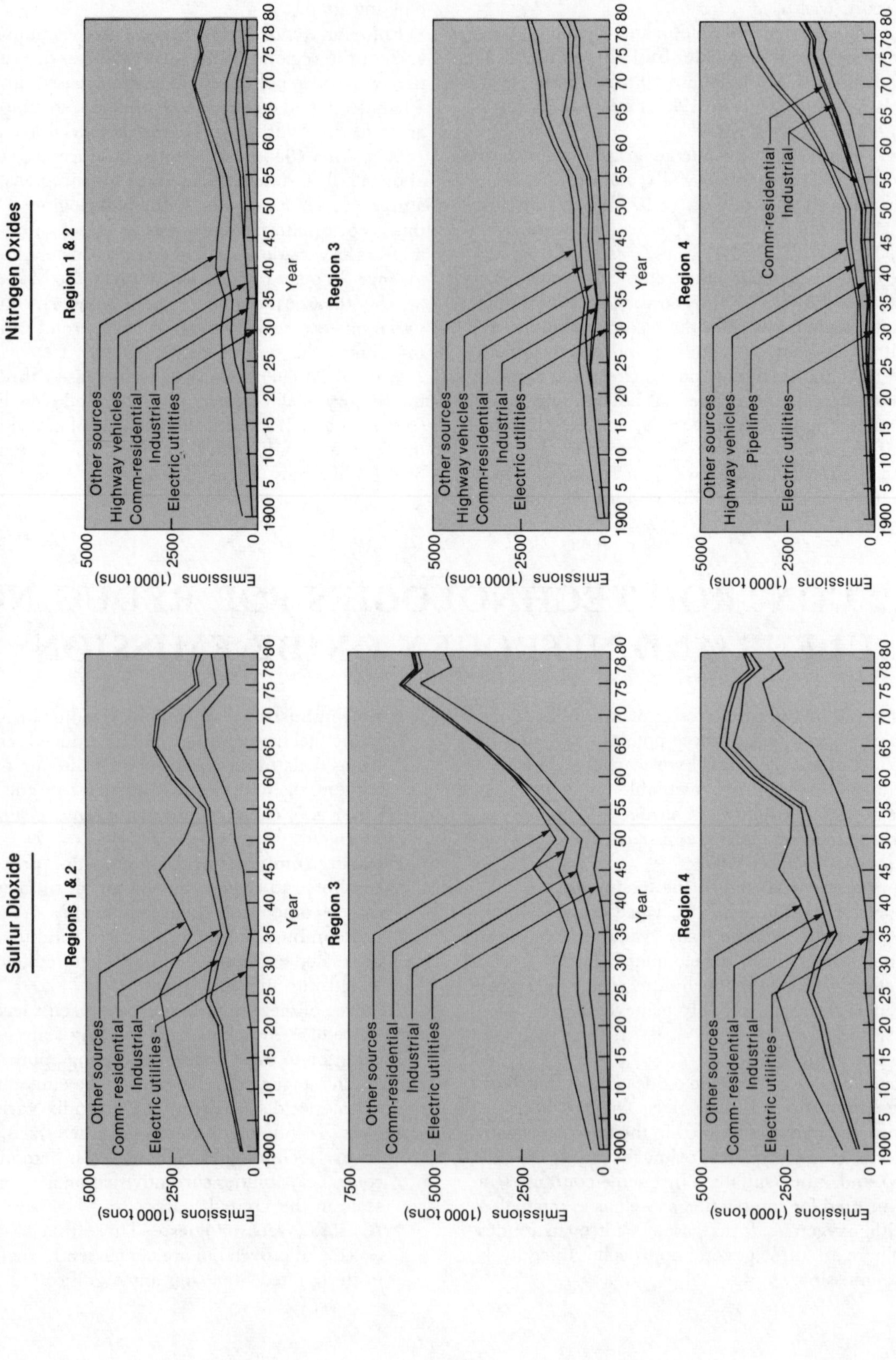

Figure A-2.—Regional SO₂ and NOₓ Emissions by Source Category From 1900 to 1980—Continued

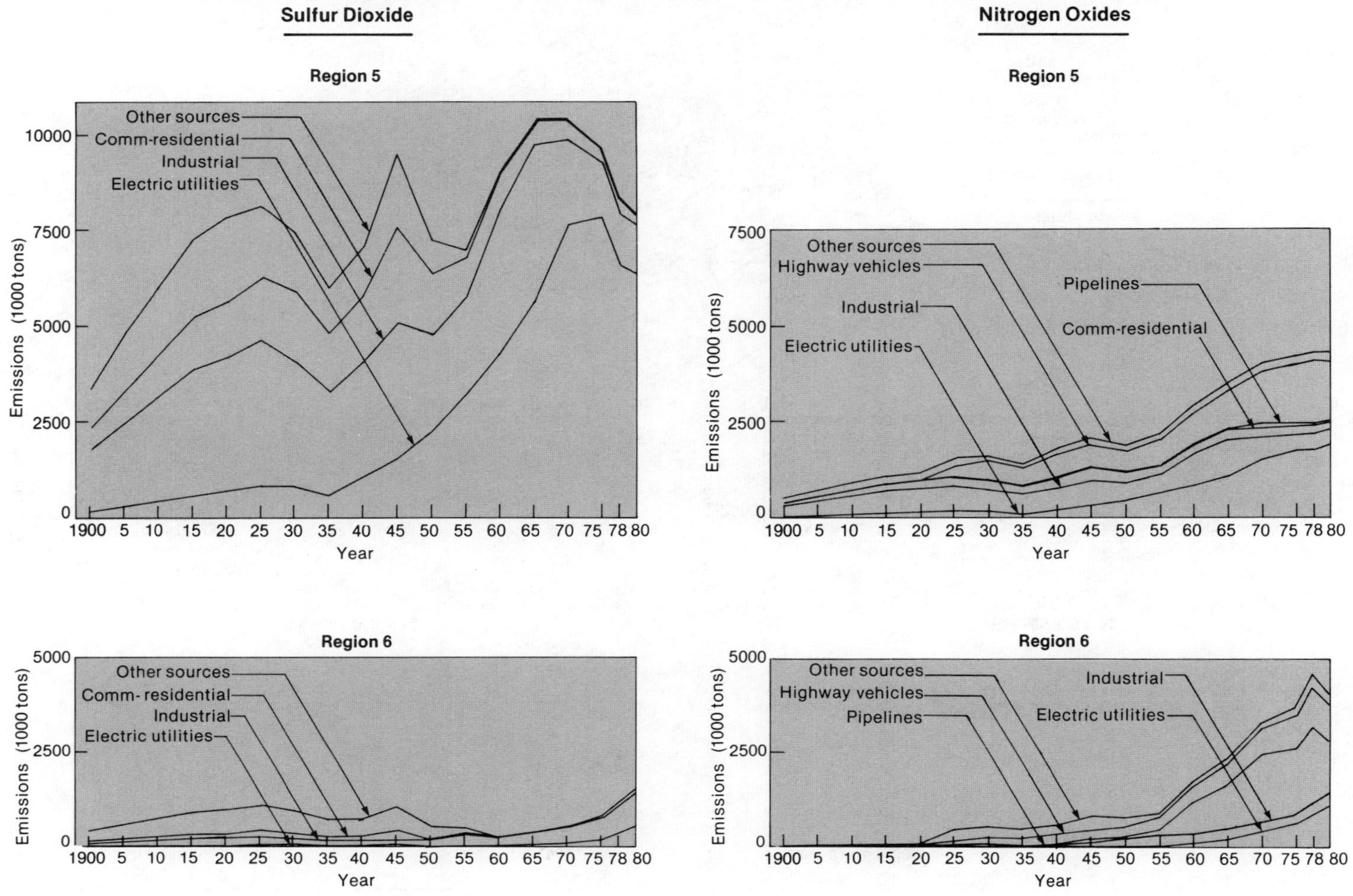

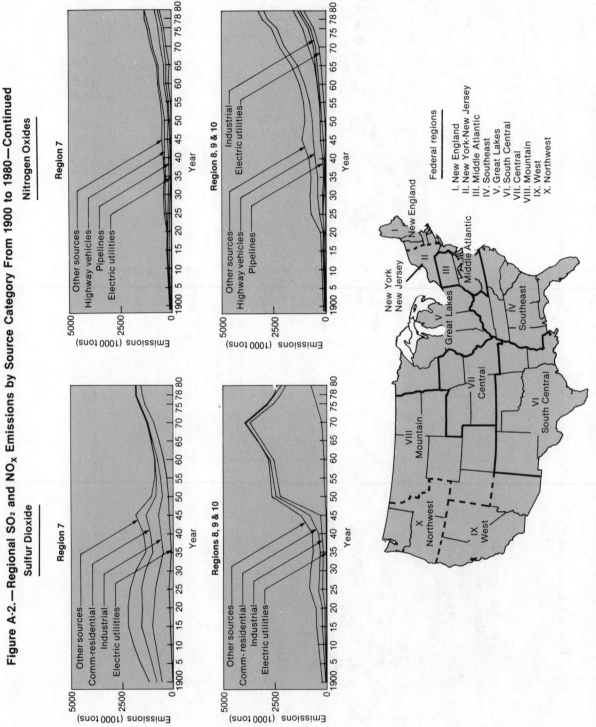

Figure A-2.—Regional SO₂ and NOₓ Emissions by Source Category From 1900 to 1980—Continued

NOTE: Emission estimates for years prior to 1950 may not account for all emissions due to data which were unavailable. The industrial category includes industrial boilers, cement plants, and copper smelters. The emissions from the latter are unaccounted for prior to 1950.

- **Emerging technologies.**—Those still primarily in the R&D phase, but have undergone testing on at least a pilot scale.*

Control approaches also differ widely in the amount of emissions reductions they are capable of achieving and in their cost effectiveness. Each technology is most cost effective in a particular range of emissions reductions. For instance, the precombustion approach of physical coal cleaning is technically feasible only for SO_2 reductions of less than 40 percent. On the other hand, the postcombustion approach of flue-gas desulfurization is cost effective in the 50- to 95-percent SO_2 removal range. The control technique appropriate for a given facility thus depends a great deal on the level of reduction desired.

Table A-3 presents summary information on the control technologies described in this appendix. Due to site-specific conditions, the removal efficiency levels given are intended for approximation only.

---

*This typology is used to characterize technologies in *Emissions, Costs and Engineering Assessment,* Work Group 3B, "United States-Canada Memorandum of Intent on Transboundary Air Pollution, 1982."

Controlling Sulfur Dioxide Emissions

Precombustion Approaches

FUEL-SWITCHING

Sulfur dioxide is formed when sulfur, an element naturally present in coal and oil, is oxidized during the combustion process. The greater the concentration of sulfur in the fuel being burned, the greater the production of SO_2 gas. One way to reduce SO_2 emissions is, therefore, to use fuels with lower concentrations of sulfur.

The amount of emissions reductions attainable by fuel-switching at a given plant depends on: 1) the amount of sulfur in the fuel currently being used, and 2) the amount of sulfur in the fuel available for replacement. The sulfur content of coal currently being used for electricity generation varies considerably, from about 0.2 to 5.5 percent sulfur by weight (from about 0.4 to 10 lb SO_2 per million Btu of coal).[3]

---

[3]*Steam Electric Plant Factors* (Washington, D.C.: National Coal Association, 1978).

Table A-3.—Overview of Control Technologies

Control technology	Reduction efficiencies (percent)	Revenue Requirements (mills/kWh)	Stage of development
Sulfur dioxide:			
Fuel-switching	30-90%	0-7	In use
Physical coal cleaning	5-40	1-5	In use
Chemical coal cleaning	60-85	NA	Emerging
Wet flue gas desulfurization	70-95	10-17	In use
Dry flue gas desulfurization	40-90	9-15	In use
Regenerable flue gas desulfurization	70-90	12-25	Available
Oil desulfurization:			
Indirect	30-40	4-6	In use
Direct	70-90	NA	In use
Nitrogen oxides:			
Low-NO$_x$ burner—commercial	30-50	0-3	In use
Low-NO$_x$ burner—developmental	50-80	0-3	Emerging
Thermal DeNox	50-65	NA	In use
Flue gas treatment without catalyst	35-40	NA	Available
Flue gas treatment with catalyst	80-90	NA	Available
Combined sulfur dioxide/nitrogen oxides:			
Limestone injection multistage burner:			
Sulfur dioxide	50-90	3-5	Emerging
Nitrogen oxides	50-70	3-5	Emerging
Fluidized bed combustion:			
Sulfur dioxide	<90	NA	Emerging
Nitrogen oxides	20-30	NA	Emerging

SOURCE: Office of Technology Assessment, primarily from EPA estimates.

The two principal components of the costs of fuel-switching are: 1) the "fuel-price differential," i.e., the difference in price between the high- and low-sulfur fuel; and 2) the type of fuel-handling facilities, boilers, and emissions control devices at the plant. Low-sulfur coal is typically more expensive than high-sulfur coal, especially in the East and Midwest.

Figures A-3 and A-4 illustrate the cost differences between high- and low-sulfur coal. Figure A-3 shows the costs of a high-sulfur, Illinois coal at various distances away from the mine. Similar costs are presented for an Appalachian low-sulfur coal in figure A-4. The costs of the low-sulfur coal are shown to be 50 percent higher than the high-sulfur coal even in the areas closest to the mines. The cost differential confronting specific utility plants will vary considerably, depending on site-specific factors and market arrangements.[4]

Many Western low-sulfur coals contain more ash than Eastern high-sulfur coals and can potentially emit greater amounts of particulates. Therefore, particulate emissions control devices (electrostatic precipitators or baghouses) generally have to be upgraded if low-sulfur fuels are used at existing plants. Fuel-handling facilities may also have to be altered because Western coals are often more difficult to pulverize than Eastern coals. In addition, certain kinds of boilers are designed to burn coal with very specific characteristics (e.g., energy yield, ash, and moisture content). These boilers would have to be modified to burn low-sulfur coal efficiently or derated (i.e., produce less electricity). The capital costs of upgrading particulate controls, fuel-handling facilities, and boilers are relatively minor compared to the increased fuel costs involved in fuel-switching. One estimate of the cost of achieving a 6-million-ton SO_2 emissions reduction by fuel-switching at the 50 largest emitters is $1.4 billion per year (1982 dollars), or about $250 per ton of SO_2 removed.[5]

There are 217 billion tons of "compliance" coal (i.e., capable of meeting an SO_2 emissions rate limitation of 1.2 pounds per million Btu (lb/MMBtu) without the application of control technologies) in the demonstrated reserve base.[6] This quantity of coal could support U.S. production for a period of about 50 years (assuming 50 percent recoverability and 3 percent annual growth in consumption). Therefore, achieving substantial emissions reductions through fuel-switching would not be constrained by the resource base over the near future.

However, 85 percent of the Nation's "compliance" reserves are located West of the Mississippi, while 63 percent of coal consumption and 72 percent of coal pro-duction occurs East of the Mississippi.[7] In order to be viable, a large-scale emissions reduction program relying primarily on fuel-switching would have to significantly expand Western coal production and transportation capacity.*

COAL CLEANING: PHYSICAL OR CHEMICAL

The second precombustion approach involves physically or chemically treating coal to remove some of the sulfur it contains. Sulfur in coal exists in two major forms: inorganic and organic. Inorganic or "pyritic" sulfur can be removed relatively inexpensively by exploiting differences in the physical properties of pyrite and coal particles. Organic sulfur is chemically bound to the carbon molecules of coal, and can be removed only by breaking the bonds through some chemical process. These chemical processes are less developed and more expensive than the physical processes that remove pyritic sulfur, but their sulfur removal potential is higher.**

Physical Coal Cleaning.—Physical coal cleaning (often called coal washing) takes advantage of differences in the sizes, densities, and surface properties of pyrite and coal particles. The first step of the cleaning process is to separate raw coal into different size ranges. Breakers and crushers are used to separate the softer coal from the harder rock and other debris contained in the coal entering the treatment plant. After breaking and crushing, the coal is typically filtered through screens to divide it into coarse, intermediate, and fine size ranges.

The method used to extract the pyritic sulfur from the coal depends on the size of particles. Coarse and intermediate size particles allow differences in the specific gravity of pyritic sulfur and coal particles to be used (pyrite has a specific gravity of 5—i.e., is five times heavier than water; coal is approximately 1.4). The coal mixture is immersed in a fluid, where the heavier pyritic particles sink and the lighter particles float. The coal product and refuse material can then be removed separately.

Fine mineral particles cannot be effectively separated by the specific gravity techniques. Physical coal cleaning

---

[4]E. H. Pechan & Associates, information supplied to OTA, October 1981.

[5]PEDCo Environmental Inc., Acid Rain: Control Strategies for Coal-Fired Utility Boilers—Volume I, Summary Report, prepared for the Department of Energy, May 1981, tables 3-1 and 3-2.

[6]E. H. Pechan & Associates, information supplied to OTA, April 1982.

[7]U.S. Department of Energy, Energy Information Administration, Coal Production—1979, DOE/EIA-0118(79), Apr. 30, 1981.

*See Office of Technology Assessment, Direct Use of Coal, OTA-E-86, April 1979; OTA, An Assessment of Development and Production Potential of Federal Coal Leases, OTA-M-150, December 1981, especially ch. 12. For an account of the socioeconomic effects of the decline of coal production, see T. R. Ford (ed.), The Southern Appalachian Region, A Survey (Lexington, Ky.: University of Kentucky Press, 1960).

**For a survey of coal-cleaning techniques, see James D. Kilgroe, "Coal Cleaning for Sulfur Cioxide Emission Control," paper submitted to the Acid Rain Conference, Springfield, Va., Apr. 8-9, 1980. The description of physical coal cleaning in this section relies heavily on Kilgroe's paper. Other surveys of coal-cleaning techniques can be found in EPA-450/3-81-004, Control Techniques for Sulfur Oxide Emissions From Stationary Sources, 2d ed., April 1981; and EPA-600/7-78-002, Engineering/Economic Analyses of Coal Preparation With SO_2 Cleanup Processes, January 1978.

Figure A-3.—Cost of Illinois High-Sulfur Coal 1980 (delivered prices in nominal cents per million Btu)

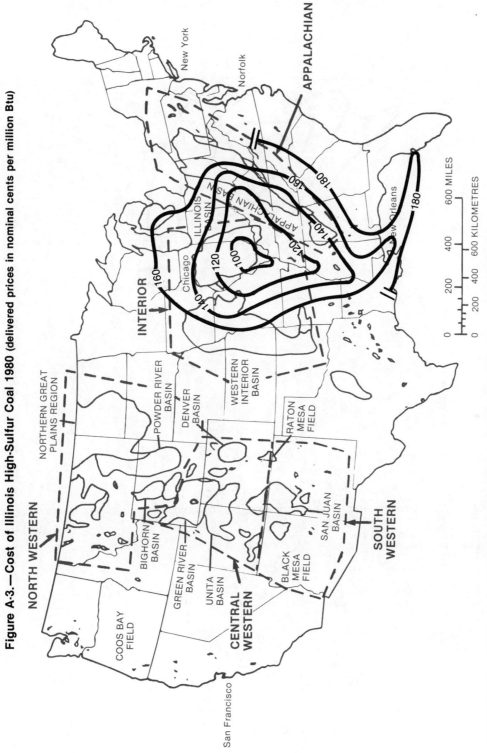

SOURCES: FPC Form 423. P. Averitt, *Coal Resources of the United States, Jan. 1, 1974,* U.S. Geological Survey Bulletin 1412, at 5, 1975.

Figure A-4.—Cost of Eastern Kentucky/West Virginia Low-Sulfur Coal, 1980
(delivered prices in nominal cents per million Btu)

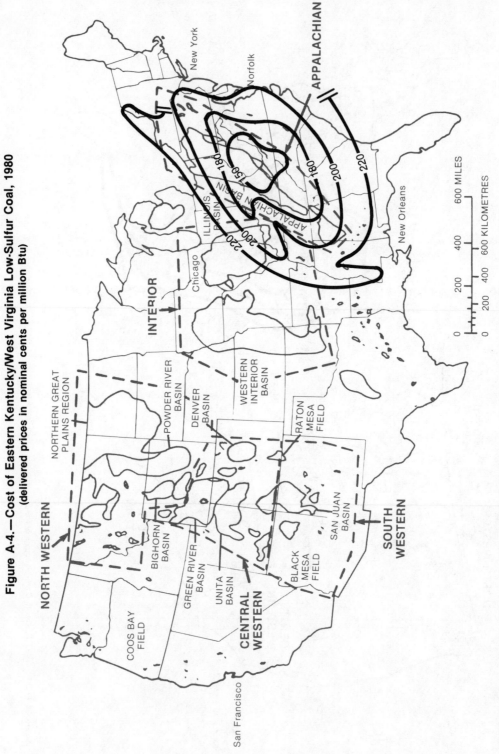

SOURCES: FPC Form 423. P. Averitt, *Coal Resources of the United States, Jan. 1, 1974,* U.S. Geological Survey Bulletin 1412, at 5, 1975.

of fine particles relies on a process in which the raw coal particles are treated with a chemical that, because of differences in surface properties, adsorbs differently on the surface of coal particles than other substances in the mixture. Air bubbles introduced into the chamber attach to the coal particles and carry the coal to the surface, where they can be skimmed off. The pyrite and other particles sink, and are removed separately.

Table A-4 shows the extent to which coal produced for the utility market by eight Eastern and Midwestern coal-producing States is physically cleaned. One-third of the coal produced by these States for utility was washed in 1979, resulting in an estimated 1.8-million-ton reduction in the potential SO_2 emissions (approximately equivalent to a 10-percent reduction in the potential SO_2 emissions).[8]

The emissions reduction potential of physical coal cleaning depends primarily on: 1) the initial sulfur level in the raw coal, 2) the ratio of pyritic to organic sulfur, and 3) the coal-cleaning technique used. Pyritic sulfur accounts for between 30 and 70 percent of the total sulfur content of coal.[9] Higher sulfur coals tend to have a larger proportion of pyritic sulfur than lower sulfur coals. Consequently, the higher the sulfur content of coal, the greater the percentage removal possible through this process. Table A-5 shows the results of an analysis prepared for the Environmental Protection Agency (EPA) on the potential for sulfur removal by coal cleaning in eight Eastern and Midwestern States.[10] As the first

[8]Versar, Inc., *Coal Resources and Sulfur Emission Regulations: A Survey of Eight Eastern and Midwestern States,* prepared for EPA, PB81-240319, May 1981.
[9]James D. Kilgroe, "Coal Cleaning for Sulfur Dioxide Emission Control," paper submitted to the Acid Rain Conference, Springfield, Va., Apr. 8-9, 1980.
[10]Versar, op. cit.

column of the table shows, reductions of between 8 and 33 percent are attainable. The second column lists the SO_2 emissions rate (in lb/MMBtu) achievable after coal washing.

Table A-6 shows the costs and emissions reduction potential of requiring all coal to be cleaned before its use. An additional reduction in SO_2 emissions of about 2.5 million tons could be achieved from the coals produced by these eight States (equivalent to a 17-percent reduction of emissions from coal produced by these States). As the table shows, coal cleaning is associated with a wide range of costs—from a low of $224/ton of SO_2 removed in Indiana to a high of over $3,000/ton removed in southern West Virginia (in 1982 dollars). Cleaning high-sulfur coals—those with the largest emissions reduction potential—is in general more cost effective than cleaning lower sulfur coals. The regionwide average cost (not including southern West Virginia and Virginia) is about $505/ton of SO_2 removed. Coal cleaning adds between $4 and $9/ton to the price of coal, and between 2 and 4 mills/kWh in annual revenue requirements.[11] This compares with an average price of residential electricity of about 50 to 60 mills/kWh.[12]

A Department of Energy contractor has assessed the costs and emissions reduction potential of washing the coal delivered to the 50 largest emitters in the United States. SO_2 removal efficiencies range from 3 to 34 percent. Costs range from $4 to $7/ton of coal cleaned, $170 to $4,900/ton of SO_2 removed, and from 0.8 to 4.4 mills/kWh (1980 dollars). Cleaning the coal used by these 50

[11]Ibid.
[12]U.S. Department of Energy, Energy Information Administration, *1980 Annual Report to Congress, Volume II,* DOE/EIA-0173-80/2.

Table A-4.—Reductions in 1979 SO₂ Emissions Achieved by Cleaning Utility Coal From Eight States

Region and State in which coal was mined	Coal delivered to utilities in 1979 (10³ tons)	Utility coal cleaned in 1979 (percent)	Sulfur content of coal (expressed as 10³ tons SO₂)		Average SO₂ reduction by coal cleaning in 1979 (percent)
			As mined (10³ tons)	As delivered (10³ tons)	
Northern Appalachia:					
Pennsylvania......................	47,400	30	2,100	1,860	12
Ohio	38,300	11	2,750	2,670	3
Northern West Virginia	31,300	23	1,760	1,690	4
Southern Appalachia:					
Southern West Virginia..............	17,500	9	300	290	1
Virginia	13,400	7	280	270	1
Eastern Kentucky...................	68,600	22	1,630	1,570	4
Eastern Midwest:					
Western Kentucky	38,100	34	2,880	2,600	13
Indiana...........................	25,300	52	1,620	1,410	13
Illinois	49,500	72	3,570	2,780	22
Alabama:					
Alabama..........................	14,600	32	460	440	5
Eight-State total/average...........	344,000	33	17,350	15,580	10

SOURCE: Versar, Inc., *Coal Resources and Sulfur Emission Regulations: A Survey of Eight Eastern and Midwestern States,* prepared for EPA, PB 81-240319, May 1981.

Table A-5.—Average SO₂ Emission Reductions and Emission Rate Potentials for Coal From Eight States (1979 data)

Region and State	Average emission reduction using physically cleaned coal[a] (percent)	Average emission potential (lb SO₂/MMBtu)	Number of washability samples
Northern Appalachia:			
Pennsylvania	33.2	4.0	170
Ohio	25.9	5.8	90
Northern West Virginia......	28.9	4.9	30
Southern Appalachia:			
Southern West Virginia	10.1	1.4	16
Virginia	7.6	1.1	8
Eastern Kentucky	15.9	2.3	13
Eastern Midwest:			
Western Kentucky	31.5	6.6	37
Indiana....................	26.4	5.9	21
Illinois	29.3	6.6	40
Alabama	10.8	2.0	10

[a]Coal crushed to 1/12 inch top size and separated at 1.6 specific gravity.

SOURCE: Versar, Inc., *Coal Resources and Sulfur Regulations: A Survey of Eight Eastern and Midwestern States*, prepared for EPA, PB 81-240319, May 1981.

Table A-6.—Typical Cost Effectiveness of Additional Coal Cleaning for Eight Eastern and Midwestern States

Region and State	Additional annual SO₂ reduction[a] 10³ ton	Percent	Levelized cost of cleaning (1982 $/clean ton)	Cost effectiveness (1982 $/ton SO₂ removed) Without benefits	With benefits
Northern Appalachia:					
Pennsylvania	450	24	$6.90	$476	$301
Ohio	720	27	8.36	369	233
Northern West Virginia	250	15	6.70	564	398
Eastern Midwest:					
Western Kentucky	530	20	5.44	243	101
Indiana	170	12	3.79	224	49
Illinois	210	5	5.64	330	155
Southern Appalachia:					
Southern West Virginia	—	0	6.70	c	c
Virginia........................	—	0	7.09	c	c
Eastern Kentucky	150	9	8.45	991	680
Alabama	65	15	6.51	845	437
Eight-State total/average[d]	2,545	16	6.56	505	294

[a]Over current practice.
[b]Of raw coal.
[c]These coals typically have a cost effectiveness exceeding $3,000/ton.
[d]Averages do not include States where insufficient data are given.

SOURCE: U.S. Environmental Protection Agency, draft memorandum, Coal Cleaning Background Paper, May 19, 1983. (Note: this memo has not been formally released by the U.S. Environmental Protection Agency and should not be construed to represent Agency policy.)

plants is estimated to yield a 1.5-million-ton reduction in SO₂ emissions (about 7 percent of total SO₂ emissions in the Eastern United States) at an average annual cost of $870 million, or $580/ton of SO₂ removed.[13] This study does not account for the emissions reductions or costs of coal used by these utilities that is currently being cleaned.

Coal cleaning has several benefits in addition to reduced SO₂ emissions. First, cleaning reduces the ash content of coal, reducing ash disposal requirements at

the power facility. Second, the removal of impurities (sulfur, ash, and others) increases the "heating value" (energy per unit of weight) of coal. Increased heating value reduces coal transportation costs and pulverization requirements at the plant. Finally, because cleaning creates a fuel with more uniform characteristics (e.g., ash, moisture, sulfur, and energy content), increased efficiency of boiler operation is possible.[14] These benefits

---

[13]PEDCo, op. cit., May 1981.

[14]*Engineering/Economic Analyses of Coal Preparation With SO₂ Cleanup Processes*, U.S. Environmental Protection Agency, EPA-600/7-78-002, January 1978; see also, *Cost Benefits Associated With the Use of Physically Cleaned Coal*, prepared by PEDCo, EPA-600/7-80-105, May 1981.

can in many instances offset a large portion of the costs of coal cleaning.

Physical coal cleaning may produce a substantial amount of solid waste. The cleaning process causes approximately one-fourth of the mined material to be discarded as waste.[15] Moreover, some coal (approximately 5 to 10 percent of the energy value) is lost in the process of removing impurities.[16]

Chemical Coal Cleaning.—Chemical coal cleaning can remove higher percentages of sulfur contained in coal because it can in some cases remove organic as well as pyritic sulfur. These processes, however, have only been successfully operated at the laboratory scale, and are estimated to be 5 to 10 years away from commercial viability. Chemical coal-cleaning processes vary widely from relatively simple methods that use chemical solutions to leach sulfur and other impurities out of coal, to processes such as solvent-refined coal, which alters the characteristics of coal so much that it is usually considered a coal-conversion process.[17]

Two of the chemical coal-cleaning processes receiving the greatest amounts of current research attention are the Meyers process and microwave desulfurization. The Meyers process, developed by TRW, Inc., is a chemical leaching process that combines coal with a ferric sulfate or sulfuric acid solution to remove sulfur. This process can remove 80 to 99 percent of the pyritic sulfur in coal (larger removal efficiencies than physical coal cleaning), but cannot remove organic sulfur.[18]

One of the several coal-cleaning processes that remove organic as well as pyritic sulfur is microwave desulfurization. Developed by General Electric, this process begins by wetting crushed coal with a sodium hydroxide solution; the mixture is then briefly irradiated with microwave energy. During irradiation, the sodium hydroxide reacts with pyritic and organic sulfur to form sodium sulfide. The coal is immersed in water to remove the sulfur-laden sodium sulfide, and the process is repeated again. Laboratory tests have achieved **total** sulfur removals in excess of 90 percent.[19]

Because chemical coal-cleaning techniques are in the early stages of development, costs are difficult to estimate. It is not yet clear whether chemical coal cleaning will be economically competitive with flue-gas desulfurization (described under ''Postcombustion Approaches'') in the future. Chemical coal cleaning can be expected to produce the same side effects—waste disposal requirements, removal of ash and other impurities, increased heating value, and improved boiler efficiency—as physical coal cleaning.

OIL DESULFURIZATION

Oil desulfurization is a widely applied method for reducing SO_2 emissions. The primary method is called hydrodesulfurization; oil is treated with hydrogen, which partially removes the sulfur by combining with it to form hydrogen sulfide gas. Oil is first distilled to separate the crude into various petroleum products. Most of the sulfur concentrates in the heavier residues. The lighter fractions, or distillate, are redistilled under a vacuum. In one variant of hydrodesulfurization, referred to as the indirect method, the second distillate is hydrotreated (i.e., reacted with hydrogen) to remove the sulfur as hydrogen sulfide gas. The product is reblended with the vacuum residue to yield low-sulfur fuel oil. This method can reduce the sulfur content by 30 to 42 percent.[20]

In another variation of hydrodesulfurization, referred to as the direct method, the residue from distillation is hydrotreated, and then reblended with the distillate to form a lower sulfur fuel, or both the residue and distillate from vacuum distillation are separately hydrotreated before reblending. This technique can achieve a degree of desulfurization as high as 70 to 90 percent, but is not yet commercially available. Indirect hydrodesulfurization is presently the predominant method for producing low-sulfur (less than 1 percent sulfur) fuel oil from high-sulfur crudes. Both the indirect and direct methods are similar to coal cleaning in that the higher the degree of desulfurization, the higher the costs. Estimated costs for desulfurizing oil containing 3-percent sulfur content to 1-percent sulfur content, range from $17 to $40/ton in 1980 prices, depending on the choice of process.[21]

Disadvantages of hydrodesulfurization are the high investment and operating costs, and the high energy requirements. Since fuel oil combustion is not expected to increase significantly in the United States, the present desulfurization capacity is expected to remain at current levels for the near future.

Combustion Alteration Approaches

LIMESTONE INJECTION MULTISTAGE BURNER (LIMB)

Many in the United States consider the LIMB to be one of the most promising control technologies under development today. The technique controls **both** SO_2

[15]Kilgroe, op. cit.

[16]*Control Techniques for Sulfur Oxide Emissions From Stationary Sources,* EPA-450/3-81-004, December 1979. See also PEDCo, op. cit.

[17]Work Group 3B, op. cit.

[18]Versar, Inc., *Technology Assessment Report for Industrial Boiler Applications: Coal Cleaning and Low Sulfur Coal,* prepared for EPA, EPA-600/7-79-178C, December 1979.

[19]Ibid.

[20]N. Elam and Trichen Consultants, Ltd., *Present and Future Levels of Sulfur Dioxide Emissions in Northern Europe,* Swedish Ministry, June 1979.

[21]Ron Jones, Director, Environmental Affairs, American Petroleum Institute, Washington, D.C., personal communication.

and NO_x emissions. The LIMB is based on the use of staged burner techniques for NO_x control, in combination with sorbent (normally limestone) which is injected through the burners for SO_2 control. SO_2 reacts with the limestone to form solid calcium sulfate.

This technology is still under development; its removal efficiencies and costs are very uncertain at this time. Planning goals established by EPA set objectives of 50 to 70 percent removal of SO_2 and NO_x, at a capital cost of $30 to $40/kW.[22] If these goals are achieved, the LIMB would offer substantial cost improvements over existing technologies. It is very possible that the LIMB, because it may be retrofitted into existing plants at a competitive cost, may emerge as a particularly attractive control technology option. However, EPA plans to limit the LIMB research program to basic bench- and large pilot-scale R&D through 1985, since funding is unavailable for Government sponsorship of a full-scale demonstration at this time.[23]

FLUIDIZED BED COMBUSTION

Another technique that removes SO_2 during the combustion process is fluidized bed combustion. For this process, crushed coal is fed into a bed of inert ash mixed with limestone or dolomite. The bed is held in suspension ("fluidized") by the injection of air from the bottom of the bed. SO_2, formed during combustion, reacts with the limestone or dolomite to form solid calcium sulfate, which can be removed from the boiler without interrupting the combustion process.

Fluidized bed combustion can remove up to 90 percent of the SO_2. Available estimates, though preliminary, show the cost effectiveness of fluidized bed combustion to be about equal to conventional boilers using flue-gas desulfurization.[24] Further research is still needed before large-scale use could be justified; however, for small facilities (up to 250 MW), fluidized bed combustion is a feasible method today. Oil may also be burned in a fluidized bed, but no such plant is yet in operation.

Aside from lower emissions, fluidized bed boilers have the advantages of greater energy efficiency, lower combustion temperatures keeping the formation of nitrogen oxides down, and smaller boiler size. Fluidized bed boilers can burn both high- and low-sulfur coals.

Postcombustion Approaches

FLUE-GAS DESULFURIZATION

Flue-gas desulfurization (FGD) technology removes the SO_2 produced during combustion by spraying the exhaust gases in the stack with a chemical absorbent, typically lime or limestone. This process is popularly referred to as "scrubbing." Of the three types of FGD systems—wet, dry, and regenerable—wet processes are most widely used. Presently there are over 100 scrubbers using all three methods in operation in the United States.

WET SCRUBBERS

The most common absorbents used for wet scrubbing are lime and limestone. The absorbent is dissolved or suspended in water to form a slurry that can then be sprayed or forced into contact with escaping gases. The slurry converts SO_2 into calcium sulfite and calcium sulfate (gypsum) solids. Limestone scrubbing is the simplest, cheapest, and most developed SO_2 wet-removal process available.

Technology to wet-scrub the flue gas with a lime or limestone slurry has been commercially available for about 10 years. As of March 1981, 5.1 percent of installed generating capacity (and 14 percent of coal-fired capacity) was controlled by wet scrubbers. By 1990, the figure is projected to increase to 9.4 percent of installed capacity.[25]

Wet lime or limestone scrubbers can remove between 70 to 90 percent of the SO_2 formed during combustion. With the addition of another chemical—adipic acid—removal efficiencies can be increased to 95 percent, while limestone requirements can be reduced by up to 15 percent.[26] However, adipic acid additives may present additional sludge disposal problems.

A Tennessee Valley Authority (TVA) study conducted in 1980 estimated the capital costs of a wet limestone system using low-sulfur Western coal (0.7 percent sulfur, 9,700 Btu/lb) to be $168 to $176/kW. For high-sulfur Eastern coal (3.5 percent sulfur, 11,700 Btu/lb) capital costs range from $236 to $244/kW. These estimates are based on costs for a new 500-MW plant, operating at a 63-percent lifetime capacity. The range in cost estimates is due to variations in bids from different con-

[22]James Abbott and Blair Martin, U.S. Environmental Protection Agency, Research Triangle Park, N.C., personal communication.
[23]Julian Jones, U.S. Environmental Protection Agency, Research Triangle Park, personal communication.
[24]Work Group 3B, op. cit.

[25]U.S. Environmental Protection Agency, "EPA Utility FGD Survey: October-December 1980," EPA-600/7-81-012b, January 1981.
[26]U.S. Environmental Protection Agency, Research Summary: Controlling SO2, Office of Research and Development, August 1980.

tractors and the specific considerations for each site. Annual revenue requirements from the TVA study range from 10.5 to 10.9 mills/kWh for low-sulfur coal and 16.4 to 16.7 mills/kWh for high-sulfur coal.[27]

The annual revenue requirements for FGD units depend on several factors, including coal sulfur content, size of the unit, age of the plant, and desired percentage reduction. The costs per ton of sulfur dioxide removed by scrubbers rise steeply as the uncontrolled emission rate drops. For example, removing 90 percent of the sulfur from a coal emitting 2 lb of sulfur dioxide per million Btu is about 75 percent more expensive (on a dollar/ton basis) than scrubbing a 4 lb/million Btu coal for the same size unit. Likewise, scrubbing a 1 lb/million Btu coal is about 75 percent (or more) costlier than scrubbing a 2 lb/million Btu coal in a similar unit.

Costs for retrofitting a scrubber onto an existing plant depend on the lifespan of the plant; the shorter the remaining lifetime of the plant, the higher the annual revenue requirements to recover the capital costs of the FGD. Also, because of economies of scale in construction, retrofitting a scrubber onto a larger unit is less expensive than onto smaller ones. Units smaller than about 100 MW are typically quite expensive to retrofit with scrubbers.

Operating problems associated with wet systems are corrosion/erosion of metal surfaces, scaling (where hard sulfate and sulfite deposits form on equipment), and plugging (where soft deposits form). Ways of minimizing these problems are currently being researched. In addition, operation of wet scrubbers requires approximately 3 to 5 percent of a plant's energy output.[28]

The major environmental disadvantage of wet FGD systems is that they produce large amounts of sludge. Limestone scrubbing produces a compound (mainly calcium sulfite and sulfate) that has the consistency of toothpaste, making it difficult to dewater, store, and handle. The total amount of FGD waste produced in a typical 1,000-MW plant burning 3.5 percent sulfur coal is about 225,000 tons annually. A recent report concluded that in the future the United States will produce more sludge from FGD scrubbing than from treating municipal sewage.[29]

Sludge may, however, be chemically treated to reduce its water content and improve its compressive strength. Forced oxidation converts the waste calcium sulfite to calcium sulfate, which precipitates as large crystals with better settling characteristics. Other means of improving the sludge's properties, such as fixation with lime and fly ash, are still being developed.

Another problem associated with sludge disposal is the leaching of toxic metals from the residual fly ash into nearby ecosystems. EPA is currently conducting research on the characteristics of leaching of metal compounds from sludge disposal sites to evaluate the seriousness of the problem.[30]

DRY PROCESSES OF FGD

Dry scrubbers are a new and fast growing segment of the FGD market. The process involves injection of a lime slurry or soda ash solution into a spray dryer concurrently with the flue gas. The lime or sodium carbonate reacts with the SO_2 to form a dry, solid product which is subsequently collected along with the fly ash in an electrostatic precipitator or fabric filter (baghouse).

Dry scrubbers offer several advantages over wet scrubbing. Although they generate more waste than wet systems, they produce a dry waste product that is easier to handle and recycle than wet sludge, and involve simpler equipment, less maintenance, lower capital costs, and lower energy requirements. In addition, dry systems require less water than wet systems, and thus are especially desirable in Western areas of the United States where water supplies are limited.[31]

There are, however, some disadvantages to using a dry scrubber over a wet system. First, dry systems require lime, which is more expensive than limestone. Second, dry scrubbers are in the early stages of commercialization and have not demonstrated as high a degree of removal as wet scrubbers. Their use has generally been limited to medium- and low-sulfur coals. However, pilot demonstration and commercial plant tests have shown sulfur removal efficiencies exceeding 90 percent for high-sulfur coal.

As of October 1983, six dry scrubber systems were in operation, five at industrial plants, and one at a utility plant generating 430 MW of electricity. Four more units will be installed on utility boilers in 1984, and approximately 16 units have been ordered for industrial use.[32] A TVA study estimates that capital costs for dry FGD systems range from $144 to $160/kW for low-sulfur Western coal, and from $180 to $188/kW for high-sulfur Eastern coals. Annual revenue requirements are estimated to range from 8.7 to 9.8 mills/kWh for Western low-sulfur coal, and 14.5 to 14.9 mills/kWh for high-sulfur coal. These annual costs are between 10 and 25 percent lower than wet systems, as reported by the same TVA study. An EPA survey of dry systems sold to util-

[27]T. A. Burnett, et al., "Spray Dryer FGD: Technical Review and Economic Assessment," Tennessee Valley Authority, presented at U.S. Environmental Protection Agency Sixth FGD Symposium, Houston, Tex., Oct. 28-31, 1980.

[28]W. Nesbit, "Scrubbers: The Technology Nobody Wanted," *EPRI Journal*, vol. 7, No. 8, October 1982.

[29]U.S. Environmental Protection Agency, *Sulfur Emissions: Control Technology and Waste Management*, Office of Research and Development, May 1982.

[30]Work Group 3B, op. cit.

[31]EPA-450/3-81-004, op. cit.

[32]Theodore Brna, U.S. Environmental Protection Agency, Research Triangle Park, N.C., personal communication.

ities, however, suggests that actual capital costs might be lower. Reported capital costs for these systems range from $80 to $130/kW.[33]

EPA is currently conducting research on the use of other dry injected minerals to be used in place of lime. If the research results are successful, dry scrubbing costs could be considerably lower than wet systems.

REGENERABLE PROCESSES

Major research efforts by various Government agencies have gone into regenerable FGD processes, which reclaim the SO_2 in powerplant flue gases using chemicals to produce a marketable product. The major benefit of regenerable control systems is that the captured sulfur can be sold, avoiding waste-disposal problems associated with wet and dry processes. Eight regenerable FGD systems are currently operating in the United States, accounting for about 8 percent of the total FGD-controlled electricity generation. The most prominent regenerable FGD process in use in the United States is the Wellman-Lord process. It involves scrubbing the exhaust gas with sodium sulfite solution, resulting in sodium sulfite-bisulfite, which is then heated to give off concentrated SO_2 gas that can be used to produce either sulfuric acid or elemental sulfur. This process is already in use by the New Mexico Public Service Co. One disadvantage of this process is its high energy requirements, which are approximately 8 to 12 percent of boiler energy input.[34]

Other regenerable systems under development are the Magnesia scrubbing process, which produces sulfuric acid, and the Rockwell process, which produces sulfur. Unfortunately regenerable processes cost approximately 30 to 50 percent more than nonrecoverable processes.

Controlling Nitrogen Oxides Emissions

Oxides of nitrogen are formed during combustion by two processes. Like sulfur dioxide, NO_x are formed as a result of the oxidation of nitrogen present in the fuel ("fuel NO_x"). NO_x are also formed by the oxidation of nitrogen in the surrounding air ("thermal NO_x"). Both processes are controlled by the amount of oxygen present; additionally, the thermal NO_x formation is controlled by temperature. The proportion of thermal to fuel NO_x produced during combustion varies from fuel to fuel. For coal, the Electric Power Research Institute estimates that 20 to 40 percent of NO_x emissions are "thermal" and 60 to 80 percent are "fuel."[35]

NO_x emissions, being dependent on the amount of oxygen present and the temperature of the combustion process, can be most directly controlled by modifying combustion conditions. The majority of NO_x control techniques focus on the combustion process. Postcombustion techniques (flue-gas treatment) are also being developed to achieve even lower emission rates. Today the two most promising combustion technologies for reducing NO_x emissions are certain types of fluidized bed combustion units, for plants up to 250 MW, and the low-NO_x burner. One precombustion technique, the denitrogenation of fuel oil, is being researched, but will not be discussed because of its early stage of development and limited potential.

Combustion Modifications

Thermal NO_x formation can be minimized by regulating the combustion temperature through delayed mixing of fuel and air in the combustion chamber. Limiting fuel NO_x is somewhat different, requiring control of the fuel-air ratio throughout the entire combustion process. Two of the major techniques used in combustion modification, **low excess air** (LEA) and **low-NO_x burners,** are presented below. Other combustion modification techniques include: staged combustion (off-stoichiometric firing), overfire air, flue-gas recirculation, low air preheat, and water injection.[36]

LEA involves reducing the combustion air to the minimum amount required for total combustion. Thus, less oxygen is available for the formation of both thermal and fuel NO_x. LEA requires no new hardware and can achieve emissions reductions merely through changes in operating practices. Also, the reduced airflow can improve boiler efficiency.

The second-generation, low-NO_x burners under development, which employ a staged combustion process, have been shown to significantly reduce the formation of both fuel and thermal NO_x in experimental systems and limited boiler applications. During the first stage of combustion, less air is supplied to the burner than is required to completely burn the fuel. Fuel-bound nitrogen is then released—but as nitrogen gas, because it cannot be oxidized. The subsequent addition of air causes the remaining fuel to be burned.

The amount by which NO_x emissions can be reduced depends on very site-specific factors, including the type of fuel burned, the type of boiler in use, and the age of the plant. Installed on an existing coal-fired plant which does not control NO_x emissions, the low-NO_x burner can reduce NO_x emissions by as much as 50 percent. Potential NO_x emissions reductions from retrofitting an oil-fired burner range from 60 to 80 percent.[37]

[33]U.S. Environmental Protection Agency, "Survey of Dry SO_2 Control Systems, III," EPA-600/7-81-097.

[34]EPA-450/3-81-004, op. cit.

[35]Ralph Whitaker, "Trade-offs in NO_x Control," *EPRI Journal,* vol. 7, No. 1.

[36]*An Analysis of the Economic Incentives To Control Emissions of Nitrogen Oxides From Stationary Sources,* EPA-600/7-79-178f, January 1981, p. A3.

[37]EPA-600/7-79-178f, op. cit.

The low-NO$_x$ burner can achieve emissions reduction at relatively low cost. Capital costs for coal-fired plants are approximately $1 to $5/kW if integrated into new boilers, and $2 to $10/kW if retrofitted onto existing plants.[38]

Potential problems such as corrosion and high maintenance requirements could delay large-scale use of the low-NO$_x$ burner. Retrofitting old boilers can be difficult, but NO$_x$ controls on new boilers can be made an integral part of boiler design without adding substantially to cost.

Another combustion modification approach for the control of NO$_x$ is the LIMB, which is discussed in further detail in the section on combustion alteration approaches for SO$_2$. EPA research goals for the LIMB are to achieve a 50- to 70-percent removal of SO$_2$ and NO$_x$, at a cost of $30 to $40/kW; however, the LIMB is not expected to be commercially available for about 3 to 5 years.[39]

Postcombustion Approaches

FLUE-GAS TREATMENT

Flue-gas treatment (FGT) is an emerging postcombustion process for high levels of NO$_x$ removal. FGT has been developed and applied extensively in Japan for use on oil-fired boilers. But due to its operational complexities and high costs for use on coal-fired boilers, FGT has not become as popular as the low-NO$_x$ burner in the United States.

At least 50 different types of FGT technologies are available today. Of these, selective catalytic reduction (SCR) achieves the highest reductions. SCR is a dry process, produces no solid waste, and in most cases can be retrofitted to existing burners. In SCR, flue gases are mixed with ammonia and then passed over a catalyst. The catalyst assists in the reaction of ammonia and NO$_x$ to form nitrogen gas and water vapor. While 90-percent NO$_x$ removal during combustion is possible, 80-percent removal is preferable in order to minimize capital and operating costs and maximize the burners' reliability and lifespan. One estimate places the costs of FGT at between $75 and $100/kW for a 60- to 80-percent reduction in NO$_x$ emissions.[40]

Two problems associated with SCR are the disposal of spent catalysts, such as vanadium and titanium, and the condensation of bisulfate and bisulfite residuals onto equipment.[41]

---

[38]Ibid.

[39]James Abbott and Blair Martin, U.S. Environmental Protection Agency, Research Triangle Park, N.C., personal communication.

[40]*EPRI Journal*, op. cit.

[41]J. D. Mobley, *Assessment of NO$_x$ Flue Gas Treatment Technology*, U.S. Environmental Protection Agency, Research Triangle Park, presented at Symposium of Stationary Combustion NO$_x$ Control, Denver, Colo., October 1980.

A.3 ALLOCATION OF SULFUR DIOXIDE EMISSIONS REDUCTIONS AND THE COSTS OF CONTROL

Introduction

The costs and distributional consequences of various control strategies are important factors in decisions about controlling transported air pollutants. Costs are affected both by the amount of emissions to be eliminated, and by the manner in which emissions reductions are to be achieved. For a given emissions reduction **strategy,** the greater the reduction, the greater the cost. For a given emissions reduction **target,** alternative implementation strategies may entail different costs, i.e., one strategy may be more cost effective than another.

Alternative control strategies may also have different distributional consequences. Certain approaches assign a greater share of the emissions reduction burden to one region or State or economic sector than to others. This section examines the **costs and distributional conse-** **quences** of various emissions reduction strategies, concentrating on emissions reductions in the **Eastern 31-State region.** Due to analytical limitations, only the costs of reducing **sulfur dioxide** (SO$_2$) emissions from **utilities** are presented.

SO$_2$ emissions for 1980 are estimated to be about 26 million tons nationwide and about 22 million tons in the Eastern 31 States. Fossil fuel combustion by electric utilities accounts for about 17 million tons or 65 percent of the national total. In the Eastern 31 States, utilities produce 70 percent of the regional SO$_2$ emissions, or about 16 million tons. Under current regulations, EPA-approved State implementation plans (SIPs) require utilities to reduce these emissions by approximately 1 million tons.

OTA has estimated the cost of further reducing utility SO$_2$ emissions in the 31-State region below the SIP-

Figure A-5.—Comparison of Utility SO₂ Control Costs

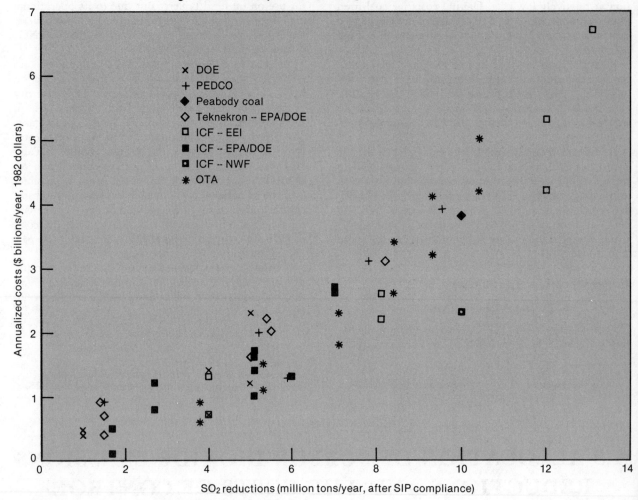

SOURCE: Office of Technology Assessment from references listed in text.

compliance level under several different control strategies. The model used in generating these estimates is described briefly at the end of this section.*

The Costs of Various Levels of Emissions Reductions

To illustrate how the extent of emissions reductions affects the costs of controlling emissions, figure A-5 displays estimates of 31-State aggregate control costs

made by OTA and several other groups.** Costs are presented for reducing SO₂ emissions from utilities only, and are in 1982 dollars. To reduce emissions by approximately 5 million tons beyond SIP compliance, the vari-

---

*This analysis uses the AIRCOST model, run by E. H. Pechan & Associates, Inc. AIRCOST was modified from a larger model used in several earlier major assessments, including the New Source Performance Standards (NSPS) review, the Ohio River Basin Energy Study (ORBES), and the Acid Rain Mitigation Study (ARMS).

Most of these cost estimates are cited in "Costs To Reduce Sulfur Dioxide Emissions," Department of Energy, DOE/PE-0042, 1982. DOE adjusted each estimate using consistent economic assumptions. Cost estimates are also included from: "Summary of Acid Rain Analyses Undertaken by ICF for the Edison Electric Institute, National Wildlife Federation, and Environmental Protection Agency," prepared by ICF, Inc., for the Edison Electric Institute, 1982; and Chris Farrand, Peabody Coal Co., testimony before the Senate Environment and Public Works Committee, October 1981. OTA estimates are based on analyses prepared by E. H. Pechan & Associates, 1983. The PEDCo study was prepared for DOE, the Teknekron analysis was prepared for EPA and DOE, and the ICF analyses were performed for EPA, DOE, the Edison Electric Institute, and the National Wildlife Federation. OTA's estimates are presented as the costs of reductions **beyond SIP compliance. The Peabody, PEDCo, and DOE estimates are reductions below actual 1980 emissions, and the ICF and Teknekron model estimates are displayed as emissions reductions below projected 1990 emissions levels.

ous estimated annual costs range from about $1 to $2 billion per year. For reductions of 8 million tons beyond SIP compliance (about 55 to 60 percent below current utility emissions), the range increases to $2 to $3.5 billion annually. The largest emissions reduction calculated—a 13-million-ton reduction below projected 1990 levels—is estimated to cost approximately $7 billion per year.

Table A-7 displays OTA's control cost estimates for a series of emission rate limitations ranging from 0.8 to 2.5 lb of SO_2 emitted per million Btu (MMBtu) of fuel burned. Eastern 31-State emissions reductions range from 4.6 million to 11.4 million tons per year, including reductions already required under current law. However, the **costs** presented consider only those reductions that would be required beyond SIP compliance.

For each emission rate limitation, two sets of cost estimates are presented. The cost estimates in the top half of the table assume that each utility chooses the least expensive control method among those applicable to plant conditions. This typically results in a statewide mix of coal washing, switching to (or blending with) lower sulfur fuels, and wet and dry scrubbers. Cost estimates presented in the bottom half of table A-7 assume that the legislation mandates the use of pollution control technologies such as wet scrubbers. Several recent bills have included such a control technology restriction to minimize job dislocations among high-sulfur coal

miners. (Section A.5 of app. A discusses the magnitude of potential coal production and related employment changes due to acid rain control legislation.)

As expected, costs increase as emissions reduction requirements increase. As shown in the top-half of table A-7, the "least-cost" method of control ranges from less than $1 billion annually to eliminate less than about 5 million tons per year, to between $4 and $5 billion to eliminate 11.4 million tons.* Moreover, the marginal costs of control increase when larger emissions rollbacks are required. That is, the cost of eliminating an additional 1 million tons of SO_2 per year is greater for an increase from 8 million to 9 million tons (approximately $700 million per year) than for an equal increase from 7 million to 8 million tons (approximately $450 million per year).

As shown in the bottom half of table A-7, mandating the use of control technology to achieve all required emissions reductions increases the cost of control. For emissions reductions in the range of 5 million tons per year, such a requirement about doubles control costs. For greater levels of emissions reductions (9 million to

---

*All cost estimates are first-year, annualized costs in 1982 dollars. Capital costs and interest payments are spread evenly over each year of the life of the investment. Because fuel and operation and maintenance costs can vary from year to year (i.e., real energy and labor costs might either increase or decrease over the next two decades), **current** fuel and operation and maintenance costs (rather than an average based on assumed trends) are added to capital costs to calculate yearly total control costs.

Table A-7.—Costs of Reducing SO₂ Emissions in the Eastern 31 States (exludes costs to meet current SIPs or to offset future emissions growth; all costs in 1982 dollars)

A. Assuming each utility chooses the most cost-effective control method:

Emission rate limitation (lb SO₂/MMBtu)	Emissions reduction (million tons SO₂)	Total cost (billions of dollars/yr)	Average cost of reductions ($/ton)	Marginal cost of reductions[a] ($/ton)
2.5	4.6	$0.6-0.9	$170-240	$320
2.0	6.2	1.1-1.5	200-280	440
1.5	8.0	1.8-2.3	260-330	700
1.2	9.3	2.6-3.4	310-400	740
1.0	10.3	3.2-4.1	350-440	830
0.8	11.4	4.2-5.0	400-480	1,320

B. Assuming utilities are required to install control technology (wet scrubbers):

Emission rate limitation (lb SO₂/MMBtu)	Emissions reduction (million tons SO₂)	Total cost[b] (billions of dollars/yr)	Average Cost of reductions ($/tons)	Increased costs due to control technology requirement[c] (billions of dollars/yr)	(percent increase)
2.5	4.6	1.4	360	0.7	110
2.0	6.2	2.0	380	1.0	90
1.5	8.0	3.1	430	1.2	70
1.2	9.3	4.0	480	1.4	55
1.0	10.3	4.8	510	1.6	50
0.8	11.4	5.9	570	1.8	40

[a]Cost (in dollars per ton) to achieve the next increment of reductions.
[b]Assumes statewide emissions reductions are from those utility plants that can install scrubbers most cost effectively. Old and small units are exempt from the requirement to install scrubbers, but equivalent emissions reductions are obtained from other plants within each State.
[c]Compared to "least cost" estimate in part A of this table.
SOURCE: Office of Technology Assessment, based on analyses by E. H. Pechan & Associates, Inc.

11 million tons per year), mandating the use of scrubbers increases total control costs by about 50 percent.

State-by-State Emissions Reductions and Costs of Control Strategies

Thus far, only aggregate, regional control cost estimates have been presented. Costs of control would vary considerably from State to State, depending on each State's emissions reduction requirements, and the costs of available emissions reductions in each State. The specific control strategy chosen affects both regional costs and their State-by-State distribution.

Actual State-level costs are determined by: 1) the amount of reductions allocated to each State, which depends on the chosen control strategy; and 2) the costs of available emissions reduction opportunities in each State, which depend on the type and number of electric-generating plants in service, and their levels of current emissions. States which already have relatively low utility emissions rates may not have as many opportunities to use less expensive control options as States with higher emissions rates. The latter States may be able to achieve relatively large reductions at lower costs per ton.

Table A-8 presents data on utility SO_2 emissions and electricity generation. The first column displays 1980 utility SO_2 emissions by State; the second column ranks the 30 highest emitting States according to these emissions. States that generate more electricity from fossil-fuel-fired utilities would be expected to emit more SO_2 (all other factors being equal); thus, columns 3 and 4 present 1980 fossil-fuel-generated electricity and corresponding rank for the top 30 States. The last two columns present average SO_2 emissions **rates**—the quantity of SO_2 emitted per million Btu of fuel burned, and the corresponding rank of States with average utility emissions rates greater than or equal to 1.2 lb/MMBtu. In general, the higher the emissions rate, the greater the opportunity for reducing emissions and the lower the cost per ton of SO_2 removed.

However, statewide average emissions rates mask the variation among plants within a given State. Table A-9 examines the potential for reducing utility SO_2 emissions in each State in greater detail. The table displays the percentage of utility emissions that could be eliminated by mandating various emissions rate limitations, ranging from 1.0 to 4.0 lb of SO_2 per million Btu of fuel burned. These estimates are calculated by assuming no facility may exceed the specified emissions rate.

Table A-10 displays the average cost, in dollars per tons of SO_2 removed, for reducing utility SO_2 emissions by 50 percent in each of the Eastern 31 States. While much of the State-level variation is due to differences

in emissions rates, considerable variation results from such other factors as distance from low-sulfur coal supplies, dependence on oil, and size and age of the utility plants.

Comparison of Alternative Approaches to Emissions Reductions

OTA has analyzed a number of approaches to allocating an 8-million-ton reduction of utility SO_2 emissions among the Eastern 31 States. The regional costs and distributional consequences of eight different allocation formulae—in terms of the reductions allocated to each State and the cost of achieving those allocated reductions—are discussed below.

Table A-11 presents the overall cost of these eight alternative allocation approaches for the 31-State region. The costs are shown to range from a low of $1.8 billion to $2.3 billion per year for reductions based on a maximum emissions rate (1.5 lb of SO_2 per MMBtu) to a high of $3.7 billion to $3.9 billion per year for an allocation formula based on total SO_2 emissions per land area. Each approach eliminates about 8 million tons of SO_2 per year; future emissions growth—estimated to be about 1 million to 2.5 million tons per year by 1995—is not offset. Cost to achieve emissions reductions already required under current regulations (SIPs) are not included.

Table A-12 shows the State-by-State emissions reductions required under each allocation approach; table A-13 estimates State-average control costs, expressed as a percentage of residential electricity costs. Some States are consistently allocated relatively large costs—in particular, Georgia, Indiana, Kentucky, Missouri, New Hampshire, Ohio, Pennsylvania, and West Virginia. For other States—e.g., Delaware, New Jersey, and Rhode Island—control costs are strongly influenced by the allocation approach used. The approaches that allocate the widest State-by-State variations in required emissions reductions—e.g., those based on emissions per person or land area—cause State-level costs to vary a great deal. In these cases, some States are allocated very large costs and others incur no costs at all.

These estimates illustrate that both the regional and State-by-State costs of control depend on the way in which emissions reductions are allocated to States. Therefore, the choice of allocation policy involves both the **political** issue of who should bear the burden of reducing emissions as well as the national **economic** issue of total cost.

A later section of this appendix (A.4) discusses an alternative method of allocating control costs. A trust fund based on a tax on emissions or electricity generation could be established to help pay for part of the costs of

Table A-8.—Fossil-Fuel-Fired Electric Utilities: SO₂ Emissions, Electricity Generated, Average SO₂ Emission Rate, 1980

State	Utility SO$_2$ emissions		Electricity generation (fossil-fuel-fired)		SO$_2$ emission rate	
	10^3 tons/yr	Rank (top 30)	10^9 kWh/yr	Rank (top 30)	lb/MMBtu	Rank (top 30)
Alabama	543.1	12	45.4	17	2.3	12
Alaska................	11.7		2.6		0.6	
Arizona	87.5	27	27.0	20	0.6	
Arkansas	26.6		10.2		0.5	
California	77.9		89.6	4	0.2	
Colorado..............	77.5		21.2	28	0.7	
Connecticut	32.1		12.6		0.5	
Delaware	52.5		6.7		1.5	21
District of Columbia......	4.6		0.7		1.0	
Florida	725.9	10	79.0	5	1.7	18
Georgia...............	736.7	9	50.5	14	2.9	7
Hawaii................	41.6		6.5		1.2	28
Idaho.................	0.0		0.0		0.0	
Illinois................	1,125.6	5	75.7	6	2.7	9
Indiana	1,539.6	2	70.1	8	4.2	2
Iowa	231.3	18	18.3		2.2	13
Kansas	150.1	23	25.1	22	1.0	
Kentucky	1,007.5	6	54.2	12	3.6	5
Louisiana	24.8		45.8	16	0.1	
Maine	16.3		2.1		1.4	24
Maryland..............	223.2	19	20.0	30	2.1	14
Massachusetts	275.5	17	31.6	19	1.8	16
Michigan	565.4	11	57.9	11	1.8	16
Minnesota	177.4	21	21.0	29	1.5	21
Mississippi............	129.2	24	18.5		1.3	27
Missouri	1,140.5	4	48.4	15	4.5	
Montana	23.4		5.5		0.7	
Nebraska	49.5		9.3		1.0	
Nevada	39.5		11.7		0.6	
New Hampshire	80.5	30	5.1		2.9	7
New Jersey	110.2	26	22.1	27	0.9	
New Mexico...........	84.6	28	24.6	23	0.6	
New York	480.3	14	63.2	9	1.4	24
North Carolina..........	435.4	15	60.8	10	1.5	21
North Dakota...........	82.5	29	11.8		1.2	28
Ohio	2,171.6	1	108.1	3	3.8	3
Oklahoma.............	37.7		43.3	18	0.2	
Oregon	3.3		0.8		0.7	
Pennsylvania	1,466.1	3	109.7	2	2.5	11
Rhode Island	5.2		1.0		1.0	
South Carolina	213.1	20	21.5	26	1.9	15
South Dakota...........	28.6		2.8		1.7	18
Tennessee	933.7	8	51.0	13	3.7	4
Texas	302.8	16	201.9	1	0.3	
Utah	22.1		11.3		0.4	
Vermont	0.5		0.0		1.2	28
Virginia...............	163.7	22	21.9	25	1.4	24
Washington	69.4		7.3		1.7	18
West Virginia...........	944.2	7	70.4	7	2.7	9
Wisconsin	485.7	13	26.0	21	3.4	6
Wyoming	120.9	25	22.8	24	1.0	
National totals.........	17,378.5		1,754.4		1.9	

SOURCE: E. H. Pechan & Associates, Inc., "Estimates of Sulfur Oxide Emissions From the Electric Utility Industry," prepared for the Environmental Protection Agency, 1982.

Table A-9.—SO₂ Emission Reductions Achieved by Emission Rate Limitations
(percent reduction in 1980 utility SO₂ emissions)

State	SO₂ emissions (10³ tons)	Percent reduction with emission limit (lb SO₂/MMBtu)						
		1.0	1.2	1.5	2.0	2.5	3.0	4.0
Alabama	543	57	49	38	24	11	4	0
Alaska	12	51	44	37	25	12	0	0
Arizona	88	0	0	0	0	0	0	0
Arkansas	27	5	2	0	0	0	0	0
California	78	0	0	0	0	0	0	0
Colorado	77	1	0	0	0	0	0	0
Connecticut	32	0	0	0	0	0	0	0
Delaware	52	37	30	20	7	0	0	0
District of Columbia	5	0	0	0	0	0	0	0
Florida	726	50	44	34	23	16	10	3
Georgia	737	65	58	48	32	17	6	0
Hawaii	42	31	22	9	0	0	0	0
Idaho	0	3	0	0	0	0	0	0
Illinois	1,126	67	63	58	50	42	34	20
Indiana	1,540	76	72	66	55	45	35	19
Iowa	231	58	51	47	39	31	24	12
Kansas	150	53	47	38	23	8	5	0
Kentucky	1,008	72	66	58	45	36	28	15
Louisiana	25	0	0	0	0	0	0	0
Maine	16	29	15	9	4	0	0	0
Maryland	223	54	46	35	18	4	0	0
Massachusetts	276	44	36	24	6	0	0	0
Michigan	565	48	39	31	20	10	1	0
Minnesota	177	42	34	25	14	5	0	0
Mississippi	129	58	53	45	32	19	9	0
Missouri	1,141	78	74	68	59	51	43	28
Montana	23	11	6	0	0	0	0	0
Nebraska	49	21	14	5	0	0	0	0
Nevada	39	0	0	0	0	0	0	0
New Hampshire	80	65	58	48	30	20	11	0
New Jersey	110	37	32	24	17	11	6	0
New Mexico	85	13	0	0	0	0	0	0
New York	480	51	44	34	18	8	3	0
North Carolina	435	32	19	4	0	0	0	0
North Dakota	82	24	13	3	0	0	0	0
Ohio	2,172	74	69	62	51	41	32	19
Oklahoma	38	0	0	0	0	0	0	0
Oregon	3	0	0	0	0	0	0	0
Pennsylvania	1,466	62	55	45	30	17	8	0
Rhode Island	5	0	0	0	0	0	0	0
South Carolina	213	50	42	30	12	2	0	0
South Dakota	29	40	29	13	0	0	0	0
Tennessee	934	73	67	59	49	40	30	16
Texas	303	10	4	0	0	0	0	0
Utah	22	0	0	0	0	0	0	0
Vermont	1	17	5	0	0	0	0	0
Virginia	164	27	15	4	0	0	0	0
Washington	69	41	29	12	0	0	0	0
West Virginia	944	64	57	50	39	29	19	7
Wisconsin	486	72	67	60	50	40	31	13
Wyoming	121	11	6	1	0	0	0	0
United States	17,379	61	55	47	36	27	19	10

SOURCE: E. H. Pechan & Associates, Inc., "Estimates of Sulfur Oxide Emissions From the Electric Utility Industry," prepared for the Environmental Protection Agency, 1982.

Table A-10.—Statewide Average Cost of Reducing Utility SO₂ Emissions by 50 Percent
(dollars/ton SO₂ removed, 1982 dollars)

Alabama	300-500
Arkansas	>1,500
Connecticut	>1,500
Delaware	750-1,000
District of Columbia	>1,500
Florida	350-450
Georgia	400-550
Illinois	250-350
Indiana	150-200
Iowa	100-250
Kentucky	300-450
Louisiana	1,000-1,500
Maine	1,000-1,500
Maryland	550-600
Massachusetts	950-1,000
Michigan	300-450
Minnesota	500-700
Mississippi	250-300
Missouri	<150
New Hampshire	500-600
New Jersey	700-800
New York	700-800
North Carolina	750-900
Ohio	200-300
Pennsylvania	450-500
Rhode Island	>1,500
South Carolina	450-800
Tennessee	<150
Vermont	—[a]
Virginia	900-1,100
West Virginia	450-500
Wisconsin	<150
31-State region	320-410

[a]$/ton costs not estimated.

SOURCE: Office of Technology Assessment, based on analyses by E. H. Pechan & Associates, Inc.

Table A-11.—Regional Costs of Alternative Approaches to Allocating an 8-Million-Ton Reduction in SO₂ Emissions (Eastern 31-State control region, all costs in 1982 dollars)

Allocation approach[b]	SO₂ reduction (million tons/yr)	Regional costs[a] (billions of dollars/yr)	($/ton)
I. Allocation based on *utility* SO₂ emissions:			
1. 50% reduction	8	2.3-2.9	320-410
2. 1.5 lb/MMBtu rate limitation	8	1.8-2.3	255-325
3. Lower of:			
1.2 lb/million Btu rate limitation or 50% reduction	7.5	1.8-2.4	275-370
4. 1.3 lb/million Btu average	8	1.8-2.4	260-340
5. 11 lb/MWhr (total) average	8	1.9-2.5	270-350
II. Allocation based on *total* SO₂ emissions:			
1. 35% reduction	7.6	2.6-3.1	385-465
2. 16 tons/square mile	8	3.7-3.9	560-585
3. 200 lb/person	8	2.6-3.0	370-415

[a]Costs are calculated on the basis of emissions reductions below SIP compliance levels.
[b]Alternative approaches explained in text.

SOURCE: Office of Technology Assessment, based on analyses by E. H. Pechan & Associates, Inc.

Table A-12.—Emissions Reductions Required by Alternative Allocation Approaches

	I: Formulae based on utility SO$_2$ emissions (percent below 1980 emissions)										II: Formulae based on total SO$_2$ emissions (percent below 1980 emissions)					
	50% reduction		1.5 lb/MMBtu cap		Lower of: 1.2 lb/MMBtu cap, 50% reduction		1.3 lb/MMBtu avg.		11 lb/MWhr avg.		35% reduction		16 tons/mi^2		200 lb/person	
State	Utility	Total	Utility	Total	Utility	Total	Utility	Total	Utility	Total	Utility	Total	Utility	Total	Utility	Total
Alabama	50	35	38	27	48	35	42	30	20	14	48	35	4	3	65	46
Arkansas	50	13	35	9	35	9	35	9	35	9	>100	35	35	9	35	9
Connecticut	50	22	0	0	0	0	0	0	0	0	78	35	0	0	0	0
Delaware	50	24	44	21	44	21	44	21	44	21	73	35	>100	70	90	43
District of Columbia	50	15	0	0	0	0	0	0	15	4	>100	35	>100	93	0	0
Florida	50	33	34	22	43	28	24	16	26	17	52	35	21	14	16	10
Georgia	50	43	47	41	50	43	53	47	51	44	39	35	0	0	38	33
Illinois	50	38	58	44	50	38	51	39	47	36	45	35	50	38	27	21
Indiana	50	38	65	50	50	38	67	52	72	55	45	35	93	71	90	69
Iowa	50	35	46	32	50	35	40	28	46	32	49	35	0	0	15	10
Kentucky	50	44	58	52	50	44	62	56	66	59	38	35	47	42	71	64
Louisiana	50	4	0	0	0	0	0	0	0	0	>100	35	0	0	0	0
Maine	50	8	8	1	15	2	8	1	0	0	>100	35	0	0	0	2
Maryland	50	33	34	22	45	30	38	25	20	13	53	35	75	50	4	16
Massachusetts	50	40	24	19	35	28	25	20	27	22	43	35	77	61	20	0
Michigan	50	31	31	19	39	24	28	17	25	15	56	35	0	0	0	0
Minnesota	50	34	24	16	33	23	13	9	2	1	51	35	0	0	0	0
Mississippi	50	22	44	20	50	22	0	0	20	9	77	35	0	0	24	11
Missouri	50	43	67	59	50	43	69	61	73	64	39	35	16	14	67	59
New Hampshire	50	43	47	41	50	43	53	46	57	49	40	35	3	3	3	3
New Jersey	50	19	24	9	32	12	0	0	0	0	88	35	>100	55	0	0
New York	50	25	33	17	43	22	7	3	1	0	68	35	31	16	1	2
North Carolina	50	36	4	2	18	13	11	8	8	6	48	35	0	0	3	2
Ohio	50	41	62	50	50	41	65	53	69	57	42	35	91	75	69	56
Pennsylvania	50	36	44	32	50	36	48	34	51	37	48	35	88	64	54	39
Rhode Island	50	17	0	0	0	0	0	0	0	0	>100	35	0	0	0	0
South Carolina	50	32	29	19	41	27	32	21	0	0	53	35	0	0	6	4
Tennessee	50	43	59	51	50	43	63	55	61	53	40	35	43	37	63	54
Vermont	50	3	0	0	4	0	0	0	0	0	>100	35	0	0	0	0
Virginia	50	22	3	1	15	6	5	2	2	1	77	35	2	1	2	1
West Virginia	50	43	49	43	50	43	51	44	56	49	40	35	74	64	90	78
Wisconsin	50	38	60	45	50	38	60	46	55	42	45	35	0	0	32	25
Eastern 31-States	50	37	50	37	47	35	50	37	50	37	48	35	50	37	50	37

SOURCE: Office of Technology Assessment, based on analyses by E. H. Pechan & Associates, Inc.

Table A-13.—Costs of Alternative Allocation Approaches
(estimated percentage increase in residential electricity rates, assuming all emissions reductions from utilities)

	50% reduction (utility)	1.5 lb/MMBtu cap	1.2 lb/MMBtu cap or 50% reduction	1.3 lb/MMBtu average	11 lb/MWhr average	35% reduction (total)	16 tons/Mi²	200 lb/person
Alabama	***	*	**	*	*	**	—	****
Arkansas	*	—	*	—	—	***	—	—
Connecticut	*	—	—	—	—	**	—	—
Delaware	*	*	*	*	*	****	******	*****
D.C.	******	—	—	—	****	******	******	—
Florida	***	*	**	*	*	***	*	*
Georgia	*****	*****	*****	*****	*****	****	—	****
Illinois	**	***	**	***	**	**	**	******
Indiana	***	****	***	*****	*****	***	******	******
Iowa	**	*	**	*	*	**	—	*
Kentucky	***	****	***	*****	****	*****	***	*****
Louisiana	*	—	—	—	—	*****	—	—
Maine	**	*	*	*	—	*****	—	—
Maryland	***	**	**	**	*	***	*****	—
Massachusetts	**	*	*	*	*	**	*****	—
Michigan	***	*	**	*	*	***	—	—
Minnesota	***	**	**	—	*	****	—	*
Mississippi	**	*	**	—	—	****	*	—
Missouri	**	****	**	****	****	*	*	****
New Hampshire	****	****	****	****	****	****	—	*
New Jersey	*	*	*	—	—	****	*****	—
New York	*	*	*	*	—	***	*	—
North Carolina	****	*	**	*	*	****	—	*
Ohio	****	*****	****	*****	*****	***	******	****
Pennsylvania	***	***	***	***	***	***	******	****
Rhode Island	****	—	—	—	—	*****	—	—
South Carolina	****	*	***	*	—	****	—	*
Tennessee	*	*	*	**	*	*	*	**
Vermont	*	—	—	—	—	*	—	—
Virginia	***	*	*	*	*	*****	******	******
West Virginia	*****	*****	*****	*****	*****	****	******	******
Wisconsin	*	*	*	*	*	*	—	*
31-State region	2.4-3.1%	1.9-2.5%	1.9-2.6%	2.0-2.6%	2.0-2.6%	2.8-3.3%	4.0-4.2%	2.8-3.2%

—	= No reduction required
*	= 0–2%
**	= 1–3%
***	= 2–4%
****	= 3–6%
*****	= 5–10%
******	= > 10%

SOURCE: Office of Technology Assessment, based on analyses by E. H. Pechan and Associates, Inc.

control. Costs could then be distributed to a larger group than those required to reduce emissions under each of the scenarios discussed below.

Key aspects of each allocation approach—including its rationale, costs, and distributional consequences—are outlined below.

1. **Equal percentage reduction in each State—utility emissions only.**

    Description: Each State is required to reduce its utility SO₂ emissions by an equal percentage.

    Rationale: Requiring an equal percentage reduction in utility SO₂ emissions distributes **relative** emissions reductions fairly uniformly among States.

Formula for achieving an 8-million-ton reduction: Eliminating 50 percent of 1980 utility emissions in each of the Eastern 31 States.

Cost: Reducing utility SO₂ emissions by 50 percent in each State is estimated to cost $2.3 to $2.9 billion annually, at an average cost of $320 to $410 per ton of SO₂ removed (1982 dollars).

Distributional consequences: This formula requires an equal percentage reduction from each State regardless of: 1) the relative costs of emissions control, or 2) the stringency of the State's existing emissions regulations. Five States—Arkansas, Connecticut, Louisiana, Maine, and Rhode Island—would not be able to reduce utility emissions by the necessary 50 percent without setting extremely stringent emission rate limitations (less than 0.4 lb/MMBtu of SO_2).

2. **Utility emission rate limitation (limiting emissions per fuel burned).**
Description: This approach sets some maximum emissions limits (an emissions "cap") for each fossil-fuel electric-generating plant. In this case, the limit is an emissions rate specifying the amount of allowable emissions per quantity of fuel burned.
Rationale: Setting an emissions cap would require emissions reductions in States with powerplants emitting over a certain rate. It would thus target States with plants emitting large quantities of SO_2 per quantity of fuel burned, but not penalize States simply for generating large quantities of electricity.
Formula for achieving an 8-million-ton reduction: Limiting emissions rates for all plants in the Eastern United States to 1.5 lb of SO_2 per MMBtu of fuel burned.
Cost: Estimated annual costs under this approach are $1.8 to $2.3 billion, at an average cost of $255 to $325/ton.
Distributional consequences: The largest costs and percentage reductions are distributed to States whose plants emit relatively large amounts of pollutants per unit of energy consumed—e.g., Missouri, Indiana, Ohio, and Tennessee. States with plants emitting at low rates (usually through the use of less polluting fuels, e.g., oil and natural gas)—e.g., Louisiana, Arkansas, and Connecticut—are allocated the smallest reductions.

3. **Utility emission rate limitation, with a maximum reduction of 50 percent below current utility emissions.**
Description: This approach modifies the cap approach by limiting any State's required reductions to 50 percent of 1980 utility emissions.
Rationale: By placing a ceiling on reductions, this approach reduces the impact on those States most heavily targeted under a cap approach. It reduces regional variations in cost by setting a maximum relative reduction requirement for all States.
Formula for achieving a 7.5-million-ton reduction: A cap of 1.2 lb of SO_2 per MMBtu, with a maximum reduction of 50 percent below 1980 emissions for each State. An alternative method of stating the formula is a 50-percent reduction in a State's 1980 utility emissions, but requiring no existing source to reduce emissions below 1.2 lb of SO_2 per MMBtu. Thus, the formula achieves less than the 8-million-ton reduction of the first allocation approach.

Cost: This approach is estimated to cost between $1.8 and $2.4 billion per year, at an average cost of $275 to $370/ton.
Distributional consequences: By placing a limit on percentage reductions, this approach lessens the impact on States required to reduce the most under a cap approach. The States that benefit by this approach as compared to a simple emissions cap are Indiana, Kentucky, Missouri, and Ohio.

4. **Average utility emissions per fuel burned.**
Description: Each State is required to achieve a specified **average** utility emissions rate. Under this averaging approach, some plants within a State are allowed to exceed the specified emissions rate (unlike the cap case) as long as the State has compensating plants emitting below the rate.
Rationale: Unlike the cap, the average emission rate approach gives credit to States with plants emitting below the specified emissions rate.
Formula for achieving an 8-million-ton reduction: Each State is required to eliminate sufficient emissions to achieve a statewide utility emissions average of 1.3 lb of SO_2 per MMBtu of fuel burned (based on 1980 emissions).
Cost: This strategy is estimated to cost $1.8 to $2.4 billion per year at an average cost of $260 to $340/ton.
Distributional consequences: Emissions reductions are allocated in a manner similar to the cap case. States in which a substantial number of plants emit at rates below the specified average (e.g., New York, Minnesota, and Misissippi) would tend to prefer the average rate approach over the cap; States in which most plants emit at rates well above the average used for allocation (e.g., Missouri and Kentucky) would tend to favor the cap over the average (assuming that identical regional reductions are required).

5. **Average utility emissions per total electricity ouput.**
Description: This approach allocates emissions reductions on the basis of the amount of SO_2 emitted per unit of electricity generated by **all** plants, including hydroelectric and nuclear powerplants.
Rationale: Allocating emissions reductions on the basis of **total** electricity generation gives credit to those States that generate electricity with fuels that do not produce SO_2 emissions.
Formula for achieving an 8-million-ton reduction: States are required to reduce utility emissions to meet an average rate of 11 lb of SO_2 per megawatt-hour of **total** electricity output.
Cost: This approach is estimated to range in cost from $1.9 to $2.5 billion annually, at an average cost of $270 to $350/ton of SO_2 reduced.

Distributional consequences: This approach favors States in which relatively high proportions of electricity produced by hydroelectricity or nuclear power—e.g., Alabama, Maine, Maryland, Minnesota, and New York.

6. **Equal percentage reductions in each State—total SO₂ emissions.**

Description: Each State is required to reduce total SO_2 emissions (i.e., emissions from all sectors, not just utility emissions) by an equal percentage from some baseline level.

Rationale: Each State participates equally in reducing aggregate emissions.

Formula for achieving a 7.6-million-ton reduction: Each State reduces total 1980 SO_2 emissions by 35 percent.

Cost: This approach is estimated to cost $2.6 to $3.1 billion annually, at an average cost of $385 to $465/ton of SO_2 removed.

Distributional consequences: This allocation formula requires an equal percentage reduction in each State regardless of relative costs of emissions control or stringency of the State's existing emissions regulations. Those States: 1) with the highest proportion of emissions from sources that are difficult to control (e.g., certain industrial processes and small residential, commercial, or industrial boilers), and 2) that have relatively low SO_2 emission rates, would incur the highest per-ton costs. This includes such States as Louisiana, Maine, Rhode Island, and Virginia.

7. **Total emissions per land area.**

Description: This approach is based on emissions densities, i.e., the amount of SO_2 emitted per unit of land area. Emissions densities are calculated from an area's **total** emissions, rather than just its utility emissions.

Rationale: To the extent that acid deposition is produced by local sources, limiting the density of SO_2 emissions would help to limit the amount of sulfur deposited in the surrounding area.

Formula for achieving an 8-million-ton reduction: Reductions are allocated by setting a maximum average emissions density of 16 tons of SO_2 per square mile.

Cost: This approach would cost $3.7 to $3.9 billion per year, at an average cost of $560 to $585/ton of SO_2 removed.

Distributional consequences: The States with the highest emissions densities, and thus the largest proportional reductions and costs under this approach, are Delaware, D.C., Indiana, Massachusetts, Ohio, Pennsylvania, and West Virginia.

8. **Total emissions per person.**

Description: Emissions reductions are calculated on the basis of the amount of pollution emitted per person residing in the State. Reductions are based on the region's **total** emissions, not just utility emissions.

Rationale: Giving credit to States with lower emissions-to-population ratios takes into account a wide range of factors, including reliance on clean fossil fuel combustion, non-SO_2-emitting electricity generation, higher energy efficiency, and presence of fewer SO_2-producing industrial activities.

Formula for achieving an 8-million-ton reduction: Reductions are allocated according to an average rate of 200 lb of SO_2 per capita.

Cost: The costs of this approach are estimated to range from $2.6 to $3.0 billion annually, with an average cost of $370 to $415/ton of SO_2 reduced.

Distributional consequences: Those States with a relatively high proportion of total SO_2 emissions to the population supported by emissions-generating activities (both industrial and electricity generation) are allocated the largest reductions. These States include Indiana, Kentucky, Missouri, Ohio, Tennessee, and West Virginia.

Comparison of Utility Estimates of Emissions Reductions Costs to Various Regional-Model Estimates

The Edison Electric Institute (EEI) requested its member utilities to estimate the cost of implementing a control proposal reported by the Senate Committee on Environment and Public Works during the 97th Congress (S.3041, reintroduced as S.768 during the 98th Congress). The acid rain control sections of this bill would require eliminating about 9 million to 10.5 million tons of SO_2 per year in the Eastern 31-State region—8 million tons per year allocated to States based on utility SO_2 emission rates and an additional 1 million to 2.5 million tons per year to offset expected emissions growth by 1995.* (S.768 was subsequently amended to require an additional 2-million-ton emissions reduction.)

---

*The amount by which a State must reduce its SO_2 emissions was determined by the following formula: Calculate the difference between a State's 1980 utility emissions and the emissions that would result if no electric-generating plant in that State emitted SO_2 at a rate greater than 1.5 lb/MMBtu. Repeat this calculation for the Eastern 31-State region as a whole. The State's proportion of the total regional difference, multiplied by 8 million tons, is the amount of SO_2 emissions that must be eliminated in that particular State. Any additional growth in emissions due to new facilities or increased use of existing ones by 1995 must also be offset.

Twenty-four utilities responded, accounting for about 3.5 million tons (about 45 percent) of the 8-million-ton reduction specified by the bill.[42] Table A-14 compares these cost estimates to regional model-based estimates prepared for EPA[43] and OTA.* In general, the utilities projected higher costs than the model-based statewide averages. The OTA estimates are typically higher than the EPA estimates. There are several reasons for these differences. First, some of the utilities surveyed have higher SO_2 emissions rates than the statewide average. As a result, these utilities will have higher emissions reduction costs than the statewide averages estimated by the models.

Second, EEI, EPA, and OTA used different accounting procedures. One major difference is the number of years over which capital costs are averaged. The EEI estimates reported in table A-14 are averaged ("levelized") over 5 years;* both EPA and OTA average capital costs over time periods equivalent to the life of the facility (about 20 years). The shorter averaging time makes the utility estimates of annual costs somewhat higher.

The estimates also make different assumptions about scrubber costs, low-sulfur coal prices, and the choice of control method. Some utilities project scrubber capital costs about equal to the average costs assumed by the models (about $150 to $250 per kilowatt of generating capacity); however, several estimate costs almost twice as high. EEI assumes that most of the emissions reduction would occur through scrubbing, whereas the model used by EPA projects that most emissions reductions would be achieved by fuel-switching at a considerable cost savings over scrubbing. The OTA model calculates a fairly even mix of scrubbing and fuel-switching to achieve the required emissions reductions, with costs typically between the EPA and utility estimates.

Overview of Model Used in Cost Analyses

OTA's cost estimates are based on a computer model that calculates the cost of reducing emissions at each major utility generating unit in the 31-State region

[42]National Economic Research Associates, Inc., "A Report on the Results From the Edison Electric Institute Study of the Impacts of the Senate Committee on Environment and Public Works Bill on Acid Rain Legislation" (S.768), 1983.

[43]ICF, Inc., "Analysis of a Senate Emission Reduction Bill" (S.3041). Prepared for EPA, 1983.

*OTA's cost estimates are from the AIRCOST model, E. H. Pechan & Associates. These estimates include the costs of emissions reductions required to offset future emissions growth, based on projections prepared for the United States-Canada Memorandum of Intent, the Edison Electric Institute, and EPA.

*EEI also reports utility estimates of rate increases based on first-year revenue requirements; though typically about 25 percent higher than the 5-year averages, these are not representative of average costs for the life of the program.

(about 2,000 units in about 900 powerplants). For each unit, the model determines the combination of emissions reduction measures that minimizes the costs of complying with a series of alternative emissions rate limitations, ranging from SIP compliance to a 0.4 lb SO_2/MMBtu limit. Emissions reduction opportunities are then ranked on the basis of costs per ton of SO_2 removed. For each alternative rate limitation, the model considers the costs of the following control options for each **unit:**

For coal-fired powerplant emissions:
- blending presently used coals with low-sulfur coals,
- switching to low-sulfur coals,
- physical coal cleaning to reduce the sulfur contents of presently used coals,
- installing dry scrubbers in conjunction with either current or alternative coal types, and
- installing wet scrubbers in conjunction with either current or alternative coal types.

For plants burning residual oil:
- switching to a lower sulfur oil.

These results are in turn used to generate State and regional cost estimates of various emissions reduction measures. These costs can be calculated in two ways:

1. **State Least Cost:** Reduction opportunities are selected in ascending order of per-ton costs **within each State** until the reduction target is achieved. Trading of emissions reductions among sources is allowed within States, but not among States. This approach assumes a "perfect market" for the exchange of emissions reductions obligations throughout the State and provides a lower bound model estimate.

2. **Plant Cap:** Each plant is required to comply with a specified emissions limit. This approach to estimating costs chooses the least-cost approach at each plant, but assumes no trading of reduction obligations among plants or States.

The cost model considers only SO_2 emissions **from utilities.** No estimates of the cost of reducing emissions of NO_x, nor estimates for controlling SO_2 or NO_x from the industrial sector, are calculated. Furthermore, **existing** utilities are the only sources considered, and are assumed to be operating at their current level of capacity utilization. The OTA analysis assumes that all reductions occur immediately, without accounting for new plants being built, or old plants being retired. Finally, the model does not include the following possible control alternatives:

1. early retirement of major sources,
2. energy conservation,
3. selective use of lower emitting plants, and
4. advanced control technologies.

In calculating cost increases, OTA's model assumes that each plant chooses the most cost-effective method of reducing emissions. However, State regulatory poli-

Table A-14.—Comparison of Estimates of Residential Electricity Rate Increases
(8-million-ton SO₂ reduction program, plus offsets for future growth)

I. Utilities located in single States			
Florida:	Florida Power & Light Co.		5%
	Tampa Electric Co.		23%
	Statewide averages	EPA: 2–3%, OTA:	3–7%
Illinois:	Illinois Power Co.		18%[b]
	Central Illinois P.S.		21%
.	Statewide averages	EPA: 1–2%, OTA:	2–11%
Indiana:	Public Service Indiana		25%
	Indianapolis P. & L.		26%[b]
	Statewide averages	EPA: 7–8%, OTA:	8–13%
Massachusetts:	New England Power Co.		4%
	Statewide averages	EPA: 1%, OTA:	0–5%
Michigan:	Detroit Edison		12%
	Statewide averages	EPA: 2–4%, OTA:	2–6%
Missouri:	Union Electric Co.		18%
	Statewide averages	EPA: 5–7%, OTA:	8–21%
North Carolina:	Duke Power Co.		4%
	Statewide averages	EPA: 1–2%, OTA:	2–5%
Ohio:	Cincinnati G. & E.		14%
	Statewide averages	EPA: 6–7%, OTA:	8–12%
Pennsylvania:	Pennsylvania Electric		20%
	Pennsylvania P. & L.		10%
	Statewide averages	EPA: 3–5%, OTA:	3%
Wisconsin:	Wisconsin Power & Light		11.3%
	Wisconsin Electric Power		12.3%
	Statewide averages	EPA: 5–6%, OTA:	11–12%

II. Multi-State utilities:

Florida, Georgia, Mississippi:

The Southern Company		12%	
Statewide averages:		EPA	OTA
	FL	2–3%	3–7%
	GA	4–5%	9–12%
	MS	3%	5–20%

Virginia, West Virginia

VEPCO		6%	
Statewide averages:		EPA	OTA
	VA	1–2%	2–7%
	WV	5–6%	10–13%

Indiana, Kentucky, Michigan, Ohio

American Electric Power (AEP)		18% (6–38%)[b]	
Statewide averages:		EPA	OTA
	IN	7–8%	8–13%
	KY	4–6%	5–9%
	MI	2–4%	2–6%
	OH	6–7%	8–12%

[a]Estimates are for a control program requiring SO₂ emissions reductions in the Eastern 31-State region such that 1995 emissions are 8 million tons below 1980 levels. Emission limits for each State are allocated by a 1.5 lb SO₂/MMBtu emission rate limitation for utilities. Including reductions to offset future growth, about 9 to 10.5 million tons of SO₂ per year must be eliminated from existing sources.

[b]For these utilities, about one-third to one-half of capital costs are for new utility construction to replace prematurely retired plants, or to compensate for electricity losses due to scrubbers.

SOURCE: Compiled by Office of Technology Assessment. See text for references.

cies can affect this choice—and hence the costs—in ways not treated by the model. For example, in most States, "automatic fuel adjustment clauses" allow utilities to pass on increased fuel costs due to fuel-switching to consumers within a few months. However, for emissions controls requiring capital investment, such as scrubbers, most States require utilities to wait until the equipment becomes operational before charging ratepayers. This practice may create a bias against capital investment in pollution control equipment in utility management decisionmaking, and increase a plant's lifetime control costs.

The model used by OTA also assigns all control costs to the State whose utility owns the facilities required to reduce emissions. The accuracy of this assumption depends on the policy chosen for allocating costs. To relieve utilities or States that are allocated particularly large emissions reductions, costs could be shared by electricity consumers in other areas.

A.4 ALTERNATIVE TAX STRATEGIES TO HELP FUND ACID RAIN CONTROL

Several acid rain control bills introduced during the 98th Congress proposed establishing a trust fund to help finance the costs of emissions reductions for controlling acid deposition. The proposals were based on one of two alternative approaches for raising revenues: a tax on pollutant emissions, or a tax on electricity generation. Each of these approaches could be implemented in several ways.

This section considers two alternative **pollution** taxes: 1) a tax on both sulfur dioxide (SO_2) and nitrogen oxides (NO_x), and 2) a tax on SO_2 emissions only. Both apply to nationwide pollutant emissions. The section analyzes the distribution of the two taxes by emissions source, and the electricity portion of the tax by State, and compares them to two **electricity-based** approaches: 1) a tax on total electricity generation, and 2) a tax on nonnuclear electricity generation.

All four tax schemes are possible alternatives to requiring those sources that must reduce emissions to pay the entire costs of control. Funds raised by a tax can be used to pay part or all control costs. A pollution tax would apportion control costs to a larger group of emitters, not just those required to reduce emissions. However, because so few sources are actually monitored, such an approach would be administratively complex. An electricity tax would also distribute control costs to a larger group of emitters, but is not directly related to actual emissions. However, because electricity generation is carefully monitored, this approach would be much easier to implement.

The analyses presented below are approximate, intended to illustrate the relative distribution of costs for raising an arbitrary $5 billion per year under each approach. The actual amount of the tax, and to some extent the distribution of the tax, varies with each specific control plan and trust-fund design.

Distribution of Emissions, Tax Rates, and Tax Revenues by Source

About 90 to 95 percent of the Nation's manmade SO_2 emissions originate from utility and industrial sources. About 95 percent of the Nation's manmade NO_x emissions originate from utility, industrial, and transportation sources. Emissions from these sectors can be considered the potentially "taxable" pollutant inventory (though in practice assessing emissions from all sources in each category with sufficient accuracy for tax purposes would be difficult). Emissions from residential, commercial, and other small dispersed sources are not considered taxable for this analysis.

For example, to raise $5 billion per year, by deriving two-thirds of the revenues from SO_2 and one-third from NO_x emissions,* the tax must be set at about $135/ton of SO_2 and $85/ton of NO_x emitted. A tax on SO_2 emissions alone must be set at about $200/ton. These rates are based on 1980 taxable emissions; revenues from a fixed tax rate would increase as emissions increase, and would decrease if acid rain control legislation were enacted. To raise $5 billion per year through taxes on electricity generation, the following rates must be set: 2.2 mills/kWh for all electricity generated and 2.5 mills/kWh for nonnuclear electricity only. Total revenues in future years would follow changes in electricity demand.

Table A-15 displays each sector's contribution to an acid rain control trust fund based on the above rates. The two-pollutants tax (i.e., on both SO_2 and NO_x) would raise about $2.8 billion (55 percent) from utilities, about $1.4 billion (30 percent) from industry, and

---

*About twice as much precipitation acidity currently originates from sulfur compounds as from nitrogen compounds in the Eastern United States.

Table A-15.—Annual Contribution to Acid Rain Control Trust Fund From Alternative Tax Approaches (billions of dollars/yr, see text for explanation of alternative taxes)

	Emissions tax (before control– 1980 emissions)		Emissions tax (after control– 1995 emissions)		Electricity tax	
	SO_2 & NO_x	SO_2 only	SO_2 & NO_x	SO_2 only	Total electricity	Nonnuclear electricity
Electric utilities...........	2.8	3.5	1.8	1.6	5.0	5.0
Industry	1.4	1.5	1.6	1.8	0.0	0.0
Transportation	0.8	0.0	0.9	0.0	0.0	0.0
Total United States......	5.0	5.0	4.3	3.4	5.0	5.0

SOURCE: Office of Technology Assessment, based on data from Emissions, Costs and Engineering, Work Group 3B, United States-Canada Memorandum of Intent on Transboundary Air Pollution, June, 1982 and the Statistical Year Book of the Electric Utility Industry, Edison Electric Institute, 1980.

$0.8 billion (15 percent) from transportation sources. If only SO_2 were taxed, about 70 percent of the fund would come from utilities and about 30 percent from industry.

The third and fourth columns in table A-15 estimate tax revenues in 1995 **after** a hypothetical acid rain control program, assuming that the tax rates remain unchanged. Utility SO_2 emissions in the Eastern 31 States are assumed to be 10 million tons below 1980 levels. All other emissions are assumed to grow at rates calculated from emissions projections developed under the *United States-Canada Memorandum of Intent on Transboundary Air Pollution*. The share of annual trust fund revenues derived from utilities would decline to about 40 percent of the total for the two-pollutants tax, and to about 45 percent of the total for the SO_2 tax. Because total nationwide pollutant emissions decline, the total tax collected drops by 15 and 30 percent, respectively.

A tax on electricity generation (either total or nonnuclear) is assumed to come entirely from the utility sector (i.e., industrial generation of electricity for internal use is not taxed).

Geographic Distribution of Electricity Rate Increases

Table A-16 presents State-by-State costs of the alternate tax approaches for the **electric utility sector only.** Costs to industry are often borne by consumers from a much larger area than the State in which the industry is located, since many manufactured goods are distributed nationwide. A tax on mobile source emissions (e.g., a sales or registration tax) would be distributed on a roughly per-capita basis.

The large variation in current pollution emission rates among utility plants would cause a **pollution tax** to distribute costs unevenly both within a State and from State to State. As shown in table A-16, though a pollution tax to raise $5 billion per year would increase average residential electricity rates by about 2 percent, State-average increases would range from virtually no increase to about 9 percent. Because utilities emit a larger share of nationwide SO_2 than NO_x emissions, electricity rate increases are typically somewhat lower for a tax on both SO_2 and NO_x emissions (col. 1) than on SO_2 emissions only (col. 2).

Assuming that emissions reductions are achieved,* Eastern States would experience smaller rate increases due to the pollution tax in 1995 (cols. 3 and 4) than in 1980. Western-State rate increases would be higher in 1995 than in 1980 due to projected increased emissions. The tax rate is assumed to be indexed to inflation, so that rate changes shown in 1995 are due solely to emissions changes and not to changes in the price of electricity.

The last two columns of table A-16 estimate residential rate increases from a **fixed kilowatt-hour tax on all electricity,** and on nonnuclear electricity, generated in each State. State-to-State variations are due solely to differences in the average electricity rate currently paid by consumers in each State. Large percentage increases imply low current rates for electricity. Nationwide, the rate increases from a tax on electricity generation are greater than for a pollution tax under which a significant share of the total $5 billion per year tax comes from other sectors. However, in several Midwestern States (e.g., Indiana, Kentucky, Missouri, and Ohio) with high rates of pollutant emissions, an electricity tax would be less costly than an emissions tax during the years before emissions reductions are achieved.

---

*Eastern 31-State utility SO_2 emissions in 1995 are assumed to be 10 million tons below 1980 levels. Reductions in each State are allocated based on utility SO_2 emissions in excess of 1.2 lb/MMBtu of fuel burned.

Table A-16.—50-State Taxes Raising $5 Billion per Year During the Early 1980's

	Average residential electricity rate increase (percent) from alternative tax approaches					
	Emissions tax (before control– 1980 emissions)		Emissions tax (after control– 1995 emissions)		Electricity tax	
	SO_2 & NO_x	SO_2 only	SO_2 & NO_x	SO_2 only	Total electricity	Nonnuclear electricity
Alabama	2.0	2.5	1.3	1.2	4.0	3.1
Alaska	0.9	1.4	1.2	1.8	4.0	4.4
Arizona	0.7	0.7	1.0	0.9	3.1	3.5
Arkansas..............	0.6	0.5	0.5	0.3	4.4	3.0
California	0.2	0.2	0.3	0.2	3.0	3.3
Colorado	1.3	1.2	1.7	1.5	3.7	4.0
Connecticut	0.3	0.3	0.3	0.3	2.5	1.5
Delaware	1.4	1.8	1.0	1.0	2.4	2.7
District of Columbia......	2.2	2.7	2.3	2.7	4.5	5.0
Florida...............	1.7	2.2	1.2	1.2	3.1	2.9
Georgia	3.5	4.5	1.8	1.7	4.2	4.1
Hawaii	0.8	1.1	1.1	1.4	1.8	2.0
Idaho	0.0	0.0	0.0	0.0	8.2	9.2
Illinois	2.9	3.6	1.5	1.2	3.6	2.9
Indiana	5.9	7.7	2.3	1.8	3.8	4.3
Iowa..................	3.0	3.5	1.9	1.6	3.6	3.6
Kansas	1.8	2.0	2.4	2.6	3.7	4.1
Kentucky..............	5.7	7.3	2.6	2.2	4.5	5.0
Louisiana	0.5	0.2	0.6	0.2	4.2	4.7
Maine.................	0.4	0.6	0.4	0.6	3.3	1.6
Maryland..............	1.8	2.3	1.1	1.2	3.6	2.6
Massachusetts..........	1.6	2.1	1.1	1.3	2.9	2.9
Michigan	2.5	3.0	1.9	1.7	4.3	3.8
Minnesota.............	1.8	2.0	1.6	1.3	3.8	2.9
Mississippi	2.1	2.6	1.3	1.1	4.0	4.5
Missouri	6.6	8.8	2.3	1.9	4.1	4.6
Montana	0.9	0.9	1.3	1.1	6.4	7.2
Nebraska..............	1.3	1.3	1.7	1.7	4.7	3.4
Nevada	1.0	0.9	1.4	1.1	3.9	4.4
New Hampshire	2.9	3.6	1.6	1.4	2.9	3.3
New Jersey	0.8	0.9	0.7	0.6	2.6	2.1
New Mexico	1.0	0.9	1.3	1.2	2.9	3.3
New York..............	0.7	0.9	0.4	0.5	2.1	2.0
North Carolina	1.8	2.1	1.7	1.7	3.7	3.9
North Dakota	1.9	2.0	2.5	2.6	4.1	4.6
Ohio..................	4.5	5.9	1.9	1.6	3.3	3.6
Oklahoma	0.6	0.3	0.9	0.5	4.5	5.0
Oregon	0.1	0.1	0.1	0.1	7.2	6.9
Pennsylvania	2.7	3.5	1.5	1.5	3.1	3.2
Rhode Island	1.3	1.5	1.5	1.5	3.0	3.3
South Carolina	1.4	1.7	1.0	0.9	3.6	2.4
South Dakota	1.1	1.1	1.4	1.4	3.6	4.1
Tennessee	5.3	7.0	2.2	2.0	4.9	5.5
Texas.................	0.7	0.5	0.9	0.7	3.7	4.1
Utah..................	0.8	0.6	1.1	0.8	3.6	4.1
Vermont	0.1	0.0	0.1	0.0	3.5	0.9
Virginia	1.2	1.4	1.1	1.2	3.3	2.5
Washington	0.5	0.7	0.7	0.9	9.5	10.5
West Virginia	4.1	5.1	2.3	2.0	4.2	4.7
Wisconsin..............	4.1	5.2	1.9	1.5	4.4	3.6

SOURCE: Based on data from Emissions, Costs and Engineering, Work Group 3B, United States-Canada Memorandum of Intent, June 1982, and the Statistical Year Book of the Electric Utility Industry, Edison Electric Institute, 1980.

A.5 OTHER EMISSION SECTORS

This section addresses major nonutility sources of SO_2 and NO_x emissions. It presents estimates of current emissions, potential emissions reductions, and control costs, where possible, for: 1) industrial and large commercial boilers, 2) industrial process emitters (e.g., smelters and petroleum refineries), and 3) mobile sources. Together, these source categories account for approximately 30 to 35 percent of SO_2 and 65 to 70 percent of NO_x emissions in the continental United States.

In general, data needed to estimate emissions from these sources are scanty and of questionable accuracy. In addition, emissions control methods, particularly for industrial processes, are in earlier stages of development than for utilities. Consequently, the estimates of emissions, potential emissions reductions, and estimated control costs presented in this section are subject to greater uncertainty than those presented earlier for the utility sector.

Industrial and Commercial Boilers

Industrial and large-commercial boilers emitted about 3.5 million tons of SO_2 in 1980; table A-17 provides State-by-State emissions estimates for these sources. Two estimates are presented; one is calculated from State-level fuel deliveries, the other from data reported to EPA.[44] Though the national totals are quite close, the difference at the State-level is often quite large. Largest emitting States were New York (about 350,000 to 450,000 tons), Ohio (about 300,000 to 400,000 tons), and Pennsylvania (about 250,000 to 300,000 tons); nine additional States had nonutility boiler emissions greater than about 100,000 tons of SO_2 per year.

Table A-17 also indicates the percentage of this sector's 1980 emissions that would have to be eliminated under various emission rate limitations. In comparison to the utility sector, SO_2 emission rates from industrial and commercial boilers are relatively low. Thus, control strategies based on emission rate limitations would reduce emissions from this sector by a smaller proportion than comparable controls on the utility sector. For example, an emission rate limitation of 1.5 lb of SO_2 per million Btu would eliminate slightly over a quarter of this sector's 1980 emissions (slightly under 1 million tons of SO_2 annually); an identical cap on utility emissions would eliminate slightly less than half of that sector's SO_2 emissions (about 8 million tons of SO_2 annually).

The lower SO_2 emission rates from nonutility boilers are due to the lower sulfur content of the fuels burned. A 1979 Department of Energy (DOE) survey[45] found that natural gas (which emits almost no SO_2) supplied about 32 percent of the energy requirements of industrial boilers. Coal and oil each accounted for about 17 percent of boiler fuels (as compared to 58 and 12 percent, respectively, of fuels used by utilities). The remainder came from such fuels as wood, bark, coke oven gas, and paper-pulping liquor.

Many nonutility boilers are capable of burning a wide variety of fuel types. Thus, if emissions controls were required for nonutility boilers, reductions in SO_2 emissions could be met by substituting lower sulfur fuels or even changing fuel types. Boilers currently burning high-sulfur oil might switch to low-sulfur oil. Natural gas, which accounted for over 30 percent of commercial and industrial boiler fuel use in 1979, might also be substituted, Federal and State regulations permitting.

For boilers equipped to burn coal, available strategies for reducing emissions include switching to lower sulfur coal, and cleaning exhaust gases with scrubbers. Switching to low-sulfur oil or gas may be possible in many cases, but would probably not be as cost effective as low-sulfur coal. Table A-18 estimates per-ton costs associated with three fuel-switching and two scrubber-installation scenarios.

Industrial Processes*

Industrial processes are estimated to account for approximately 15 to 20 percent of the SO_2 emitted nationwide and about 7 to 12 percent of those emitted in the Eastern 31-State region of the United States. Less than 5 percent of U.S. NO_x emissions came from industrial processes. Data on emission rates for individual sources are scanty. Moreover, relatively little literature is available on the technical feasibility and costs of controlling emissions from these sources. Consequently, emissions and control cost estimates are subject to greater uncertainty than those associated with utility, industrial, and commercial boiler operations. A study produced for OTA by Energy & Resource Consultants, Inc., provides preliminary estimates of SO_2 emissions and control costs for five major industrial sectors: 1) pulp and paper,

[44]Data are from EPA's National Emission Data System, analyzed for OTA by E. H. Pechan & Associates, Inc.

[45]U.S. Department of Energy, Energy Information Administration, "Survey of Large Combustors: Report on Alternative-Fuel Burning Capabilities of Large Boilers in 1979," DOE/EIA-0304.
*This subsection is based primarily on: "An Assessment of Reducing Emissions in Five Critical Industries for the Purpose of Acid Deposition Mitigation," Energy & Resource Consultants, Inc., contractor report submitted to the Office of Technology Assessment, 1982.

Table A-17.—Potential SO₂ Reductions From Nonutility Boilers

State	Nonutility boiler SO₂ emissions (thousand tons/yr)		Percent reduction in emissions with emission limit (lb/MMBtu)				
	U.S./Canada[a]	NEDS[b]	1.0	1.2	1.5	2.0	2.5
Alabama	86	119	51	44	35	23	15
Arizona	9	4	32	29	27	22	15
Arkansas	32	7	0	0	0	0	0
California	56	153	15	6	3	2	1
Colorado	24	19	16	13	10	6	5
Connecticut	34	14	1	1	1	1	1
Delaware	26	20	3	2	1	0	0
District of Columbia	8	14	11	4	2	1	0
Florida	97	97	48	41	31	17	9
Georgia	44	66	56	48	38	22	10
Idaho	11	5	22	16	8	0	0
Illinois	188	111	45	40	34	26	19
Indiana	290	129	59	53	45	35	28
Iowa	57	56	72	67	59	47	35
Kansas	11	0	0	0	0	0	0
Kentucky	66	32	52	46	41	33	27
Louisiana	76	78	13	11	10	7	6
Maine	65	93	59	51	38	19	2
Maryland	56	23	0	0	0	0	0
Massachusetts	58	33	0	0	0	0	0
Michigan	154	122	50	43	35	26	21
Minnesota	44	49	47	38	26	14	7
Mississippi	48	46	0	0	0	0	0
Missouri	55	17	40	35	28	20	15
Montana	25	9	80	77	71	65	60
Nebraska	4	4	34	29	20	11	6
Nevada	2	2	15	10	5	0	0
New Hampshire	10	20	51	43	29	7	0
New Jersey	74	78	0	0	0	0	0
New Mexico	2	9	58	53	48	40	33
New York	334	455	14	7	5	3	2
North Carolina	116	130	47	37	24	7	1
North Dakota	13	5	32	19	9	4	4
Ohio	310	403	70	66	61	53	46
Oklahoma	15	13	32	27	20	8	5
Oregon	25	14	0	0	0	0	0
Pennsylvania	254	314	12	11	10	7	6
Rhode Island	8	4	7	0	0	0	0
South Carolina	84	76	45	35	22	8	1
South Dakota	3	2	19	13	6	0	0
Tennessee	83	97	50	44	37	27	21
Texas	106	121	5	3	1	0	0
Utah	16	16	27	18	7	1	0
Vermont	5	2	39	30	17	0	0
Virginia	142	129	49	40	27	10	1
Washington	41	28	24	18	13	9	7
West Virginia	84	94	57	50	41	31	22
Wisconsin	107	150	60	55	49	38	30
Wyoming	30	32	45	36	24	7	2
National totals	3,491	3,514	37	32	26	18	13

SOURCES: Office of Technology Assessment, based on: [a]Emissions, Costs and Engineering Assessment, Work Group 3B, United States-Canada Memorandum of Intent on Transboundary Air Pollution, June 1982; and [b]EPA's National Emissions Data System.

Table A-18.—Representative Costs for Reducing SO₂ Emissions From Coal-Fired Industrial Boilers

Industrial strategies	$/ton SO₂ removed (1982 dollars)
Shift from high[a]- to low[b]-sulfur coal ..	$ 250–$550
Shift from high- to medium[c]-sulfur coal..........................	300–500
Shift from medium- to low-sulfur coal..........................	400–1,000
Shift from unscrubbed high to scrubbed high sulfur[d]	800–1,000
Shift from unscrubbed medium to scrubbed medium sulfur[d]	1,200–2,000

[a]About 3 to 5 lb SO₂/MMBtu.
[b]About 1.5 to 2.5 lb SO₂/MMBtu.
[c]About 0.8 to 1.3 lb SO₂/MMBtu.
[d]Based on the costs of retrofitting a scrubber on a 170 MMBtu/hr coal-fired industrial boiler.

SOURCE: Analysis of Senate Emission Reduction Bill (S-3041). Report prepared for EPA by ICF, Inc., 1983.

2) cement, 3) sulfuric acid production, 4) iron and steel, and 5) nonferrous metal smelting. Emissions estimates (but not control costs) are also presented for petroleum refining.

Table A-19 presents estimates of SO₂ emissions from these six industries: 1) by EPA region for the 31 Eastern States, 2) for the remainder of the United States, and 3) for the Nation overall. In nearly all cases, SO₂ emissions have been estimated indirectly, by applying an **emissions factor** to estimated plant production or production capacities derived from industry surveys. For the cement and pulp and paper industries, in particular, the wide variability in potential emissions per unit of production capacity leads to a range of emissions estimates. Estimates for the iron and steel industry are derived from actual output levels, and are presented for years of differing iron and steel production, to illustrate the effects of production levels on emissions. Where available, estimates of emissions calculated for other studies are also included to further demonstrate the significant uncertainties in these estimates.

Production processes for five of these industries were examined in some detail to determine how much SO₂ could feasibly be eliminated from their emissions, and at what cost. As presented in table A-20, rough estimates show that about 1 million tons of SO₂ could be eliminated from process emissions in the Eastern 31-State region, at widely differing cost levels. Slightly more than half these emissions—primarily from sulfuric acid plants and coke ovens—could be eliminated at average costs of $500/ton or less; an additional 300,000 tons might be eliminated from cement plant emissions at an average cost of approximately $1,000/ton. However, estimates of potential emissions reductions, and associated costs, for several of these industries are based on tech-

nologies that are theoretically feasible but not commercially proven. The computation methods used to derive cost estimates mask significant variations from plant to plant within each industry; only in the pulp and paper industry was sufficient information available to present a range of per-ton cost estimates, based on differences in plant sizes, economies of scale, and differing production processes in use—the average per-ton cost of control is estimated to be $2,600, ranging from $450 to $14,800/ton of SO₂ removed.

Only the cement industry, of the five surveyed, was found to emit substantial quantities of NO$_x$—approximately 120,000 tons in the Eastern 31-State region, and 80,000 tons in the Western portion of the United States.

Mobile Sources*

Automobiles and other mobile sources produce substantial amounts of two pollutants, NO$_x$ and hydrocarbons (HC). NO$_x$ and HC are the primary pollutants that react in the atmosphere to form ozone and other oxidants. NO$_x$ can also be converted to nitrates, a component of acid deposition.

Many recent studies suggest that ozone and ozone precursors (NO$_x$ and HC) are transported long distances. The highest concentrations of ozone do not necessarily occur where emissions densities are greatest (i.e., in cities), but, because of chemical transformations over time, at locations that are several hours downwind.

The extent to which mobile sources contribute to acid deposition is uncertain. Tailpipe emissions may not disperse sufficiently to reach the mixing layer of the atmosphere, where they are readily transported and transformed into acid compounds. However, mobile sources have been linked to increases in acid deposition in urban areas, e.g., the Los Angeles Basin.[46]

Current Emissions: Mobile sources account for major portions of both NO$_x$ and HC emissions nationwide, and a very small portion of SO₂ emissions. As of 1978, mobile sources contributed 40 percent of national NO$_x$ emissions (10.3 million tons), approximately 38 percent of total HC emissions (11.8 million tons), and 3 percent of national SO₂ emissions (0.9 million tons).[47]

Of NO$_x$ emissions from mobile sources, approximately 40 percent came from automobiles, 10 percent

---

*This subsection is based on: M. P. Walsh, "Motor Vehicle Emissions of Nitrogen Oxides," contractor report submitted to the Office of Technology Assessment, 1981.

[46]PEDCo Environmental, Inc., and Faul W. Spaite Co., *Perspective on the Issue of Acid Rain*, DOE contract No. DE-AC21-81MC16361, June 1981.

[47]*National Air Pollutant Emission Estimates, 1970-1978*, Office of Air Quality Planning and Standards, U.S. Environmental Protection Agency, EPA-450/4-80-002, January 1980.

Table A-19.—SO₂ Emissions From Industrial Processes (estimates for 1980 in thousand tons/yr)

EPA region	Pulp and paper[a,c]	Cement[a]	Sulfuric[a,b] acid	Iron and steel Coke[a] ovens only	Iron and steel Total[a,b]	Petroleum[b] refineries	Copper[a] smelting
I	7 (3–15)	3 (2–4)	1	4	—	0	0
II	7 (3–17)	36 (24–52)	8–22	7	20	42	0
III	10 (4–22)	84 (57–130)	12–22	66	165	79	0
IV	63 (23–140)	96 (58–120)	130–270	15	36	29	7
V	6 (3–15)	110 (75–160)	16–37	68	180	170	72
VI (partial)	18 (7–40)	13 (8–18)	39–83	0	0	105	0
VII (partial)	1 (1–4)	63 (43–95)	5–11	1	1	8	0
Eastern 31-States	110 (43–250)	410 (270–580)	210–450	160	250–400	430	79
West	26 (17–57)	240 (150–310)	53–160	16	23–26	565	1,380
United States total	150 (66–340)	650 (410–890)	263–610	180	280–400	1,000	1,460

NOTE: Summed estimates have slight discrepancies from combining several sources of data.

SOURCES:

[a]Energy and Resource Consultants, Inc., "Background Documentation SO$_x$ and NO$_x$ Emissions From Five Industrial Process Categories," OTA contractor report, 1982.

[b]Work Group 3B, "Emissions, Costs and Engineering Assessment." Report prepared under the Memorandum of Intent on Transboundary Air Pollution signed by the United States and Canada, 1982.

[c]Mitre Corp. estimates published in "Background Document on SO$_x$ and NO$_x$ Emissions From Five Industrial Process Categories." States within EPA regions: I—Maine, Vermont, Massachusetts, New Hampshire, Connecticut, Rhode Island; II—New York, New Jersey; III—Pennsylvania, Maryland, Delaware, West Virginia; IV—Florida, Kentucky, Tennessee, North Carolina, South Carolina, Mississippi, Alabama, Georgia; V—Minnesota, Wisconsin, Indiana, Ohio, Michigan; VI—Arkansas, Louisiana; VII—Iowa, Missouri.

**Table A-20.—Potential SO₂ Emissions Reductions and Control Costs
for Industrial Processes**

	Pulp and paper	Cement	Sulfuric acid	Coke[a] ovens	Other iron[a] and steel	Copper[b] smelting
Total United States						
Current emissions (10³ tons)	150	650	610	230	120	1,460
Potential emissions reductions (10³ tons)	130[c]	520[d]	510[e]	185[f]	27[g]	350[h]
Eastern 31 States						
Potential emissions reductions (10³ tons)	110	330	360	170	24	0
$/ton	2,600[i]	1,000	550	300	>3,000	—
West						
Potential emissions reductions (10³ tons)	20	190	150	15	3	350
$/ton	2,600[i]	1,000	500	300	>3,000	200

[a]Emissions estimates for the iron and steel industry are based on 1976 production levels rather than 1980 levels due to the depressed production rates in 1980.
[b]Emissions estimates for copper smelting assume that all smelters still operational are producing at near-full capacity.
[c]Assumes that exhaust gases from recovery boilers are scrubbed with a removal efficiency of 85 percent.
[d]Assumes that wet scrubbers are installed on cement kilns, with an 80-percent removal efficiency. This is not a commercially proven technology.
[e]Assumes sodium sulfite scrubbing to achieve a 3 lb/ton of acid emissions limit.
[f]Assumes coke oven gas desulfurization with 90-percent removal efficiency.
[g]Assumes that wet scrubbers are installed on sinter plants with a 90-percent removal efficiency.
[h]Based on the use of double contact acid plants at the Phelps-Dodge Ajo and Douglas smelters in Arizona.
[i]Estimates range from $450 to $14,800/ton.

SOURCE: Energy and Resource Consultants, Inc., OTA contractor report, 1982.)

from light-duty trucks, 25 percent from heavy-duty trucks, and 25 percent from other mobile sources such as trains and off-highway vehicles. Of HC emissions, 60 percent came from automobiles, somewhat greater than 10 percent each for light- and heavy-duty trucks, and 15 percent from other mobile sources. State-level estimates of NO_x emissions from mobile sources are shown in table A-2; NO_x emissions from highway vehicles alone—about 75 percent of total mobile source emissions—are presented in table A-21.

Trends in Highway Vehicle Emissions

Since 1940, nationwide NO_x emissions have approximately tripled; a fourfold increase in the number of motor vehicles since 1945 contributed significantly to this dramatic growth rate.[48] In addition, NO_x emissions per mile driven increased during the late 1960's and early 1970's, due to the technologies used to implement the first generation of HC and carbon monoxide (CO) emissions control standards. Between 1970 and 1978, HC emissions from highway vehicles decreased

by about 10 percent, from 11.3 million to 10.2 million tons, while NO_x emissions increased by 25 percent, from 5.8 million to 7.4 million tons.[49]

During the same period, vehicle miles traveled in the United States increased by about 37 percent, showing some decline in NO_x emission rates due to controls mandated by the Clean Air Act. Since the late 1970's, overall amounts of NO_x emissions from motor vehicles have also begun to decrease slightly as the proportion of NO_x-controlled vehicles in the United States increases.

To estimate future NO_x emissions levels for highway vehicles, OTA has projected three alternative travel scenarios for 1995: a no-growth, a low-growth, and a medium-growth case. Estimates of vehicle-miles traveled under the three scenarios were then used to project nationwide 1995 NO_x emissions from highway vehicles under a variety of control standards. Table A-22 summarizes the effects of the various growth cases and emissions standards on 1995 NO_x emissions projections.

Two cases have been selected from among the 18 projected emissions levels to represent a likely lower and upper bound for emissions estimates. The lower-bound

[48]*Nitrogen Oxides*, National Academy of Sciences, 1977, and *MVMA Motor Vehicle Facts and Figures '81*, September 1981.

[49]*National Air Pollutant Emissions Estimates, 1970-1978*, U.S. Environmental Protection Agency, EPA-450/4-80-002, January 1980.

Table A-21.—1980 U.S. NO$_x$ Emissions From Highway Vehicles (10^3 tons)

Eastern region		Western region	
State	NO$_x$	State	NO$_x$
Alabama	127	Alaska	13
Arkansas	74	Arizona	87
Connecticut	87	California	696
Delaware	20	Colorado	87
District of		Hawaii	20
Columbia	13	Idaho	33
Florida	328	Kansas	74
Georgia	194	Montana	27
Illinois	281	Nebraska	54
Indiana	174	Nevada	27
Iowa	80	New Mexico	47
Kentucky	120	Oklahoma	120
Louisiana	100	Oregon	80
Maine	33	South Dakota	27
Maryland	13	Texas	482
Massachusetts	154	Utah	40
Michigan	281	Wyoming	20
Minnesota	120		
Mississippi	74		
Missouri	154		
New Hampshire	27		
New Jersey	221		
New York	341		
North Carolina	187		
Ohio	321		
Pennsylvania	308		
Rhode Island	27		
South Carolina	107		
Tennessee	147		
Vermont	13		
Virginia	127		
West Virginia	54		
Wisconsin	147		
31 + D.C. total	4,454	West total	1,934
		U.S. total	6,388

SOURCE: Michael P. Walsh, "Motor Vehicle Emissions of Nitrogen Oxides," OTA contractor report, Nov. 30, 1981.

Table A-22.—1995 Highway Vehicle NO$_x$ Emission Projections

Emissions standards			1995 nationwide emissions (1,000 tons)		
Auto[a]	Light truck[a]	Heavy truck[b]	No growth	Low gowth[c]	Medium growth[d]
1.0	1.2	1.7	3,067	3,759	4,767
1.0	1.2	4.0	3,633	4,608	5,725
1.0	1.2	6.0	4,104	5,287[a]	6,487
1.5	1.7	6.0	4,764	6,052	7,514
2.0	2.3	10.7	5,868	7,469	9,193[b]
None	None	None	7,950	9,880	12,438

[a]Grams/mile.
[b]Grams/brake horsepower-hour.
[c]Low growth:
  Autos and light trucks grow 1% per year.
  Heavy gasoline trucks decline 2% per year.
  Heavy diesel trucks grow 4% per year.
[d]Medium growth:
  Autos and light trucks grow 3% per year.
  Heavy gasoline trucks decline 2% per year.
  Heavy diesel trucks grow 5% per year.

SOURCE: Michael P. Walsh, "Motor Vehicle Emissions of Nitrogen Oxides," OTA contractor report, Nov. 30, 1981.

scenario assumes low growth, retention of the 1.0 gram per mile (gpm) automobile standard currently in effect for 1981 and later model cars, and a tightening of light- and heavy-duty truck standards to 1.2 gpm and 6.0 grams per brake horsepower-hour respectively, as the 1977 Clean Air Act Amendments require. By 1995, this would result in a 21-percent reduction from current NO_x mobile-source emissions.

The upper-bound scenario assumes medium growth, retention of the current light- and heavy-truck standards rather than any tightening, and a rollback of the automobile standard to 2.0 gpm. This would result in a 37-percent increase in NO_x mobile-source emissions over 1980. Assuming a low-growth scenario with these same emissions standards would result in only a 12-percent NO_x increase over 1980 levels.

Costs of Automobile Emissions Controls

Estimates of the costs and fuel-economy implications of emissions controls are highly controversial. The Bureau of Labor Statistics has estimated that between 1975 and 1979, pollution control devices have increased the cost of new automobiles by about $165—approximately 10 percent of the total cost increase for new cars during the same 5 years. EPA and manufacturers' estimates of the costs[50] of meeting statutory automobile emission standards of 0.4 gpm HC, 3.4 gpm CO, and 1.0 gpm

NO_x are presented in table A-23. Control cost estimates vary widely; the General Motors' (GM) estimate of $720/car is about double that of EPA, and is 50 percent higher than Ford's. Differences in technology among manufacturers, and the difficulty of allocating the costs of multipurpose components to particular objectives (e.g., emissions reductions, as opposed to the resulting improvements in fuel economy or vehicle performance), probably account for a substantial amount of the variation. The differences narrow when NO_x controls are looked at alone: Ford, EPA, and Chrysler show only a $27/vehicle spread in estimates of savings associated with a change in standards from 1 to 2 gpm NO_x—ranging from $48 to $75/vehicle. GM's estimate is still substantially higher, at $188/vehicle.

Inspection and maintenance (I/M) programs offer an alternative approach to reducing NO_x emissions from mobile sources. A recent study concluded that adding NO_x testing to an existing I/M program for HC and CO would add about $4/inspected vehicle, and that having 20 percent of the vehicles repaired (at an average cost of $50 each) could result in about a 10-percent reduction in NO_x emissions.[51] An EPA analysis concluded that the cost-effectiveness of an I/M program for NO_x control would range from $400 to $500/ton of NO_x eliminated if added to an existing HC/CO program, or $1,700 to $2,700/ton if started up exclusively for NO_x control.[52]

---

[50]"The Cost of Controlling Emissions of 1981 Model Year Automobiles," U.S. Environmental Protection Agency, June 1981; testimony by Michael Walsh before the Health and Environment Subcommittee, U.S. House of Representatives, Sept. 21, 1981; and letter from Betsy Ancker-Johnson, General Motors to Douglas Costle, U.S. Environmental Protection Agency, Sept. 22, 1980.

[51]"A Study of the Relationship Between Motor Vehicle Emissions and Attainment of National Ambient Air Quality Standards," Part 1: Nitrogen Dioxide, SRI International, February 1981.

[52]Internal EPA memo, Tom Cackette to Michael P. Walsh, Jan. 9, 1981.

Table A-23.—Costs of Emissions Controls for Automobiles

Autos	Cost differential per vehicle: 1983 cars v. uncontrolled[a]	NO_x costs per vehicle: 1 gpm v. uncontrolled[b]	NO_x costs per vehicle: 1 v. 2 gpm
EPA	370[c]	$123	50
Ford	500	167	48[d]
GM	725	242	188
Chrysler	—	—	75

[a]1983 car costs are based on emissions standards of 0.41 HC/3.4 CO/1.0 NO_x grams per mile.
[b]Assumes that emission control costs of 1983 cars are equally divided between HC, CO, and NO_x.
[c]EPA estimates that this would drop to $330 by 1988 as systems are refined.
[d]Assumes that 60 percent of cost estimated by Ford for CO, high altitude and NO_x control—$80 per car—is attributable to NO_x control. This is a high estimate, based on Chrysler's estimate that 60 percent of its costs for CO and NO_x control is due to NO_x alone.
SOURCE: Michael P. Walsh, "Motor Vehicle Emissions of Nitrogen Oxides," OTA contractor report, Nov. 30, 1981.

A.6 POTENTIAL SECONDARY ECONOMIC EFFECTS OF EMISSIONS CONTROL PROGRAMS

Emissions controls and the associated costs are likely to have the greatest effects on three sectors of the economy: high-sulfur coal mining, industries that depend heavily on electricity consumption, and the electric utility industry. This section discusses ways in which these industries might be affected by a major program to reduce sulfur dioxide (SO_2) emissions in the Eastern United States.

Potential effects on the coal industry are quantified on the basis of several hypothetical SO_2 emissions reduction scenarios; qualitative estimates of the degree of vulnerability are provided for electricity-intensive industries and the electric utility industry. However, it should be noted that both the degree and nature of the potential impact on these sectors would depend on the type and magnitude of the chosen control program, the way in which reductions are allocated, and the way in which control costs are allocated. Thus, the discussions provided below are intended to give only a general indication of these sectors' relative vulnerability to the effects of emissions controls.

Coal Production and Related Employment

Coal Reserves and Current Production

Many legislative proposals for controlling acid rain have focused on reducing SO_2 emissions in the Eastern United States. Emissions reductions designed to control acid rain might cause significant shifts in the coal market by increasing the value of low-sulfur coals as compared to high-sulfur coals. Because the sulfur content of coal varies from region to region throughout the United States, any emission reduction strategy that relies even in part on "switching" to lower sulfur coals can potentially affect the regional distribution of coal production and employment. Social dislocations could accompany these changes in the coal market, as some areas experience rapid economic growth while others decline.

Figure A-6 shows the location of the Nation's coal deposits. Three factors influence regional coal **production** from these reserves: 1) mine-mouth prices (the cost of production), 2) transportation costs (the distance between the mine and the consumer), and 3) fuel characteristics (primarily a coal's energy value and sulfur con-

tent).[53] Acid rain control measures would affect the existing production patterns by increasing the value of low-sulfur coal relative to high-sulfur coal, all other factors remaining equal.

Table A-24 displays the distribution of each State's coal reserves by sulfur content category. Figure A-7 shows a distinctive difference in the sulfur content of coal reserves between the Eastern and Western United States. A large majority (74 percent) of coal reserves in the Eastern United States are high in sulfur (greater than 2.0 pounds per million Btu (lb/MMBtu) of SO_2). By contrast, the majority (72 percent) of Western reserves are low in sulfur (less than 1.2 lb/MMBtu). The two significant Eastern exceptions to this pattern are Kentucky and West Virginia, both of which have significant quantities of reserves above and below 1.2 lb/MMBtu.

Table A-25 displays each State's coal production for the utility market. The first column presents each State's coal production, in millions of tons, **for the utility market** in 1980. The second column shows what proportion of that production would not allow utilities to comply with a 1.2 lb/MMBtu SO_2 emission limit without applying control technologies. The third column presents the percentage of this "noncompliance" coal sold on the spot market, i.e., sales not covered by a long-term contract between a utility and a mining company. Noncompliance coal sold on the spot market is likely to be most vulnerable to more stringent SO_2 regulations. The final column shows the portion of noncompliance coal exported to other States—an indicator of the potential efficacy of State-level policies designed to minimize coal market disruptions.

---

[53]For a discussion of the factors affecting the choice of coal, see Congressional Budget Office, *The Utility Industry, the Coal Market, and the Clean Air Act,* April 1982; and Martin Zimmerman, *The U.S. Coal Industry: The Economics of Public Choice* (Cambridge, Mass.: MIT Press, 1981).

*The degree to which contracts constrain fuel-switching is a major uncertainty in this analysis. In 1980, 88.5 percent of coal purchased was purchased on contract. It is not clear whether changes in environmental regulations would absolve purchasers of their contractual obligations. A contract can contain provisions (e.g., "force majeure" clauses) which directly address the obligations of parties in the event of changes in environmental regulations. Buyer or seller could be relieved of all or part of the contractual obligations. See Scott, "Coal Supply Agreements," 23 *Rocky Mountain Law Institute* 107 (1979).

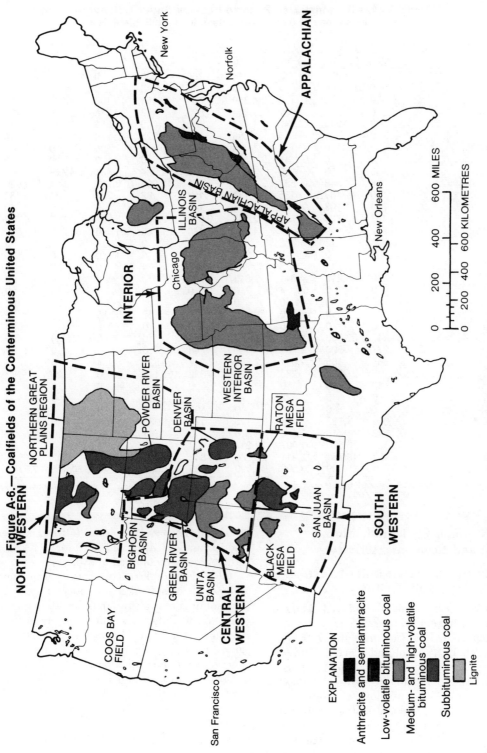

Figure A-6.—Coalfields of the Conterminous United States

EXPLANATION

Anthracite and semianthracite

Low-volatile bituminous coal

Medium- and high-volatile bituminous coal

Subbituminous coal

Lignite

SOURCE: P. Averitt, *Coal Resources of the United States, Jan. 1, 1974,* U.S. Geological Survey Bulletin 1412, at 5, 1975.

Table A-24.—Demonstrated Reserve Base by Sulfur Category
(quantities in millions of tons, sulfur categories in lb SO_2/MMBtu)

State	<0.9	0.9-1.2	1.3-1.5	1.6-2.0	2.1-3.0	3.1-4.0	4.1-5.0	5.1-6.0	>6.0	Total
Alabama	5	1,775	1,712	1,074	1,756	438	0	0	0	6,760
Georgia	0	0	4	0	0	0	0	0	0	4
Illinois	0	0	0	4,359	1,581	3,151	3,107	14,248	41,260	67,705
Indiana	0	212	992	1,304	503	453	2,018	1,976	3,161	10,621
Kentucky	0	10,210	3,846	1,473	410	749	1,556	7,524	8,472	34,240
Maryland	0	1	5	296	65	175	178	107	0	826
Michigan	0	0	0	0	95	0	26	0	7	128
North Carolina	0	0	11	0	0	0	0	0	0	11
Ohio	0	0	0	0	1,119	1,294	6,684	4,429	5,509	19,035
Pennsylvania	16	568	587	1,992	8,581	12,203	3,757	1,684	1,039	30,428
Tennessee	0	189	135	154	154	62	234	31	39	998
Virginia	784	1,469	458	561	148	118	0	0	0	3,538
West Virginia	3,407	13,724	2,932	2,791	6,029	3,084	3,535	355	4,128	39,985
Eastern U.S. total	4,212	28,149	10,681	14,005	20,440	21,726	21,096	30,353	63,616	214,277
Alaska	5,805	18	332	0	0	0	0	0	0	6,155
Arizona	0	0	0	399	25	0	0	0	0	424
Arkansas	0	11	23	260	43	74	0	0	0	411
Colorado	7,800	2,212	4,841	213	1,150	0	0	0	0	16,215
Idaho	0	0	4	0	0	0	0	0	0	4
Iowa	0	0	0	0	0	0	0	71	2,127	2,199
Kansas	0	0	0	0	0	190	123	210	472	995
Missouri	0	0	0	0	0	0	518	0	5,559	6,077
Montana	84,247	32,786	1,410	1	1,527	0	0	0	499	120,469
New Mexico	1,277	508	2,701	7	48	0	0	0	0	4,541
North Dakota	564	165	1,961	2,908	2,244	1,524	604	0	0	9,971
Oklahoma	8	750	280	26	332	144	0	21	83	1,644
Oregon	12	0	0	6	0	0	0	0	0	17
South Dakota	0	0	193	74	0	99	0	0	0	366
Texas	0	0	0	0	12,693	0	0	0	0	12,693
Utah	399	4,733	158	0	178	1,033	0	0	0	6,502
Washington	843	16	0	578	0	143	0	0	0	1,580
Wyoming	33,527	8,560	1,007	24,214	2,606	4	0	0	95	70,014
Western U.S. total	134,482	49,761	12,911	28,685	20,845	3,212	1,246	302	8,835	260,279
United States	138,694	77,909	23,592	42,690	41,285	24,938	22,341	30,655	72,451	474,556

SOURCE: Adapted for Office of Technology Assessment by E. H. Pechan & Associates from U.S. Department of Energy, Demonstrated Reserve Base of Coal in the United States on Jan. 1, 1979, DOE/EIA-0280(79), May, 1981.

Changes in Regional Coal Production, Employment, and Economic Activity

METHODS OF PROJECTING REGIONAL COAL PRODUCTION

This appendix projects regulation-induced changes in regional coal production using results from a computer model modified by ICF, Inc., from the DOE National Coal Model. ICF's Coal and Electric Utilities Model (CEUM) makes it possible to compare: 1) projected regional coal production in 1990 (and 2000) assuming that current SO_2 emissions standards are maintained, to 2) projected regional coal production in 1990 (and 2000) if significant SO_2 emissions reductions, designed to control acid rain, are required. The ICF model has been used to project the effects of acid rain control proposals by: the Environmental Protection Agency, the Department of Energy, the Edison Electric Institute, and the National Wildlife Federation, and

National Clean Air Coalition. ICF did not perform the model analyses discussed here for OTA, but for the other groups mentioned above.

CEUM is a "least-cost optimization model" that chooses the combination of scrubbers, coal washing, and low-sulfur coal substitution or blending that minimizes the utility industry's emissions reduction costs.[54] Changes in utility coal consumption patterns alter regional patterns of coal production. These projected production shifts form the basis for OTA's estimates.

This report uses four ICF SO_2 emissions reduction scenarios, and their attendant regional coal production scenarios, to analyze the potential magnitude of coal market impacts:

1. **Scenario I:** a 5-million-ton decrease in utility SO_2

---

[54]For a description of ICF's Coal and Electric Utilities Model see the executive summary in ICF, Inc., *Capabilities and Experience in the Coal and Electric Utility Industries*, May 1981.

Figure A-7.—Demonstrated Reserve Base by Sulfur Content

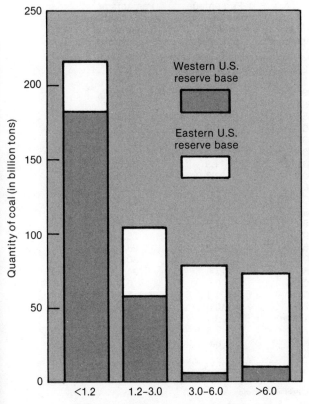

SOURCES: Office of Technology Assessment; and E. H. Pechan Associates, 1982.

emissions by 1990, allocated according to a "regional (31-State) least cost" approach;

2. **Scenario II:** a 10-million-ton reduction of SO_2 emissions by 1990, allocated according to utility emissions in excess of an emissions rate of 1.2 lb/MMBtu;

3. **Scenario III:** a 13-million-ton reduction by 1990, allocated according to a formula similar to (2) above; and

4. **Scenario IV:** a 10-million-ton reduction, allocated according to a "regional least cost" approach, showing regional coal production shifts out to 2000.[55]

---

[55]Scenario I was performed by ICF for DOE and EPA. See *Alternative Strategies for Reducing Utility SO_2 and NO_x Emissions,* draft report, September 1981. Scenarios II and III were performed by ICF for the Edison Electric Institute. See the EEI memo dated Feb. 8, 1982, on ICF analysis of the Mitchell Bill (S.1706). Scenario IV was performed by ICF for the National Wildlife Federation and National Clean Air Coalition. See *Cost and Coal Production Effects of Reducing Electric Utility Sulfur Dioxide Emissions,* Nov. 14, 1981.

The model cannot predict how various acid rain proposals would, in practice, be implemented. These scenarios merely illustrate the potential magnitude and direction of coal market shifts associated with various reductions in SO_2 emissions, when costs to the utility industry are minimized. Some analysts assert that the ICF model seriously underestimates the probable extent of fuel-switching, while others suggest that its fuel-switching estimates are overstated.*

In addition, changes in model assumptions cause future coal production estimates to vary considerably. OTA considers that the chosen scenarios reasonably represent the relative magnitude of fuel-switching and scrubber use.

Several important factors that might influence the accuracy of ICF's projections are:

- **Innovation in pollution control technology:** The likely extent of fuel-switching depends on the cost of that approach as compared to other emission reduction options. The ICF model reflects the best available estimates of current costs for various control options. If innovations were to significantly reduce the costs of control technology relative to fuel-switching, smaller changes in regional coal production would accompany any given level of emissions reductions.

- **Utility regulatory policy:** State regulatory policies may make certain emissions reduction options more attractive to utilities. For instance, provisions that allow utilities to pass increased fuel costs through to consumers without undergoing a rate hearing may make fuel-switching more attractive to utility managers than the ICF model would suggest.** The final section of this appendix addresses potential effects of State regulatory policies in greater detail.

- **Transportation costs:** Railroad rates govern the penetration of low-sulfur Western coal into Eastern and Midwestern utility markets. A rapid escala-

---

*For analyses asserting that ICF underestimates fuel-switching, see the testimony of Chris Farrand of Peabody Coal Co. on S.1706 to the Committee on Environment and Public Works, U.S. Senate, Oct. 29, 1981. If this is the case, the projections presented here have underestimated the magnitude of regional redistribution of production.

On the other hand, utility analyses of how this bill would be implemented for their systems show little evidence of potential coal market disruptions. An analysis by American Electric Power (the Nation's largest utility and coal consumer) states that only 4 of their 27 units would switch to lower sulfur fuels, while the others would retrofit scrubbers or be retired. See AEP, "Economic Impact Summary of Mitchell Bill (S.1706) on Customers of the AEP System," Feb. 23, 1982.

**Many public utility commissions do not allow utilities to earn a return on capital investment (e.g., a scrubber) until it becomes operational. Thus, because changes in fuel prices can be passed on immediately to consumers, utilities might prefer fuel-switching. This could be counteracted somewhat by provisions allowing utilities to earn cash returns on "construction work in progress" before the equipment becomes operational. The final section of this appendix surveys and discusses State regulatory policies for public utilities in the Eastern United States.

Table A-25.—Coal Production for the Domestic Utility Market

State	1980 production for utility market (millions of tons)	Percentage noncompliance[a]	Percentage noncompliance sold on spot market	Percentage noncompliance exported to other States
Alabama	15.8	82.5%	17.3%	10.1%
Arizona	10.5	0.0	0.0	0.0
Colorado	13.6	7.1	0.4	2.8
Illinois	53.4	99.9	6.6	66.0
Indiana	27.3	99.9	8.3	22.1
Iowa	0.4	95.9	14.5	0.0
Kansas	0.7	100.0	29.3	81.7
Kentucky	112.4	89.9	16.5	72.9
East	73.9	83.2	19.0	75.1
West	38.5	100.0	11.8	68.7
Maryland	1.2	100.0	22.8	24.7
Missouri	5.0	100.0	6.9	33.5
Montana	27.9	63.6	0.0	51.9
New Mexico	17.0	69.8	0.3	1.2
North Dakota	15.3	99.2	13.6	20.8
Ohio	34.3	100.0	18.9	26.5
Oklahoma	2.7	98.6	17.3	98.6
Pennsylvania	50.9	99.1	29.9	30.1
Tennessee	7.6	86.7	17.6	34.6
Texas	27.0	100.0	0.0	0.0
Utah	8.5	20.0	1.1	7.1
Virginia	13.8	87.5	10.6	71.0
West Virginia	53.1	81.3	8.1	39.4
North	30.8	97.8	7.5	46.1
South	22.3	58.5	8.8	30.1
Wyoming	89.7	16.6	0.9	9.9

[a]"Noncompliance" coal is defined as coal that would not permit utilities to comply with an emissions limit of 1.2 lb of SO_2/MMBtu without applying control technologies.

SOURCE: From DOE/EIA Form 423 data, supplied to OTA by E. H. Pechan & Associates.

tion in Western rail rates could raise the delivered price of Western coal, thereby reducing the magnitude of regional shifts.

• **Electricity growth rates:** While the rate of growth in electricity demand should not significantly affect the extent of fuel-switching as opposed to other control options, projected increases in the amount of coal produced by 1990 are highly dependent on assumptions about the rate of growth in electricity demand.

FORECASTING COAL MINE EMPLOYMENT AND ECONOMIC CHANGES

OTA combined production estimates from the ICF model with coal-miner productivity and income data to project the effects of acid rain control scenarios on regional employment and economic activity. Employment in the coal-mining industry is determined by two factors: the level of coal production (tons of coal) and the rate of worker productivity (tons of coal produced per miner). Historically, employment levels have been affected more by changes in productivity than by changes

in production.*** Therefore, employment forecasts must provide for uncertainties about future productivity levels. This analysis presents projected coal-mine employment changes as ranges reflecting different assumptions about future productivity levels: a lower bound of a 10-percent decline from 1979 productivity levels and an upper bound of a 30-percent increase.*

***Over the period 1960 to 1970, coal-mine employment **declined** from 190,000 to 144,000, a 3-percent average annual decrease. Over the same period, coal production **increased** from 434 million to 613 million tons, an average annual increase of 4 percent. The discrepancy between employment and production trends is accounted for by increases in average coal-miner productivity during this period. The average coal production per miner increased from about 12 to about 18.5 tons per day—an average annual increase of nearly 4 percent. The increasing proportion of surface mining—from 32 percent of annual production (or 139 million tons) in 1960 to 44 percent (or 270 million tons) in 1970 —accounts for some of the gains, since the average surface miner produces about three times as much coal per day as the average underground miner.

*These productivity ranges have been chosen somewhat arbitrarily. The 30-percent increase in productivity was chosen as one bound because it reflects the historical maximum. The 10-percent decrease was chosen to account for factors that may contribute to decreased productivity, such as more stringent mine health and safety or surface reclamation regulations, or a shift from surface to underground mining. After a steady decline over the past 12 years, productivity is finally beginning to rise again, but future trends are uncertain. For a discussion of factors affecting worker productivity in coal mining see Office of Technology Assessment, *Direct Use of Coal,* OTA-E-86, April 1979, ch. IV. See also Electric Power Research Institute, *The Labor Outlook for the Bituminous Coal Mining Industry,* EPRI EA-1477, final report, August 1980.

These employment projections are combined with miner income data to estimate the ''direct'' income effects of acid rain controls.

However, direct income effects do not reflect the full impact of changes in coal-mine employment. Economic activities dependent on the coal-mining industry, such as rail transport and retail services to coal-mine industry employees, are also affected. These indirect economic effects are likely to be quite significant, but are extremely difficult to estimate. Indirect effects include reduced employment, reduced income to the employed, or some combination of both. In this analysis, direct income effects are combined with an income ''multiplier'' —a **very rough** approximation of the regional economic activity that depends indirectly on coal mining—to derive ''total'' income effects of acid rain control scenarios.**

PROJECTED PATTERNS OF CHANGE

Table A-26 summarizes how 5-, 10-, and 13-million-ton SO_2 emissions reductions might affect regional coal production, employment, and economic activity. Several generalizations emerge from the analysis. First, the model projects significant growth in coal production nationwide (about 60 percent) between 1979 and 1990. Second, regulations designed to control acid rain, even those calling for the largest emissions reductions, do not alter the projected increases in **national** production. Even with the additional costs of acid rain controls, coal is projected to retain its competitive advantage over other fuels.

Third, while acid rain control measures are not projected to change **nationwide** production levels, the ICF model projects a **redistribution** of coal production among regions. Regions with low-sulfur reserves are projected to experience production growth beyond what would occur under current regulations. On the other hand, between 1979 and 1990, production in regions with high-sulfur reserves is projected to decline below currently projected 1990 levels, and—in the case of the 10-million-ton and greater reductions of SO_2 emissions—below 1979 production levels as well. The projected redistributions increase in magnitude as SO_2 emissions reductions increase, but by less than linear proportions.* Figure A-8 shows the projected change in regional coal production from 1979 to: 1) 1990 levels,

assuming no change in SO_2 standards; and 2) 1990 levels, assuming a 10-million-ton decrease in SO_2 emissions.**

The areas most likely to experience significant growth in production are southern West Virginia, eastern Kentucky, and the regions west of the Mississippi (particularly Colorado). The regions most likely to experience significant production declines include northern West Virginia, Ohio, western Kentucky, and Illinois. However, available model projections for 2000 suggest that production declines below current levels may be reversed in the decade following 1990. Production levels are projected to rebound due to general trends in the energy market, such as growth in utility demand, and to the fact that an increasing number of new plants regulated under New Source Performance Standards will come online after 1990.

Employment patterns are projected to correspond to changes in production. However, uncertainties regarding future productivity trends create a larger range of uncertainty for employment effects than for production effects. The loss of portions of the market for high-sulfur coal could reduce employment opportunities in Midwestern and northern Appalachian regions by about 10 to 40 percent of projected 1990 coal-mining work force levels under current emissions standards. The areas of northern West Virginia, Ohio, western Kentucky, and Illinois are projected to experience actual employment decreases below 1979 levels for emissions reductions of 10 million tons and greater.

Future employment changes would be accompanied by proportional changes in direct miner income and total monetary effects. For **each** of the high-sulfur coal regions of northern Appalachia and the Midwest, these costs range from $250 million to $500 million in **direct** annual income losses to miners, and from $600 million to $1,100 million in **total** (direct plus indirect) annual monetary losses. The coal-related **benefits** in central Appalachia range from $400 million to $550 million annually in direct income gains, and total annual income gains of $750 million to $1,100 million. Estimates of benefits in the West range from $100 million to $150 million in direct income gains and total income gains of $500 million to $750 million per year. All estimates are in 1981 dollars. These figures, particularly in the case of total monetary impacts, must be considered very rough estimates.

Changes in coal-related employment and income may cause some additional community-level social and economic repercussions. In areas projected to experience significant declines in employment, decreases in tax rev-

---

**To arrive at employment estimates, OTA divides projected production increases by State-by-State productivity data developed from DOE data. These employment changes are then combined with miner salary data to arrive at direct income effects. Indirect economic impacts were estimated using an ''economic base technique.'' For each State, multipliers were developed by calculating the ratio of income derived from the ''base'' or ''primary'' sector to income derived from the ''service'' or ''secondary sector.''

*As emissions reduction requirements increase beyond a certain level, the proportion of reductions that are projected to be met by ''fuel-switching'' decreases relative to the proportion met by scrubbers.

**Of the 90 million tons of annual production lost by the Eastern and Midwestern high-sulfur coal market by 1990, about 50 million tons is gained by Eastern low-sulfur producers and 40 million tons by Western producers.

Table A-26.—Summary Table of Regional Coal Market Effects of Acid Rain Control Legislation

5-million-ton sulfur dioxide emission reduction	10-million-ton sulfur dioxide emission reduction	13-million-ton sulfur dioxide emission reduction
North Appalachia Region (Maryland, northern West Virginia, Ohio, and Pennsylvania)		
Under current environmental regulations, annual coal production is projected to increase approximately 10 percent between 1979 and 1990; under a 5-million-ton acid rain control program no change in production is projected over this period. Employment opportunities foregone are projected to range from 6,300 to 9,100 jobs (a 10-percent reduction); because there is no projected production change, employment changes from 1979 levels will be a function of productivity changes only. Direct income opportunities foregone by the regional economy are projected to be $160 million to $230 million; total income opportunities lost could range from $450 million to $640 million.	Under a 10-million-ton acid rain control program, production is projected to decrease by about 10 percent between 1979 and 1990. Employment is projected to be 15 percent (9,800 to 14,100 jobs) less than it would have been under the 1990 base case; projected employment changes from 1979 levels range from no change to a 30-percent (23,000 job) decrease. Direct income opportunities foregone range from $250 million to $360 million; total income foregone ranges from $630 million to $910 million. Available projections for the year 2000 suggest these declines may only be temporary.	Under a 13-million-ton acid rain control program, production is projected to decrease by about 13 percent between 1979 and 1990. 1990 employment levels are projected to be 20 percent (12,700 to 16,500 jobs) less than what they would have been in 1990 under current regulations, and 14 to 35 percent (10,800 to 26,100 jobs) below 1979 employment. Direct income opportunities foregone range from $330 million to $470 million; total income foregone is projected to be $810 million to $1,170 million.
Central Appalachia Region (eastern Kentucky, southern West Virginia, Tennessee, and Virginia)		
Under current environmental regulations, annual coal production is projected in increase by about 50 percent between 1979 and 1990; under a 5-million-ton acid rain control program, a 62-percent increase is projected over this period. Employment is projected to be about 10 percent (8,800 to 12,700 jobs) greater than it would have been in 1990 under current regulations; projected employment changes from 1979 levels range from 25- to 80-percent (21,800 to 69,900 jobs) increase. Direct annual income opportunities created in this region range from $230 million to $330 million; total annual income created ranges from $450 million to $640 million.	Under a 10-million-ton acid rain control program, production is projected to increase 70 percent between 1979 and 1990. 1990 employment levels are projected to be about 15 percent (15,000 to 21,700 jobs) greater than they would have been in 1990 under current regulations, and 38 to 99 percent (33,200 to 86,500 jobs) greater than 1979 employment levels. Direct income opportunities created are projected to be $390 million to $560 million; total income generated ranges from $1,030 million to $1,490 million.	Under a 13-million-ton emission reduction, production is projected to increase 75 percent between 1979 and 1990. 1990 employment levels are projected to be 16 percent (17,300 to 25,000 jobs) greater than what they would have been in 1990 under current regulations, and 40 to 100 percent (35,800 to 90,000 jobs) above 1979 levels. Direct income opportunities created by the projected increase in coal production range from $440 million to $640 million; total income generated ranges from $1,200 million to $1,700 million.

Table A-26.—Summary Table of Regional Coal Market Effects of Acid Rain Control Legislation (continued)

5-million-ton sulfur dioxide emission reduction	10-million-ton sulfur dioxide emission reduction	13-million-ton sulfur dioxide emission reduction
Midwest Region (Illinois, Indiana, and western Kentucky)		
Under current environmental regulations, annual coal production is projected to increase 31 to 34 percent between 1979 and 1990; under a 5-million-ton reduction, production is projected to increase 12 percent over this period. 1990 employment levels are projected to be 16 percent (5,400 to 7,700 jobs) less than what they would have been in 1990 under current regulations, and between a 13-percent (4,200-job) decrease and a 25-percent (8,000-job) increase from 1979 levels. Direct income opportunities foregone range from $140 million to $200 million; total income foregone ranges from $370 million to $530 million.	Under a 10-million-ton acid rain control program, production is projected to decrease 10 percent between 1979 and 1990. 1990 employment levels are projected to be 33 percent (10,500 to 15,200 jobs) below what they would have been in 1990 under current regulations, and 6 to 35 percent (1,900 to 11,300 jobs) less than 1979 employment. Direct income opportunities foregone are projected to range from $270 million to $390 million; total income foregone ranges from $770 million to $1,100 million. Projections for the year 2000 suggest these declines may be reversed in the period 1990 to 2000.	Under a 13-million-ton sulfur dioxide emission reduction, production is projected to decrease by 17 percent between 1979 and 1990. Employment is projected to be 38 percent (12,100 to 17,400 jobs) below what it would have been in 1990 without an acid rain control program; projected employment decreases from 1979 levels range from 13 to 40 percent (4,200 to 12,900 jobs). Direct income opportunities foregone range from $310 million to $480 million; total income foregone ranges from $870 million to $1,200 million.
The Western United States		
Under current environmental regulations, annual coal production is projected to increase approximately 138 percent between 1979 and 1990; under a 5-million-ton acid rain control program, production is projected to increase 145 percent over this period. 1990 employment levels are projected to be 3 percent (1,200 to 1,700 jobs) higher than what they would have been in 1990 under current regulations, and 80 to 160 percent (16,600 to 32,900 jobs) above 1979 levels. Direct income opportunities created by acid rain controls are projected to range from $30 million to $40 million; total income benefits are projected to be $120 million to $170 million.	Under a 10-million-ton acid rain control program, production is projected to increase 158 percent between 1979 and 1990. 1990 employment is projected to be 13 percent (4,600 to 6,700 jobs) greater than what it would have been in 1990 in the absence of acid rain controls, and between 95 and 180 percent (19,100 to 36,300 jobs) greater than 1979 levels. Increases in direct income opportunities range from $120 million to $170 million; total income increases are projected to range from $510 million to $740 million.	Under a 13-million-ton sulfur dioxide emission reduction, production is projected to increase 165 percent between 1979 and 1990. Acid rain controls are projected to increase employment opportunities by 20 percent (6,800 to 9,800 jobs) over what they would have been in 1990 without any change in environment regulations. 1990 employment levels are projected to be 105 to 196 percent (21,000 to 39,300 jobs) greater than 1979 levels. Direct income opportunities created in the region are projected to range from $180 million to $250 million; total income benefits range from $750 million to $1,100 million.

SOURCE: Office of Technology Assessment, based on coal production estimates from ICF, Inc.

Figure A-8.—Regional Coal Production: Effects of a 10-Million-Ton Sulfur Dioxide Emission Reduction

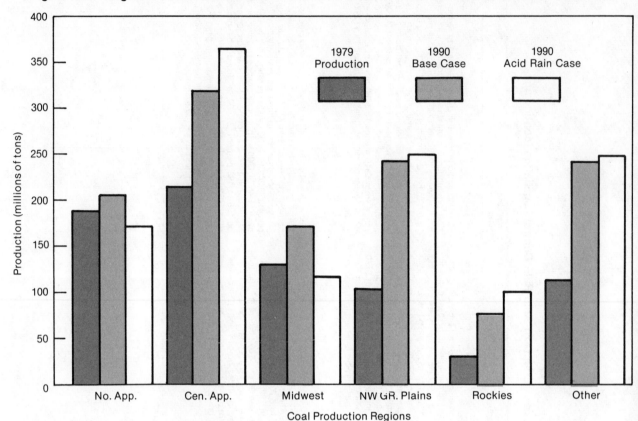

SOURCE: Office of Technology Assessment, adapted from ICF, Inc.

enues could cause the quantity or quality of community services to decline. In areas projected to experience rapid increases in employment, the capacity of communities to provide adequate health care, housing, education, etc., may be strained.

RESULTS OF OTHER STUDIES

The United Mine Workers (UMW) has also calculated the potential effects of a 10-million-ton reduction in SO₂ emissions, allocated as in OTA's Scenario II. The UMW analysis presents three sets of estimates of effects on mineworker employment and economic activity in **high-sulfur coal areas only,** assuming that fuel-switching would account for 50, 75, or 100 percent of the required reductions. However, the UMW analysis made no calculation of gains in employment and economic activity in low-sulfur coal areas, or of the **net** effects of the 10-million-ton emissions cutbacks.

Table A-27 shows the UMW projections of job losses, direct annual economic losses, and total annual economic losses for the three levels of fuel-switching. Using a DOE estimate that between 50 and 75 percent of the

reductions required under a major acid rain control program would be met by fuel-switching, the UMW calculated that between 40,000 and 60,000 coal mining jobs would be lost in high-sulfur coal areas, producing direct annual income losses of $1.1 billion to $1.6 billion, and total economic losses ranging between $3.0 billion and $4.6 billion.[56]

For comparison, OTA estimates of the net effects of the 10-million-ton reduction on high-sulfur coal areas are also presented in table A-27. Two factors must be considered in comparing these estimates:

1. OTA used projections of increases in coal production, including increases due to construction of new electricity plants, through 1990, and compared them to projections of how further emissions controls would affect these new production levels. UMW estimates are calculated from 1981 production levels, assuming that **no changes in production** occur up to the time that controls would be implemented.

---

[56]United Mine Workers, "Employment Impacts of Acid Rain," June 1983.

Table A-27.—Employment and Economic Effects on High-Sulfur Coal-Producing Areas of a 10-Million-Ton Reduction in SO₂ Emissions— Comparison of UMW and OTA Analyses

	UMW estimates percent of emissions reductions achieved through fuel switching			OTA estimates	
	50	75	100	Change from 1990 base case[a]	Change from actual 1979 levels
Employment losses[b]	40,000	60,000	80,000	23,000-33,000	9,000-38,000
Direct annual economic losses (millions 1981 dollars)[c]............	$1,100	$1,600	$2,100	$600-$800	$200-$1,100
Total annual economic losses ...	$3,000	$4,600	$6,100	$1,600-$2,300	$600-$2,700

[a]OTA assumes, based on ICF analyses, that the requisite emissions reductions will be met by a combination of fuel-switching and scrubbers. The base case assumes no change in environmental regulations.
[b]These employment losses occur over the period required to implement the pollution reductions. The ranges reflect uncertainty in future productivity levels. OTA bounds employment and economic estimates by assuming that productivity might rise as much as 30 percent or decrease by as much as 10 percent between 1979 and 1990.
[c]Annual monetary estimates assume implementation of emissions reductions over 10 years, and that shifts in coal production are distributed equally over that period.

SOURCE: Office of Technology Assessment, basesd on coal production estimates by ICF, Inc.

2. In the OTA estimates, employment losses in high-sulfur coal areas are partially compensated for by employment gains. Thus, the OTA estimates are of the **net effects** in **high-sulfur coal-producing regions.** No projected employment increases are figured into the UMW analysis.

OTA's best estimates of potential effects on high-sulfur coal regions show employment impacts about half as large as those estimated by UMW, assuming 50 to 75 percent fuel-switching.* The most pessimistic of the OTA estimates—38,000 jobs lost from actual 1979 levels—approximates the low-end UMW figure of 40,000.

Possible means of preventing or decreasing coal miner unemployment that may ensue from acid rain control legislation are discussed in chapter 7 under question 8. They include mandating control technologies to achieve emissions reductions, thereby prohibiting fuel switching and employing section 125 of the Clean Air Act to restrict coal consumption to "local or regional" coals.

The **net** effect of acid rain legislation on nationwide coal production, employment, and economic activity, however, also includes the offsetting increases in employment and economic activity in low-sulfur coal regions. When these are considered in **aggregate**, OTA estimates that no significant changes in employment and economic activity result from control-induced production changes.

Electricity-Intensive Industries

OTA used 1979 and 1980 data from the U.S. Census Bureau's *Annual Survey of Manufacturers* to assess the electrical energy dependency of approximately 450 types of industries.[57] Specific industries for which electricity represents 4 percent or more of the total value of shipments, and/or 10 percent or more of the total "value added,"* are listed in table A-28. The 17 industries identified in the table are largely concentrated in the areas of primary metals; chemicals—particularly industrial inorganic chemicals; and stone, clay, and glass products. The identified industries account for a disproportionate share of U.S. industrial electricity use—although they account for only 2 percent of total value of shipments and 2 percent of total value added by American manufacturers, they purchase approximately 25 percent of the electricity sold to industry, and account for about 16 percent of utility revenues from industrial electricity sales.

Five of these industrial categories—electrometallurgical products, primary zinc, primary aluminum, alkalies and chlorine, and industrial gases—are especially electricity intensive; the cost of purchased electricity equals about 40 percent or more of their total value added, and about 10 to 25 percent of their total value of shipments. These industries might be considered most

---

*UMW's estimate of 40,000 to 60,000 jobs lost is compared to OTA's estimate of 23,000 to 33,000. Although the estimation procedures differ somewhat, both estimates calculate changes from a hypothetical base case, and thus come closest to providing a reliable basis for comparison.

[57]U.S. Department of Commerce, Bureau of the Census, *1980 Annual Survey of Manufacturers: Fuels and Electric Energy Consumed,* August 1982.
*"Total value added" is the difference between the value of goods and the value of the materials purchased to manufacture them.

Table A-28.—Statistics on Electricity-Intensive Industries

Industry	SIC code	Value of shipments (10⁶ 1980$)	Electricity purchased (10⁶ kWh)	Electricity cost as percent of:		Electricity rate ¢/kWh (1982$)	Ratio to industrial average rate (3.84¢/kWh)
				Value added	Value of shipments		
Cotton seed oil mills...............	2074	1,033.7	540.7	10.7	2.0	4.61	1.20
Manufactured ice	2097	169.6	460.7	15.6	11.0	4.70	1.23
Particle board	2492	512.4	825.1	11.4	4.8	3.44	0.90
Alkalies and chlorine	2812	1,354.1	10,679.5	45.5	19.6	2.89	0.75
Industrial gases	2813	1,539.6	11,958.6	42.4	24.5	3.66	0.95
Other industrial inorganic chemicals	2819	12,095.9	37,092.0	13.9	7.5	2.86	0.75
Carbon black.....................	2895	498.0	540.4	13.3	3.5	3.78	0.99
Reclaimed rubber	3031	38.3	75.4	12.2	7.8	4.62	1.20
Cement, hydraulic	3241	3,962.4	9,237.9	15.3	8.2	4.08	1.06
Lime	3274	598.8	813.8	10.8	5.1	4.38	1.14
Mineral wool	3296	2,235.4	2,703.5	7.3	4.0	3.82	0.99
Electrometallurgical products	3313	1,249.3	6,814.3	42.0	13.8	2.94	0.77
Malleable iron foundries	3322	521.2	1,015.5	11.9	7.0	4.17	1.09
Primary zinc.....................	3333	413.1	1,487.8	51.7	8.3	2.67	0.70
Primary aluminum	3334	6,979.9	72,279.1	39.3	15.6	1.75	0.47
Other primary nonferrous metals	3339	1,906.6	4,279.4	15.6	5.1	2.66	0.69
Carbon and graphite products	3624	1,183.3	2,171.8	7.5	4.2	2.64	0.69

SOURCE: U.S. Census Bureau, *1980 Annual Survey of Manufacturers: Fuels and Electric Energy Consumed,* August 1982.

sensitive to potential increases in the cost of electrical power resulting from further control of SO_2 emissions. For all five of these industries, a substantial proportion of production occurs in the 31 Eastern States.

Primary zinc is the most concentrated industrial category—only five producers currently operate in the United States. The three largest manufacturers are located in Pennsylvania, Illinois, and Tennessee, and account for approximately three-quarters of the Nation's current production. The zinc industry appears to be particularly vulnerable to increases in the cost of production —U.S. annual production capacity fell from about 1 million tons to 300,000 tons over the past decade, and foreign producers have captured a substantial share of domestic sales.[58]

Primary aluminum, by far the largest of these industries, is produced in 13 of the 31 Eastern States. Although two non-Eastern States—Texas and Washington—currently have the largest production capacities, the Eastern United States currently accounts for about 60 pecent of national production capabilities. Major producers in the region include: Alabama, Arkansas, Indiana, Kentucky, Louisiana, Missouri, New York, Ohio, and Tennessee.[59]

Production of alkalies and chlorine is about equally divided between the Eastern and Western regions of the United States. Louisiana accounts for nearly one-quarter of national output; the 17 other Eastern States in

which these chemicals are produced together account for a slightly smaller proportion of production.[60] Alabama, New York, Michigan, and West Virginia are the fifth, sixth, eighth, and ninth largest producing States in the country, respectively.

Information on the distribution of industrial gas production is limited, due in part to confidentiality requirements for protecting individual manufacturers. Available data indicate that Texas and California were the highest producing States in the late 1970's, and show substantial amounts of production in the following Eastern States: Alabama, Delaware, Illinois, Louisiana, New Jersey, New York, Ohio, Pennsylvania, and Tennessee.[61]

Over 90 percent of U.S. electrometallurgical products (i.e., specialized metal alloys made with such metals as molybdenum, manganese, and chromium) were produced in the 31 Eastern States in 1981. Ohio accounted for about one-third of national production; six additional States—Alabama, Kentucky, New York, South Carolina, Tennessee, and West Virginia—together accounted for slightly under one-half of national production. The industry is highly vulnerable to foreign competition, as countries with deposits of the necessary ores are rapidly developing their own production capabilities.[62]

[58]Personal communication, James Kennedy, Bureau of Industrial Economics, U.S. Department of Commerce, October 1983.
[59]Ibid.

[60]Personal communication, Frank Maxey, Bureau of Industrial Economics, U.S. Department of Commerce, October 1983.
[61]Ibid.
[62]Personal communication, Tom Jones, Bureau of Mines, U.S. Department of the Interior, December 1983.

Uncertainties about how utilities might apportion control-related increases in electricity rates make it difficult to assess the likely extent of financial effects on electricity-intensive industries. As shown in columns 3 and 6 of table A-28, many of these industries are large-scale electricity consumers, and pay relatively low electricity rates. If control costs were apportioned to users primarily on the basis of current rates (i.e., increasing existing rates by a uniform **percentage** for all users), effects on these industries, although potentially significant, would not be disproportionate to cost increases undergone by all electricity consumers. However, if control costs were apportioned primarily on the basis of electricity consumption (i.e., increasing existing rates by a uniform mill/kWh fee for all users), percentage rate increases would be highest for those industries currently paying low electricity rates. Effects could be particularly severe for those industries having both low rates and high electricity dependency—primary aluminum, alkalies and chlorine, electrometallurgial products, and primary zinc.

*Utilities in the Eastern 31 States**

The amount of SO_2 that an individual utility must eliminate from its emissions is, of course, the primary determinant of the effect of acid rain control legislation on a given company's finances. Such factors as each utility's ability to raise capital to cover construction costs and regulatory policies in any given State further determine a utility's ability to pay for required reductions without adverse financial effects.

To address the utility sector's vulnerability to further emissions reductions, this section will: 1) present 1980 State-average SO_2 emissions rates for coal- and oil-burning plants to indicate the potential extent of additional control requirements, 2) use available financial indicators for 1980 to assess the health of each State's utility sector, 3) assess the implications of State regulatory policies in 1980-81 for utility finances, and 4) integrate the first three types of information in concluding observations, identifying areas of particular vulnerability, where possible.

Current Emission Rates and Generating Capacities

Figures A-9 and A-10 rank States in the Eastern United States according to their coal- and oil-fueled electrical generating capacities, and by average 1980 emis-

sion rates for all coal- or oil-fueled plants in the State. The greater a State's dependence on either of these fossil fuels, and the higher its average SO_2 emission rate, the greater the likelihood that proposed emissions controls would require additional utility expenditures to reduce emissions. States with the greatest probability of extensive expenditures for emissions control appear in the upper left portion of each table; those with the least, appear at the bottom right. Overall, emission rates for coal-fired utilities are substantially higher than for oil-fired facilities; thus, many more States would be exposed to significant control expenditures on the basis of current utility coal combustion than oil combustion. Detailed estimates of SO_2 emissions reductions required, by State, under a number of alternative control scenarios, are provided in section A.3 of this appendix.

Utility Financial Positions

Ultimately, a utility recoups its emission-reduction expenditures by selling power to customers in its service area, or to other utilities. However, a utility must shoulder the burden of pollution control expenditures from the time they are made until it is allowed to begin charging customers for them. Substantial capital investment is required to retrofit existing powerplants with emissions control devices, or to build newer, cleaner powerplants. Capital investment may also be necessary to modify existing powerplant operations to permit the burning of low-sulfur fuel. The utility's capacity to **finance** these expenditures depends in large part on its ability to attract investment capital.

To place the potential capital-raising burden associated with acid rain control into perspective, estimated costs of major control programs can be compared to actual utility construction expenditures. Over 5 years (1978 through 1982), electric utilities spent approximately $180 billion (1982 dollars) for construction in the United States;[63] potential construction costs of major acid rain control proposals over a similar 5-year period might range from about 5 to 20 percent of this figure, depending on the particular proposal. Control costs would constitute a higher proportion of construction expenditures for particular States and/or utilities from which large emission reductions would be required. Such capital-raising burdens may be particularly critical for those utilities already scheduled to replace or retire a substantial proportion of plants over the period in which further emissions controls would be implemented.

A number of indicators are in use to assess utilities' competitive positions in capital markets, and no single measure of financial well-being can adequately charac-

*This section based primarily on Kathleen Cole, Duane Chapman, and Clifford Rossi, ''Financial and Regulatory Factors Affecting the State and Regional Economic Impact of Sulfur Oxide Emissions Control,'' prepared for the Office of Technology Assessment, U.S. Congress, August 1982.

[63]Merrill Lynch, Pierce, Fenner & Smith, Inc., ''Utility Industry, A Statistical Review (Preliminary),'' April 1983.

Figure A-9.—Coal-Based Generating Capacities and SO₂ Emissions Rates

Coal dependency
(Share of total electric-generating capacity)

←────────────────────

	>2/3 coal capacity	1/3 to 2/3 coal capacity	<1/3 coal capacity
>3 lbs.	Missouri (4.6)[a] Indiana (4.2) Ohio (3.9) Kentucky (3.6)	Wisconsin (3.6) New Hampshire (3.6) Illinois (3.1)	Florida (3.5)
2–3 lbs.	Georgia (2.9) West Virginia (2.7)	Pennsylvania (2.8) Delaware (2.4) Iowa (2.3) Alabama (2.3) Michigan (2.0) South Carolina (2.0)	New York (2.8) Maryland (2.5) Mississippi (2.3)
<2 lbs.		Minnesota (1.6) North Carolina (1.5)	Massachusetts (1.6) Virginia (1.4)

Average SO₂ emission rates from coal-fired utilities (lb per million Btu) ↑

[a]Numbers in parentheses are State-average SO₂ emission rates for coal-burning plants, expressed in lbs. of SO₂ per million Btu.

SOURCE: Office of Technology Assessment, from E. H. Pechan & Associates, Inc., and K. Cole, et al., "Financial and Regulatory Factors Affecting the State and Regional Economic Impact of Sulfur Oxide Emissions Control," OTA contractor report, August 1982.

Figure A-10.—Oil-Based Generating Capacities and SO₂ Emissions Rates

Oil dependency
(Share of total electric-generating capacity)

←────────────────────

	1/2 oil capacity	1/4 to 1/2 oil capacity	<1/4 oil capacity
>1.5 lbs.	New Hampshire (2.1) Massachusetts (1.8) Florida (1.6)	South Carolina (2.0)	Mississippi (2.7) Georgia (1.9)
1–1.5 lbs.	Maine (1.4) New York (1.3) Delaware (1.1) Vermont (1.1) Rhode Island (1.0)	Arkansas (1.5) Maryland (1.3)	Minnesota (1.5) Alabama (1.5) Virginia (1.4) Wisconsin (1.2) Ohio (1.2) Missouri (1.1) North Carolina (1.1) Indiana (1.1) Kentucky (1.1) Louisiana (1.0)
<1 lb.	New Jersey (0.7) Connecticut (0.5)	Pennsylvania (0.8)	Illinois (0.8) Iowa (0.8) Michigan (0.8)

Average SO₂ emission rates from coal-fired utilities (lb per million Btu) ↑

[a]Numbers in parentheses are State-average SO₂ emission rates for oil-burning plants, expressed in lbs. of SO₂ per million Btu.

SOURCE: Office of Technology Assessment, from E. H. Pechan & Associates, Inc., and K. Cole, et al., "Financial and Regulatory Factors Affecting the State and Regional Economic Impact of Sulfur Oxide Emissions Control," OTA contractor report, August 1982.

terize a utility's prospects. However, two major financial criteria were selected to describe utility financial conditions at the State level: 1) return on common equity (ROCE), and 2) bond ratings. The first represents common stockholders' net earnings during a given year—indicating the utility's **current** profitability. The second represents experts' judgments about the utility's **long-term** ability to reliably repay debt. The lower a utility's bond rating, the higher the interest rate it will need to offer to induce investors to purchase bonds.

Table A-29 categorizes States according to 1980 data on whether more than 50 percent of their electrical power was generated by utilities with: 1) bond ratings of A or better, and 2) ROCEs above the 1980 national median of 11.1 percent per year. Column A lists States meeting both of these criteria; these States may be considered to have a relatively healthy investor-owned electric utility sector. Column D lists States that met neither of the above criteria. These eight States may be regarded as particularly vulnerable to measures requiring utilities to generate additional capital for pollution-control purposes. Columns B and C show States failing to meet either of the two criteria.

Utilities may be at greater risk from capital-raising needs if control-related expenditures must be added to

significant amounts of non-control-related construction—either to replace retired plants or to accommodate increasing electricity demand—during the period in which further controls would be implemented. While increasing demand for electricity could, in itself, positively influence utilities' positions in capital markets, requirements for replacing retired plants carry high capital costs without necessarily enhancing utility positions. States in which more than 20 percent of current generating capacity is scheduled for replacement by 1995 include: Arkansas, District of Columbia, Maryland, Massachusetts, New York, and Rhode Island.[64]

State Regulatory Policies

Public utility commissions (PUCs) in each State make numerous regulatory decisions that affect a utility's ability to pass on costs associated with emissions control. PUC regulatory policies vary widely from State to State;[65] they may also change over time in response to

[64]Personal communication, E. H. Pechan, from U.S. DOE Generating Unit Reference File (1981).
[65]Sally Hindman, Duane Chapman, and Kathleen Cole, *State Regulatory Policies for Privately Owned Electric Utilities in 1981,* University Research Group on Energy, New York State College of Agriculture and Life Sciences, Cornell University, Ithaca, N.Y., October 1982.

Table A-29.—Summary of 1980 Utility Financial Conditions by State[a]

A. High bond, high ROCE	B. High bond, low ROCE
States in which more than 50 percent of generated power was from utilities with bond ratings of Aa or A, and ROCEs of 11.1 percent or lower: (national median):	States in which more than 50 percent of generated power was from utilities with bond ratings of Aa or A, and ROCEs below the national median:
Iowa Kentucky Maryland[b] Massachusetts[b] Minnesota Mississippi New Jersey Wisconsin	Delaware Illinois Indiana New York[b] Rhode Island[b] South Carolina
C. Low bond, high ROCE	**D. Low bond, low ROCE**
States in which more than 50 percent of generated power was from utilities with bond ratings of Baa or lower, and ROCEs above the national median:	States in which more than 50 percent of generated power was from utilities with bond ratings of Baa or lower, and ROCEs below the national median:
Alabama Georgia Louisiana Missouri New Hampshire North Carolina Ohio West Virginia	Arkansas[b] Connecticut Florida Maine Michigan Pennsylvania Vermont Virginia

[a]Based on data from 106 surveyed utilities in the Eastern 31-State region. Extremely small utilities, utilities with no generating capacities (electricity distributors), and utilities with no coal or oil generating capacities have been excluded.
[b]States in which more than 20 percent of current generating capacity is scheduled for replacement by 1995.

SOURCE: Office of Technology Assessment; adapted from K. Cole, et al., "Financial and Regulatory Factors Affecting the State and Regional Economic Impact of Sulfur Oxide Emissions Control," OTA contractor report, August 1982.

changing economic and political conditions. Imposing stricter emissions controls at the Federal level might induce considerable changes in affected States' utility regulations; thus, current regulations may not reliably indicate how State-level policies would influence utility finances. However, to demonstrate the range of current regulatory conditions, survey information on five major regulatory policies for each of the Eastern 31 States during 1980-81 is outlined in table A-30.

Two of the surveyed policies directly concern the delay required before adjustments in utility costs can be passed on to consumers. Each involves short-term delays—the number of months required, on average, for State utility commissions to rule on requests for rate increases (col. 4), and the number of times per year that utilities are allowed to adjust electricity rates according to changes in fuel costs (col. 3). The frequency of allowable fuel cost adjustments is particularly significant to those utilities for which switching to more expensive, low-sulfur coal or oil is a potential means of meeting more stringent emissions limits.

Three of the policies assessed in table A-30 affect the manner in which utility rates are calculated. PUCs must determine a total amount of utility expenses and costs, or calculated **revenue requirements,** allowed to be passed on to consumers, in order to set a utility's electricity rates. One major component of these costs is the return on capital investments. The first column of table A-30, "allowed return on common equity" or ROCE, shows the maximum return to investors allowed by each State, calculated as a percentage of a utility's assets, or rate base. The second column of the table, "amount of CWIP allowed in rate base," indicates the extent to which "construction work in progress" (CWIP) is considered a part of the utility's assets for ratemaking purposes.

Table A-30.—Major State Regulatory Policies

State	Allowed ROCE (median: 14.25)	Amount of CWIP allowed in rate base	Frequency of adjustment for fuel price changes	Average number of months for rate decisions (median: 8.5)	Type of test year
Alabama	12.85	100%	Quarterly	6	Historical
Arkansas	15.0	100%[a]	Monthly	10	Historical
Connecticut	14.8	0	Monthly	5	Historical
Delaware	15.0	100%	Monthly	7	Forecast
Florida	15.5	Varies	Monthly	8	Forecast
Georgia	13.33	Varies	Quarterly	6	Forecast
Illinois	16.5	Varies	Irregular-as needed	11	Forecast
Indiana	15.83	0	Quarterly	6	Historical
Iowa	13.35	0	Monthly	12	Historical
Kentucky	14.25	100%	Monthly	10	Historical
Louisiana	14.33	100%	Monthly	12	Historical
Maine	15.13	0	Quarterly	9	Historical
Maryland	14.0	100%	Monthly	7	Forecast
Massachusetts	14.31	0	Quarterly	6	Historical
Michigan	13.25	100%	Monthly	9	Forecast
Minnesota	14.0	100%	Monthly	12	Forecast
Mississippi	12.85	Varies	Monthly	6	Forecast
Missouri	13.71	0	No clause	11	Historical
New Hampshire	14.75	0	Quarterly or monthly	6	Historical
New Jersey	14.0	Varies	Irregular-as needed	8	Forecast
New York	15.5	Small %[b]	Monthly	11	Forecast
North Carolina	13.87	100%	3/year	7	Historical
Ohio	15.86	Varies	Biannually	9	Forecast
Pennsylvania	15.63	Small %	Yearly	9	Forecast
Rhode Island	14.13	0	Quarterly	8	Historical
South Carolina	13.88	100%	Biannually	12	Historical
Vermont	14.5	Small %	No clause	21	Historical
Virginia	15.0	100 %	Biannually	5	Historical
West Virginia	14.0	Varies	Biannually	10	Historical
Wisconsin	12.72	0	Monthly	8.5	Forecast

[a]CWIP to be in service within 1 year is allowed.
[b]"Small %" indicates that less than 10% of CWIP is allowed.

SOURCE: K. Cole, et al., "Financial and Regulatory Factors Affecting the State and Regional Economic Impact of Sulfur Oxide Emissions Control," Office of Technology Assessment contractor report, August 1982.

If a State allows construction work in progress (CWIP) to be included in the rate base, utilities begin to earn returns on control-related expenditures as soon as they are made; if not, capital improvements must be financed by the utility until the scrubber or other plant modification is actually operating—a period of up to 4 or more years. For utilities in weak financial positions, the ability to recoup expenditures during a planning and construction period of 4 years or longer may be a significant factor in deciding what means to use to comply with stricter emissions controls. Consequently, States allowing little or no CWIP in the rate base may make capital-intensive approaches to SO_2 abatement less attractive, especially to financially troubled utilities. Such utilities could choose to switch to higher priced, lower sulfur fuels, even when costs for doing so are higher over the long run. Although State PUCs vary considerably in their CWIP expenditure policies, decisions on whether to allow CWIP in the rate base are often made on a case-by-case basis, except in States where allowing CWIP is prohibited by statute. Some analysts consider that States are considerably more likely to allow CWIP for pollution control expenditures to enter a utility's rate base.[66]

It should be noted, however, that some PUCs choose to substitute higher allowed rates of return for allowing CWIP in the rate base as a means of increasing utility revenues during periods of construction activity. For example, table A-30 shows that the States of Indiana, Maine, New York, and Pennsylvania allowed rates of return to exceed 15 percent in 1980, while including little or no CWIP in the rate base. Available data did not permit OTA to estimate the probable effects of such a substitution on control choices.

Finally, the kind of "test year" selected to provide data on expenses and costs (col. 5) can also influence calculated revenue requirements. In times of rising costs, historical test years may tend to understate utility expense estimates, while forecast test years can allow for the projected effects of inflation.

State regulatory policies for 1980-81 are, of course, an imperfect indicator of the probable regulatory climate over the decade or more required to implement further SO_2 restrictions. Public utility commissions could respond to control requirements by adopting policies more favorable to capital construction or fuel-switching, particularly in States burdened with large SO_2 reduction requirements. Such responses are virtually impossible to predict, however; PUCs are affected by a broad array of political and institutional conditions, and must, in their regulatory decisionmaking, balance consumer and producer interests. Concurrently, coal-producing

States could constrain utility options for meeting tougher emissions standards by requiring continued use of in-State produced coal. Despite these uncertainties, the information provided in table A-30 can be used as a general barometer of the favorableness or unfavorableness of a State's current regulatory climate.

Combined Indicators

In this section, the three sets of State-level indicators surveyed above—1980 utility emission rates from coal- and oil-burning plants, measures of short- and long-term utility profitability for 1980, and State regulatory policies for 1980-81—are integrated to provide an overall picture of **current** utility-sector vulnerability to stricter emissions control. It is important to note, however, that this provides only a surrogate for assessing the financial effects of controls **at the same time they would be implemented.** In addition, changes in such factors as demand for electricity, financial viability of nonfossil fuel electricity generation, interest rates, inflation, and the price of coal, oil, and gas could greatly affect the relative vulnerability of the region's utility companies.

Eight States are identified in table A-29 as having financially weak utilities—Arkansas, Connecticut, Florida, Maine, Michigan, Pennsylvania, Vermont, and Virginia. Three of these States have coal-fired utility emission rates of at least 2 lb SO_2/MMBtu: Florida (3.5), Pennsylvania (2.8), and Michigan (2.0). However, less than a third of Florida's electricity-generating capacity is coal-fired; more than half depends on oil, with 1980 SO_2 emissions averaging 1.6 lb/MMBtu. When emission rates from **all** utility fuel sources are considered, only Pennsylvania is among the upper 15 States in the region, ranking 11th with an average rate of 2.5 lb SO_2/MMBtu.

Pennsylvania utilities may also be of particular concern due to current State regulations governing fuel cost increases and calculated revenue requirements. While Florida and Michigan utilities are allowed monthly fuel cost adjustments, those in Pennsylvania are allowed only one per year.

Utilities in Michigan are allowed relatively low ROCEs, while 100 percent of CWIP is allowed in the rate base; both Florida and Pennsylvania allow above-average ROCEs, but Florida allows "varying" amounts of CWIP in the rate base, while Pennsylvania includes only small portions of CWIP. The remaining five States in the "highly vulnerable" category rank so low in current emissions as to make the probable effect of additional control requirements on their utility sectors quite small.

Utilities in an additional eight States are characterized in table A-29 as having above-average rates of return and relatively low bond ratings for 1980 (col. C), sug-

---

[66]Personal communication, Michael Foley, National Association of Regulatory Utility Commissioners, September 1983.

gesting potential concerns for long-term profitability. Four of these States combine heavy reliance on coal-fired plants with high average SO_2 emission rates from these plants: Georgia (2.9 lb/MMBtu), Missouri (4.6), Ohio (3.9), and West Virginia (2.7). A fifth State, New Hampshire, relies on oil-fired plants for more than half its generating capacity, and has an average oil-fired emissions rate of 2.1 lb/MMBtu.

Six States are identified in table A-30 as having relatively high bond ratings, but low rates of return, for 1980. Of these, Indiana combines strong coal dependency with a very high coal-fired, SO_2 emissions rate (4.2 lb/MMBtu), while Illinois has both moderate coal dependency and a relatively high emissions rate (3.1 lb/MMBtu).

Appendix B
Effects of Transported Pollutants

B.1 AQUATIC RESOURCES AT RISK

Extent of Resources at Risk*

Scientists are concerned that acid deposition may be damaging substantial numbers of U.S. and Canadian lakes and streams. As part of its assessment of transported air pollutants, OTA contracted with The Institute of Ecology (TIE) to:

- describe **mechanisms** by which acid deposition may be affecting sensitive lakes and streams;
- provide an **inventory of Eastern U.S. lakes and streams considered to be sensitive** to acid deposition;
- estimate the **number of lakes and streams** in these sensitive regions **that have been affected and/or altered by acidic deposition;** and
- examine three scenarios for future sulfate deposition levels to the year 2000, and **project effects on sensitive aquatic resources.**

Because of scientific uncertainties and data limitations, none of these tasks can be addressed at this time with a high degree of accuracy. Each of these topics is the subject of active research under the National Acid Precipitation Assessment Program (NAPAP). To illustrate, the estimates of the numbers of lakes and streams sensitive to acid deposition are based on eight separate water quality surveys conducted at different times using nonuniform procedures. NAPAP is currently planning to undertake a national survey—sampling several thousand water bodies over a much wider geographic area—to provide a more complete picture of the current magnitude of the problem.

Because of the large area of a typical watershed, most of the acid ultimately deposited in lakes and streams comes from water that runs off or percolates through the surrounding land mass, rather than from precipitation falling directly on water bodies. The amount of acidifying material that actually enters a given lake or stream is determined primarily by the soil and geologic conditions of the surrounding watershed. When the two major chemical components of acid rain—nitric acid and sulfuric acid—reach the ground, they may react with soils is a variety of ways.** For example, soils can neutralize the acids, exchange nutrients and trace metals for components of the acids, and/or hold sulfuric acid.

Most soils contain amounts of counterbalancing (neutralizing) substances such as bicarbonate that may be available to "buffer" acid inputs. Such nutrients as calcium and magnesium, when present in soils, may be leached by acidic deposition and enter water bodies, while acidity remains in the soil. When soils are highly acidic, similar leaching of toxic metals such as aluminum can occur, which may cause damage to aquatic life in lakes and streams. In addition, the soils of some watersheds are able to retain sulfuric acid to varying degrees. For these areas, deposited sulfuric acid will not pass into lakes and streams until the "adsorption capacity" of the soils is exceeded.

The extent to which such reactions actually occur depends on a number of geologic and soil conditions. Where slopes are relatively steep, and soils are thin, less opportunity exists for acid precipitation to infiltrate soil

---

*This section adapted from: The Institute of Ecology, "Regional Assessment of Aquatic Resources at Risk From Acidic Deposition," OTA contractor report, 1982.

**For current attempts to assess the effects of acid deposition on aquatic ecosystems, sulfuric acid is considered the principal substance of concern. The importance of atmospheric inputs of nitric acid to aquatic systems is still uncertain because the nitric acid can be used as a plant nutrient. Although nitric acid deposition may influence spring acidification (depression of pH) due to snowmelt, it is unlikely to have an appreciable effect on midsummer acidity.

layers and react chemically with soil components. Further, the composition of soils—the availability of neutralizing material, exchangeable elements, or sulfuric acid adsorption capacity—also affects their overall ability to mitigate acid deposition inputs to water bodies. Watersheds in a number of regions are believed to provide aquatic resources with virtually complete protection from current levels of acid deposition. In other regions, however, watersheds have little capacity to neutralize acidic substances, and much of the acid in precipitation in these regions moves through the watershed into lakes and streams.

Under unaltered conditions, virtually all lakes and streams also have some acid-neutralizing capacities. Like soils, their waters contain such substances as bicarbonate, which neutralize the entering acids. **Alkalinity levels,** which are expressed in **microequivalents per liter of water** (μeq/l), measure the acid-neutralizing capacity of lakes and streams. Lakes and streams defined as very sensitive to acidic inputs have alkalinity levels of 0 to 40 μeq/l, while a lake with high capacity for acid neutralization can measure over 500 μeq/l.* If the surrounding watershed contains little neutralizing material, natural alkalinity levels in lakes and streams may be quite low, making these aquatic resources highly sensitive to even low levels of acidic inputs.

When acids enter a lake or stream, available neutralizing substances are consumed, and alkalinity levels are depressed. As water bodies become acidified, aquatic plant and animal populations may be altered. A lake or stream is considered to be acidified when no neutralizing capacity is left. Such bodies of water have been measured as having **negative** alkalinity levels as great as –100 μeq/l.

A multistep process was employed to develop an inventory of sensitive (but not necessarily altered) lakes and streams in the Eastern United States. TIE (adapting a procedure developed by Oak Ridge National Laboratory) first used data on soil, watershed, and bedrock characteristics in 27 Eastern States to generate a list of individual counties whose freshwater resources were likely to be sensitive to acidic deposition. The list of counties was then aggregated into 14 acid-sensitive regions (fig. B-1). Using U.S. Geological Survey maps, the contractor systematically sampled each region to esti-

Figure B-1.—Areas Sensitive to Acid Rain (shaded grey)

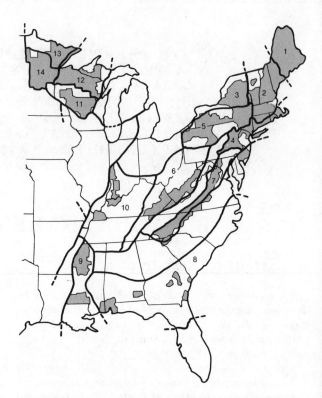

Lake and stream sampling areas modified from Braun (1950) and Fenneman (1938). Region numbers correspond to those shown in table B-1.

mate its **total** number of lakes greater than 15 acres in size, and **total** miles of first- and second-order streams.** The results show an estimated 17,000 lakes and 117,000 miles of first- and second-order streams in the 14 sensitive regions (table B-1).

Of this total number of lakes and streams in the sensitive regions, only a portion may be considered sensitive to acid inputs. Local variations in geology, soil conditions, and runoff patterns cause alkalinity levels of lakes and streams **within a sensitive region** to range from less than zero μeq/l (acidified) to over 500 μeq/l (acid resistant). Regional water quality surveys*** were used to estimate the percentage of the lakes and streams in the 14 regions that can be considered sensitive to acid

---

*Reports by J. R. Kramer (3), H. Harvey, et al. (4), and others have divided the spectrum of their sensitivity measure into a series of intervals referred to as sensitivity classes or categories. Each approach differed slightly from the others, leading the authors of the U.S.-Canada Aquatic Impacts Assessment Subgroup (5) to propose the following classification for lakes:

Class		Alkalinity (μeq/l)
I	Acidified	<0
II	Extreme sensitivity	0-39
III	Moderate sensitivity	40-199
IV	Low sensitivity	200-499
V	Not sensitive	≥500

**The smallest unbranched tributary of a stream is a first-order stream; the junction of two first-order streams produces a second-order stream segment.

***Eight surveys of lake and stream water quality were used to evaluate the regional sensitivity of aquatic ecosystems to acid deposition. Regional estimates are based on measurements from about 40 New England streams (6), 430 Adirondack lakes (7), 45 Pennsylvania streams (8), 40 streams in North Carolina and Virginia (9), 360 lakes in Wisconsin (10) and Minnesota (11), and 40 Wisconsin streams (12).

**Table B-1.—Total Estimated Lake and Stream Resources in the Acid-Sensitive
Regions of the Eastern United States (see fig. B-1)**

Region	Sensitive area (mi²)	Total lakes Number	Total lakes Acres	Total streams (mi) 1st order	Total streams (mi) 2d order
1. Eastern Maine	26,398	1,425	582,825	9,714	3,485
2. Western New England	29,666	1,543	763,785	15,308	4,569
3. Adirondacks	14,066	1,139	231,217	5,289	3,024
4. East Pennsylvania/ South New England	20,947	1,320	118,800	8,400	2,556
5. West New York/Pennsylvania	25,051	376	16,920	7,114	1,678
6. Appalachian Plateau	16,190	13	29,510	7,350	2,299
7. Blue Ridge/Great Smoky Mountains	20,964	126	14,868	10,901	3,396
8. Coastal Plain	9,264	241	8,917	1,547	713
9. Lower Mississippi	13,075	170	56,610	5,374	1,255
10. Indiana/Kentucky	8,603	9	603	2,805	989
11. Central Wisconsin	12,141	583	187,726	2,683	728
12. Wisconsin/Michigan Highlands	19,229	5,307	801,357	5,037	1,737
13. Northeast Minnesota	10,560	1,637	473,093	1,637	475
14. Central Minnesota	18,870	3,170	323,340	4,831	2,529
Totals	245,024	17,059	3,609,571	87,990	29,433

SOURCE: "Regional Assessment of Aquatic Resources at Risk From Acidic Deposition," prepared for OTA by The Institute of Ecology, June 1982.

deposition, using a 200-μeq/l alkalinity level as the cut-off point between sensitive and nonsensitive lakes and streams. Results show an estimated 9,400 lakes and 60,000 miles of streams that are **currently sensitive to** further acid inputs (tables B-2 and B-3).

To estimate the portion of these sensitive lakes and streams that **already have been altered** by acidic deposition, TIE compared data on the distribution of alkalinity levels for two distinct geographic areas: 1) regions with little neutralizing capacity that currently receive high (resource-affecting) levels of acidic deposition; and 2) geologically similar areas of northwestern Ontario and northern Minnesota having little neutralizing capacity, but that receive negligible amounts of acid deposition. The difference between the two distributions provides an estimate of the proportion of lakes and streams that can be considered "acid-altered," rather than simply sensitive. Only lakes with alkalinity levels less than 40 μeq/l and streams with less than 100 μeq/l—already acidified or extremely sensitive to further alteration—are considered in these calculations. Calculations using this approach show an estimated 3,000 lakes and 23,000 miles of streams with alkalinity levels that can be described as already acid-altered. This corresponds to 18 percent of the lakes and 20 percent of the streams located within the 14 sensitive areas (see tables B-4 and B-5).

Finally, TIE employed a simple model to estimate the effects on aquatic resources of three possible future acid deposition scenarios. As an underlying assumption, the model uses an empirical measure to project changes in lake and stream alkalinities given a change in sulfate

deposition. This measure—the "alkalinity impact parameter"—is based on both limited observations of alkalinity changes through time in areas where sulfate deposition has been increased or reduced, and on current theory about the processes involved.* Although not yet fully tested, the model suggests that lake and stream alkalinities are likely to respond to future **changes** in sulfate deposition. The model **cannot** address further changes in lake and stream water quality that might occur if deposition **remains constant** over the next several decades.

For scenario I, a 10-percent **increase** in sulfate deposition by 2000, the model projects that 5 to 15 percent (depending on the region) of the most sensitive lakes and streams worsen in condition—becoming either "acidified" or "extremely sensitive" to acid inputs.

---

*An empirical "alkalinity impact parameter" (AIP) can be defined as the ratio of observed **changes in lake and stream alkalinity levels** to **changes in sulfate loadings.** When sulfate retention by the watershed approaches zero, nitrate uptake by plants is high, and further losses of nutrient cations—e.g., calcium and magnesium—are low or negligible, acidity (H_2SO_4) **directly** affects alkalinity (HCO_3), and the expected AIP is 2. For the case in which some neutralization of acid input occurs in the watershed, the AIP would be less than 2; during the very early stages of acidic deposition, it should approach zero. Where soils have high sulfate adsorption capacity, the AIP would also approach zero during the early stages of an acidification process; later, if acid deposition to the watershed is decreased, some of the sulfate previously retained can be washed from the soil, and AIP values could exceed 2. Calculations using an AIP of greater than 2 were not considered, since many of the watersheds in the regions mapped as sensitive for this study have low sulfate adsorption capacities.

The importance of atmospheric deposition of calcium and magnesium as potential neutralizing agents has been considered. For the areas examined, calcium and magnesium deposition appear to be only one-tenth the magnitude of sulfate deposition; therefore, its role has been considered negligible for the present calculations.

Table B-2.—Estimated Lake Resources at Risk in the Acid-Sensitive Regions of the Eastern United States

Region	Sensitive area (mi²)	Total number lakes	Percentage of lakes <200 µeq/l	Calculated number of lakes at risk
1. Eastern Maine	26,398	1,425	(80)[a]	1,140
2. Western New England	29,666	1,543	(80)[a]	1,234
3. Adirondacks	14,066	1,139	80	911
4. East Pennsylvania/ South New England	20,947	1,320	(80)[a]	1,056
5. West New York/Pennsylvania	25,051	376	(80)[a]	301
6. Appalachian Plateau	16,190	13	—[b]	—
7. Blue Ridge/Great Smoky Mountains	20,964	126	—	—
8. Coastal Plain	9,264	241	—	—
9. Lower Mississippi	13,075	170	—	—
10. Indiana/Kentucky	8,603	9	—	—
11. Central Wisconsin	12,141	583	(42)[c]	245
12. Wisconsin/Michigan Highlands	19,229	5,307	42	2,228
13. Northeast Minnesota	10,560	1,637	48	786
14. Central Minnesota	18,870	3,170	(48)[d]	1,522
Totals	245,024	17,059		9,423

[a] In the absence of other data, alkalinities from the Adirondacks have been used.
[b] No estimate is being made for regions with fewer than 250 lakes.
[c] In the absence of other data, alkalinities from north Wisconsin have been used.
[d] In the absence of other data, alkalinities from north Minnesota have been used.

SOURCE: "Regional Assessment of Aquatic Resources at Risk From Acidic Deposition," prepared for OTA by The Institute of Ecology, June 1982.

Table B-3.—Estimated First- and Second-Order Stream Resources at Risk in the Acid-Sensitive Regions of the Eastern United States

Region	Sensitive area (mi²)	Total streams (mi) 1st order	2d order	Percentage of stream <200 µeq/l	Calculated total miles of: 1° streams at risk	2° streams at risk
1. Eastern Maine	26,398	9,714	3,485	81	7,868	2,823
2. Western New England	29,666	15,308	4,569	56	8,573	2,559
3. Adirondacks	14,066	5,289	3,024	(56)[a]	2,962	1,693
4. East Pennsylvania/South New England	20,947	8,400	2,556	38	3,192	971
5. West New York/Pennsylvania	25,051	7,114	1,678	61	4,340	1,024
6. Appalachian Plateau	16,190	7,350	2,299	(61)[b]	4,484	1,402
7. Blue Ridge/Great Smoky Mountains	20,964	10,901	3,396	64	6,977	2,173
8. Coastal Plain	9,264	1,547	713	(43)[c]	665	307
9. Lower Mississippi	13,075	5,374	1,255	(43)[c]	2,311	540
10. Indiana/Kentucky	8,603	2,805	989	(43)[c]	1,206	425
11. Central Wisconsin	12,141	2,683	728	43	1,154	313
12. Wisconsin/Michigan Highlands	19,229	5,037	1,737	13	655	226
13. Northeast Minnesota	10,560	1,637	475	(13)[d]	213	62
14. Central Minnesota	18,870	4,831	2,529	(13)[d]	628	329
Totals	245,024	87,990	29,433		45,228	14,847

[a] In the absence of other data, alkalinities from west New England and west New York/Pennsylvania have been used.
[b] In the absence of other data, alkalinities from west New York/Pennsylvania have been used.
[c] In the absence of other data, alkalinities from central Wisconsin have been used.
[d] In the absence of other data, alkalinities from northern Wisconsin have been used.

SOURCE: "Regional Assessment of Aquatic Resources at Risk From Acidic Deposition," prepared for OTA by The Institute of Ecology, June 1982.

Table B-4.—Estimates of Extremely Sensitive or Acidified Lake Resources[a] in the Eastern United States

Region	Total number of lakes	1980 number of lakes with alkalinities <40 μeq/l	Historic number of lakes with alkalinities <40 μeq/l	1980 number of acid-altered lakes <40 μeq/l
1. Eastern Maine	1,425	456	43	413
2. Western New England	1,543	494	46	448
3. Adirondacks	1,139	456	34	422
4. East Pennsylvania/ South New England	1,320	423	40	383
5. West New York/Pennsylvania	376	150	11	139
6. Appalachian Plateau	13	—	—	—
7. Blue Ridge/Great Smoky Mountains	126	—	—	—
8. Coastal Plain	241	—	—	—
9. Lower Mississippi	170	—	—	—
10. Indiana/Kentucky	9	—	—	—
11. Central Wisconsin	583	134	17	117
12. Wisconsin/Michigan Highlands	5,307	1,220	159	1,061
13. Northeast Minnesota	1,637	49	49	0
14. Central Minnesota	3,170	95	95	0
Totals	17,059	3,477	494	2,983

Total number of lakes altered, Class I and II: 2,983.
Percentage of lakes altered: 18%.
[a]Lakes with alkalinity less than 40 μeq/l, based on using 1980 calculated alkalinity depression and "historic" area alkalinity distributions as a control.
SOURCE: "Regional Assessment of Aquatic Resources at Risk From Acidic Deposition," prepared for OTA by The Institute of Ecology, June 1982.

Table B-5.—Estimates of Extremely Sensitive or Acidified Stream Resources[a] in the Eastern United States

Region	Total stream miles	1980 miles with alkalinities <100 μeq/l[b]	Historic stream miles with alkalinities <100 μeq/l	Acid-altered stream miles <100 μeq/l
1. Eastern Maine	13,199	3,746	816	2,930
2. Western New England	19,877	5,641	1,228	4,413
3. Adirondacks	8,313	3,060	514	2,546
4. East Pennsylvania/South New England	10,956	3,109	677	2,432
5. West New York/Pennsylvania	8,792	3,237	543	2,694
6. Appalachian Plateau	9,649	2,738	596	2,142
7. Blue Ridge/Great Smoky Mountains	14,297	4,058	884	3,174
8. Coastal Plain	2,260	482	140	342
9. Lower Mississippi	6,629	1,412	410	1,002
10. Indiana/Kentucky	3,794	809	234	575
11. Central Wisconsin	3,411	726	211	515
12. Wisconsin/Michigan Highlands	6,774	418	418	0
13. Northeast Minnesota	2,112	130	131	0
14. Central Minnesota	7,360	455	455	0
Totals	117,423	30,021	7,257	22,765

[a]Streams with alkalinity less than 100 μeq/l, based on 1980 calculated alkalinity depression and "historic" area alkalinity distributions as a control.
[b]A higher alkalinity level was used to denote extreme sensitivity for streams than for lakes.
SOURCE: "Regional Assessment of Aquatic Resources at Risk From Acidic Deposition," prepared for OTA by The Institute of Ecology, June 1982.

Under scenario II, which provides for a 20-percent **decrease** in sulfate deposition by 2000, 10 to 25 percent of the most sensitive lakes and streams are estimated to experience some recovery—i.e., "acidified" aquatic resources become "extremely sensitive" **or** "extremely sensitive" resources become "moderately sensitive." Scenario III, which involved a 35-percent **decrease** in sulfate deposition by the year 2000, is estimated to result in some recovery for 14 to 40 percent of the most sensitive aquatic resources.*

Figures B-2 and B-3 summarize the projected effects of scenarios I, II, and III on lakes and streams in a number of the sensitive areas. Each bar graph illustrates scenarios I, II, and III in that order. The two figures show the **sum of the calculated shifts to or from the most sensitive resource categories,** expressed as a percent of the **total** lake or stream resource in each area. The short, solid portion of each bar represents a highly probable response; the shaded portion of each bar represents the upper bound of the probable response.

Scenario III (a 35-percent reduction in sulfate deposition by 2000) appears likely to result in relatively significant responses for the total resource. Recovery for lakes is projected to range from a few to about 30 percent in each area, and up to 20 percent for streams, with the greatest recovery in areas of highest current deposition.

While the model indicates some important prospects for recovery, it cannot address certain long-term consequences of acidification. Soils that may have been depleted of such nutrients as calcium and magnesium by acid deposition might take a great deal longer to recover normal nutrient levels than water bodies take to regain equilibrium alkalinity levels. If the soil's ability to mitigate acid deposition recovers slowly, "acid shock" episodes to water bodies from such events as spring snowmelt may persist for some time. The magnitude of such consequences is unpredictable at this time.

Lastly, some discussion of the implications of these results for biological responses in aquatic systems is required. Scientists are gradually developing an understanding of how fish and other aquatic life are affected by acid-induced alterations of their environments. Thus, predictive statements about changes in water quality over some period of abatement represent the first step in making predictive statements about the potential recovery of aquatic life.

*Because the TIE model is most applicable to those lakes and streams in the acid-altered (Class I: < 0 μeq/l) and extremely sensitive (Class II: 0 to 40 μeq/l) categories, TIE used transfers into and out of each of these categories as the measure of change for aquatic resources in response to altered deposition. To correct for differences in alkalinity distributions between streams and lakes, a defined portion of the streams in Class III (40 to 100 μeq/l) was included in the TIE calculations.

Figure B 2.—Lake Model Projections

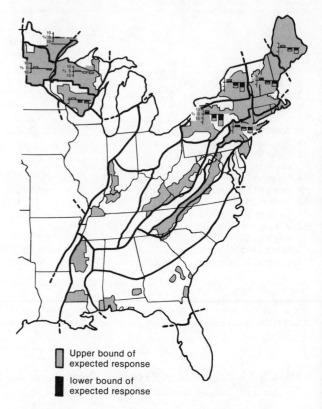

■ Upper bound of expected response

■ lower bound of expected response

(Where there is no black band, the lower bound is zero)

Bar-graphs show the percent increase (or decrease) by the year 2000 in lakes classed as "acidified" or "extreme" for the three deposition scenarios I (a 10-percent increase in deposition), II (a 20-percent decrease), and III (a 35-percent decrease), represented by the bars, in that order from left to right.
SOURCE: "Regional Assessment of Aquatic Resources at Risk From Acidic Deposition," prepared for OTA by The Institute of Ecology, June 1982.

Effects of Acid Deposition on Aquatic Life

Losses of fish populations attributed to the effects of acid deposition have received a great deal of public attention; however, the available evidence indicates that acidic waters also affect many other forms of aquatic life, from single-celled algae to large aquatic plants to amphibians such as frogs and salamanders. Adverse effects on aquatic plants and animals can affect the availability of food to other animals such as fish, aquatic birds, and mammals.

Fish **reproduction** requires water pH levels of above 4.5, according to numerous laboratory studies and field surveys (13). The International Joint Commission has recommended a water quality standard of greater than

Figure B 3.—Stream Model Projections

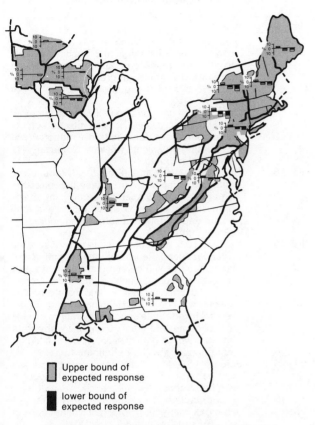

■ Upper bound of
expected response

■ lower bound of
expected response

(Where there is no black band, the lower bound is zero)

Bar-graphs show the percent increase (or decrease) by
the year 2000 in lakes classed as "acidified" or
"extreme" for the three deposition scenarios I (a 10-
percent increase in deposition), II (a 20-percent decrease),
and III (a 35-percent decrease), represented by the bars,
in that order from left to right.

SOURCE: "Regional Assessment of Aquatic Resources at Risk From Acidic
Deposition," prepared for OTA by The Institute of Ecology, June 1982.

pH 6.5 for successful fish reproduction. Death of **adult**
fish does not generally occur until the pH is less than
5.0. Rapid decreases in stream and lake pH due to
spring snowmelt and release of acid accumulated over
the winter can be detrimental if they coincide with sensitive periods of the fish reproductive cycle. Several
reports have documented sudden fish kills in both rivers
and lakes associated with springtime pH depressions
(14).

Survival of fish in water of low pH is influenced by
temperature, presence of metals such as aluminum,
hardness of the water, and type of acid input. Aluminum increases the sensitivity of fish to low pH levels
(15). Increases in the concentration of aluminum are
correlated with decreasing pH. Fish mortalities have
been documented as a result of increased aluminum con-

centrations, increased acidity, and the combination of
these two factors. The hardness of the water (mineral
content) increases the ability of fish to withstand low
pH; fish communities disappear from soft waters at
higher pH than they do from hard waters (16).

A recent inventory (1980) (17) of the New York State
Adirondacks (one of the largest sensitive lake districts
in the Eastern United States receiving significant
amounts of acid deposition) indicates that the brook
trout fishery has been most severely affected by acidification. At least 180 former brook trout ponds in the Adirondacks will no longer support populations. A survey
of 214 Adirondacks lakes in 1975 revealed that 52 percent had surface pH levels below 5.0, and that 90 percent of these were entirely devoid of fish life. Some of
these lakes had been surveyed between 1929 and 1937,
when only 4 percent (or 10 lakes) were below pH 5.0
and devoid of fish; over the intervening forty years entire fish communities of brook trout, lake trout, white
sucker, prawn bullhead, and several cyprinid species
were eliminated (18).

Similar losses of fish species have been observed in
acidic lakes in the La Cloche mountain range of Ontario, Canada (19). These field studies performed over
time show that species vary in their susceptibility to declining pH, and that the mechanisms by which individual species are eliminated are complex. In Nova Scotia
there are nine rivers with pH less than 4.7 which previously had salmon that can no longer sustain trout or
salmon reproduction (20). Losses to brook trout populations in the Great Smoky Mountain National Park have
also been associated with the acidity of streams and aluminum concentrations (21).

In the field, mass mortalities of fish have been observed during the spring due to the "acid shock" from
high concentrations of pollutants in snowmelt. Elevated
concentrations of aluminum mobilized from the soils by
strong acids present in snowmelt water are thought to
be a contributing factor to such large-scale fish mortality
(22). Increases in juvenile salmon mortality in Nova
Scotia hatcheries have also been associated with snow-
melt-induced pH depressions (23).

Field surveys and laboratory experiments have shown
amphibian populations, such as frogs and salamanders,
to be extremely sensitive to changes in pH. Many species breed in temporary pools that may be formed from
low-pH meltwater in spring. Because of the great vulnerability of their habitat to pH depressions, damage
to amphibian populations may be one of the earliest consequences of acidification of freshwaters. Experiments
have shown correlations between pH and both mortality
and embryo deformity in frog and salamander populations (24).

Numerous invertebrate animals are known to be affected by the acidification of water, although individual

species may vary greatly in sensitivity. Of these, shell-bearing organisms and molting crustaceans appear to be the most sensitive to low pH (25). No molluscs are known to inhabit waters of pH lower than 6.0, while most crustaceans (e.g., crayfish) are absent from waters of pH below 4.6 (26). Aquatic insects exhibit a wide range of sensitivities to pH (27).

Single-celled algae are a basic constituent of the aquatic food chain. Studies have shown that as pH decreases, significant changes occur in the species and diversity of algae that predominate (28). As lakes or streams acidify, acid-tolerant algae proliferate (29). This group of algae is not readily edible by zooplankton, the animals that link algae and smaller fish in the food chain. However, a recent study suggests that algal species have some capability to adapt to acidic environments over the long term. This may explain the observation that a group of relatively recently acidified lakes in Norway have less diverse algae than natural historically acidic lakes (30).

Changes in algae community structure induced by acidification may also alter zooplankton community structure. Acidification of lakes is accompanied by changes in abundance, diversity, and seasonality of zooplankton which may reflect changes in their food base (algae), predators (fish), and/or complex changes in water chemistry. Since both population density and average size of the animals are reduced, food availability to fish and other animals may be reduced (31).

Limited findings from New York State suggest that acid-tolerant algae may cover submerged aquatic plant communities in acidic lakes, thereby preventing them from receiving the sunlight necessary for growth (32). Studies of Swedish lakes and preliminary information from New York, Nova Scotia, and Ontario have shown that acidification tends to cause decline of aquatic plants and replacement by growths of sphagnum mosses on lake and river bottoms (33). Sphagnum moss creates a unique habitat which is considered unsuitable for some species of bottom-dwelling invertebrates or for use as fish spawning and nursery grounds (34). Dense sphagnum beds may also reduce the appeal of freshwater lakes and rivers for recreational activities.

A number of studies have also found that acidic waters are more favorable to fungi than to normal bacterial populations. In many Scandinavian lakes studied to date, an increase in bottom accumulation of organic matter has been observed. This has been attributed to a shift in dominance from bacteria to fungi, which are less effective at decomposing organic material and which delay the recycling of nutrients (35).

Table B-6 and figure B-4 summarize the effects of decreasing pH on aquatic organisms. Table B-6 describes biological processes affected in different orga-

Table B-6.—Effects of Decreasing pH on Aquatic Organisms

pH	Effect
8.0-6.0	In the long run, decreases of *less than one-half of a pH unit* in the range of 8.0 to 6.0 are likely to alter the biotic composition of lakes and streams to some degree. However, the significance of these slight changes is not great. Decreases of *one-half to one pH unit* (a threefold to tenfold increase in acidity) may detectably alter community composition. Productivity of competing organisms will vary. Some species will be eliminated.
6.0-5.5	Decreasing pH from 6.0 to 5.5 will reduce the number of species in lakes and streams. Among remaining species, significant alterations in the ability to withstand stress may occur. Reproduction of some salamander species is impaired.
5.5-5.0	Below pH 5.5, numbers and diversity of species will be reduced. Reproduction is impaired and many species will be eliminated. Crustacean zooplankton, phytoplankton, molluscs, amphipods, most mayfly species, and many stone fly species will begin to be eliminated. In contrast, several invertebrate species tolerant to low pH will become abundant. Overall, invertebrate biomass will be greatly reduced. Certain higher aquatic plants will be eliminated.
5.0-4.5	Below pH 5.0, decomposition of organic detritus will be impaired severely. Most fish species will be eliminated.
4.5 and below	In addition to exacerbation of the above changes, many forms of algae will not survive at a pH of less than 4.5.

SOURCE: International Joint Commission, Great Lakes Advisory Board (1979), after Hendrey, 1979.

nisms as the pH of water decreases. Figure B-4 displays the percent of each of 7 major categories (taxonomic groups) remaining as pH decreases. For example, at pH 7, 100 percent of normal mollusc species are present. As pH decreases, the number of species remaining decreases rapidly. At a pH of 5.5, all mollusc species have disappeared.

B.1 References

1. Braun, E. L., *Deciduous Forests of Eastern North America* (Philadelphia, Pa.: The Blakiston Co., 1950).
2. Fenneman, N. M., *Physiography of the Eastern United States* (New York: McGraw-Hill Book Co., 1938).
3. Kramer, J. R., "Geochemical and Lithological Factors in Acid Precipitation," USDA Forest Service General Technical Report NE-23, 1976.
4. Harvey, H. H., Pierce, R. C., Dillon, P. J., Kramer, J. P., and Whelpdale, D. M., "Acidification in the Canadian Aquatic Environment: Scientific Criterion for Assessing Effects of Acidic Deposition on Aquatic Ecosystems"

Figure B-4.—Relative Number of Taxa of the Major Taxonomic Groups as a Function of Acidity

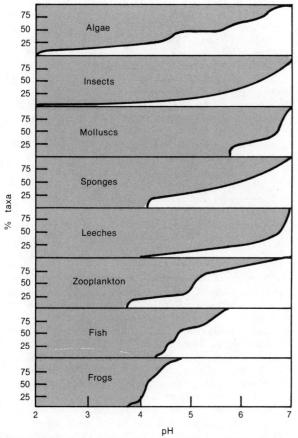

SOURCE: *Impact Assessment*, Work Group 1, United States - Canada Memorandum of Intent on Transboundary Air Pollution, Final Report, January 1983.

(Ottawa, Ontario, Canada: National Research Council Canada, NRCC No. 18475, 1981).

5. U.S.-Canada Memorandum of Intent on Transboundary Air Pollution, "Impact Assessment, Work Group I," Phase II Interim Working Paper (Washington, D.C., and Ottawa, Ontario, Canada, 1981).

6. Haines, T. A., "Effects of Acid Rain on Atlantic Salmon Rivers and Restoration Efforts in the United States," *Proceedings of the Conference on Acid Rain and the Atlantic Salmon, Portland Maine, November 22-23, 1980*, International Atlantic Salmon Foundation Special Publication Series No. 10, March 1981 (New York: IASF, 1981).

7. Pfeiffer, M. H., and Festa, P. J., "Acidity Status of Lakes in the Adirondack Region of New York in Relation to Fish Resources. Progress Report" (Albany, N.Y.: New York State Department of Environmental Conservation, 1980).

8. Arnold, D. E., "Vulnerability of Lakes and Streams in the Middle Atlantic States to Acidification," Interim Progress Report (University Park, Pa.: Cooperative Fisheries Research Unit, Pennsylvania State University, 1981).

9. Hendrey, G. R., Galloway, J. N., Norton, S. A., Schofield, C. L., Shaffer, P. W., and Burns, D. A., "Geological and Hydrochemical Sensitivity of the Eastern United States to Acid Precipitation" (Corvallis, Oreg.: U.S. EPA Environmental Research Lab, EPA-600/3-80-024, 1980).

10. Eilers, J. (with 12 other authors), "Acid Precipitation Investigation for Northern Wisconsin," Progress Report (Duluth, Minn.: Wisconsin DNR, Rhinelander; and U.S. EPA-ERL, 1979).

11. Glass, G. E., and Loucks, O. L. (eds.), "Impacts of Airborne Pollutants on Wilderness Areas Along the Minnesota-Ontario Border," EPA-600/3-80-044 (Duluth, Minn.: U.S. EPA Environmental Research Lab, 1980).

12. Andrews, L. M., and Threinen, C. W., "Surface Water Resources of Oneida County" (Madison, Wis.: Wisconsin Conservation Department Report, 1966); and Klick, T. A., and Threinen, C. W., "Surface Water Resources of Jackson County, Lake and Stream Classification Project" (Madison, Wis.: Department of Natural Resources, 1968).

13. Beamish, R. J., "Acidification of Lakes in Canada by Acid Precipitation and the Resulting Effects on Fishes," *Water, Air, Soil Pollut.* 6:501-514, 1976; and EIFAC (European Inland Fisheries Advisory Commission), "Water Quality Criteria for Freshwater Fish, Report on Extreme pH Values and Inland Fisheries," *Water Res.* 3:593-611, 1969.

14. Harvey, H. H., "The Acid Deposition Problem and Emerging Research Needs in the Toxicology of Fishes," Proc. 5th Annual Aquatic Toxicity Workshop, Hamilton, Ontario, Nov. 7-9, 1978, *Fish. Mar. Serv. Tech. Rep.* 862:115-128, 1979.

15. Davis, J. M., External Review Draft, Research Triangle Park, N.C., U.S. Environmental Criteria and Assessment Office, 1980; and Dickson, W., "Some Effects of the Acidification of Swedish Lakes," *Verh. Int. Verein. Limnol.* 20:851-856, 1978.

16. Leivestad, H., Hendrey, G., Muniz, I. P., and Snekvik, E., "Effects of Acid Precipitation on Freshwater Organisms," *Impact of Acid Precipitation on Forest and Freshwater Ecosystems in Norway*, F. Braekke (ed.), SNSF Project, NISK 1432 Aas-NLH, Norway, 1976.

17. Pfeiffer, M. H., and Festa, P. J., "Acidity Status of Lakes in the Adirondack Region of New York in Relation to Fish Resources," Progress Report, Department of Environmental Conservation, New York State, Albany, 1980.

18. Schofield, C. L., "Lake Acidification in the Adirondack Mountains of New York: Causes and Consequences," *Proc. 1st Int. Symp. on Acid Precipitation and the Forest Ecosystem*, USDA Forest Service General Technical Report NE-23, 477, 1976.

19. Beamish, R. J., "The Loss of Fish Populations From Unexploited Remote Lakes in Ontario, Canada, as a Consequence of Atmospheric Fallout of Acid," *Water Res.* 8:85-95, 1974; Beamish, R. J., "Acidification of Lakes in Canada by Acid Precipitation and the Resulting Effects on Fishes," *Water, Air, Soil Pollut.* 6:501-514, 1976;

and Beamish, R. J., and Harvey, H. H., "Acidification of the La Cloche Mountain Lakes, Ontario and Resulting Fish Mortalities," *J. Fish. Res. Board Can.* 29:1131-1143, 1972.
20. Watt, W. D., "Present and Potential Effects of Acid Precipitation on the Atlantic Salmon in Eastern Canada," *Acid Rain and the Atlantic Salmon,* Special Publications Series of the International Atlantic Salmon Foundation, No. 10, 1981.
21. Herrmann, R., and Baron, J., "Aluminum Mobilization in Acid Stream Environments, Great Smoky Mountains National Park, U.S.A.," *Proc. Int. Conf. Ecol. Impact of Acid Precipitation,* D. Drablos and A. Tollan (eds.), SNSF Project, Norway, 1980.
22. Muniz, I. P., and Leivestad, H., "Acidification—Effects on Freshwater Fish," *Proc. Int. Conf. Ecological Impact Acid Precipitation,* D. Drablos and A. Tollan (eds.), SNSF Project, Norway, 1980; and Schofield, C. L., and Trojnar, J. R., "Aluminum Toxicity to Brook Trout (*Salvelinus fontinalis*) in Acidified Waters," *Polluted Rain* (New York: Plenum Press, 1980).
23. Farmer, G. J., Goff, T. T., Ashfield, D., and Samant, H. S., "Some Effects of the Acidification of Atlantic Salmon Rivers in Nova Scotia," *Can. Tech. Rep. Fish. Aquat. Sci.,* No. 972, 1980.
24. Pough, F. H., "Acid Precipitation and Embryonic Mortality of Spotted Salamanders, *Ambystoma Maculatum*," *Science* 192:68-70, 1976; and Stirjbosch, H., "Habitat Selection of Amphibians During Their Aquatic Phase," *Oikos* 33:363-372, 1979.
25. Okland, K. A., "Ecology and Distribution of Acellus Aquaticus (L) in Norway, Including Relation to Acidification in Lakes," SNSF Project, IR 52/80, 1432 Aas-NLH, Norway, 1980; and Wiederholm, T., and Eriksson, L., "Benthos of an Acid Lake," *Oikos* 29:261-267, 1977.
26. Okland, J., "Om Fursuring av Vassdrag og Betydningen av Surhetsgraden (pH) for Fiskens Naeringsdyr: Ferskvann," *Fauna* 22:140-147, 1969; and Svardson, G., "Inform. Inst. Freshw. Res. Drottingholm" (Cited in Almer, et al., 1978), 1974.
27. Almer, B., Dickson, W., Ekstrom, C., and Hornstrom, E., "Sulfur Pollution and the Aquatic Ecosystem," *Sulfur in the Environment: Part II Ecological Impacts,* J. O. Nriagu (ed.) (New York: John Wiley & Sons, Inc., 1978).
28. Kwiatkowski, R. E., and Roff, J. C., "Effects of Acidity on Phytoplankton and Primary Production of Selected Northern Ontario Lakes," *Can. J. Bot.* 54:2546-2561, 1976.
29. Dickson, W., "Some Effects of the Acidification of Swedish Lakes," *Verh. Int. Verein. Limnol.* 20:851-856, 1978; and Yan, N. D., "Phytoplankton of an Acidified, Heavy

Metal-contaminated Lake Near Sudbury, Ontario, 1973-1977," *Wat. Air Soil Pollut.* 11:43-55, 1979.
30. Raddum, G. G., Hobaek, A., Lomsland, E. R., and Johnson, T., "Phytoplankton and Zooplankton in Acidified Lakes in South Norway," *Ecol. Impact of Acid Precipitation,* D. Drablos and A. Tollan (eds.), SNSF Project, Norway, 1980.
31. Yan, N. D., and Strus, R., "Crustacean Zooplankton Communities of Acidic, Metal-contaminated Lakes Near Sudbury, Ontario," *Ont. Min. Env. Tech. Rep.,* LTS 79-4, 1979.
32. Hendrey, G. R., and Vertucci, F., "Benthic Plant Communities in Acidic Lake Colden, New York: *Sphagnum* and the Algal Mat," *Proc. Int. Conf. Ecological Impact Acid Precipitation,* D. Drablos and A. Tollan (eds.), SNSF Project, Norway, 1980.
33. Harvey, H. H., Pierce, R. C., Dillon, P. J., Kramer, J. P., and Whelpdale, D. M., *Acidification in the Canadian Aquatic Environment: Scientific Criterion for an Assessment of the Effects of Acidic Deposition on Aquatic Ecosystems,* Nat. Res. Coun. Canada Report No. 18475, 1981; Hendrey, G. R., and Wright, R. F., "Acid Precipitation in Norway: Effects on Aquatic Fauna," Proc. 1st Spec. Symp. on Atmospheric Contribution to the Chemistry of Lake Waters, Int. Assoc. Great Lakes Res., Orillia, Ontario, Sept. 28-Oct. 1, 1975, *J. Great Lakes Res. 2,* Suppl. 1:192-207, 1976; Kerekes, J. J., "Summary of the 1980 Environmental Contaminants Control Fund Investigation in the Calibrated Watersheds Study in Kejmkujik National Park," unpublished manuscript, Canadian Wildlife Service, Halifax, Nova Scotia, 1981; and Grahn, O., "Macrophyte Succession in Swedish Lakes Caused by Deposition of Airborne Acid Substances," *Proceedings of the First International Symposium on Acid Precipitation and the Forest Ecosystem,* L. S. Dochinger and T. A. Seliga (eds.), Ohio State University, May 12-15, 1975, USDA Forest Service General Technical Report NE-23, Upper Darby, Pa., Forest Service, U.S. Department of Agriculture, Northeastern Forest Experiment Station, 1976.
34. Hultberg, H., and Grahn, O., "Effects of Acid Precipitation on Macrophytes in Oligotrophic Swedish Lakes," *Proc. First. Specialty Symposium on Atmospheric Contribution to the Chemistry of Lake Waters, Internat. Assoc. Great Lakes Res. Sept. 28-Oct. 1, 1975.*
35. Bick, H., and Drews, E. F., "Self Purification and Silicate Communities in an Acid Milieu (Model Experiments)," *Hydrobiologia* 42:393-402, 1973; and Traaen, T. S., and Laake, M., "Microbial Decomposition and Community Structure as Related to Acidity of Fresh Waters—An Experimental Approach," SNSF Project, Norway, 1980.

B.2 TERRESTRIAL RESOURCES AT RISK*

The Effects of Ozone on Agricultural Productivity

For over two decades, ozone has been known to harm crops (27).** Alone, or in combination with sulfur dioxide (SO_2) and nitrogen oxides (NO_x), it causes up to 90 percent of the Nation's air pollution-related crop losses (29). Previous studies estimated that 2 to 4 percent of total U.S. crop production was lost annually, using limited available data and assuming that all areas of the United States just met the current ozone standard. These efforts were limited by the unavailability of field-generated data on crop loss, insufficient data on ozone levels in various parts of the country, and a lack of integration with available crop distribution and productivity data.

OTA's analysis uses National Crop Loss Assessment Network (NCLAN) field-experiment data on the effects of ozone on crops (28), in combination with more recent crop and ozone data, to estimate the effects of ozone on U.S. corn, wheat, soybean, and peanut production.

The selected crops range in susceptibility to ozone from sensitive (peanut) to sensitive/intermediate (soybean) to intermediate (wheat) to tolerant (corn). Among major U.S. agricultural commodities, these four crops represent 62 percent of the acres harvested and 63.5 percent of the dollar value. The analysis compared county-level agricultural data with estimated county-level nonurban ozone concentrations derived from measurements at approximately 300 selected monitoring stations. Actual 1978 crop yields were assumed to represent potential yields minus reductions in productivity due to current levels of atmospheric pollutants including ozone. Data from controlled field experiments were used to develop dose-response functions relating ozone level to crop productivity. The functions were then used to estimate potential gains in productivity achievable by reducing ozone levels to an estimated natural "background" concentration of 25 parts per billion (ppb).

The assessment estimates that in 1978, corn yields would have increased by 2.5 percent, wheat by 6 percent, soybeans by 13 percent, and peanuts by 24 percent if ozone levels had been reduced to natural background levels. As measured by 1978 crop prices, this represents about $2 billion of agricultural productivity.

---

*This section adapted from: Oak Ridge National Laboratory, Environmental Sciences Division, "An Analysis of Potential Agriculture and Forest Impacts of Long-Range Transport Air Pollutants," OTA contractor report, 1983.

**Citation numbers are keyed to Reference list at back of this section.

Of the estimated dollar impact, soybeans represent 69 percent, corn 17 percent, wheat 6 percent, and peanuts 8 percent. The Corn Belt States of Illinois, Iowa, and Indiana, plus Missouri, Arkansas, Minnesota, Ohio, Kentucky, North Carolina, and Virginia were estimated to have experienced the greatest agricultural effect.

Crop Response Data

Crop response data were obtained from the 1980 NCLAN Annual Report (77), or from earlier experiments using the methods later adopted for the NCLAN project (22,24,25). Test plants were grown in uniform, open-top field chambers and exposed to carefully controlled ozone levels. Yield data from plants receiving charcoal-filtered air (25 ppb ozone) were used as controls. Three sets of soybean data, four sets of wheat data, and one set each for corn and peanuts were used to estimate quantitative relationships between ozone levels and crop damage.

Crop Yield Data

The Census of Agriculture, conducted approximately every 5 years by the Department of Commerce, develops an extensive national inventory based on responses to mail questionnaires. The 1978 Census of Agriculture provided county-level yield statistics for the surveyed crops. The analysis averaged winter and spring wheat yields together, and excluded sweet corn production from corn yields.

Ozone Data

The U.S. Environmental Protection Agency (EPA) provided estimates of seasonal ozone concentrations for the analysis (75). EPA selected approximately 300 from a total of over 500 EPA monitoring stations as regionally representative and free from urban influence. Stations and observations were screened to eliminate those with few or unrepresentative readings. The monitoring stations are irregularly distributed, and large areas of the country lack monitoring data for rural areas. The available data were used to estimate values for counties without monitoring data using a statistical-averaging procedure called kriging. Seasonal averages were calculated as the mean of the growing season months appropriate for each crop (wheat, April-May; corn, peanuts, June-August; and soybeans, June-September). The EPA estimates of average ozone concentration during June to September 1978 are show in chapter 4 (fig. 15).

Regional Impacts

Figures B-5 through B-8 show the general pattern of productivity gains for each crop as potential yield increases (i.e., bushels/acre). Table B-7 summarizes these yield increases (as percentage increases), and their market value at 1978 average crop prices, by State. However, these dollar values do not reflect the potential price effect of the projected yield increases. Since increasing crop production would tend to lower crop prices, the dollar values in table B-7 should only be considered a surrogate for ozone-related crop damage; the dollar values allow comparisons of yield increases across all four crops, as well as comparisons of potential State-level productivity increases.

Projections of Economic Effects If Ozone Levels Are Reduced in the Future

If ozone levels are reduced, the cost of producing an ozone-sensitive crop will decrease, because the same amount of land, fertilizer, labor, etc., will result in greater crop yields. But the economic effects of reducing ozone levels also depend on how farmers and consumers react to these changes. Farmers could, for example, choose to grow the same amounts of these crops as before, reducing their inputs of land, fertilizer, and labor. Alternatively, they could increase their production, making greater crop supplies available in the marketplace, though presumably at somewhat reduced crop prices.

Analysts at the U.S. Department of Agriculture (USDA) used two econometric models to estimate how OTA's projected yield increases might affect farmers and consumers (80). The models assessed the potential effect of eliminating half the manmade ozone over a 10-year period (i.e., reducing ozone concentrations to the midpoint between measured 1978 levels and the estimated natural background level of 25 ppb by the early 1990's).

One of the models focuses primarily on domestic agricultural trends and policies; it projected that increasing the productivity of these three crops would cause supplies to increase moderately. However, it also projected these increases to cause proportionately larger declines in crop prices, reducing net farm income significantly, while inducing only marginal declines in the Consumer Price Index for food. The second model was designed primarily to assess international trends in agricultural production. While it also projected a moderate increase in U.S. supplies of corn, wheat, and soybeans, changes in production levels had significantly different economic repercussions. Estimated price reductions and supply increases were approximately in balance; supply increases outweighed price declines for corn and soybeans,

while price declines were proportionately larger than supply increases for wheat. Gross farm receipts for the three crops overall were estimated to increase slightly. The two models provide a qualitative perspective on the complex relationship between pollution and the agricultural sector of the economy; the economic effect of potential ozone reductions depends heavily on both farmer response and Federal agricultural policy.

Effects of Acid Rain on Agricultural Crops

Because several major U.S. agricultural regions experience elevated levels of acid deposition, researchers are attempting to determine whether acid deposition affects crop productivity. Crops are more likely to be damaged through direct contact with acid deposition on aboveground portions of plants than through soil-related effects. However, some soil-mediated effects—e.g., changes in nutrient availability, microbial activity, or metal toxicity—might also be important.

Research on how acid deposition affects crops has advanced about as far as research on ozone effects in the late 1960's. Acid deposition is a mixture of chemicals; plants respond not only to the hydrogen ions (acidity) but also to sulfate and nitrate ions that can act as fertilizers. Moreover, some researchers hypothesize interactions with other physical and biotic causes of plant stress (e.g., air pollution and pests), but little definitive evidence exists on which to base conclusions.

Mechanisms of Acid Rain Effect on Vegetation

No direct, visible injury to vegetation **in the field** has been demonstrated to result from exposure to ambient acid deposition. Rather, information about effects comes from a wide variety of approaches involving, in most instances, some form of rain "simulation." Adding sulfate and nitrate to soil-plant systems can have both positive and negative effects. Each system's response is affected by: 1) precedent conditions (e.g., soil nutrient status, plant nutrient requirements, plant sensitivity, and growth stage); and 2) the total loading or deposition of the critical ions (nitrate, sulfate, and hydrogen ions).

Concentrations of hydrogen ions equivalent to those measured in highly acidic rainfall events (i.e., pH less than about 3), have caused tissue lesions on a wide variety of plant species in greenhouse and laboratory experiments. This visible injury is reported to occur at a threshold of between pH 2.0 and 3.6. No evidence at the present time suggests that hydrogen ion inputs have any beneficial effect.

Table B-7.—Estimated Crop Gains (percentage increase and millions of 1978 dollars) Due to Ozone Reduction—Based on 1978 Crop and Ozone Data

	Wheat		Corn		Soybeans		Peanuts	
	Percent increase	Millions of dollars	Percent increase	Millions of dollars	Percent increase	Millions of dollars	Percent increase	Millions of dollars
Alabama	8.0	—	2.7	1	13.3	28	19.5	21
Alaska	—	—	—	—	—	—	—	—
Arizona	—	—	—	—	—	—	—	—
Arkansas	5.6	1	4.5	—	18.8	132	—	—
California	—	—	2.3	2	—	—	—	—
Colorado	7.6	12	3.0	5	—	—	—	—
Connecticut	—	—	0.0	—	—	—	—	—
Delaware	2.0	—	3.0	1	12.0	6	—	—
Florida	—	—	1.2	—	9.2	5	14.9	5
Georgia	8.0	1	2.7	5	15.8	29	22.3	72
Hawaii	—	—	—	—	—	—	—	—
Idaho	—	—	—	—	—	—	—	—
Illinois	5.3	5	2.6	68	13.0	262	—	—
Indiana	5.2	3	3.0	42	13.7	123	—	—
Iowa	5.9	—	2.3	73	11.3	200	—	—
Kansas	4.8	33	2.8	10	9.9	17	—	—
Kentucky	3.7	1	2.4	6	12.8	30	—	—
Louisiana	7.3	—	2.3	—	10.8	54	—	—
Maine	—	—	—	—	—	—	—	—
Maryland	2.0	—	3.4	4	14.1	11	—	—
Massachusetts	—	—	—	—	—	—	—	—
Michigan	4.0	2	1.6	7	6.3	9	—	—
Minnesota	4.9	3	1.1	15	9.6	76	—	—
Mississippi	6.7	—	3.7	—	18.0	89	—	—
Missouri	4.5	4	2.7	11	12.7	120	—	—
Montana	0.9	—	—	—	—	—	—	—
Nebraska	6.2	13	2.1	32	8.4	21	—	—
Nevada	6.3	—	—	—	—	—	—	—
New Hampshire	—	—	—	—	—	—	—	—
New Jersey	3.0	—	1.9	—	9.4	3	—	—
New Mexico	10.2	2	3.6	—	—	—	—	—
New York	5.5	—	2.1	2	—	—	—	—
North Carolina	7.2	1	4.1	10	20.6	48	35.9	34
North Dakota	5.3	—	0.7	—	—	—	—	—
Ohio	4.6	5	2.8	22	12.1	97	—	—
Oklahoma	4.7	17	3.0	—	17.9	6	26.3	10
Oregon	1.5	—	—	—	—	—	—	—
Pennsylvania	5.6	1	2.5	7	10.1	2	—	—
Rhode Island	0.0	—	—	—	0.0	—	—	—
South Carolina	8.3	—	4.1	2	21.7	37	35.9	2
South Dakota	5.4	3	1.3	5	8.1	6	—	—
Tennessee	4.9	1	2.9	3	13.2	43	—	—
Texas	7.3	12	2.9	7	11.5	12	12.7	10
Utah	7.8	—	3.7	—	—	—	—	—
Vermont	—	—	—	—	—	—	—	—
Virginia	3.2	—	3.6	4	19.1	15	38.9	21
Washington	1.9	—	—	—	—	—	—	—
West Virginia	3.9	—	2.1	—	—	—	—	—
Wisconsin	6.6	—	2.3	15	12.0	5	—	—
Wyoming	7.5	1	3.0	—	—	—	—	—
United States	5.3	125	2.4	361	13.0	1,485	23.8	175

SOURCE: Oak Ridge National Laboratory, 1983.

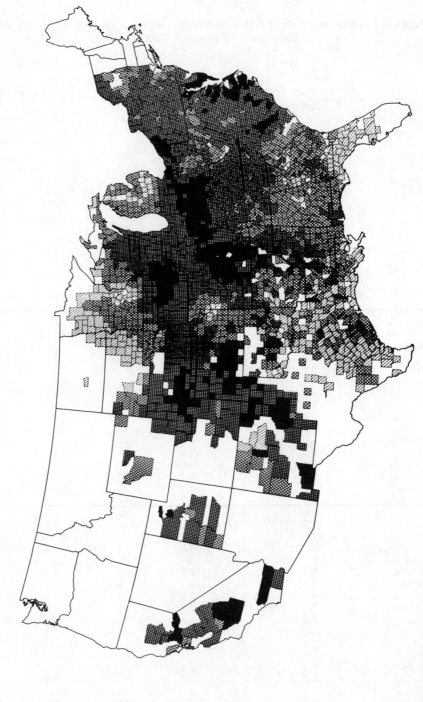

Figure B-5.—Corn: Crop Yield Gains (kg/ha) With Ozone Control
(based on 1978 agriculture census and 1978 ozone (EPA))

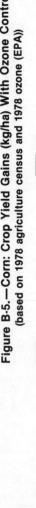

1-50 KG/HA

51-100 KG/HA

101-200 KG/HA

201-300 KG/HA

SOURCE: Oak Ridge National Laboratory, 1983.

Figure B-6.—Soybeans: Crop Yield Gains (kg/ha) With Ozone Control
(based on 1978 agriculture census and 1978 ozone (EPA))

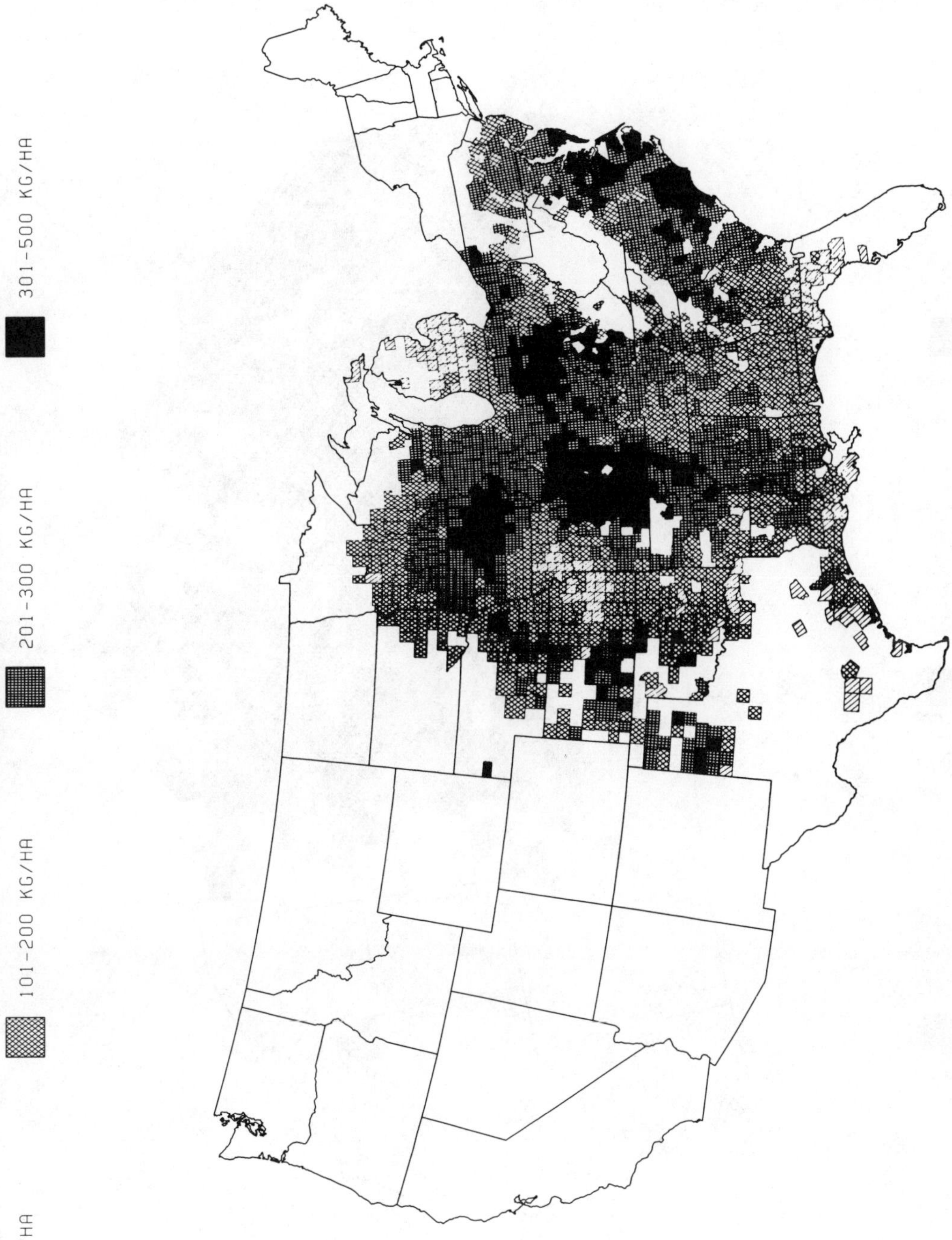

1-100 KG/HA

101-200 KG/HA

201-300 KG/HA

301-500 KG/HA

SOURCE: Oak Ridge National Laboratory, 1983.

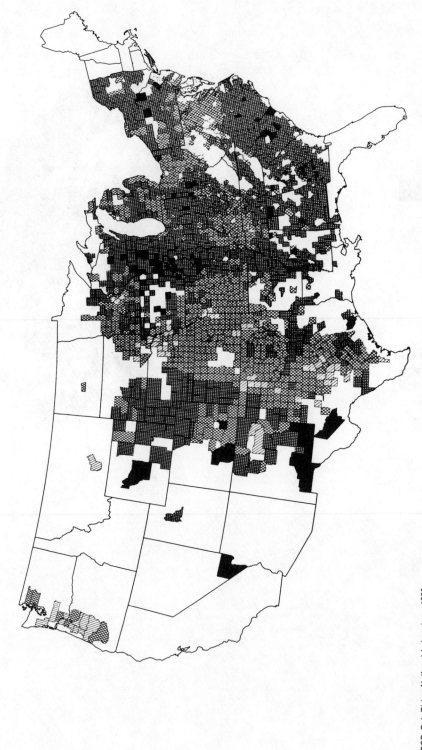

Figure B-7.—Wheat: Crop Yield Gains (kg/ha) With Ozone Control
(based on 1978 agriculture census and 1978 ozone (EPA))

1-50 KG/HA   51-100 KG/HA   101-200 KG/HA   201-400 KG/HA

SOURCE: Oak Ridge National Laboratory, 1983.

Figure B-8.—Peanuts: Crop Yield Gains (kg/ha) With Ozone Control
(based on 1978 agriculture census and 1978 ozone (EPA))

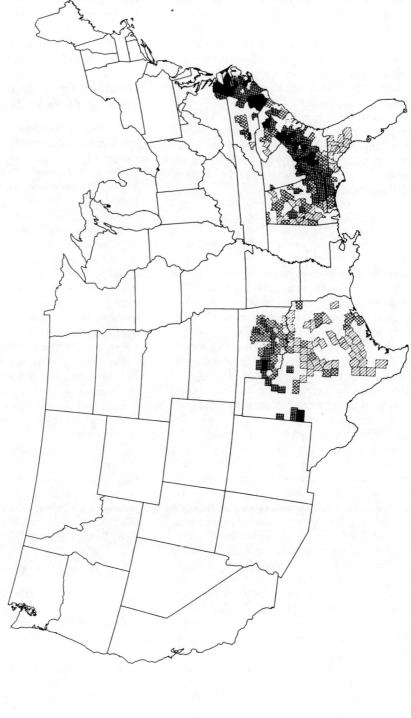

1-250 KG/HA

250-500 KG/HA

501-1000 KG/HA

1001-1500 KG/HA

SOURCE: Oak Ridge National Laboratory, 1983.

Recent research has found that vegetation is extremely responsive to the sulfur and nitrogen inputs in acid precipitation. Evidence from studies of field-grown soybeans (34) and forest tree species (2,119) indicate an apparent positive growth response to the sulfur and nitrogen in simulated acid rain. Other work suggests that sulfur may have been a limiting factor in the nutrition of experimental lettuce plots (37).

Pollutant deposition theoretically could affect soil-plant systems over the long term through potential soil changes—e.g., loss of calcium and magnesium or release of toxic metals. However, since croplands are heavily managed and fertilized, such soil-related effects due to acid deposition are unlikely.

Results of Field and Laboratory Studies

Several investigators have performed dose-response experiments on a variety of plant species. Thresholds for direct, visible injury to greenhouse foliage subjected to simulated acid rain typically are about pH 3.1 (36). However, field trials using the same treatment solutions under both greenhouse and field situations yield significantly different estimates of species sensitivity.

Experimental evidence suggests that a plant's "wetability" is an important factor in its response to acid deposition. Comparisons between studies of relatively wetable, nonwaxy bean cultivars (19,38,83) and studies of very waxy citrus leaves (26) show that the bean cultivars have a threshold of between pH 3.1 and 3.5 for developing foliar lesions, while a greater than 400-times increase in hydrogen ion concentration—to near pH 2.0—is required to induce visible symptoms in the citrus leaves. Waxy leaves appear to minimize the contact time for acid solutions. Table B-8 summarizes results of field experiments that applied simulated acid rain to nine crops: alfalfa, beet, corn, fescue, kidney bean, mustard green, radish, soybean, and spinach. The table lists effects on crop growth or yield rather than visible injury. No consistent trends are observed. For example, experiments on different types of soybeans resulted in positive, negative, and no growth effects. For both alfalfa and mustard green, altering the chemical composition of the acid rain simulant (but keeping the pH constant) drastically altered experimental results. Further complicating interpretation of these data, research has shown that the experimental procedures used to apply acid rain simulants also can affect results (18).

To summarize available information on how acid deposition affects crops: 1) visible injury thresholds for acid precipitation lie between pH 2.0 and 3.6, depending on species, and may vary from pH 3.0 to 3.6 within the same species (e.g., bean); 2) total dose of hydrogen ions appears to be most clearly related to visible injury; and 3) growth effects in the absence of visible injury have

been reported at a threshold of between pH 3.5 and 4.0, but sulfur and nitrogen in the precipitation may cause positive net growth effects, depending on soil nutrient status, buffering capacity, other growth conditions, and plant nutrient requirements.

Relationship of Acid Rain to Overall Crop Damage From Pollutants

Because acid deposition occurs throughout the Eastern United States and Canada, vegetation is commonly exposed both to gaseous pollutants such as ozone and sulfur dioxide, and to wet deposition of acidic substances. Little information is available to evaluate how plants respond to the combined effects of wet- and dry-deposited pollutants.

The foliage of vegetation is wetted by rain, fog, or dew formation during significant portions of the growing season in midlatitude temperate climates. During these periods, leaf surfaces more readily take up dry-deposited gases. For example, researchers found that as SO_2 dissolved in the dew on leaf surfaces, the acidity of the dew increased, suggesting the potential for dry-deposited acidic pollutants to react directly with wet vegetation surfaces (103).

Preliminary work suggests that acid deposition may interact with other pollutants. One researcher observed a significant growth reduction at harvest in plants intermittently exposed to ozone in addition to receiving four weekly exposures to rainfall of pH 4.0 (85). Another demonstrated that ozone depresses both growth and yield of soybeans under three different acid rain treatments, and that the depression was greatest with the most acidic rain (36). Experiments on field-grown soybeans found that simulated acid precipitation (pH 3.1) appeared to lessen plant response to SO_2 (34). The mechanisms of interaction are currently under investigation, but unknown.

Effects of Multiple Pollutants on Forests

One-third of the total land area of the United States is forested; two-thirds of that area—approximately 400 million acres—is classed as commercial timberland. Nearly three-quarters of the country's commercial timberland is located in the Eastern United States, distributed about equally between the North and South sections (fig. B-9). Nearly 80 percent of New England, and greater than 40 percent of the Atlantic Coast States, are forested.

Scientists have recently discovered productivity declines in several tree species throughout the Eastern United States from New England to Georgia. Acid dep-

Table B-8.—Field Research on Effects of Acid Precipitation on Crop Growth and Yield

Species/variety	Test pH	As compared to:	Effect
Alfalfa	3.0, 3.5,	Control: 5.6	No effect on yield
	4.0[a]	Control: 5.6	No effect; 9% greater yield
Beet	2.7, 3.1, 4.0	Ambient: 4.06	Lower number of marketable roots
	5.7	Ambient: 4.06	10% greater shoot growth, 16% greater yield
Corn	3.0, 3.5	Control: 5.6	No effect on yield or growth
	4.0	Control: 5.6	9% lower yield, no effect on growth
Fescue	3.0	Control: 5.6	No effect on yield
	3.5, 4.0	Control: 5.6	19%, 24% greater yield
Kidney bean	3.2	Control: 6.0	No effect on yield or growth
Mustard green	3.0[a], 4.0[a]	Control: 5.6	No effect; 31 to 33% lower yield
	3.5	Control: 5.6	No effect on yield
Radish "Champion"	2.8	Control: 5.6	13 to 17% higher root weight
	3.5	Control: 5.6	7 to 11% higher root weight
	4.2	Control: 5.6	3 to 7% higher root weight
	5.6	Ambient: 3.8	No effect; 12% lower root weight
Radish "Cherry Belle"	3.0, 4.0	Control: 5.6	No effect on yield or growth
	3.5[a]	Control: 5.6	No effect; 25% greater yield
Radish "Cherry Belle"	2.7, 3.1, 4.0	Control: 5.7	No effect on yield or growth
Soybean "Amsoy"	2.3	Ambient: 4.1	No effect on yield, lower pods/plant
	2.7	Ambient: 4.1	11% lower seed weight, lower seeds and pods/plant
	3.1, 4.0	Ambient: 4.1	No effect on yield or growth
Soybean "Amsoy"[b]	2.7[a]	Control: 5.6	3 to 11% lower yield
	3.3[a]	Control: 5.6	7 to 17% lower yield
	4.1[a]	Control: 5.6	8 to 23% lower yield
Soybean "Beeson"	2.8	Control: 4.0	32% greater yield, 17% greater seed size
	3.4	Control: 4.0	No effect on yield, 8% smaller seed size
Soybean "Davis"	2.8, 3.2, 4.0	Control: 5.3	No effect on yield or growth
	2.4, 3.2, 4.1	Control: 5.4	No effect on yield or growth
Soybean "Wells"	3.06	Control: 5.6	No effect on yield, 4% greater weight/seed
	5.6	Ambient: 4.1	No effect on yield, 4% greater weight/seed
Soybean "Williams"	2.8	Control: 4.0	No effect on yield, 17% smaller seed size
	3.4	Control: 4.0	No effect on yield, 22% greater seed size
Spinach	3.0, 3.5, 4.0	Control: 5.6	No effect on yield or growth

[a]Different acid rain simulants or treatment methods produced different results.
[b]See reference 18 to text of this section.

SOURCE: Modified from U.S. Environmental Protection Agency, "Effects on Vegetation," *The Acid Deposition Phenomenon and Its Effects, Critical Assessment Review Papers*, Public Review Draft, 1983, except as noted above.

osition, ozone, heavy-metal deposition, drought, severe winters or a combination of these are possible causes under investigation.

By coring trees and measuring the thickness of annual growth rings, scientists have observed marked reductions in productivity beginning about 1960 in red spruce, shortleaf pine, and pitch pine. Corings from about 30 other species at 70 sites throughout the East are currently being analyzed to determine the geographic extent and severity of the problem. Routine measurements of tree growth by the U.S. Forest Service have shown productivity declines in loblolly pine and shortleaf pine during the 1970's in the Piedmont region of South Carolina and Georgia. Again, the cause of these declines is not yet known, but air pollution is a possible factor.

Air pollutants can influence plant health through a complex process that depends not only on the level of pollution and duration of exposure but also on environmental factors that influence the plant's overall response as a living organism under stress. As with all stress-inducing agents, air pollutants may initiate changes within plant metabolic systems that cause extensive physiological modifications; sufficient change may lead to visible symptoms. In some instances, adding low pollutant levels to a plant's environment may induce a fertilizer-like response. This phenomenon has been analyzed in agronomic crops; however, no studies have shown beneficial effects on natural ecosystems.

Continual exposure to pollutants such as ozone and sulfur dioxide can cause tree death. Other contributing or mitigating factors also may be involved (i.e., abiotic or biotic disease-inducing agents or insect attack). Depending on the tree species, the seasonal stage of growth, pollutant dose, and environmental conditions, many forms of injury, varying widely in impact, may occur. A given plant may exhibit symptoms of acute and chronic injury simultaneously. However, injury does not necessarily imply damage (i.e., economic loss).

Figure B-9.—Percent of Land Area Capable of Commercial Timber Production[a]

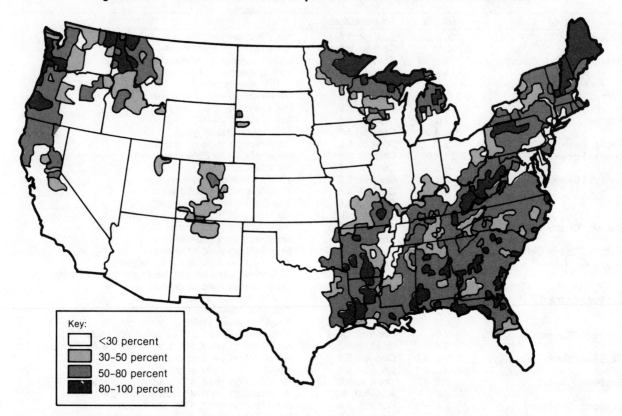

Key:
- ☐ <30 percent
- ▨ 30–50 percent
- ▩ 50–80 percent
- ■ 80–100 percent

[a]The U.S. Forest Service defines commercial timberland as lands capable of producing greater than 20 cubic feet of industrial roundwood per acre per year, in natural stands.
SOURCE: Oak Ridge National Laboratory from U.S. Forest Service inventory data.

The potential effects of acid deposition and gaseous pollutants (e.g., ozone) on forest productivity can be discussed only qualitatively at present. Figure B-10 summarizes the various mechanisms by which such a combination of pollutants might affect forest productivity. The top part of the diagram illustrates positive and negative effects on exposed vegetation; the bottom part of the diagram illustrates positive and negative effects on vegetation through soil processes. For example, each of the gaseous pollutants—ozone, SO_2, and NO_x—has a predominantly negative effect on vegetation. Acid deposition may have both positive and negative effects—fertilizing the soil with sulfur and nitrogen, but potentially leaching nutrients from leaves and releasing toxic aluminum from the soil.

Figure B-10 shows the **net** effect on the growth of vegetation as the sum of a series of positive and negative effects. Site-specific factors that control plant responses to any individual mechanism are likely to determine the net effect on plant productivity, assuming that different mechanisms do not interact to produce additional effects.

The greatest potential for negative pollutant impacts on trees appears to occur in the commercial forests of the Southeastern Coastal Plain, the Mississippi River Valley, the Appalachian Mountain chain, and the upper Ohio River Valley. These regions experience both high concentrations of ozone and elevated levels of acid deposition. In each of these areas, nitrogen inputs to forests would be expected to partially offset negative impacts, while sulfur inputs currently exceed forest growth requirements and probably have neither a significant positive or negative influence at this time.

To summarize the potential for long-term forest-productivity effects from both acid deposition and gaseous pollutants, at the present time OTA can state only that such interactions might occur and that their probability of occurrence is greatest in those regions of the Eastern United States outlined above. The mechanisms involved and the relative importance of those mechanisms to forest growth response must be studied further in order to better describe and eventually quantify these potential effects.

Figure B-10.—Schematic Representation of the Potential Effects of Air Pollutants (acid deposition, ozone, and other gases) on Forest Growth

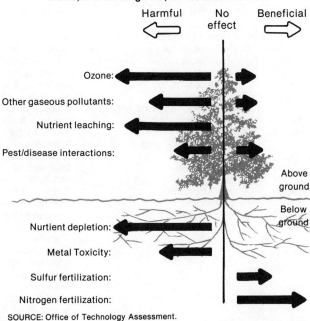

SOURCE: Office of Technology Assessment.

Implications of Potential Forest Productivity Declines Due to Air Pollution

If air pollution is shown to significantly affect the productivity of commercially forested timber species, potential long-term effects on forestry and related industries could be of concern. OTA used in-house information and analyses to identify significant factors about the current forest industry and how it might be affected by potential forest productivity declines due to air pollution.

It is estimated that improved management practices on suitable lands could double sustainable timber harvest levels on over 90 percent of forestland in the Eastern United States. Thus, significant **potential** for offsetting future forest productivity declines exists.

However, if timber harvest levels do not increase, potential forest-productivity losses due to air pollution could be of particular significance for regional timber markets in the South. Lack of softwood reforestation on many private nonindustrial forest lands over the past two decades may decrease softwood-timber harvests in the South, beginning about 1995. Timber supplies in the Northeastern United States appear to be adequate for the foreseeable future. Productivity declines, whether of regional or local scale, could threaten the economic viability of individual lumbermills and papermills. Significant reductions in harvests over a sustained period

could cause mill closures; papermills are particularly vulnerable, since they represent large capital investments, and must operate very close to capacity (in general, over 90 percent) to break even.

Potential losses in timber production in the Northeast and South, if realized, could alter opportunities to increase forest-product exports, and could, at the extreme, result in increasing imports of timber from the Canadian Northwest.

Effects of Ozone on Forest Productivity

Considerable literature is available to describe ozone effects on forest vegetation. Most studies examined **foliar (leaf) injury** rather than yield loss. Table B-9 lists tree species that have been determined to be sensitive, of intermediate sensitivity, and tolerant of ozone. However, researchers caution against overreliance on these relative rankings, because the individual experiments varied in study methods used (exposure chamber, ambient air), age of trees, and type of response measured (injury, growth).

Most of the few studies examining **yield loss** exposed forest tree seedlings to ozone under controlled laboratory or greenhouse conditions. One field study, how-

Table B-9.—Relative Susceptibility of Trees to Ozone Damage

Sensitive	Intermediate	Resistant
Tree-of-Heaven	Boxelder	Balsam fir
juneberry	eastern redbud	white fir
white ash	Japanese larch	sugar maple
swamp ash	incense cedar	Norway maple
honey locust	sweetgum	European white birch
European larch	knobcone pine	flowering dogwood
tulip poplar	lodgepole pine	European beech
jack pine	short leaf pine	American holly
coulter pine	South Florida slash pine	black walnut
Jeffrey pine	sugar pine	western juniper
Austrian pine	pitch pine	swamp tupelo
ponderosa pine	eastern white pine	Norway spruce
monterey pine	Scotch pine	white spruce
loblolly pine	Torrey pine	blue spruce
Virginia pine	scarlet oak	red pine
American sycamore	pin oak	digger pine
Japanese poplar	black oak	Rocky Mountain Douglas fir
black cottonwood	common lilac	common pear
quaking aspen	Chinese elm	shingle oak
white oak		bur oak
European mountain ash		English oak
lilac		northern red oak
		black locust
		redwood
		giant sequoia
		northern white cedar
		American basswood
		littleleaf linden
		eastern hemlock

SOURCE: D. D. Davis and H. D. Gerhold, "Selection of Trees for Tolerance of Air Pollutants," *Better Trees for Metropolitan Landscapes Symposium Proceedings,* U.S. Forest Service General Technical Report, NE-22:61-66, 1976.

ever, has measured yield reductions in mature white pine in the Blue Ridge Mountains of Virginia.

The study compared annual radial-increment growth in tolerant, intermediate, and sensitive varieties of white pine (*Pinus strobus*) (6). Observed within-species variations in ozone-induced foliar injury were used to classify trees into the three sensitivity categories. The trees were then compared to determine how much less growth had occurred in the sensitive and intermediate varieties than in their tolerant counterparts. Growth in the sensitive and intermediate varieties was reduced by 45 percent and 15 percent for 1 year (1978), by 40 percent and 20 percent over a 10-year period (1968-78), and by 28 percent and 15 percent over a 25-year cumulative period. These figures may be conservative, as they are based on comparisons to ozone-tolerant tree growth in areas of known ozone occurrence (50 to 75 ppb, 7-hour average, May-September yearly).

Several field studies related significant changes in forest **ecosystem response** to ambient oxidant concentrations (88). The San Bernardino Mountain Study documented mortality of sensitive ponderosa (*Pinus ponderosa*) and Jeffrey (*P. Jeffreyi*) pines after bark beetles infested air-pollution-stressed trees (63,65). Air pollu-

tion stress appears to be shifting forest species composition toward more tolerant species such as white fir. Other examples of shifts in species composition associated with oxidants or mixtures of air pollutants also have been reported (21,60).

Fate and Effects of Acid Deposition in Forest Ecosystems

Upon entering a forest ecosystem, acidic pollutants such as sulfate and nitrate become part of a chemical system regulated by a variety of natural processes. The chemical constituents of acid deposition should be viewed as an addition to the hydrogen, sulfate, and nitrate ions produced and cycled naturally within forest ecosystems.

This section discusses ways in which atmospherically deposited hydrogen, sulfate, and nitrate ions could affect forest nutrient cycles. The section also examines the fate and effects of deposition **in excess** of amounts that can be biologically used, or chemically trapped or neutralized by forest soils.

Effects on Forest Sulfur and Nitrogen Status

Acid deposition contains readily usable forms of the essential plant nutrients sulfur and nitrogen. Nitrogen-deficient forests are common throughout the United States, but sulfur-deficient forests are much less common, occurring primarily in the Pacific Northwest (98,99,114,120).

Atmospheric inputs of nitrate and ammonium could improve nitrogen nutrition substantially in forests of the North Central and Northeastern States, especially in areas near the eastern Great Lakes. In most areas of the West, atmospheric nitrogen inputs are much less significant when compared to the total nitrogen requirements of Western forests.

The sulfur deposited in some forested areas of the Western United States may be less than that required for optimal growth, but data to quantify how widely this occurs are scanty. Much of the Eastern United States appears to receive inputs equal to or in excess of tree sulfur requirements. Moreover, trees require nearly 15 times as much nitrogen as sulfur, on a weight basis, to synthesize protein. The ratio of nitrogen to sulfur in atmospheric deposition is far from this ideal value throughout the United States, with greater amounts of sulfur than nitrogen deposited over most of the Eastern United States. Thus, it would appear that substantially greater quantities of sulfur are being deposited than can be used as fertilizer over the long term, and that many forests would have to be heavily fertilized, or otherwise enriched in nitrogen, to benefit at all from sulfur deposition (99).

Forests do not depend entirely on atmospheric inputs to meet nutrient requirements, as they recycle nutrients —e.g., by reclaiming them from decomposing leaves. When atmospheric nutrient inputs fail to meet growth requirements and soil-available nutrient supplies are low (as is often the case for nitrogen), recycling processes within forest ecosystems and nutrient translocation from one part of a tree to another help supply nutrients to growing tissues. Thus, while increased atmospheric nitrogen and sulfur inputs might benefit forests limited in those nutrients, under undisturbed conditions atmospheric inputs do not have to equal plant uptake to maintain site fertility. However, to maintain site fertility in **harvested** forests, inputs must compensate for the amount of nutrients removed by logging.

Effects on Forest Cation Nutrient Status

In addition to supplying some nutrients, acid deposition (and naturally produced acids) can **remove** other nutrients stored in leaves, the litter layer on the forest floor, or the soil. The hydrogen ions (i.e., the "acidity") of acid deposition can **replace** or "leach" **nutri-ent cations,** * removing these essential nutrients from the forest ecosystem.

Acid deposition can remove essential nutrient cations (e.g., calcium) **directly** from tree foliage. If the rate of nutrient loss is greater than can be replaced through the roots, nutrient deficiency will result. Scientists do not know which tree species are most susceptible to foliar nutrient loss, or the level of acid deposition at which such loss becomes harmful. For any given species, the rate of loss probably depends on both the total **amount** and **concentration** of acid-producing substances (sulfate and nitrate) deposited on leaf surfaces.

Nutrient leaching from soils is somewhat different. No cation leaching will occur unless the acid-producing substances can travel freely through the ecosystem (47). Since forest nitrogen deficiencies are very common and nitrate is taken up readily by forest vegetation (1,74), atmospheric nitrate inputs are unlikely to be mobile enough to leach significant amounts of nutrient cations from most forest soils. Sulfate, the other major acid-producing substance in rainfall, can travel through many types of forest soils and is, therefore, of greater concern.

While acid deposition can accelerate cation leaching rates, the **magnitudes** of these increases must be compared to losses from natural leaching processes. The relative importance of deposition-induced leaching depends on: 1) the amount of acid input at a given site, 2) the rate of soil leaching by natural processes (8,10,66), and 3) the ability of soils to buffer against leaching (e.g., by "adsorbing" or trapping sulfate onto their surfaces) (46). Furthermore, a number of variables govern how accelerated leaching ultimately affects forest cation nutrient status, most notably: 1) the amount of exchangeable cations, 2) the rate at which nutrients are replaced through mineral weathering (74,91), 3) forest cation nutrient requirements, and 4) management practices such as harvesting (44).

If the quantities of soil cation reserves within a forest ecosystem are large relative to leaching rates (e.g., in calcareous soils), a doubling or tripling of leaching rates due to acid rain probably would be of little consequence. If reserves are small (e.g., in highly weathered soils), doubling or tripling of leaching rates may have long-term significance. Soils in which current input levels of acid deposition can significantly deplete nutrient reserves over less than many decades are probably rare, however. Nonetheless, given a **sufficiently large input** for a **sufficient amount of time,** acid rain must eventually deplete these reserves.

Currently, few forests of the United States have cation deficiencies, although notable exceptions are known in certain forests of the Northeast (90). An intensive

---

*Nutrients that have the same chemical charge as hydrogen ions, e.g., calcium, magnesium, and potassium.

study of a central Adirondack Mountain forest indicates that atmospheric sulfate deposition has increased rates of soil nutrient-cation leaching substantially (66). Since these soils are quite low in available cation reserves, the researchers concluded that, "Chronic leaching by [sulfuric acid] combined with internally generated organic acids may represent a real threat to the nutrient status of many Adirondack forest soils" (66). However, the authors acknowledge that total soil cation reserves and weathering rates (or rates at which these reserves become available to trees) are unknown, and that a complete assessment must encompass these factors. Acid rain itself may cause soil weathering rates to increase, potentially offsetting accelerated nutrient leaching to some extent.

Effects of Aluminum Mobilization

Soil scientists have long known that soils release aluminum under sufficiently acid conditions (5,121). Aluminum is also known to be toxic to plant roots in sufficient concentrations, either killing them directly or interfering with nutrient uptake (especially phosphorus and calcium) (71,73). Researchers recently found a marked increase in soil aluminum concentrations over a 13-year period in a beech and Norway spruce forest soil at the Solling site in West Germany (58,101). They attributed the change to a combination of natural acidifying processes within the forest ecosystem and atmospheric acid inputs. Furthermore, the authors believe that aluminum levels have become toxic to tree roots, posing a situation with "serious consequences for forestry in Central Europe."

The findings of these West German researchers are cause for concern, but they may not apply to all forest types. Acid and sulfate inputs are very high at the Solling site, as would be necessary to further acidify a soil that was initially very acid. Moreover, species vary widely in their susceptibility to aluminum toxicity.*

Similar declines have been observed in red spruce in the Northeastern United States. However, recent work fails to support the soil aluminum hypothesis in these cases. Specifically, researchers found no changes in soil pH over a 15-year period (1965-80) and no relationship between tree vigor and root or foliar aluminum concentration. The causes for the decline in red spruce are unknown as of this writing. Acid rain, aluminum concentrations, and forest decline, but acid rain (perhaps via other mechanisms) remains one of several working hypotheses under investigation.

*Researchers report great variations in toxicity thresholds among several tree species, ranging from 10 mg/l Al in solution for a poplar hybrid to 80 to 120 mg/l in oak, birch, and pine (61). Others report Al concentrations in "equilibrium soil solution" (i.e., solution obtained after extraction of soil with water for 24 hr) of less than 3 mg/l (101). More recently, Al concentrations of nearly 20 mg/l in soil solutions were reported from the spruce stand at Solling (58).

It must be emphasized that acid rain effects are site-specific, depending on the amount of acid input and on the vegetation, soils, and nutrient status of the site receiving such inputs. Forest ecosystems in **general** cannot be expected to respond to acid rain in any single way.

The Regional Distribution of Soils at Risk From Acid Deposition

Analysts have proposed and used several sets of sensitivity criteria to define geographical regions most susceptible to acid deposition effects. Each set is based on scientific concepts that aim at particular target organisms or ecosystems (e.g., forests or aquatic ecosystems). Those directed toward aquatic effects emphasize bedrock geology (31,67), while those directed toward soils effects emphasize cation exchange capacity (CEC) and base saturation (52,59).

Scientists at Oak Ridge National Laboratory have classified unmanaged (i.e., forest or range) soils according to their sensitivity to three types of acid-deposition-induced changes: 1) losses of essential nutrients such as calcium and magnesium, 2) release of toxic metals such as aluminum, and 3) further acidification.

The classification scheme uses three soil properties: 1) whether the soil adsorbs (chemically traps) sulfate; 2)the soil's cation exchange capacity (CEC);** and 3) the PH (acidity) of the soil, which also indicates base saturation, i.e., the relative proportion of basic cations (nutrients such as calcium and magnesium) to acidic cations (hydrogen and aluminum).

Table B-10 outlines the relative sensitivities of various soil types; figures B-11 and B-12 describe the chemical exchanges that acid deposition produces in each of these soils. Figure B-13 maps the extent and location of these soils in the Eastern United States. The three types of potential soil changes attributable to acid deposition are discussed separately below.

RELEASE OF ALUMINUM

As shown in table B-10, soils that are naturally acidic (i.e., pH below about 5) and that do not adsorb sulfate, are considered most likely to release toxic metals such as aluminum. Figure B-11 illustrates the mechanism schematically. Sulfate and hydrogen ions from acid deposition reach the soil layer. Because the soil does not trap sulfate, the sulfate is free to move through the soil. The associated hydrogen ion can either: 1) travel with the sulfate, or 2) be exchanged on the soil surface for a base cation (e.g., calcium or magnesium) or an acid

**The total amount of cations (positively charged ions such as calcium, magnesium, aluminum, and hydrogen) the soil can hold.

Table B-10.—Theoretical Sensitivities of Forest Soils to Acid Deposition

Soil properties		Terrestrial sensitivity to:		
pH	CEC[a]	Base cation loss	Soil acidification (surface soils)	Al solubilization
I. Non-sulfate-absorbing soils				
1. >6	High	High	Low	Low
2. >6	Low	High	Low-moderate	Low-moderate
3. 5-6	High	High	Moderate	Moderate
4. 5-6	Low	High	High	Moderate
5. <5	High	Moderate	Moderate	High
6. <5	Low	Moderate	Moderate	High
II. Sulfate-absorbing soils				
7. >6	High	Moderate	Low	Low
8. >6	Low	Moderate	Low-moderate	Low
9. 5-6	High	Low	Moderate	Low
10. 5-6	Low	Low	High	Low
11. <5	High	Low	Moderate	Low
12. <5	Low	Low	Moderate	Low

[a]Cation Exchange Capacity (CEC).
[b]High CEC = above 9.0 meq/ml, low CEC = below 9.0 meq/ml.
SOURCE: Oak Ridge National Laboratory, 1983.

cation (aluminum or another hydrogen ion). Because aluminum both dissolves most easily and is most plentiful in acid soils (fig. B-11c), these soils release the greatest amounts of aluminum.

Figure B-12 illustrates soil processes in sulfate-adsorbing soils. Because these soils can trap both sulfate and the associated hydrogen ion from acid deposition, less aluminum is released.

Figure B-13 shows the distribution of soils considered susceptible to aluminum release, based on county-level soil data. The medium-grey areas are the naturally acid, nonsulfate adsorbing soils discussed above. These cover New England, and parts of northern New York State, the upper Midwest, and the South. Acid soils that can adsorb sulfate are shaded as light grey. These cover large areas of the South and South Central States. Because soils classified as adsorbing sulfate often do so only in deeper soil layers, the surface layers in these regions still might be susceptible to aluminum release.

SOIL ACIDIFICATION

Soils thought to be sensitive to further acidification are moderately acid (pH about 5 to 6) with low CEC. Such soils occur to a very minor extent in those regions receiving significant inputs of acid deposition. As shown as the darkest areas on figure B-13, these soils predominate in scattered counties east of the Mississippi (i.e., counties in Illinois, Indiana, Georgia, and Tennessee). Other areas of the East receiving higher deposition levels (e.g., parts of the Adirondacks) probably have some soils of this type, but not in sufficient quantities to constitute a county's predominant soil type.

For these moderately acidic soils, concerns over further acidification include: 1) potential effects on soil biota, 2) release of aluminum if acidity increases to below a pH of about 5, and 3) the loss of nutrients from these soils, as discussed below.

NUTRIENT DEPLETION

As shown in table B-7, those soils most susceptible to nutrient cation (calcium, magnesium, and potassium) loss are soils with a moderate to high pH that do not adsorb sulfate. Again, figures B-11 and B-12 show the mechanisms of nutrient loss. As sulfate and associated hydrogen ions enters the soil layer, the hydrogen ions can be exchanged for base cations. Sulfate-adsorbing soils trap hydrogen ions (fig. B-12), while lower pH soils (e.g., fig. B-11c) exchange most of the hydrogen ions for aluminum and remove fewer nutrient cations.

Of the soils listed as most susceptible to nutrient loss in table B-9, only the moderate pH, nonsulfate adsorbing soils with low CECs have **both** a high potential for nutrient loss and low enough nutrient levels so that this loss might be significant. These are the same soils discussed above as being susceptible to further acidification, and are shown on figure B-13 as the darkest regions.

Though listed as only moderately susceptible to nutrient loss in table B-10, naturally acid, nonsulfate-adsorbing soils typically have the lowest quantities of stored nutrient cations. Some of these areas may have such low nutrient levels that further loss might affect forest productivity. Such areas might be located within the medium-grey regions shown in figure B-13; how-

Figure B-11.—Schematic Diagrams of Soil Leaching in Non-Sulfate-Adsorbing Soils

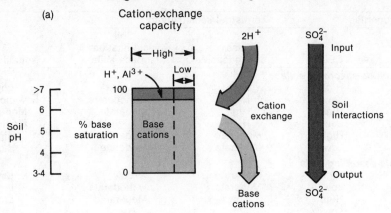

(a)

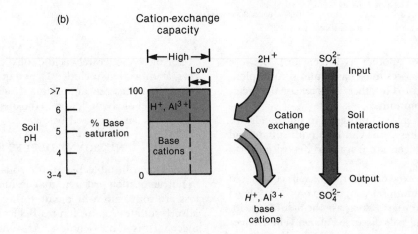

(b)

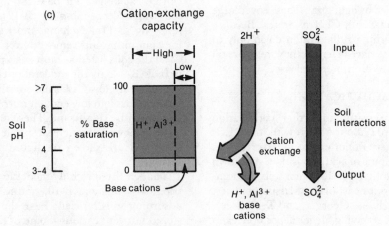

(c)

SOURCE: Oak Ridge National Laboratory, 1983.

Figure B-12.—Schematic Diagrams of Soil Leaching in Sulfate-Adsorbing Soils

(a)

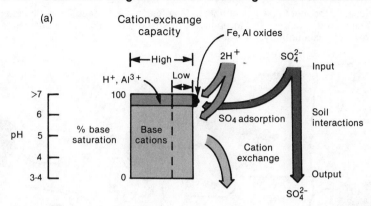

(b)

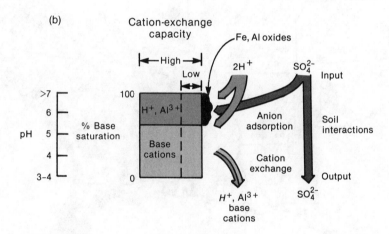

(c)

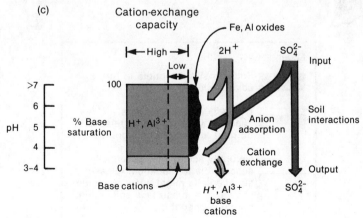

SOURCE: Oak Ridge National Laboratory, 1983.

Figure B-13.—Soil Sensitivity to Acid Deposition (nonagricultural)

Forested and range areas with soils thought to be susceptible to the effects of acid deposition. Shaded areas represent counties in which a susceptible soil type predominates. The three levels of shading correspond to different soil types, and potential effects, rather than to degrees of susceptibility.

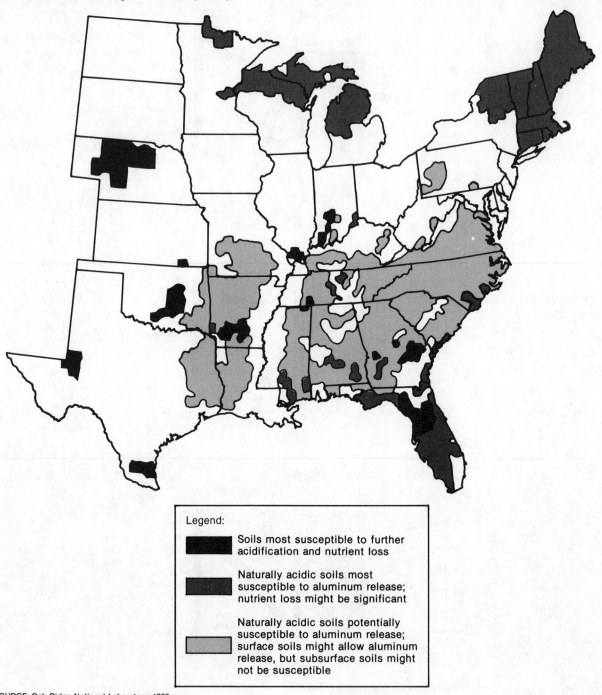

Legend:

Soils most susceptible to further acidification and nutrient loss

Naturally acidic soils most susceptible to aluminum release; nutrient loss might be significant

Naturally acidic soils potentially susceptible to aluminum release; surface soils might allow aluminum release, but subsurface soils might not be susceptible

SOURCE: Oak Ridge National Laboratory, 1983.

ever, whether nutrient loss rates exceed natural replacement rates from weathering is unknown.

B.2 References

(Numbers are keyed to citations in text)

1. Abrahamson, G., "Acid Precipitation, Plant Nutrients, and Forest Growth," *Ecological Impact of Acid Precipitation,* D. Drablos and A. Tollan (eds.) (Mysen, Norway: Johs. Grefslie Trykkeri A/S, 1980).
2. Abrahamson, G., and Dollard, G. J., "Effects of Acidic Precipitation on Forest Vegetation and Soil," *Ecological Effects of Acid Precipitation,* G. Howells (ed.) (La Jolla, Calif.: Electric Power Research Institute, EPRI 50A77-403, 1979).
3. American Phytopathology Society, "Glossary of Air Pollution Terms and Selected Reference List," *Phytopathol. News* 8:5-8, 1974.
4. Andersson, F., Fagerstrom, T., and Nilsson, S. I., "Forest Ecosystem Responses to Acid Deposition—Hydrogen Ion Budget and Nitrogen/Tree Growth Model Approaches," *Effects of Acid Precipitation on Terrestrial Ecosystems,* T. C. Hutchinson and M. Havas (eds.) (New York: Plenum Press, 1980).
5. Bache, B. W., "The Acidification of Soils," *Effects of Acid Precipitation on Terrestrial Ecosystems,* T. C. Hutchinson and M. Havas (eds.) (New York: Plenum Press, 1980).
6. Benoit, L. F., "Ozone Effects on Long-term Growth and Reproduction in Eastern White Pine," M.S. thesis, Virginia Polytechnic Institute and State University, Blacksburg, Va., 1981.
7. Brennan, E., and Davis, S. H., "Air Pollution Damage to Austrian Pine in New Jersey," *Plant Dis. Rep.* 51:964-967, 1967.
8. Cole, D. W., and Johnson, D. W., "Atmospheric Sulphate Additions and Cation Leaching in a Douglas-Fir Ecosystem," *Water Resour. Res.* 13:313-317, 1977.
9. Cost, N. D., "Forest Statistics for the Mountain Region of North Carolina, 1974," USDA Forest Service Resource Bulletin SE-31 (Southeast Forest Experiment Station, Asheville, N.C.), 1975.
10. Cronan, C. W., Reiners, W. A., Reynolds, R. L., and Lang, G. E., "Forest Floor Leaching: Contributions From Mineral, Organic, and Carbonic Acids in New Hampshire Subalpine Forests," *Science* 200:309-311, 1978.
11. Davis, D. D., and Coppolino, J. B., "Relationship Between Age and Ozone Sensitivity of Current Needles of Ponderosa Pine," *Plant Dis. Rep.* 58(7):660-663, 1974.
12. Davis, D. D., and Gerhold, H. D., "Selection of Trees for Tolerance of Air Pollutants," *Better Trees for Metropolitan Landscapes Symposium Proceedings,* U.S. Forest Service General Technical Report NE-22:61-66, 1976.
13. Davis, D. D., and Wood, F. A., "The Relative Susceptibility of Eighteen Coniferous Species to Ozone," *Phytopathology* 62:14-19, 1972.
14. Dochinger, L. S., "Effects of Nutrition on the Chlorotic Dwarf Disease of Eastern White Pine," *Plant Dis. Rep.* 48:107-109, 1964.
15. Evans, L. S., Hendrey, G. R., Stensland, G. J., Johnson, D. W., and Francis, A. J., "Acidic Precipitation: Consideration for an Air Quality Standard," *Water Air Soil Pollut.* 16:469-509, 1981.
16. Evans, L. S., Lewin, K. F., and Cunningham, E. A., "Effects of Simulated Acid Rain on Yields of Field-grown Radishes and Garden Beets," *Am. Chem. Soc.,* Division of Environmental Chemistry, 21:82-87, 1981.
17. Evans, L. S., Lewin, K. F., and Cunningham, E. A., "Effects of Simulated Acid Rain on Yields of Field-grown Radishes and Garden Beets," *Agriculture and the Environment* 7:285-298, 1982.
18. Evans, L. S., Lewis, K. F., Patti, M. J., and Cunningham, E. A., "Comparison of Experimental Designs To Determine Effects of Acidic Precipitation on Field-grown Soybeans," *A Specialty Conference on Atmospheric Deposition,* Air Pollution Control Association, SP-49, 1982.
19. Evans, L. S., Gmur, N. F., and DaCosta, F., "Leaf Surface and Histological Perturbations of Leaves of *Phaseolus vulgaris* and *Helianthus annuus* After Exposure to Simulated Acid Rain," *Am. J. Bot.* 64:903-913, 1977.
20. Harward, M. E., and Riesenauer, H. M., "Movement and Reactions of Inorganic Soil Sulfur," *Soil Sci.* 101:326-335, 1966.
21. Hayes and Skelly, J. M., "Transport of Ozone From the Northeast United States Into Virginia and Its Effects on Eastern White Pine, *Plant Dis. Rep.* 61:778-782, 1977.
22. Heagle, A. S., Philbeck, R. B., and Knott, W. M., "Thresholds for Injury, Growth and Yield Loss Caused by Ozone on Field Corn Hybrids," *Phytopathology* 69:21-26, 1979.
23. Heagle, A. S., Philbeck, R. B., Feicht, P. G., and Ferrell, R. E., "Response of Soybeans to Simulated Acid Rain in the Field,"*J. Environ. Qual.* (submitted) 1983.
24. Heagle, A. S., Spencer, S., and Letchworth, M. B., "Yield Response of Winter Wheat to Chronic Doses of Ozone," *Can. J. Bot.* 57:1999-2005, 1979.
25. Heagle, A. S., and Heck, W. W., "Field Methods To Assess Crop Losses Due to Oxidant Air Pollutants," *Assessment of Losses Which Constrain Production and Crop Improvement in Agriculture and Forests,* P. S. Teng and S. V. Krupa (eds.), Proceedings of the E. C. Stakman Commemorative Symposium, Misc. Publ. # 7, Agricultural Experiment Station, University of Minnesota, 1980.
26. Heagle, A. S., Heck, W. W., Knott, W. M., Johnston, J. W., Stanel, E. P., and Cowling, E. B., *Responses of Citrus to Acidic Rain From Simulated SRM Fuel Exhaust Mixtures and Exhaust Components,* Internal Report, (Raleigh, N.C.: North Carolina State University, 1978).
27. Heck, W. W., Mudd, J. B., and Miller, P. R., "Plants and Microorganisms," *Ozone and Other Photochemical Oxidants,* (Washington, D.C.: National Academy of Science, 1977).

28. Heck, W. W., Taylor, O. C., Adams, R., Bingham, G., Miller, J., Preston, E., and Weinstein, L., "Assessment of Crop Loss From Ozone," *J. Air Pollut. Control Assoc.* 32:353-361, 1982.

29. Heck, W. W., Larsen, R. I., and Heagle, A. S., "Measuring the Acute Dose-response of Plants to Ozone," *Assessment of Losses Which Constrain Production and Crop Improvement in Agriculture and Forests,* P. S. Teng and S. V. Krupa (eds.), Proceedings of the E. C. Stakman Commemorative Symposium, Misc. Publ. # 7, (Agricultural Experiment Station, University of Minnesota, 1980).

30. Heggestad, H. E., and Bennett, J. H., "Photochemical Oxidants Potentiate Yield Losses in Snap Beans Attributable to Sulfur Dioxide," *Science* 213:1008-1010, 1981.

31. Hendrey, G. R., Galloway, J. N., Norton, S. A., Schofield, C. L., Burns, D. A., and Schaffer, P. W., "Sensitivity of the Eastern United States to Acid Precipitation Impacts on Surface Waters," *Ecological Impact of Acid Precipitation,* D. Drablфs and A. Tollan (eds.) (Mysen, Norway: Johs. Grefslie Trykkeri A/S, 1980).

32. Hibben, C. R., "Ozone Toxicity to Sugar Maple," *Phytopathology* 59:1424-1428, 1969.

33. Hibben, C. R., "Plant Injury by Oxidant-type Pollutants in the New York City Atmosphere," *Plant Dis. Rep.* 53:544-548, 1969.

34. Irving, P. M., "Response of Field-grown Soybeans to Acid Precipitation Alone and in Combination With Sulfur Dioxide," Ph. D. dissertation, University of Wisconsin, Milwaukee, 1979.

35. Irving, P. M., and Miller, J. E., "Productivity of Field-grown Beans Exposed to Acid Rain and Sulfur Dioxide Alone and in Combination," *J. Environ. Qual.* 10:473-478, 1981.

36. Jacobson, J. S., Troiano, J., Colavito, L. J., Heller, L. I., and McCune, D. C., "Polluted Rain and Plant Growth," *Polluted Rain,* T. Y. Toribara, M. W. Miller, and P. E. Morrow (eds.) (New York: Plenum Publishing Corp., 1980).

37. Jacobson, J. S., "The Influence of Rainfall Composition on the Yield and Quality of Agricultural Crops," *Proceedings of the International Conference on Ecological Impact of Acid Precipitation,* Sandefjord, Norway, Mar. 11-14, 1980.

38. Jacobson, J. S., and Van Leuken, P., "Effects of Acid Precipitation on Vegetation," *Proceedings of the Fourth International Clean Air Congress,* Tokyo, 1977.

39. Jensen, K. F., "Response of Nine Forest Tree Species to Chronic Ozone Fumigation," *Plant Dis. Rep.* 57:914-917, 1973.

40. Jensen, K. F., "Air Pollutants Affect the Relative Growth Rate of Hardwood Seedlings," U.S. Forest Service Research Paper NE 470 (N.E. Forest Experimental Station, Broomall, Pa., 1981).

41. Johnson, A. H., Siccama, T. G., Wang, D., Turner, R. S., and Barringer, T. H., "Recent Changes in Patterns of Tree Growth Rate in the New Jersey Pinelands: A Possible Effect of Acid Rain," *J. Environ. Qual.* 10(4):427-430, 1981.

42. Johnson, A. H., Siccama, T. G., Wang, D., Barringer, T. H., and Turner, R. S., "Decreases in Stream pH and Tree Growth Rates in the New Jersey Pinelands: A Possible Link to Acid Rain," *J. Environ. Qual.* 10:427-430, 1981.

43. Johnson, A. H., Siccama, T. G., Turner, R. S., and Lord, D. G., "Assessing the Possibility of a Link Between Acid Precipitation and Decreased Growth Rates of Trees in the Northeastern United States," *Proceedings of the American Chemical Society* (in press), Las Vegas, Nev.

44. Johnson, D. W., "Acid Rain and Forest Productivity," *Proceedings of the International Union of Forestry Research Organizations (IUFRO),* Kyoto, Japan, Division I, Ibaraki, Japan, 1981.

45. Johnson, D. W., "The Natural Acidity of Some Unpolluted Waters in Southeastern Alaska and Potential Impacts of Acid Rain," *Water Air Soil Pollut.* 16:243-252, 1981.

46. Johnson, D. W., and Cole, D. W., "Sulfate Mobility in an Outwash Soil in Western Washington," *Water Air Soil Pollut.* 7:489-495, 1977.

47. Johnson, D. W., and Cole, D. W., "Anion Mobility in Soils: Relevance to Nutrient Transport From Terrestrial Ecosystems," *Environ. Int.* 3:79-90, 1980.

48. Johnson, D. W., Cole, D. W., Gessel, S. P., Singer, M. J., and Minden, R. V., "Carbonic Acid Leaching in a Tropical, Temperate, Subalpine and Northern Forest Soil," *Arct. Alp. Res.* 9:329-343, 1977.

49. Johnson, D. W., Hornbeck, J. W., Kelly, J. M., Shank, W. T., and Todd, D. E., "Regional Patterns of Soil Sulfate Accumulation: Relevance to Ecosystem Sulfur Budgets," *Atmospheric Sulfur Deposition: Environmental Impact and Health Effects,* D. S. Shriner, C. R. Richmond, and S. E. Lindberg (eds.) (Ann Arbor, Mich.: Ann Arbor Science, 1980).

50. Karnosky, D. F., "Threshold Levels for Foliar Injury to *Populus Tremuloides* by Sulfur Dioxide and Ozone," *Can. J. For. Res.* 6:166-169, 1976.

51. Kender, W. J., and Spierings, F., "Effects of Sulfur Dioxide, Ozone, and Their Interactions on 'Golden Delicious' Apple Trees," *Neth. J. Plant Pathol.* 81:149-151, 1975.

52. Klopatek, J. M., Harris, W. F., and Olson, R. J., "A Regional Ecological Assessment Approach to Atmospheric Deposition: Effects on Soil Systems," *Atmospheric Sulfur Deposition: Environment Impact and Health Effects,* D. S. Shriner, C. R. Richmond, and S. E. Lindberg (eds.) (Ann Arbor, Mi.: Ann Arbor Science, 1980).

53. Knight, H. A., and McClure, J. P., "North Carolina's Timber, 1974," USDA Forest Service Resource Bulletin SE-33 (Southeast Forest Experimental Station, Ashville, N.C., 1975).

54. Kress, L. W., and Skelly, J. M., "Growth Impact of Long Term, Low Concentration Exposure of Several Tree Species to Air Pollution," *Plant Dis.* (in press).

55. Kress, L. W., Skelly, J. M., and Hinkleman, K. H., "Growth Impact of O_3, NO_2, and/or SO_2 on *Pinus Taeda,*" *Env. Monitor. and Assess.* (in press), 1982.

56. Larsen, R. I., and Heck, W. W., "An Air Quality Data Analysis System for Interrelating Effects, Standards, and Needed Source Reductions: Part 3, Vegetation Injury," *J. Air Pollut. Control Assoc.* 26:325-333, 1976.

57. Lee, J. J., and Neely, G. E., "CERL-OSU Acid Rain Crop Study Progress Report," Air Pollution Effects Branch, Corvallis Environmental Research Laboratory, 1980.

58. Matzner, E., and Ulrich, B., "Effect of Acid Precipitation on Soil," *Beyond the Energy Crisis: Opportunity and Challenge,* R. A. Fazzolare and C. B. Smith (eds.) (Oxford, England: Pergamon Press, 1981).

59. McFee, W. W., "Sensitivity of Soils to Acidification by Acid Precipitation," *Atmospheric Sulfur Deposition: Environmental Impact and Health Effects,* D. S. Shriner, C. R. Richmond, and S. E. Lindberg (eds.) (Ann Arbor, Mich.: Ann Arbor Science, 1980).

60. McClenahan, J. R., "Community Changes in the Deciduous Forest Exposed to Air Pollution," *Can J. Forest Research* 8:432-438, 1978.

61. McCormick, L. H., and Steiner, K. C., "Variations in Aluminum Tolerance Among Six Genera of Trees," *For. Sci.* 24:565-568, 1978.

62. Miller, Paul R. (ed.), "Effects of Air Pollutants on Mediterranean and Temperate Forest Ecosystems," USDA Forest Service Technical Report PSW-43, 1980.

63. Miller, P. R., "Oxidant-Induced Community Change in a Mixed Conifer Forest," *Air Pollution Damage to Vegetation,* J. A. Nagegela (ed.), Advances in Chemistry Services 122 (Washington, D.C.: American Chemical Society, 1973).

64. Miller, P. R., and McBride, J. R., "Effects of Air Pollutants on Forests," *Response of Plants to Air Pollution,* J. B. Mudd and T. T. Kozlowski (eds.) (New York: Academic Press, 1975).

65. Miller, P. R., and Elderman, M. J., "Photochemical Oxidant Air Pollution Effects on a Mixed Conifer Ecosystem," Ecological Research Series, EPA, 600-3-77-104, 1977.

66. Mollitor, A. V., and Raynal, D. J., "Acid Precipitation and Ionic Movements in Adirondack Forest Soils," *Soil Sci. Soc. Amer. J.* 46:137-141, 1982.

67. Norton, S. A., "Sensitivity of Aquatic Systems to Atmospheric Deposition," *Atmospheric Sulfur Deposition: Environmental Impact and Health Effects,* D. S. Shriner, C. R. Richmond, and S. E. Lindberg, (eds.) (Ann Arbor, Mich.: Ann Arbor Science, 1980).

68. Odum, E. P., *Fundamentals of Ecology,* 3d ed. (Philadelphia, Pa.: W. B. Saunders Co., 1971).

69. Olson, R. J., Emerson, C. J., and Nungesser, M. K., "GEOECOLOGY: A County-level Environmental Data Base for the Coterminous United States" (Oak Ridge, Tenn.: Oak Ridge National Laboratory, ORNL/TM-7351, 1980).

70. Olson, R. J., Johnson, D. W., and Shriner, D. W., "Regional Assessment of Potential Sensitivity of Soils in the Eastern United States to Acid Precipitation" (Oak Ridge, Tenn.: Oak Ridge National Laboratory, ORNL/TM-8374, 1982).

71. Pratt, P. F., "Aluminum," *Diagnostic Criteria for Plants and Soils,* H. D. Chapman (ed.) (Abilene, Tex.: Quality Printing Co., Inc., 1965).

72. Puckett, L. J., "Acid Rain, Air Pollution, and Tree Growth in Southeastern New York," *J. Environ. Qual.* 11:376-381, 1982.

73. Ragland, J. L., and Coleman, N. T., "Influence of Aluminum on Phosphorus Uptake by Snap Bean Roots," *Soil Sci. Soc. Am. Proc.* 26:88-90, 1959.

74. Raynal, D. J., Leaf, A., Marion, P. D., and Wang, C. J. K. (eds.), "Effects of Acid Precipitation on a Forest Ecosystem" (Syracuse, N.Y.: State University of New York, 1980).

75. Reagan, J. A., EPA, personal communication to OTA, 1983.

76. Reinert, R. A., Shriner, D. S., and Rawlings, J. O., "Responses of Radish to All Combinations of Three Concentrations of Nitrogen Dioxide, Sulfur Dioxide, and Ozone," *J. Environ. Qual.* 11:52-57, 1982.

77. Research Management Committee (RMC), *The National Crop Loss Assessment Network (NCLAN): 1980 Annual Summer Report* (Corvallis, Oreg.: Corvallis Environmental Research Laboratory, EPA, 1981).

78. Roman, J. R., and Raynal, D. J., "Effects of Acid Precipitation on Vegetation," *Effects of Acid Precipitation on a Forest Ecosystem,* D. J. Raynal, A. L. Leaf, P. D. Marion, and C. J. K. Wang (eds.) (Syracuse, N.Y.: State University of New York, 1980).

79. Rosenquist, I. Th., *Sur Jord/Surt Vann* (Oslo, Norway: Ingeniorforlaget, 1977).

80. Salathe, L., and Maxwell, D., USDA, personal communication to OTA, 1982.

81. Santamour, F. S., Jr., "Air Pollution Studies on *Platanus* and American Elm Seedlings," *Plant Dis. Rep.* 53:482-484, 1969.

82. Seip, H. M., "Acidification of Freshwater—Sources and Mechanisms," *Ecological Impact of Acid Precipitation,* D. Drabløs and A. Tollan (eds.) (Mysen, Norway: Johs. Grefslie Trykkeri A/S, 1980).

83. Shriner, D. S., "Effects of Simulated Acidic Rain on Host-parasite Interactions in Plant Diseases," *Phytopathology* 68:213-218, 1978.

84. Shriner, D. S., "Terrestrial Vegetation-Air Pollutant Interactions: Non-gaseous Pollutants, Wet Deposition," *Air Pollutants and their Effects on Terrestrial Ecosystems,* A. H. Legge and F. V. Krups (eds.), in press (New York: John Wiley, 1983).

85. Shriner, D. S., "Interactions Between Acidic Precipitation and SO$_2$ or O$_3$: Effects on Plant Response," *Phytopathology News* (Abstract) 12:152, 1978.

86. Shriner, D. S., and Johnston, J. W., "Effects of Simulated, Acidified Rain on Nodulation of Leguminous Plants by *Rhizobium* Spp.," *Environ. Exp. Bot.* 21:199-209, 1981.

87. Smith, W. H., *Air Pollution and Forests: Interactions Between Air Contaminants and Forest Ecosystems* (New York: Springer-Verlag, 1980).

88. Smith, W. H., "Air Pollution: A 20th Century Allogenic Influence on Forest Ecosystems," *Effects of Air Pollutants*

on *Mediterranean and Temperate Forest Ecosystems*, P. R. Muller (ed.), U.S. Forest Service General Technical Report PSW-43, 1980.

89. Sollins, P., Grier, C. C., McCorison, F. M., Cromack, K., Jr., Fogel, R., and Fredricksen, R. L., "The Internal Element Cycle of an Old-Growth Douglas-Fir Ecosystem in Western Oregon," *Ecol. Monogr.* 50:261-285, 1980.

90. Stone, E. H., and Kszystyniak, R., "Conservation of Potassium in the *Pinus Resinosa* Ecosystem," *Science* 198:192-193, 1977.

91. Stuanes, A. O., "Release and Loss of Nutrients From a Norwegian Forest Soil Due to Artificial Acid Rain of Varying Acidity," *Ecological Effects of Acid Precipitation*, D. Drablös and A. Tollan (eds.) (Mysen, Norway: Johs. Grefslie Trykkeri A/S, 1980).

92. Tingey, D. T., and Taylor, G. E., Jr., "Variation in Plant Response to Ozone: A Conceptual Model of Physiological Effects," *Proceedings of the 32d University of Nottingham Conference of the School of Agriculture Science Symposium on Effects of Gaseous Air Pollution in Agriculture and Horticulture*, Nottingham, England, Sept. 1-5, 1980.

93. Townsend, A. M., and Dochinger, L. S., "Relationship of Seed Source and Development Stage to the Ozone Tolerance of *Acerrubrum* Seedlings," *Atmos. Environ.* 8:956-964, 1974.

94. Troiano, J., Colavito, L., Heller, L., and McCune, D., "Effect of Simulated Acid Rain and Photochemical Oxidant on Seed Development in Soybean," *Phytopathology* 71:565 (Abstract), 1981.

95. Troiano, J., Colavito, L., Heller, L., McCune, D. C., and Jacobson, J., "Effects of Acidity of Simulated Rain and Its Joint Action With Ambient Ozone on Measures of Biomass and Yield in Soybean," *Environmental and Experimental Botany* 23(2):113-119, 1983.

96. Troiano, J., Heller, L. O., and Jacobson, J. S., "Effect of Added Water and Acidity of Simulated Rain on Growth of Field-grown Radish," *Environ. Pollut.* (Series A) 29:1-11, 1982.

97. Turner, J., Johnson, D. W., and Lambert, M. J., "Sulphur Cycling in a Douglas-Fir Forest and Its Modification by Nitrogen Applications," *Oecol. Plant.* 15:27-35, 1980.

98. Turner, J., Lambert, J. J., and Gessel, S. P., "Use of Foliage Sulphate Concentrations To Predict Response to Area Application by Douglas-Fir," *Can. J. For. Res.* 7:476-480, 1977.

99. Turner, J., Lambert, M. J., and Gessel, S. P., "Sulphur Requirements of Nitrogen Fertilized Douglas-Fir," *For. Sci.* 25:461-467, 1979.

100. Ulrich, B., "Production and Consumption of Hydrogen Ions in the Ecosphere," *Effects of Acid Precipitation on Terrestrial Ecosystems*, T. C. Hutchinson and M. Havas (eds.) (New York: Plenum Press, 1980).

101. Ulrich, B., Mayer, R., and Khanna, P. K., "Chemical Changes Due to Acid Precipitation in a Loess-Derived Soil in Central Europe," *Soil Sci.* 130:193-199, 1980.

102. U.S. Department of Agriculture (USDA), *Agricultural Statistics 1980*, Washington, D.C., 1980.

103. Unsworth, M. H., and Fowler, D., "Field Measurements of Sulfur Dioxide Fluxes to Wheat," *Atmosphere-Surface Exchange of Particulate and Gaseous Pollutants, 1974* (Springfield, Va.: National Technical Information Service, CONF-740921, 1976).

104. U.S. Congress, Office of Technology Assessment, *Wood Use: U.S. Competitiveness and Technology*, OTA-ITE-210, August 1983.

105. USDA-Forest Service (USDA), "The Outlook for Timber in the United States," Forest Resource Report No. 20 (Washington, D.C.: U.S. Government Printing Office, 1973).

106. USDA-Forest Service (USDA), "An Analysis of the Timber Situation in the United States, 1952-2030" (review draft copy) (Washington, D.C.: U.S. Government Printing Office, 0-620-222/3720, 1980).

107. U.S. Environmental Protection Agency, "Effects on Vegetation," *The Acidic Deposition Phenomenon and Its Effects, Critical Assessment Review Papers* (public review draft), 1983.

108. Ward, M. M., "Variation in the Response of Loblolly Pine to Ozone," M.S. thesis, Virginia Polytechnic Institute and State University, Blacksburg, Va., 1980.

109. Weaver, J. R., and Clements, F. E., *Plant Ecology*, 2d ed. (New York: McGraw-Hill, 1938).

110. West, D. C., McLaughlin, S. B., and Shugart, H. H., "Simulated Forest Response to Chronic Air Pollution Stress," *J. Environ. Qual.* 9:43-49, 1980.

111. Wiklander, L., "The Acidification of Soil by Acid Precipitation," *Grundforbattring* 26:155-164, 1974.

112. Wiklander, L., "Interaction Between Cations and Anions Influencing Adsorption and Leaching," *Effects of Acid Precipitation on Terrestrial Ecosystems*, T. C. Hutchinson and M. Havas (eds.) (New York: Plenum Press, 1980).

113. Wilhour, R. G., "The Influence of Ozone on White Ash (*Fraxinus Americana L.*)," Ph. D. thesis, Pennsylvania State University, University Park, Pa., 1970.

114. Will, G. M., and Youngberg, C. T., "Sulfur Status of Some Central Oregon Pumice Soils," *Soil Sci. Soc. Am. J.* 41:132-134, 1978.

115. Wood, F. A., "The Relative Sensitivity of Sixteen Deciduous Tree Species to Ozone," *Phytopathology* 50:579 (Abstract), 1970.

116. Wood, F. A., and Coppolino, J. B., "The Influence of Ozone on Selected Woody Ornamentals," *Phytopathology* 51:133 (Abstract), 1971.

117. Wood, F. A., and Coppolino, J. B., "The Influence of Ozone on Deciduous Forest Tree Species," *Effects of Air Pollutants on Forest Trees*, VII International Symposium of Forest Fume Damage Experts, 1972.

118. Wood, F. A., and Davis, D. D., "Sensitivity to Ozone Determined for Trees," *Sci. Agric.* 17:4-5, 1969.

119. Wood, T., and Bormann, F. H., "The Effects of an Artificial Acid Mist Upon the Growth of *Betula Alleghaniensis* Britt.," *Environ. Pollut.* 7:259-268, 1974.

120. Youngberg, C. T., and Dyrness, C. T., "Biological Assay of Pumice Soil Fertility," *Soil Sci.* 97:391-399, 1966.

121. Yuan, T. L., "Some Relationships Among Hydrogen, Aluminum, and pH in Solution and Soil Systems," *Soil Sci.* 97:391-399, 1963.

B.3 MATERIALS AT RISK

Air pollutants are one of a number of environmental factors—including humidity, temperature fluctuations, sunlight, salts, and micro-organisms—known to cause materials damage. Studies have demonstrated that a broad range of materials, including building stone, rubber, zinc, steel, paint, leather, textiles, paper, and photographic materials are affected by such pollutants as sulfur oxides (SO_x), nitrogen oxides (NO_x), and ozone. For most of the materials under discussion, SO_x (i.e., sulfur dioxide and its transformation products, including sulfates and sulfuric acid) are the chief anthropogenic cause of damage; however, rubber is affected chiefly by ozone, while ozone and NO_x have the greatest effect on textile dyes. Table B-11 summarizes the types of damage that occur to various categories of materials, as well as natural causes of deterioration, methods of measurement, and available mitigation measures.

Pollutants generally damage materials in ways that are not qualitatively different from the weathering effects caused by the natural environment. Consequently, estimating how much of observed damage is contributed by pollution sources is extremely difficult. The diverse pollutant mix characteristic of heavily industrialized urban areas—where greatest amounts of materials damage would be expected—increases the difficulty of pinpointing the cause and mechanisms of damage. In addition, environmental legislation and changes in manufacturing processes have caused pollution patterns to change over time; in particular, concentrations of large particulates have decreased dramatically over the last decade. As a result, pollutant-atmospheric conditions that may have contributed significantly to such notable effects as the deterioration of sculptural stone may no longer prevail in the United States. Finally, the relative contribution of local v. transported pollutants to observed materials damage is unknown. However, since both pollution sources and quantities of sensitive materials tend to be concentrated in urban areas, most researchers consider that local-scale pollutants account for the bulk of currently recognized materials damage.

Two kinds of materials damage are of concern: 1) damage to culturally significant structures and monuments, and 2) damage to reparable or replaceable "common construction" material items. The effects of air pollutants on unique or historically important statuary, monuments, buildings, or other artifacts are often irreparable; consequently, their cost to society cannot be described completely in monetary terms. Damages to sculptural stone and bronze, and to historic buildings constructed of such sensitive materials as marble, sandstone, and limestone, are frequently of this nature.

Pollution-induced damages to replaceable materials, and their economic costs, are potentially quantifiable. However, a great deal of information must be taken into account in estimating pollution-related losses. Since those damages tend to be similar in form to other environmental damages to materials, they are likely to affect the **rate** at which preventive, mitigative, or replacement activities occur, but not to be their sole cause. Little information is available on how pollutant-related damages affect normal maintenance and repair activities. Analysts also need information on the amount of materials damage for which specified pollutant levels are responsible. Most of our knowledge about the rates at which specified pollutant levels cause individual materials to deteriorate is based on field and laboratory experiments using small samples of materials rather than measurements from actual structures. Knowledge about pollutant-material interaction is further limited by the failure of many studies to consider (and measure) important environmental factors. Moreover, estimates of the total quantities of materials exposed and their distribution are limited, so that little information is available to evaluate the **extent** or the **economic consequences** of such damage over large geographic areas. Information gaps in each of these areas have, to date, prevented investigators from developing reliable estimates of the overall economic effects of materials damage.

Other factors that may affect how much damage takes place, and about which little is currently known, are: 1) microclimatic variations, 2) the physical placement of materials, and 3) chemical and physical variations in seemingly similar materials. For example, rain may wash sulfate and nitrate particles from exposed surfaces and remove the build-up of soluble pollutant-material residues, while the particles that remain on rain-sheltered surfaces may cause greater damage. Variations in the properties of stone might cause samples from even the same quarry to deteriorate at significantly different rates under similar atmospheric exposure conditions.

Several laboratory and field experiments have estimated "dose-response" relationships for a limited number of specific pollutant-material interactions. Greatest amounts of data are available on the effects of SO_x on such metals as zinc and steels under different weather/atmospheric conditions. Sulfur oxides corrode metals; the solubility of a given metal, and its ability to form stable, protective metal oxide coatings when exposed to the atmosphere, determine its ability to withstand corrosion. Metal corrosion always requires moisture, and tends to accelerate above critical humidity levels that range from 60 to 80 percent, depending on the particular metal.

Table B-11.—Air Pollution Damage to Materials

Materials	Type of impact	Principal air pollutants	Other environmental factors	Mitigation measures
Metals	Corrosion, tarnishing	Sulfur oxides and other acid gases	Moisture, air, salt, particulate matter	Surface plating or coating, replacement with corrosion-resistant material, removal to controlled environment
Building stone	Surface erosion, soiling, black crust formation	Sulfur oxides and other acid gases	Mechanical erosion, particulate matter, moisture, temperature fluctuations, salt, vibration, CO_2, micro-organisms	Cleaning, impregnation with resins, removal to controlled environment
Ceramics and glass	Surface erosion, surface crust formation	Acid gases, especially fluoride-containing	Moisture	Protective coatings, replacement with more resistant material, removal to controlled atmosphere
Paints and organic coatings	Surface erosion, discoloration, soiling	Sulfur oxides, hydrogen sulfide	Moisture, sunlight, ozone, particulate matter, mechanical erosion, micro-organisms	Repainting, replacement with more resistant material
Paper	Embrittlement, discoloration	Sulfur oxides	Moisture, physical wear, acidic materials introduced in manufacture	Synthetic coatings, storing controlled atmosphere deacidification, encapsulation, impregnation with organic polymers
Photographic materials	Microblemishes	Sulfur oxides	Particulate matter, moisture	Removal to controlled atmosphere
Textiles	Reduced tensile strength, soiling	Sulfur and nitrogen oxides	Particulate matter, moisture, light, physical wear, washing	Replacement, use of substitute materials, impregnation with polymers
Textile dyes	Fading, color change	Nitrogen oxides, ozone	Light, temperature	Replacements, use of substitute materials, removal to controlled environment
Leather	Weakening, powdered surface	Sulfur oxides	Physical wear, residual acids introduced in manufacture	Removal to a controlled atmosphere, consolidated with polymers, or replacement
Rubber	Cracking	Ozone	Sunlight, physical wear	Add antioxidants to formulation, replace with more resistant materials

SOURCE: U.S. Environmental Protection Agency, "The Acidic Deposition Phenomenon and Its Effects," Critical Assessment Review Papers, vol. II, EPA-600/8-83-016B, May 1983.

However, results from certain recent studies suggest that the rate of pollutant-induced corrosion depends most on "time-of-wetness"[1]—i.e., the relative length of time a metal surface is wet (e.g., from morning dew).

Studies have shown that current ambient concentrations of sulfur dioxide (SO_2) can accelerate the corrosion of exposed ferrous metals, and that higher relative humidities significantly increase the extent of SO_2-induced corrosion. However, most uses of ferrous metal products involve the application of such protective coatings as paint and zinc, or the addition of protective alloys. Zinc coatings, used primarily for galvanizing steel, are also corroded by atmospheric SO_2 concentrations, potentially allowing steel underneath to rust, and accelerating maintenance or replacement.

---

[1]J. E. Yocum and N. S. Baer, "Effects on Materials," *The Acidic Deposition Phenomenon and Its Effects, Critical Assessment Review Papers,* public review draft, U.S. Environmental Protection Agency, 1983.

The extent of zinc corrosion at given ambient SO_2 levels depends on such climatic factors as relative humidity, windspeed, and time-of-wetness; and on the surface geometry of the product. The economic importance of zinc has caused its reaction to sulfur pollutants to be extensively studied. A number of researchers have developed dose-response estimates for zinc coatings. For example, figure B-14 shows an experimental estimate of the difference between rates of zinc corrosion for large sheets of roofing and siding and those for wire fencing, under different environmental conditions. Rates for galvanized wire and fencing are approximately double those of galvanized sheet exposed to the same environment. The figure suggests that differences between relative humidities in various areas of the country are more significant to corrosion rates than differing SO_2 levels. One researcher has calculated that, for an area with an average humidity of 70 percent, rust could first appear on fencing after 10 years at SO_2 concentrations of 80

Figure B-14.—Estimated Corrosion Rates for Zinc Coatings on Galvanized Steel

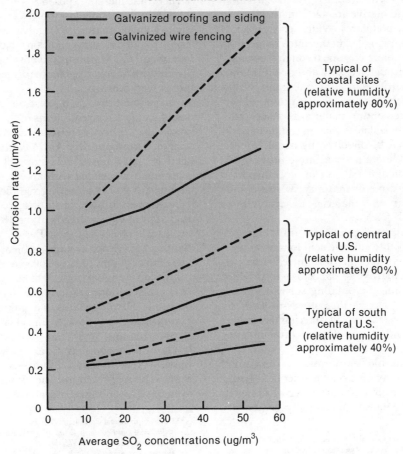

SOURCE: Derived from equations in: "Review of the National Ambient Air Quality Standards for Sulfur Oxides: Assessment of Scientific and Technical Information," U.S. Environmental Protection Agency, 1982.

$\mu g/m$ (the primary ambient air quality standard), as opposed to an interval of about 30 years required for rust to appear in the absence of SO_2. First rust would occur later on most products, depending on the surface geometries and/or coating thicknesses involved.[2]

A variety of paints has been found to be susceptible to SO_2-induced damage. However, the available evidence suggests that climate tends to play a far more significant part in determining deterioration rates than SO_x concentrations. Sulfur oxides appear to accelerate normal erosion processes in paint, and to interfere with drying processes of certain paints. Experiments have found that oil-based paints are the most susceptible to damage, probably because they use extenders that react readily with acidic pollutants. No recent studies of the effects of pollutants on paints are available; a limited number of earlier studies were performed during the early 1970's under atmospheric/pollutant conditions that may differ substantially from current ones.

Extensive qualitative information is available on the effects of SO_x on stone and masonry. In general, the greater the porosity or permeability of stone and masonry, the greater its vulnerability. Such carbonate stones as limestone and marble are particularly sensitive to damage from acidic pollutants. Water serves as a medium for bringing acidifying pollutants into contact with these materials. Crumbling of stone through ''normal'' deterioration (i.e., through freezing and thawing) may further expose stone surfaces to sulfur pollutants. Sulfur oxides react with calcite, the major constituent of carbonate stone and a cementing material in some sandstones, to form calcium sulfate. Calcium sulfate deposits can form crusts and/or be dissolved by runoff waters, washing away or eroding a layer of stone in the process. Alternatively, calcium sulfate can be transported into the body of the stone or masonry, where it may crystallize and cause the material to crumble or fragment.

In addition, bacteria on the surface of buildings convert atmospheric SO_2 into sulfuric acid for use as a digestive fluid. This fluid can react with the calcium carbonate in limestone, marble, or sandstone to produce calcium sulfate, eroding the building surface when it flakes off or dissolves. The various processes have the same net effect: accelerated stone weathering that causes statues to lose detail and reduces the structural integrity of stone buildings.

A recent study of marble deterioration in the United States has measured decay rates on the order of 2.0 mm/100 years; however, studies of more reactive stones in European cities have yielded substantially greater deterioration rates. Ongoing investigations of 3,900 marble tombstones located in 21 U.S. National Cemeteries are developing data on marble decay in headstones exposed to the environment for 1 to 100 years. Since the marble for these tombstones is supplied from only a few quarries, the effects of climatic and pollutant conditions on a relatively standardized stone can be examined across several regions. Preliminary results show the size of grain in the marble, total amount of precipitation, and local air quality to be significant factors affecting decay.

Efforts to estimate aggregate materials damage to the Eastern United States, whether in physical or economic terms, are hampered by the lack of available information on the distribution of sensitive materials throughout the regions subject to elevated pollution levels. Materials at risk may not be distributed simply as a function of population density; limited field surveys suggest that the period of settlement and urban development, and the local availability of particular materials, also may be influential. For example, a recent field survey of the quantities of paint, galvanized steel, and structural concrete exposed to different concentrations of SO_2 in the greater Boston area suggests that substantially smaller quantities of galvanized steel may be exposed to atmospheric conditions than generally has been assumed.[3] OTA attempts to develop regional materials inventories and/or reliable surrogates for estimation purposes were unsuccessful.

An estimate of U.S. historic resources exposed to elevated ambient concentrations of SO_2 has been prepared under the *United States-Canada Memorandum of Intent on Transboundary Air Pollution*.[4] Using data from the National Register of Historic Places, which includes sites either associated with an event or person, having architectural or engineering significance, or potentially contributing to historic studies, researchers estimated that approximately 16,800 of the 18,300 sites registered as historic places in the 31 Eastern States are in counties that experience average ambient SO_2 concentrations less than 60 $\mu g/m^3$. About 900 sites experience SO_2 concentrations ranging from 60 to 80 $\mu g/m^3$, and about 600 sites are in counties experiencing concentrations above 80 $\mu g/m^3$. Historic places in eight States—Maine, New Hampshire, New York, Pennsylvania, West Virginia, Illinois, Indiana, and Ohio—are exposed to the highest levels of SO_2 concentrations. However, only in two States—New York and Illinois—are more than 20 percent of the registered historic places exposed to annual average SO_2 concentrations above 80 $\mu g/m^3$. While such

[2]U.S. Environmental Protection Agency, *Review of the National Ambient Air Quality Standards for Sulfur Oxides: Assessment of Scientific and Technical Information*, OAQPS Staff Paper, EPA-45015-82-007, 1982.

[3]TRC Environmental Consultants, *Air Pollution Damage to Man-Made Materials: Physical and Economic Estimates* (Palo Alto, Calif.: Electric Power Research Institute, EPRI EA-2837, 1983).

[4]''Impact Assessment,'' Work Group 1, *U.S.-Canadian Memorandum of Intent on Transboundary Air Pollution*, January 1983.

a survey can be helpful in indicating an area's relative exposure to potential damages, the ambient SO_2 levels chosen to categorize levels of exposure are arbitrary, representing convenient indicators rather than some known threshold below which materials damage would not take place.

Predicting human responses is perhaps the most significant difficulty in estimating the consequences of pollution-induced materials damage. Individuals confronted with obvious deterioration may choose to ignore it, accelerate cleaning, painting, or replacement, or substitute a less susceptible material. Unless the damage causes some change in the material's utilization or results in some cost to owners, it will have no measurable economic significance. For example, metal guardrails on highways are likely to suffer damage from air pollutants; however, highway accidents generally restrict a guardrail's useful life to a greater extent than does air pollution. Ozone causes rubber and other elastomers to lose elasticity prematurely, and become brittle. Consequently, automobile tires and other exposed products are routinely manufactured with antioxidant agents—the cost of these additives, rather than a shortening of usable life, represents this economic effect of air pollution.

Since the early 1970's, a number of studies have calculated annual costs of materials damage due to air pollutants by *estimating amounts of damage* and deriving some monetary equivalent for these damages. While the availability of dose-response relationships for certain pollutant-material interactions permit this type of analysis, the uncertainties involved are quite large. Moreover, such studies still must rely on broad hypotheses about material exposure and individual economic behavior.

For example, a recent study estimated the amount by which materials damage would be reduced if European OECD member countries decreased SO_x emissions by about 20 percent and 50 percent from projected emissions of about 24 million tons in 1985.[5] Estimates were made only for corrosion to zinc and galvanized steel, and for damage to paint coatings. The study assumed that each of these materials was used in proportion to the population, using OECD annual statistics on the use of paint and of zinc for galvanizing in member countries. Galvanized materials were assumed to be unpainted initially; sheet and products manufactured from sheet were assumed to be painted, and wire replaced, after some corrosion occurred. Repainting was

assumed to occur at the economically optimal time; however, materials older than 25 years were excluded, and no consideration was given to withdrawal of materials prior to that time. These assumptions yielded an estimate that costs of damage would be reduced by $450 million annually (1979 dollars) if emissions were reduced by about 20 percent, and by $960 million annually if emissions were reduced by about 50 percent, by 1985.

A recent study commissioned by EPA's Office of Air Quality Planning and Standards used microeconomic and statistical techniques—rather than physical dose-response approaches—to estimate pollution-related economic losses from materials damage.[6] The method statistically estimates how much of the observed variations in expenditures for goods and services sensitive to differing air pollution levels is due to a variety of economic and climatological factors, and how much of the remaining variation can be attributed to differing SO_2 levels. This methodology has the advantage of taking into account a wider variety of potential responses to pollution-related damages (e.g., relocating, substituting pollution-resistant materials, doing nothing) than studies assuming that all perceived damages would be remedied by repair or replacement. The study has the further advantage of taking into account costs due to air pollution, but not perceived as such—e.g., accelerated depreciation of machinery. However, such statistical methods can show only that a **correlation** exists between pollution and the materials-related costs, and cannot prove that pollution causes the economic effect.

The EPA-sponsored study calculated the value of reducing SO_2 levels nationwide from the primary NAAQS (365 $\mu g/m^3$, 24-hour averaging time) to a hypothetical secondary standard of 260 $\mu g/m^3$ (24-hour averaging time).* Calculations of benefits were made for households in 24 standard metropolitan statistical areas for electric utility maintenance; for agriculture; and for six selected industries for which adequate economic data were available—1) meat products, 2) dairy products, 3) paperboard containers and boxes, 4) fabricated structural metal products, 5) metal forging and stampings, and 6) metalworking machinery.** Results were then

[5]Organization for Economic Cooperation and Development (OECD), *The Costs and Benefits of Sulphur Oxide Control: A Methodological Study* (Paris: OECD, 1981).

[6]E. H. Manuel, Jr., et al., "Benefits Analysis of Alternative Secondary National Ambient Air Quality Standards for Sulfur Dioxide and Total Suspended Particulates," produced by Mathtech, Inc., under contract to U.S. Environmental Protection Agency, OAQPS, Research Triangle Park, N.C., 1982.
*The current secondary standard—1,300 $\mu g/m^3$, 3-hour averaging time—was found to be less restrictive, for most locations, than the primary standard. Using statistical averaging techniques to match 3-hour to 24-hour standards, only 5 counties in the country (out of 182 counties for which air quality data were available) would require additional controls to meet the secondary standard, as compared to the primary standard.
**These industries correspond to Standard Industrial Classification (SIC) codes 201, 202, 265, 344, 346, and 354.

extrapolated to households throughout the United States, comparable manufacturing sectors, and electric utility operation and maintenance. The study concluded that reducing SO_2 emissions in urban areas to meet the 260 $\mu g/m^3$ standard would create benefits of approximately $300 million annually for about half of the households and 7 to 9 percent of the producing sector*

*The study defines the "producing sector" to include agriculture, forestry, and fisheries; mining and construction; manufacturing; transportation, communication, and utilities; commercial and services; government; and other.

in the United States. These results cannot be extrapolated to provide estimates of benefits to the Nation overall; the lack of necessary data precludes analyzing the remainder of the Nation's economy in this manner.

B.4 VISIBILITY IMPAIRMENT*

Introduction

An observer's perception of "visibility" integrates several factors—general atmospheric clarity or haziness, the total distance over which objects can be seen, their apparent color and contrast with the sky, and discerned details of line, texture, and form. Visibility degradation is one of the most obvious effects of air pollution. The present Clean Air Act (CAA) addresses the impairment of visual range in pristine areas, atmospheric discoloration, and the presence of actual smoke plumes ("plume blight"). The reduction in visibility from many and diverse sources spreading over a large area—regional haze—has not yet been addressed. Regional haze reduces visibility in all directions from an observer, is relatively homogeneous, and can occur on a geographic scale ranging from a city to a multi-State region. Haze conditions can reduce contrast, cause distant objects to disappear, and nearby objects to appear discolored and "flattened," add brown or grey discoloration to the atmosphere, and decrease the number of stars visible in the night sky.

Visibility impairment is of concern both for esthetic reasons (especially in areas of great natural beauty) and practical concerns (transportation operations). Limited studies suggest that actual measurements of visibility correlate with: 1) perceived air quality, and 2) perceived property values in Los Angeles and the rural Southwest. Preliminary attempts to quantify visitors' "willingness-to-pay" to preserve scenic vistas have been quite variable. The major effects of visibility on transportation are related to air traffic. Available data show that episodic regional haze over large segments of the East tends to curtail some segments of general aviation air-

craft and slow commercial, military, and other instrument flight operations on the order of 2 to 12 percent of the time during the summer. The Federal Aviation Administration (FAA) restricts visual flight operations when visibility falls below 3 miles. Table B-12 summarizes efforts to characterize the social, economic, and psychological value of various levels of visibility.

A variety of natural and anthropogenically produced particles are capable of interfering with the passage of light and contributing to regional haze. Liquid or solid particles** ranging from 0.005 micrometer (μm) to coarse dusts on the order of 100 μm can either scatter or absorb light, reducing visibility through the extinction of light. Theoretical and empirical results provide strong evidence that visibility reduction caused by urban and regional haze normally is controlled by **fine particles,** primarily sulfates (smaller than 2.5 μm in diameter). The only important situations in which **large particles** dominate are such naturally occurring phenomena as precipitation, fog, and dust storms, or manmade phenomena like construction, agricultural and forest slash-burning, and open-pit mining.

Factors Affecting Visibility

Natural

Natural causes of impaired visibility include dust, fog, low clouds, precipitation, elevated humidity, seaspray, volcanic emissions, and forest fires. Humidity is a particularly significant visibility determinant, as it not only reduces visibility levels in itself, but also affects the visibility-reducing properties of other airborne materials. At high humidity levels, fine airborne particles take up

*This appendix is based primarily on the OTA background paper "Review of the Long-Range Transport of Sulfate Contribution to Visibility Impairment," by Brand L. Niemann, 1983.

Nitrogen dioxide is the only **gaseous pollutant in the atmosphere capable of contributing to the extinction of light; however, its concentrations are rarely large enough to result in a substantial contribution.

Table B-12.—Summary of Qualitative Evidence for Visibility-Related Values

Effect of increased visibility	Affected groups	Averaging times[a]	Supporting observation
Transportation:			
More efficient, lower risk operations, visual approach permitted	Airport users, operators civilian and military	1-3 hr. readings	Visual approaches permitted when visibility >3-5 miles; airport specific (FAA, 1980b)
Increased opportunity to operate aircraft	General aviation aircraft (noninstrument capable pilots, aircraft)	1-3 hr. readings	VFR permitted when visibility >3 miles (FAA, 1980a)
Aesthetic:			
1) Social criteria:			
Decreased perception of air pollution	Substantial percentage of general population; urban areas	Daily to annual	Perception of air pollution in Los Angeles significantly related to visibility for all averaging times (Flachbert and Phillips, 1980). Perception, annoyance significantly related to particulate matter (Schusky, 1966)
Options values; maintaining or increasing opportunity to visit less impaired natural and urban settings	Outdoor recreationists, campers, tourists	Daily, peak visitation in summer months	Aggregate of activity values in iterative bidding studies suggests importance of options values (Rowe and Chestnut, 1981)
Improved view of night sky	Amateur astronomers, other star watchers	Nightly	Decrease in star brightness by fine particles (Leonard, et al., 1977)
2) Economic criteria:			
Increased property values	Home owners	Long term	Property values related to perception of air pollution, hence visibility (Rowe and Chestnut, 1981; Brookshire, et al., 1979)
Enhanced enjoyment (user or activity values) of environment in:			
a) Urban settings	Urban dwellers	Long term	Willingness to pay for increased visibility in urban (Brookshire, et al., 1979) and nonurban settings (Rowe, et al., 1980)
b) Natural settings	Outdoor recreationists, campers, residents of nonurban areas	Daily, peak visitation in summer months	
3) Psychological criteria:			
Existence values; maintaining pristine environments	General population	Long term	Existence values may far outweigh activity or user values (Rowe and Chestnut, 1981)
Less concern over perceived health effects	General population, urban areas	Daily to long term	About two-thirds of bid for improved visibility in Los Angeles was related to concern over potential health effects (Brookshire, et al., 1979)

[a]Represents EPA staff judgment of most important averaging time based on supporting observation. Because averaging times are related it is difficult to specify single (long or short) averaging time as most significant. Perception of visibility is essentially instantaneous.

SOURCE: U.S. Environmental Protection Agency, "Review of the National Ambient Air Quality Standards for Particulate Matter," EPA-450/5-82-001, January 1982.

water directly from the atmosphere; this can cause fine-particle scattering to increase by a factor of 2 as relative humidity increases from 70 to 90 percent. The annual mean relative humidity is greater than 70 percent east of the Mississippi, and greater than 80 percent in Maine and several Atlantic coastal areas. Dense fog is, of course, most frequent in coastal and mountainous areas, with the northern Appalachian mountains, northern California coast, and Nantucket Island showing 50 to 80 days/year of dense fog. Blowing dust is a significant cause of visibility impairment only in the southern Great Plains and Western desert regions.

On a regional or national basis, the frequency of relevant meteorological phenomena has been determined by the National Oceanic and Atmospheric Administration (NOAA) and individual researchers. However, reports from **individual** sites usually have not included information on the occurrence of these natural phenomena during impaired visibility. Without such information, it is difficult to evaluate how much of observed visibility degradation is due to natural causes.

Manmade

Anthropogenic particles contributing to reduced visibility originate from stationary and mobile sources and may be emitted directly or formed in the atmosphere through transformation of such gaseous pollutants as SO_2. The origin and composition of fine particles (less than 2.5 μm) is generally different than that of large or coarse particles. Fine particles tend to originate from the condensation of materials produced during combustion (e.g., lead) or atmospheric transformation of gases (e.g., sulfates). (See app. C, "Atmospheric Chemistry.") Atmospherically formed fine particles—particularly sulfates—can circulate in moving air masses, and subsequently be dispersed over large geographic areas far from source regions. Since larger particles settle out most rapidly, elevated levels of coarse particles usually occur only near strong emissions sources.

Evidence for Anthropogenically Caused Decrease in Visibility

Both current and historical data bases can provide insight into the relationship between manmade air pollution and visibility degradation.

Current information on amounts and location of SO_2 and NO_x emissions can be related to the monitoring data for air concentrations and deposition of sulfates and nitrates. In conjunction with meteorological data and visibility measurements, this information allows detailed analysis of factors contributing to short-term (e.g., seasonal) changes in visibility.

Historical visibility data can be used to infer long-term trends in air quality, because changing patterns of visibility reflect variation in natural and anthropogenic emissions and meteorology over the long term.

General Conclusions

Based on: 1) current assessments of natural sulfur sources and regional fine-particle levels, 2) long-term historical visibility data in the Northeast from 1889 to 1950, and 3) examination of airport visibility trends after deleting data potentially influenced by natural sources (fog, precipitation, blowing dust), anthropogenic sulfate levels appear to be the dominant component of Eastern regional haze. Investigations over the past decade, using a variety of data bases, show several areas of agreement:

- Examination of airport data, pollution measurements, and satellite photography indicates that region-scale hazy air masses move across the Eastern United States and cause significant visibility reduction in areas with little or no air pollutant emissions. In addition, aircraft measurement of the plumes of large powerplants, smelters, and major urban areas have tracked the visibility impairment by sources for 30 to 125 miles downwind.

- Light scattering by anthropogenic particulate pollution—of which fine sulfate particles are the most important—appears to be the predominant cause of Eastern regional haze. Recent studies indicate that sulfate in the Eastern United States is responsible for about 70 percent of visibility impairment in the summer, and 50 percent on an annual basis. Nitrates rarely contribute substantially to visibility degradation in the East, while carbon particles appear more important within urban areas than in suburban or rural areas.

- Contributions to visibility degradation in the West appear to be more varied. Depending on the site analyzed, substantial contributions have been shown for nitrates, carbon, sulfates, and dust. Analyses of the relationship between copper-smelter emissions and regional visibility degradation in the Southwest, however, have shown correlations between SO_2 emission levels and the percent of time during which reduced visibility occurs.

- Currently highest average visual ranges for the United States occur in the mountainous Southwest (annual visibility generally greater than 70 miles). Annual median visibilities east of the Mississippi and south of the Great Lakes are less than 15 miles, with the Ohio River Valley showing the lowest visibility range (fig. B-15). While some of this difference stems from lower relative humidity levels in the West, a more important factor is the higher regional fine-particulate loadings in the East (e.g.,

Figure B-15.—Median Yearly Visual Range (miles) for Suburban and Nonurban Areas

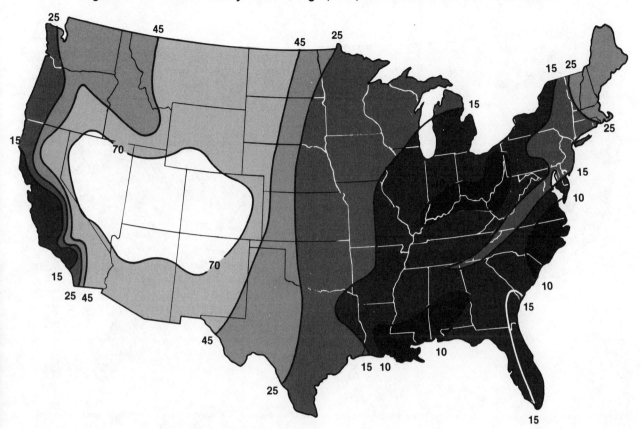

Data from 1974–76, estimated from visual observations and other methods.

SOURCE: J. Trijonis and R. Shapland, *1979: Existing Visibility Levels in the U.S.: Isopleth Maps of Visibility in Suburban/Nonurban Areas During 1974-76,* EPA 450/5-79-010, U.S. Environmental Protection Agency, Research Triangle Park, N.C.

about 25 $\mu g/m^3$ in the summer) than in the West (about 4 $\mu g/m^3$ in the summer). (See fig. B-16.)

- National visibility maps show that summertime visibility is much lower than annual-average visibility levels in the East, and that the largest regional gradients in visibility are found in California. In California, the two major pockets of impaired visibility (Los Angeles Basin and southern San Joaquin Valley) are due more to local- or medium-range transport than to long-range transport, while in the East, the major area of impaired visibility (Ohio River Valley) is undoubtedly related to the high density of SO_2 emissions. The cause of pockets of impaired visibility found in the Gulf and mid-Atlantic coasts is less apparent, but probably reflects a combination of natural and anthropogenic factors.

- Trend analyses of visibility at Eastern airports for the period of 1950-80 indicate that while winter-time visibilities improved in some Northeastern lo-

cations, overall regional visibility declined until 1974, then slightly improved. However, summertime, often the best season for visibility in the 1950's, is currently marked by the worst episodic regional haze conditions.* (See fig. B-17.)

- From the early 1960's through the mid-1970's, U.S. control programs resulted in substantial reductions in total suspended particles (TSP) and SO_2 levels in most of the more polluted urban areas. However, during this same period, available information suggests that Eastern U.S. regional concentrations of summertime fine particles, particularly sulfates, increased.

---

*While quantities of smaller particles (less than 0.1 μm) are sometimes present in polluted air masses, they are relatively ineffective at scattering light; larger particles are effective light-scatterers, but are rarely present in sufficient concentrations to affect visibility substantially.

Figure B-16.—Airborne Fine-Particulate Concentrations (μg/m³) (summer 1977-81)

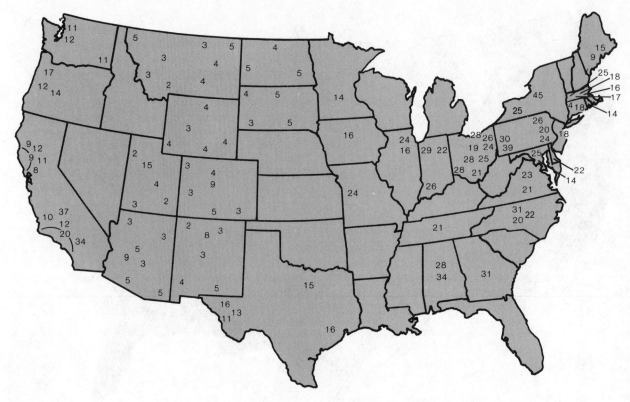

SOURCE: Composite map based on data from 3 networks: EPA's Inhalable Particulate Network, EPA's Western Fine Particle Data Base, and EPRI SURE network.

Mechanisms of Visibility Degradation

In a completely ''pure'' atmosphere, visual ranges across the horizon can extend up to 200 miles; such conditions are occasionally approached on clear days in the Southwestern United States. The extent of visibility degradation is determined both by the **size and concentration** of particles in the atmosphere. For example, adding 10 μg/m³ of **coarse** particles—greater than 2.5 μm in diameter—to clean air would reduce visibility moderately, from 130 km to about 108 km. If, however, the particles were **very small** (in the optically critical size range of 0.1 to 1.0 μm), the addition of 10 μg/m³ would reduce visibility significantly, from 130 km to about 44 km. (Table B-13 shows how the relative contribution of fine and coarse particles varies from location to location.)

Adding even low **concentrations** of substances to pristine environments has a profound effect on visibility. The addition of 1 μg/m³ of fine particles to a clean atmosphere can reduce visual ranges by about 30 percent. As the atmosphere is degraded, each additional incre-

ment of particulate matter has a smaller effect on visibility—adding 1 μg/m³ of fine particles to an atmosphere with a 20-mile visual range reduces visibility by only 3 percent (see fig. B-18).

Two fine-particle components, hygroscopic (water-absorbing) sulfates and elemental carbon, generally tend to be most important in reducing visibility. In the East, sulfate compounds are the predominant component in the fine particles causing light **scattering** over wide regions, while elemental carbon accounts for most light **absorption** in urban areas.

Fine particles between 0.1 and 2.0 μm diameter are the most efficient at scattering light, and appear to account for the bulk of visibility degradation due to light scattering.* Sulfates and nitrates, the transformation products of SO_2 and NO_x, exist in the atmosphere primarily as particles ranging from 0.1 to 1.0 μm in size before being deposited to the earth in wet or dry form.

---

*Recent evidence suggests that at least some of the difference may be due to shorter and less frequent episodes of elevated humidity during the 1950's than occurred in the 1970's. C. Sloane, ''Summertime Visibility Declines: Meteorological Influences,'' *Atmospheric Environment* 17(4):763-74, 1983.

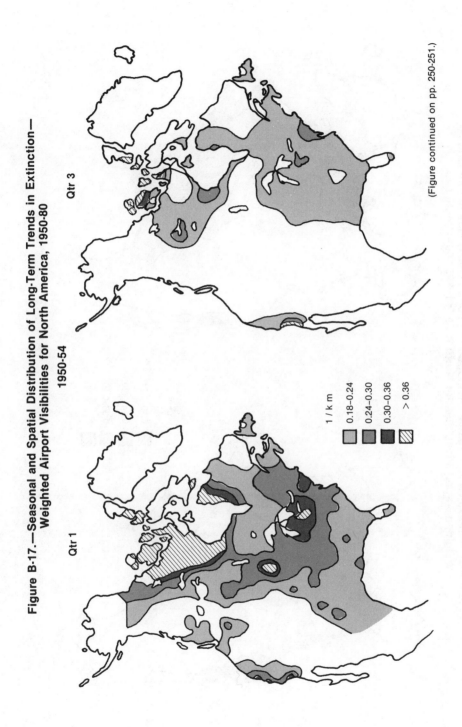

Figure B-17.—Seasonal and Spatial Distribution of Long-Term Trends in Extinction— Weighted Airport Visibilities for North America, 1950-80

Qtr 3

1950-54

Qtr 1

1 / k m

0.18–0.24
0.24–0.30
0.30–0.36
> 0.36

(Figure continued on pp. 250-251.)

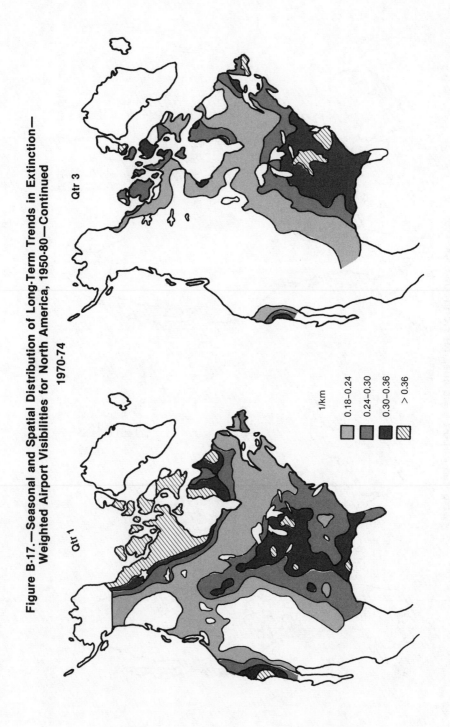

Figure B-17.—Seasonal and Spatial Distribution of Long-Term Trends in Extinction—Weighted Airport Visibilities for North America, 1950-80—Continued

Figure B-17.—Seasonal and Spatial Distribution of Long-Term Trends in Extinction—
Weighted Airport Visibilities for North America, 1950-80—Continued

1976-80

Qtr 1

Qtr 3

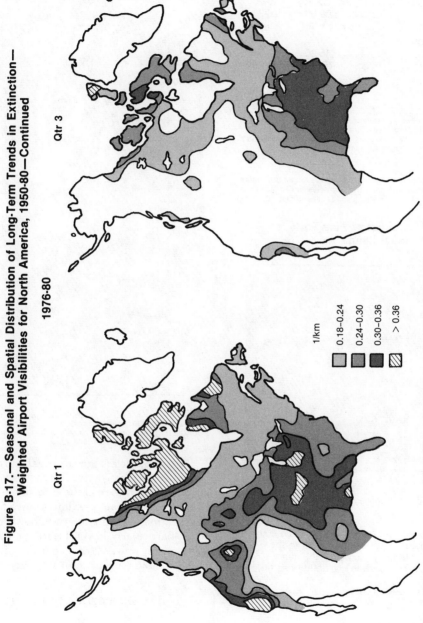

1/km

0.18–0.24

0.24–0.30

0.30–0.36

> 0.36

SOURCE: "Impact Assessment," Work Group I, United States - Canada Memorandum of Intent on Transboundary Air Pollution, June 1982.

Table B-13.—Characterization of Airborne Particulate-Matter Concentrations, 1977-81[a]

Long-term (6-12 months) average	TSP[b]	FP[c] (<2.5 μm)
Eastern locations:		
Undisturbed	30-40	15-20
Downtown	60-90	20-30
Industrial	60-110	25-45
Arid Western locations:		
Undisturbed	15-20	3-5
Downtown	75-130	15-25
West coast:		
Los Angeles area	90-180	30-40
Pacific Northwest	45-95	15-25

[a]The data used from the three networks include: EPA's Inhalable Particulate Network, 35 urban sites, April 1980-March 1981; EPA's Western Fine Particle Data Based, 40 nonurban sites, Summer 1980-Spring 1981; Electric Power Research Institute SURE data base, 9 rural sites, 15 months, 1977-1978.
[b]Total suspended particulates.
[c]Fine particulates.

SOURCE: Pace, T. G. (1981). Characterization of Particulate Matter Concentrations. Memorandum to John Bachmann, Strategies and Air Standards Division, Office of Air Quality Planning and Standards (Dec. 30, 1981).

Figure B-18.—The Effect of Fine Particles on Visual Range

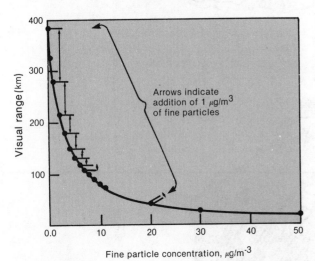

In clean areas (where visual range is greater than 200 km), adding small quantities of fine particles to the atmosphere degrades visibility markedly; the same increment added to an area with low visibility has little effect.
SOURCE: U.S. Environmental Protection Agency, Protecting Visibility, An EPA Report to Congress, 1979.

The strong light-scattering properties of sulfate and nitrate particles are due to their affinity for water vapor; moreover, the greater the relative humidity of the atmosphere, the greater the capacity of sulfate particles to scatter light, especially when relative humidities rise above 70 percent (see fig. B-19).

Figure B-19.—The Relationship Between Relative Humidity and Light Scattering by Aerosol Sulfate

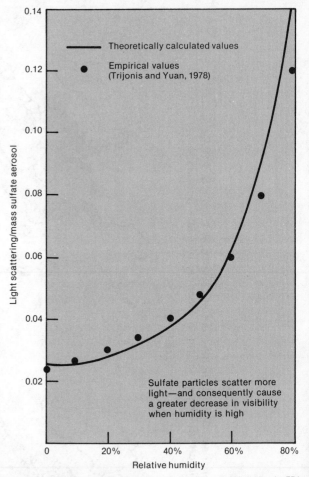

SOURCE: U.S. Environmental Protection Agency, Protecting Visibility, An EPA Report to Congress, 1979.

Carbon particles appear to be the major pollutant involved in absorbing light. In urban settings, where concentrations of carbon particles tend to be relatively high, light absorption can be as important a factor in visibility degradation as light scattering; however, on a regional scale, particularly in rural settings, particle scattering accounts for upwards of 75 percent of light **extinction** —the standard measure of visibility degradation.

Measurement Techniques

The physics and chemistry of light scattering and absorption is well understood. A variety of techniques is available to measure scattering and absorption with reasonable accuracy. The simplest of these involves estimation of visual range, using objects at specified distances from an observer as reference points for estimating the distance beyond which distinct visual phenomena cannot be observed. Such estimates are inherently imprecise, and can be affected by such subjective factors as the observer's visual acuity.* However, the availability of such observations for a wide variety of sites over a multiyear period—visual ranges have been recorded on a daily basis at hundreds of U.S. and Canadian airport sites in urban, suburban, and rural locations since 1948—makes this data base indispensable for performing time-trend analyses of visibility. Comparisons of historical patterns for visibility in the Eastern United States such as those in figure B-17 necessarily derive from such data.

Telephotometry provides statistical measurements analogous to perceived visual ranges, while affording greater precision. The technique involves the use of a telescope capable of measuring the contrast between the brightness of a faraway object and the horizon sky surrounding it. In addition, direct measurements of the portion of a light source lost to atmospheric interference are made with such devices as sun photometers, instruments to measure direct solar radiation intensity, and integrating nephelometers. This last device passes a light source through a given air sample to determine how much light scattering occurs. While nephelometers are not capable of measuring light absorption, and may distort measurements as a consequence of air sample manipulation, they are currently a widely used method of measuring visibility, and are the primary means available for determining how individual pollutants or pollutant mixes affect visibility. The nephelometer has been the basis for most of the experimental data relating cause and effect in visibility degradation studies.

No single measurement technique is adequate at present for assessing all significant factors involved in visibility impairment. The most productive areas of recent research have involved comparing two or more of the available monitoring techniques at selected sites or in new networks where fine particulate and meteorological measurements are made concurrently.

Until recently, visual-range/pollutant-concentration studies dominated the visibility literature; a number of studies completed over the past few years, however, have relied on nephelometer and related measurements to determine correlations with pollutant levels. Imprecision may be introduced into either of these analytical techniques by discrepancies between pollution- and visibility-monitoring locations, as well as by limitations in measurement techniques mentioned above. However, a large group of studies have found consistent patterns pointing to sulfates as the major cause of regional-scale visibility degradation.

Key Studies

A description of some of the key studies will illustrate three different ways researchers have used incomplete data to examine the visibility/sulfate relationship:
- the integrated use of multiple data bases,
- specific case studies, and
- modeling efforts.

Use of Multiple Data Bases: "Capita"

The most extensive analyses of spatial and temporal patterns of visibility impairment in the Eastern United States have been performed by the Center for Air Pollution Impact and Trend Analysis (CAPITA).[7] The CAPITA analyses have used four historical data bases: airport visual range at 147 U.S. and 177 Canadian sites from 1948 to 1980; Blue Hill Observatory visual-range data (3 mountaintops—32, 72, and 107 km from the observatory) for 1889 to 1959; the NOAA/WMO** turbidity network of 25 to 35 sites during 1960 to 1975; and direct solar radiation intensity measurements at Madison, Wis., from 1920 to 1978. Significant findings of the trend analysis were:
- the region of lowest visibility in the 1970's was along the Ohio River Valley;
- the strongest increase in haziness occurred in the summer season in the States adjacent to the Great Smoky Mountains (a decrease in annual average visibility of 15 to 6 miles since 1948);
- around the Great Depression, the visibility at Blue Hill, Mass., improved, and two peaks of haziness around 1910-20 and 1940-50 coincide with two peaks of coal- and wood-burning. Likewise, a strong peak in turbidity corresponding to a decrease in visibility was present in the Madison, Wis., data coinciding with the increase in national coal consumption. However, direct cause-effect relationships have not been established; and
- regional visibility in Eastern Canada and in both the Eastern and Western United States apparently has improved somewhat since 1972, but not to pre-1960 levels; whether this improvement relates to more favorable meteorology or reflects the slight reduction achieved in particulate and SO_2 emissions in the last 10 years is unclear.

---

*Prior to 1970, observations beyond 15 miles were not reported at most stations in the Mideastern States. The coarseness of distant observations increases with distance due to fewer available targets. Visibilities greater than 15 miles are now estimated in multiples of 5 miles.

---

[7]R. B. Husar, et al., "Spatial and Temporal Pattern of Eastern United States Haziness: A Summary," report prepared by the Center for Air Pollution Impact and Trend Analysis, Washington University, St. Louis, Mo., for the U.S. Environmental Protection Agency, 1981.

**National Oceanic and Atmospheric Administration/World Meteorological Organization.

Case Studies: Southwestern United States

A number of factors combine to make visual ranges in the "four corners" region of the Southwestern United States a promising means of assessing the effects of sulfates on visibility. Pollutant concentrations and relative humidity levels in most parts of Arizona, New Mexico, Colorado, and Utah tend to be quite low; consequently, visibility levels are among the highest known throughout the United States, and changes in pollutant concentrations make significant differences in perceived visual ranges. In addition, over 90 percent of the region's sulfur emissions come from a single industry—copper smelters—which experienced a total shutdown during 1967-68, and a partial shutdown in 1980. However, ambient sulfate levels have not been monitored extensively in the region, as they have in the Eastern United States. Thus, while airport visual ranges show marked increases in these four States during the two copper-smelter shutdowns, relationships between sulfate and visibility have been difficult to establish.

Initial investigations found substantial decreases in sulfate levels at monitoring sites both near major smelting operations, and at remote areas up to 300 miles from the major smelting area in southeast Arizona, during the 1967-68 shutdown.[8] Visibility conclusions from this study have been criticized on the basis that sufficient data were lacking to document a consistent sulfate/visibility relationship. During a second strike in the summer of 1980, mean sulfate concentrations dropped to one-third of normal levels within 60 miles of the smelter; between 60 and 400 miles away, sulfate levels were about half of nonstrike conditions. Trajectory analyses of sulfate episodes in both the northern Great Plains and Grand Canyon areas show that some ultra-long-range transport from southern California occurs.

To further test the sulfate/visibility hypothesis, and to extend the information base on Southwestern visibility, an OTA contractor analyzed visual range and sulfate concentration data in 22 case studies covering pollution episodes and nonepisode periods before, during, and following the two shutdown periods. In addition, the RCDM long-range-transport model was used to estimate sulfate levels more generally over the "four corners" region, and to provide preliminary estimates of the extent of sulfate contributions from sources outside the four-State region for the period 1979-81. The analysis strongly confirms the relationship among copper smelter emissions, sulfate levels, and visual ranges; in addition, it suggests that substantial portions of the sulfate levels measured during the 1980 shutdown can be traced to more distant sources, primarily those in southern California.

Modeling: Extinction Budget

While there are limitations in the use of regression models for determining extinction budgets and aerosol/visibility relationships, these techniques show that overall, sulfates account for over half (53 percent) of the extinction budget, nitrates account for only 8 percent, and a significant part of the budget is not accounted for at most of the sites analyzed. The nitrate contribution to the extinction budget is very uncertain (but small) due to uncertainties in the conventional nitrate filter-concentration measurements. More comprehensive studies of the extinction budget are needed, using special air quality and visibility measurements rather than relying on conventional air quality monitoring and airport data.

Sulfate was known to contribute significantly to light extinction 10 years ago. Subsequent efforts to determine the relative importance of nitrate and carbon to visibility impairment were hampered by measurement techniques and inherent spatial (urban v. rural) and temporal (seasonal) variability. There still is not enough high-quality data of nonsulfate measurements to generate complete regional budgets of the various pollutants' contribution to visibility impairment. Most recent information suggests that carbon may contribute to light extinction in heavily urban areas, such as Houston (17 to 24 percent of light extinction[9]), Denver (about 40 percent of light extinction[10]), and New York (35 percent of light extinction[11]). Nitrate is an important factor in the West—e.g., in Riverside, Calf., it is responsible for about 20 to 25 percent of light scattering.[12] Nonetheless, at most Eastern U.S. sites, sulfate is the single most important pollutant responsible for visibility degradation. Under typical Eastern summertime conditions, sulfate accounts for 70 percent or more of light extinction in the Great Smoky Mountains,[13] the Shenandoah Valley,[14] and Detroit.[15] On an annual basis, sulfates contribute an average of about 50 percent to visibility impairment in the Eastern United States.[16]

[9]T. G. Dzubay, R. K. Stevens, C. W. Lewis, D. H. Hern, W. J. Courtney, J. W. Tesch, and M. A. Mason, "Visibility and Aerosol Composition in Houston, Tex.," Environ Sci. Technol. 16:514-525, 1982.

[10]P. J. Groblicki, G. T. Wolff, and R. J. Countess, "Visibility-Reducing Species in Denver 'Brown Cloud'—I. Relationships Between Extinction and Chemical Composition," Atmos. Environ. 15:2473-2483, 1981.

[11]G. T. Wolff, P. J. Groblicki, S. H. Cadle, and R. J. Countess, "Particulate Carbon at Various Locations in the United States," Particulate Carbon: Atmospheric Life Cycle, G. T. Wolff and R. L. Klimisch (eds.) (New York: Plenum Press, 1982).

[12]J. N. Pitts, Jr., and D. Grosjean, "Detailed Characterization of Gaseous and Size-Resolved Particulate Pollutants at a South Coast Air Basin Smog Receptor Site" (Springfield, Va.: National Technical Information Service, #PB 302 294, 1979).

[13]M. A. Ferman, G. T. Wolff, and N. A. Kelly, "The Nature and Source of Haze in the Shenandoah Valley/Blue Ridge Mountains Area," J. Air Pollution Control Assoc. 31:1074-1082, 1981.

[14]R. K. Stevens, T. G. Dzubay, C. W. Lewis, and R. W. Shaw, Jr., "Source Apportionment Methods Applied to Determination of the Origin of Ambient Aerosols That Affect Visibility in Forested Areas," Atmos. Environment (in press).

[15]Wolff, et al., op. cit.

[16]U.S. Environmental Protection Agency, Protecting Visibility, An EPA Report to Congress, EPA 450/5-79-008, Research Triangle Park, N.C., 1979.

[8]J. C. Trijonis, "Visibility in the Southwest: An Exploration of the Historical Data Base," Atmos. Environ. 13:833-43, 1979.

B.5 HUMAN HEALTH RISKS*

Sulfur Oxides

National Ambient Air Quality Standards (NAAQS) have been established for gaseous sulfur dioxide (SO_2), recognizing that it is harmful to human health in high concentrations. The current primary standard for SO_2 is 365 $\mu g/m^3$ (24-hour average concentration), a level considered to pose no significant health risk. Though currently unregulated, concern also exists about health risks from **sulfate** particles—e.g., sulfuric acid and ammonium sulfate—that form through reactions between SO_2 and other substances in the atmosphere. Because these particles are extremely small (mostly under 1 μm in diameter), they can be transported over long distances in the atmosphere and can readily be inhaled into the deep passages of the lung.

Acute exposures to sulfates (greater than 315 $\mu g/m^3$) constrict lung passages and lengthen lung clearance-times in humans and laboratory animals; chronic exposure of laboratory animals to sulfuric acid mist produced evidence of the onset of chronic lung disease. In addition, numerous epidemiological studies have found correlations between ambient sulfate concentrations and mortality rates. Adverse effects at current ambient levels (less than about 25 $\mu g/m^3$) have not been directly observed.

Researchers at Brookhaven National Laboratory (under contract to OTA) have estimated that about 2 percent (a range of 0 to 5 percent) of the deaths per year in the United States and Canada might be attributable to atmospheric sulfur-particulate pollution. The range reflects uncertainties within the scientific community about the causal relationship between air pollution and mortality. Some researchers conclude there is a negligible effect at prevailing sulfate concentrations, while others have found a significant association with mortality.

Sulfur Dioxide

SO_2 emissions currently are regulated under the NAAQS of the Clean Air Act (CAA); the primary standard for SO_2 is 365 $\mu g/m^3$ (24-hour average concentration). Air pollution episodes characterized by particulates and very high levels of SO_2 have resulted in increased deaths in people with preexisting heart and lung disease. Changes in the function of the lungs have been seen in sensitive groups at concentrations above

5,220 $\mu g/m^3$. Recently, a study of asthmatics has shown that constriction of bronchial passages during periods of moderate exercise can occur at concentrations as low as 1,300 and 260 $\mu g/m^3$.[17]

Experimental Evidence of Sulfate-Related Health Damages

Once in the atmosphere, SO_2 is converted into sulfate particles. Two main types of sulfate particles are known to be produced: sulfuric acid (H_2SO_4) and ammonium sulfate [$(NH_4)2SO_4$]. Both types of particles are extremely small and may be inhaled deep into the lung. The high acidity of sulfuric acid particles make them of primary concern for medical researchers, although ammonia in human breath may neutralize sulfuric acid. Ammonium sulfate has not produced the pulmonary effects in animal and clinical studies that are seen with sulfuric acid mist.

In laboratory experiments, acute exposures to **high** concentrations of sulfuric acid particles have a variety of adverse health effects. Concentrations of about 750 $\mu g/m^3$ have irritated eyes and temporarily decreased vision; concentrations of 350 $\mu g/m^3$ have increased breathing rates and altered lung function in asthmatics. Changes in lung clearance rates have been observed in healthy nonsmokers at concentrations of 100 $\mu g/m^3$. Populations at special risk from particulate sulfates are the elderly and adults with preexisting chronic heart or lung disease. Children also appear to be especially susceptible to increased lower respiratory-tract illness and decreased lung function. However, there is no direct evidence showing detectable effects on human health from maximum likely environmental concentrations of sulfate particles **alone,** although laboratory and chemical studies have verified that these small sulfate particles concentrate deeper in the lung than larger inhaled particles. In addition, there is evidence that acid sulfates (and SO_2) render lung tissues more susceptible to the carcinogenic effects of polycyclic organic matter.

Evidence of Sulfate-Particulate-Related Health Damages

Substantial evidence has been gathered over more than 30 years indicating injury from some aspect of the sulfate-particulate mix in air pollution. At high exposure levels, sulfur-particulate air pollution can aggravate

---

*This appendix is based primarily on the OTA background paper "Long-Range Transport Air Pollution Health Effects," Biomedical and Environmental Assessment Division, Brookhaven National Laboratory, 1982.

[17]D. Sheppard, A. Saisho, J. A. Nodel, and H. A. Boushey, "Exercise Increases Sulfur Dioxide-Induced Bronchoconstriction in Asthmatic Subjects," *Am. Rev. Resp. Dis.* 123:486, 1981.

asthma, chronic bronchitis, and heart disease.[18] There also is evidence that sulfur-particulate air pollution causes increased acute respiratory disease in children.

Many analyses of cities with different air pollution levels, comparing death rates among specific population groups, or cohorts, have shown strong correlations between pollution levels and mortality. Evidence is strongest for correlation between acute episodic effects and severe air pollution incidents; evidence of long-term effects at comparatively low levels of pollution is more limited and more controversial.

Nonetheless, scientists generally have been unable to attribute effects to any **single** element of the pollution mix. During the early 1970's, evidence seemed to point to sulfate particles as the health-damaging agent in the sulfate-particulate mix. More recent evidence suggests that the **combination** of sulfates and other associated particles such as metallic ions, nitrates, and fine soot particles may cause the observed effects.

Quantitative Estimates of Health Damages From Long-Range Transport Air Pollutants

To derive quantitative estimates of damage caused by long-range pollution transport, Brookhaven National Laboratory used sulfate concentrations as an **index** of the sulfur-particulate air pollution mix, acknowledging that its use in this manner remains controversial, but it is the best indicator of health risk currently available. Several reports have discussed problems with the use of the sulfate surrogate model. They indicate that other surrogates, e.g., respirable particles, may prove better but, at this time, the sulfur surrogate still remains a reasonabale choice, and possibly the best choice, for air pollution health effects risk assessment. A detailed study by the Harvard School of Public Health for DOE concluded that a fine particulate (FP) measure would be preferable, but "in the absence of FP data, . . . sulfates may be applied with caution."[*] The contractor used a previously developed health-damage function that specifically addresses uncertainties in knowledge by projecting a range of mortality estimates for a given population exposure level.[**]

The health-damage function used is essentially a compilation of expert opinion about the relationship between sulfate pollution and premature mortality (e.g., due to aggravation of preexisting respiratory or cardiac problems). The range reflects a controversy over the validity of epidemiological (i.e., statistical) studies indicating a relationship between mortality and air pollution levels. It includes estimates from scientists who believe there is a negligible effect at prevailing sulfate concentrations as well as those believing there is a significant association.

These studies, carried out and extensively examined over the past decade, examine mortality statistics from areas of the country exposed to different levels of air pollution. The value of these studies is that they examine human health directly, without the necessity of extrapolating from animal studies or small samples of people. They indicate that there are regional differences in mortality, and that regional patterns of mortality are similar to air pollution patterns. While it is possible that factors not considered in these analyses may be more important than the sulfur-particulate mix, none have been demonstrated to date. Such studies are most useful for examining the potential effects of chronic, low-level exposure—what might be happening and what might result from future air pollution levels.

The mortality estimates developed for OTA assume that there is no damage threshold (i.e., minimum exposure level at which air pollution begins to affect mortality). If there is a threshold—which available medical evidence neither confirms nor refutes—the mortality estimates will decrease.

Sulfate-concentration data were derived from SO_2 emission inventories developed for the OTA study, using the Regional Climatological Dispersion Model (RCDM-2) developed at the University of Illinois—one of the models evaluated by the U.S.-Canadian Work Group on Transboundary Air Pollution. Population estimates and projections were derived from the U.S. Census Bureau and Canadian Ministry of Industry, Trade, and Commerce data.

Figure B-20 displays current State-by-State sulfate-exposure levels weighted by population. The map shows that some of the Northeastern States with the highest population density (e.g., New York, Pennsylvania, and Ohio) also are exposed to the highest ambient sulfate concentrations.

Estimates of excess deaths due to sulfate-particulate air pollution were made for: 1) 1980 population levels using 1978 emissions data; 2) populations in 2000, as-

[18]Environmental Protection Agency, "Review of the National Ambient Air Quality Standards for Particulate Matter: Draft Staff Paper," Strategies and Air Standards Division OAQPS/EPA/RTP, January 1982; Lester B. Lave and E. P. Seskin, *Air Pollution and Human Health*, 1977, Johns Hopkins University Press, Baltimore, Md.; Frederica Perera and A. K. Ahmed, *Respirable Particles: Impact of Airborne Fine Particulates on Health and the Environment* (Cambridge, Mass.: Ballinger Publishing Co., 1979).

[*]Spengler Final Report to DOE, October 1983, p. 5, and contribution of Spengler and Evans at DOE/HERAP Workshop on Health Effects of Air Pollution, Brookhaven National Laboratory, August 1982.

[**]The function, developed by Morgan et al., is a probabilistic one with a 90-percent confidence interval of 0-11 excess deaths per 100,000 person-μg/m^3 sulfate exposure (i.e., deaths that would not occur in the absence of sulfate). M. G. Morgan, S. C. Morris, A. K. Meier, and D. L. Shenk, "A Probabalistic Methodology for Estimating Air Pollution Health Effects From Coal-Fired

Power Plants," *Energy Systems and Policy* 2:287-310, 1978. The current range of scientific judgment on the issue has not narrowed, but still spans the range of the 1978 subjective distribution (Morgan, M., et al., *Technological Uncertainty in Policy Analysis*, Report to the National Science Foundation, August 1982).

Figure B-20.—Population Exposure to Airborne Sulfate (an indicator of potential health effects from sulfates and other airborne particulates in each State)

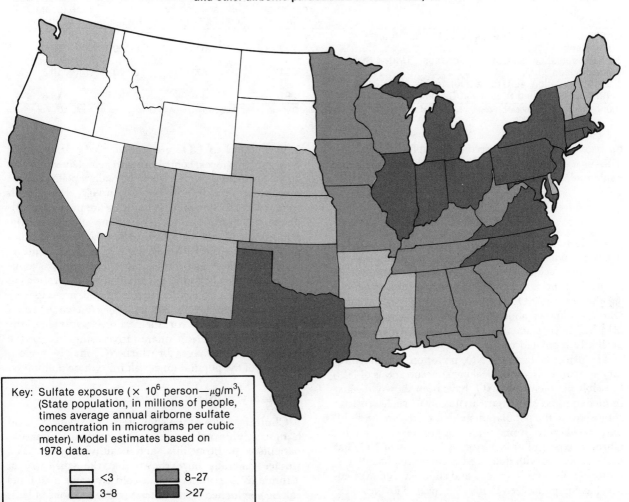

Key: Sulfate exposure ($\times$ 10^6 person—$\mu g/m^3$). (State population, in millions of people, times average annual airborne sulfate concentration in micrograms per cubic meter). Model estimates based on 1978 data.

- ☐ <3
- ▨ 3-8
- ▧ 8-27
- ▓ >27

SOURCE: Brookhaven National Laboratory, Biomedical and Environmental Assessment Division, "Long Range Transport Air Pollution Health Effects," OTA contractor report, May 1982.

suming that total emission levels are held constant at 1978 levels; and 3) populations in the year 2000, assuming that sulfate-particulate levels are reduced by 30 percent from 1978 levels. Results of these three scenarios are presented in table B-14.

Total pollutant emissions in the United States and Canada have been estimated to result in about 50,000 premature deaths under the first scenario, increasing 1978 mortality rates by about 2 percent—an amount approximately equivalent to the number of deaths at-

tributable to infectious lung diseases. While increases in population by 2000 would cause 1978 emissions levels to induce slightly higher levels of premature deaths (scenario 2), a 30-percent decrease in the overall sulfate-particulate mix by 2000 is estimated to reduce the number of deaths annually attributable to air pollution to about 40,000, or 1.6 percent of the total mortality rate.

Estimating mortality attributable to pollution exposure does not necessarily imply that the mortality impacts are the most significant. Mortality dose-response

Table B-14.—Summary of Scenario Results

Scenario	Population (millions)	Excess deaths total (10^3 deaths)	Range	Rate (deaths/10^5 population)
1. 1980 population, 1978 emissions, United States and Canada	249	51	0-150	20.4
2. 2000 population, emissions unchanged, United States and Canada	291	57	0-170	19.8
3. 2000 population, sulfate-particulate mix 30% below 1978 levels, United States and Canada	291	40	0-120	13.8

SOURCE: Brookhaven National Laboratory, Biomedical and Environmental Assessment Division, "Long Range Transport Air Pollution Health Effects," OTA contractor report, May 1982.

functions are used because the available data on morbidity (illness) are inadequate for detailed epidemiological analyses.

Nitrogen Oxides

The term nitrogen oxides (NO_x) refers to a number of compounds—NO, NO_2, and such secondary byproducts as nitric acid, nitrate aerosols, and nitrosamines*— all of which have the potential to affect human health. Of the several NO_x compounds, by far the greatest amount is known about the effects of NO_2, a pollutant that has been studied over the past 30 years and is presently regulated under NAAQS.

The principal target of NO_x pollution is the respiratory system. Episodic or peaking concentrations of NO_2 (possibly augmented by NO) have been shown to cause immediate and short-term irritation to such sensitive subgroups of the population as asthmatics and individuals recovering from acute respiratory infections. Chronic exposure to lower concentrations of NO_2 has been associated with increased occurrence of acute respiratory infections in infants and children. Some scientists have hypothesized that such repeated low-level exposures also are associated with chronic lung disease and increased "aging" of the lung in adolescence and adulthood.

Health effects directly attributable to NO_2 generally are considered to result from **localized** sources of pollution. Combustion of coal, oil, and gasoline is estimated to be responsible for local outdoor concentrations of NO_x 10 to 100 times naturally occurring background levels in areas of high emissions.** Indoor sources of NO_x, such as gas cooking stoves, some home heating systems, and cigarette smoking, also are known to contribute to population exposure, and in some cases may exceed outdoor concentrations of NO_x.

---

*These secondary byproducts are produced from photochemical transformation of NO and NO_2 in the atmosphere; nitrosamine formation has been theoretically suggested but not conclusively proven.

**Mobile-source combustion was estimated to contribute 44 percent of anthropogenically produced NO_x for 1976 in the United States, while stationary-source combustion accounted for 56 percent. USEPA, *Air Quality Criteria for Oxides of Nitrogen*, June 1979, pp. 1-2 and 1-3.

Byproducts of NO_x are known to be transported over long distances, contributing to acid deposition and ozone formation. Some of these secondary pollutants are more toxic on a per-unit basis than NO_2; however, it is not currently known whether they are present in sufficient concentrations—or persist long enough—in the atmosphere to endanger human health. Recent studies performed for the EPA and the National Academy of Sciences suggest that nitrosamines and similar chemical species may be found in sufficient concentrations in polluted **urban** air near certain industrial areas to warrant concerns for health. Not enough is known yet about the effects of NO_x, or their concentrations in the atmosphere, to permit quantitative estimation of the health-related damages for which NO_x may be responsible, or of the population at risk from these pollutants.

Summary of Medical Research

Clinical studies of the **short-term** effects of NO_x on human volunteers have been conducted on asthmatics, patients with bronchitis, and healthy subjects. The studies generally have shown that the sensitivity of asthmatics to irritants such as cold air or air pollutants can be heightened by short-term concentrations of NO_2 as low as 940 $\mu g/m^3$ (the primary NAAQS for NO_2 is 100 $\mu g/m^3$ annually; there is no shorter term standard). Recovery from these effects tends to be rapid, and it is not known whether repeated exposures of this kind have any cumulative effects or predispose the lungs to permanent damage. Most studies do not show increased sensitivity or irritation in either healthy or bronchitic subjects when NO_2 concentrations are at or below 2,820 $\mu g/m^3$.

Laboratory experiments have tested the reactions of animal tissues to similar and higher concentrations of NO_2. These experiments have provided significant insight into the mechanisms that govern human reactions to NO_2 exposures, and suggest more serious consequences of long-term human exposure to NO_2 than have appeared in short-term clinical studies.

Prolonged exposure to NO_2 has been observed to cause damage to lung tissue in laboratory animals. The principal consequences of such damage appear to be development of emphysema-like conditions and reductions in resistance to respiratory infection. For a fixed dosage, greater concentrations have been shown to cause greater increases in mortality rates for animals exposed to respiratory infection than greater duration of exposure. This suggests that fluctuating levels of NO_2, such as are found in community air, may prove more toxic than sustained levels of the gas.

Epidemiological studies of populations of children exposed to NO_2 concentrations, primarily via indoor air pollution, confirm laboratory findings of reduced resistance to respiratory infection in exposed animals. Children exposed to additional quantities of NO_2 (and possibly NO) from gas stove combustion—in particular, infants under the age of 2—show significantly greater incidence of acute respiratory illness and changes in lung function than counterparts living in homes with electric stoves. Similar findings have not been observed in adults.

Indirect Health Effects of Acid Precipitation

Acidified waters are known to be capable of dissolving toxic metals—e.g., aluminum, copper, lead, and mercury—and releasing such toxic substances as asbestos, from soils and rocks in watersheds and lakes, and from drinking water distribution systems. Researchers are attempting to determine the extent to which the total body burden of these substances in humans might result from acidic deposition, as opposed to direct inhalation or occupational exposure.

No direct relationship has yet been established between acid deposition and degradation of drinking-water quality. Potentially harmful levels of asbestos and lead, however, have been found in "aggressive" (i.e., corrosive) acidified waters in the Eastern United States. Scientists have encountered difficulty in pinpointing the direct source of concentrations of toxic materials found in acidic tap waters. Acidic precipitation can scavenge toxic materials from the **atmosphere** during rainfall events, leach them from soils and rocks as they pass through the **watershed,** or leach them from **pipes and conduits** used to distribute water to users.

The aggressiveness of **municipal** water supplies can be monitored and corrected fairly easily. A recent amendment to the National Interim Primary Drinking Water Regulations has established the initial steps in a corrosion control program.[19] Public water systems are now required to identify the presence of specific mate-

rials (e.g., lead and cadmium) within the distribution system and to monitor corrosiveness characteristics for at least 1 year. Also, the types of materials used in the distribution system and home plumbing must be reported.

A recent study sponsored by EPA[20] of 119 surface water supplies in the 6 New England States indicates that 84 to 92 percent of the water bodies are highly aggressive. Anti-corrosion treatment is currently practiced in specific areas (e.g., Boston) where acid precipitation is known to affect water quality.[*] However, aggressive well water in rural areas where soils have little capacity to counteract acid deposition is more difficult to detect and mitigate, and potential health effects remain of concern.

Asbestos

Asbestos occurs widely in natural rock formations throughout the east and west coasts of the United States. In addition, asbestos fibers are mixed in concentrations of 10 to 25 percent with cement to reinforce pipe used to distribute water supplies. While studies have shown that water can corrode asbestos-cement materials and release fibers into the drinking water, data showing a direct association between precipitation pH and asbestos content of drinking water are not available. However, preliminary estimates of asbestos in drinking water from asbestos/cement distribution pipes suggest that approximately 11 percent of the total U.S. population is exposed to asbestos concentrations greater than 10 million fibers/liter.[21]

Correlations between above-average incidence of certain abdominal cancers and elevated concentrations of asbestos in drinking water recently have been found in the San Francisco Bay area, where abundant natural supplies of asbestos occur in bedrock.[22] EPA has used data from studies of workers exposed to airborne asbestos to estimate that one additional cancer will be caused for every 100,000 people exposed to drinking water containing 300,000 asbestos fibers/liters for 70 years.[**]

[19]Environmental Protection Agency, Interim Primary Drinking Water Regulations; Amendment. Final Rule, Fed. Reg. 45(168): 57332-57357, Aug. 27, 1980.

[20]Floyd B. Taylor, "Impact of Acid Rain on Water Supplies in Terms of EPA Drinking Water Regulations," *Proceedings of the American Water Works Association,* Las Vegas, June 1983, in press.
[*]Boston has a high percentage of lead service lines and plumbing. During 1976-77, prior to pH adjustment, 44 percent of the top water samples exceeded the maximum contaminant level (MCL) of 0.05 mg/l lead.
[21]J. R. Millette, M. F. Pansing, and R. L. Boone, "Asbestos-Cement Materials Used in Water Supply," *Water Engineering and Management,* 128:48, 51, 60, 97, 1981.
[22]M. S. Kanarek, P. M. Conforti, L. A. Jackson, R. C. Coper, and J. C. Murchio, "Asbestos in Drinking Water and Cancer Incidence in the San Francisco Bay Area," *Am. J. Epidemiol.,* 112:54-72, 1980.
[**]Federal Register 44(191):56634, Oct. 1, 1979.

Lead

Lead enters aquatic ecosystems from wet and dry precipitation, mineral erosion, street runoff, leaded gasoline, and municipal and industrial discharge, as well as from corrosion of lead in pipes and plumbing systems. Corrosion of lead from lead-containing materials is facilitated by waters of low pH (less than 6.5)—especially when the waters are also of low alkalinity. Individual water samples in isolated areas characterized by low pH values have shown lead concentrations of up to 100 times the 50 μg/l ambient water quality standard.[23] Early morning water samples from New England distribution systems showed 7 percent exceeded the standard for lead.[24]

While elevations in human blood lead levels will result directly from ingesting contaminated drinking water, the human body also absorbs lead from a number of other sources, including food, ambient air, cigarettes, paint, dust, and dirt.*

Mercury

Studies in Scandinavia, Canada, and the United States have found correlations between elevated levels of mercury in fish and increasing acidity of lake and stream habitats. However, no cases of mercury poisoning are known to be associated with freshwater fish in the United States. Lakes in acid-sensitive regions of Minnesota, Wisconsin, and in the Adirondacks of New York have yielded fish with mercury concentrations above the FDA public health standard of 0.5 ppm.[25] [26] Studies are currently under way to assess correlations between observed mercury levels and lake pH levels.

A number of recent efforts to neutralize acidic lakes through the application of lime appear to be successful in reducing mercury levels in fish. Favorable results have been reported for various locations in Sweden, and for Nelson Lake in Ontario, Canada.[27]

Other Metals

Acidified waters are known to leach substantial amounts of **aluminum** from watersheds, and the solubility of aluminum increases as pH decreases below 6.0. Concentrations of aluminum in acidified well water in the United States have been found as high as 1.7 mg/l, which could represent a substantial portion of an individual's daily aluminum intake. Little is known about the toxicity of aluminum to most human populations; no restrictions have been established in the United States on aluminum concentrations in drinking waters or foods.

Several studies have shown, however, that elevated aluminum concentrations may be toxic to individuals with impaired kidney function—e.g., water containing more than 50 μg/l of aluminum is thought to be unsafe for dialysis treatment. Sixty-one percent of surface water samples in New England contained aluminum equal to or greater than 100 μg/l; 24 percent exceeded 200 μg/l.[28]

For normal human beings, **copper** deficiency is more widespread than copper toxicity. A limit of 1 mg/l for copper concentration in U.S. drinking water has been set on the basis of taste; no regulatory limit exists for copper concentrations in food. Acidic waters have been shown to be capable of corroding copper from pipes in household distribution systems—elevated copper levels have been reported in several drinking water samples from sensitive areas of the Adirondacks.[29] Additionally, a recent survey of New England distribution systems showed 29 percent of early morning water samples exceeded the standard for copper.[30] While several cases of copper toxicity have been reported in the United States among individuals with Wilson's disease, a once-fatal disorder of copper metabolism, the hazard to the general population from currently observed copper levels appears quite small.

In its natural state, **cadmium** occurs as an impurity in zinc, copper-zinc, or lead-zinc deposits. In concentrated or pure form it is very toxic. Little evidence of cadmium corrosion from galvanized pipe or plumbing alloys currently exists, although studies of municipal wa-

[23]P. Mushak, *Multimedia Pollutants: Report to the National Commission on Air Quality*, Contract No. 232-AQ-6981, 1981; G. W. Fuhs and R. A. Olsen, "Technical Memorandum: Acid Precipitation Effects on Drinking Water in the Adirondack Mountains of New York State," New York State Dept. of Health, Albany, N.Y., 1979.

[24]Taylor, F. B., op. cit.

*EPA has defined approximately 2.5 million people—inner-city children under 5 and pregnant women—as being at special risk from elevated levels of lead in the bloodstream. While aggressive drinking waters can leach lead from pipes and contribute to lead levels in the blood, such effects may constitute a greater threat to **rural** populations using acidified groundwaters than to urban populations using waters that can be treated readily. Preliminary investigations in the New York State Adirondacks region have found isolated cases of human exposure to lead-contaminated drinking water resulting in lead concentrations in blood as high as 59 μg/dl. (Blood lead levels should be maintained below 30 μg/dl to avoid deleterious health effects.) New York State Department of Health, Technical Memorandum: "Lead Poisoning Related to Private Drinking Water Sources," Oct. 23, 1981.

[25]*Acid Precipitation in Minnesota*, Minnesota Pollution Control Agency, Minnesota Department of Natural Resources, Minnesota Department of Health, Jan. 26, 1982, pp. 7-67; Letter from G. Wolfgang Fuhs, Director, New York State Department of Health, to Congressman Toby Moffett, July 16, 1980, p. 3.

[26]Personal communication, James Wiener, U.S. Fish and Wildlife Service, La Crosse Field Research Station, La Crosse, Wis., May 1982.

[27]"The Role of Clouds in Atmospheric Transport of Mercury and Other Pollutants," G. H. Tomlinson, R. J. P. Brouzes, R. A. N. McLean, and John Kadlecek, in *Ecological Impact of Acid Precipitation*, Proceedings of an International Conference, Sandefjiord, Norway, Mar. 11-14, 1980, Oslo-As.

[28]Taylor, F. B., op. cit.

[29]G. W. Fuhs and R. A. Olson, "Technical Memorandum: Acid Precipitation Effects on Drinking Water in the Adirondack Mountains of New York," New York State Department of Health, Albany, 1979.

[30]Taylor, F. B. op. cit.

ter systems have shown levels to occasionally exceed the U.S. health standard of 10 $\mu g/l$. The concentrations found in drinking water, however, represent only a minute fraction of the amounts known to cause acute cadmium poisoning or chronic health effects under industrial exposure conditions. Based on the infrequent occurrence of cadmium in drinking water at levels above 10 $\mu g/l$, such exposures are not considered a threat to many people.

B.6 ECONOMIC SECTORS AT GREATEST RISK FROM CONTROLLING OR NOT CONTROLLING TRANSPORTED POLLUTANTS

Throughout this report, five sectors of the U.S. economy have been identified as sensitive to the potential effects of decisions to control or not to control transported air pollutants: 1) farming and agricultural services, 2) forestry and related products, 3) coal mining, 4) freshwater fishing-related recreation, and 5) the electric utility industry. This appendix presents information about the magnitude and geographic distribution of these activities in the Eastern 31-State region. OTA assembled data from the Department of Labor, the U.S. Fish and Wildlife Service, and the Edison Electric Institute to estimate levels of economic activity for each, and levels of participation, where appropriate, in recent years. These tabulations are of **total** income, expenditures, employment, and resource utilization for a given sector. They are provided to indicate the **relative importance** of each sector to the economy and people of the Eastern 31-State region, not as estimates of the number of people or amount of economic activity that might be affected by decisions regarding transported air pollutants.

The amount of available information on the potential effect of controlling or not controlling transported air pollutants varies substantially among sectors. Moreover, for sectors dependent on resources potentially susceptible to transported pollutants, reliable estimates of the financial losses associated with resource damage cannot presently be attempted, even for resources for which damages can be estimated. Estimates of losses in crop production from ozone, and of the potential susceptibility of aquatic resources and forests to acid deposition, are provided in chapters 3 and 5, and are treated in detail in appendix B, section 2. Estimates of the economic effects of emissions control on coal mining and electric utilities, and of the coal-mining employment effects of emissions controls, are also presented in chapters 3 and 5, and detailed in appendix A. In general, the costs associated with emissions controls are better known than those associated with potential resource damage. As the available measures of potential effects are expressed in different forms, and represent disparate levels of knowledge, they cannot be compared directly across the five sectors. However, the importance of the **economic sectors themselves** can be compared, both in monetary and participatory terms, as well as among sectors and States.

Table B-15 presents State-by-State estimates of the personal **income** and expenses for which the five sectors directly account, in millions of dollars and as a percentage of the state total. U.S. Department of Labor data on wages, salaries, and proprietary income, averaged over the years 1978-80, are presented for farming and agricultural services, forestry and related products, and coal mining. Freshwater fishing-related recreation expenses are compiled from U.S. Fish and Wildlife Service survey data on expenditures for travel, lodging, food, fees, and light equipment used exclusively for fishing in 1980. For electric utilities, data from the Edison Electric Institute on the percentage of personal income spent on residential electricity consumption in each State are provided.

Farming- and forestry-related income each account for slightly less than 2 percent of the Eastern U.S. region total, or an average of $21.8 billion and $20.5 billion, respectively, for the 1978-80 period. Intraregional variations are significant: farming and agricultural services accounted for over 3 percent of personal income in Kentucky, Mississippi, Missouri, North Carolina, Vermont, and Wisconsin, and over 5 percent in Arkansas, Iowa, and Minnesota. Similarly, forestry, lumber, wood, and paper products accounted for over 3 percent of personal income in Alabama, Georgia, Minnesota, Mississippi, New Hampshire, South Carolina, Vermont, and Wisconsin, over 5 percent in Arkansas, and over 10 percent in Maine.

The greatest regional variation is found in the distribution of income due to coal mining, which accounted for an average of nearly $7 billion in the region during

Table B-15.—Income or Revenues From Farming, Forestry, Coal, Fishing, and Utilities
(in millions of dollars per year and percent of State total income)

Region/State	Farming and agriculture services		Forestry, lumber, wood, and paper products		Coal-mining		Freshwater fishing-related recreation		Utility revenues (residential only)	
	Income	Percent	Income	Percent	Income	Percent	Expenses	Percent	Revenues	Percent
New England:										
Maine.................	110.2	1.7	678.2	10.5	0.3	0.0	83.6	1.3	179.7	2.9
New Hampshire.........	27.3	0.5	208.1	3.6	0.0	0.0	36.2	0.6	166.8	2.9
Vermont	131.1	4.3	103.6	3.4	0.0	0.0	32.1	1.1	81.2	2.8
Massachusetts..........	48.9	0.1	687.9	1.6	0.3	0.0	86.3	0.2	830.0	1.9
Rhode Island	20.4	0.3	58.2	0.9	0.0	0.0	12.0	0.2	135.6	2.2
Connecticut	35.1	0.1	272.0	1.0	0.0	0.0	61.3	0.2	543.8	2.1
Middle Atlantic:										
New York	719.0	0.5	1,349.4	1.0	1.5	0.0	240.8	0.2	2,322.4	1.7
New Jersey.............	231.7	0.4	846.2	1.5	—	—	99.2	0.2	1,294.4	2.3
Pennsylvania	951.3	1.1	1,331.1	1.6	1,215.3	1.4	272.7	0.3	1,784.2	2.2
East North Central:										
Ohio..................	911.0	1.1	1,123.7	1.4	481.5	0.6	280.2	0.4	1,737.4	2.2
Indiana	1,017.1	2.5	641.7	1.6	210.3	0.5	268.7	0.7	839.0	2.2
Illinois	1,805.7	1.9	1,005.3	1.1	564.5	0.6	321.5	0.4	1,690.0	1.9
Michigan	779.9	1.0	767.7	1.0	1.3	0.0	394.9	0.6	1,197.4	1.7
Wisconsin	1,424.8	4.2	1,520.4	4.5	0.2	0.0	440.5	1.4	641.5	2.0
West North Central:										
Minnesota..............	1,664.0	5.3	1,109.2	3.5	1.2	0.0	383.5	1.3	504.8	1.7
Iowa..................	1,670.7	8.1	171.4	0.8	8.7	0.0	111.6	0.6	481.3	2.5
Missouri	1,308.3	3.7	416.4	1.2	54.5	0.2	301.6	0.9	807.9	2.4
South Atlantic:										
Delaware	116.2	2.3	—	—	0.0	0.0	7.8	0.2	11.6	2.3
Washington, D.C.........	3.4	0.0	0.9	0.0	—	—	3.7	0.0	229.6	1.7
Maryland	265.9	0.9	261.1	0.9	28.2	0.1	61.1	0.2	499.5	1.7
Virginia	426.4	1.2	681.8	1.9	583.7	1.6	174.1	0.5	1,075.8	3.0
West Virginia	52.8	0.5	104.6	0.9	1,747.3	15.0	100.5	0.9	266.8	2.4
North Carolina	1,410.9	3.8	984.1	2.6	3.3	0.0	209.3	0.6	1,043.7	2.9
South Carolina..........	304.2	1.7	566.3	3.1	0.6	0.0	135.7	0.8	548.4	3.1
Georgia	760.0	2.1	1,149.7	3.2	1.9	0.0	300.8	0.9	903.2	2.6
Florida................	1,564.5	2.7	736.4	1.3	1.3	0.0	483.9	0.8	2,377.3	4.1
East South Central:										
Kentucky	757.5	3.5	299.0	1.4	1,532.0	7.0	235.8	1.1	511.9	2.5
Tennessee	418.5	1.5	639.8	2.3	135.2	0.5	268.5	1.0	872.2	3.2
Alabama	661.3	2.9	979.9	4.3	389.2	1.7	285.8	1.3	765.5	3.5
Mississippi	650.9	5.0	564.3	4.4	0.1	0.0	170.3	1.4	434.5	3.5
West South Central:										
Arkansas	1,042.0	8.4	639.2	5.1	7.1	0.1	237.9	2.0	384.8	3.3
Louisiana	506.4	1.9	644.2	2.4	0.1	0.0	224.3	0.8	717.5	2.6
Eastern 31-State total	21,797.2	1.9	20,541.6	1.8	6,969.7	0.6	6,326.2	0.6	25,980.3	2.3

SOURCES: U.S. Department of Labor; U.S. Fish and Wildlife Service, Department of the Interior; Edison Electric Institute.

1978-80, or 0.6 percent of the total. Nearly two-thirds of this income was earned in Kentucky, Pennsylvania, and West Virginia; coal mining accounted for over 1 percent of personal income in Alabama, Pennsylvania, and Virginia; 7 percent in Kentucky; and 15 percent in West Virginia.

Expenditure data for electrical power show that residential consumers spent nearly $26 billion to purchase electricity in the region in 1980. In general, the proportion of income spent on electricity is higher in Southern States, reflecting greater use of electrically powered cooling equipment. As a proportion of personal income, expenditures range from a low of 1.7 percent in the District of Columbia, Maryland, Michigan, Minnesota, and New York, to a high of 4.1 percent in Florida.

Freshwater fishing accounted for expenditures of approximately $6.3 billion in the region in 1980, or 0.6 percent of the region's total personal income. States in which these expenditures exceeded 1 percent of personal income included Alabama, Arkansas, Kentucky, Maine, Minnesota, Mississippi, Tennessee, Vermont, and Wisconsin. As shown in the table, freshwater fishing generated at least $250 million in 1980 expenditures in 12 States: Alabama, Florida, Georgia, Illinois, Indiana, Michigan, Minnesota, Missouri, Ohio, Pennsylvania, Tennessee, and Wisconsin.

Table B-16 presents Department of Labor estimates of the **number of people** employed in farms and agricultural services, forestry and related products, and coal mining in 1980. In the Eastern region overall, agriculture employed slightly over 3 million people, or 4 percent of the regional total. Variations within the region are substantial—agriculture employed over 5 percent of the work force in Alabama, Indiana, Minnesota, Mississippi, Missouri, North Carolina, South Carolina, Tennessee, Vermont, and Wisconsin; and over 10 percent of the work force in Arkansas, Iowa, and Kentucky.

Total Eastern employment in forestry, lumber, wood and paper products was slightly over one million, or 1.4 percent of the regional total. These industries employed

Table B-16.—Number of People Employed in Farms and Agricultural Services, Forestry and Related Products, and Coal Mining in 1980

	Farms and agricultural services[a]		Forestry, lumber, and wood and paper products[b]		Coal mining	
	Number of people	Percent of State total	Number of people	Percent of State total	Number of people	Percent of State total
U.S. total	4,628,300	4.3	1,404,000	1.0	251,000	0.2
New England:						
Connecticut	20,436[c]	1.3	11,872	0.7	—	—
Maine	23,069	4.4	32,188	6.2	—	—
Massachusetts	25,670[c]	0.9	33,395[c]	1.2	—	—
New Hampshire	7,987	1.8	11,066[c]	2.5	—	—
Rhode Island	3,121	0.7	3,901	0.9		
Vermont	15,220	6.1	6,409	2.6	—	—
Mideast:						
Delaware	7,116	2.4	4,082[c]	1.4	—	—
District of Columbia	161	0.0	384[c]	0.1	—	—
Maryland	38,293	1.9	13,824	0.7	1,049	0.1
New Jersey	30,570	0.9	38,599	1.1	—	—
New York	117,351	1.5	64,965	0.8	—	—
Pennsylvania	118,613	2.2	63,580	1.2	37,911[c]	0.7
Great Lakes:						
Illinois	168,380	3.1	47,079	0.9	18,147	0.3
Indiana	134,314	5.3	32,791	1.3	6,060	0.2
Michigan	116,823	3.1	32,218	0.8	—	—
Ohio	154,279	3.2	52,404	1.1	15,490	0.3
Wisconsin	163,400	7.2	68,842	3.0	—	—
Plains Region:						
Iowa	177,130	12.3	8,464	0.6	—	—
Minnesota	161,453	7.6	43,415	2.0	—	—
Missouri	165,696	7.2	23,910	1.0	1,049	0.0
Southeast:						
Alabama	101,110	6.0	49,056	2.9	12,539	0.7
Arkansas	103,621	10.6	34,104	3.5	—	—
Florida	135,023	3.2	39,191	0.9	—	—
Georgia	119,319	4.6	59,375	2.3	—	—
Kentucky	154,212	10.0	16,749	1.1	47,319	3.1
Louisiana	72,610	3.9	28,516	1.5	—	—
Mississippi	104,257	9.6	31,218	2.9	—	—
North Carolina	177,556	6.1	57,191	2.0	—	—
South Carolina	76,427	5.1	30,150	2.0	—	—
Tennessee	144,397	6.7	37,106	1.7	4,184	0.2
Virginia	100,666	3.8	38,351	1.4	19,107	0.7
West Virginia	30,607	4.1	7,350	1.0	64,096[c]	8.6
Eastern 31-State total	3,010,885 (65%)[d]	4.0	1,020,724 (73%)[d]	1.4	227,252 (91%)[d]	0.3

[a]Includes farm proprietors; excludes manufacture and sale of farm equipment.
[b]Includes construction of prefabricated buildings and mobile homes; excludes manufacture of furniture, printing and publishing industries, and sale of building materials.
[c]1980 data not available for all data points—estimates may be slightly low due to use of data from mid-1970's.
[d]Figures in parentheses represent the proportion of the U.S. total employed within the Eastern 31-state region.
SOURCE: U.S. Department of Labor.

2 percent or more of the work force in Alabama, Georgia, Minnesota, Mississippi, New Hampshire, North Carolina, South Carolina, and Vermont, and 3 percent or more in Arkansas, Maine, and Wisconsin.

Employment in coal mining is the least evenly distributed of those sectors surveyed. It accounted for slightly under a quarter-million jobs, or 0.3 percent of the Eastern U.S. work force, in 1980. Coal mining employed greater than 0.5 percent of the work force in Alabama, Pennsylvania, and Virginia, and employed 3.1 and 8.6 percent of the work force in Kentucky and West Virginia, respectively. Estimates of shifts in coal mining employment that might accompany stricter SO$_2$-emissions controls are presented in appendix A.

The 1980 National Survey of Fishing and Hunting conducted by the Fish and Wildlife Service is the basis for estimates in table B-17 of the number of participants in freshwater fishing in the Eastern region. Counting only in-state fishing participants, to avoid double counting, over 21 million people are estimated to have taken part in freshwater fishing, devoting an average of somewhere between 11 and 21 days per year to this form of recreation. Counting only in-State residents, Florida, Georgia, Illinois, Michigan, Minnesota, New York, Ohio, Pennsylvania, and Wisconsin each had over a million freshwater-fishing participants; when out-of-State anglers are included, Alabama, Indiana, Kentucky, Missouri, North Carolina, and Tennessee are added to this list.

Table B-17.—Number of Residents and Nonresidents Participating in Freshwater Fishing in 1980[a]

	Number of residents	Total number of participants
Alabama	874,952	1,117,099
Arkansas	574,351	895,619
Connecticut	271,488	307,217
Delaware	30,221	35,136
District of Columbia	10,361	15,006
Florida	1,193,583	1,550,406
Georgia	1,117,544	1,253,265
Illinois	1,264,434	1,401,922
Indiana	913,212	1,111,095
Iowa	592,242	646,180
Kentucky	734,630	1,052,587
Louisiana	752,110	955,567
Maine	214,505	364,062
Maryland	268,716	321,687
Massachusetts	333,680	414,012
Michigan	1,292,682	1,666,295
Minnesota	1,175,026	1,639,131
Mississippi	538,349	689,901
Missouri	998,667	1,230,423
New Hampshire	115,357	224,998
New Jersey	229,175	383,375
New York	1,036,257	1,225,313
North Carolina	927,341	1,096,338
Ohio	1,412,022	1,500,525
Pennsylvania	1,168,907	1,400,689
Rhode Island	60,143	72,633
South Carolina	490,089	639,259
Tennessee	903,633	1,161,467
Vermont	113,256	182,753
Virginia	637,681	823,369
West Virginia	341,293	416,874
Wisconsin	1,109,738	1,674,219
Eastern 31-State total ..	21,760,645	[b]

[a]Does not include fishing in the Great Lakes.
[b]Total not calculated due to potential double-counting of participants.

SOURCE: U.S. Fish and Wildlife Service, Department of the Interior.

Atmospheric Processes

C.1 ATMOSPHERIC CHEMISTRY*

The atmosphere is a mixture of chemicals—some of natural origin, some anthropogenically generated, and some that are produced by nature as well as by man. These chemicals can react with each other to varying degrees under varying conditions. Because the atmosphere is dynamic, the particular chemical environment it represents is different for every location, every season, and every meteorological condition.

Both acid deposition and ozone are produced by transported air pollutants. The dominant precursors of acid deposition are sulfur dioxide (SO_2) and nitrogen oxides (NO_x). Ozone formation involves NO_x and reactive hydrocarbons (RHC). Anthropogenic sulfur oxides (SO_x) are produced primarily by burning such sulfur-containing fossil fuels as coal and oil. Nitrogen oxides also result from the burning of fossil fuel by utility, industrial, and mobile sources. Anthropogenic hydrocarbon emissions result primarily from petroleum refining and storage, other industrial process emissions, and mobile sources.

After release into the atmosphere, the particular sequence of changes a pollutant undergoes depends on the physical and chemical characteristics of the air mass in which it travels. Ultimately, though, because the atmosphere is 20 percent oxygen, emitted SO_x and NO_x will oxidize** and can form acid when combined with water. This can occur while the pollutants are in the air, or following deposition on the Earth. The acids formed may subsequently be neutralized if appropriate chemical species are available.

Which of many chemical routes is actually followed depends on: 1) the initial concentrations of all pollutants; and 2) a number of physical factors, such as wind speed, air turbulence, sunlight intensity, temperature, and rainfall frequency.

While scientists know a great deal about individual

chemical reactions and specific physical processes, they cannot precisely characterize the detailed path of a pollutant from its origin or "source" to its removal or "sink." Reactions can occur when pollutants exist as gases, are dissolved in liquids, or adhere to particles. In general, gas-phase reactions predominate in the transformation of NO_x and the production of ozone, while all three phases—gas, liquids, and solids—are presently believed to play a part in SO_x transformations under different atmospheric conditions. Nonetheless, the key atmospheric reactions involved in producing acid deposition and ozone have some common features and are closely interrelated.

Energy from sunlight triggers chemical reactions that transform SO_x and NO_x (which includes NO and NO_2) into sulfuric and nitric acid, respectively. Such "photochemical" processes, which also form ozone, require the presence of RHC. For example, hydroxyl (OH) radicals—a very reactive chemical species—initiate the gas phase transformation of SO_2 to sulfuric acid. Since concentrations of OH depend, in turn, on concentrations of ozone, NO_x, and RHC, as well as on sunlight intensity, the atmospheric chemistry of ozone, NO_x, SO_2, and RHC must be considered together. Altering the concentrations of any one of these will affect pollutant transformation and deposition rates.

Deposition of Sulfur and Nitrogen

In the East, approximately two-thirds of the acid deposited results from sulfur compounds, and one-third results from nitrogen compounds. Over much of the West, NO_x emissions play a relatively greater role in acidification than in the East. To become acids, emitted SO_2 and NO_x must be oxidized either: 1) in the gas phase, 2) after absorption into water droplets, or 3) after dry deposition on the ground.

These materials can be deposited on the ground *unchanged* (as primary gaseous pollutants), or in a *transformed* state (as secondary pollutants). Transformed pollutants can be deposited in *wet* form (as rain, fog, or snow), or *dry* form (due to particles containing these materials settling out). The amount of time a pollutant remains in the atmosphere, and therefore, how far it

---

*This appendix is based on the OTA contractor report, "An Assessment of the Atmospheric Chemistry of Oxides of Sulfur and Nitrogen: Acid Deposition and Ozone," by B. J. Finlayson-Pitts and J. N. Pitts, Jr., 1982.

**Oxidation is the process of adding oxygen to a chemical. Oxidizing agents or "oxidants" are chemicals that supply the extra oxygen needed to convert SO_2 to sulfate, or NO_x to nitrate. When sulfate and nitrate combine with water, sulfuric acid and nitric acid are formed unless neutralized by other chemicals present.

is transported, depends significantly on its chemical form. For example, SO_2 gas is dry-deposited at a greater rate than sulfate particles (products of oxidation). If SO_2 is quickly converted to sulfate, a smaller fraction of emitted sulfur will be deposited locally, in the absence of precipitation. The rate of conversion of SO_2 to sulfate depends on the chemical composition of the atmosphere. The frequency and intensity of precipitation controls the rate of wet sulfur deposition.

Dry deposition is believed to occur at a fairly constant rate over time (i.e., a certain percentage of the SO_2 in the air is dry-deposited each hour), but varies somewhat over different terrain. Wet deposition is episodic, and the amount deposited varies considerably even within a rainfall event. For example, a short rain may deposit heavy doses if pollutants are concentrated— e.g., if they have been forming and accumulating in the air over time. Without sufficient time for pollutant concentrations to accumulate and be transformed, a second rain in quick succession may deposit little new acid material. The product of concentration times rainfall determines the *total* dose of wet-deposited acidic material.

For this reason, acid fogs (recently identified in the Los Angeles basin) may expose the area to a very high *concentration* of acid (a large quantity of acid per amount of water), but significantly smaller *amounts* of acid may be deposited than would occur from a rainfall. On an annual basis, the contribution to total acid loadings depends on the percent of time that fog covers an area. Particularly in high-altitude regions (e.g., the Northern Appalachian mountains) where cloud cover and fog persist for about 50 percent of the time, precipitation may account for less acid deposition than fog. The relative effect of high acid concentrations (but low total doses) as compared to high total doses of acid (at low concentrations) depends on the nature of the receptor or ecosystem in question. (See app. B, ''Aquatic Resources, Terrestrial Ecosystems, and Materials.'')

In general, areas *close* to emission sources receive significant proportions of their pollution from steady dry deposition of SO_2. In locales *remote* from emission regions, much of the SO_2 available for dry deposition has been depleted or converted to secondary pollutants. In these areas, wet deposition delivers a greater share of the total pollutant dose than does dry deposition (see fig. C-1). Over most of the nonremote Eastern United States, the contribution from wet and dry deposition is estimated to be about equal. Air over any particular area will carry some residual pollution from distant areas, as well as infusions received from more recently passed areas. The continued replenishment and depletion of pollutants along the path of an air mass makes precise source-receptor relationships extremely difficult to determine.

Atmospheric Chemistry of the Oxides of Sulfur

About 26 million tons of manmade SO_2 are emitted in the continental United States. About 22 million of these tons are emitted in the Eastern 31-State region. The oxidation of natural sulfur compounds could contribute significantly to atmospheric SO_2 concentrations in regions where natural emissions are high (e.g., from volcanoes, or some types of marshes) and manmade emissions are low. However, on a nationwide basis, less than 5 to 10 percent of sulfur emissions are attributed to natural sources.

The following discussion of the various fates of emitted SO_2 is summarized in figure C-2. One way in which sulfate is formed involves SO_2 gas interacting with OH radicals in a *homogeneous gas phase reaction*—i.e., the reactants are all in the gas phase. Because OH is highly reactive with many atmospheric components, each OH radical has a short lifetime in the atmosphere. Sunlight is necessary for triggering the chain reaction leading to OH production. Consequently, the greatest quantity of SO_2 gas is oxidized by OH radicals during periods of intense sunlight—i.e, at midday, and in the summer. The maximum rate at which this reaction converts SO_2 to sulfate is estimated to be about 1 to 4 percent per hour. However, field experiments show conversion rates significantly greater (10 to 30 percent per hour) than homogeneous gas-phase reaction rates. Therefore, significant quantities of sulfate must be produced by aqueous (liquid) phase reactions or heterogeneous reactions involving two phases (i.e., reactions of gases on either liquid droplets or solid particles).

In *aqueous phase reactions,* SO_2 is dissolved in water droplets, where oxidants convert the SO_2 to sulfate. There is little agreement as to which oxidizing agent (the candidates include dissolved oxygen, ozone, metals, hydrogen peroxide, free radicals, and NO_x) is most important under particular conditions. The rate of each oxidizing process may depend on the acidity of the solution; the relative importance of particular oxidizing agents may, therefore, change as acid is formed and the pH* of the water droplet decreases. As acidity increases, SO_2 is also less easily dissolved, which slows down some aqueous phase reactions significantly. (For example, the presence of nitrate compounds can increase the acidity of droplets, allowing less SO_2 to dissolve; the presence of ammonia in the atmosphere can buffer such increases in acidity, allowing more SO_2 to dissolve.) Current research suggests that the major aqueous phase oxidation route for SO_2 under typical ambient conditions is

---

*pH is related to acidity. Decreasing pH corresponds to increasing acid. The pH scale is not linear; a drop of one pH unit reflects a tenfold increase in acidity. Compared to a pH of 7 (neutral), a solution of pH 6 is 10 times more acid, pH 5 is 100 times more acid, and pH 4 is 1,000 times more acid.

Figure C-1.—The Effects of Time and Distance on Conversion and Deposition of Sulfur Pollution

Sulfur can be deposited in both its emitted form, sulfur dioxide (lighter shading), and as sulfate, after being chemically transformed in the atmosphere (darker shading). Both compounds can be deposited in either dry or wet form. The relative amount of sulfur deposited in these forms varies with distance from emission sources. Dry deposition predominates in areas close to emission sources. Wet deposition is responsible for a larger percentage of pollutant load in areas distant from source regions.

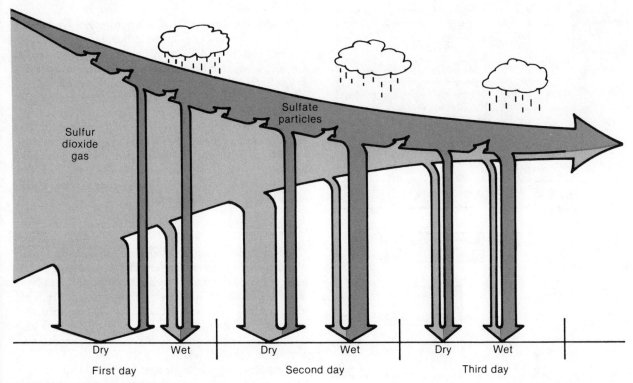

SOURCE: Office of Technology Assessment.

the reaction with the oxidant hydrogen peroxide, because this reaction occurs quickly and appears to be relatively independent of pH.

A variety of measurements indicate that SO_2 gas can be adsorbed onto particles (e.g., carbon soot in plumes) and then oxidized to sulfate. These types of *heterogeneous reaction* rates may be particularly significant in urban plumes.

Gas phase, liquid phase, and heterogeneous reactions may all be important under differing atmospheric conditions. For example, if there is no condensed water and the concentration of particulate surfaces is low, gas phase oxidation will predominate during daylight hours. However, if clouds or fog are present, oxidation in the aqueous phase can predominate. In either case, heterogeneous reactions on surfaces may also be important if sufficient surfaces associated with particulates are available. Such conditions are most likely near an emissions source—e.g., in a powerplant plume.

Overall, current estimates based on empirical observation and model results suggest that homogeneous gas-phase reactions account for 25 to 50 percent of sulfate formed, and aqueous phase reactions account for the remaining 50 to 75 percent on a regional scale. SO_x can be converted to sulfate quickly in the aqueous phase or in concentrated plumes (e.g., more than 10 percent per hour) or slowly (e.g., less than 1 percent per hour in the dry winter) in the gas phase. Thus, SO_x are available for atmospheric transport for periods of 1 day to about a week, and will travel varying distances depending on meteorology and precipitation frequency. The form in which it is deposited depends on the chemistry described above. Ultimately, dry-deposited SO_2 and sulfate may also produce acid on the surface of the Earth following oxidation and combination with available water (e.g., dew).

Atmospheric Chemistry of Oxides of Nitrogen

Manmade NO_x emissions result both from nitrogen bound in fuels and from compounds formed from nitrogen and oxygen in the air during combustion. Anthro-

Figure C-2.—Schematic Diagram of Possible Fates of Emitted Sulfur Dioxide Gas

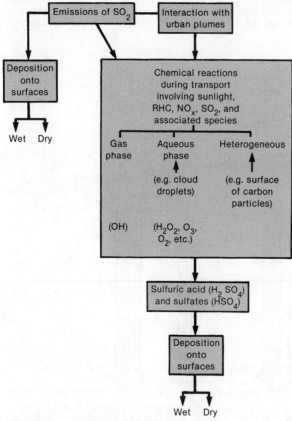

SOURCE: Office of Technology Assessment, modified from Finlayson-Pitts and Pitts, OTA contractor report, 1982.

pogenic sources emitted about 21 million tons of NO_x in the continental United States during 1980. About 14 million tons were emitted in the Eastern 31-State region. Additionally, natural sources produce several forms of nitrogen compounds, primarily from soil processes, organic decay, and lightning. Natural sources of reactive NO_x emissions are estimated to produce less than 15 percent of total NO_x emitted in the Eastern United States. In North America as a whole, the natural background of NO_x may represent 5 to 35 percent of the total NO_x produced.

Gas phase reactions of NO_x have been studied for a number of years because of their role in forming ozone in photochemical smog. The importance of NO_x as a source of acid has only been investigated more recently.

Both ozone and nitric acid formation involve RHCs. The homogeneous gas phase reaction leading to nitric acid (involving the OH radical) occurs about 10 times as rapidly as the corresponding reaction with SO_2. Consequently, nitric acid formation and deposition should occur at distances closer to the source, constituting more

of a local phenomenon than sulfuric acid deposition. A recent modeling study of a very polluted area, the Los Angeles basin, suggests that 40 percent of emitted NO_x are transformed into nitric acid over the course of 1 day. Similar rapid conversion occurs in plumes from the northeast moving over the Atlantic Ocean, a much less polluted area.

In addition to nitric acid, other nitrogen-containing species are formed in polluted atmospheres—e.g., peroxyacetylnitrate (PAN), a nitrogen-containing chemical known to be toxic to plants. In the winter, when PAN is less likely to be decomposed by heat, it may serve as a reservoir for NO_x, allowing substantial transport before either decomposition or deposition occurs.

Recent experimental evidence indicates that uncatalyzed aqueous phase reactions of NO_x compounds are too slow to be important under most atmospheric conditions. However, catalyzed aqueous reactions (e.g., due to the presence of metals or surfaces) may proceed quickly and therefore be important.

Ozone

Ozone is regulated by National Ambient Air Quality Standards under the current Clean Air Act, and has been the focus of most oxidant control studies. NO_x react with sunlight and hydrocarbon-produced radicals to form ozone. Because ozone as well as its precursors can travel substantial distances, ozone concentrations downwind of emissions sources commonly exceed natural background levels.

Naturally produced hydrocarbons, including terpenes from pine trees, and methane from termites and wetland areas, can play a role in forming ozone. Also, additions of ozone from the upper atmosphere (the stratosphere) will contribute directly to observed levels. Such natural contributions can result in ozone concentrations on the order of 10 to 50 parts per billion (ppb), with common background measurements of about 20 to 30 ppb. At midlatitudes in the summer, natural ozone is augmented by photochemical ozone produced when pollutant precursors react with sunlight. (See app. B, "Terrestrial Resources at Risk From Ozone and Acid Deposition," for seasonal ozone levels throughout the United States.) Recent evidence[2] suggests that air masses with very low concentrations of NO_x and RHC (by air quality standards) produce high ozone values in the mountains of Colorado—up to or exceeding the ozone standard. Such concentrations may be quite common in the rural Midwestern and Eastern United States; high ozone levels may be produced at these sites, especially during the summer.

---

[2]F. C. Fehsenfeld, M. J. Ballinger, S. C. Liu, et al., "A Study of Ozone in the Colorado Mountains," *Journal of Atmospheric Chemistry*, in press.

Some of the secondary pollutants (e.g., nitrous acid and formaldehyde) formed along with ozone can themselves facilitate further ozone production. These secondary pollutants can remain in a stagnant air mass overnight and react in the presence of sunlight the next morning.

IMPLICATIONS FOR CONTROL STRATEGIES

A nonreactive primary pollutant such as carbon monoxide (CO) emitted in an urban atmosphere does not, on the time scale of 1 day, undergo significant chemical reactions during diffusion, dispersion, and transport processes. For this pollutant, reducing emissions by 50 percent will reduce CO concentrations in ambient air by 50 percent. Thus, in California's South Coast Air Basin, although the number of vehicle miles traveled has increased substantially over the last decade, exhaust emission controls put on light-duty vehicles have reduced ambient CO levels..

However, primary pollutant emissions that can react relatively rapidly in the air to form secondary pollutants present an entirely different situation. Oxides of nitrogen and RHCs react in the presence of sunlight to form ozone and a host of other secondary pollutants such as formaldehyde, PAN, hydrogen peroxide, nitrous acid, and nitric acid, along with respirable particles. In such a complex system, the effect of reducing emissions is not as easy to determine as in the case of CO, i.e., it may not be "linear."

The term "linear" is used in connection with acid deposition to indicate that a given percentage reduction (or increase) in emissions would cause the same percentage change in acid deposition at a specific location. However, a number of factors may cause emissions reductions (of SO_x, NO_x, or RHC) at one location to result in reductions in acid deposition that are *not* directly proportional at a particular site downwind. For example, introducing fresh supplies of NO_x and RHC (either individually or together) between controlled sources and a receptor could increase or decrease quantities of acid (both nitric acid and sulfuric acid) deposited at that site. In addition, the relative rates at which the various chemicals are deposited (e.g., SO_2 v. sulfate) may also influence the effect of emissions reductions on acid deposition at a particular location.

One of two possible fates occurs to sulfur and nitrogen pollutants: 1) oxidation to sulfuric and nitric acids (or sulfates or nitrates), followed by deposition at the Earth's surface; or 2) deposition in their emitted form (i.e., unchanged). In the latter case, chemical oxidation on the Earth's surface may cause the same net result—i.e., acidification.

Elevated concentrations of oxidizing chemicals such as ozone and hydrogen peroxide are found in atmospheres containing anthropogenic emissions. However, it is possible that at certain times and places, the amount of SO_2 or NO_x may exceed the supply of available oxidants in the atmosphere; when the supply is exhausted, additional acid cannot be made in the air until more oxidants become available. This would tend to delay acid deposition until the pollutants travel further downwind. Such conditions of "saturation" are thought to be episodic, and can generally be discounted in regional descriptions of transport and deposition.

Until recently, it had been assumed that "natural" water would have an acidity level, or pH, of about 5.6 (a pH of 7.0 being neutral, 0 to 7 being acidic, and 7 to 14 basic), due to atmospheric carbon dioxide dissolved in it. However, even "clean" atmospheres contain a host of other chemical constituents as well, which can interact to produce solutions more or less acidic than a pH of 5.6. For example, it has been shown recently that rainwater pHs of less than 5 might be expected in "clean air" environments under certain conditions when naturally produced sulfur and chlorine compounds are present (e.g., in coastal environments).

In determining whether the oxidation of SO_x and NO_x will actually cause acids to be deposited, the availability of neutralizing species such as ammonia and calcium (e.g., from windblown dust) must also be considered. Sufficient quantities of neutralizing species will reduce the actual acid formed in the atmosphere. Thus, while two sites may be subjected to identical concentrations of anthropogenically produced sulfate and nitrate, quite different levels of acid may be deposited if significant concentrations of neutralizing species are available at one location, but not at the other.

The ultimate effect of the deposited compounds, however, is of prime concern. Nonacidic sulfates are probably less damaging to *materials* than acid sulfates. However, these compounds could eventually act to acidify a *natural ecosystem*. For example, if ammonia combines with sulfates, the deposition will not be acidic. Yet ammonia, when used by plants and micro-organisms in soils, produces acidity, which can subsequently affect soils, lakes, and streams.

Altering Emissions of Primary Pollutants

Characterizing the "chemical soup" of the atmosphere at any specific location requires integrated information on the concentrations of all pollutants, the availability of oxidants, the predominance of gas or aqueous phase chemistry, and detailed meteorological information. The complexities involved in the various chemical and physical processes allow OTA to make only a very general description of the effect of changing emissions of various pollutants. The discussion refers to regional-level response over time, and should not be interpreted as applying to particular episodic events or specific receptor sites.

REDUCING REACTIVE HYDROCARBON EMISSIONS

If NO_x concentrations remain at a fixed level, reducing RHC emissions subsequently reduces ozone concentrations, by decreasing production of the free radicals necessary for ozone production. The peak ambient concentrations of ozone are then expected to be lower.

The only mechanism for producing *nitric acid* believed to be significant in urban areas and powerplant plumes is the oxidation of NO_2 by the hydroxyl radical (and possibly by ozone) to produce other oxides of nitrogen which then form nitric acid. Reducing concentrations of RHC would lower the concentrations of the free radicals as well as of ozone; this should slow down the rate at which NO_x is oxidized to nitric acid. This slowing could in turn cause nitric acid formation and deposition over a larger geographical area, but at lower concentrations.

Reducing RHC emissions will similarly reduce the rate of gas phase oxidation of SO_2. The rate of liquid phase oxidation by hydrogen peroxide may also decrease because its formation rate is proportional to the concentration of OH radicals. The effect on other liquid phase transformations of SO_2 are difficult to assess but are currently thought to be insignificant.

REDUCING NITROGEN OXIDES EMISSIONS

The question of how decreasing NO_x emissions while keeping RHC emissions constant would affect ozone levels is much more controversial than questions associated with the effects of RHC control. This is because the effect of reducing NO_x emissions depends on the resulting *ratio* of hydrocarbons to NO_x. Figure C-3 shows how ozone levels change with varying levels of NO_x and hydrocarbon emissions. Thus, when the ratio of RHC/NO_x is greater than indicated by the diagonal line in figure C-3 (i.e., for the right lower portion of the diagram), reducing NO_x emissions reduces ozone concentrations. However, at lesser ratios (i.e., for the upper left of the diagram), reducing NO_x emissions while holding RHC levels constant, leads to increases in ozone concentrations.*

Figure C-3 implies that in the vicinity of emissions centers like downtown Los Angeles, where the RHC/NO_x ratio is less than that of the diagonal line, reducing NO_x emissions might increase ozone concentrations slightly. However, over an entire air basin, including regions several hundred kilometers downwind, reduc-

---

*Peak ozone levels decrease because at higher NO_x concentrations, a larger portion of the available free radicals react with NO_2 to form nitric acid, and become unavailable for the chain reactions leading to ozone formation.

ing NO_x emissions should decrease ozone concentrations overall. Since NO_2 is the sole precursor to anthropogenic ozone, this must hold true over a large region.

Because NO_x concentrations affect the availability of hydroxyl radicals, decreasing NO_x emissions may change the oxidation rate of SO_2. The change probably also depends on the RHC/NO_x ratio, but is poorly understood at present. However, reducing NO_x concentrations, regardless of the ambient hydrocarbon concentration, decreases the NO_x available for nitric acid formation and deposition.

REDUCING REACTIVE HYDROCARBON AND NITROGEN OXIDES EMISSIONS SIMULTANEOUSLY

Smog chamber and modeling studies (fig. C-3) show that simultaneous control of both RHC and NO_x—keeping their concentration ratio constant—would reduce ozone concentrations. As mentioned above, less nitric acid formation is also expected since the reduced NO_x limits how much acid can be formed. In this case, the oxidation rate of SO_2 is also likely to be reduced.

REDUCING SULFUR DIOXIDE EMISSIONS (ALONE)

Available knowledge of atmospheric chemistry suggests that if: 1) there is no shortage of oxidizing agents (i.e., saturated conditions do not prevail); 2) levels of RHC and NO_x remain constant; and 3) deposition processes and meteorology remain constant, reducing SO_2 emissions will reduce the total amount of acid formed in the atmosphere. Furthermore, given these conditions, a decrease in SO_2 emissions should decrease the atmospheric formation of sulfuric acid by an approximately equal proportion.

REDUCING SULFUR DIOXIDE EMISSIONS CONCURRENTLY WITH REACTIVE HYDROCARBONS AND NITROGEN OXIDES

There are substantial uncertainties in even qualitatively predicting how simultaneously reducing SO_2, NO_x, and RHC emissions from given sources would affect acid deposition at a distant receptor site. Altering the concentrations of RHC and NO_x in an urban plume that interacts with SO_2 from a powerplant plume may well alter the amount of acid deposition at a particular downwind location, but the meteorological and chemical factors involved are so complex that no reliable quantitative estimates can be made at the present time.

For example, changing RHC and NO_x emissions *without* changing SO_2 emissions could affect the deposition of sulfuric acid at a given location by changing the concentrations of available oxidants needed for converting SO_2 to sulfate. Further effects could arise if alterations in RHC and NO_x concentrations affected the pH

Figure C-3.—Typical Ozone Concentrations Formed From RHC-NO$_x$ Mixtures

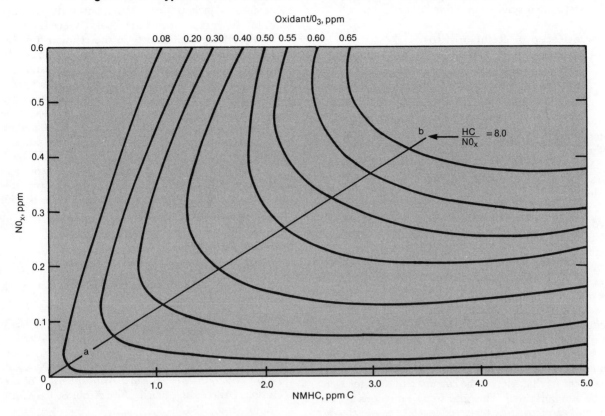

Oxidant/O$_3$ isopleths derived from combined use of smog chamber and photochemical modeling techniques.

SOURCE: *Air Quality Criteria for Ozone and Other Photochemical Oxidants*, U.S. Environmental Protection Agency, Research Triangle Park, EPA-600/8-78-004, April 1979.

of existing cloud droplets, e.g., through the formation and dissolution of nitric acid in the cloud. For the aqueous phase oxidation of SO$_2$, in which the major processes are pH-dependent, changes in cloud acidity levels could change the rate of sulfuric acid formation.

If the net result of changed RHC and NO$_x$ emissions is faster conversion of SO$_2$, sulfuric acid will form and be deposited closer to sources. If the concentrations of RHC and NO$_x$ are altered such that less oxidizing material is initially available, sulfuric acid is deposited further from emission sources. Therefore, alterations in the rate of oxidation could change the amount of acid deposition to a specific location, but not the *total* amount of sulfur deposited (e.g., the sum of SO$_2$ and sulfates) over the entire downwind area. The sulfur emitted will eventually return to the surface at some point. If NO$_x$ and RHC emissions are decreased such that their ratio remains constant while SO$_2$ emissions are decreased, total deposition of both sulfuric and nitric acid will decrease and total ozone production will decrease.

INCREASE NITROGEN OXIDES, HOLDING HYDROCARBON AND SULFUR DIOXIDE EMISSIONS CONSTANT

This scenario is likely to occur without major changes in current air pollution control regulations. Future increases in NO$_x$ levels are projected (primarily from utilities and the industrial sector), while SO$_2$ emissions are projected to remain fairly constant or increase slightly over the next 20 years (see app. A). Chamber studies show that increasing NO$_x$ from very low levels, holding RHC levels constant, causes *peak* ozone concentrations to increase. As NO$_x$ levels are further increased, ozone concentrations reach a maximum and then decrease with further increases in NO$_x$ (see fig. C-3).

The concentrations of other nitrogenous pollutants such as nitrous acid also generally increase with increased NO$_x$. Increasing NO$_x$ emissions while SO$_2$ emissions are held constant will augment local acid deposition due to nitric acid. Since emitted NO$_x$ are oxidized more readily than SO$_2$ in the gas phase, increasing NO_x concentrations may expand the geographical area over which sulfur deposition occurs.

Source-Receptor Relationships

A major goal of atmospheric science is to predict for a given pollution source, the dose of pollutants at a specific location downwind, and how changes in that source's emissions would change the pollutant burden at the receptor site. Source-receptor relationships are determined by the location and nature of the primary pollutant emissions (e.g., SO_2, NO_x, RHC) and by associated meteorological, chemical, and physical processes that occur as the pollutants travel from the source to the receptor. Current long-range transport models that incorporate sophisticated meteorology (i.e., those used in the Canadian-American Work Group effort under the Memorandum of Intent) attempt to simulate chemical conversions of SO_2 to sulfate by assuming that the complex set of chemical processes will balance out over time and distance to approximate a constant average rate of transformation. This simplifying assumption makes regional-scale calculations tractable; crude source regions and receptor regions can be identified for sulfur compounds. Because they are linear models, reducing emissions in source regions results in a proportional reduction of deposition in receptor regions. These models appear to characterize the *current* situation for wet deposition fairly well. They use actual emissions as input, and can reproduce observed levels of regional wet sulfate deposited within a factor of 2.

The first attempt to incorporate multiple chemical reactions involving NO_x, SO_x, and RHC into a long-range transport model—called the Rohde model—contains 19 chemical equations but virtually no meteorology. Three of the equations concern sulfuric or nitric acid production. Sixteen of the equations describe the gas phase photochemistry associated with the RHC/NO_x systems, ozone, hydroxyl radical, and hydrogen peroxide—all compounds involved in actually forming the acid. *All* of the aqueous and heterogeneous phase reactions are combined into one simplified equation.

This model assumes that dry deposition decreases in proportion to emissions. However, it predicts that reducing emissions might cause wet deposition to decline less than proportionally—e.g., a response 60 percent as great.*

Recently, a Committee of the National Academy of Sciences altered the chemistry in the Rohde model to incorporate new laboratory results. It found that the new assumptions greatly reduced the nonlinearity in the rela-

tionship between ambient SO_2 concentrations and ambient sulfate concentrations. Using currently available data, the NAS report concludes that, "there is no evidence for strong nonlinearity in the relationships between long-term average emissions and deposition."[3]

Very specific source-receptor relationships cannot be defined unless the behavior of all other pollutants is known. Given the complexity of the atmospheric chemistry alone, as well as the need to develop detailed emission inventories (especially for NO_x and RHC), and inherent meteorological variability, it is unlikely that a definitive model integrating SO_2, NO_x, and RHC will be developed in the next decade or two. Decisions to control or not to control precursor emissions over this time period will have to be made without the benefit of such precise information.

Selected References

The following list of references includes recent review articles and several very recent key papers that may not be included in the review articles cited.

Barrie, L. A., "The Prediction of Rain Acidity and SO_2 Scavenging in Eastern North America," *Atmospheric Environment* 15:31-41 (1981).

Calvert, J. G. (ed.), *Acid Precipitation: SO_2, NO, and NO_2 Oxidation Mechanisms: Atmospheric Considerations* (Ann Arbor, Mich.: Ann Arbor Science Publishing, Inc., 1982).

Calvert, J. G., and Stockwell, W. R., "The Mechanism and Rates of the Gas Phase Oxidations of Sulfur Dioxide and the Nitrogen Oxides in the Atmosphere," *Acid Precipitation: SO_2, NO, and NO_2 Oxidation Mechanisms: Atmospheric Considerations* (Ann Arbor, Mich.: Ann Arbor Science Publishing, Inc., 1982).

Chamberlain, J., Foley, H., Hammer, D., MacDonald, G., Rothaus, O., and Ruderman, M., "The Physics and Chemistry of Acid Precipitation," Technical Report No. JSR-81-25, prepared for the U.S. Department of Energy, September 1981.

Chameides, W., and Davis, D. D., "The Free Radical Chemistry of Cloud Droplets and Its Impact Upon the Composition of Rain," *J. Geophys. Res.* 486, 1982.

Charlson, R. J., and Rodhe, H., "Factors Controlling the Acidity of Natural Rainwater," *Nature* 295, 683 (1982).

Eldred, R. A., Ashbaugh, L. L., Cahill, R. A., Flocchini, R. G., and Pitchford, M. L., "Sulfate Levels

*See appendix C.2, "Source-Receptor Relationships," for further explanation. Note that OTA specified the model with conservative assumptions; subsequent runs using different background concentrations for pollutants over time show that wet deposition may respond more directly to emissions reductions.

[3]*Acid Deposition, Atmospheric Processes in Eastern North America*, Committee on Atmospheric Transport and Chemical Transformation in Acid Precipitation, National Research Council (Washington, D.C.: National Academy Press, 1983).

in the Southwest During the 1980 Copper Smelter Strike," paper submitted to *Science*.

Electric Power Research Institute, *Aircraft Measurements of Pollutants and Meteorological Parameters During the Sulfate Regional Experiment (SURE) Program*, EPRI Report EA-1909 (Palo Alto, Calif.: Electric Power Research Institute, 1981).

Finlayson-Pitts, B. J., and Pitts, J. N., Jr., "The Chemical Basis of Air Quality: Kinetics and Mechanisms of Photochemical Air Pollution and Application to Control Strategies," *Advan. Environ. Sci. Technol.* 7, 975 (1977).

Graedel, T. E., and Weschler, C. J., "Chemistry Within Aqueous Atmospheric Aerosols and Raindrops," *Rev. Geophys. Space Phys.* 19, 505 (1981).

Hegg, D. A., and Hobbs, P. V., "Oxidation of Sulfur Dioxide in Aqueous Systems With Particular Reference to the Atmosphere," *Atmos. Environ.* 12, 241 (1978).

Hoffman, M. R., and Jacob, D. J., "Kinetics and Mechanisms of the Catalytic Oxidation of Dissolved Sulfur Dioxide in Aqueous Solution: An Application to Nighttime Fog Water Chemistry," *Acid Precipitation: SO_2, NO, and NO_2 Oxidation Mechanisms: Atmospheric Considerations* (Ann Arbor, Mich.: Ann Arbor Science Publishers Inc., 1982).

Larson, T. B., "Secondary Aerosol: Production Mechanisms of Sulfate Compounds in the Atmosphere," *Ann. N.Y. Academy of Sciences* 338, 12 (1980).

Martin, L. R., "Kinetic Studies of Sulfite Oxidation in Aqueous Solutions," *Acid Precipitation: SO_2, NO, NO_2 Oxidation Mechanisms: Atmospheric Considerations* (Ann Arbor, Mich.: Ann Arbor Science Publishers, Inc., 1982).

National Research Council, *Acid Deposition, Atmospheric Processes in Eastern North America*, Committee on Atmospheric Transport and Chemical Transformation in Acid Precipitation (Washington, D.C.: National Academy Press, 1983).

Oppenheimer, M., "The Relationship of Sulfur Emissions to Sulfate in Precipitation," *Atmos. Environ.*, in press.

Platt, U., and Perner, D., "Detection of NO_3 in the Polluted Troposphere by Differential Optical Absorption," *Geophys. Res. Lett.* 1, 89 (1980).

Platt, U., Perner, D., and Kessler, C., "The Importance of NO_3 for the Atmospheric NO_x Cycle From Experimental Observations," paper presented at the 2d Symposium on the Composition of the Nonurban Troposphere, Williamsburg, Va., May 25-28, 1982.

Platt, U. F., Pitts, J. N., Jr., Biermann, H. W., and Winer, A. M., "Spectroscopic Measurements of the Nitrate Radicals at Four Rural Sites in Southern California: Implications for Acid Precipitation," manuscript in preparation.

Rahn, K. A., "Elemental Traces and Sources of Atmospheric Acidity for the Northeast—A Statement of New Evidence," Statement of Nov. 3, 1981; "Tracing Sources of Acid Rain Causes Big Stir," note in "Research News" section of *Science*, February 1982.

Rodhe, H., Crutzen, P., and Vanderpol, A., "Formation of Sulfuric and Nitric Acid in the Atmosphere During Long Range Transport," *Tellus* 33, 132, 1981.

Russell, A. G., McRae, G. J., and Cass, G. R., "Acid Deposition of Photochemical Oxidation Products—A Study Using a Lagrangian Trajectory Model," paper presented at the 13th International Technical Meeting on Air Pollution Modeling, Toulon, France, Sept. 14-18, 1982.

Spicer, C. W., "The Distribution of Oxidized Nitrogen in Urban Air," *Scie. Total Environ.* 24, 183 (1982).

Tuazon, E. C., Winer, A. M., and Pitts, J. N., Jr., *Environ. Sci. Technol.* 15, 1232, 1981.

U.S. Environmental Protection Agency, "The Acidic Deposition Phenomenon: Transformation Processes," chapter A-5 in the Critical Assessment Document entitled "The Acidic Deposition Phenomenon and Its Effects," draft copy, May 10, 1982.

Waldman, J. M., Murger, J. W., Jacob, D. J., Flagan, R. C., Morgan, J. J., and Hoffmann, M. R., "Chemical Composition of Acid Fog," *Science*, in press.

C.2 SOURCE-RECEPTOR RELATIONSHIPS

Introduction

Broad regions of North America receive acidic deposition both in wet form—acid rain—and as dry deposition of acidic substances. Because acidifying substances reach the Earth from the atmosphere both through removal by rainfall and as directly deposited gases and particles from the air, the term acid rain is misleading. The acidity of rainfall per se is generally considered less significant than the quantity of "acid-producing" substances added to the environment—onto soils, vegetation, and materials, and, after passing through watersheds, into lakes and streams. The term acid-producing substances as used in this report refers to sulfur oxides (SO_x) and nitrogen oxides (NO_x) and other substances that have the *potential* for producing acidity, although they may not be deposited in an acid form. For example, sulfate can be deposited in a neutral form—ammonium sulfate—but end up as sulfuric acid by the time it reaches a lake or stream if the ammonium is used by plants in the watershed.

The chain of physical and biological processes from emissions of pollutants to eventual deposition of acid-producing substances in the environment is complex and not fully understood. However, several lines of evidence can be combined to express the *likely* relationship between emissions and deposition.

Acid deposition results from both local and distant sources of SO_x and NO_x. Current scientific understanding suggests that reducing sulfur dioxide (SO_2) emissions throughout the Eastern 31-State region would reduce the deposition of acid-producing substances; but that this will occur in the areas *sensitive* to acid deposition cannot be stated with certainty. For the *Eastern United States,* no other control strategy offers greater potential for reducing acid deposition than reducing SO_2 emissions. While curbing other pollutant emissions could be considered simultaneously, and might ultimately be necessary to achieve a desired level of deposition reduction, most scientists would focus initial attempts to control acid deposition on SO_2.

By considering preliminary information drawn from several alternative approaches, one can piece together a *plausible* relationship between pollutant emissions and deposition of acid-producing substances. This appendix addresses four key issues. The discussion begins with regional-scale deposition of acidifying substances, and then identifies the major constituents of deposition and the relative magnitude of current sources. Model-based estimates of how pollutant emissions from parts of the Eastern United States affect deposition in other areas

are then discussed. Two complementary modeling approaches are used to estimate the magnitude of potential reductions in acid-producing substances reaching the environment due to reductions in SO_2 emissions. Finally, the analysis addresses the question of whether these potential reductions in acid-producing substances might be enough to meet "target" deposition rates to protect sensitive resources.

Current Deposition of Acid-Producing Substances

The best information on patterns of acidic deposition—both its chemical composition and spatial distribution over affected parts of North America—comes from monitoring networks collecting rainfall samples. Though wet deposition may account for only about half the deposited SO_x and NO_x,* dry-deposited gaseous and particulate pollutants are not monitored extensively enough to determine their precise distribution. This discussion focuses primarily on acid-producing substances deposited through precipitation.

The balance of chemical species originating from such natural sources as seaspray, windblown soil, and carbon dioxide in the air, and such manmade sources as SO_x and NO_x pollutants, determine the acidity of rainfall. Rainfall acidity can be decreased either by removing acid-producing substances, or by adding acid-neutralizing substances. The major acid-producing substances in rainfall in the Eastern United States are SO_x and NO_x from both natural and manmade sources. However, the presence of these substances in rainfall does not necessarily indicate acidity since they can be counterbalanced by such airborne acid-neutralizing substances as calcium and magnesium from soil and ammonium from natural sources and fertilizers.

Patterns of acidity, sulfate, and nitrate deposition in rainfall over Eastern North America are mapped in figures C-4 through C-6. Figure C-4 presents the deposition of hydrogen ions—the substance actually measured to determine acidity. More than 40 milliequivalents per square meter per year ($meq/m^2/yr$) of hydrogen ions are

---

*Most long-range transport air pollution models estimate that dry deposition is about equal to wet deposition when averaged over the Eastern United States. The ratio of dry to wet deposition varies with distance away from sources of pollution, with ratios on the order of 8 to 12 in areas with high SO_2 concentrations, to about 0.2 to 0.4 in the Adirondack Mountains (D.Fowler, "Removal of Sulphur and Nitrogen Compounds From the Atmosphere," Ecological Impact of Acid Precipitation, SNSF project, October 1980. A.H. Johannes, et al., "Relationships Between Wet Deposition, Dry Deposition and Throughfall Chemistry," Air Pollution Control Association Annual Meeting, New Orleans, June 1982.

Figure C-4.—Hydrogen Ion in Precipitation, 1980 (annual deposition in milliequivalents per square meter)

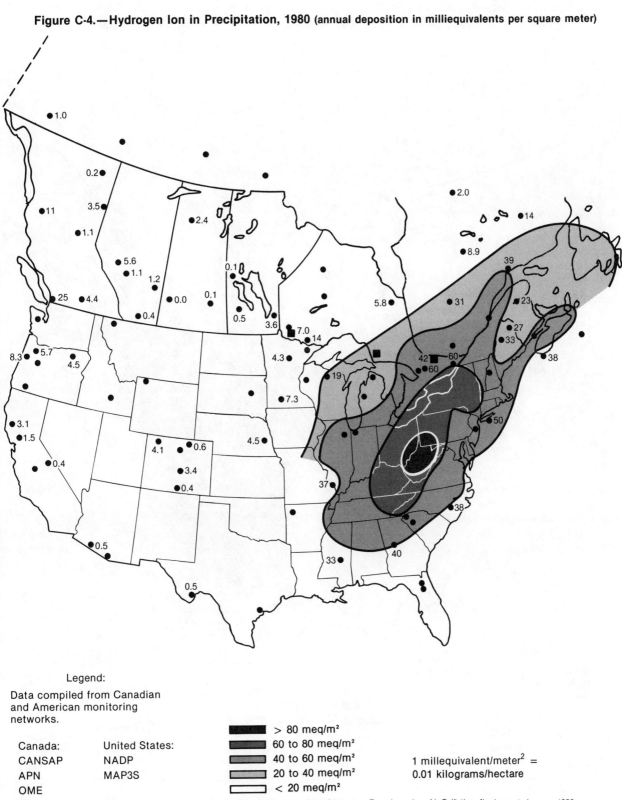

Legend:

Data compiled from Canadian and American monitoring networks.

Canada:	United States:
CANSAP	NADP
APN	MAP3S
OME	

> 80 meq/m²
60 to 80 meq/m²
40 to 60 meq/m²
20 to 40 meq/m²
< 20 meq/m²

1 milliequivalent/meter² = 0.01 kilograms/hectare

SOURCE: Impact Assessment, Work Group 1, United States-Canada Memorandum of Intent on Transboundary Air Pollution, final report, January 1983.

Figure C-5.—Sulfate in Precipitation, 1980 (annual deposition in milliequivalents per square meter)

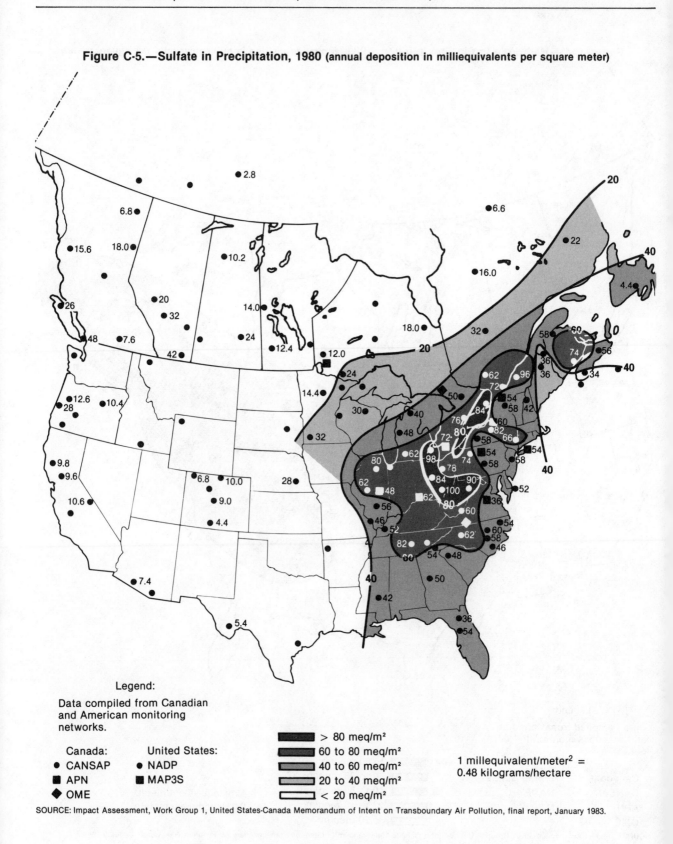

Legend:

Data compiled from Canadian and American monitoring networks.

Canada: United States:
● CANSAP   ● NADP
■ APN   ■ MAP3S
◆ OME

> 80 meq/m²
60 to 80 meq/m²
40 to 60 meq/m²
20 to 40 meq/m²
< 20 meq/m²

1 millequivalent/meter² = 0.48 kilograms/hectare

SOURCE: Impact Assessment, Work Group 1, United States-Canada Memorandum of Intent on Transboundary Air Pollution, final report, January 1983.

Figure C6.—Nitrate in Precipitation During 1980
(weighted by precipitation-milliequivalents per square meter)

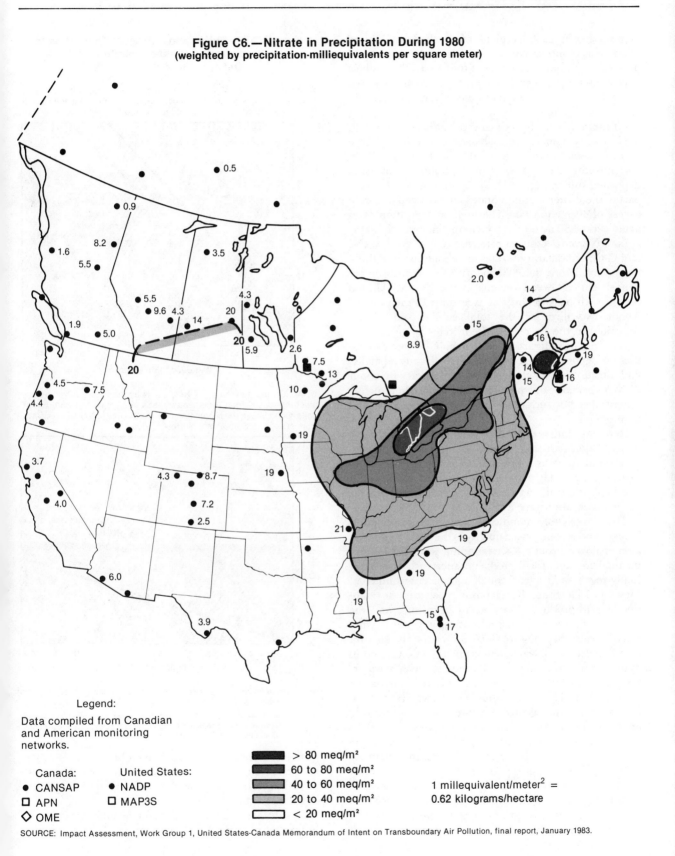

Legend:

Data compiled from Canadian and American monitoring networks.

Canada:
● CANSAP
□ APN
◇ OME

United States:
● NADP
□ MAP3S

> 80 meq/m²
60 to 80 meq/m²
40 to 60 meq/m²
20 to 40 meq/m²
< 20 meq/m²

1 millequivalent/meter² = 0.62 kilograms/hectare

SOURCE: Impact Assessment, Work Group 1, United States-Canada Memorandum of Intent on Transboundary Air Pollution, final report, January 1983.

deposited over broad regions of the Eastern United States, in contrast to deposition rates under 10 meq/m²/yr throughout much of the West. The highest deposition rates exceed 80 meq/m²/yr, and are centered around eastern Ohio, western Pennsylvania, and northern West Virginia.

Of the major acid-producing substances in rainfall, only two originate in substantial amounts from manmade sources in the Eastern United States: sulfates and nitrates. The patterns of deposited acidity and deposited sulfate (fig. C-5), are quite similar. A larger part of the Eastern United States receives deposition in excess of 40 meq/m²/yr. The highest deposition rates again exceed 80 meq/m²/yr, centered in about the same region. Nitrate deposition patterns are similar (figs. C-5 and C-6), but deposition rates are about one-half those for sulfur. More than 20 meq/m²/yr of nitrates are deposited over broad regions of the Eastern United States, with peak deposition exceeding 40 meq/m²/yr. About two-thirds of the total sulfate and nitrate deposited in the Eastern United States is sulfate.

By comparing figures C-4 through C-6, one can see that the deposition of *acid-producing substances* (sulfate and nitrate) exceeds the deposition of *acidity by about 25 to 50 percent;* this portion of the sulfate and nitrate is neutralized by such other constituents as calcium and ammonium.

Reducing sulfate deposition might be the most likely way to begin reducing the deposition of acidity, given that about twice as much sulfate as nitrate is present in rainfall. Similar patterns are assumed to occur for dry deposition of acid-producing substances, but far fewer observations are available to substantiate this.

The most significant indicator for assessing alterations in lake- and stream-water quality is the acidity of water after it flows through a surrounding watershed—i.e., the total amount of acid-producing substances that eventually reach and travel through aquatic environments. Figure C-7 illustrates the relationship between the quantity of acid-producing substances in rainfall and the quantity of acid-producing substances in water flowing out of a watershed. Figure C-7A shows that the amount of sulfate leaving a watershed is about equal to, and in many cases greater than, the amount entering a watershed in rainfall, when averaged over a period of one or several years. That more sulfur leaves a watershed than enters from rainfall is probably due to the amounts that enter as dry-deposited gases and particles.

For nitrogen-containing substances such as nitrate and ammonium (as shown in fig. C-7B), the picture is different. Only about one-third of the nitrogen entering a watershed from *rainfall* leaves the watershed. If the nitrogen input from dry deposition is included, the ratio of nitrogen leaving to nitrogen entering a watershed becomes even lower. As discussed in the forest

Figure C-7.—Sulfur and Nitrogen: Quantities in Precipitation Versus Quantities in Outflow From Watersheds

A: Annual input of SO_4^{2-} – S by precipitation versus the leaching losses from forest watersheds and lysimeters with forest soils. Solid line is the regression line, dotted line is the 1:1 line.

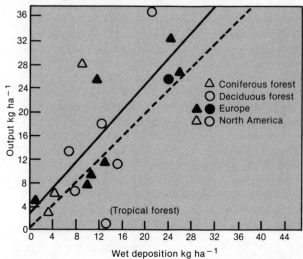

B: Annual input of $(NH_4^+ + NO_3^-)$ – N by precipitation versus the leaching losses from forest watersheds and lysimeters with forest soils. Solid line is the regression line, dotted line is the 1:1 line. Data from studies in Europe and North America.

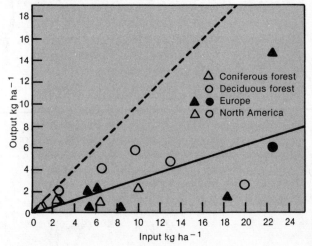

NOTE: Solid line is the regression line, dotted line is the 1:1 line. Data from studies in Europe and North America.

SOURCE: G. Abrahamsen, "Acid Precipitation, Plant Nutrients, and Forest Growth" (1980). Ecological Impact of Acid Precipitation, Proceedings of an International Conference.

resources section, these results might be expected—while both nitrogen and sulfur are essential nutrients for forest growth, most eastern forests require far greater inputs of nitrogen than sulfur.

In summary, about twice as much sulfate is generally present in rainfall as nitrate. When considering the acid-producing substances that *travel through the environment* (and effects such as altered lake- and stream-water quality), sulfate may predominate even more. This can vary from region to region, and certainly varies for short periods. For example, the nitrate component of spring snowmelt can be as great as or even greater than sulfate levels in some watersheds. However, over broad regions on an annual time scale, sulfates comprise a much larger share of acid-producing substances than nitrates.

Manmade and Natural Source Contributions to Acidic Deposition

Relatively low background levels of acidic deposition are thought to originate from natural sources (and possibly global-scale transported air pollutants), when averaged over large regions (e.g., the Eastern United States or the North American Continent). This "natural background" deposition of wet sulfur in North America (excluding Mexico) has been estimated to be about 4 to 10 meq/m².[4] This is about 20 to 40 percent of the *average* sulfur deposition from precipitation over all of North America. Natural sources contribute relatively smaller proportions in areas of highest deposition. Averaged over Eastern North America (east of the Mississippi and south of James Bay in Canada), natural background sources might contribute about 12 to 25 percent of the total. Another group has estimated natural sources of sulfur to be about 5 to 10 percent of manmade sources in this same region.[5] Over parts of the Eastern United States, where wet sulfur deposition exceeds 50 meq/m² and is as high as 80 meq/m² in some areas, the natural background contributes even less.

This natural background comes from several different sources: Husar estimates that 6 percent of the wet sulfur deposition in North America originates from seaspray. The Electric Power Research Institute (EPRI) has estimated that about 5 percent of SO_2 emissions originate from natural, biological sources.[6] In addition, geologic sources such as volcanoes are thought to contribute to natural background.

When averaged over the North American Continent, the acid-producing *potential* of manmade SO_2 emissions far exceeds total wet sulfur deposition. The over 30 million tons of SO_2 emitted by manmade sources in North America is 2.5 times total wet sulfur deposition and 6 to 10 times the natural background. The portion of manmade sulfur that is not deposited in rainfall is either deposited dry or exported off the continent.

Natural background is estimated to contribute similar proportions of total wet nitrate deposition—about 20 to 40 percent when averaged over the North American Continent, and about 10 to 25 percent when averaged over Eastern North America.

The Relationship Between Current Emissions and Deposition

One of the major controversies in the acid rain debate is the effect that pollutant emissions from any source (or group of sources) will have on ambient air quality and pollutant deposition at some other location. The relationship between emissions and deposition is determined by a complex chain of chemical and physical processes that occur as primary pollutants (e.g., SO_2) are emitted, transformed into secondary pollutants (e.g., sulfates), transported, and finally deposited.

Computer models, called transport models, are used to mathematically *simulate* the transformation, transport, and deposition processes. Models describing long-range transport of SO_x have been available for several years; preliminary models of NO_x transport are just now being developed. Transport models are the only practical procedure available to estimate the relationship between areas of origin and areas of deposition for long-range transport pollutants, unless newly developed tracer techniques prove reliable. Large-scale regional transport cannot now be measured directly for the large number of sources of emissions and deposition regions of interest, and under the variety of meteorological conditions needed to perform the analysis.

The major long-range transport (LRT) models describing SO_x transport incorporate six atmospheric processes:

1. release of emissions,
2. horizontal transport and dispersion,
3. vertical mixing of pollutants in the atmosphere,
4. chemical transformation,
5. dry deposition, and
6. wet deposition.

The models themselves are composed of submodels which simulate chemical and physical processes within these broader categories. The main data requirements of LRT models are: emissions inventories of pollutants, meteorological data, ground cover data, and a host of values (parameters) representing chemical reaction rates and other physical processes.

Eight LRT models were evaluated under the U.S.-Canada Memorandum of Intent (MOI) on Transboundary Air Pollution;[7] results indicate that the models

[4]R. B. Husar and J. M. Holloway, "Sulfur and Nitrogen Over North America," presented at 1982 Stockholm Conference on Acidification of the Environment.

[5]*Atmospheric Sciences and Analysis*, Work Group 2, United States-Canada Memorandum of Intent on Transboundary Air Pollultion, Final Report, November 1982.

[6]Electric Power Research Institute, "Biogenic Sulfur Emissions in the SURE Region" EA-1516, 1980.

[7]*Atmospheric Sciences and Analysis*, op. cit.

appear to reproduce large-scale patterns of observed wet sulfur deposition. However, the size and quality of the data base precludes a complete evaluation of LRT models at this time.*

This section presents modeling results to provide a *plausible* description of the current relationship between sources and deposition of SO$_x$ in the Eastern United States. This is only one of the acid-producing substances currently deposited; however, as discussed earlier, sulfate is currently the major acid-producing substance in precipitation.

The model used in this analysis is the Advanced Statistical Trajectory Regional Air Pollution Model (ASTRAP) developed by Argonne National Laboratory under DOE and EPA funding. The ASTRAP model includes several components of the source-receptor relationship not included in the other models.**

OTA has used another model that incorporates more realistic atmospheric chemistry and considers the effects of co-pollutants such as NO$_x$ and hydrocarbons (but at the expense of sophisticated meteorology), to assess how the simplifying chemical assumptions used in ASTRAP might affect its resulting projections. This comparison indicates that the ASTRAP model might adequately represent dry deposition of sulfur, but that variations in ambient concentrations of other pollutants might significantly affect wet sulfur deposition. (These results are discussed in the preceding subsection, "Atmospheric Chemistry.")

Because of its sophisticated treatment of the regional patterns of emissions and meteorology, the ASTRAP model can be used to investigate the *current* relationship between regions of SO$_2$ emissions and regions of sulfur deposition. The model is best used in a relative sense—e.g., estimating the proportion of deposition one region contributes to another—rather than for projecting the magnitude of deposition quantitatively. Again the following discussion of sulfur deposition describes the general pattern of current relationships, and must not be interpreted as making quantitative predictions.

Acid deposition has often been characterized as "acid in Adirondack lakes from powerplants in Ohio." The ASTRAP model can be used to show that such statements are overly simplistic: pollutants do travel from one region to another, but in *all* directions, not just west to east. In addition, while pollutants can travel long distances, emissions *within* a region contribute a large share to total deposition in that region.

To illustrate these points, figure C-8 divides eastern North America into four regions. The intersection of the regions has been chosen to correspond to the area of peak wet sulfur deposition in 1980. Figure C-8 also displays the percentage of SO$_2$ emitted in each region, and the percentage of total sulfur deposited (as simulated by ASTRAP) in each of the regions. Sulfur dioxide emissions are roughly comparable in the northeastern region (I), southeastern region (II), and southwestern region (III). Emissions in the northwestern region (IV) are over twice the amount of any of the other regions. Deposition is lowest in the southern regions (II and III) and highest in the northern regions (I and IV).

Figures C-9 through C-12 show model-based estimates of: 1) the percentage of each region's deposition originating from *within* its borders, and from each of the *other* regions; and 2) for deposition originating *outside* a region, the percentage of deposition traveling less than 500 km, 500 to 1,000 km, 1,000 to 1,500 km, and greater than 1,500 km.

For example, figure C-9 illustrates these relationships in region I (the northeastern region). The pie chart in the upper right projects that approximately 80 percent of the deposition comes from emissions in two regions—from within its own borders and from the northwestern region in about equal amounts. The bar graphs placed in regions II, III, and IV illustrate each region's contribution to deposition in the northeastern region, according to its distance from the sources of emissions. For example, the bar graph in the lower right shows model estimates that 40 percent of the deposition coming from the southeastern region travels less than 500 km to its eventual area of deposition in the northeast; another 40 percent travels between 500 to 1,000 km; and the remainder travels over 1,000 km.

Figures C-9 through C-12 demonstrate the following general observations:

1. All regions contribute to deposition in all other regions.
2. At the spatial scale used in this analysis, each region generates as much or more of its own deposition as any other single region contributes to it.
3. Substantial quantities of deposition originate from sources over 500 km away.
4. Pollutants are transported further from west to east and south to north than from east to west or north to south.

---

*Even if the models were "perfect," one would expect the model simulations to deviate from the observations since the latter are influenced by both the factors treated in the model and the factors that are not treated (e.g., small-scale precipitation variations). In addition, part of the difference between model simulations and observations is due to the inherent variability of the real world. The model is of necessity designed to simulate an average of the observations while the monitoring data base at this time is insufficient to calculate a representative average (i.e., the average over a number of years with similar emissions, meteorological conditions, etc.).

**The ASTRAP model includes: the ability to account for seasonal differences (the ASTRAP model simulates January and July average conditions); release height of emissions; the use of detailed meteorological data; consideration of vertical atmospheric processes in addition to horizontal movement; wet deposition rates that vary with rainfall intensity; and dry deposition rates that vary temporally and spatially. The other models evaluated include some of these components, but ASTRAP is the only model that includes all of them.

Figure C-8.—1979 Sulfur Dioxide Emissions and Estimated Sulfur Deposition—Percent Contributed and Received in Four Subregions Covering the Eastern Half of the United States

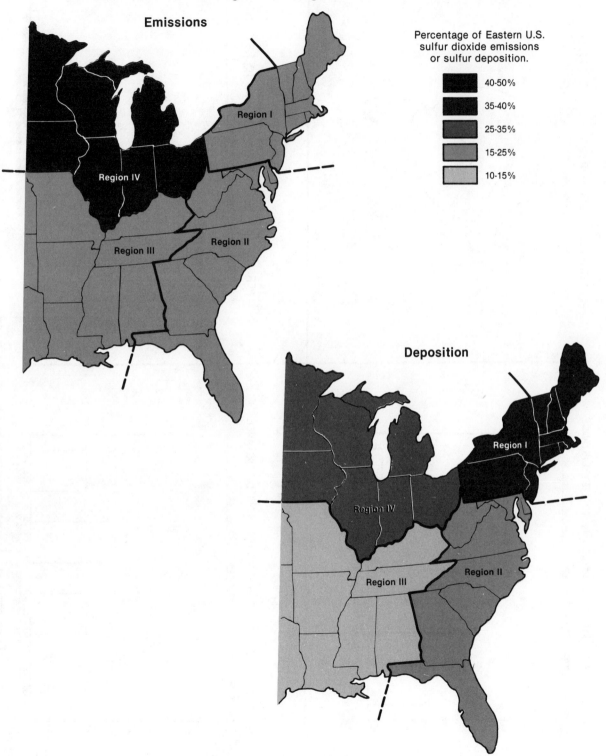

SOURCE: J. Shannon, personal communication, Argonne National Laboratory and E. H. Pechan & Associates, Inc., 1982.

Figure C-9.—Deposition in Region I

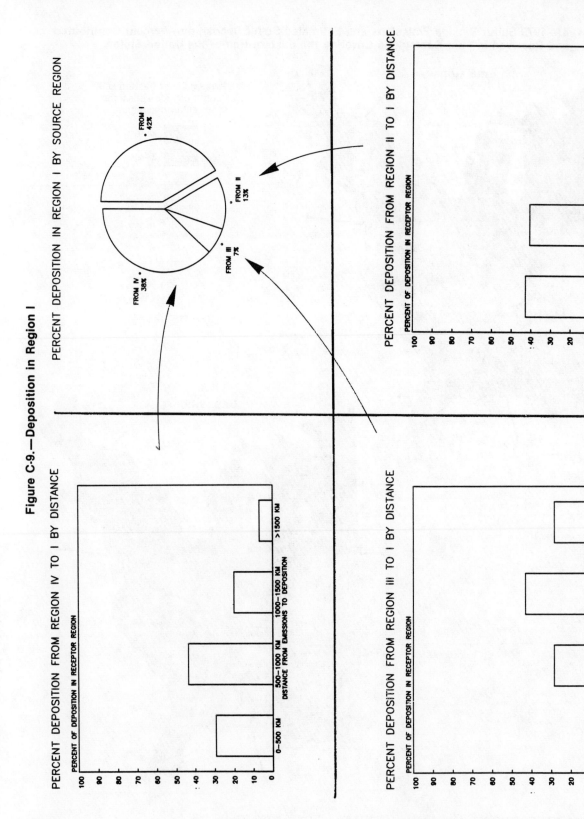

SOURCE: J. Shannon, personal communication, Argonne National Laboratory and E. H. Pechan & Associates, Inc., 1982.

Figure C-10.—Deposition in Region II

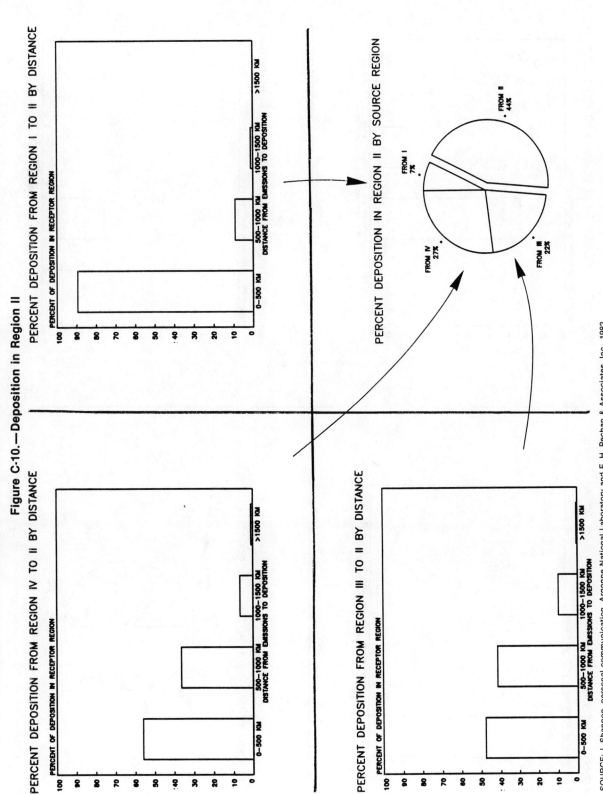

SOURCE: J. Shannon, personal communication, Argonne National Laboratory and E. H. Pechan & Associates, Inc., 1982.

Figure C-11.—Deposition in Region III

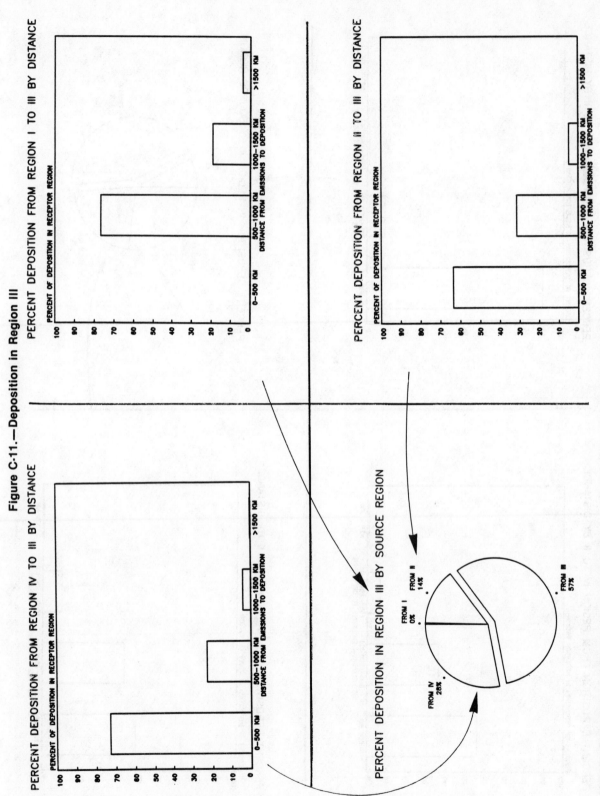

SOURCE: J. Shannon, personal communication, Argonne National Laboratory and E. H. Pechan & Associates, Inc., 1982.

Figure C-12.—Deposition in Region IV

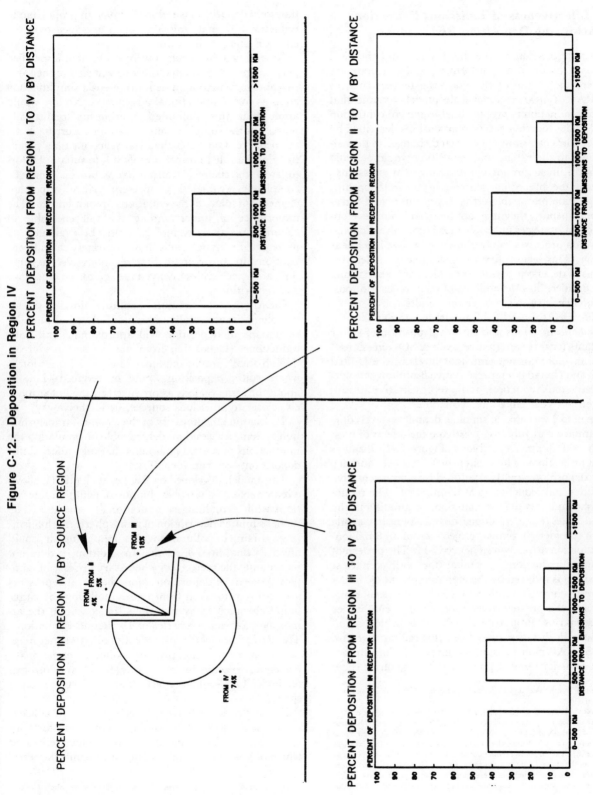

SOURCE: J. Shannon, personal communication, Argonne National Laboratory and E. H. Pechan & Associates, Inc., 1982.

The Effectiveness of Emissions Reductions for Achieving Deposition Reductions

Assumptions concerning the physical and chemical processes involved in transforming SO_2 to sulfate are inherent in the use of regional-scale models such as ASTRAP. *Linear* regional-scale models assume that sulfate production is proportional to the concentration of SO_2. The source-receptor relationships described by these models can simulate expected changes in deposition only to the extent that deposition would actually change in linear proportion to changes in emissions.

While the preceding source-receptor relationships may provide reasonable estimates of inter- and intra-region transport, they may not be reliable for developing control strategies unless chemical transformation and deposition processes can be shown to behave in a linear manner. This section first discusses linear model projections of the effects of different emissions scenarios and then considers how the addition of more realistic atmospheric chemistry might alter the results.

OTA used the ASTRAP model to simulate atmospheric concentrations and surface deposition of sulfur pollutants for three alternative levels of SO_2 emissions.[*] These include: current emissions levels in the United States and Canada; a representative 8-million-ton-per-year emissions reduction; and a representative 10-million-ton-per-year emissions reduction.[**]

The model was used to simulate deposition levels during January and July, to investigate the effects of both winter and summer conditions. Figure C-13 displays model projections of how extensively both wet and dry sulfur deposition would be reduced by a representative 10-million-ton reduction in SO_2 emissions. The reductions shown apply only to emissions originating in the United States (i.e., deposition from emissions in Canada are not considered). Similar projections for an 8-million-ton reduction are shown in figure C-14. The pattern of deposition reductions is similar for both scenarios. Deposition is reduced by the greatest percentage in the Midwest—the region with both the highest current emissions and the greatest reduction requirements under both scenarios. Proportional reductions in deposition decline with distance away from this region. Because the ASTRAP model assumes a linear relationship between emissions and deposition, both scenarios show

that *total* deposition is reduced almost in proportion to reductions in total emissions when averaged over the entire Eastern United States.

Assuming a linear relationship—i.e., that a specified percentage reduction in emissions will lead to the same percentage reduction in deposition—is a simplification adopted for computational advantages. No one would argue that this simplified relationship realistically represents the complex transformations occurring in the atmosphere. Over 100 chemical reactions may potentially play a role in transforming SO_2 to sulfate. Unfortunately, the chemical transformation process cannot be completely evaluated at present, since important elements of many of the equations are not known. The importance of understanding the full ensemble of chemical reactions cannot currently be evaluated. A more pertinent question is: how accurately can a linear relationship approximate these reactions over the large time and space scales involved in *regionwide* emissions and deposition?

Clearly the total amount of sulfur emitted to the atmosphere is eventually deposited; thus, ultimately, reductions in deposition will approximate emissions reductions. (Deposition from natural sulfur sources, though small, would remain.) The crucial question is *where* sulfur deposition would be reduced—i.e., in about the same regions as predicted by the linear models, closer to emissions sources, or further away?

To examine the linearity of the chemical transformation system, a second model, capable of simulating the interactions of several pollutants that may affect sulfur deposition, was run for OTA.[8]

This model, developed by Rodhe, et al. (1981), allows a reasonable qualitative evaluation of pollutant interactions while remaining computationally tractable. The model's limited description of atmospheric mechanisms (e.g., mixing of pollutants with surrounding air) could affect its quantitative results. In addition, it does not incorporate the meteorology necessary to describe complex patterns of deposition. Nonetheless, it represents a useful step forward from linear modeling, by simulating chemical transformations that occur in the atmosphere, through a series of 19 chemical equations. The Rodhe model can provide a qualitative picture of how changes in other primary pollutant emissions—principally reactive hydrocarbons (RHC) and nitrogen oxides (NO_x)—might affect downwind sulfur deposition.

Dry sulfur deposition depends highly on the concentration of SO_2 in the atmosphere. Changing the concentrations of RHC and NO_x might alter the rate at which SO_2 is converted to sulfate, and change the reser-

---

[*]Personal communication, J. Shannon, Argonne National Laboratory, December 1981.

[**]Senate bills S.1706 and S.1709 (97th Congress) were two of the earliest legislative proposals to control acid deposition. S.1706 (introduced by Senator Mitchell of Maine) and S.1709 (introduced by Senator Moynihan of New York) were both referred to the Senate Committee on Environment and Public Works October 1981. The State-level reductions specified by these bills were used as the basis for the 10- and 8-million-ton reduction scenarios, respectively. These scenarios assume that reductions in emissions from each point source within a State are proportional to the reduction assigned that State in the OTA analysis of these bills.

---

[8]Perry J. Samson, "On the Linearity of Sulfur Dioxide to Sulfate Conversion in Regional-Scale Models," OTA contractor report, June 1982.

Figure C-13.—Estimated Deposition Following a 10-Million-Ton-per-Year Reduction in Sulfur Dioxide Emissions

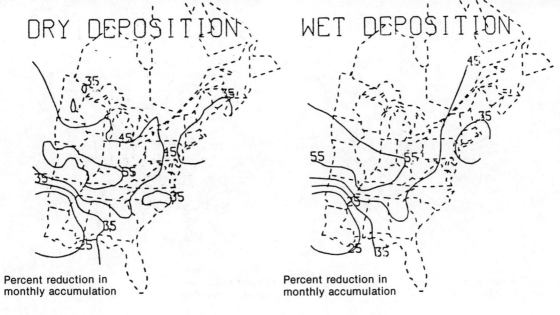

Percent reduction in
monthly accumulation

Percent reduction in
monthly accumulation

January

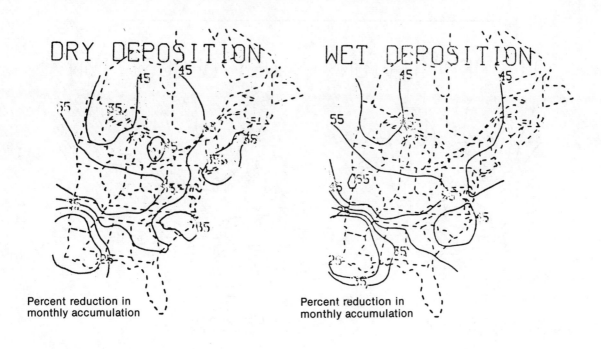

Percent reduction in
monthly accumulation

Percent reduction in
monthly accumulation

July

NOTE: Emissions reductions allocated by S. 1706, 97th Congress. Estimates of deposition based on model results using OTA emissions analysis.
SOURCE: Jack Shannon, Argonne National Laboratory (ASTRAP model).

Figure C-14.—Estimated Deposition Following an 8-Million-Ton-per-Year Reduction in Sulfur Dioxide Emissions

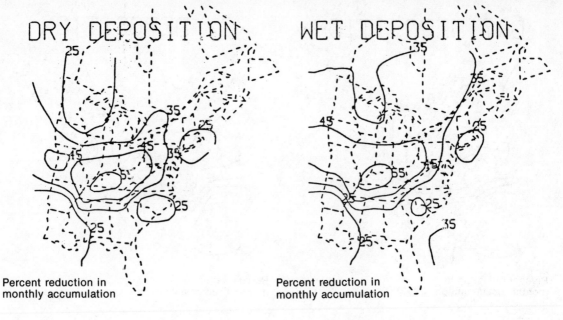

January

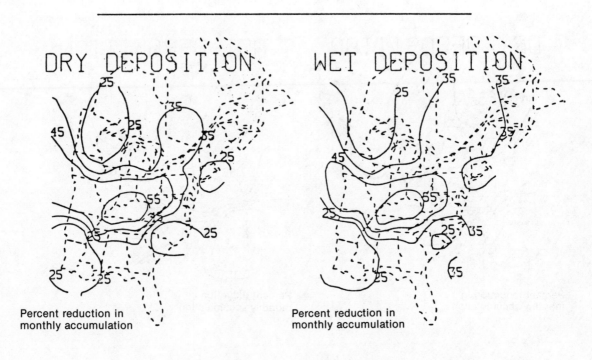

July

NOTE: Emissions reductions allocated by S. 1706, 97th Congress. Estimates of deposition based on model results using OTA emissions analysis.

SOURCE: Jack Shannon, Argonne National Laboratory (ASTRAP model).

voir of SO_2 available for dry deposition. However, the model simulations indicate that dry sulfur deposition is fairly insensitive to the NO_x and RHC mixture in the atmosphere. Figure C-15 illustrates this by showing how much dry sulfur deposition changes per unit change of primary pollutant concentrations as a function of time downwind of a source region, as predicted by the Rodhe model. It shows that, of the three pollutants considered, SO_2 has by far the greatest effect on dry sulfur deposition. In addition, the figure shows that, for pollutant travel times of less than 2 days, a given percentage reduction in emissions appears to reduce *dry* sulfur deposition comparably. Thus, since most dry deposition occurs within this time period, omitting co-pollutants and assuming a linear relationship in regional-scale models such as ASTRAP may be a reasonable assumption for predicting changes in the dry sulfur component of deposition.

Wet sulfur deposition may respond to changes in pollutant emissions differently than dry deposition. As shown in figure C-16, changing the initial amounts of SO_2 by 50 percent might result in roughly a 30-percent change in wet sulfur deposition.* One must keep in mind that these results are highly dependent on the model's approximation of chemical transformations in clouds. Because such processes cannot yet be simulated in detail, the accuracy of this result cannot be evaluated at this time.

However, like dry deposition, wet sulfur deposition is affected more by changes in SO_2 concentration than by changes in other pollutant concentrations. Nonetheless, it should be noted that wet sulfur deposition is relatively sensitive to changes in RHC. Reducing RHC emissions could decrease wet sulfur deposition, although the effect would not be as pronounced as equivalent reductions in SO_2. The sensitivity of wet sulfur deposition to changes in NO_x concentrations is less pronounced, but in the opposite direction—i.e., reducing NO_x emissions might lead to a small increase in wet sulfur deposition. However, this increase might be offset by decreased dry sulfur deposition and reductions in nitrate deposition.

The Rodhe model is not intended to estimate pollutant deposition quantitatively. It was employed to evaluate pollutant interactions qualitatively and assess how they might affect dry and wet sulfur deposition. The results suggest that *wet* sulfur deposition is relatively sensitive to the mix of RHC and NO_x, while *dry* sulfur deposition is not.

An analysis performed by a committee of the National Research Council/National Academy of Sciences[9] (NAS) came to a similar conclusion. This committee slightly modified the Rodhe model used by OTA to reflect some recent laboratory results and to change some assumptions about mixing of chemicals in the atmosphere. Their results suggest that the role of NO_x and RHC are somewhat less important than indicated by the "worst-case" assumptions used by OTA.

Both the OTA and NAS analyses suggest that if reducing *total* sulfur deposition is a desired goal, reducing SO_2 emissions would likely be an effective strategy. The NAS report concludes,

> If we assume that all other factors, including meteorology, remain unchanged, the annual average concentration of sulfate in precipitation at a given site should be reduced in proportion to a reduction in SO_2 and sulfate transported to that site from a source or region of sources. If ambient concentrations of NO_x, nonmethane hydrocarbons, and basic substances (such as ammonia and calcium carbonate) remain unchanged, a reduction in sulfate deposition will result in at least as great a reduction in the deposition of hydrogen ion.

"Target" Deposition Rates To Protect Sensitive Resources

The previous discussion considered only the extent to which decreasing SO_2 emissions by 8 million and 10 million tons per year in the Eastern 31-State region would reduce total sulfur deposition. No attempt was made to relate these estimates to preventing potential damage to sensitive resources. At least three separate groups have estimated deposition "targets"—i.e., levels of deposition below which sensitive lakes and streams are not expected to further acidify.**

The Impact Assessment Working Group established under the U.S.-Canada Memorandum of Intent on Transboundary Air Pollution suggested the first of these targets.[10] Both the U.S. and Canadian members agreed that for North America:

> There have been no reported chemical or biological effects for regions currently receiving loadings of sulphate in precipitation at rates less than about 20 kg/ha-yr [kilograms per hectare per year]. Evidence of chemical change exists for some waters in regions currently estimated or measured to be receiving about 20-30 kg/ha-yr sulphate in precipitation . . . . Long-term chemical

---

*This estimate is for: 1) relatively high initial concentrations of pollutants, such as those found in the Ohio River basin during pollution episodes, and 2) an "average" rainfall event (1 hour at 1 mm/hr) 24 hours downwind of the source.

[9]NRC/NAS, *Acid Deposition: Atmospheric Processes in Eastern North America*, National Academy Press, Washington, D.C., 1983.

**OTA estimates of the effects of changes in deposition on acid-altered aquatic resources are presented in app. B. Rather than presenting specific deposition targets to prevent acidification of sensitive resources, the effects of three scenarios of changes in wet sulfur deposition are discussed.

[10]*Impact Assessment*, Work Group 1, U. S.-Canada Memorandum of Intent on Transboundary Air Pollution, Final Report, January 1983.

Figure C-15.—Changes in Wet Sulfur Deposition

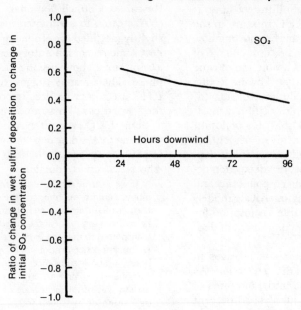

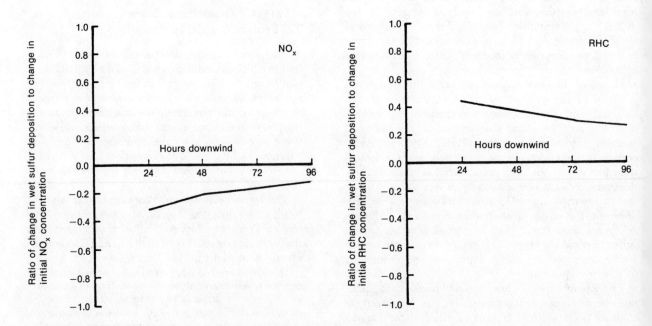

The curves project the changes in potential *wet* sulfur deposition resulting from a unit change in the initial concentrations in the primary pollutants. Changes in deposition are plotted as a function of time downwind from the source region. These estimates assume a precipitation rate of 1 mm/hr at a given time.

SOURCE: Perry Samson, OTA contractor reort, 1982.

Figure C-16.—Changes in Dry Sulfur Deposition

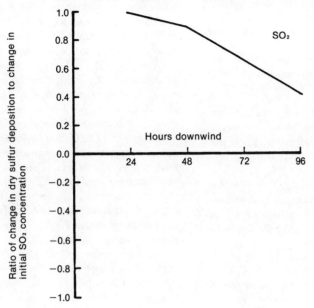

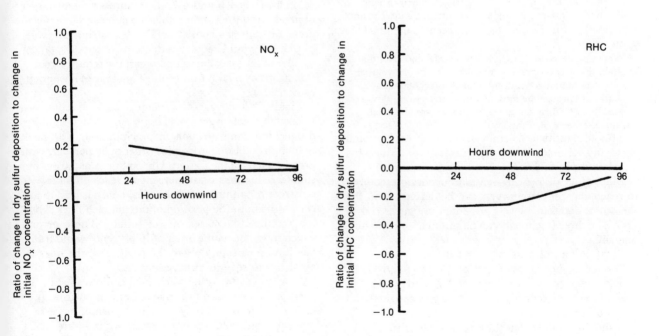

The curves project the changes in potential *dry* sulfur deposition resulting from a unit change in the initial concentrations in the primary pollutants. Changes in deposition are plotted as a function of time downwind from the source region.

SOURCE: Perry Samson, OTA contractor report, 1982.

and/or biological effects and short-term chemical effects have been observed in some low alkalinity surface waters experiencing loadings greater than about 30 kg/ha-yr. Based on these observations, the Canadian members of the group proposed that

... deposition of sulfate in precipitation be reduced to less than 20 kg/ha-yr [about 18 lbs/acre-yr] in order to protect all but the most sensitive aquatic ecosystems in Canada.

The U.S. members concluded that based on the current status of scientific understanding about the mechanisms that lead to surface water alteration, "it is not now possible to derive quantitative loading/effects relationships."

A recently published National Research Council/National Academy of Sciences (NAS) report uses the acidity of precipitation, rather than the concentration of sulfates, to specify a level that would protect sensitive freshwater ecosystems.[11] NAS states:

It is desirable to have precipitation with pH values no lower than 4.6 to 4.7 throughout such areas, the value at which rates of degradation are detectable by current survey methods. In the most seriously affected areas (average precipitation pH of 4.1 to 4.2), this would mean a reduction of 50 percent in deposited hydrogen ions.

Evans, Hendrey, Stensland, Johnson, and Francis presented a third estimate in a recent paper.[12] This group states:

For aquatic ecosystems, current research indicates that establishing a maximum permissible value for the volume weighted annual H^+ concentration of precipitation at 25 ueq/l may protect the most sensitive areas from permanent lake acidification. Such a standard would probably protect other systems as well.

This last estimate is quite similar to the National Academy estimate; a H^+ concentration of 25 ueq/l is equal to a pH of 4.6.

Maps of the decrease in *wet sulfur deposition* required to reach each of these targets can be derived from the measured deposition levels presented in figures C-4 to C-6. The three statements can be summarized into four plausible targets:

1. 20 kg/ha (42 meq/m²) wet sulfate,
2. average precipitation pH of 4.6 (25 ueq/l H^+),
3. average precipitation pH of 4.7, and
4. 50-percent reduction in H^+ (hydrogen ion) deposited in rainfall.

It should be noted that these target values all use wet deposition as a surrogate for total (wet plus dry) deposition, because of the larger data base from which to draw comparisons to ecological effects.

Several assumptions are required for calculating the reductions in sulfate deposition necessary to reach the last three target values. First, if wet sulfate levels are reduced, a corresponding quantity of hydrogen ions (in absolute units, *not* percentage) must be eliminated to preserve the required charge balance. Second, one must assume that other ions, especially neutralizing ions such as calcium and ammonium, will remain at constant levels. Both assumptions are reasonable simplifications given the current chemical constituents in rainfall.

Figures C-17 to C-20 present maps of the percentage decrease in wet sulfur deposition required to reach the four deposition targets. These figures are derived from 1980 data—a year in which the annual precipitation was about average in most regions. Figure C-17 estimates regional wet sulfur-deposition reductions needed to meet the first target value (20 kg/ha wet sulfate). Figure C-17 shows that to reach this target, wet sulfur deposition would have to be reduced by about 50 percent in the areas of heaviest deposition, and by over 30 percent across broad regions of the Eastern United States.

Figures C-18 and C-19 show the wet sulfate-deposition reductions needed to meet target values of average rainfall pH of 4.6 and 4.7. The more stringent target of pH 4.7 requires greater than 70-percent decreases in areas of highest deposition. The less stringent target of pH 4.6 would require reductions about 10 percent smaller in the peak deposition areas; the required reduction drops by a larger percentage in areas of lower deposition.

Figure C-20 displays wet sulfate deposition reductions needed to meet target 4—a 50-percent reduction in hydrogen ion concentration in precipitation. The peak reductions required are on the order of 50 percent, with broad regions of the Eastern United States requiring wet sulfate reductions of 40 percent to reach this target.

Errors in sampling and chemical analysis lead to uncertainty about the position of the mapped lines showing required decreases of wet sulfate. These errors, which might be on the order of 10 percent, would translate into uncertainty about the position of the lines by about 50 to several hundred km.

Year-to-year weather variations could also shift the position of the lines on the maps. For comparison, projections of decreases in wet sulfur deposition necessary to meet target values 3 and 4 are shown in figures C-21 and C-22. These projections are based on 1979 data, rather than on 1980 data. For both target calculations, the 1979 data show *lower* required reductions, with the peak reductions shifted to the northeast. It is not possible to determine how much of the difference is attributable to sampling error, the smaller number of sampling stations operating in 1979, or differences in weather patterns.

[11]NRC/NAS, *Atmosphere-Biosphere Interactions: Toward a Better Understanding of the Ecological Consequences of Fossil Fuel Combustion*, National Academy Press, Washington, D.C., 1981.

[12]L. S. Evans, et al., "Acidic Deposition: Considerations for an Air Quality Standard," *Water, Air and Soil Pollution* 16, 1981, pp. 469-509.

Figure C-17.—Target Value: Wet Sulfate Loadings of 20 kg/ha-yr

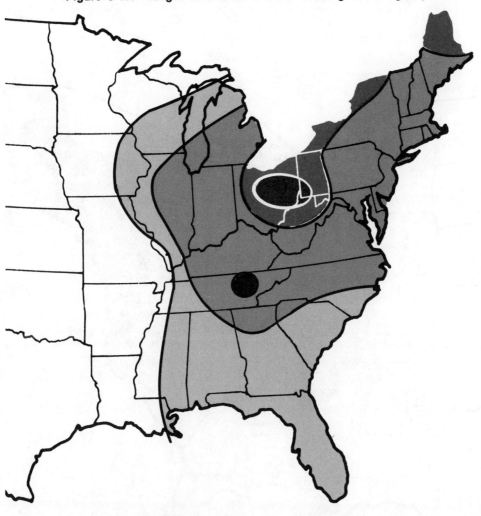

Estimated percent reduction in wet sulfate deposition necessary to reduce wet sulfate loadings
to less than or equal to 20 kg/ha-yr (1980 data)

Key:
- 0–20% reduction
- 20–40% reduction
- 40–50% reduction
- ≥ 50% reduction
- - - limited data

SOURCE: Office of Technology Assessment.

Figure C-18.—Target Value: Average Precipitation pH of 4.6

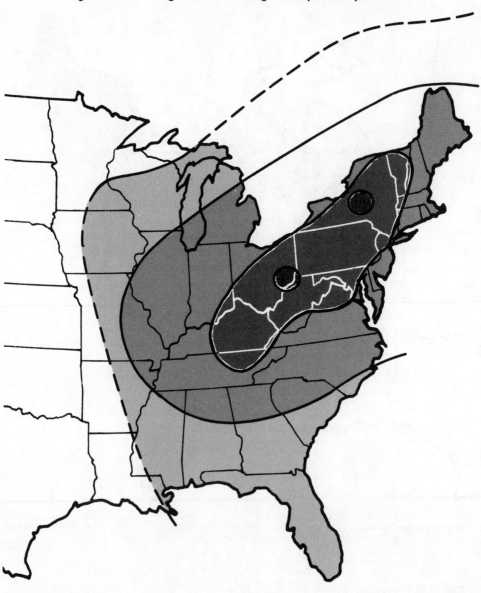

Estimated percent reduction in wet sulfate deposition necessary to increase pH to 4.6 or greater (1980 data).

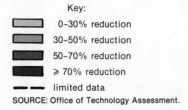

Key:
0–30% reduction
30–50% reduction
50–70% reduction
≥ 70% reduction
limited data

SOURCE: Office of Technology Assessment.

Figure C-19.—Target Value: Average Precipitation pH of 4.7

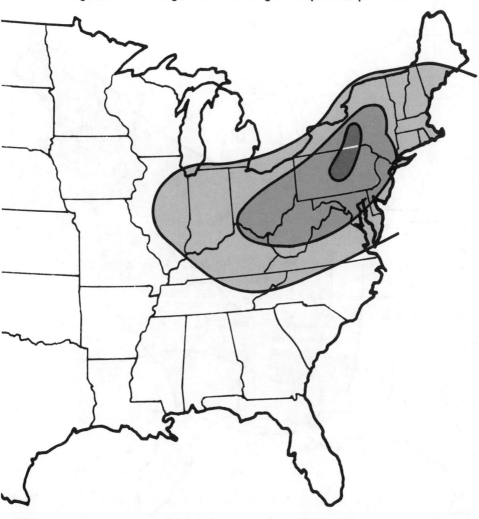

Estimated percent reduction in wet sulfate deposition necessary to increase pH to 4.7 or greater (1980).

Key:
50–70% reduction
70–80% reduction
≥ 80% reduction
limited data

SOURCE: Office of Technology Assessment.

Figure C-20.—Target Value: 50% Reduction in Hydrogen Ion Deposition

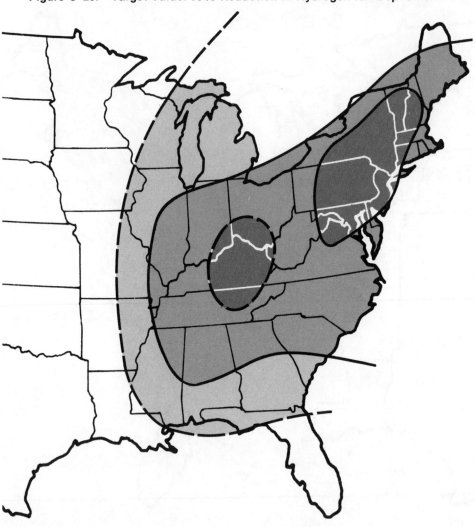

Estimated percent reduction in wet sulfate deposition so that hydrogen ion deposition is reduced by 50 percent (1980 data).

Key:

30–40% reduction

40–50% reduction

≥ 50% reduction

— — — limited data

SOURCE: Office of Technology Assessment.

Figure C–21.—Target Value: Average Precipitation pH of 4.7

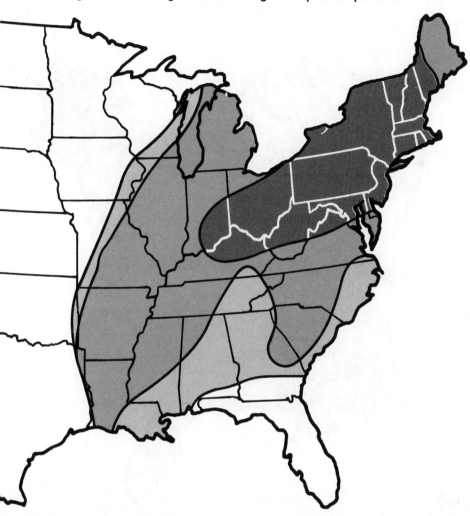

This figure illustrates the estimated percent reduction in wet sulfate deposition necessary to reach the same target value as in fig. C-19—average precipitation pH of 4.7 or greater—however, the estimates are based on 1979 data.

Key:

■■■■ 1–20% reduction

■■■■ 20–40% reduction

■■■■ > 40% reduction

SOURCE: Office of Technology Assessment.

Figure C-22.—Target Value: 50% Reduction in Hydrogen Ion Deposition

This figure illustrates the estimated percent reduction in wet sulfate deposition necessary to reach the same target value as in fig. C-20—i.e., a 50-percent reduction in hydrogen ion deposition—however, the estimates are based on 1979 data.

Key:

1–20% reduction

20–40% reduction

> 40% reduction

SOURCE: Office of Technology Assessment.

As figures C-17 through C-22 illustrate, the range of reductions required to reach each of the four targets—and the same target in two successive years—varies considerably. However, these figures permit some general *qualitative* statements to be made about the wet sulfate reductions needed to reach the suggested targets.

In regions of highest deposition, target deposition reductions range from 50 to 80 percent. For New England, deposition reductions required to reach the targets vary from about 30 to 70 percent. For sensitive areas south of the peak deposition region (e.g., the southern Appalachians in Tennessee), wet sulfur-deposition reductions needed to reach the targets are on the order of 20 to 50 percent. In the upper Midwest (e.g., the lake regions of Wisconsin and Minnesota), deposition would have to be reduced by 0 to 40 percent to reach the targets.

The previous section characterized the uncertainties inherent in using models to predict deposition reductions resulting from emissions reductions. Plausible model-based estimates of how much *both* wet and dry sulfur deposition might be reduced by an 8-million to 10-million-ton-per-year reduction in SO_2 emissions were presented. Because the deposition targets are expressed as decreases in wet sulfur deposition, and due to the large uncertainties in both sets of analyses, the deposition reductions that might result from reducing SO_2 emissions can only be compared tentatively to the deposition reductions required to meet targets for protecting sensitive resources. In areas of highest deposition, for example, western Pennsylvania, the suggested target reductions to protect sensitive resources *might not* be achievable with an 8-million to 10-million-ton reduction in SO_2 emissions; in areas of lower deposition, such as northern New England, the southern Appalachians and the upper Midwest, the target deposition reductions *might* be achievable with SO_2 emissions reductions of this magnitude.

Thus, the uncertainties about reaching target deposition levels are greater in those areas that receive most of their sulfur deposition in wet form (e.g., the Adirondack Mountains). As discussed above, for a given level of SO_2 emissions reductions, the reduction in wet deposition may be *less* than for dry deposition. Moreover, changes in wet sulfur deposition resulting from a given change in SO_2 emissions may also depend on levels of such co-pollutants as NO_x and RHC.

Existing Domestic and International Approaches

D.1 INTERSTATE AND INTERNATIONAL PROVISIONS OF THE CURRENT CLEAN AIR ACT

Provisions in the existing Clean Air Act (CAA) address both interstate and transboundary pollution; however, the **effectiveness** of these statutory mechanisms is subject to question. The act also provides affected parties with a means to seek remedy for interstate pollution not adequately regulated by existing control programs. It does not directly provide other nations a means of remedy for transboundary (international) pollution; however, actions taken by the previous administration under the act's international provision may have created a right to legal recourse. In addition, avenues other than the CAA could potentially be pursued to remedy transboundary pollution.

Interstate Pollution Control and the Clean Air Act

The Environmental Protection Agency (EPA) and the courts have taken action under the interstate provisions of the CAA to abate interstate air pollution resulting from **local sources.** However, considerable uncertainty exists over how these provisions should be interpreted with regard to **longer range** transported air pollutants. EPA currently takes the position that analytical techniques addressing transported pollutants are not reliable for regulatory purposes; the courts have yet to rule on this issue. The statutory language of the interstate provisions does not provide a direct means of controlling acidic deposition.

The NAAQS SIP Process

The CAA requires that States adopt implementation plans to: 1) attain and maintain national ambient air quality standards (NAAQS) within their borders and 2) prevent significant deterioration (PSD) in areas already meeting NAAQS. Section 110(a)(2)(E) also specifically requires that State implementation plans (SIPs) include provisions prohibiting any stationary source from emitting pollutants that would prevent attainment and maintenance of NAAQS or interfere with PSD measures in **another** State. The Administrator may not approve a SIP that does not comply with these interstate control requirements.

Utility of the Interstate Provision for Controlling Transported Air Pollutants

LIMITATIONS OF SECTION 110(a)(2)(E)

Section 110(a)(2)(E) has several limitations for controlling interstate pollution: It applies only to **air** pollution, and offers no direct means of controlling acidic **deposition.** It gives little guidance as to how much interstate air pollution is prohibited, and does not outline the level of proof of causation required to substantiate regulation by EPA. As written, the section leaves open such questions as: 1) whether pollution must be linked to individual **sources** to justify control, and 2) whether analytical techniques (including models) that estimate the relationship between emissions from "source" regions and the resulting air quality of "receptor" regions can be used to justify regulating individual sources. Finally, the section applies only to stationary sources; it does not control mobile-source emissions.

THE INTERSTATE PROVISION AS APPLIED BY EPA

Since section 110(a)(2)(E) was enacted in 1977, EPA has initiated no review of SIPs to assess their compliance with the provision. The agency has issued no regulations to spell out how a State can determine if its SIP complies with section 110(a)(2)(E). EPA has reviewed and approved a number of revisions to SIPs since 1977, but the agency has not articulated definitive policies for determining whether an individual source relaxation complies with section 110(a)(2)(E). Current EPA procedures, however, limit the scope of SIP review to that portion of the plan undergoing revision. Hence, where SIP revisions propose emissions relaxations for individual plants, EPA considers only the local air quality impact resulting from the change in emissions for these plants.

EPA also has taken the position that there are no **adequate** tools to assess long-range transport effects, and EPA practices reflect this position. First, in reviewing emissions limitations with respect to the interstate provisions, the agency only considers impacts that can be estimated by models approved under its modeling guideline. This effectively limits consideration of impacts to within 50 km of the source, because there are no **approved** models to estimate long-range transport impacts. Second, the agency does not consider potential impacts of the transformation products of the pollutant for which a SIP relaxation is being considered. For example, the agency reviews the interstate effect of a sulfur dioxide emissions relaxation solely for its impact on sulfur dioxide air concentrations in downwind states. However, sulfur dioxide also is transformed to particulate sulfates in the atmosphere. Sulfates cause visibility degradation, and contribute to total suspended particulates (TSP), for which there are national air quality standards. EPA does not consider the effect of increased sulfur dioxide emissions on total suspended particulate levels or on visibility.

REMEDIES FOR INTERSTATE POLLUTION UNDER THE CLEAN AIR ACT

CAA currently contains two means of remedy for interstate air pollution. The first relies on general **judicial** review provisions under section 307 allowing litigants to challenge EPA actions. The second initially relies on **administrative** review provisions under section 126, allowing States and political subdivisions to petition EPA on matters dealing specifically with inter-

state pollution. Since 1977, a number of suits and petitions have been filed under these provisions of the act to remedy interstate air pollution. Early actions sought remedy for interstate air pollution in situations where pollutants were traceable to individual sources in the near vicinity. In later actions, attention has shifted from the "local-source problem" and focused on interstate pollution allegedly caused by long-range transport.

JUDICIAL REMEDIES: SECTION 307 SUITS INVOLVING THE TRANSPORTED AIR POLLUTANTS

States and other litigants seeking remedies for interstate pollution have challenged EPA approval of SIP revisions for single sources under section 307 of the act. In these suits, litigants have attempted to obtain judicial review of EPA's practice of not addressing regional emissions through the SIP process. They also have attempted to compel EPA to use models and other techniques to assess long-range transport effects.

Litigants have advanced the following reasons for challenging EPA approval of the SIP revisions: 1) the Administrator failed to properly review the long-range effects of the individual source for which a relaxation was approved; 2) EPA failed to consider the air quality impacts of the transformation products of sulfur dioxide; and 3) the Administrator failed to review the whole SIP to determine whether the cumulative emissions of sources governed by the SIP do not cause pollution in violation of section 110(a)(2)(E).

SECTION 126: THE ADMINISTRATIVE PETITION PROCESS

Section 126 is a companion section to 110(a)(2)(E). It requires States to provide notice to nearby States of sources that "may significantly contribute" to air pollution in excess of NAAQS. In addition, it provides an administrative remedy for interstate pollution through petition to the EPA Administrator. The section provides in part that:

> . . . a State or political subdivision may petition the Administrator for a finding that any major source emits or would emit any air pollutants in violation of the prohibition of section 110(a)(2)(E)(i).

Within 60 days of receipt of a petition, the act requires the Administrator to hold a public hearing and either make such a finding or deny the petition.

PETITIONS UNDER SECTION 126 SEEKING REMEDY FOR TRANSPORTED AIR POLLUTANTS

States seeking remedy for interstate pollution caused by the long- range transport of emissions from multiple sources have filed section 126 petitions in tandem with suits under section 307. At least nine petitions of the State of New York, and the petitions of Pennsylvania and Maine, have been consolidated into a single proceeding, which places before EPA the gamut of issues involved in the long-range transport controversy.

The consolidated petitions claim that sulfur dioxide and particulates emitted by sources governed by SIPs in Illinois, Indiana, Kentucky, Michigan, Ohio, West Virginia, and Tennessee are causing interstate pollution in violation of section 110(a)(2)(E). The petitioners allege that such pollution prevents attainment and maintenance of NAAQS for both total suspended particulates and sulfur dioxide, and interferes with PSD requirements. Petitioners further allege that the conversion of sulfur dioxide to particulate sulfates contributes to the aforementioned problems and, in addition, that sulfates present a hazard to health and cause acid rain, resulting in damage to aquatic and terrestrial ecosystems. Maine specifically claims that transformed products of sulfur dioxide cause visibility degradation in the mandatory Class I area of Acadia National Park in violation of the act. These three States have asked that EPA review the SIPs for long-range transport effects and have requested major reductions in emissions in the Eastern United States.

These States have presented extensive information on: the air quality problems and alleged environmental problems resulting from acid rain in their States; air quality data and modeling results allegedly demonstrating that interstate pollution contributes significantly to these problems; air quality models and analytical techniques available to assess the long-range transport of air pollutants; the relative stringency of emissions controls in the Midwestern States versus New York, Pennsylvania, and Maine; and finally, the different levels of emissions limitations that petitioners claim are needed to control interstate pollution.

Extensive comments have been filed concerning the information presented by the petitioners and the issues raised. Although the New York-Pennsylvania-Maine petitions were filed between fall, 1980, and summer, 1981, as yet, EPA has issued no preliminary findings in the proceeding. Six Northeastern States recently sued EPA (March 1984) to rule on the outstanding petitions, but no court action has yet been taken.

REVIEW AND REMEDIES UNDER SECTION 307, SIP CHALLENGES, AND SECTION 126 PETITIONS

A recent court ruling suggests that the types of review obtainable under judicial and administrative remedy provisions may differ. EPA has asserted, and the Second Circuit Court of Appeals has ruled, that EPA is not required to review the whole SIP for its compliance with the Act when it reviews proposed revisions amending only portions of the SIP. Accordingly, plaintiffs might not be able to obtain review of an implementation plan as a whole in the context of SIP revisions for individual sources. Thus, section 126 administrative proceedings may be the only way for States to seek remedy for pollution caused by cumulative emissions from all stationary sources regulated by a SIP.

It is not clear what relief the petitioners could win in the suits pending before the courts or in the section 126 proceedings before the agency; however, a wide range of results is possible. Neither route offers a means to compel direct control of acidic deposition. Litigants under section 307 seeking EPA review of SIP relaxations might obtain court decisions requiring the agency to consider long-range transport effects using "state-of-the-art" techniques. The scope of the New York-Pennsylvania-Maine section 126 petitions is wider; the petitioners could, if successful, win a reversal of EPA SIP review policies, leading EPA to require broad-scale reductions in emissions of sulfur dioxide and particulates from Midwestern States.

An appeal from **any** EPA determination on the New York-Pennsylvania-Maine section 126 petition could come before the District of Columbia Court of Appeals. Thus, in the absence of further congressional direction to EPA and the courts on long-range transported pollutants, the appeals court could become the arbiter of pollution-transport controversies between the Midwestern and Northeastern States.

Control of Transboundary Pollution: The U.S.-Canadian Context

The problems of interstate and transboundary pollution control are strongly linked. Winds that transport pollutants over State lines can also carry them across the border between Canada and the United States, from both sides. A number of mechanisms are currently in place for resolving transboundary pollution issues. Means of control are potentially available: 1) through a bilateral accord, 2) under the CAA, and 3) under both domestic common law and international law. The efficacy of these mechanisms to deal with transboundary pollution depends substantially on the combined commitment of the United States and Canada to control such pollution.

Diplomatic/Legal Context of the U.S.-Canadian Transboundary Air Pollution Issue

The United States and Canada have a long history of cooperation concerning environmental affairs and joint commitments to principles for controlling transboundary pollution. Beginning with the Boundary Waters Treaty of 1909, the two countries have expended considerable efforts to negotiate and/or arbitrate transboundary pollution problems, most recently in negotiations culminating in the 1978 Great Lakes Water Quality Agreement. Both the U.S. Congress and the executive branch have made repeated commitments to bilateral research, consultation, and negotiations on transboundary air pollution, as well as to the multilateral Declaration of the U.N. Conference on the Human Environment (Stockholm Declaration 1972), and the 1979 Economic Commission for Europe's "Convention on Long-Range Transboundary Air Pollution."

No agreement between the United States and Canada directly governs transboundary air pollution; however, cooperative activities have culminated in a Memorandum of Intent.[1] Under the Memorandum the two countries have agreed to begin negotiations to reach a bilateral accord. The Memorandum also states the two countries' commitments to take interim control actions. Although the status of the Memorandum is unclear, it does not appear to be legally binding on Canada or the United States. Its force derives from the good intentions of both countries.

The MOI also established several Work Groups to prepare technical information as a background for conducting negotiations. Final drafts of three Work Group reports—impact assessment, atmospheric sciences and analysis, and emissions costs and engineering assessment—were released in February 1983.

U.S. Government officials state that reasonable progress toward reaching a bilateral accord is being made. However, many Canadian officials are dissatisfied with the progress made in the negotiations and, in 1982, threatened to withdraw from the talks altogether.[2] Federal and provincial Ministers of the Environment have recently pledged to reduce sulfur dioxide emissions 50 percent (from 1980 levels) in Eastern Canada by 1994 and have urged the United States to do the same. Acidic precipitation resulting from the long-range transport of air pollution has emerged as one of the most significant bilateral issues between Canada and the United States.

Transboundary Pollution Control Under the Clean Air Act

SECTION 115

Congress adopted section 115 of CAA to provide a mechanism for dealing with transboundary air pollu-

tion. The section is invoked by the Administrator of EPA on his own initiative or at the request of the Secretary of State. The Secretary must allege, or the Administrator must determine, that pollution emitted in the United States **causes** or **contributes** to air pollution that "may reasonably be anticipated to endanger public health or welfare in a foreign country." The section provides that the Administrator can make such a determination "upon receipt of reports, surveys or studies from any duly constituted international agency"; however, it does not specify how the Secretary of State will be apprised of a problem.

Once the Secretary of State has requested the Administrator to activate the section 115 process, or the Administrator has made a finding of "endangerment," the statute requires the Administrator to give formal notice to the Governor(s) of the State(s) in which the emissions causing the pollution originate. The Administrator must take this step, however, only if he "determines the foreign country receiving the pollution has given the United States essentially the same rights with respect to the prevention or control of air pollution occurring in that country as is given that country by [section 115]." Thus the Administrator must make a determination of reciprocity to trigger the mandatory duty under section 115.

Section 115 relies on the SIP revision process as the means to abate international pollution prohibited by the section. Section 115 provides that notice given to the governor constitutes a finding with respect to section 110(a)(2)(E)—i.e., that the State implementation plan is inadequate to comply with the requirements of the CAA and must be revised.

UTILITY OF SECTION 115 FOR CONTROLLING TRANSPORTED AIR POLLUTANTS

Section 115 can be construed to permit the control of transboundary pollution caused by acidic deposition. However, the language of section 115 provides no guidelines on how to implement the section. It does not detail the procedures for the Administrator to follow in identifying which State or States are the source of the transboundary emissions, and offers no guidance on allocating control responsibilities when emissions from more than one State create transboundary problems. The legislative history of section 115 is also silent on these issues.

EPA's current practices for reviewing the SIP control of interstate pollution, if applied to transboundary pollution, would limit the efficacy of section 115 for controlling possible acidic deposition and air pollution in Canada. As yet, EPA has not chosen to activate the transboundary pollution control provision of the act.

---

[1]Memorandum of Intent between the Government of Canada and the Government of the United States of America concerning Transboundary Air Pollution, Aug. 5, 1980.

[2]L., Mosher, "Congress May Have to Resolve Stalled U.S.-Canadian Acid Rain Negotiations," *National Journal*, Mar. 13, 1982, p. 456; "Canada May End Talks With U.S. for Accord to Combat Acid Rain," *The Wall Street Journal*, June 16, 1982, pp. 1-7, col. 3.

ACTIVITY UNDER SECTION 115

The Mitchell Request.—The Canadian Clean Air Act was amended by unanimous vote in both Houses of Parliament in December 1980 to provide clear authority for the Canadian Federal Government to take steps to control the emission of pollutants affecting another country. The amendment was designed primarily to allow "mutual recourse between Canada and the United States."

On December 23, 1980, Senator George Mitchell of Maine sent letters to the Administrator of EPA and the Secretary of State calling their attention to the recently enacted legislation, and to reports prepared by the International Joint Commission (IJC) and the U.S.-Canada Research Consultation Group on Long-Range Transboundary Air Pollution (RCG). The Senator reviewed the information in the reports and concluded his letters with a strongly worded request that action be taken under section 115.

The Costle Response: Determination To Activate Section 115.—In January 1981, Administrator Costle of EPA responded to the Mitchell request and sent letters to both the Senator and the Secretary of State announcing his findings.[3] He found, based on his review of the IJC reports and CAA, that section 115 could be activated to control acidic deposition in Canada. He also determined that the Canadian Clean Air Act provides Canada with authority to give the United States essentially the same rights as Canada under section 115, and that at present Canada was so interpreting the act. He noted that this second aspect of EPA's determination is necessarily a dynamic one and would continue to be influenced by Canadian actions. Thus, having made the requisite determination to activate section 115, the Administrator instructed EPA staff to begin work to identify which States should receive formal notification, and to lay the groundwork to assist those States in appropriately revising their SIPs.

There have been no indications that the work initiated by Administrator Costle is proceeding under the present EPA administration. As yet, section 115 notification has not been given to any State, and EPA appears not to have continued the process leading up to notification. EPA has issued no statement, however, that reverses the Costle determination. No court has yet reviewed the legal significance of Costle's action.

Remedies for Transboundary Pollution

RECOURSE UNDER THE CLEAN AIR ACT

The initial decision to activate section 115 clearly is discretionary. Thus, the statute does not explicitly pro-

vide a course of action that Canada or others could pursue in domestic courts to remedy transboundary pollution. An argument can be made, however, that the actions of former Administrator Costle "activated" section 115 and created a legal obligation for the present Administrator to revise SIPs to control acidic deposition in Canada.

Section 304 of CAA authorizes "any person" to bring suit to compel the Administrator to perform nondiscretionary duties under the act. Under this citizen suit provision a number of different groups could bring suit to compel action under section 115—among them are environmental organizations and Northeastern States that might "benefit" from activation of the section. The eligibility of Canada or the Province of Ontario to bring suit is less clear. Section 302(e) does not specifically mention foreign governments, and the issue of whether foreign governments are considered to be "persons" under sections 302(e) and 304 remains unsettled.[4] However, standing to sue would not be a barrier to litigation by plaintiffs having interests similar to those of Ontario or Canada.

If a suit were initiated under section 304 to compel the present Administrator to notify States under section 115 to revise their SIPs, a court could be faced with the question of whether Costle's determinations were arbitrary and capricious, or in excess of statutory authority and, as such, unlawful. The present Administrator would have the burden of convincing a court that the previous Administrator's determinations were invalid. Since the statute gives the Administrator great discretion, and courts as a rule defer to administrative determinations, this would be a difficult burden to overcome.

RECOURSE THROUGH DIPLOMATIC CHANNELS

The Canadian Government could choose to link the transboundary issue to other areas of bilateral concern in an effort to encourage adoption of policies to reduce the long-range transport of air pollution. Canada is an important ally and neighbor. The United States's involvement with Canada is probably greater than with any other foreign country. The two-way trade is about $77 billion, which is greater than that between the United States and all the countries of the European Community. The two countries are allies in NATO and

---

[3]Letters from Douglas Costle, EPA Administrator, to Edmund Muskie, Secretary of State, Jan. 13, 1981; and to Senator George Mitchell, Jan. 15, 1981.

[4]It can be argued that foreign governments are considered to be "persons" under secs. 302(e) and 304. Sec. 302(e) could be construed as inclusive of possible litigants rather than defining the complete set. Such a construction was placed on a similarly worded definition under the antitrust laws and thus the definition in the statute was not a mandate to reverse the longstanding presumption that foreign nations are entitled to sue in courts of the United States *Pfizer, Inc.* v. *Government of India* 434 U.S. 308 (1978). Accordingly the Court in *Pfizer* found that India was a "person" within the meaning of sec. 4 of the Clayton Act in spite of the fact that the section did not include foreign governments in the list of those authorized to sue.

have a unique military joint command, the North American Air Defense Command.

RECOURSE UNDER DOMESTIC COMMON LAW AND INTERNATIONAL LAW

In theory, domestic common law and international law also provide a means of legal recourse should Canada or others be dissatisfied with U.S. control efforts.

In practice, however, domestic common law may not, and international law does not, provide an effective means to compel U.S. control efforts. In the case of domestic common law, recent court decisions as well as problems surrounding proof-of-causation may limit the use of this avenue; in the case of international law, there are no effective means to enforce legal doctrines.

D.2 INTERNATIONAL PROGRAMS FOR CONTROLLING EMISSIONS OF SULFUR DIOXIDE

As in the United States, air quality laws in Western Europe, Canada, and Japan focus primarily on ambient concentrations of air pollutants within the locale of emission sources, rather than on pollutant deposition. However, over the past decade, increasing awareness of acid deposition as a potential problem has led several countries to develop and adopt further control policies. Working within the existing regulatory framework for controlling sulfur dioxide (SO_2), Canada, West Germany, and the Scandinavian countries have initiated further SO_2 emissions limitations and restricted the level of sulfur in fuel in order to address acid deposition.

European nations have established extensive cooperative monitoring programs to gather information on the nature and extent of acid deposition and other transported air pollutants. Some accords dealing with transboundary pollution have been reached, and negotiations are in progress in others.

This appendix describes the international organizations and accords that deal with transboundary pollutants. In addition, it outlines the existing policies of the countries of Scandinavia, the United Kingdom, West Germany, Canada, and Japan concerning acid rain and transboundary air pollution.

International Organizations and Accords Dealing With Transboundary Pollution

Considerable international effort has been expended to address transboundary air pollution and acid rain over the last decade. At the urging of the Scandinavian countries, transboundary pollution problems have been discussed in such international forums as the U.N. Economic Commission for Europe (ECE), the European Economic Community (EEC), and the Organization for

Economic Cooperation and Development (OECD); these organizations have also launched research efforts to study the problem. In March 1984, Environmental Ministers from nine European nations and Canada signed an agreement to reduce national sulfur dioxide emissions at least 30 percent by 1993 in an effort to curb transboundary air pollution. The countries signing the agreement—referred to as the "30 percent Club"—were Canada, Austria, Denmark, West Germany, Finland, France, the Netherlands, Norway, Sweden, and Switzerland. They also agreed to urge that other signatories to the Convention on Long Range Transboundary Air Pollution of the UN Economic Commission for Europe (ECE) take similar action.

Economic Commission for Europe (ECE) and the Convention on Long-Range Transboundary Air Pollution

The ECE, comprised of all European United Nations (U.N.) members plus Canada, the United States, and the U.S.S.R., is one of five regional economic commissions of the U.N. It began to address the transboundary pollution issue as early as 1969, when a working group on air pollution recommended reducing SO_2 emissions. ECE negotiations began in 1977, with Sweden and Norway pressing members to, at a minimum, hold SO_2 emissions to current levels, and to lay the groundwork for abating SO_2 levels by a fixed percentage.

In 1978, the Committee of Senior Advisors to the ECE established the Special Group on Long-Range Transboundary Air Pollution, instructing the group to draft proposals for the consideration of future senior advisory sessions. Extensive negotiation produced a convention substantially modified from that originally proposed by the Nordic countries; the modified convention was accepted at a high-level meeting of the ECE in November 1979. The ECE convention was the first multilateral agreement to address specifically the problem of transboundary air pollution caused by long-range transport, and was the first major environmental accord involving the nations of Eastern and Western Europe and North America.

The accord requires the signing countries to develop policies and strategies "as far as possible" to reduce air pollution gradually, including long-range transboundary air pollution, employing "best available technology which is economically feasible." The convention defines long-range transboundary pollution as pollution traveling to another nation from such a distance that "it is not generally possible to distinguish the contribution of individual emission sources or groups of sources." While the convention clearly addresses acid deposition, it mandates no emission limitations. Since the convention does not establish numerical goals, limits, or timetables, or contain enforcement provisions, the signing countries do not have to alter their pollution-control policies unless they choose to do so.

However, the convention is important as a basis for coherent research and international management of transboundary pollution. The signatories agreed to cooperate in conducting research on control technologies, monitoring and modeling techniques, and effects of air pollutants (e.g., sulfur compounds) on human health and the environment. The ECE countries agreed to exchange information for advancing international research efforts such as data on emissions and results of domestic research efforts, and further agreed to support the ongoing international monitoring program established by the U.N. Environment Program. This program has established monitoring sites to measure SO_2 and particulate sulfate in the air, and acidity in precipitation, with stations in some 20 European countries.

The European Economic Community (EEC)

The EEC was formed in 1957 and presently includes ten European countries of the Common Market—West Germany, France, Italy, Belgium, the Netherlands, Luxembourg, Ireland, the United Kingdom, Greece, and Denmark. The EEC was formed initially to deal with economic issues among member countries; however, it has also been used as a forum for discussing international air quality issues. While the EEC has never directly addressed the long-range transboundary air pollution issue, it has developed and issued directives dealing with SO_2 emissions generally. A directive on the sulfur content of certain liquid fuels was issued in 1975; a directive establishing health protection standards for

SO_2 was submitted to the governing Council of Ministers for approval in 1976 and was finally adopted in 1980. The standards are relatively lenient by comparison to current World Health Organization and U.S. standards. The directive requires that member countries adopt measures to meet the standards by April 1983, but allows nonattainment areas 10 years to achieve compliance.

The directive also requires countries to establish an air-quality monitoring network, and establishes common procedures for the network and for exchanging data and information. Although the EEC directive does not directly address long-range transport and acidic deposition, the resolution accompanying the directive is an indication of the EEC's awareness and concern for these issues. In language similar to the ECE Convention, the resolution states that EEC members:

. . . will endeavor, in accordance with objectives of the above mentioned Directive, and taking due account of the facts and problems involved, to limit, and, as far as possible, gradually reduce and prevent transboundary air pollution . . . .

The EEC directive is more significant as a symbol of commitment to controlling transboundary and domestic air pollution than as a means of implementing control measures for SO_2. Less than 5 percent of EEC's land mass will exceed the health standard in 1983. Despite the goals of the EEC directive, it appears to do little to further the role of either the EEC or its members in reducing and preventing transboundary air pollution.

The Organization for Economic Cooperation and Development (OECD)

The OECD was founded in 1961 as a "Western" alliance for promoting economic growth. Its members include the United States, Japan, Canada, West Germany, the United Kingdom, and the Scandinavian countries. Although all decisions within the OECD are nonbinding, the Organization has been highly influential in developing international law and policy concerning transboundary air pollution. The OECD has also produced some important research on transported air pollution.

In 1972, the OECD established the "Cooperative Technical Program to Measure the Long-Range Transport of Air Pollutants." The program measured SO_2 emissions in 11 European countries, as well as air concentrations of SO_2, particulate sulfate, and sulfate in precipitation. Computer models were used to estimate domestic and foreign contributions to each country's sulfur deposition. The effort, coordinated by the Norwegian Institute for Air Research, was among the first to rely extensively on long-range transport models; results were published initially in 1977 and in an expanded version in 1979. The study concluded that more than half of the deposition in five countries was caused by transboundary pollution.

The OECD has also produced reports on the legal aspects of transboundary pollution. By adopting the Principles Concerning Transfrontier Pollution the OECD Council urged member countries to follow guidelines in developing international law to deal with transfrontier pollution. Specifically, the Principles recommend: 1) a country in which transboundary pollution originates should address the problem as it would if the pollution occurred within its borders; 2) equal rights should be granted to foreigners in administrative and judicial proceedings; and 3) other nations should be informed of actions that a country believes might increase transboundary pollution. In addition, the Council also espoused the principle that the producers of pollution should pay for its control even when effects are felt outside the country of origin.

The Nordic Environmental Protection Convention

In 1974, Finland, Denmark, Norway, and Sweden signed the Nordic Environmental Protection Convention. The convention essentially eliminates international boundaries with respect to controlling pollution from stationary sources, and can be construed to deal with acid deposition from transboundary pollution. In many respects the Nordic Convention resembles the principles on transboundary pollution approved by the Council of OECD. It provides that permit decisions for pollution sources should weigh any adverse effects the source might have on a foreign country as though such effects would occur domestically. The Convention also adopts the principle that a foreigner has a right to institute proceedings in the country of emission concerning the permissibility of the emissions and to seek compensation for damages.

Multilateral European Monitoring Efforts

International research efforts in Europe began over a decade ago. Three monitoring networks have provided information on air and precipitation chemistry on long-range transport of air pollutants: the European Atmospheric Chemistry Network (EACN), the Organization for Economic Cooperation and Development Study on Long Range Transport of Air Pollutants (OECD/LRTAP), and the Economic Commission for Europe's cooperative program for monitoring and evaluating transported air pollutants in Europe (ECE-EMEP). The EACN, begun in 1950 by Swedish scientists, consisted at its peak of 120 stations in 12 countries

analyzing air quality and wet deposition monthly. Data from this network showed an expanding area with highly acidic precipitation and led to the creation of OECD/LRTAP, operating from 1972 to 1977.[5]

Results of OECD/LRTAP suggested that future studies should include all European countries. EMEP, organized under ECE, in cooperation with the United Nations Environment Program (UNEP) and the World Meteorological Organization (WMO), was begun in 1977. Its main objective is to "provide governments with information on the deposition and concentration of air pollutants, as well as on the quantity and significance of long-range transmission of pollutants and transboundary fluxes."[6]

About 65 stations in 20 European countries are currently in operation. The monitoring sites have been selected primarily to represent rural areas. The EMEP sampling network relies principally on 24-hour sampling of SO_2 and particulate sulfate in air, and sulfate and acidity in precipitation. In addition, nitrate and ammonium in precipitation are measured in more than half the countries. The EMEP program is projected to issue semiannual reports for several years.

Approaches to SO_2 Control in Canada, Scandinavia, West Germany, the United Kingdom, and Japan

CANADA

Acid rain has become a major public policy issue in Canada. Particularly in the Eastern Provinces, there is deep and widespread concern over the possible damage to Canadian lakes and forests, and to the extensive tourist, recreational, and forestry industries they support. Due to transboundary transport of pollutants between the United States and Canada, acid rain has become a major issue in relations between the two countries.

Total SO_2 emissions in Canada in 1980 were about 5.3 million tons a year, approximately one-fifth the amount emitted by the United States. Most of these emissions come from two source categories: nonferrous smelters and coal-fired utilities. Although utilities contribute much less to Canada's total SO_2 emissions than smelters, Canadian powerplants could have a disproportionate effect on transboundary pollution because the majority of plants are located close to the U.S. border.

Canada and the United States are formally committed to developing a bilateral strategy to control transbound-

---

[5]L. Granat, "Sulphate in Precipitation as Observed by the European Atmospheric Chemistry Network," *Atmospheric Environment* 12, 413-424, 1978.

[6]H. Douland, "European Networks—Operation and Results," *Sulfur in the Atmosphere,* Proceedings of an International Symposium in Dubrovnik, Yugoslavia, Sept. 7-14, 1977.

ary air pollution. In August 1980, the two nations signed a Memorandum of Intent (MOI) establishing five scientific and technological workgroups and pledging both countries to formal treaty negotiations. Three of the five workgroups under the MOI have completed their work and released their results on February 22, 1983.

Canadian air pollution control programs tend to be undertaken flexibly, with minimum use of formal legal measures, emphasizing government/industry cooperation instead. The legal basis for controlling air pollution in Canada lies in its Clean Air Act, most recently amended in December 1980. Although the act now provides the Canadian Federal Government with the authority to control transboundary pollution originating in Canada, the Federal role is mainly one of guidance and demonstration to the relatively autonomous Provinces.

The Canadian Clean Air Act of 1980 exhibits distinctive differences from, but important similarities to, the U.S. Clean Air Act:[7]

- The national ambient air quality objectives contained in Canada's Clean Air Act, like those of the United States, are concerned primarily with local, ground-level effects, rather than regional or long-range transport impacts.
- As in the United States, the act does not directly address sulfates and nitrates (the main components of acid deposition), because they are largely formed in the air, rather than being emitted directly.
- Unlike those of the U.S. Clean Air Act, Canada's Federal standards are only guidelines and are not binding on Provinces. The Provinces have absolute discretion in the Canadian regulatory process. The Provincial governments often negotiate with industry to attain emissions reductions. Canadian courts are not involved in this process.
- Not all Provinces of Canada have adopted ambient standards. Standards for those that have—Alberta, Manitoba, New Brunswick, Ontario, and Saskatchewan—are far more stringent than the comparable U.S. primary standards.
- Cost effectiveness is a major consideration in developing most Provincial air pollution control programs. Less costly measures, such as the use of low-sulfur coal, and dispersion techniques such as tall stacks and siting, are the major means used to avoid excessively high ambient concentrations from powerplants. No scrubbers are in use in Canada today.
- The Canadian Clean Air Act empowers the Federal Government to set national guidelines only for

new sources and pollutants determined to have health effects. These guidelines are not mandatory.
- In 1981, Canada passed a program for coal-fired powerplants analogous to U.S. New Source Performance Standards. Other new sources are not as stringently controlled; emphasis has focused on controlling existing sources.

The Canadian Parliament, in December 1980, amended the Canadian Clean Air Act to grant the Minister of the Environment authority to recommend site-specific standards for sources "that may reasonably be anticipated to constitute a significant danger to the health, safety, or welfare of persons in another country." Provinces are given the first opportunity to enforce standards to "eliminate or significantly reduce" transboundary pollution. The Government-in-Council (essentially, the Federal Cabinet) may implement the standards if the provinces have not acted expeditiously.[8]

In March 1984, federal and provincial Ministers of the Environment agreed to reduce SO_2 emissions by 50 percent in eastern Canada by 1994, using 1980 as a base case year.

Formerly, Canada had been committed to a 25 percent emissions reduction east of Saskatchewan by 1990 to be achieved primarily by controlling Ontario Hydro and the International Nickel Co. (INCO) smelters.

Ontario Hydro, the provincially controlled utility system and largest aggregate source of utility emissions in Canada, was to reduce total SO_2 and NO_x emissions 43 percent from 1982 levels.

Ontario's Government-in-Council (i.e., the Provincial Cabinet) restricted emissions from the largest single source of Canada's SO_2, INCO's massive smelters at Sudbury, Ontario, to 1,950 tons/day in 1983. This represented a decrease from a maximum of 7,200 tons per day in the late 1960's.[9]

The control measures imposed on INCO, and Ontario Hydro may be changed when implementation plans for the recent decision to reduce emissions 50 percent in eastern Canada are developed.

SWEDEN

Swedish authorities consider acidification to be the most serious environmental problem of the decade, and are continuing their efforts both in Sweden and internationally, to reduce acid deposition. Of about 85,000 Swedish lakes classified as medium to large in size, more than 18,000 are currently acidified. About 4,000 of them are very seriously acidified and have suffered extensive biological damage. In about 9,000 lakes, mainly in

[7]G. Wetstone, "Review of Approaches to Long-Range Transport Control in the United States, Canada, Europe, and Japan," report prepared by the Environmental Law Institute for the OTA, March 1981.

[8]Clean Air Act §22.1, House of Commons 1st Session, 32d Parliament, 29 Elizabeth II, 1980, Bill 151.
[9]Written communications from Bruce Jutzi, First Secretary, Embassy of Canada, Mar. 10, 1983, and Sept. 13, 1983.

southern and central Sweden, damage to fish stocks range from minor upsets in lifecycles to extinction of trout and crayfish species.[10] Swedish scientists believe that several thousand more lakes will be threatened if acid deposition continues at present rates.

Sweden has decided to control its own SO_2 emissions stringently, although it is estimated that 70 percent of Sweden's pollutant deposition originates from sources outside the country. Since the early 1970's, when the problems of acidification first attracted notice, Sweden has introduced emission controls that have lowered emissions substantially in recent years. In 1970, SO_2 emissions in Sweden totaled about 450,000 metric tons (tonnes). Currently, Sweden is emitting about 250,000 tonnes of SO_2 a year. New control limits for powerplants effective October 1, 1984, will set maximum emissions of 0.24 gram of sulfur/megajoule of fuel—about 1.1 lb SO_2/million Btu fuel burned. Nineteen of twenty-four Provinces in Sweden currently meet that standard.

In the spring of 1981, the Swedish Parliament adopted an interim measure limiting maximum emissions of sulfur from any installation to 1,600 tonnes/day. This emissions cap has required two flue-gas desulfurization (FGD) units to be installed on a 400-megawatt (MW) and 700-MW powerplant. The Swedish Parliament has set a goal of reducing industrial sulfur discharges from 200,000 tonnes of SO_2 a year to half that amount by 1985. According to Sweden's National Environmental Protection Board, emissions probably will be reduced to about 85,000 tonnes by 1985. A special committee on coal, health, and the environment is currently preparing a report expected to lead to new proposals for a much lower industrial emissions standard in the spring of 1984.

Sweden has also embarked on an ambitious liming program to restore acidified lakes. A total of 3,000 lakes, 3,000 kilometers of streams, and 500 watersheds have been limed from the program's inception through July 1983. Total program costs have reached $17 million to date, including approximately $4 million to lime 500 lakes in fiscal year 1983. The program is financed by a tax on fuel oil. Although liming has been shown to be successful in temporarily preventing acidification and restoring natural acidity to surface waters, the Swedish Government has adopted the policy that liming is a stopgap measure and cannot substitute for controlling acidifying emissions at their source.[11]

NORWAY

Norwegian officials currently consider acid deposition to be their single most significant pollution problem. Extensive acid-deposition damage has been found in Southern Norway, where recent studies of 5,000 lakes have shown losses of fish populations in 1,750 lakes, with another 900 lakes projected to undergo serious acidification. As much as 90 percent of Norway's acidic deposition has been estimated to originate from sources outside its borders—the highest estimated percentage of pollution import of any European country.[12]

Overall emissions of SO_2 have been reduced in Norway following the enactment of new fuel-sulfur limitations in the late 1970's. Under the Neighbor Act of 1961, air pollution sources are required to use fuel oil with a maximum sulfur content of 2.5 percent (about 2.7 lb SO_2/million Btu). Amendments to the act in 1977 and 1979 imposed a maximum sulfur content of 1 percent (about 1.1 lb SO_2/million Btu) for all fuel oils used by new sources or by expansions of existing sources. In addition, existing sources were required to reduce annual SO_2 emissions by 20 percent from 1977 emissions levels.[13] These more stringent requirements apply only to the nine southern and most populated counties of Norway. Further reductions in SO_2 emissions are expected over the next 5 years; however, Norwegians assert that no national-level controls will be sufficient to rectify the damage to their environment caused by acid deposition.

Norwegian concern over the effects of acid precipitation prompted major government-sponsored research beginning in 1972. The multidisciplinary research project, entitled "Acid Precipitation—Effects on Forests and Fish," culminated in an International Scientific Conference in March 1980 in Sandefjord, Norway. Norwegian officials believe that reports from this conference conclusively link emissions of SO_2 to environmental damage.

Over the past 10 years, the Norwegian Government has worked to achieve a gradual reduction of total sulfur emissions from the member countries of the ECE. This goal was most recently articulated at the Stockholm 1982 Conference by Wenche Frogn Sellaeg, Norwegian Minister of the Environment, who called for: 1) reducing sulfur emissions in the countries of Europe and North America, and 2) ensuring that no new powerplant or industrial source is constructed without effective controls on sulfur emissions.

[10]"Acidification Today and Tomorrow," Swedish Ministry of Agriculture, Environment 1982 Committee, 1982, pp. 50 and 130.

[11]Written communication from Carl Johan Liden, Counselor, Embassy of Sweden, Jan. 7, 1983.

[12]Written communication from Stein Seeberg, Counselor, Royal Norwegian Embassy, Sept. 7, 1983.

[13]"Norwegian Strategies and Policies for the Abatement of Air Pollution Caused by Sulphur Compounds," Major Government Review of 1982, Oslo, June 1982.

DENMARK

Unlike other Scandinavian countries, Denmark contains large areas with soils capable of buffering the high levels of acid deposition it receives. However, Danish researchers have found evidence of lake acidification in some poorly buffered areas. Acting on this evidence, Federal and local government officials, along with power company executives, have formed a task force to examine ways to reduce emissions of SO_2 and NO_x.

Denmark emits about 450,000 tonnes of SO_2 annually. Two-thirds of these emissions come from oil-fired powerplants and oil-heated homes. Half of all sulfur deposition in Denmark is thought to originate in other countries, principally West Germany and the United Kingdom.

Denmark is presently in the midst of major switches from oil to coal use, but this fuel change is expected to cause SO_2 emissions levels to decline. Oil containing up to 2.5 percent sulfur has met over 80 percent of Denmark's energy needs since the early 1970's. The imported coal replacing the oil will have a much lower sulfur content. However, maximum allowable sulfur levels for coals have not yet been established.[14]

Denmark's air pollution is regulated by the Environmental Protection Act of 1973. The act sets standards for maximum sulfur levels for oils at 0.8 percent for light oil and 2.5 percent for heavy oil (about 0.9 and 2.7 lb SO_2/million Btu, respectively). A stricter limit of 1.0 percent for all oil was established in the metropolitan area of Copenhagen. The act is implemented by municipal and county authorities under the guidelines of the National Agency for Environmental Protection. The act required major polluters to receive permits from the municipal or county officials.

Although Denmark is mainly concerned with reducing emissions to levels that do not contribute to adverse health conditions in the country, it is actively participating in developing international-level controls. Denmark cosponsored the draft proposal that led to the ECE Convention on Long-Range Air Pollution in November 1979.[15]

THE FEDERAL REPUBLIC OF GERMANY

West Germany is the second largest producer of SO_2 in Western Europe, and is believed to be a substantial contributor to acid deposition in Scandinavia. West Germany has established an ambitious air pollution control program. It is currently the only country in Europe to rely on scrubbers to abate sulfur pollution from new sources and presently operates eight FGD units.

Air pollution in West Germany is regulated under the Federal Emission Protection Act of 1974 (FIPA). Embodied in the Act are detailed nonbinding guidelines entitled "Technical Instructions for Air" or TA-Luft. The responsibility for meeting these requirements rests with each State or "Lander." Legislative proposals are under consideration to make the TA-Luft legally binding on the Landers.

The first phase of planned revisions to FIPA was approved by the Bundesrat on February 4, 1983. In particular, the new regulations reduce SO_2 emissions limits for new sources by about 35 to 40 percent. It is estimated that this will reduce West Germany's emissions from electricity generation by 1 million tonnes by 1988.

West Germany emitted about 3.9 million tonnes of SO_2 in 1982, primarily from coal-fired powerplants and from industries burning oil and coal. West Germany is also believed to receive substantial amounts of pollution from other nations: about half of the sulfur deposited in West Germany is estimated to be of nondomestic origin.[16]

In recent years, environmental officials and the general public have become increasingly concerned about the possible effects of acid deposition on German forests.[17] Because forestry is one of the country's leading industries, recent reports that air pollution—both local and transported—is severely damaging the nation's pine, fir, and spruce trees have aroused major concern. In response to this new evidence, the Federal Government has recently passed (July 1983) an ordinance on large firing installations to reduce total SO_2 emissions by 50 percent over the next 10 years. Additionally, West Germany has recently shifted its position from opposing international accords to promote control of transboundary air pollution to willing participation in international efforts.

UNITED KINGDOM

The United Kingdom is the largest emitter of SO_2 in Western Europe and is believed by some scientists to be the largest contributor to acid deposition in Scandinavia.[18] An OECD study concluded that the United Kingdom is a significant exporter of pollutants to downwind nations, and calculates that it is the largest contributor of acid deposition to Norway, as well as the second-largest outside contributor of acid deposition to Sweden, after West Germany.

---

[14]Written communication with Evy Jordan, Vice Consul, Royal Danish Embassy, Oct. 1, 1982.

[15]Ibid.

[16]Statement by the Federal Republic of Germany's Interior Minister at the "Conference on Acidification," Stockholm, June 27, 1982.

[17]Written communication with Detlef Boldt, Aug. 23, 1982.

[18]Elam, "Present and Future Levels of Sulfur Dioxide Emissions in Northern Europe," prepared for the Swedish Ministry of Agriculture, June 1979.

Air pollution regulations in the United Kingdom date back to the Alkali Act of 1863, and are based on the concept of regulating emissions via the ''best practicable'' means of control. The approach is designed to allow flexibility and evolving standards as control technologies improve—a wide range of emission standards are enforced by a central government inspectorate. However, for SO_2 and NO_x emissions, Britain's principal control strategy is dispersion. Backup strategies include regional use of low-sulfur fuel, coal washing, siting industrial plants in nonurban areas, and developing nuclear power. FGD is not used to control SO_2 in the United Kingdom at the present time.

Britain relies on coal to produce almost 70 percent of its electric power, and powerplants account for almost 60 percent of its total SO_2 emissions. Total SO_2 emissions in the United Kingdom have already declined during the past 10 years from 6 million to 4.5 million tonnes; they are estimated to remain about constant or possibly decrease slightly in the future.

The British Government takes the position that significant uncertainties exist about the atmospheric processes leading to acid rain formation and about its reported effects. It asserts that more research is needed before a firm case can be established for policies to further reduce SO_2 emissions. However, international action within the UNECE convention, the Stockholm 1982 Conference, and the EEC may influence future U.K. policy with regard to transported air pollutants.[19]

JAPAN

Although Japan is not typically a focus of discussion for long-range transported air pollutants, its stringent control program and success in reducing ambient concentrations make it worth noting. Japan has the most rigorous SO_2 control policies in the world. Control requirements are geared to an ambient standard of 100 $\mu g/m^3$ for a daily averaging time, compared to the U.S. standard of 365 $\mu g/m^3$. In 1981, 98 percent of the monitoring stations in Japan met that standard. In 1974,

Japan instituted an emissions fee for large SO_2 sources in polluted areas. The proceeds are used in designated areas for the medical care of patients affected by air pollution.

About 1,362 FGD units were in operation in Japan during 1982. Most are small units installed primarily on industrial plants producing chemicals or pulp and paper products. Sixty-three of the units are installed on powerplants, accounting for 40,000 MW of electrical generating capacity. Unlike the United States and West Germany, where coal-fired plants are the focus of FGD controls, 29 of the Japanese units have been installed on coal-fired boilers and 34 on oil-fired plants.[20]

According to the Japanese Government, these FGD units have not created a sludge disposal problem, because such materials as gypsum produced by scrubbers have been highly salable in Japan. The use of FGD was in fact promoted by the short supply of sulfur materials, creating a favorable market for these products. However, rapid expansion in the production of these goods has recently outstripped the market demand, which may make scrubber-byproduct disposal a land-use problem. Other countries are now beginning to follow Japanese techniques for regenerating FGD sludge.

Government subsidies and the expansion of the Japanese economy have contributed to the rapid increase of FGD use. The Government provides low-interest loans and allows accelerated depreciation for facilities that install control devices. The total investment in SO_2 control, including FGD and hydro desulfurization of oil, was about $3.7 billion in 1977 U.S. dollars.

Ambient SO_2 concentrations have declined substantially in major urban areas as a result of the abatement program. From a 1965 level of about 150 $\mu g/m^3$, the 1978 annual ambient average on a 24-hour basis dropped to about 40 $\mu g/m^3$,[21] a figure comparable to the 1978 urban ambient average in the United States.

[19]Written communication from Mike Norton, First Secretary, Embassy of Great Britain, Aug. 30, 1982.

[20]''Environment in Japan 1981,'' Environment Agency, Government of Japan, December 1981.

[21]Written communication with Seiji Ikkatai, Second Secretary, Embassy of Japan, Feb. 23, 1983.

D.3 MITIGATING THE EFFECTS OF ACID DEPOSITION ON AQUATIC ECOSYSTEMS

Introduction

Available strategies for controlling acid deposition and its ecological consequences include both further controlling pollutant emissions at their source and mitigating effects on sensitive resources—in particular, reducing the acidity of sensitive lakes and streams. Ameliorative measures such as liming affected lakes, streams, and watersheds have been proposed in several bills introduced during the 97th and 98th Congresses. Research is also underway on developing acid-tolerant strains of fish and aquatic plant life.

Proposed emissions control strategies are likely to require several years from enactment to implementation. Likewise, biological experimentation to develop acid-resistant aquatic life will require many years. Thus, few prospects exist for a short-term solution to the acid deposition problem. Alleviating the **symptoms** of the problem—decreasing the acidity of soil or water and restoring normal buffering capacity by adding lime or limestone—may save or restore many important recreational and commercial fisheries while long-term solutions are developed and implemented.

Important biological or chemical effects of acid deposition on water quality or fish populations have been reported in New York, Massachusetts, New Hampshire, Maine, Pennsylvania, West Virginia, North Carolina, and Tennessee, as well as in Ontario, Quebec, and Nova Scotia. Almost all States and Provinces in the Eastern United States and Canada are thought to contain **some** sensitive surface waters, based on analyses of their soils and geology.

The most sensitive lakes and streams generally are located in areas that receive high levels of acid deposition, have steep topography, and are covered with thin and poorly buffered soils. If these soils are depleted of their limited capacity to neutralize incoming acidity, acid accumulates in lakes and streams within the watershed, and, in turn, mobilizes toxic metals. Eventually the water body becomes unable to support its normal range of plant and animal life. Temporarily restoring the buffering capacity of a lake or stream by applying lime or limestone can often allow aquatic life to be restored. For most mitigation efforts to date, the primary objective has been to improve water quality sufficiently to maintain reproducing fisheries.

Liming has been effective in counteracting surface water acidification in parts of Scandinavia, Canada, and the United States. Although its effects are only tempo-

rary, the material is inexpensive, the dosage required fairly well known, and the technology of applying lime simple.

However, not all lakes and streams respond sufficiently to liming to reestablish aquatic life. In particular, lakes with rapid water flow in comparison to their volume (i.e., with water "retention time" of less than a year), and running waters with great variation in flow, are very difficult to lime effectively. Moreover, it is impossible to determine the effectiveness of a liming application without extensive monitoring of the chemical and biological changes that follow. The results of individual applications will remain uncertain until more is known about how liming affects various types of water bodies. On the average, however, the buffering capacity that a single application of lime restores to a lake or stream will be depleted over a period of 3 to 5 years, after which the effectiveness of the application must be reconsidered, and a decision made whether to continue mitigation efforts.

Possibly of greater concern with regard to establishing a wide-scale liming program is that scientists do not know how periodic realterations of water body chemistry through liming will affect aquatic ecosystems over the long term. For example, a number of substances that normally are found in a biologically inert form in neutral waters become unbound, or soluble, in acidified waters. If, several years after liming, the lake again begins to acidify, accumulated metals that have been rendered insoluble over a period of time may again become soluble and create a serious toxic condition. In addition, little is known about the effects of periodic or even single applications of liming on other living organisms in the water body. While liming has enhanced fish survival in a number of lakes and streams, its long-term implications for the food chain on which fish depend are uncertain.

Though it is neither possible nor desirable to lime all acid-sensitive aquatic ecosystems in the Eastern United States, liming can be an effective stopgap measure to restore or preserve water bodies of particular value from the effects of acid deposition. Some characteristics to consider in choosing which water bodies to lime are:
- the current or historic ability of the system to support a viable and important fishery;
- recreational importance and public access to the waters;
- present chemical condition, i.e., pH, alkalinity, acid loadings, watershed buffering capacity;

- physical factors—water retention time, geographic location; and
- economic constraints—costs of material, application, and frequency of reapplication.

Such characteristics must be assessed on a site-specific basis before the feasibility of liming can be determined. Figure D-1 presents a series of criteria suggested by a report to U.S. Fish and Wildlife Service for evaluating the appropriateness of liming a water body. All of these criteria must be met for liming to be an appropriate mitigating strategy.

Liming Materials

Many alkaline materials can be used to neutralize acidified surface waters. These include lye, soda ash, olivine, and lime compounds, as well as several byproducts and wastes of industries such as cement dust and sludge from water treatment plants. However, while industrial byproducts are low in price, they frequently have a high level of such impurities as heavy metals, which may exacerbate the already-elevated metal concentrations typically present in acidified waters. Lime compounds are much more chemically uniform and have been the neutralizing material of choice for the majority of water bodies.

The term "lime" is generally applied to several compounds of calcium and magnesium that are highly capable of neutralizing acid. The three most often used **calcium** compounds are limestone (calcium carbonate), quicklime (calcium oxide), and hydrated or slaked lime (calcium hydroxide). Available magnesium-based compounds include dolomite, dolomite lime, and dolomite hydrated lime. Calcium lime is used more commonly than dolomite. Dolomites have a slightly higher neutralizing value by weight than the nonmagnesium lime, but if their magnesium carbonate content is greater than 10 percent, they may dissolve too slowly to be of value in neutralizing acidified lakes and streams.

Crushed limestone, or "aglime," is currently the primary alkaline material used in experimental liming programs in the United States and Canada and in more wide-scale programs in Scandinavia. The more acidic the water, and the finer the limestone is ground, the more quickly it will dissolve. Limestone is a relatively inexpensive natural material and is less caustic than quicklime or hydrated lime. In general, limestone goes into solution more slowly than either quicklime or hydrated lime, but remains effective longer. The differences between lime and limestone are shown in figure D-2.

Response to Liming

Chemical Changes

Adding a liming agent causes the pH of the water body to rise and restores alkalinity—i.e., the ability to neutralize further acid inputs. If a very soluble base such as quicklime is added, pH rises sharply, and the highest pH is reached shortly after the treatment. In a New York State lake, for example, adding lime initially raised pH from 5 to 9—a ten-thousandfold decrease in acidity before the water body reached equilibrium at a lower pH value. The shock from such chemical changes, if too rapid, can be lethal to a variety of aquatic life, especially fish. When a less soluble agent such as limestone is added to a water body, the rise in pH is less dramatic. The pH generally will not exceed 7, even during the initial period after limestone is added. Applied as a powder or finely crushed stone, it will settle readily to the bottom and dissolve slowly.

Aluminum, manganese, and zinc frequently are found in elevated concentrations in acidified waters. High levels of copper, mercury, nickel, and iron may also be present due to leaching from surrounding soils or industrial wastes. These trace-metal concentrations generally decrease after acidified waters are limed. After experimental liming at four lakes near Sudbury, Ontario, decreases in metal concentrations ranged from 66 to 91 percent for aluminum, 23 to 73 percent for zinc, 15 to 79 percent for manganese, 32 to 95 percent for copper, 23 to 81 percent for nickel, and 15 to 89 percent for iron. Such metals will precipitate out of solution most quickly in small shallow lakes where liming agents mix thoroughly in a short time.[22] Dissolved organic material, which usually gives water a brownish tint, also will be removed as the metals precipitate out of solution. This causes the water to appear more transparent following liming.[*]

The chief agent responsible for fish mortality in acidified water bodies is aluminum released by acid percolating through watershed soils. Although aluminum is the most prevalent metal in the Earth's crust, the concentrations of soluble aluminum compounds are low in surface waters with moderate acidity levels (above pH 5.5). As surface-water pH drops to about 5, aluminum

[22]J. E. Fraser and D. L. Britt, *Liming of Acidified Waters: A Review of Methods and Effects on Aquatic Ecosystems,* U.S. Fish and Wildlife Service, Division of Biological Services, Eastern Energy and Land Use Team, FWS/OBS 80/40.13, 1982.
[*]Acidification of water bodies also may make them clearer as phytoplankton (tiny plant life) die off.

Figure D-1.—Criteria for Evaluating a Water Body for Suitability of Liming

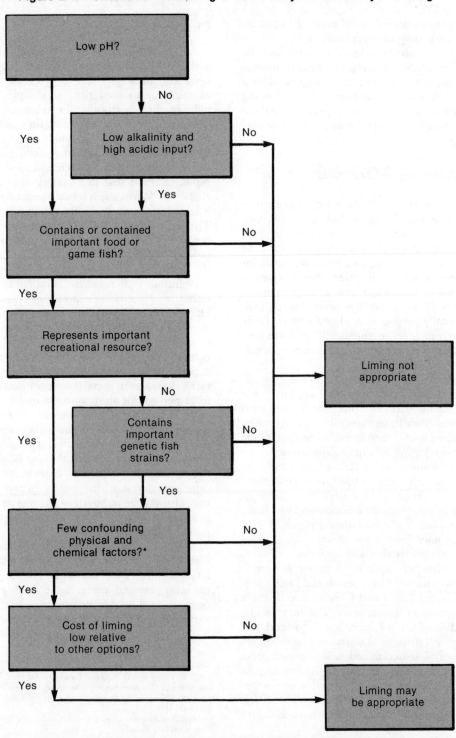

*Confounding physical and chemical factors include high flushing rates, high metal concentrations, extensive accumulations of snowpack, rapid aluminum leaching from watershed soil, predominance of soft sediments, and presence of humic substances.

SOURCE: Adapted by Office of Technology Assessment from J. E. Fraser and D. L. Britt, *Liming of Acidified Waters: A Review of Methods and Effects on Aquatic Ecosystems,* U.S. Fish and Wildlife Service, Division of Biological Services, Eastern Energy and Land Use Team, FWS/OBS 80/40.13, 1982.

Figure D-2.—Comparison of Lime and Limestone

Neutralizing materials / Characteristics	Lime		Limestone (CaCO₃)	
	Quicklime (calcium oxide)	Hydrated lime (calcium hydroxide)	Aglime (pulverized limestone)	Limestone rock
Effect on pH	Rapid rise in pH	Rapid rise in pH	Less rapid rise in pH than lime	Less rapid rise in pH than aglime
Corrosivity	Extremely caustic	Less caustic than CaO	Not caustic	Not caustic
Reactivity in water	High reactivity: less quantity required than limestone	High reactivity: less quantity required than limestone	Lower reactivity than lime[a]	Lower reactivity than lime[a]
Length of effectiveness	Short	Short	Longer than lime	Longer than lime

[a]Uncertainty exists as to whether the CaCO₃ that does not go into solution becomes reactive at a later date or becomes nonreactive.
[b]Relative neutralizing value if pure CaCO₃ is assigned a value of 100%.

SOURCE: Adapted by Office of Technology Assessment from J. E. Fraser and D. L. Britt, *Liming of Acidified Waters: A Review of Methods and Effects on Aquatic Ecosystems,* U.S. Fish and Wildlife Service, Division of Biological Services, Eastern Energy and Land Use Team, FWS/OBS 80/40.13, 1982.

becomes much more soluble and more toxic to fish. Below pH 4.5, aluminum appears to have less effect on fish, but acidity levels themselves are so high that few species can survive. If a water body of **less** than pH 5 is limed, it will pass again through the critical pH range at which aluminum is especially toxic—and for a brief time fish mortality will be of concern. As the pH increases beyond this range, the aluminum will precipitate out of solution and settle to the bottom.

The pH of surface waters will gradually decrease if significant acidic inputs continue from precipitation, streamflow, ground water infiltration, or perhaps even from the lake sediments as they use up the buffering capacity of the water above them. Liming will generally prevent acidity from increasing for about 3 to 5 years. However, once acidity increases again, aluminum and other soluble metals that have been precipitated out of the water are again "mobilized." The water may contain greater concentrations of metals following reacidification than in its original acidified state several years earlier. This is because the sediments will release both those metals initially precipitated out of solution by adding lime as well as those that entered the lake or stream and settled to the bottom while the lime provided buffering capacity. Continued liming must be timed carefully to prevent such toxicity from recurring. Table D-1 displays water quality changes in an acidified Ontario lake immediately prior to, and for 6 years following, the addition of lime.

Biological Changes

Acidification of aquatic ecosystems reduces the diversity of the normally present biological community. The total number of plant and animal species often decreases significantly. Species sensitive to acidic conditions are eliminated while tolerant species proliferate. Acidification inhibits the bacteria normally responsible for decomposition, thereby slowing the rate of nutrient cy-

Table D-1.—Changes in Chemistry of Lohi Lake, Ontario, Canada, Following Addition of Neutralizing Agents in 1973 (hydrated lime), 1974 (hydrated lime and limestone)

Parameters	1973	1974	1975	1976	1977	1978	1979
pH	4.39	6.04	6.09	6.09	5.27	4.79	4.76
Copper (mg/m³)	84	44	43	37	44	71	—
Aluminum (mg/m³)	—	140	110	120	100	160	—
Water transparency (Secchi disk, m)	8.8	5.6	5.7	5.7	6.9	9.3	7.6
Alkalinity (μeq/l)	0	46	102	44	0	0	0

SOURCE: National Research Council Canada, "Acidification in the Canadian Aquatic Environment: Scientific Criteria for Assessing the Effects of Acidic Deposition on Aquatic Ecosystems," Ottawa, Canadian Environmental Secretariat, 1981.

cling. Aluminum toxicity associated with acidification eliminates various fish species.

Liming drastically decreases the density of acid-tolerant phytoplankton (e.g., algae). Normal populations generally will be established within about a year. Normal zooplankton populations (animals that feed on the phytoplankton) may take much longer to recover. Fish populations, in turn, feed on the zooplankton; thus, several years may be required to reestablish a viable fishery. Liming experiments so far have shown enhanced survival of natural populations of brook trout in Adirondack lakes; lake trout, brook trout, and smallmouth bass in an Ontario lake; and Atlantic salmon in a Nova Scotia stream.

Biological diversity in limed water bodies might be enhanced by adding organic carbon and/or phosphorus in nutrients (organic humus or perhaps biologically treated wastewater). Phosphorus, an important element in phytoplankton nutrition, is often in short supply in acidic waters. Limited success has been reported when phosphorus was added following liming in Canadian lakes. The effect of adding organic carbon is highly speculative. If these nutrient additions prove effective in enhancing recovery of limed acidified water bodies, they could be applied at little cost.

Costs and Methods of Applying Liming Materials[23]

The techniques available for liming aquatic systems depend on the type of neutralizing material used, the availability of dispersal equipment, and the target area being limed. The major application methods used to date in the United States, Canada, and Scandinavia are outlined in figure D-3.

The accessibility of the water body may determine the appropriate liming method. For example, a remote lake can be limed only by aircraft, while an accessible water body can be limed by truck or boat. Directly liming the water body appears to be the most economically efficient technique. It is currently the most commonly used method for lakes, and is appropriate as long as the water retention time (a measure of how rapidly the lake is replenished) is longer than 1 year. If the water retention time is short, the added alkalinity will quickly leave the system (although it may neutralize water bodies downstream). Liming tributary streams might provide downstream lakes and rivers with longer term buffering capacity, and enhance fish spawning.

Researchers have yet to determine whether acidified aquatic resources may be restored more effectively by liming watersheds or lakes and streams themselves.

[23]This section is based in part on Fraser and Britt, op. cit., 1982.

However, to achieve comparable acid-neutralizing capacities in surface water, 100 times more lime must be applied to a watershed than directly to a water body. Despite this, Sweden has applied 40 percent of its total tonnage of lime on land.

For maximum effect, lime should be added shortly before critical periods of peak acidity and biological activity, i.e., during early spring, for surface waters that still support fish populations. Spring snowmelts often flow directly into water bodies without experiencing the potential neutralizing effects of soils. In much of the Eastern United States and Canada, this snowmelt has a pH of less than 4.5. The acidity that has been stored in snows throughout the winter reaches water bodies when sensitive embryos and fish fry are developing. Alternatively, liming lakes slightly later in the season, during the spring overturn, takes advantage of lake circulation patterns to enhance mixing and distribution of neutralizing agents.

Table D-2 outlines costs of limestone materials, transport, and application in Sweden in 1981. Normally, 1 to 2 tons of limestone are added per acre of surface water. The Government of Sweden has undertaken the most extensive liming program to date—3,000 lakes, 3,000 kilometers of streams, and 500 watersheds from the program's inception through July 1983. Total program costs have reached $17 million to date, including approximately $4 million to lime 500 lakes in fiscal year 1983.

Several waterway deacidification experiments have taken place in North America. Since 1973, the Ontario Ministry of the Environment has limed four acidified lakes in the Sudbury region. The treatments have been successful in returning pH to normal levels.

The most extensive program in the United States was begun by the New York State Department of Environmental Conservation in 1959. It initially targeted small, naturally acidic ponds in heavily used recreational areas, and expanded to treating selected acidified lakes with significant potential to support recreational fishing during the mid-1970's. The program is quite small in scope; only about 60 lakes in total (covering approximately 1,000 acres) have been treated to date. It has significantly improved water quality at a number of lakes and ponds, and permitted self-propagating sport fishing populations to be maintained and/or reintroduced. Costs for liming ponds and lakes under the program have ranged from approximately $50 to $300/acre for each application, depending on the size and accessibility of the water body. Between 1 and 2.2 tons of lime are normally added per acre of surface water to be treated—costs for transporting the material to the lake site constitute a significant portion of overall expenses.

Currently, only Massachusetts and New York have formal surface water mitigation projects. Since 1957,

Figure D-3.—General Comparison of the Various Liming Application Techniques

Technique	Countries employing various techniques	Receptor type	Advantages	Disadvantages
Boats	• Canada Sweden United States	• Lakes	• Simple and relatively inexpensive technique • Allows choice of elementary to sophisticated distribution options	• Application is a relatively slow process if bag dumping or slurry techniques are used • Difficult to use at remote bodies of water
Sediment injection	• Sweden	• Lakes	• Reported to be 5 to 7 times as efficient as adding lime directly to lakes on an equivalent basis	• Expensive • Need large sophisticated equipment • Only applicable to lakes accessible by roads
Truck and spreaders or blower	• Norway Sweden	• Lakes • Streams • Watershed soils	• Can distribute large amounts of lime in a relatively short period	• Can only be applied in areas accessible by roads
Aerial applications	• Canada Sweden United States	• Lakes • Streams	• Facilitates access to remote sites • Less labor • Can apply large amounts of lime in a relatively short period	• Expensive
Silos (mechanical release)	• Sweden	• Streams	• Allows for more precise maintenance of pH, since liming material is applied as needed	• Need regular maintenance, as existing silos continually break down • Overall, relatively expensive to build and maintain
Diversion wells	• Norway Sweden	• Streams	• Simple and relatively inexpensive	• Not adaptable to slow-flowing streams • Efficiency not known
Limestone barriers in streams	• Canada Sweden United States	• Streams	• Simple and relatively inexpensive technique • Once applied, the limestone is present for a relatively long time	• Technique only suitable for easily accessible sites • Technique fails during high water flows • Controversy over long-term buffering capabilities
Rotary drums filled with limestone gravel	• United States	• Streams	• Effective maintenance of stream pH because controlled by stream flow • Continual abrasion of limestone prevents coating by iron hydroxide and calcium sulfate precipitates	• Not adaptable to slow-flowing streams • Still in prototype stage, may need some design changes • Hopper reloading required, regular maintenance

SOURCE: Adapted by Office of Technology Assessment from: J. E. Fraser, D. Hinckley, R. Burt, R. Rodensky Severn, and J. Wisniewski, *Feasibility Study to Utilize Liming as a Technique to Mitigate Surface-Water Acidification* (Palo Alto, Calif.: Electric Power Research Institute, 1982), EPRI EA-2362.

Table D-2.—Range of Costs for Limestone Materials, Transport, and Application in Sweden 1981

Liming parameters	Costs
Materials:	
Bulk limestone	$20-$30/ton
Bagged limestone	$40/ton
Transport of limestone	$10-$20/ton
Application techniques:	
Truck	$4-$6/ton
Pontoon boat with blower	$10-$16/ton
Helicopter	$30-$40/ton
By hand	$20-$60/ton

SOURCE: National Fisheries Board of Sweden, *Rad och Riktinijer for Kalkning av Sjoar och Vattendrag*, Report No. 1, 1982.

Massachusetts has limed about 40 small ponds covering 2,000 acres. Funded for liming is quite limited, however, and future projects are uncertain. New York has developed a 6-year liming plan. During this time, 33 lakes will receive aglime treatments, and extensive chemical and biological monitoring will be conducted. A recent study of liming requirements in the Adirondack region of New York estimated that a 5-year program for liming all the known acidified lakes in the region would cost from $2 to $4 million per year, depending on the targeted buffering level.[24] This estimate represents

[24]F. C. Menz and C. T. Driscoll, ''An Estimate of the Costs of Liming to Neutralize Acidic Adirondack Surface Waters,'' contribution #13, Upstate Freshwater Institute, June 1983.

materials and labor only; it does not include costs for fish restocking or continued monitoring which can be considerable. Particularly in the initial stages of a liming program, frequent monitoring for chemical and biological changes in treated water bodies is necessary. Annual costs may range from $3,000 to $20,000 per lake. When a sufficient data base exists to develop a generic treatment protocol for various aquatic ecosystems—water bodies of differing geological, chemical, and biological characteristics—monitoring costs may be reduced significantly.

No direct Federal support is currently being provided to States, localities, or other organizations that undertake to treat acidified surface waters. Federal involvement in mitigation research began in 1982 under the direction of the Fish and Wildlife Service (FWS), as provided for in the National Acid Precipitation Assessment Plan.* To date, the Federal research effort has produced a technical report on liming[25] and an agenda of further research needs determined by participants in an international mitigation conference. Current plans for field research include monitoring the effects of liming on fish populations in several lakes in the Adirondack Mountains, as part of the research program on water chemistry sponsored privately by the Electric Power Research Institute. FWS is also supporting a pilot scale liming project on 10 acidified lakes in the Adirondack region in an attempt to understand the variation in response of fish populations and to evaluate the success of restocking strategies. Total Federal funding for such efforts in fiscal year 1983 amounted to about $225,000. The administration recently proposed about $5 million for liming research for fiscal year 1985. Such funding increases would permit researchers to study the effects of liming on water bodies with differing geological, chemical, and biological characteristics throughout the Eastern United States, and to investigate the effectiveness of alternative mitigation measures.

---

*Chapter 6 discusses the National Acid Precipitation Assessment Program and Federal research on mitigation techniques in greater detail.

[25]Fraser and Britt, 1982.

Index

Index